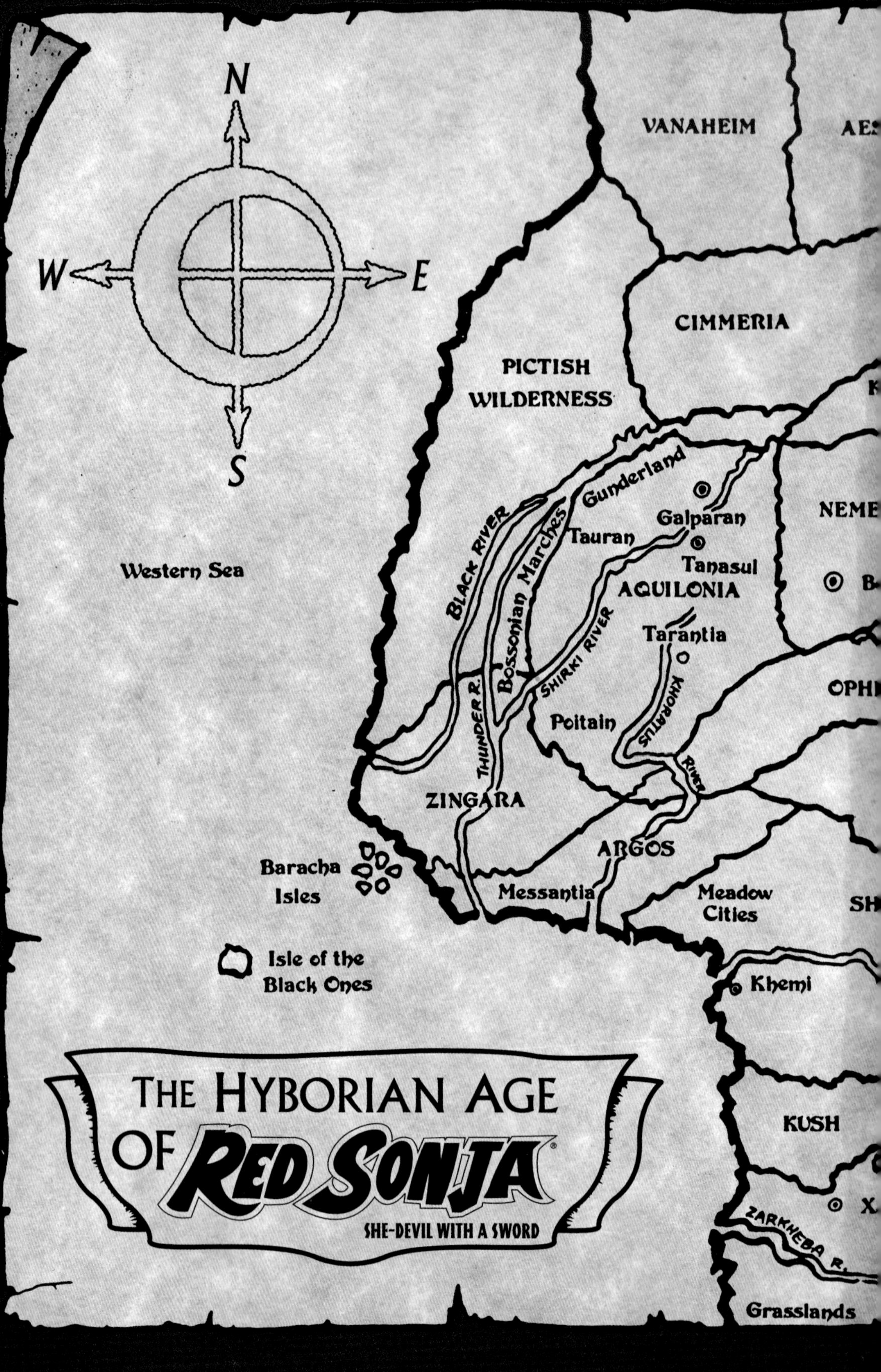

N
W
E
S
VANAHEIM
AES
CIMMERIA
PICTISH
WILDERNESS
Gunderland
Galparan
Tauran
Tanasul
AQUILONIA
NEME
Western Sea
BLACK RIVER
Bossonian Marches
SHIRKI RIVER
Tarantia
THUNDER R.
KHORATUS
RIVER
Poitain
OPH
ZINGARA
ARGOS
Baracha
Isles
Messantia
Meadow
Cities
SH
Isle of the
Black Ones
Khemi
KUSH
ZARKHEBA R.
Grasslands
THE HYBORIAN AGE
OF RED SONJA
SHE-DEVIL WITH A SWORD

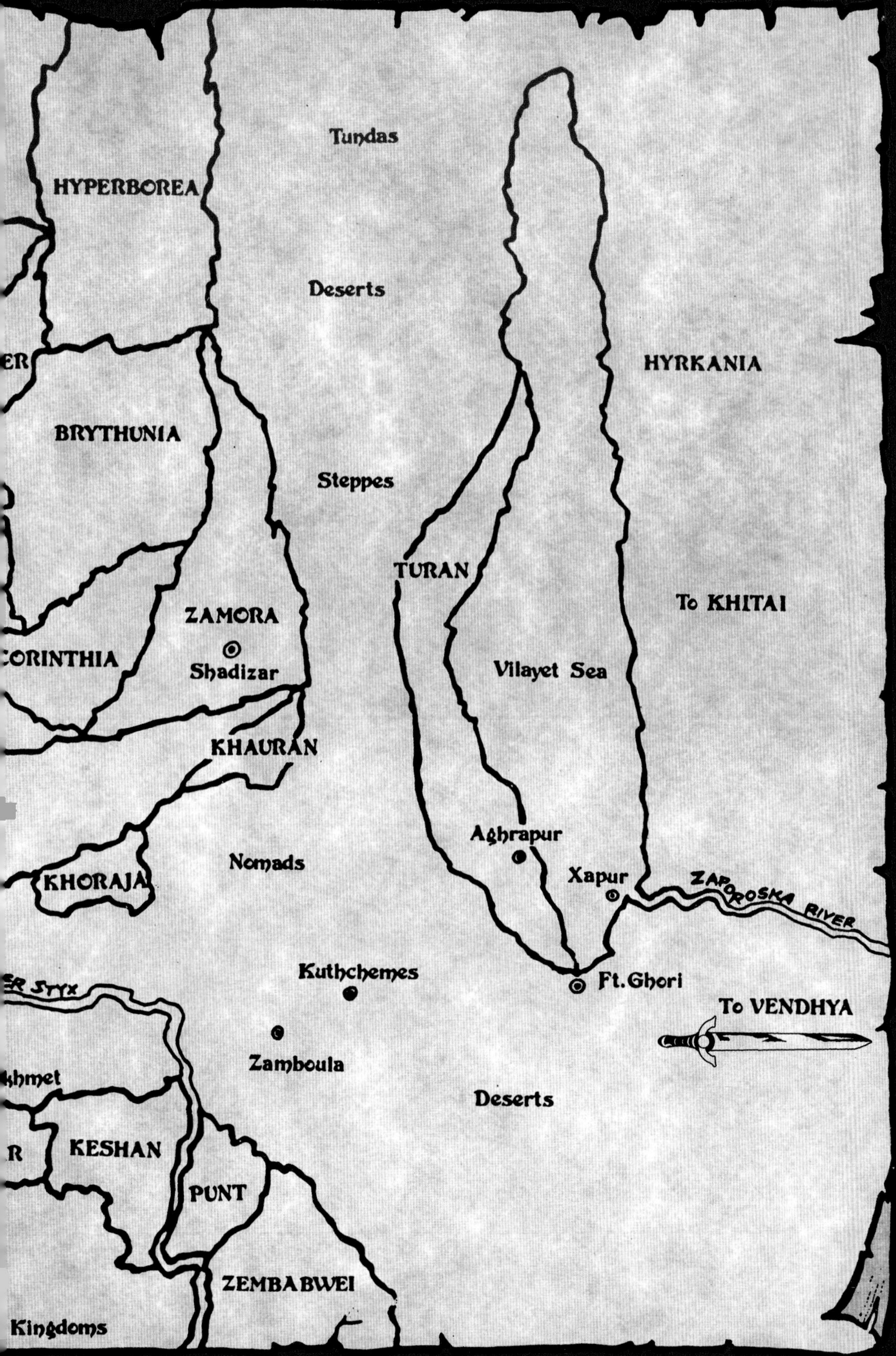

Tundas
HYPERBOREA
Deserts
ER
HYRKANIA
BRYTHUNIA
Steppes
TURAN
To KHITAI
ZAMORA
CORINTHIA
Shadizar
Vilayet Sea
KHAURAN
Aghrapur
Nomads
Xapur
KHORAJA
ZAPOROSKA RIVER
Kuthchemes
Ft. Ghori
ER STYX
To VENDHYA
Zamboula
khmet
Deserts
R
KESHAN
PUNT
ZEMBABWEI
Kingdoms

**Dynamite Entertainment Presents**

# QUEEN SONJA™

## Volume Six: HEAVY SITS THE CROWN

*written by* **Luke Lieberman**

*art by* **Milton Estevam** (#26-35) *and* **Gledson Barreto** (#35)

*colors by* **Salvatore Aiala Studios**

*cover by* **Lucio Parrillo**

*letters by* **Simon Bowland**

*based on the heroine created by*
**Robert E. Howard**

---

*This volume collects Queen Sonja issues
twenty-six through thirty-five by Dynamite Entertainment.*

---

*Executive Editor - Red Sonja*
**Luke Lieberman**

*In memory of* **Arthur Lieberman** *at Red Sonja llc.*

**Dedicated to Robert E. Howard**

**For more on Red Sonja, visit WWW.DYNAMITE.COM and WWW.REDSONJA.COM**

**DYNAMITE**®

Nick Barrucci, CEO / Publisher
Juan Collado, President / COO
Rich Young, Director Business Development
Keith Davidsen, Marketing Manager

Joe Rybandt, Senior Editor
Hannah Gorfinkel, Associate Editor
Josh Green, Traffic Coordinator
Molly Mahan, Assistant Editor

Josh Johnson, Art Director
Jason Ullmeyer, Senior Graphic Designer
Katie Hidalgo, Graphic Designer
Chris Caniano, Production Assistant

ISBN-10: 1-60690-402-7
ISBN-13: 978-1-60690-402-2
First Printing
10 9 8 7 6 5 4 3 2 1

Visit us online at **www.DYNAMITE.com**
Follow us on Twitter **@dynamitecomics**
Like us on Facebook **/Dynamitecomics**
Watch us on YouTube **/Dynamitecomics**

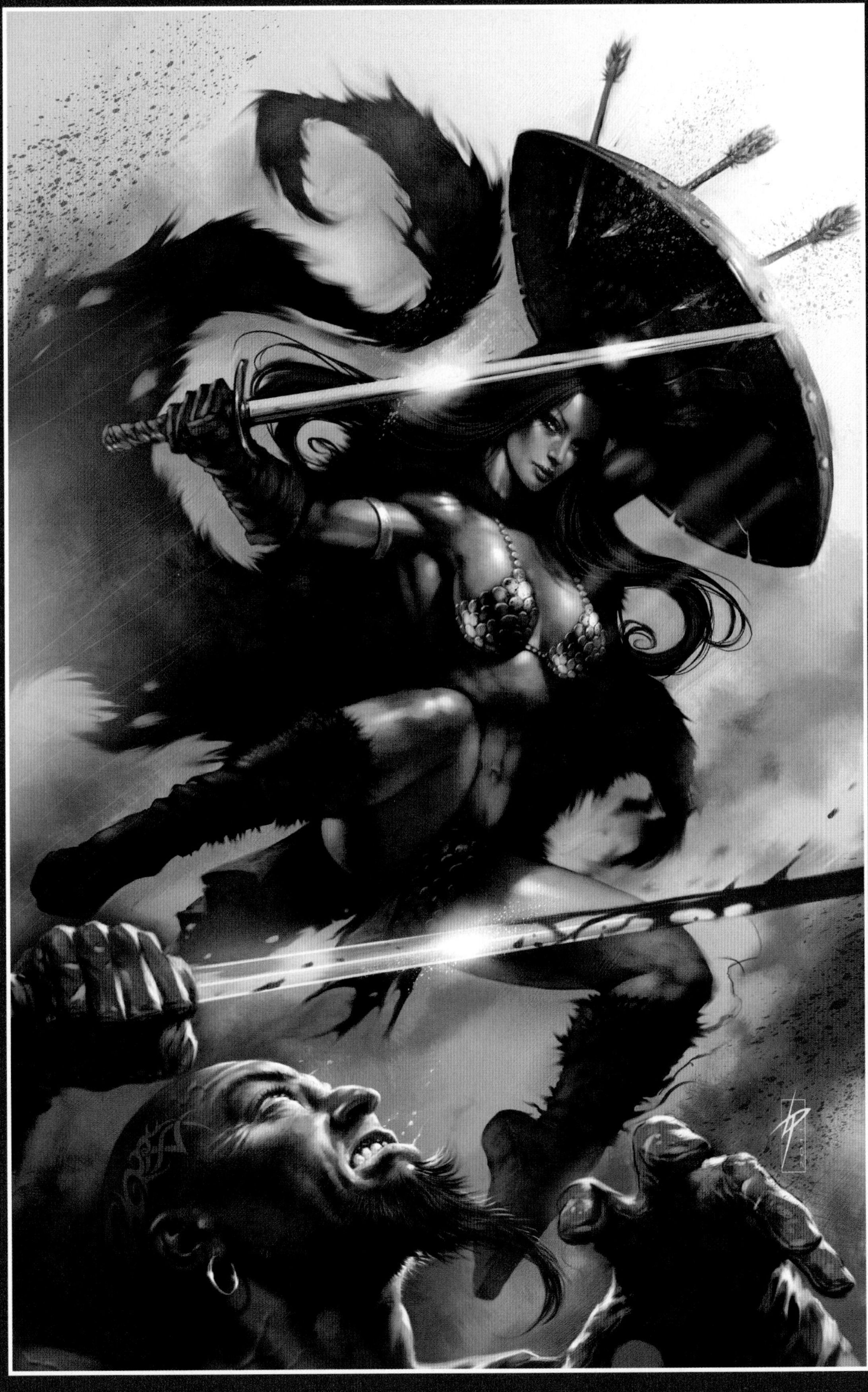

ISSUE #26 COVER BY LUCIO PARRILLO

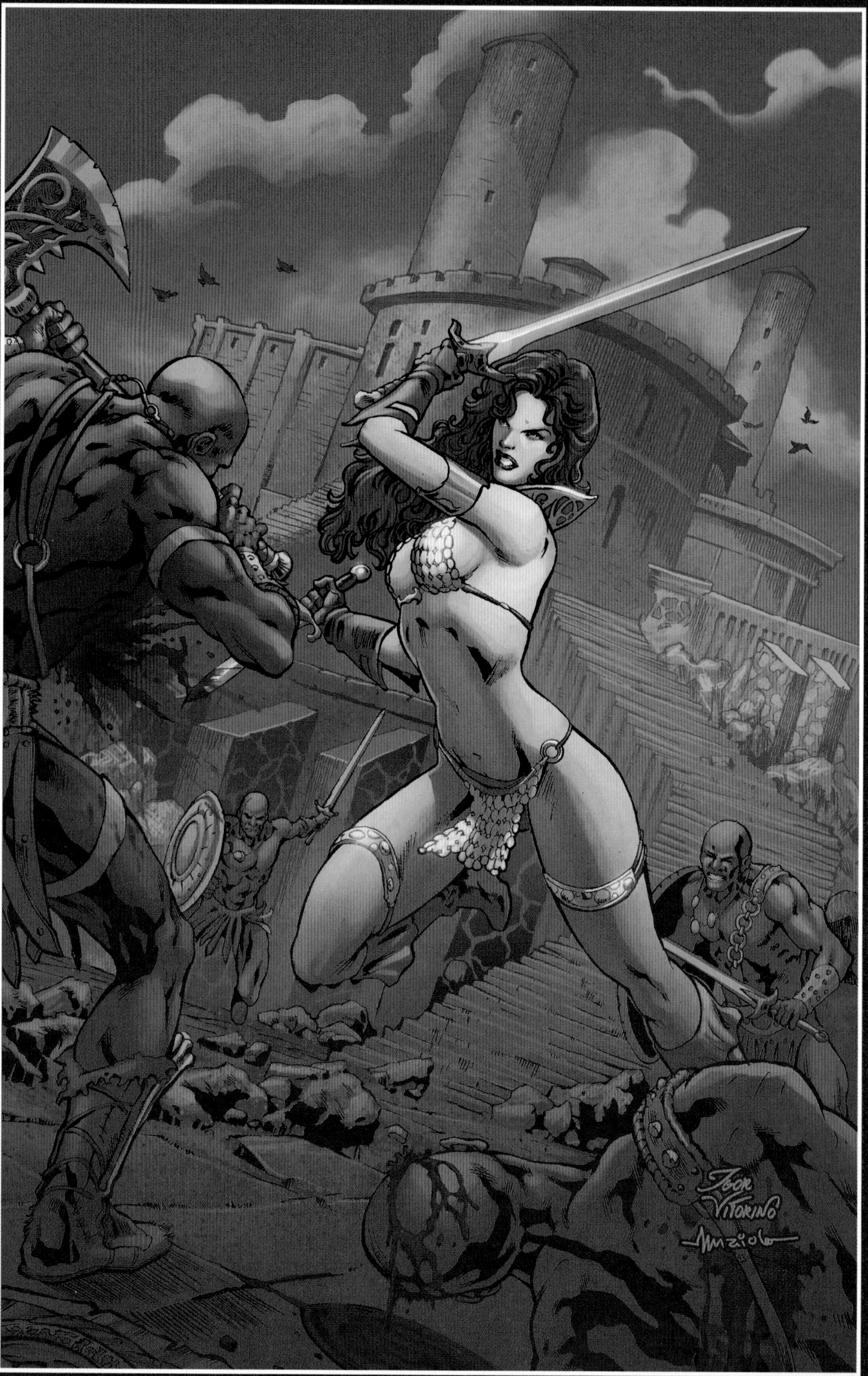
IGOR VITORINO

ISSUE #26 COVER BY IGOR VITORINO

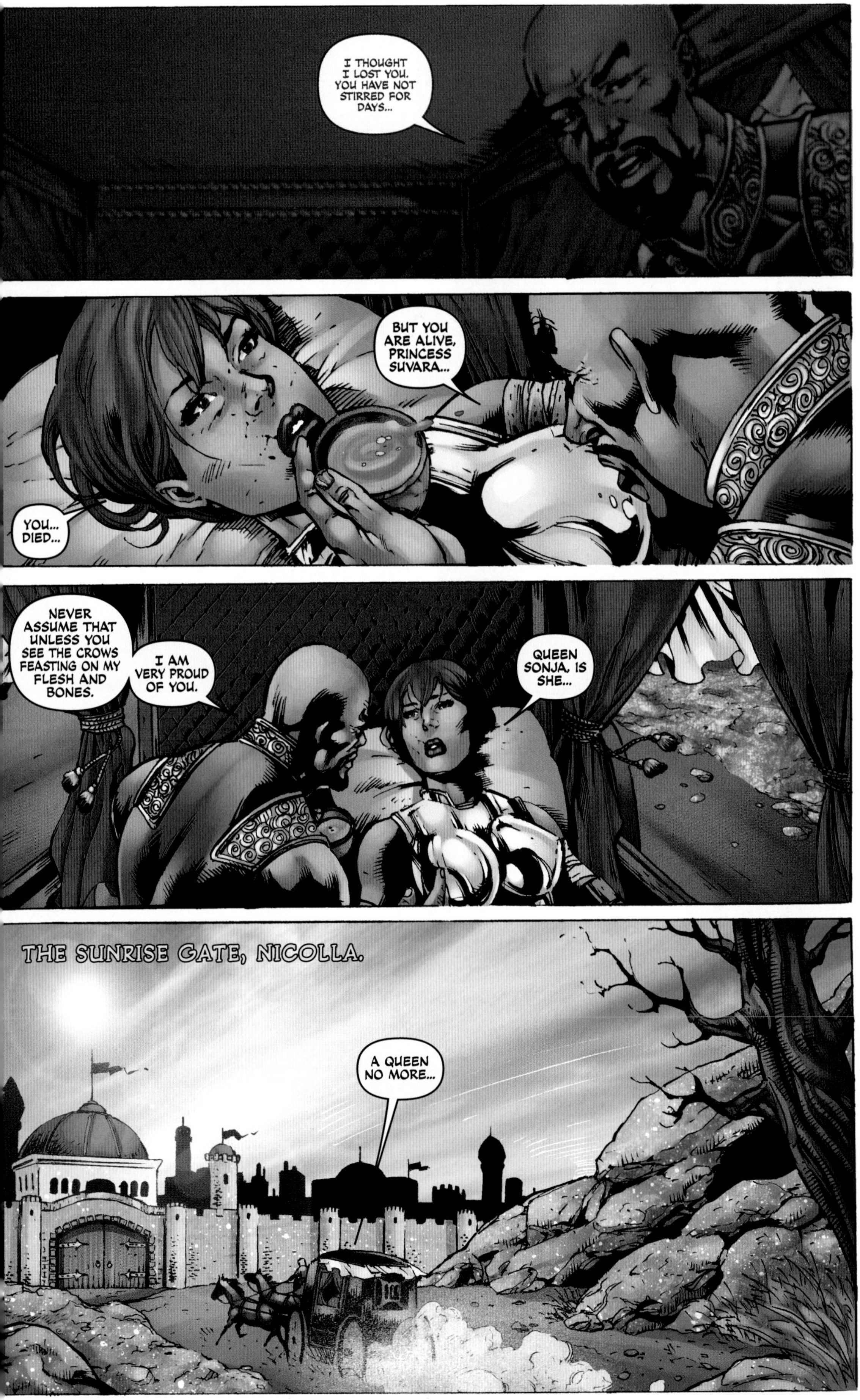
I THOUGHT I LOST YOU. YOU HAVE NOT STIRRED FOR DAYS...
BUT YOU ARE ALIVE, PRINCESS SUVARA...
YOU... DIED...
NEVER ASSUME THAT UNLESS YOU SEE THE CROWS FEASTING ON MY FLESH AND BONES.
I AM VERY PROUD OF YOU.
QUEEN SONJA, IS SHE...
THE SUNRISE GATE, NICOLLA.
A QUEEN NO MORE...

"...IT IS *EMPRESS* SONJA NOW."

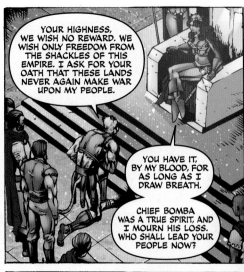

YOUR HIGHNESS, WE WISH NO REWARD. WE WISH ONLY FREEDOM FROM THE SHACKLES OF THIS EMPIRE. I ASK FOR YOUR OATH THAT THESE LANDS NEVER AGAIN MAKE WAR UPON MY PEOPLE.

YOU HAVE IT, BY MY BLOOD, FOR AS LONG AS I DRAW BREATH.

CHIEF BOMBA WAS A TRUE SPIRIT, AND I MOURN HIS LOSS. WHO SHALL LEAD YOUR PEOPLE NOW?

I SHALL HAVE THAT HONOR, YOUR HIGHNESS. I MUST GO NOW AND SEE TO THEM, BUT YOU ARE ALWAYS A WELCOME GUEST IN OUR LANDS, EMPRESS SONJA.

AND YOU AND ALL YOUR PEOPLE SHALL BE WELCOME GUESTS IN EMORA FROM NOW ON, CHIEF SOUTHPAW.

WHERE IS THE ONE THEY CALL *XANDER?*

HERE, HIGHNESS.

WHAT IS TO BE DONE WITH YOU? I SAW YOU MANY TIMES AT ANTONIOUS'S RIGHT HAND, BUT WHEN HE NEEDED YOU MOST, YOU BETRAYED HIM. EXPLAIN YOURSELF.

PRAY HIGHNESS YOU WAIT TO PASS JUDGMENT ON ME, FOR I WAS EVER LOYAL TO SOGORIA--ESPECIALLY WHEN I RODE NEXT TO ANTONIOUS.

WHO ARE YOU?

ALL WILL SOON BE CLEAR.

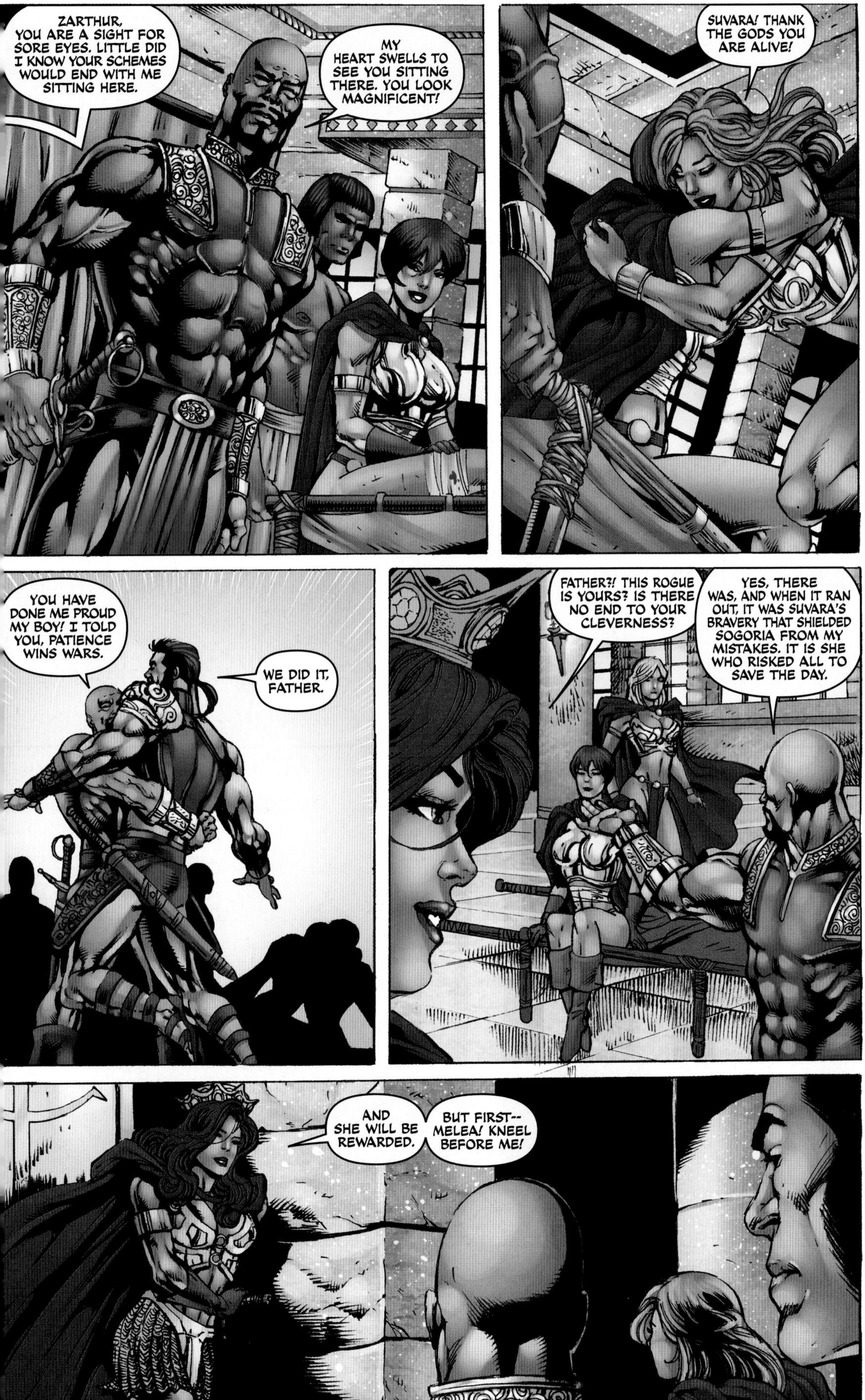
ZARTHUR, YOU ARE A SIGHT FOR SORE EYES. LITTLE DID I KNOW YOUR SCHEMES WOULD END WITH ME SITTING HERE.
MY HEART SWELLS TO SEE YOU SITTING THERE. YOU LOOK MAGNIFICENT!
SUVARA! THANK THE GODS YOU ARE ALIVE!
YOU HAVE DONE ME PROUD MY BOY! I TOLD YOU, PATIENCE WINS WARS.
WE DID IT, FATHER.
FATHER?! THIS ROGUE IS YOURS? IS THERE NO END TO YOUR CLEVERNESS?
YES, THERE WAS, AND WHEN IT RAN OUT, IT WAS SUVARA'S BRAVERY THAT SHIELDED SOGORIA FROM MY MISTAKES. IT IS SHE WHO RISKED ALL TO SAVE THE DAY.
AND SHE WILL BE REWARDED.
BUT FIRST-- MELEA! KNEEL BEFORE ME!

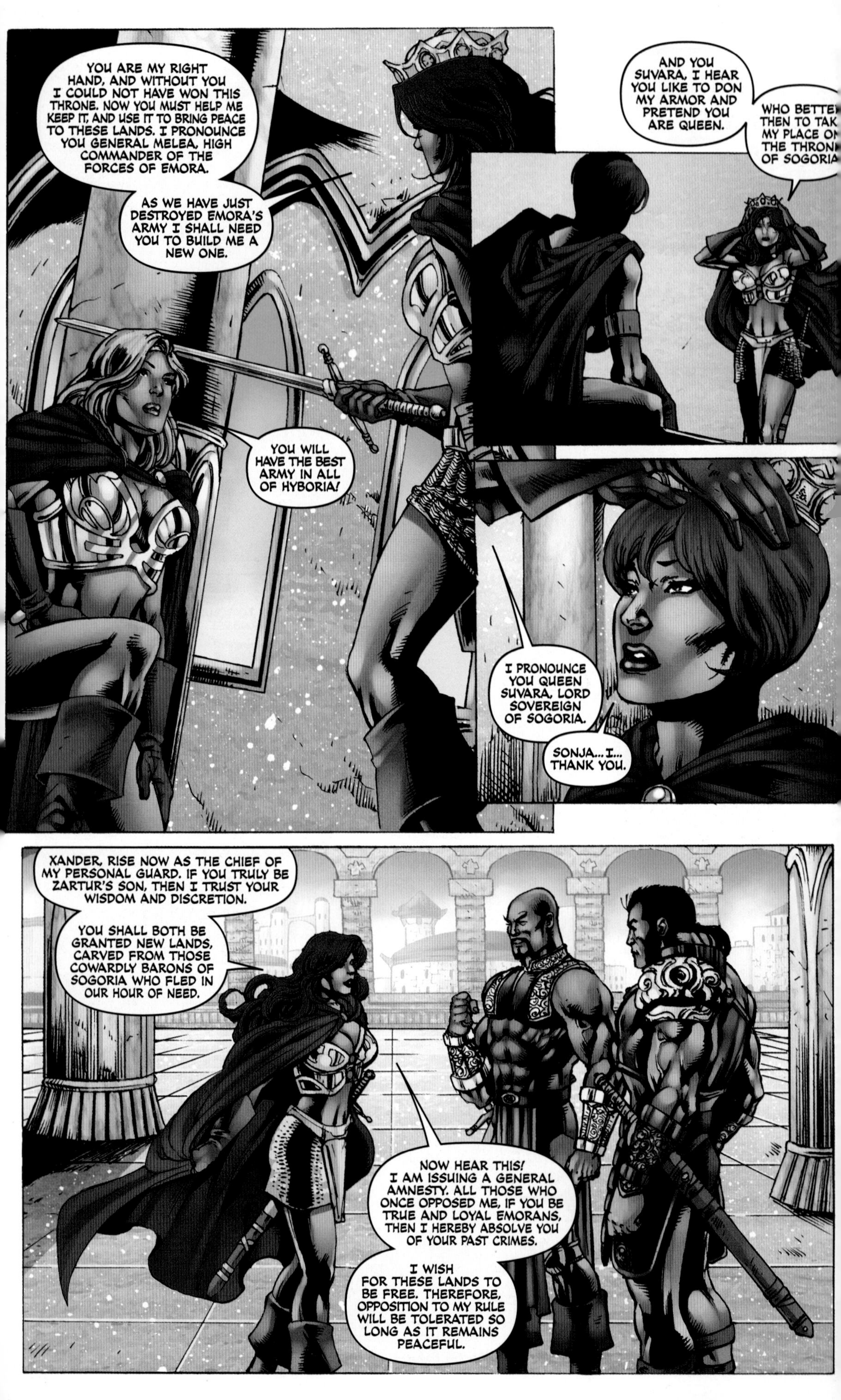
YOU ARE MY RIGHT HAND, AND WITHOUT YOU I COULD NOT HAVE WON THIS THRONE. NOW YOU MUST HELP ME KEEP IT, AND USE IT TO BRING PEACE TO THESE LANDS. I PRONOUNCE YOU GENERAL MELEA, HIGH COMMANDER OF THE FORCES OF EMORA.
AS WE HAVE JUST DESTROYED EMORA'S ARMY I SHALL NEED YOU TO BUILD ME A NEW ONE.
YOU WILL HAVE THE BEST ARMY IN ALL OF HYBORIA!
AND YOU SUVARA, I HEAR YOU LIKE TO DON MY ARMOR AND PRETEND YOU ARE QUEEN.
WHO BETTE THEN TO TAK MY PLACE O THE THRON OF SOGORIA
I PRONOUNCE YOU QUEEN SUVARA, LORD SOVEREIGN OF SOGORIA.
SONJA... I... THANK YOU.
XANDER, RISE NOW AS THE CHIEF OF MY PERSONAL GUARD. IF YOU TRULY BE ZARTUR'S SON, THEN I TRUST YOUR WISDOM AND DISCRETION.
YOU SHALL BOTH BE GRANTED NEW LANDS, CARVED FROM THOSE COWARDLY BARONS OF SOGORIA WHO FLED IN OUR HOUR OF NEED.
NOW HEAR THIS! I AM ISSUING A GENERAL AMNESTY. ALL THOSE WHO ONCE OPPOSED ME, IF YOU BE TRUE AND LOYAL EMORANS, THEN I HEREBY ABSOLVE YOU OF YOUR PAST CRIMES.
I WISH FOR THESE LANDS TO BE FREE. THEREFORE, OPPOSITION TO MY RULE WILL BE TOLERATED SO LONG AS IT REMAINS PEACEFUL.

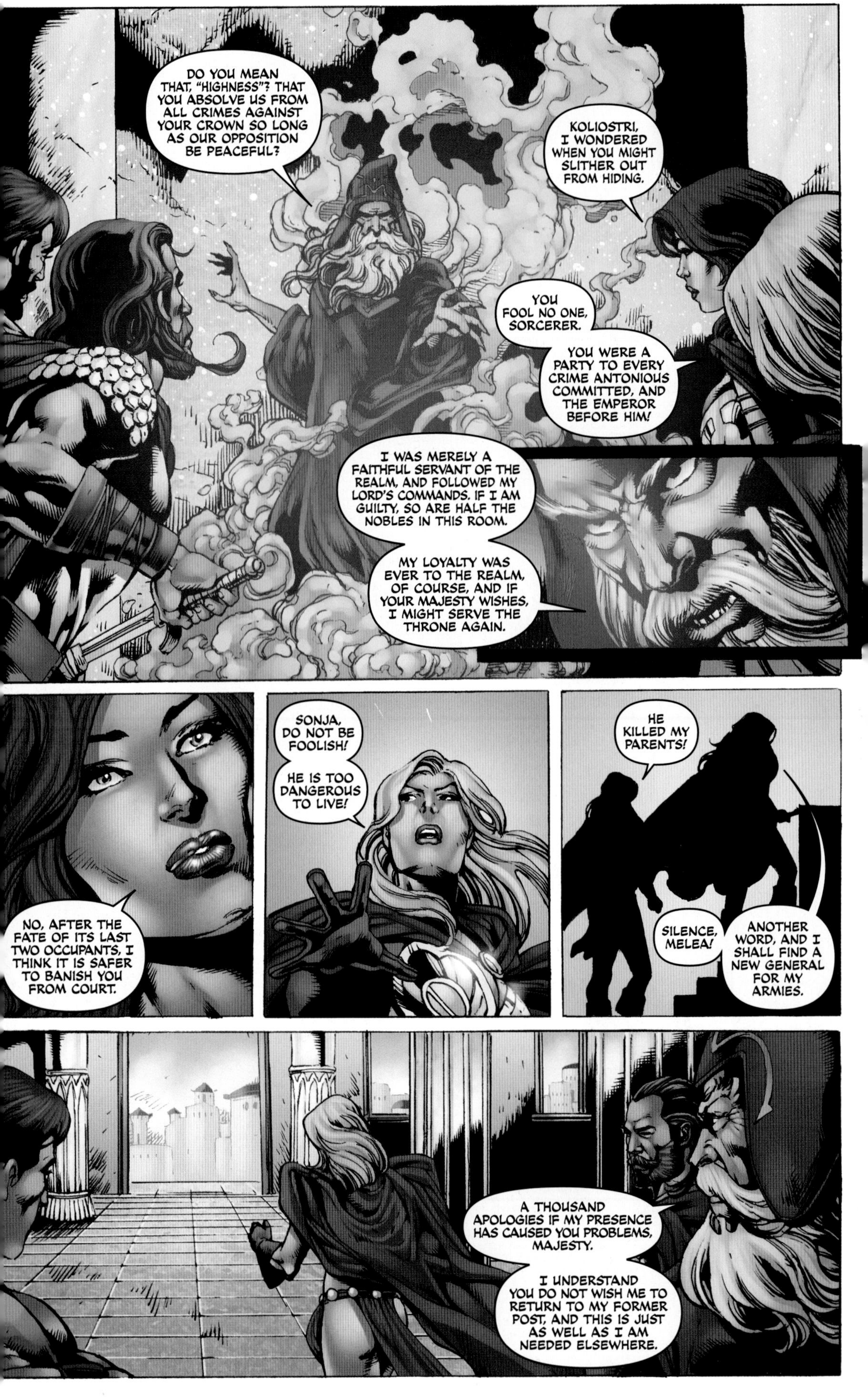
DO YOU MEAN THAT, "HIGHNESS"? THAT YOU ABSOLVE US FROM ALL CRIMES AGAINST YOUR CROWN SO LONG AS OUR OPPOSITION BE PEACEFUL?
KOLIOSTRI, I WONDERED WHEN YOU MIGHT SLITHER OUT FROM HIDING.
YOU FOOL NO ONE, SORCERER.
YOU WERE A PARTY TO EVERY CRIME ANTONIOUS COMMITTED, AND THE EMPEROR BEFORE HIM!
I WAS MERELY A FAITHFUL SERVANT OF THE REALM, AND FOLLOWED MY LORD'S COMMANDS. IF I AM GUILTY, SO ARE HALF THE NOBLES IN THIS ROOM.
MY LOYALTY WAS EVER TO THE REALM, OF COURSE, AND IF YOUR MAJESTY WISHES, I MIGHT SERVE THE THRONE AGAIN.
NO, AFTER THE FATE OF ITS LAST TWO OCCUPANTS, I THINK IT IS SAFER TO BANISH YOU FROM COURT.
SONJA, DO NOT BE FOOLISH!
HE IS TOO DANGEROUS TO LIVE!
HE KILLED MY PARENTS!
SILENCE, MELEA!
ANOTHER WORD, AND I SHALL FIND A NEW GENERAL FOR MY ARMIES.
A THOUSAND APOLOGIES IF MY PRESENCE HAS CAUSED YOU PROBLEMS, MAJESTY.
I UNDERSTAND YOU DO NOT WISH ME TO RETURN TO MY FORMER POST, AND THIS IS JUST AS WELL AS I AM NEEDED ELSEWHERE.

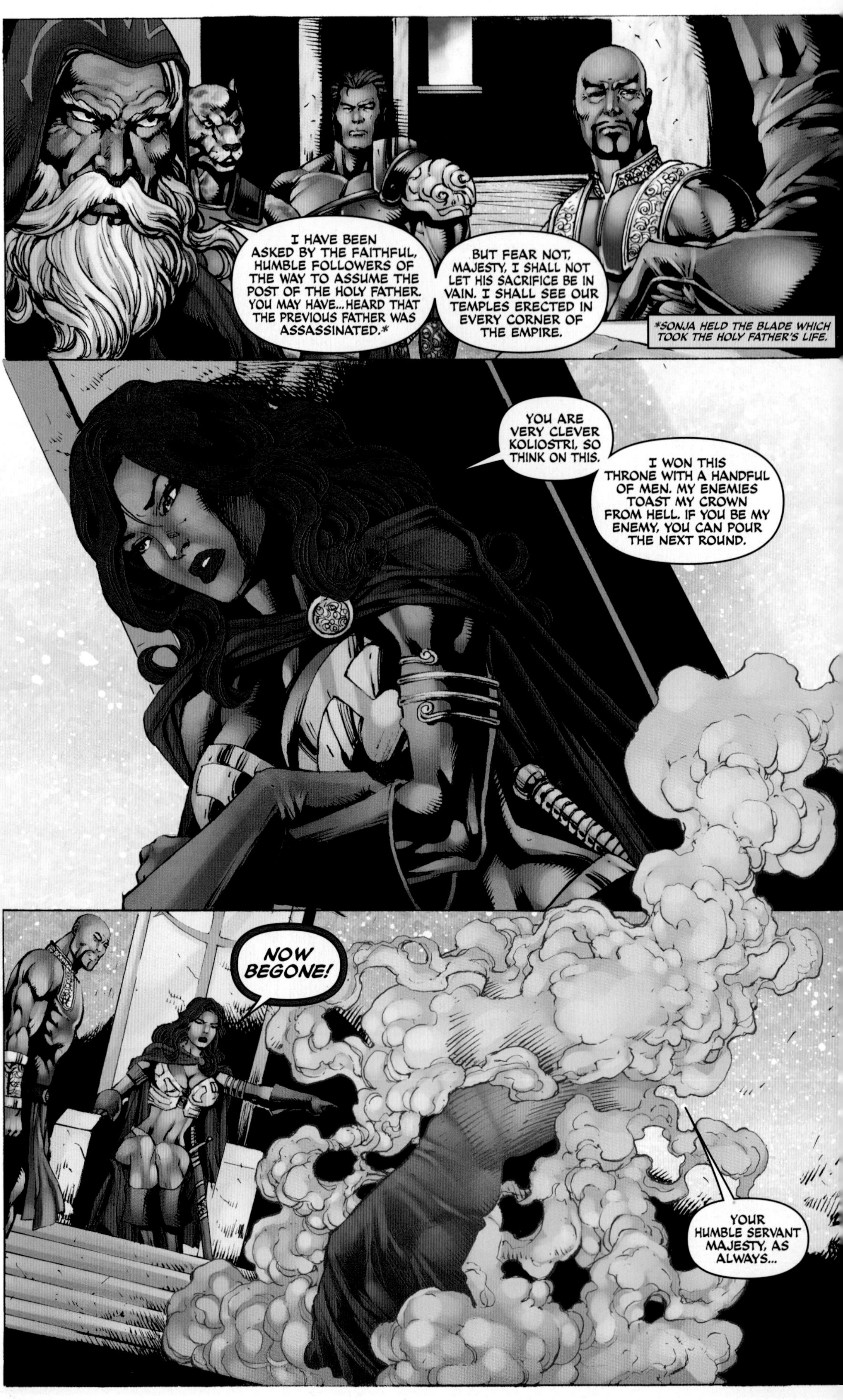
I HAVE BEEN ASKED BY THE FAITHFUL, HUMBLE FOLLOWERS OF THE WAY TO ASSUME THE POST OF THE HOLY FATHER. YOU MAY HAVE...HEARD THAT THE PREVIOUS FATHER WAS ASSASSINATED.*
BUT FEAR NOT, MAJESTY, I SHALL NOT LET HIS SACRIFICE BE IN VAIN. I SHALL SEE OUR TEMPLES ERECTED IN EVERY CORNER OF THE EMPIRE.
*SONJA HELD THE BLADE WHICH TOOK THE HOLY FATHER'S LIFE.
YOU ARE VERY CLEVER KOLIOSTRI, SO THINK ON THIS.
I WON THIS THRONE WITH A HANDFUL OF MEN. MY ENEMIES TOAST MY CROWN FROM HELL. IF YOU BE MY ENEMY, YOU CAN POUR THE NEXT ROUND.
NOW BEGONE!
YOUR HUMBLE SERVANT MAJESTY, AS ALWAYS...

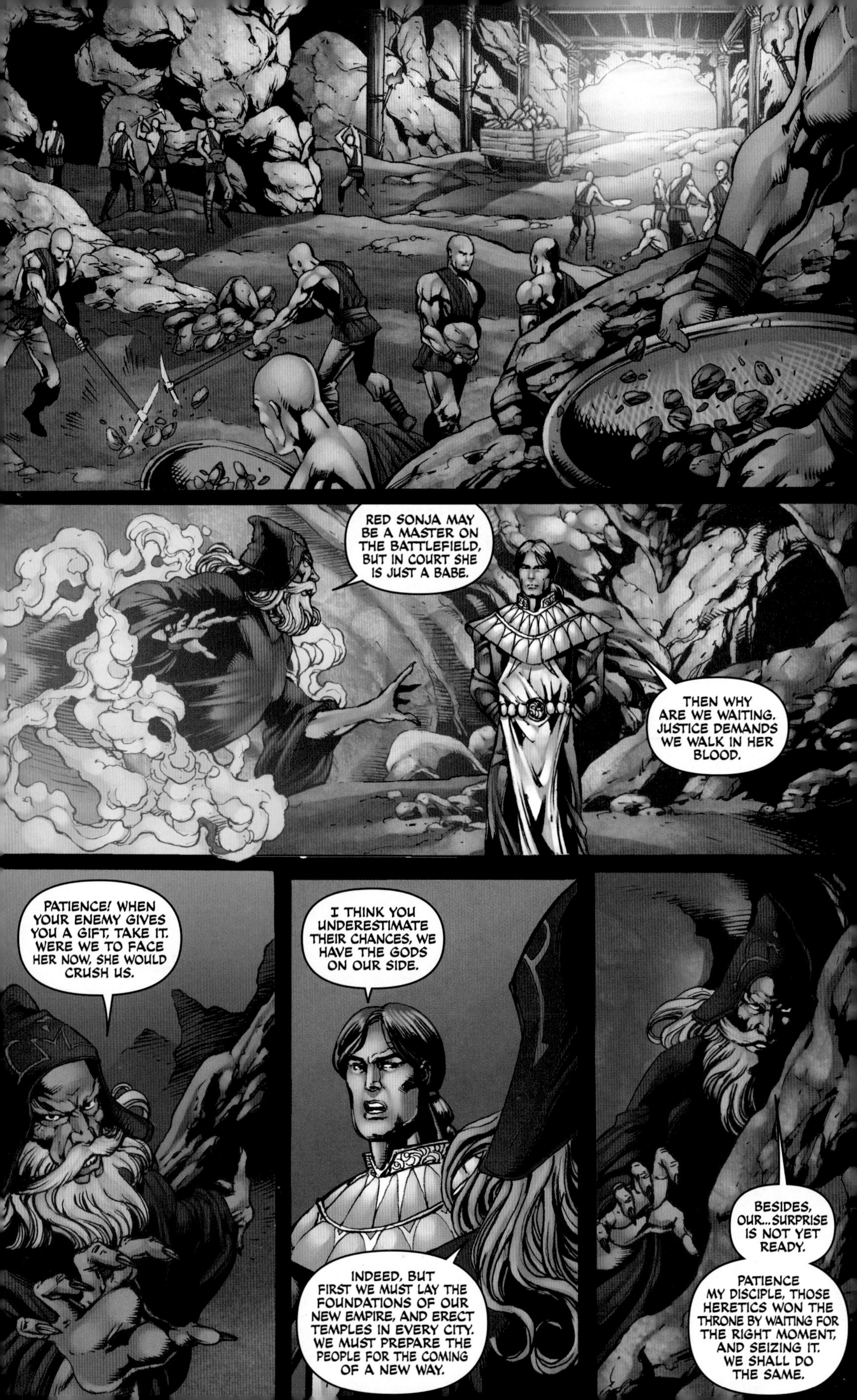
RED SONJA MAY BE A MASTER ON THE BATTLEFIELD, BUT IN COURT SHE IS JUST A BABE.
THEN WHY ARE WE WAITING. JUSTICE DEMANDS WE WALK IN HER BLOOD.
PATIENCE! WHEN YOUR ENEMY GIVES YOU A GIFT, TAKE IT. WERE WE TO FACE HER NOW, SHE WOULD CRUSH US.
I THINK YOU UNDERESTIMATE THEIR CHANCES, WE HAVE THE GODS ON OUR SIDE.
INDEED, BUT FIRST WE MUST LAY THE FOUNDATIONS OF OUR NEW EMPIRE, AND ERECT TEMPLES IN EVERY CITY. WE MUST PREPARE THE PEOPLE FOR THE COMING OF A NEW WAY.
BESIDES, OUR...SURPRISE IS NOT YET READY.
PATIENCE MY DISCIPLE, THOSE HERETICS WON THE THRONE BY WAITING FOR THE RIGHT MOMENT, AND SEIZING IT. WE SHALL DO THE SAME.

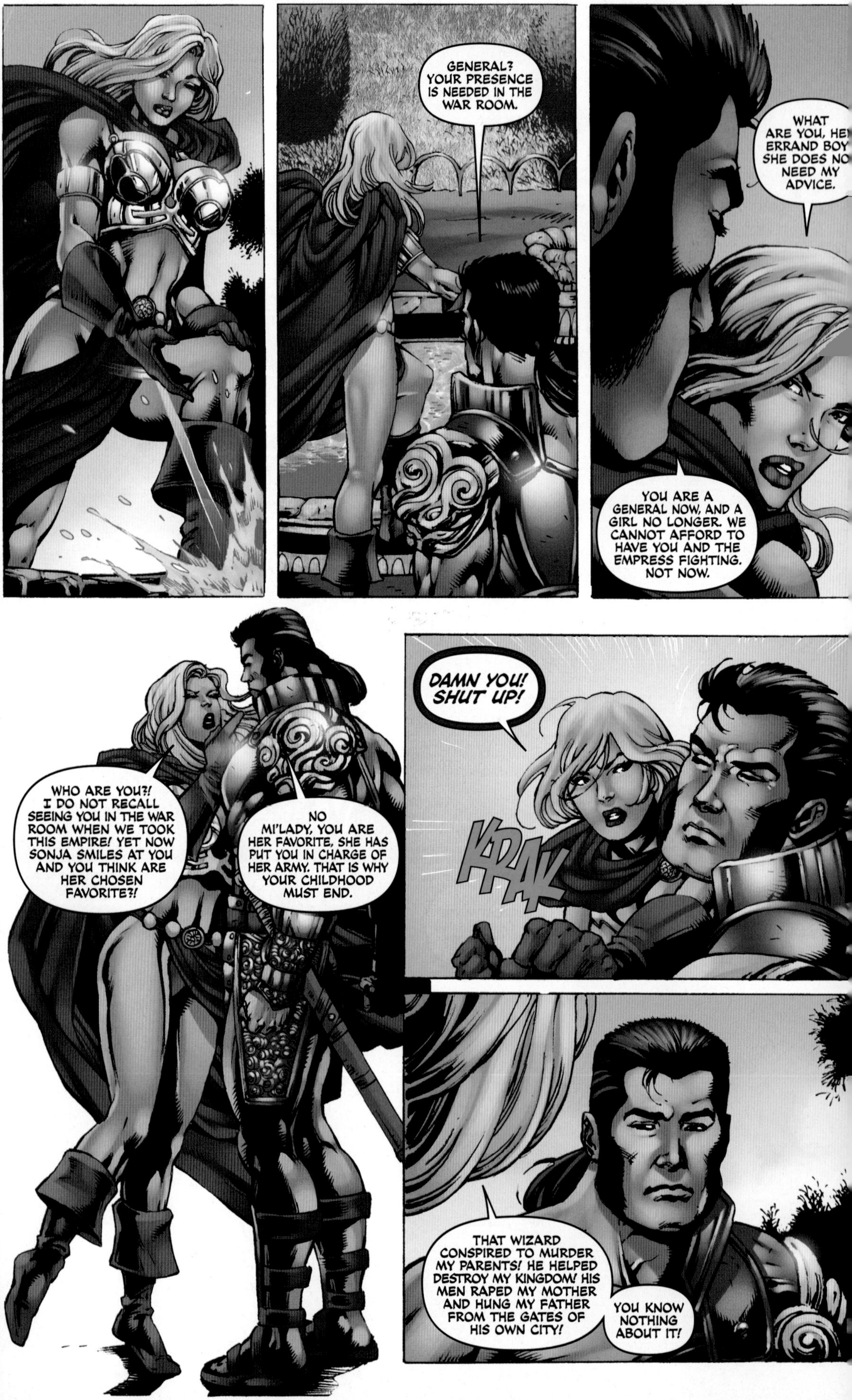
GENERAL? YOUR PRESENCE IS NEEDED IN THE WAR ROOM.
WHAT ARE YOU, HE ERRAND BOY SHE DOES NO NEED MY ADVICE.
YOU ARE A GENERAL NOW, AND A GIRL NO LONGER. WE CANNOT AFFORD TO HAVE YOU AND THE EMPRESS FIGHTING. NOT NOW.
WHO ARE YOU?! I DO NOT RECALL SEEING YOU IN THE WAR ROOM WHEN WE TOOK THIS EMPIRE! YET NOW SONJA SMILES AT YOU AND YOU THINK ARE HER CHOSEN FAVORITE?!
NO MI'LADY, YOU ARE HER FAVORITE, SHE HAS PUT YOU IN CHARGE OF HER ARMY. THAT IS WHY YOUR CHILDHOOD MUST END.
DAMN YOU! SHUT UP!
KRAK
THAT WIZARD CONSPIRED TO MURDER MY PARENTS! HE HELPED DESTROY MY KINGDOM! HIS MEN RAPED MY MOTHER AND HUNG MY FATHER FROM THE GATES OF HIS OWN CITY!
YOU KNOW NOTHING ABOUT IT!

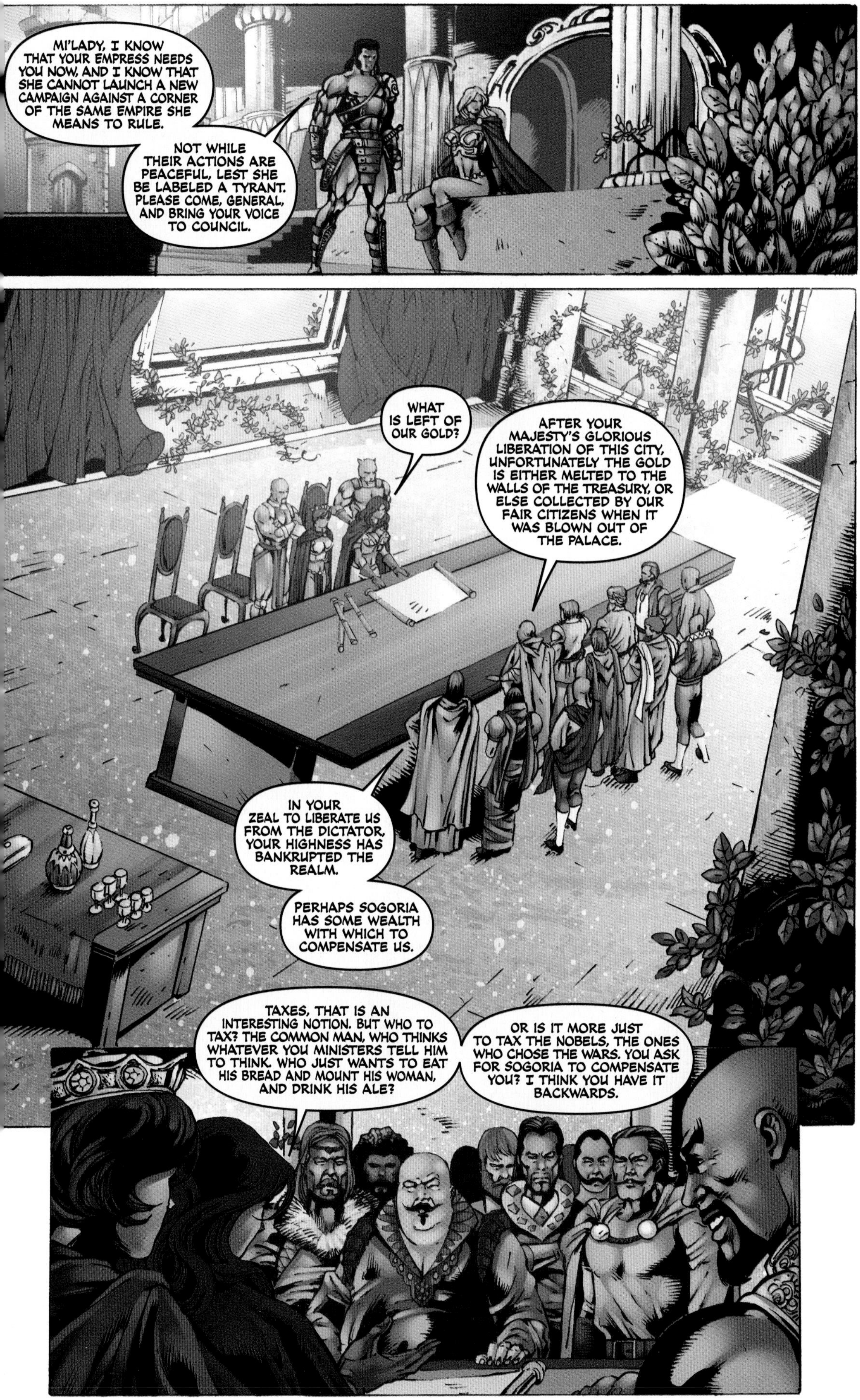
MI'LADY, I KNOW THAT YOUR EMPRESS NEEDS YOU NOW, AND I KNOW THAT SHE CANNOT LAUNCH A NEW CAMPAIGN AGAINST A CORNER OF THE SAME EMPIRE SHE MEANS TO RULE.
NOT WHILE THEIR ACTIONS ARE PEACEFUL, LEST SHE BE LABELED A TYRANT. PLEASE COME, GENERAL, AND BRING YOUR VOICE TO COUNCIL.
WHAT IS LEFT OF OUR GOLD?
AFTER YOUR MAJESTY'S GLORIOUS LIBERATION OF THIS CITY, UNFORTUNATELY THE GOLD IS EITHER MELTED TO THE WALLS OF THE TREASURY, OR ELSE COLLECTED BY OUR FAIR CITIZENS WHEN IT WAS BLOWN OUT OF THE PALACE.
IN YOUR ZEAL TO LIBERATE US FROM THE DICTATOR, YOUR HIGHNESS HAS BANKRUPTED THE REALM.
PERHAPS SOGORIA HAS SOME WEALTH WITH WHICH TO COMPENSATE US.
TAXES, THAT IS AN INTERESTING NOTION. BUT WHO TO TAX? THE COMMON MAN, WHO THINKS WHATEVER YOU MINISTERS TELL HIM TO THINK. WHO JUST WANTS TO EAT HIS BREAD AND MOUNT HIS WOMAN, AND DRINK HIS ALE?
OR IS IT MORE JUST TO TAX THE NOBELS, THE ONES WHO CHOSE THE WARS. YOU ASK FOR SOGORIA TO COMPENSATE YOU? I THINK YOU HAVE IT BACKWARDS.

FORGIVE ME, I THOUGHT YOU MEANT TO RULE EMORA, NOT SOGORIA.

FOR THAT MATTER, WHAT OF SOGORIA? WILL IT JOIN THE EMORAN EMPIRE? IF SOGORIA DOES NOT FOLLOW YOU, WHY SHOULD ANYONE?

WE DO FOLLOW HER, WE EVEN FOLLOWED HER HERE. NOW WE SHALL SEE JUSTICE, AND YOU SHALL PAY REPARATIONS TO SOGORIA, ELSE I SHALL PERSONALLY HAUL YOU TO ISSINDI TO FACE THE VICTIMS OF YOUR WARMONGERING!

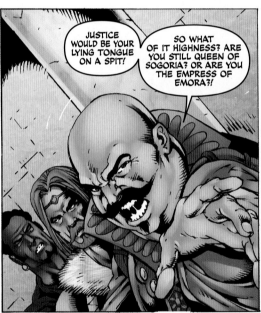

JUSTICE WOULD BE YOUR LYING TONGUE ON A SPIT!

SO WHAT OF IT HIGHNESS? ARE YOU STILL QUEEN OF SOGORIA? OR ARE YOU THE EMPRESS OF EMORA?!

I AM RED SONJA!

OH WHAT NOW, YOU THINK TO MURDER ME AS WELL? A LOYAL SUBJECT OF EMORA? THE BARON OF TRIVOL? I OWN THIS CITY! TOUCH ME, AND IT SHALL RISE UP AGAINST YOU.

I SAID, YOU SHALL LIVE SO LONG AS YOUR OPPOSITION BE PEACEFUL.

BUT SPEAK TO ME LIKE THAT AGAIN, AND I SHALL STRIP YOU NAKED IN THE STREETS AND BEAT YOU TO WITHIN AN INCH OF DEATH.

I WILL PAY NO TAXES TO YOU, WENCH, I DARE YOU TO COLLECT THEM.

MY PLEASURE.

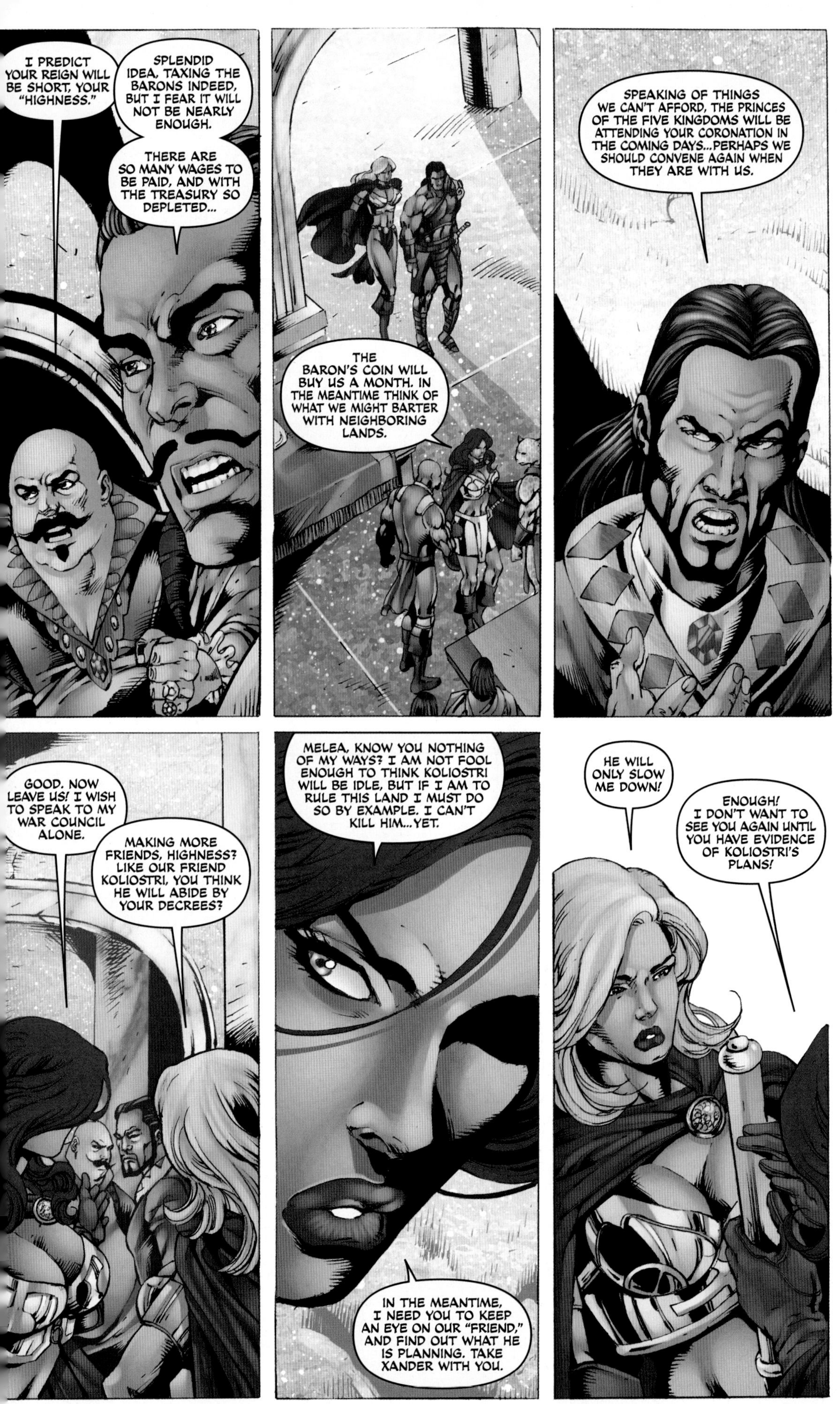
I PREDICT YOUR REIGN WILL BE SHORT, YOUR "HIGHNESS."
SPLENDID IDEA, TAXING THE BARONS INDEED, BUT I FEAR IT WILL NOT BE NEARLY ENOUGH.
THERE ARE SO MANY WAGES TO BE PAID, AND WITH THE TREASURY SO DEPLETED...
THE BARON'S COIN WILL BUY US A MONTH. IN THE MEANTIME THINK OF WHAT WE MIGHT BARTER WITH NEIGHBORING LANDS.
SPEAKING OF THINGS WE CAN'T AFFORD, THE PRINCES OF THE FIVE KINGDOMS WILL BE ATTENDING YOUR CORONATION IN THE COMING DAYS...PERHAPS WE SHOULD CONVENE AGAIN WHEN THEY ARE WITH US.
GOOD. NOW LEAVE US! I WISH TO SPEAK TO MY WAR COUNCIL ALONE.
MAKING MORE FRIENDS, HIGHNESS? LIKE OUR FRIEND KOLIOSTRI, YOU THINK HE WILL ABIDE BY YOUR DECREES?
MELEA, KNOW YOU NOTHING OF MY WAYS? I AM NOT FOOL ENOUGH TO THINK KOLIOSTRI WILL BE IDLE, BUT IF I AM TO RULE THIS LAND I MUST DO SO BY EXAMPLE. I CAN'T KILL HIM...YET.
IN THE MEANTIME, I NEED YOU TO KEEP AN EYE ON OUR "FRIEND," AND FIND OUT WHAT HE IS PLANNING. TAKE XANDER WITH YOU.
HE WILL ONLY SLOW ME DOWN!
ENOUGH! I DON'T WANT TO SEE YOU AGAIN UNTIL YOU HAVE EVIDENCE OF KOLIOSTRI'S PLANS!

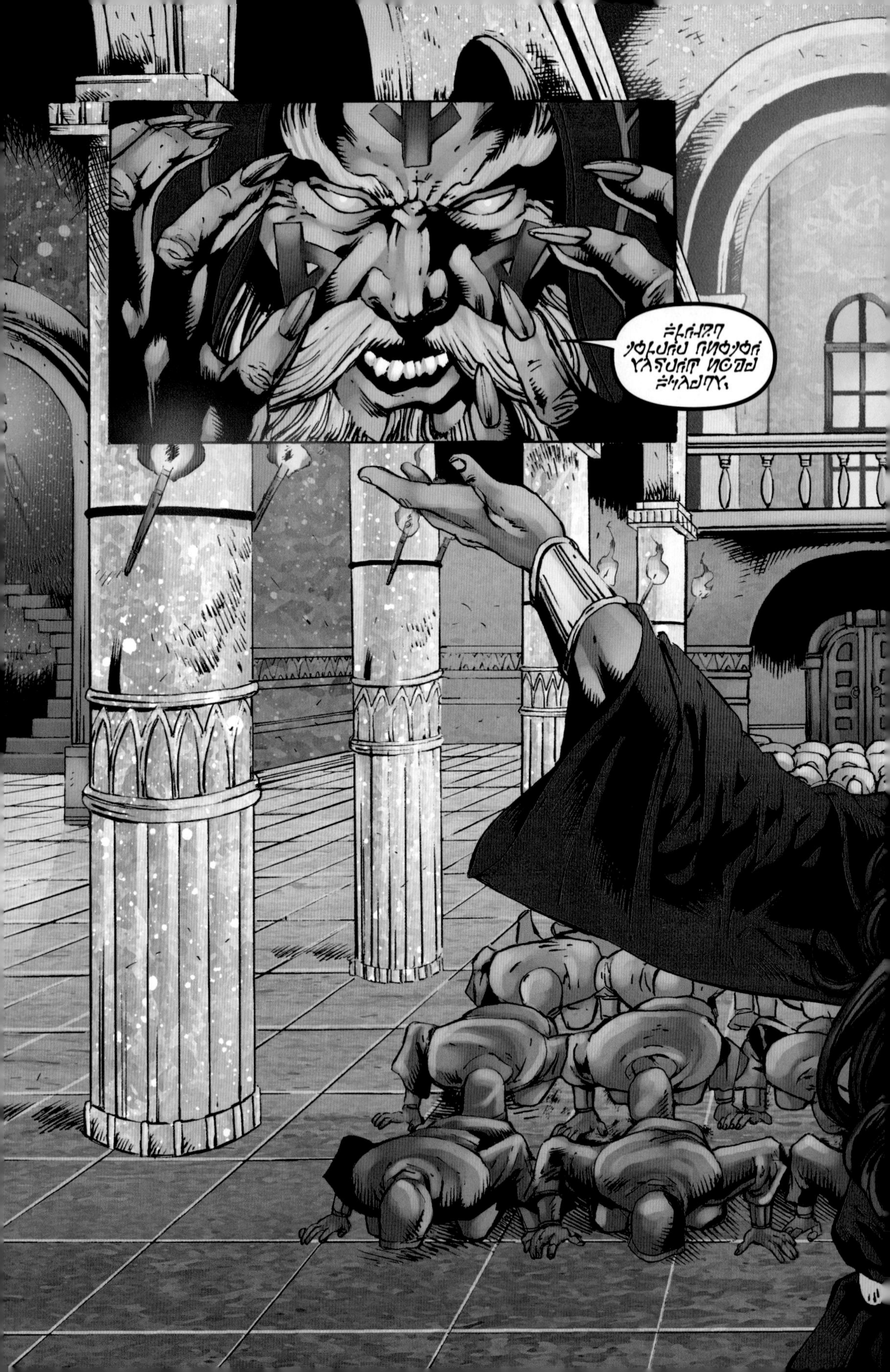

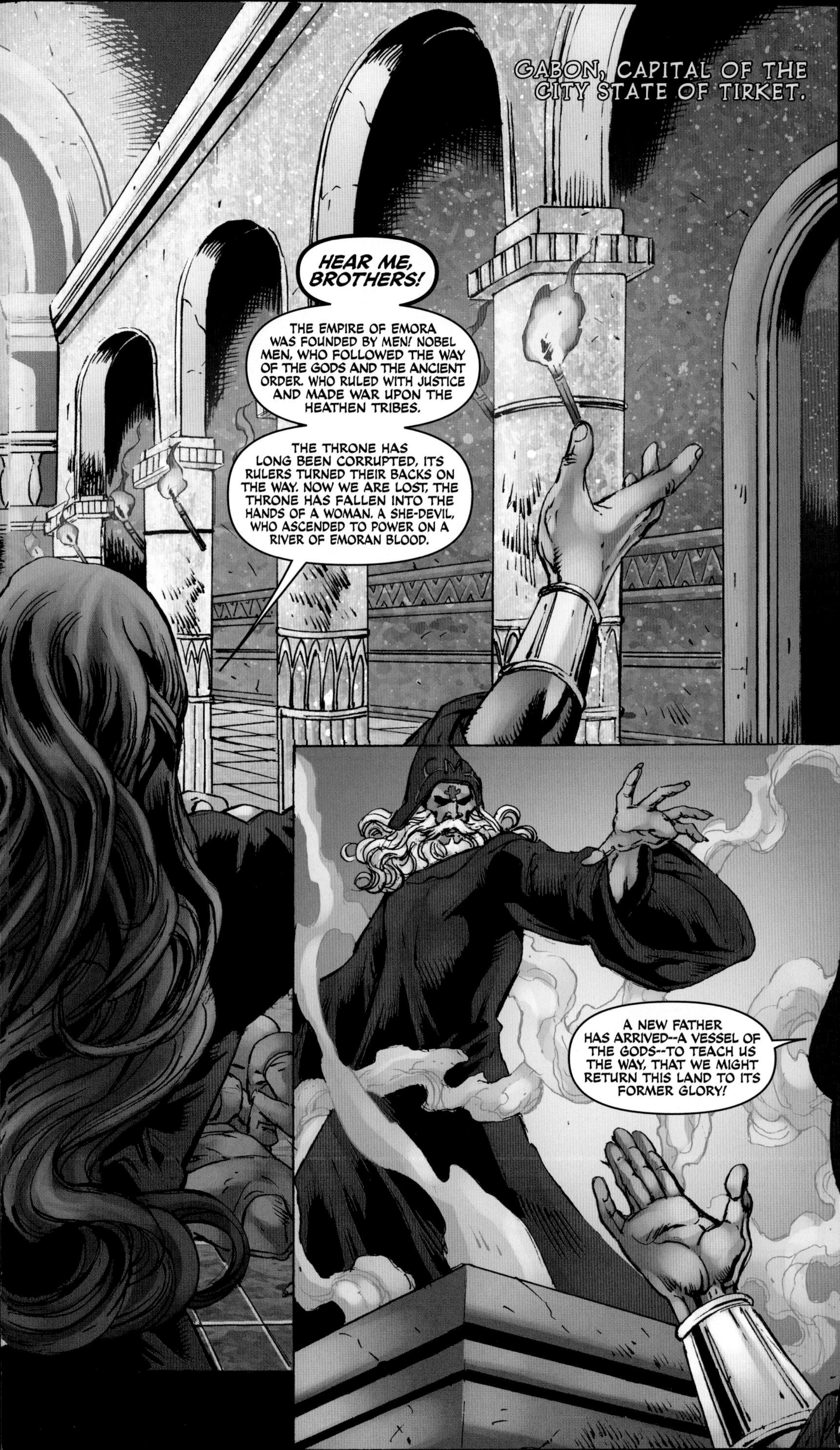
GABON, CAPITAL OF THE CITY STATE OF TIRKET.
HEAR ME, BROTHERS!
THE EMPIRE OF EMORA WAS FOUNDED BY MEN! NOBEL MEN, WHO FOLLOWED THE WAY OF THE GODS AND THE ANCIENT ORDER. WHO RULED WITH JUSTICE AND MADE WAR UPON THE HEATHEN TRIBES.
THE THRONE HAS LONG BEEN CORRUPTED, ITS RULERS TURNED THEIR BACKS ON THE WAY. NOW WE ARE LOST, THE THRONE HAS FALLEN INTO THE HANDS OF A WOMAN. A SHE-DEVIL, WHO ASCENDED TO POWER ON A RIVER OF EMORAN BLOOD.
A NEW FATHER HAS ARRIVED--A VESSEL OF THE GODS--TO TEACH US THE WAY, THAT WE MIGHT RETURN THIS LAND TO ITS FORMER GLORY!

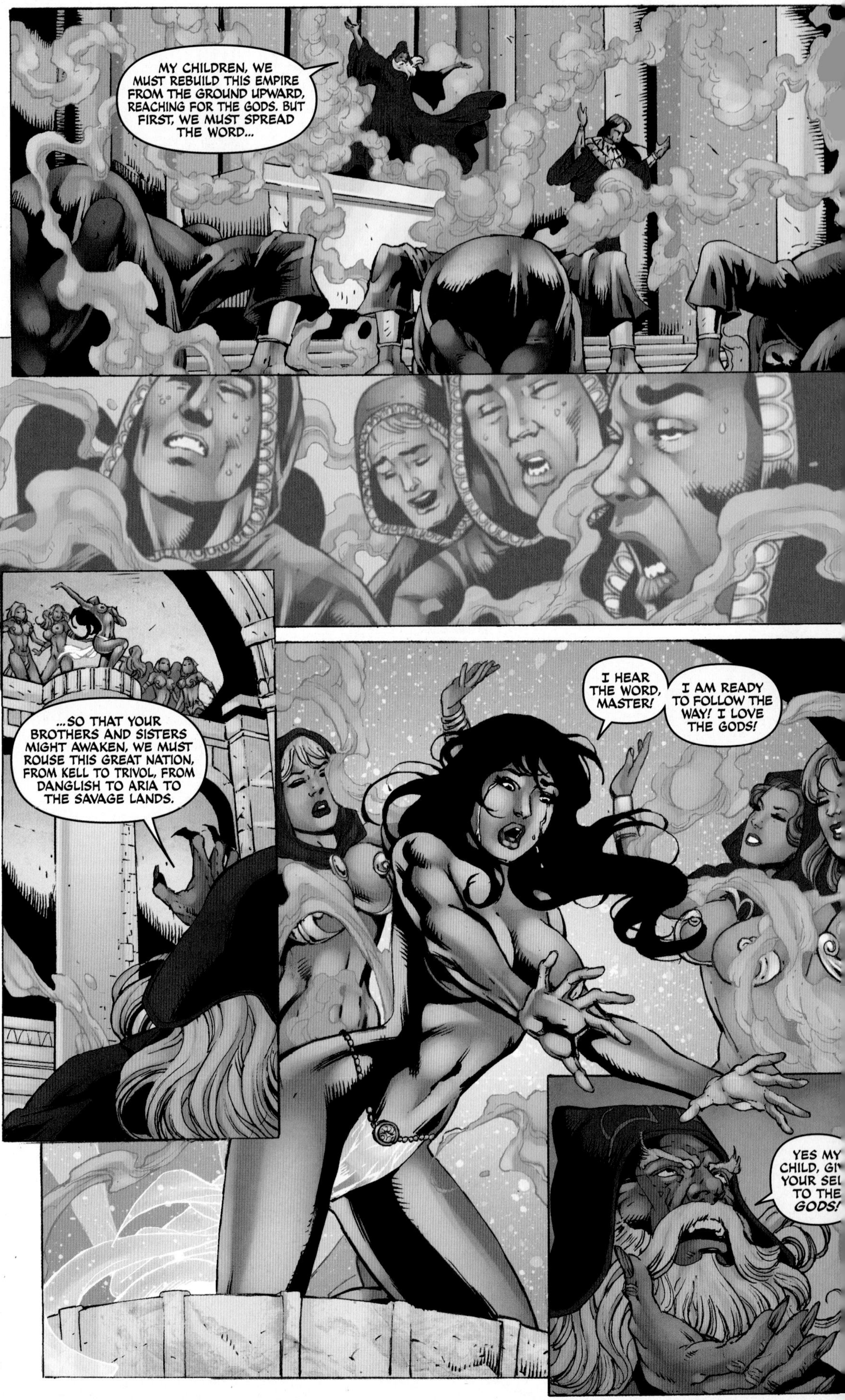
MY CHILDREN, WE MUST REBUILD THIS EMPIRE FROM THE GROUND UPWARD, REACHING FOR THE GODS. BUT FIRST, WE MUST SPREAD THE WORD...
...SO THAT YOUR BROTHERS AND SISTERS MIGHT AWAKEN, WE MUST ROUSE THIS GREAT NATION, FROM KELL TO TRIVOL, FROM DANGLISH TO ARIA TO THE SAVAGE LANDS.
I HEAR THE WORD, MASTER!
I AM READY TO FOLLOW THE WAY! I LOVE THE GODS!
YES MY CHILD, GI YOUR SE TO THE GODS!

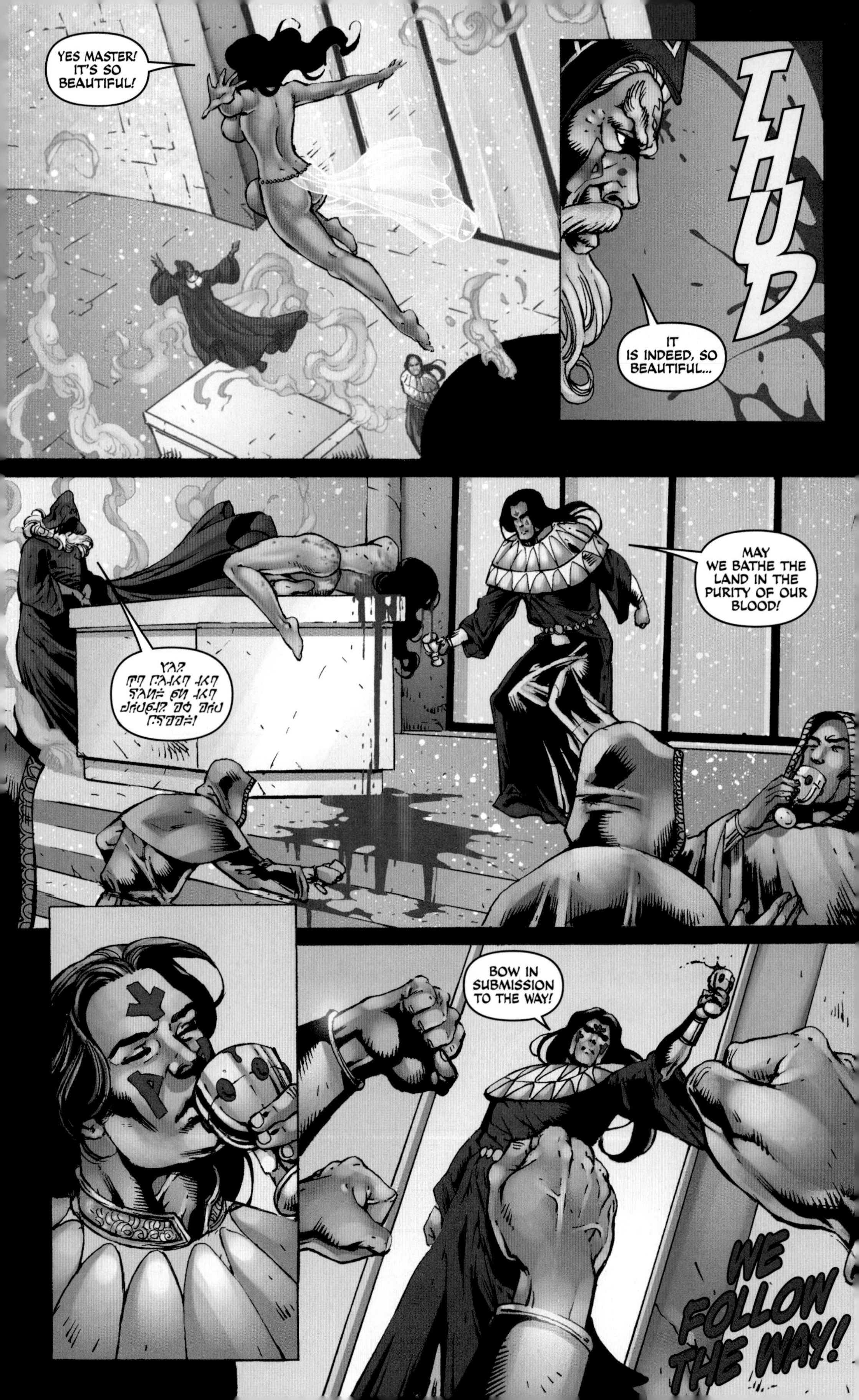
YES MASTER! IT'S SO BEAUTIFUL!
THUD
IT IS INDEED, SO BEAUTIFUL...
MAY WE BATHE THE LAND IN THE PURITY OF OUR BLOOD!
BOW IN SUBMISSION TO THE WAY!
WE FOLLOW THE WAY!

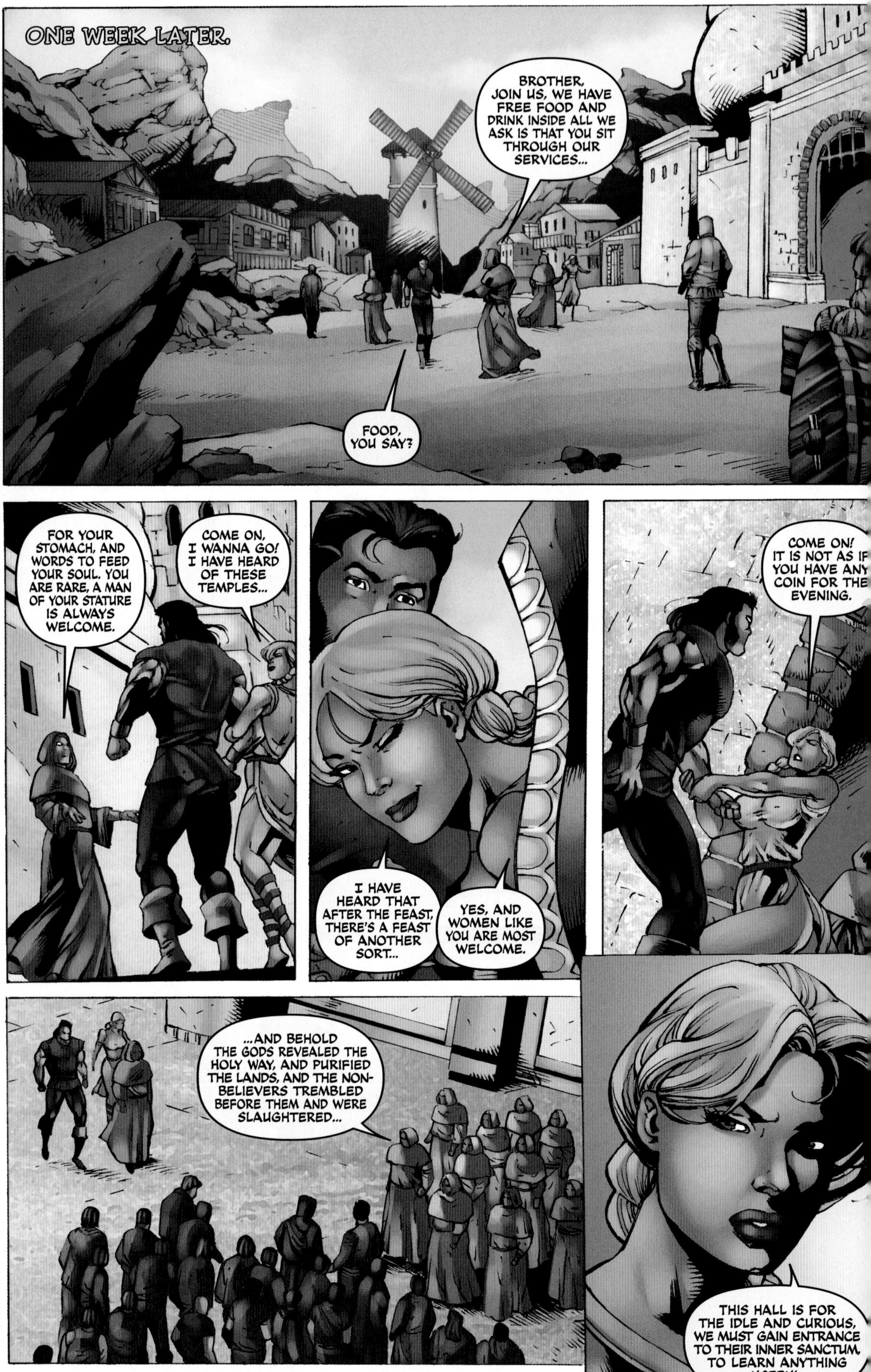
ONE WEEK LATER.
BROTHER, JOIN US, WE HAVE FREE FOOD AND DRINK INSIDE ALL WE ASK IS THAT YOU SIT THROUGH OUR SERVICES...
FOOD, YOU SAY?
FOR YOUR STOMACH, AND WORDS TO FEED YOUR SOUL. YOU ARE RARE, A MAN OF YOUR STATURE IS ALWAYS WELCOME.
COME ON, I WANNA GO! I HAVE HEARD OF THESE TEMPLES...
I HAVE HEARD THAT AFTER THE FEAST, THERE'S A FEAST OF ANOTHER SORT...
YES, AND WOMEN LIKE YOU ARE MOST WELCOME.
COME ON! IT IS NOT AS IF YOU HAVE ANY COIN FOR THE EVENING.
...AND BEHOLD THE GODS REVEALED THE HOLY WAY, AND PURIFIED THE LANDS, AND THE NON-BELIEVERS TREMBLED BEFORE THEM AND WERE SLAUGHTERED...
THIS HALL IS FOR THE IDLE AND CURIOUS, WE MUST GAIN ENTRANCE TO THEIR INNER SANCTUM, TO LEARN ANYTHING USEFUL.

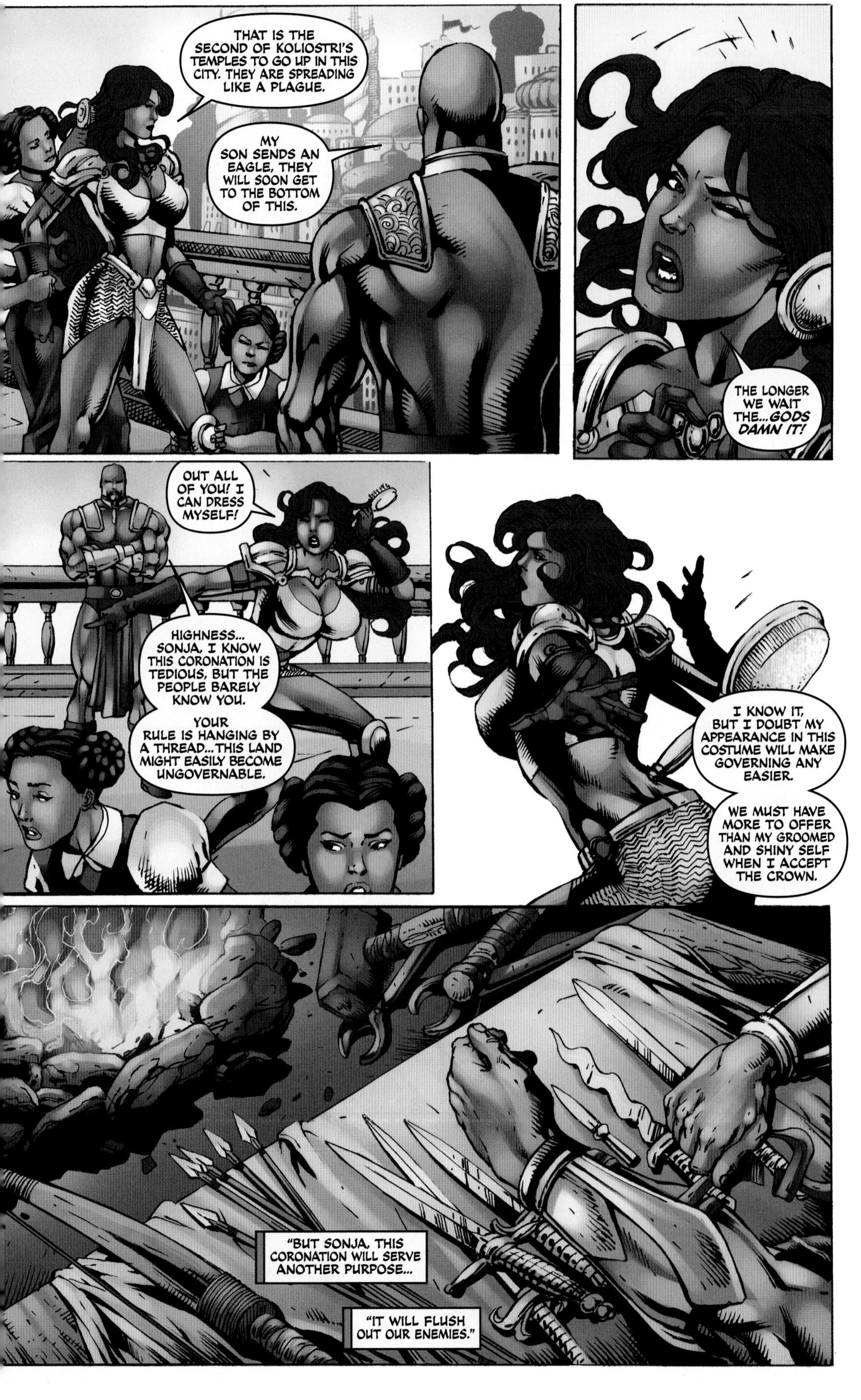
THAT IS THE SECOND OF KOLIOSTRI'S TEMPLES TO GO UP IN THIS CITY. THEY ARE SPREADING LIKE A PLAGUE.
MY SON SENDS AN EAGLE, THEY WILL SOON GET TO THE BOTTOM OF THIS.
THE LONGER WE WAIT THE...*GODS DAMN IT!*
OUT ALL OF YOU! I CAN DRESS MYSELF!
HIGHNESS... SONJA, I KNOW THIS CORONATION IS TEDIOUS, BUT THE PEOPLE BARELY KNOW YOU.
YOUR RULE IS HANGING BY A THREAD...THIS LAND MIGHT EASILY BECOME UNGOVERNABLE.
I KNOW IT, BUT I DOUBT MY APPEARANCE IN THIS COSTUME WILL MAKE GOVERNING ANY EASIER.
WE MUST HAVE MORE TO OFFER THAN MY GROOMED AND SHINY SELF WHEN I ACCEPT THE CROWN.
"BUT SONJA, THIS CORONATION WILL SERVE ANOTHER PURPOSE...
"IT WILL FLUSH OUT OUR ENEMIES."

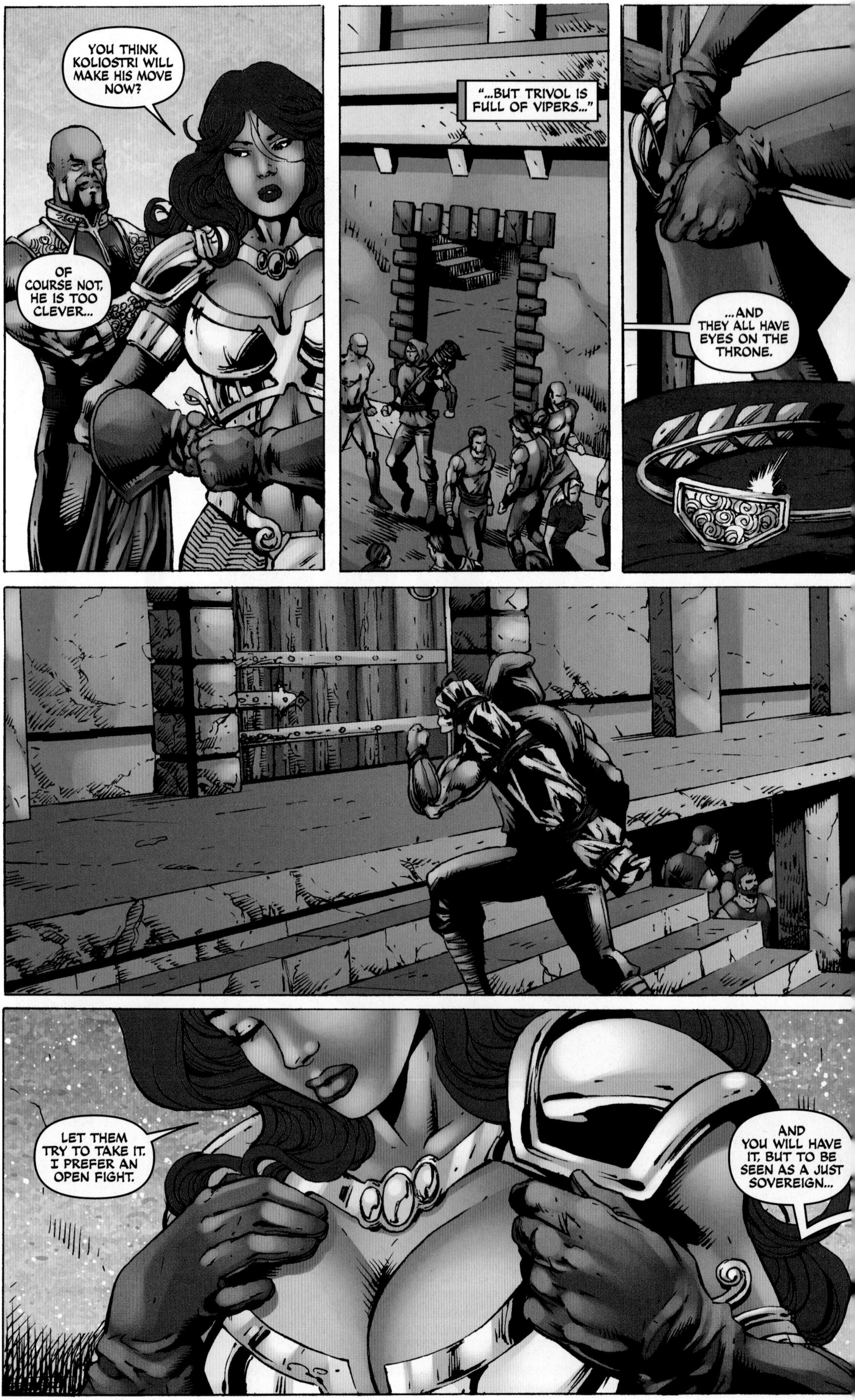
YOU THINK KOLIOSTRI WILL MAKE HIS MOVE NOW?
OF COURSE NOT, HE IS TOO CLEVER...
"...BUT TRIVOL IS FULL OF VIPERS..."
...AND THEY ALL HAVE EYES ON THE THRONE.
LET THEM TRY TO TAKE IT. I PREFER AN OPEN FIGHT.
AND YOU WILL HAVE IT, BUT TO BE SEEN AS A JUST SOVEREIGN...

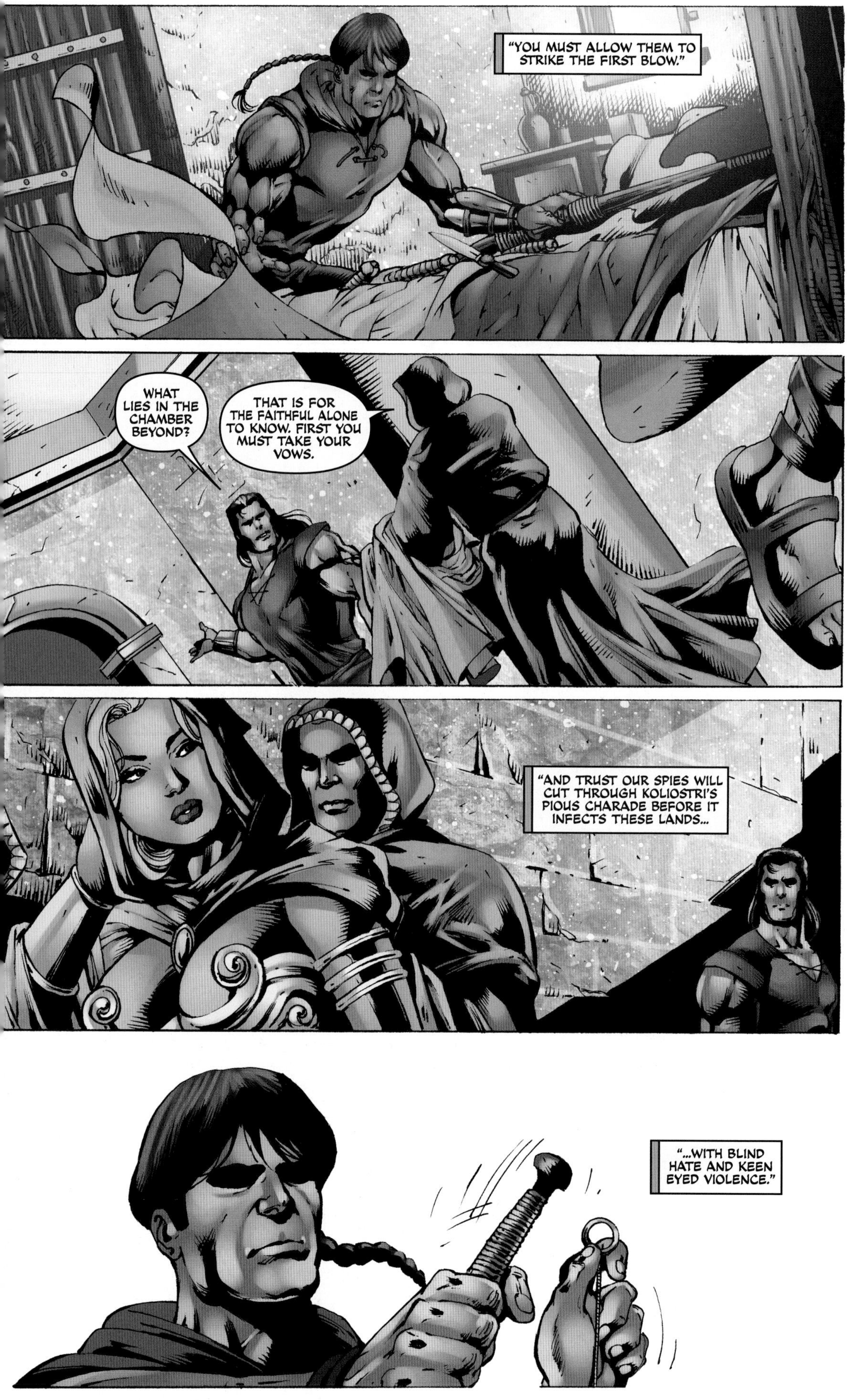
"YOU MUST ALLOW THEM TO STRIKE THE FIRST BLOW."
WHAT LIES IN THE CHAMBER BEYOND?
THAT IS FOR THE FAITHFUL ALONE TO KNOW. FIRST YOU MUST TAKE YOUR VOWS.
"AND TRUST OUR SPIES WILL CUT THROUGH KOLIOSTRI'S PIOUS CHARADE BEFORE IT INFECTS THESE LANDS...
"...WITH BLIND HATE AND KEEN EYED VIOLENCE."

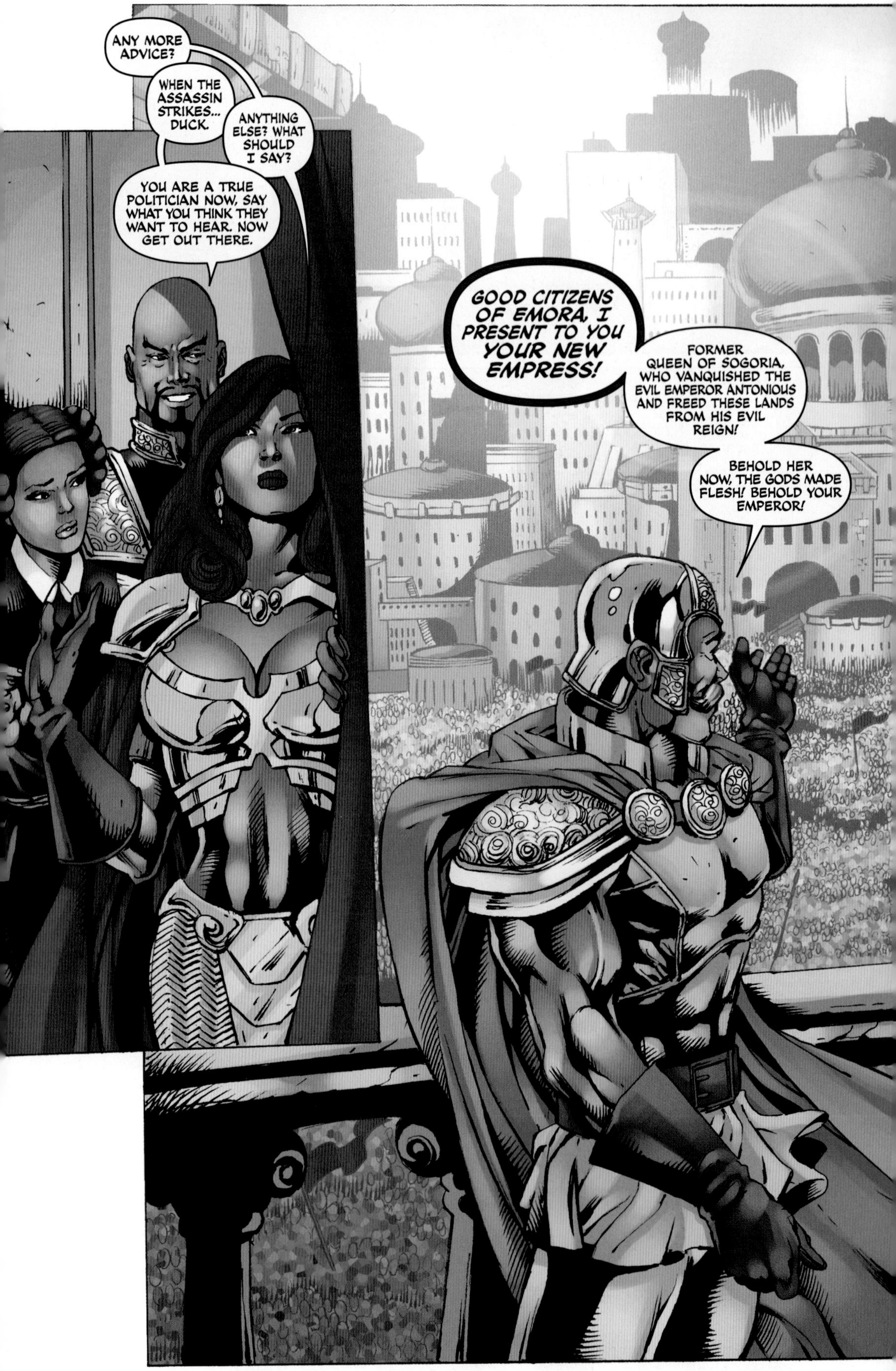
ANY MORE ADVICE?
WHEN THE ASSASSIN STRIKES... DUCK.
ANYTHING ELSE? WHAT SHOULD I SAY?
YOU ARE A TRUE POLITICIAN NOW, SAY WHAT YOU THINK THEY WANT TO HEAR. NOW GET OUT THERE.
GOOD CITIZENS OF EMORA, I PRESENT TO YOU YOUR NEW EMPRESS!
FORMER QUEEN OF SOGORIA, WHO VANQUISHED THE EVIL EMPEROR ANTONIOUS AND FREED THESE LANDS FROM HIS EVIL REIGN!
BEHOLD HER NOW, THE GODS MADE FLESH! BEHOLD YOUR EMPEROR!

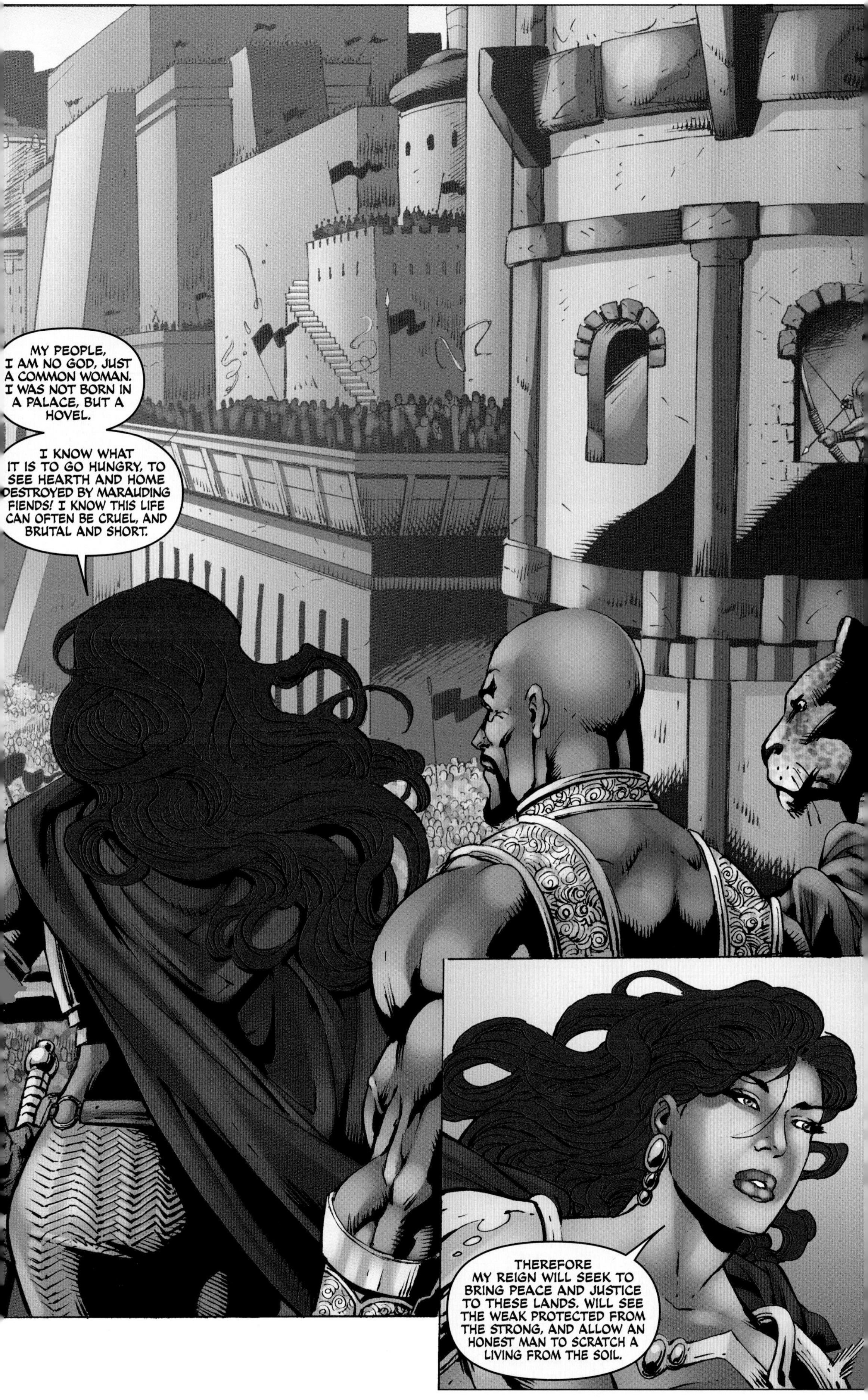
MY PEOPLE, I AM NO GOD, JUST A COMMON WOMAN. I WAS NOT BORN IN A PALACE, BUT A HOVEL.
I KNOW WHAT IT IS TO GO HUNGRY, TO SEE HEARTH AND HOME DESTROYED BY MARAUDING FIENDS! I KNOW THIS LIFE CAN OFTEN BE CRUEL, AND BRUTAL AND SHORT.
THEREFORE MY REIGN WILL SEEK TO BRING PEACE AND JUSTICE TO THESE LANDS. WILL SEE THE WEAK PROTECTED FROM THE STRONG, AND ALLOW AN HONEST MAN TO SCRATCH A LIVING FROM THE SOIL.

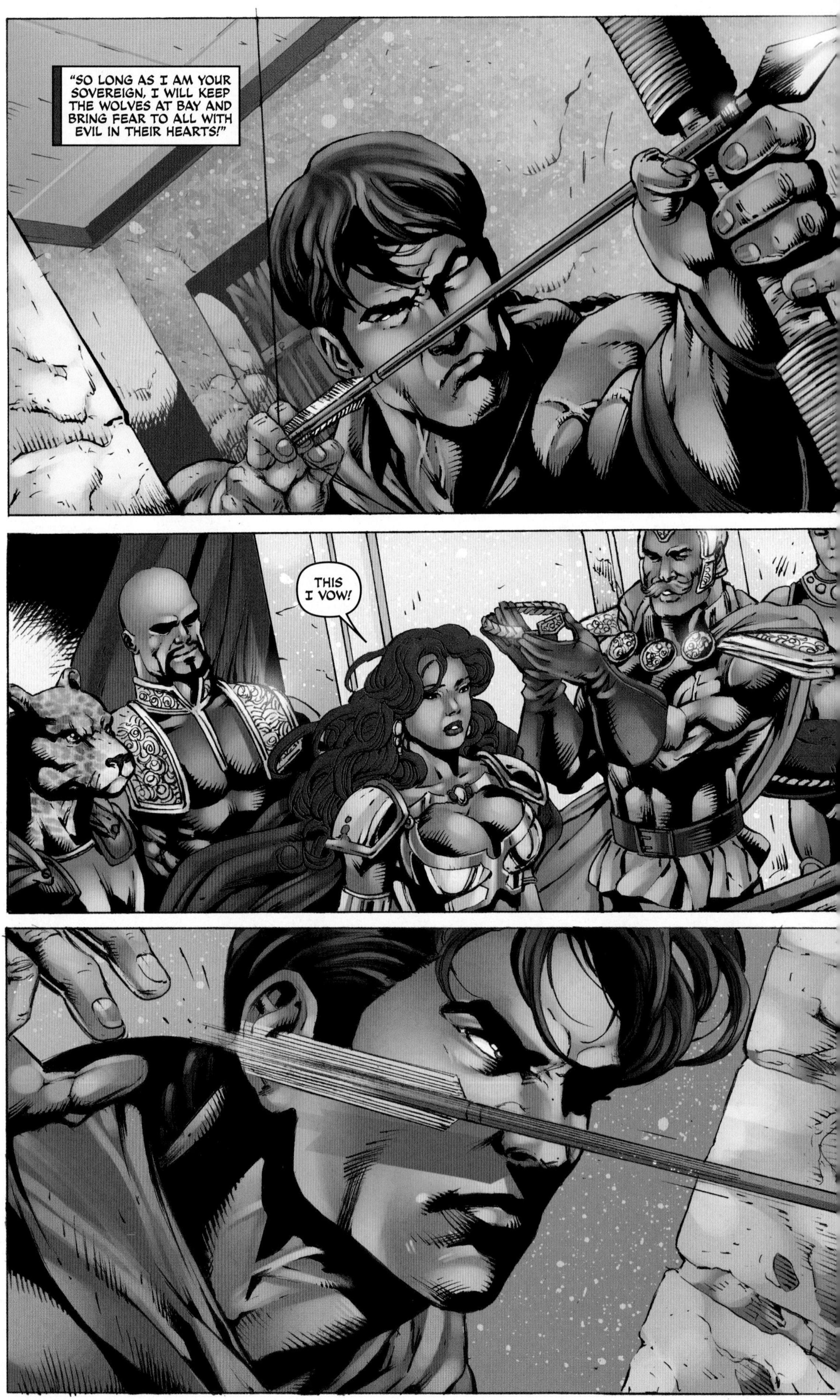
"SO LONG AS I AM YOUR SOVEREIGN, I WILL KEEP THE WOLVES AT BAY AND BRING FEAR TO ALL WITH EVIL IN THEIR HEARTS!"
THIS I VOW!

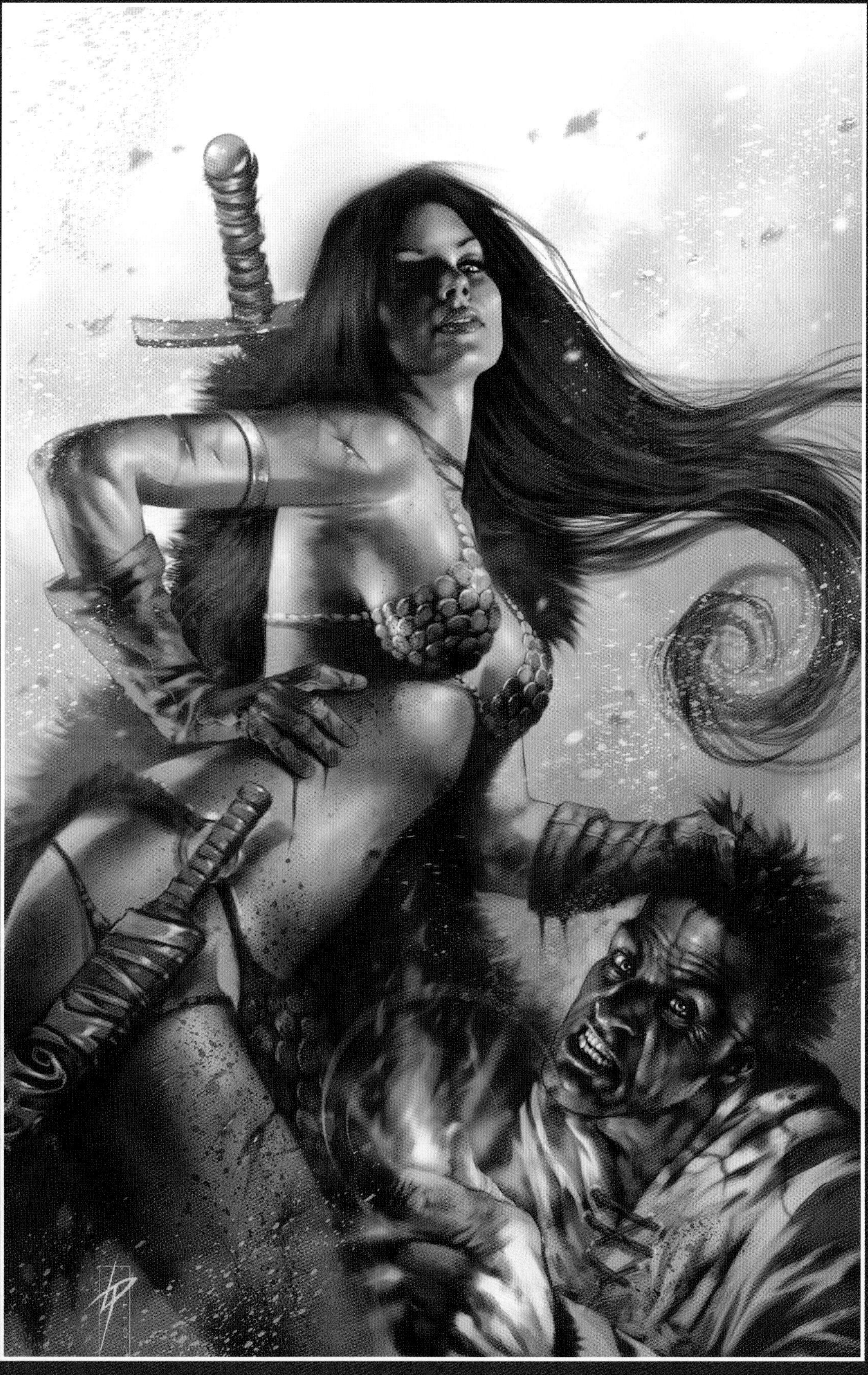

ISSUE #27 COVER BY LUCIO PARRILLO

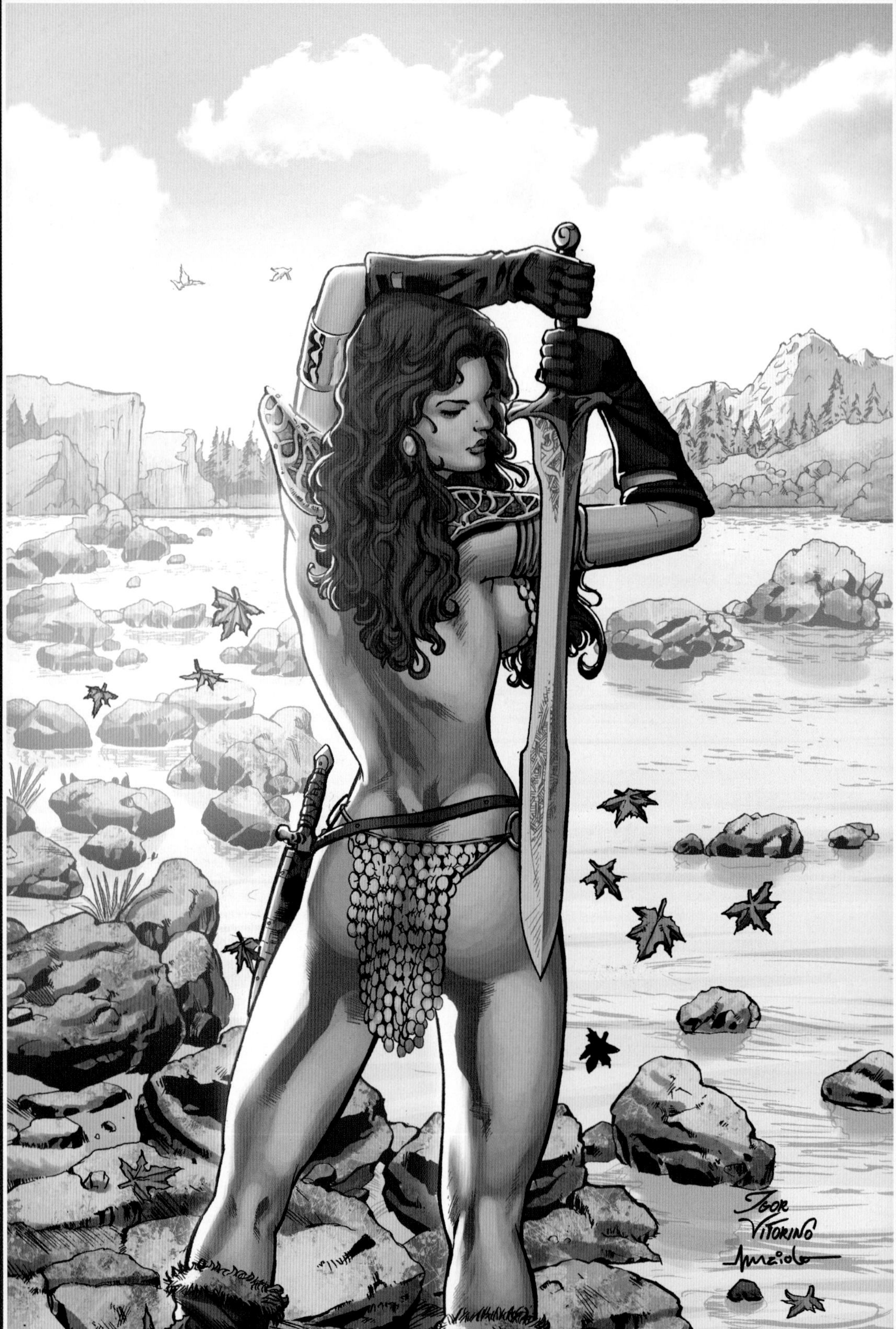
IGOR
VITORINO

ISSUE #27 COVER BY IGOR VITORINO

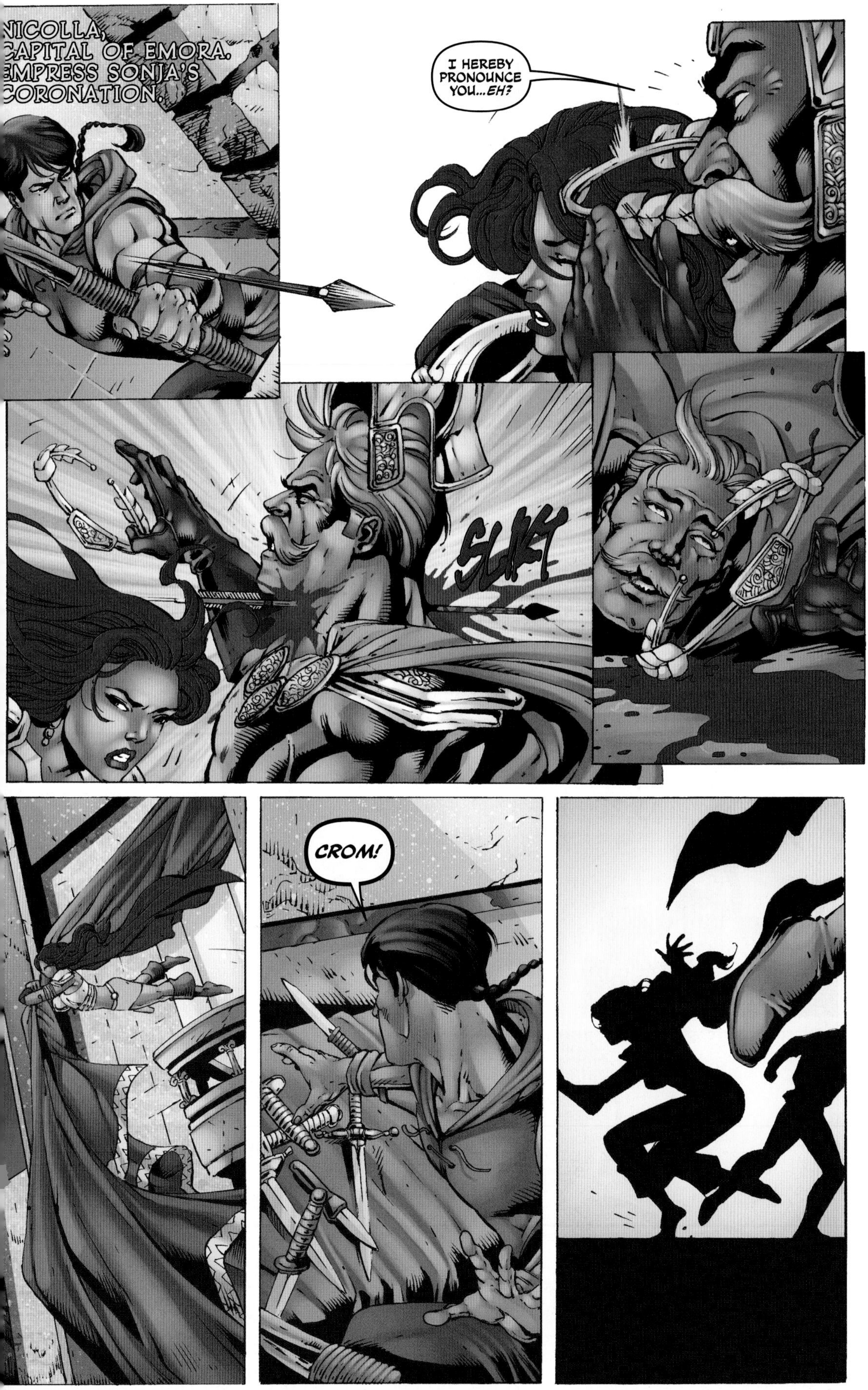
NICOLLA, CAPITAL OF EMORA. EMPRESS SONJA'S CORONATION.
I HEREBY PRONOUNCE YOU...EH?
SLIKT
CROM!

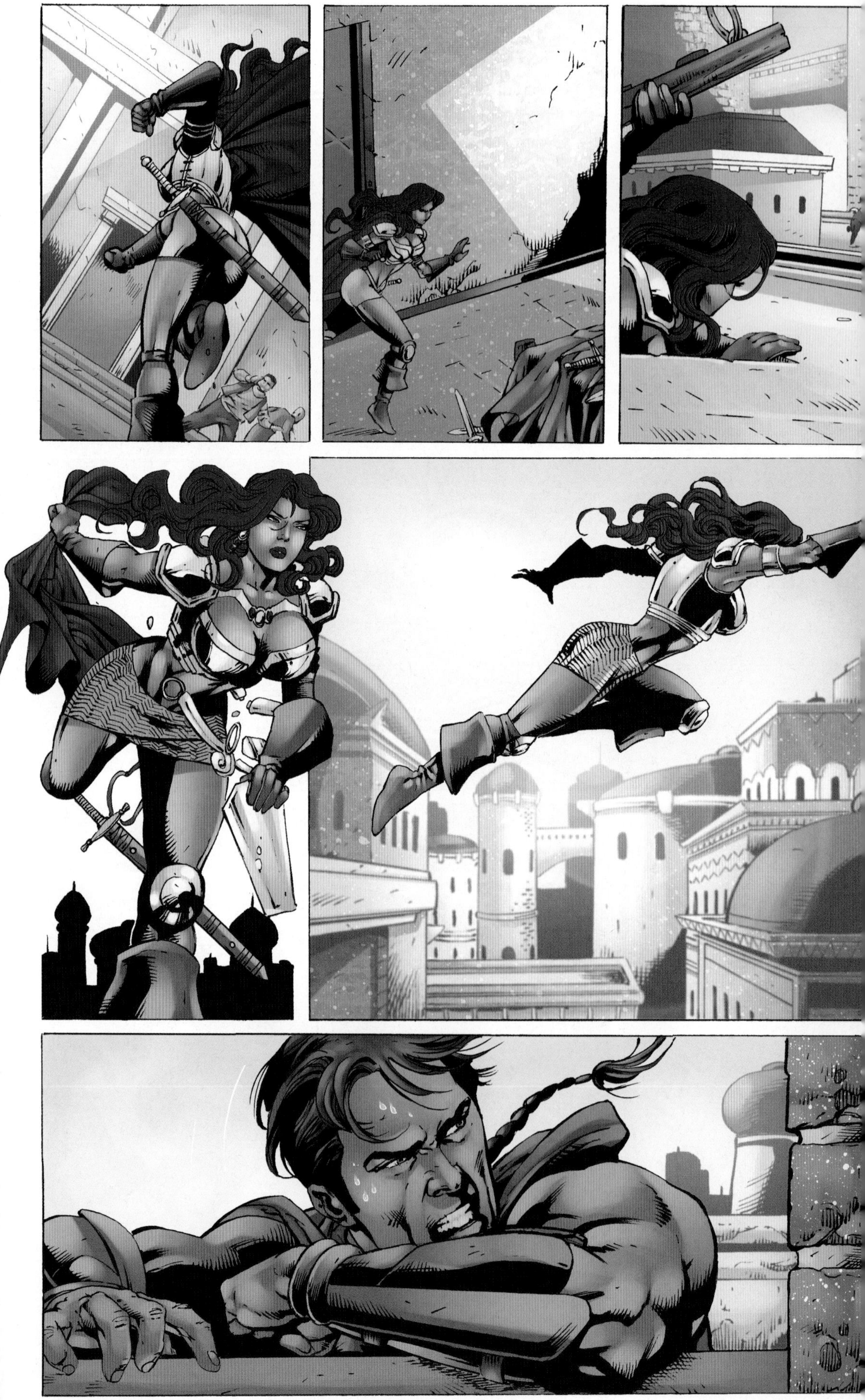

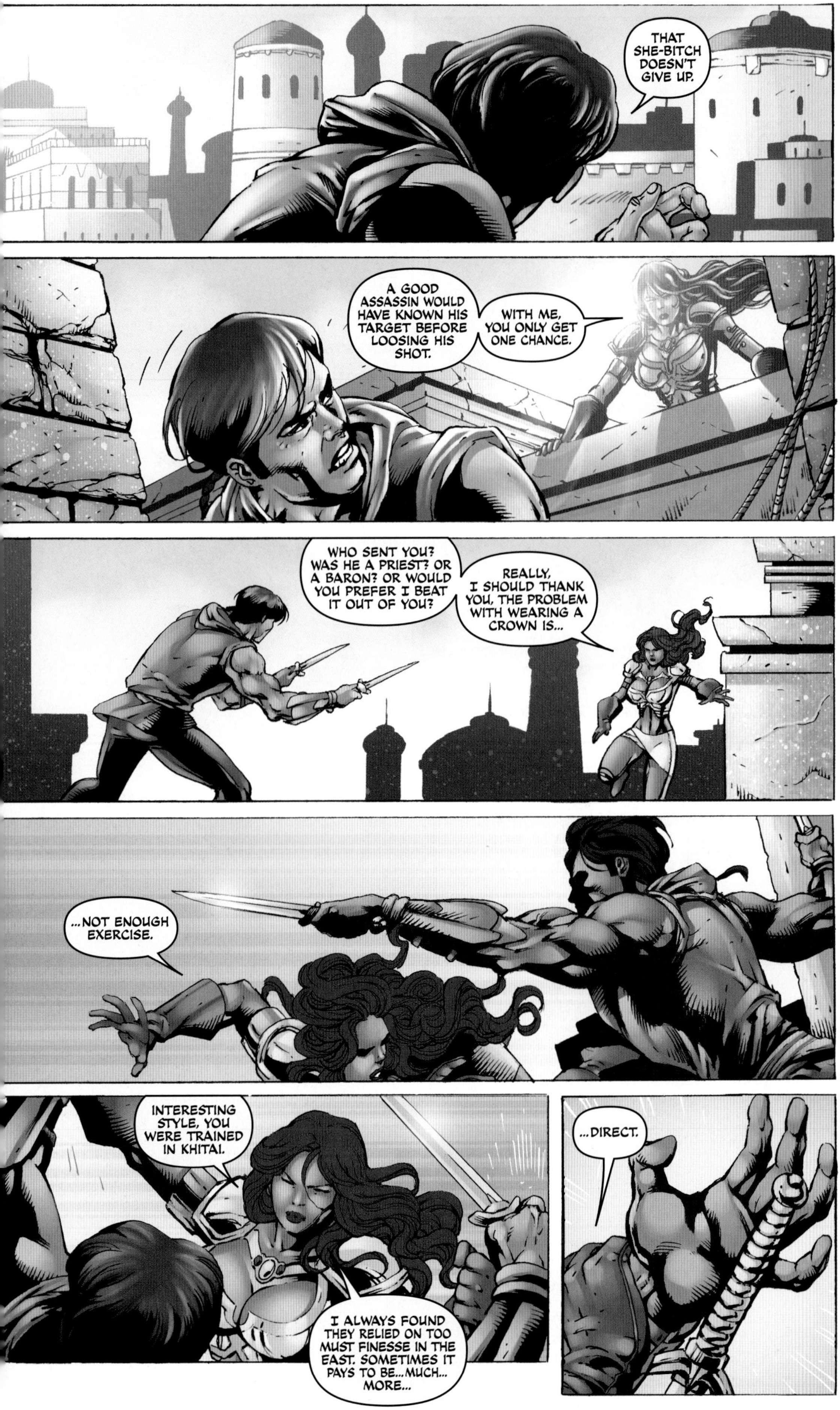
THAT SHE-BITCH DOESN'T GIVE UP.
A GOOD ASSASSIN WOULD HAVE KNOWN HIS TARGET BEFORE LOOSING HIS SHOT.
WITH ME, YOU ONLY GET ONE CHANCE.
WHO SENT YOU? WAS HE A PRIEST? OR A BARON? OR WOULD YOU PREFER I BEAT IT OUT OF YOU?
REALLY, I SHOULD THANK YOU, THE PROBLEM WITH WEARING A CROWN IS...
...NOT ENOUGH EXERCISE.
INTERESTING STYLE, YOU WERE TRAINED IN KHITAI.
I ALWAYS FOUND THEY RELIED ON TOO MUST FINESSE IN THE EAST. SOMETIMES IT PAYS TO BE...MUCH... MORE...
...DIRECT.

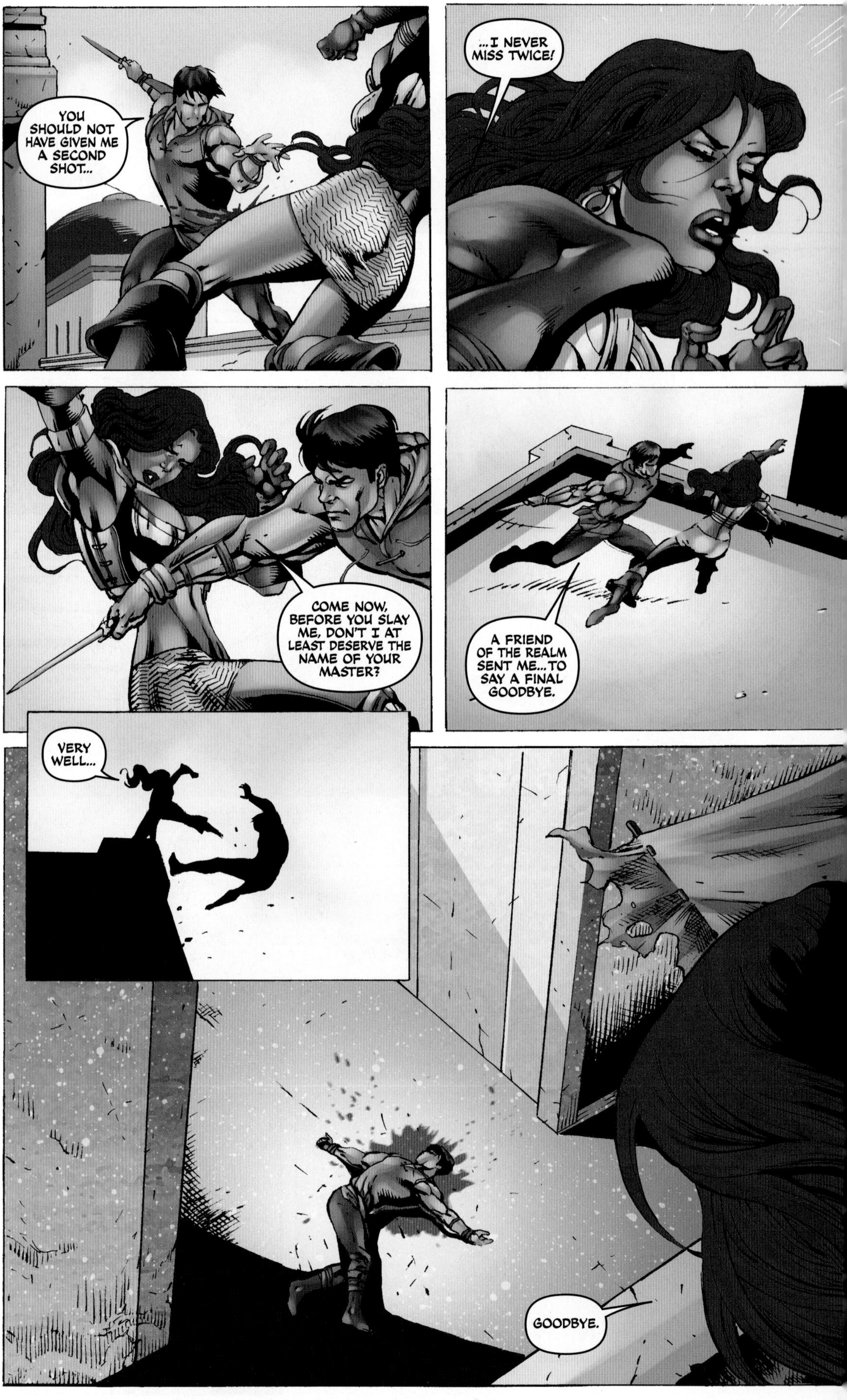
YOU SHOULD NOT HAVE GIVEN ME A SECOND SHOT...
...I NEVER MISS TWICE!
COME NOW, BEFORE YOU SLAY ME, DON'T I AT LEAST DESERVE THE NAME OF YOUR MASTER?
A FRIEND OF THE REALM SENT ME...TO SAY A FINAL GOODBYE.
VERY WELL...
GOODBYE.

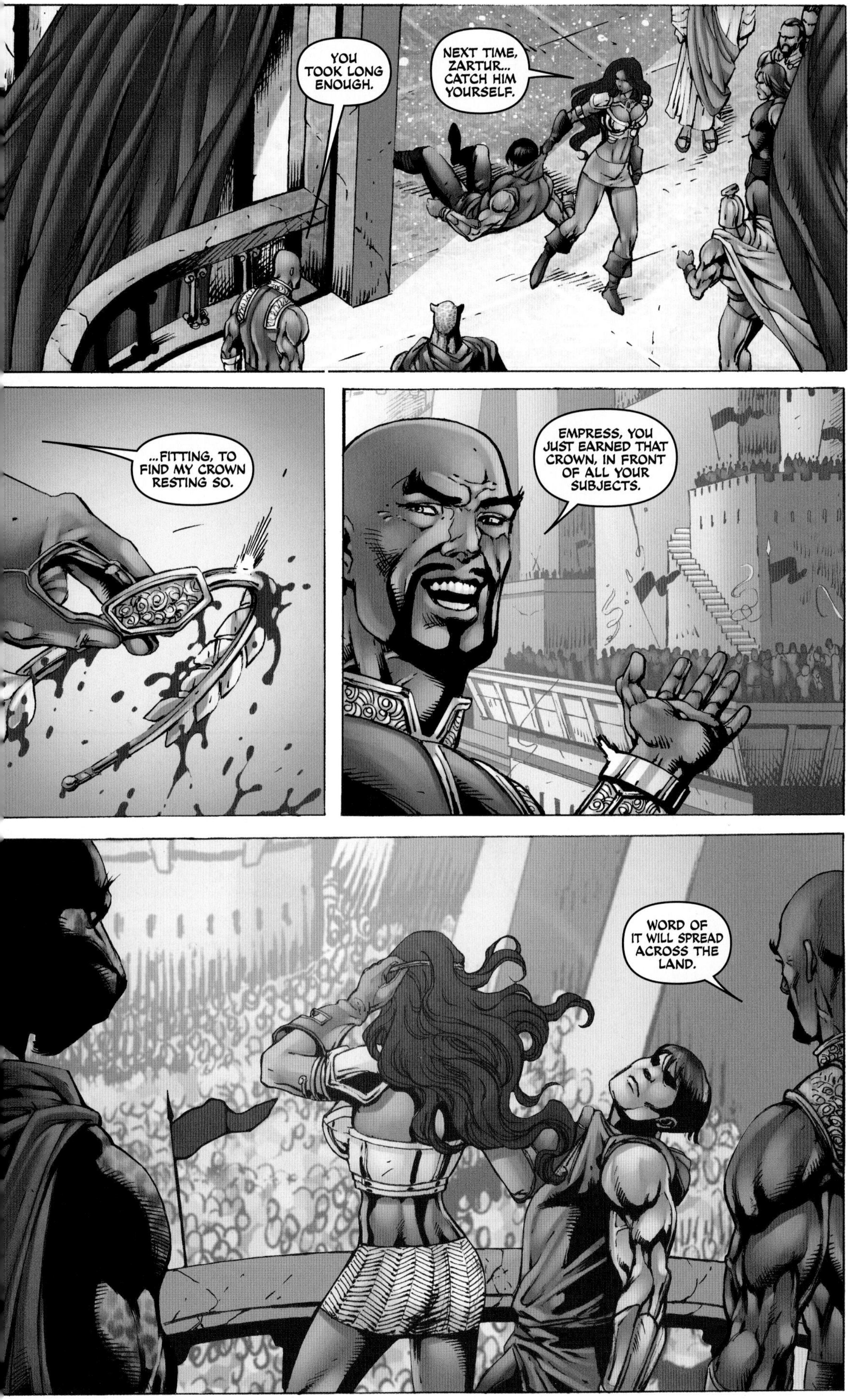

YOU TOOK LONG ENOUGH.
NEXT TIME, ZARTUR... CATCH HIM YOURSELF.
...FITTING, TO FIND MY CROWN RESTING SO.
EMPRESS, YOU JUST EARNED THAT CROWN, IN FRONT OF ALL YOUR SUBJECTS.
WORD OF IT WILL SPREAD ACROSS THE LAND.

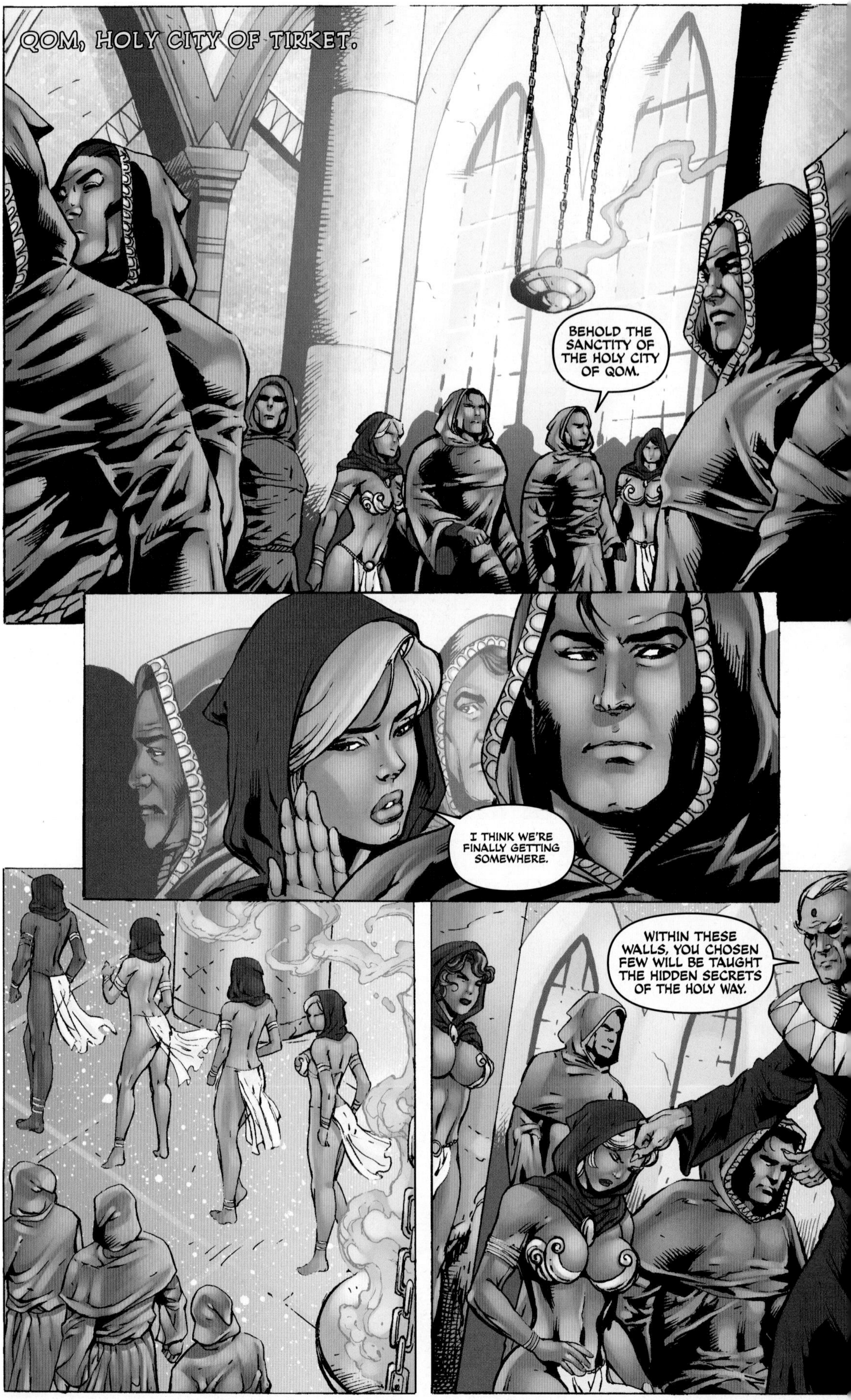
QOM, HOLY CITY OF TIRKET.
BEHOLD THE SANCTITY OF THE HOLY CITY OF QOM.
I THINK WE'RE FINALLY GETTING SOMEWHERE.
WITHIN THESE WALLS, YOU CHOSEN FEW WILL BE TAUGHT THE HIDDEN SECRETS OF THE HOLY WAY.

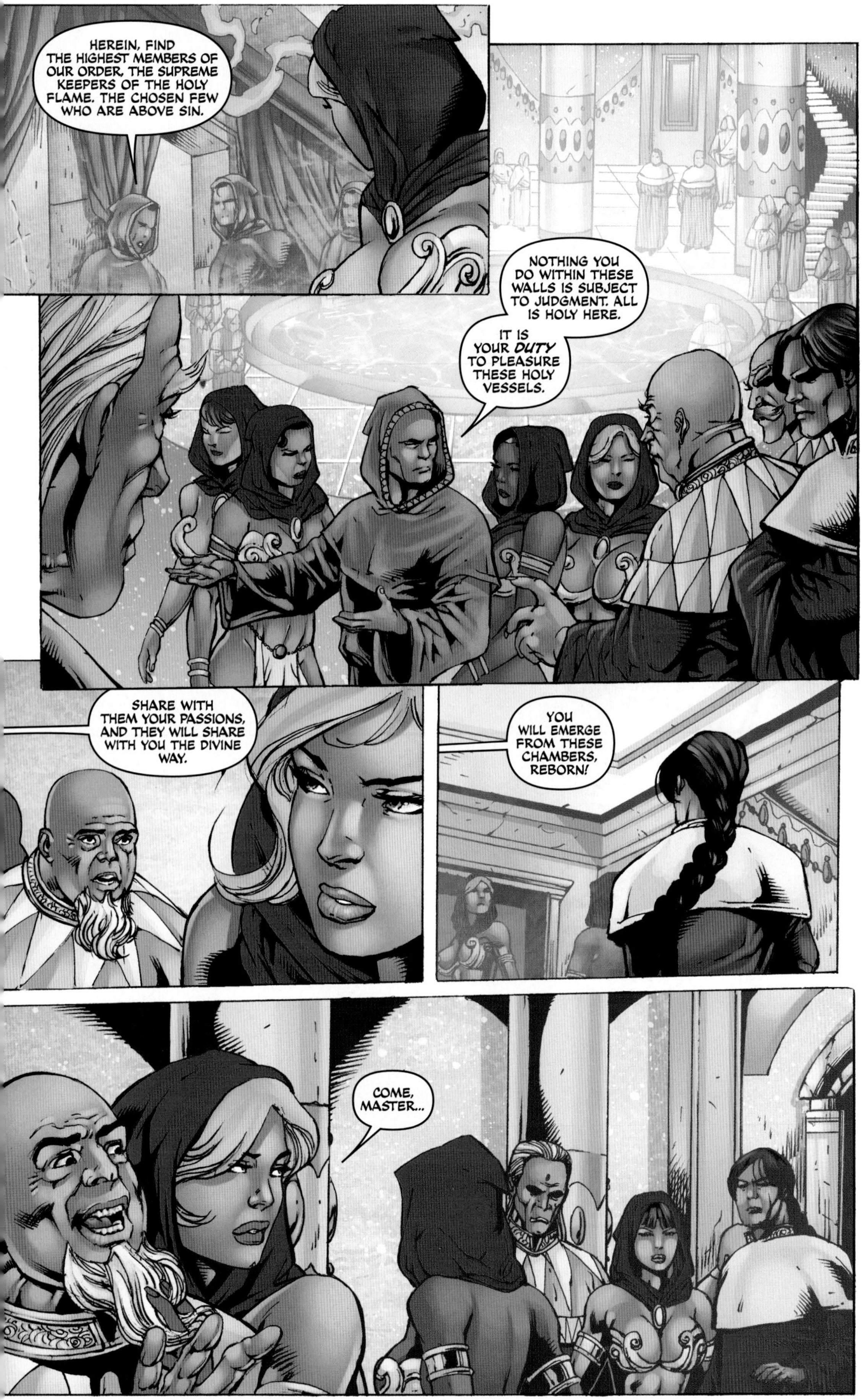
HEREIN, FIND THE HIGHEST MEMBERS OF OUR ORDER, THE SUPREME KEEPERS OF THE HOLY FLAME. THE CHOSEN FEW WHO ARE ABOVE SIN.
NOTHING YOU DO WITHIN THESE WALLS IS SUBJECT TO JUDGMENT. ALL IS HOLY HERE.
IT IS YOUR *DUTY* TO PLEASURE THESE HOLY VESSELS.
SHARE WITH THEM YOUR PASSIONS, AND THEY WILL SHARE WITH YOU THE DIVINE WAY.
YOU WILL EMERGE FROM THESE CHAMBERS, REBORN!
COME, MASTER...

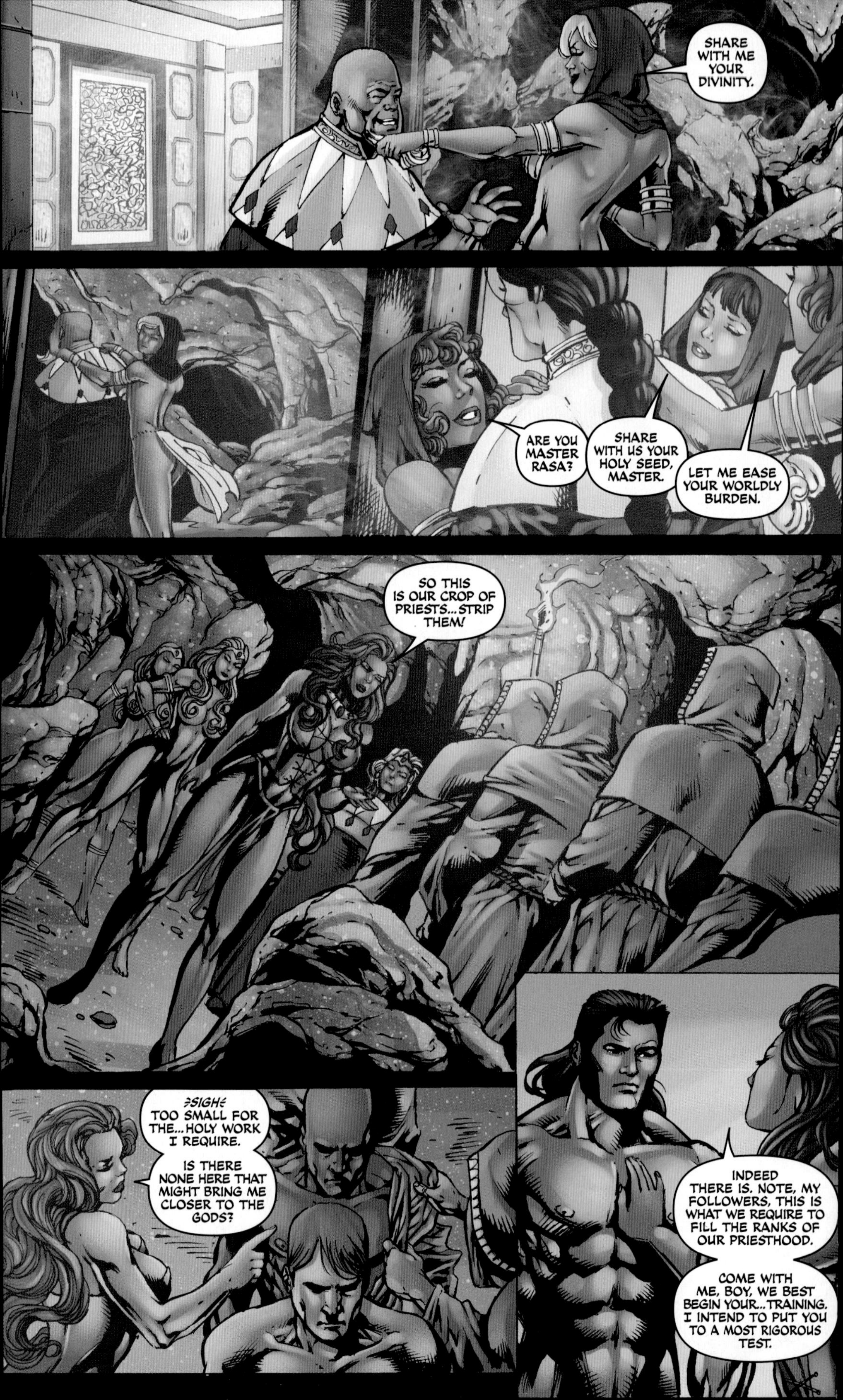
SHARE WITH ME YOUR DIVINITY.
ARE YOU MASTER RASA?
SHARE WITH US YOUR HOLY SEED, MASTER.
LET ME EASE YOUR WORLDLY BURDEN.
SO THIS IS OUR CROP OF PRIESTS...STRIP THEM!
SIGH
TOO SMALL FOR THE...HOLY WORK I REQUIRE.
IS THERE NONE HERE THAT MIGHT BRING ME CLOSER TO THE GODS?
INDEED THERE IS. NOTE, MY FOLLOWERS, THIS IS WHAT WE REQUIRE TO FILL THE RANKS OF OUR PRIESTHOOD.
COME WITH ME, BOY, WE BEST BEGIN YOUR...TRAINING. I INTEND TO PUT YOU TO A MOST RIGOROUS TEST.

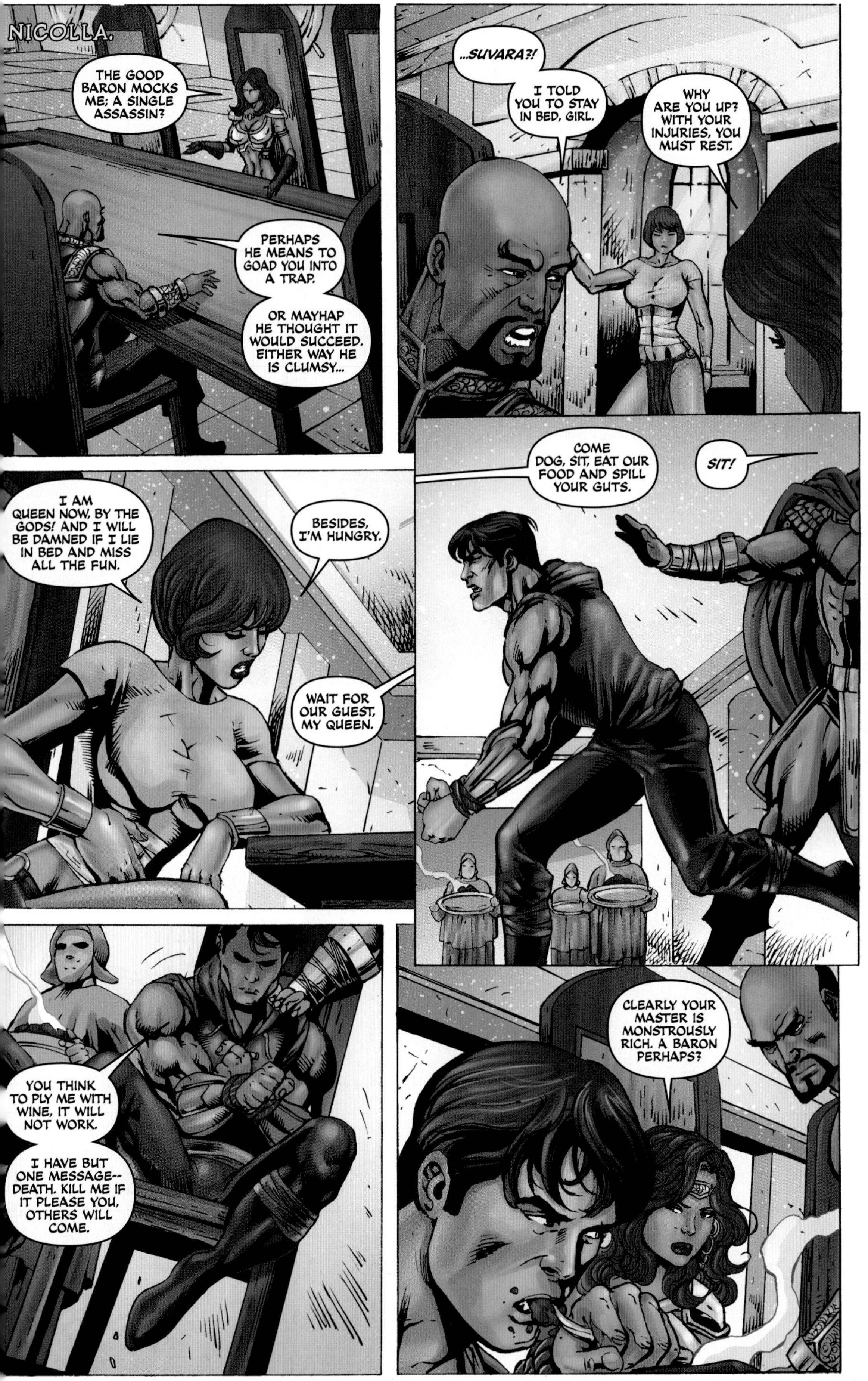
NICOLLA.
THE GOOD BARON MOCKS ME; A SINGLE ASSASSIN?
PERHAPS HE MEANS TO GOAD YOU INTO A TRAP.
OR MAYHAP HE THOUGHT IT WOULD SUCCEED. EITHER WAY HE IS CLUMSY...
...SUVARA?!
I TOLD YOU TO STAY IN BED, GIRL.
WHY ARE YOU UP? WITH YOUR INJURIES, YOU MUST REST.
I AM QUEEN NOW, BY THE GODS! AND I WILL BE DAMNED IF I LIE IN BED AND MISS ALL THE FUN.
BESIDES, I'M HUNGRY.
WAIT FOR OUR GUEST, MY QUEEN.
COME DOG, SIT, EAT OUR FOOD AND SPILL YOUR GUTS.
SIT!
YOU THINK TO PLY ME WITH WINE, IT WILL NOT WORK.
I HAVE BUT ONE MESSAGE-- DEATH. KILL ME IF IT PLEASE YOU, OTHERS WILL COME.
CLEARLY YOUR MASTER IS MONSTROUSLY RICH. A BARON PERHAPS?

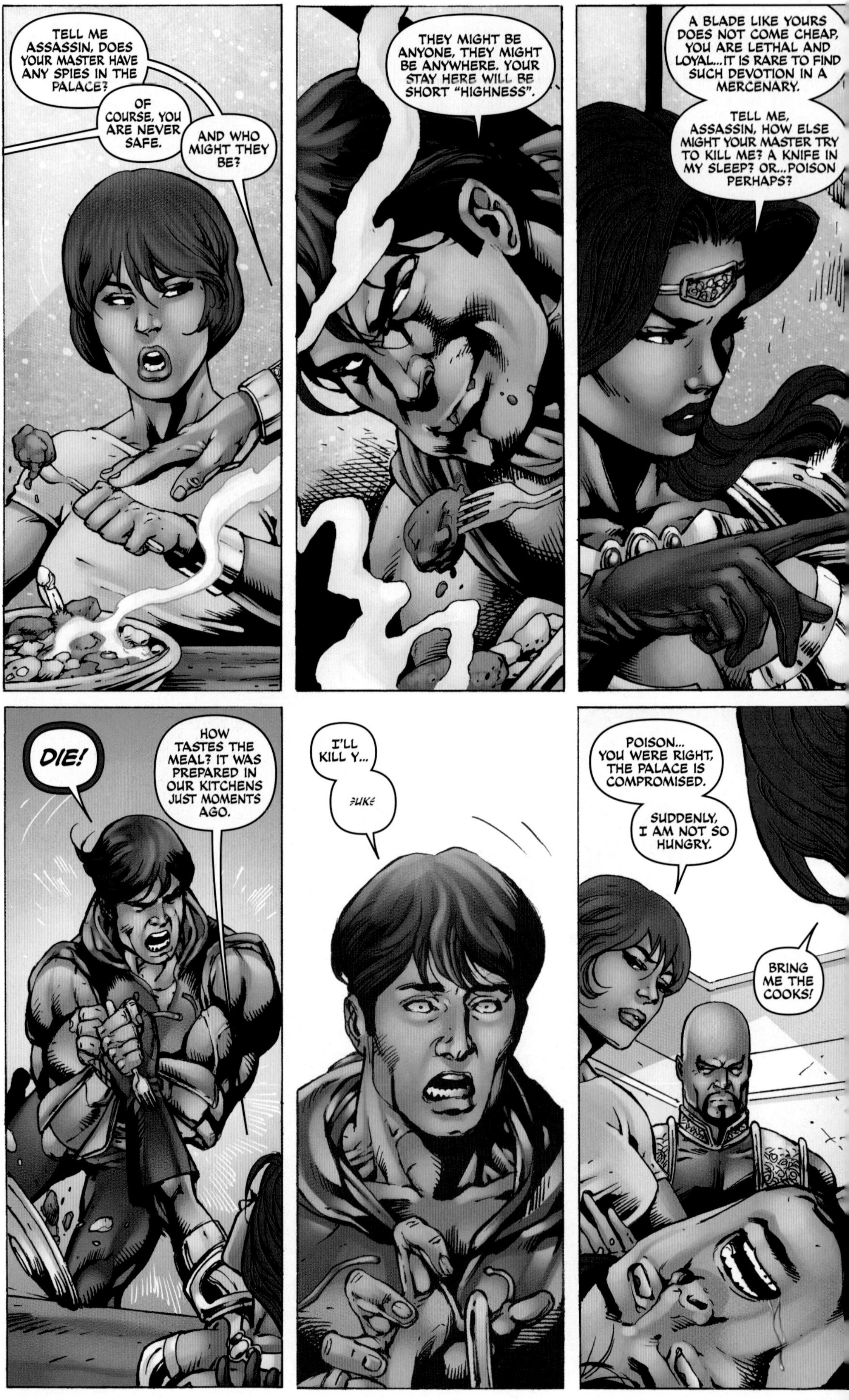
TELL ME ASSASSIN, DOES YOUR MASTER HAVE ANY SPIES IN THE PALACE?
OF COURSE, YOU ARE NEVER SAFE.
AND WHO MIGHT THEY BE?
THEY MIGHT BE ANYONE, THEY MIGHT BE ANYWHERE. YOUR STAY HERE WILL BE SHORT "HIGHNESS".
A BLADE LIKE YOURS DOES NOT COME CHEAP, YOU ARE LETHAL AND LOYAL...IT IS RARE TO FIND SUCH DEVOTION IN A MERCENARY.
TELL ME, ASSASSIN, HOW ELSE MIGHT YOUR MASTER TRY TO KILL ME? A KNIFE IN MY SLEEP? OR...POISON PERHAPS?
DIE!
HOW TASTES THE MEAL? IT WAS PREPARED IN OUR KITCHENS JUST MOMENTS AGO.
I'LL KILL Y...
UKK
POISON... YOU WERE RIGHT, THE PALACE IS COMPROMISED.
SUDDENLY, I AM NOT SO HUNGRY.
BRING ME THE COOKS!

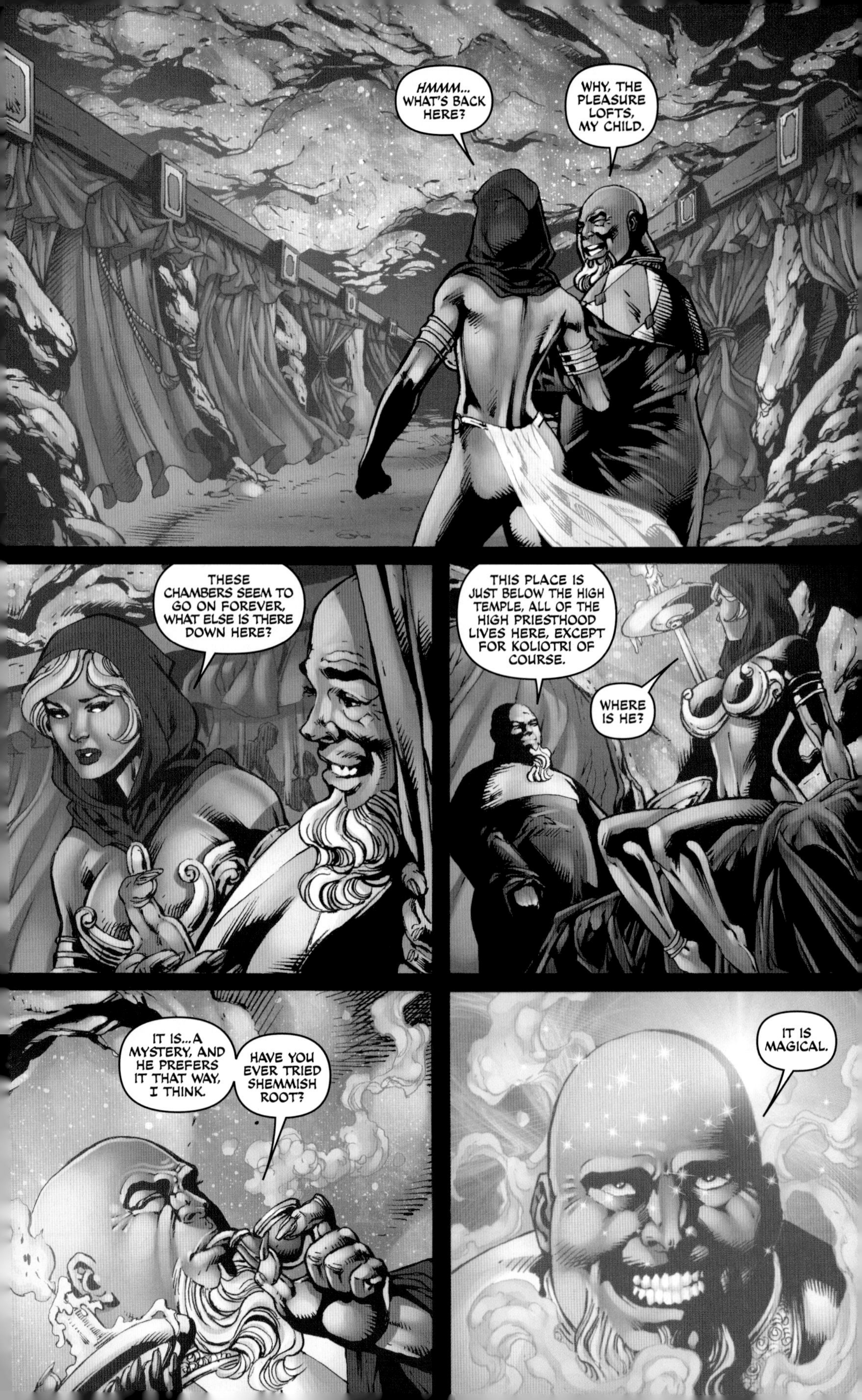
HMMM... WHAT'S BACK HERE?
WHY, THE PLEASURE LOFTS, MY CHILD.
THESE CHAMBERS SEEM TO GO ON FOREVER, WHAT ELSE IS THERE DOWN HERE?
THIS PLACE IS JUST BELOW THE HIGH TEMPLE, ALL OF THE HIGH PRIESTHOOD LIVES HERE, EXCEPT FOR KOLIOTRI OF COURSE.
WHERE IS HE?
IT IS...A MYSTERY, AND HE PREFERS IT THAT WAY, I THINK.
HAVE YOU EVER TRIED SHEMMISH ROOT?
IT IS MAGICAL.

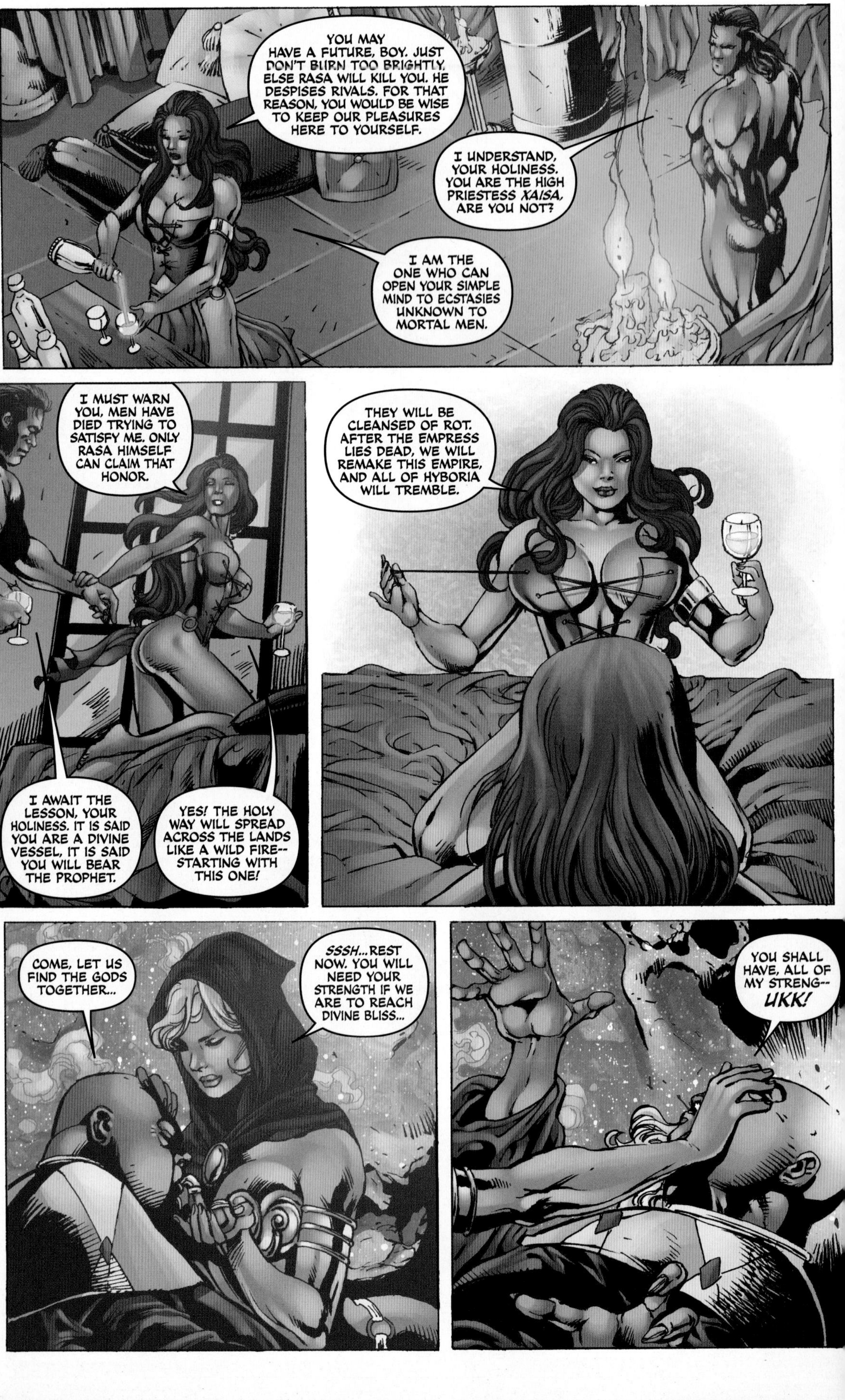
YOU MAY HAVE A FUTURE, BOY. JUST DON'T BURN TOO BRIGHTLY, ELSE RASA WILL KILL YOU. HE DESPISES RIVALS. FOR THAT REASON, YOU WOULD BE WISE TO KEEP OUR PLEASURES HERE TO YOURSELF.
I UNDERSTAND, YOUR HOLINESS. YOU ARE THE HIGH PRIESTESS *XAISA*, ARE YOU NOT?
I AM THE ONE WHO CAN OPEN YOUR SIMPLE MIND TO ECSTASIES UNKNOWN TO MORTAL MEN.
I MUST WARN YOU, MEN HAVE DIED TRYING TO SATISFY ME. ONLY RASA HIMSELF CAN CLAIM THAT HONOR.
I AWAIT THE LESSON, YOUR HOLINESS. IT IS SAID YOU ARE A DIVINE VESSEL, IT IS SAID YOU WILL BEAR THE PROPHET.
YES! THE HOLY WAY WILL SPREAD ACROSS THE LANDS LIKE A WILD FIRE-- STARTING WITH THIS ONE!
THEY WILL BE CLEANSED OF ROT. AFTER THE EMPRESS LIES DEAD, WE WILL REMAKE THIS EMPIRE, AND ALL OF HYBORIA WILL TREMBLE.
COME, LET US FIND THE GODS TOGETHER...
*SSSH*...REST NOW. YOU WILL NEED YOUR STRENGTH IF WE ARE TO REACH DIVINE BLISS...
YOU SHALL HAVE, ALL OF MY STRENG-- *UKK!*

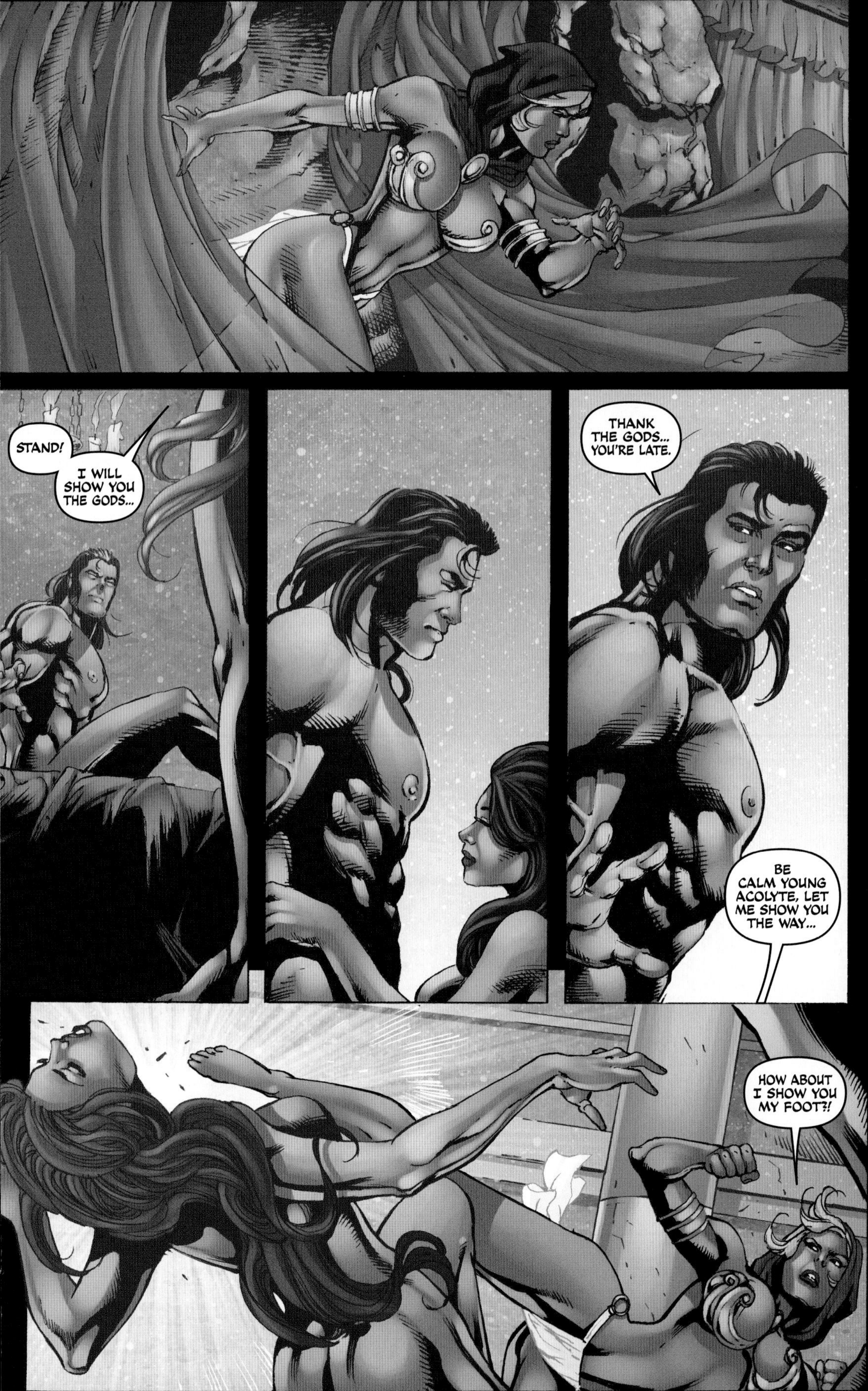
STAND!
I WILL SHOW YOU THE GODS...
THANK THE GODS... YOU'RE LATE.
BE CALM YOUNG ACOLYTE, LET ME SHOW YOU THE WAY...
HOW ABOUT I SHOW YOU MY FOOT?!

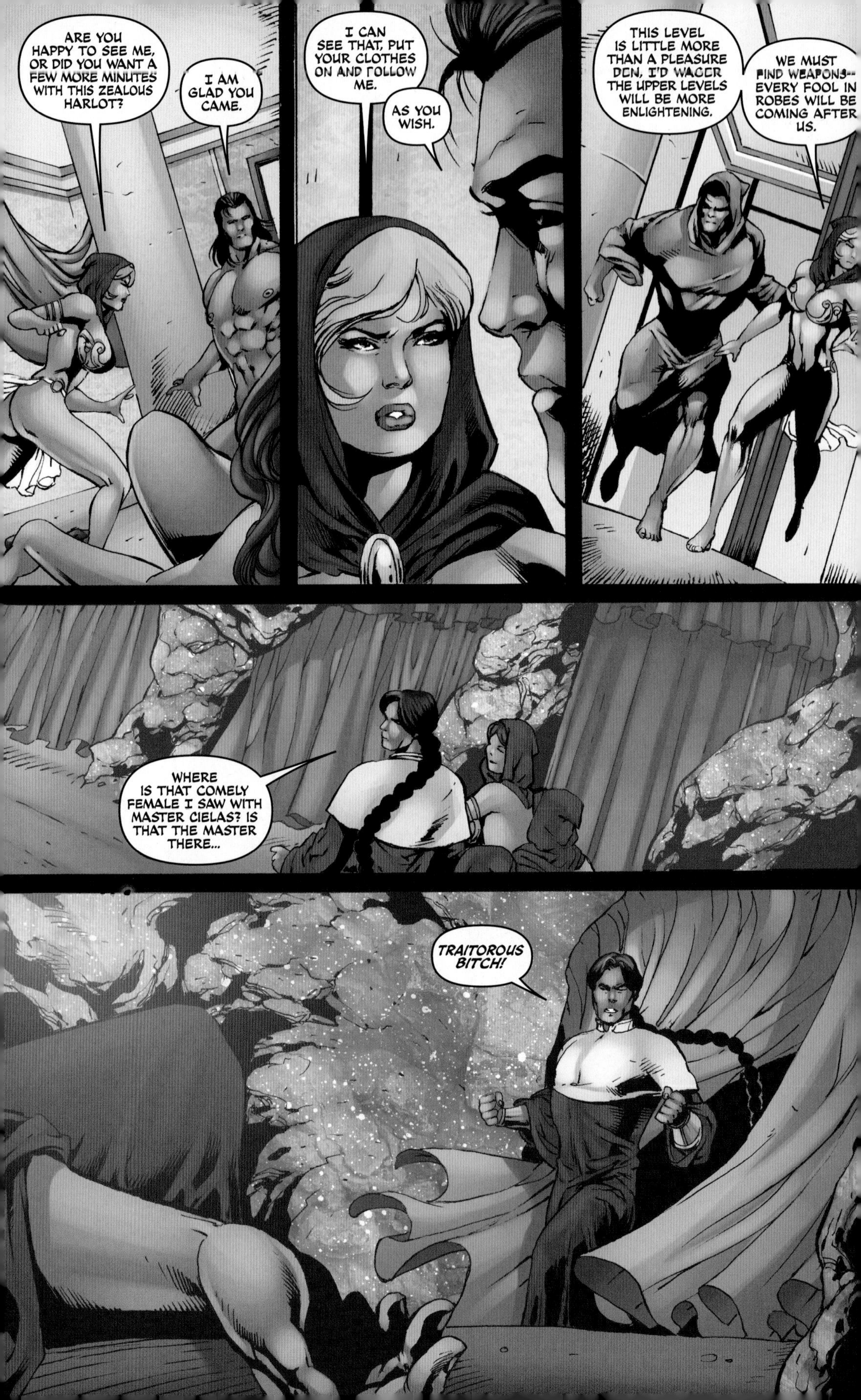
ARE YOU HAPPY TO SEE ME, OR DID YOU WANT A FEW MORE MINUTES WITH THIS ZEALOUS HARLOT?
I AM GLAD YOU CAME.
I CAN SEE THAT, PUT YOUR CLOTHES ON AND FOLLOW ME.
AS YOU WISH.
THIS LEVEL IS LITTLE MORE THAN A PLEASURE DEN, I'D WAGER THE UPPER LEVELS WILL BE MORE ENLIGHTENING.
WE MUST FIND WEAPONS-- EVERY FOOL IN ROBES WILL BE COMING AFTER US.
WHERE IS THAT COMELY FEMALE I SAW WITH MASTER CIELAS? IS THAT THE MASTER THERE...
TRAITOROUS BITCH!

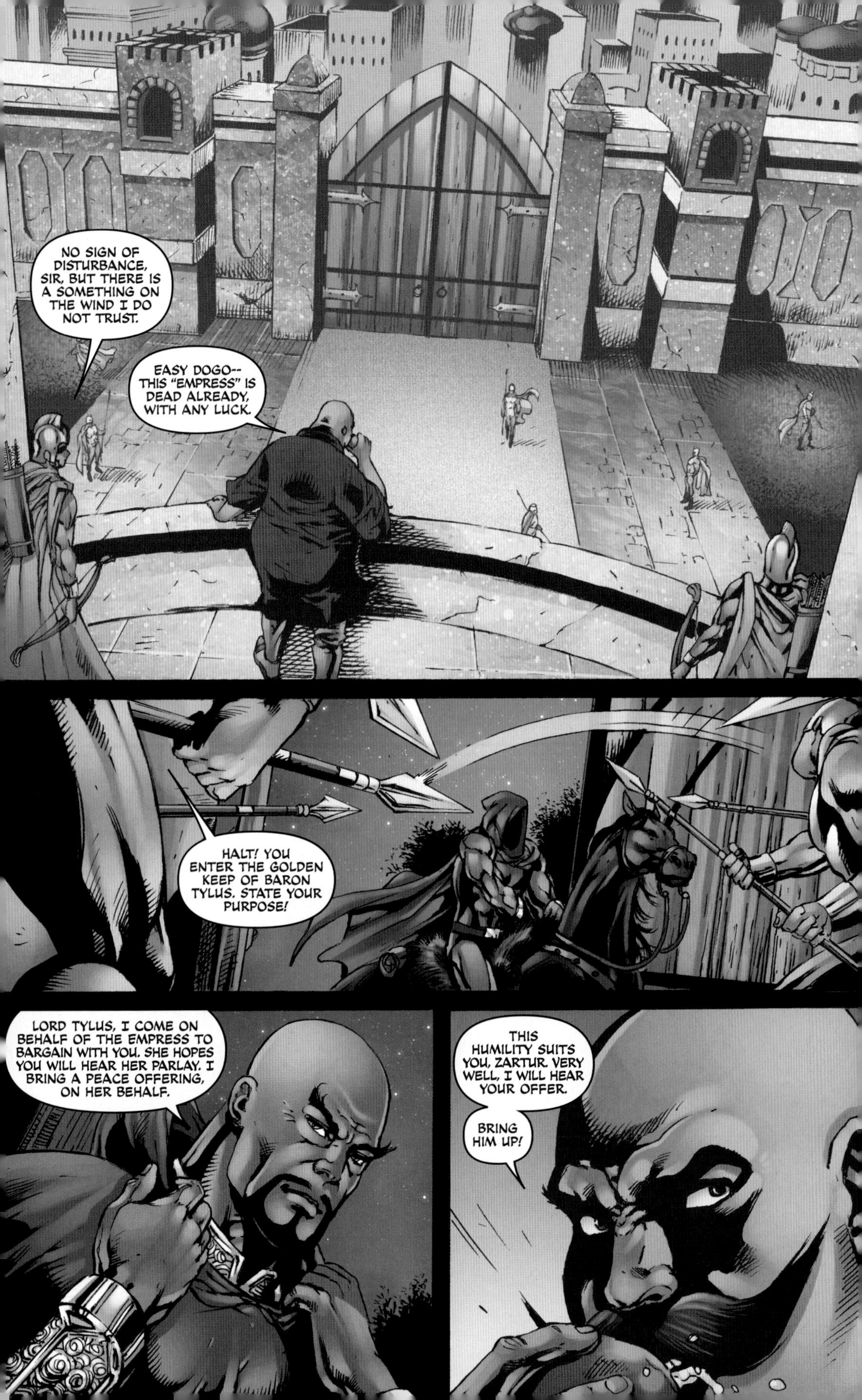
NO SIGN OF DISTURBANCE, SIR, BUT THERE IS A SOMETHING ON THE WIND I DO NOT TRUST.
EASY DOGO-- THIS "EMPRESS" IS DEAD ALREADY, WITH ANY LUCK.
HALT! YOU ENTER THE GOLDEN KEEP OF BARON TYLUS. STATE YOUR PURPOSE!
LORD TYLUS, I COME ON BEHALF OF THE EMPRESS TO BARGAIN WITH YOU. SHE HOPES YOU WILL HEAR HER PARLAY. I BRING A PEACE OFFERING, ON HER BEHALF.
THIS HUMILITY SUITS YOU, ZARTUR. VERY WELL, I WILL HEAR YOUR OFFER.
BRING HIM UP!

HE CARRIES NO WEAPONS, YOUR GRACE, BUT HE REFUSES TO ALLOW US TO OPEN HIS OFFERING.

IT IS FOR LORD TYLUS ALONE.

YOU MAY PLACE IT AT MY FEET. I HAVE HEARD MUCH OF YOU ZARTUR, IT SURPRISES ME YOU LEAVE YOUR OWN LUSH KEEP FOR ADVENTURES WITH THIS MERCENARY-TURNED-QUEEN.

I KNOW NOT HOW YOU HANDLE MATTERS IN THOSE BACKWATER WOODS YOU CALL HOME, BUT HERE WE HAVE LAW. I AM THE LAW. MY COINS WARM THE PALMS OF EVERY MAN WHO COUNTS IN THIS REALM.

HE WHO HOLDS THE GOLD MAKES THE RULES, EH?

THE EMPRESS ALSO BELIEVES IN THE LAW. HERE IS THE CHEF WHO PREPARED OUR...SUPPER, AND THE BOY WHO SERVED IT. WE FED IT TO THE ASSASSIN WHO MADE AN ATTEMPT ON SONJA'S LIFE THIS MORNING. TELL ME, LORD TYRUS, UNDER THE LAW, WHAT IS THE PUNISHMENT FOR TREASON?

YOU DARE BRING THIS ABOMINATION HERE? YOU DARE TO MOCK ME!

I SHALL SEND THE EMPRESS YOUR HEAD IN RETURN!

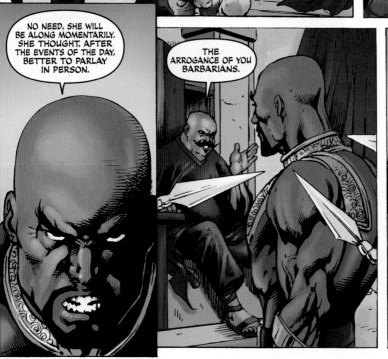

NO NEED, SHE WILL BE ALONG MOMENTARILY. SHE THOUGHT, AFTER THE EVENTS OF THE DAY, BETTER TO PARLAY IN PERSON.

THE ARROGANCE OF YOU BARBARIANS.

I ASSURE YOU, WE ARE QUITE SAFE HERE...OR AT LEAST I AM.

SURE ABOUT THAT?

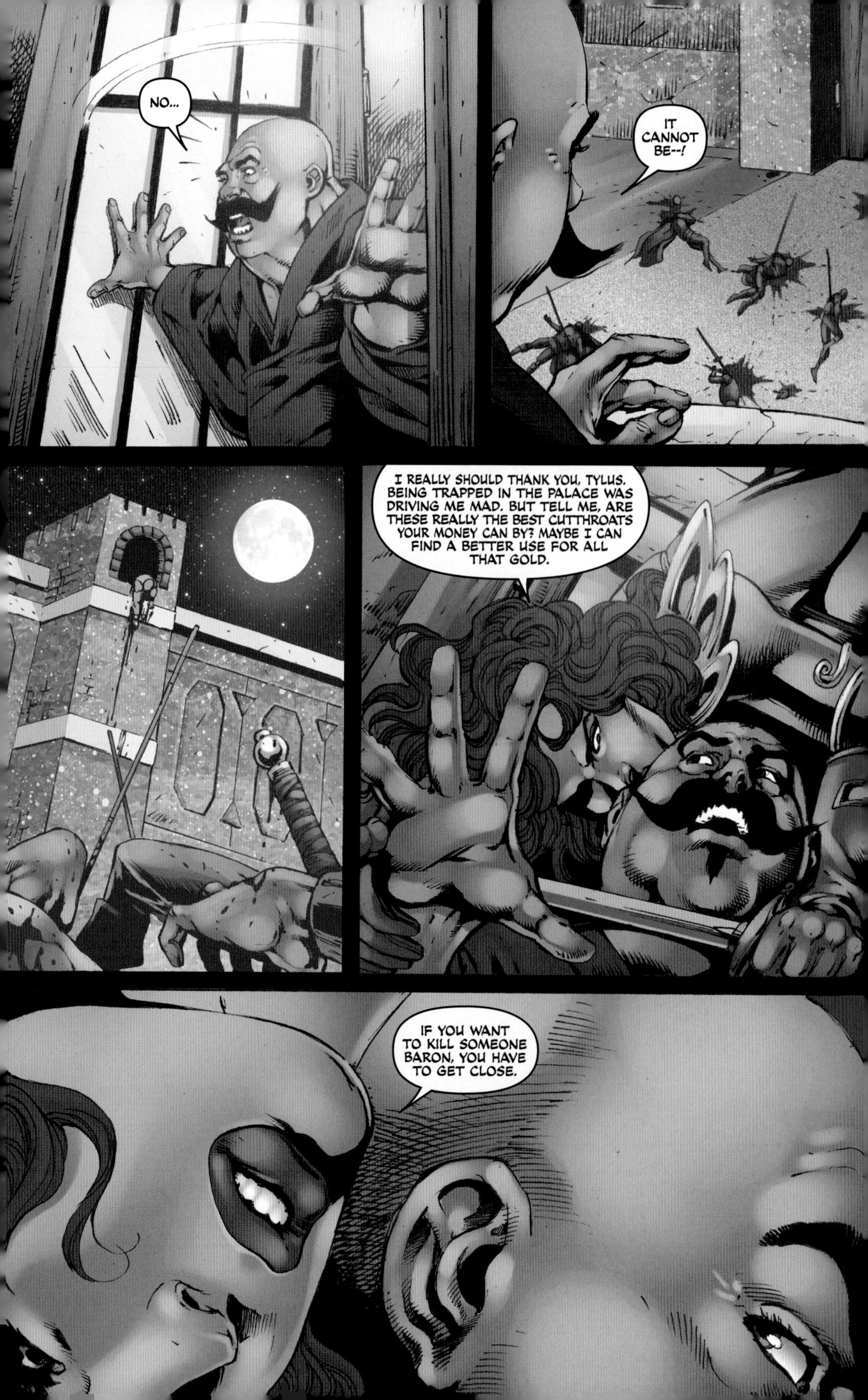

NO...
IT CANNOT BE--!
I REALLY SHOULD THANK YOU, TYLUS. BEING TRAPPED IN THE PALACE WAS DRIVING ME MAD. BUT TELL ME, ARE THESE REALLY THE BEST CUTTHROATS YOUR MONEY CAN BY? MAYBE I CAN FIND A BETTER USE FOR ALL THAT GOLD.
IF YOU WANT TO KILL SOMEONE BARON, YOU HAVE TO GET CLOSE.

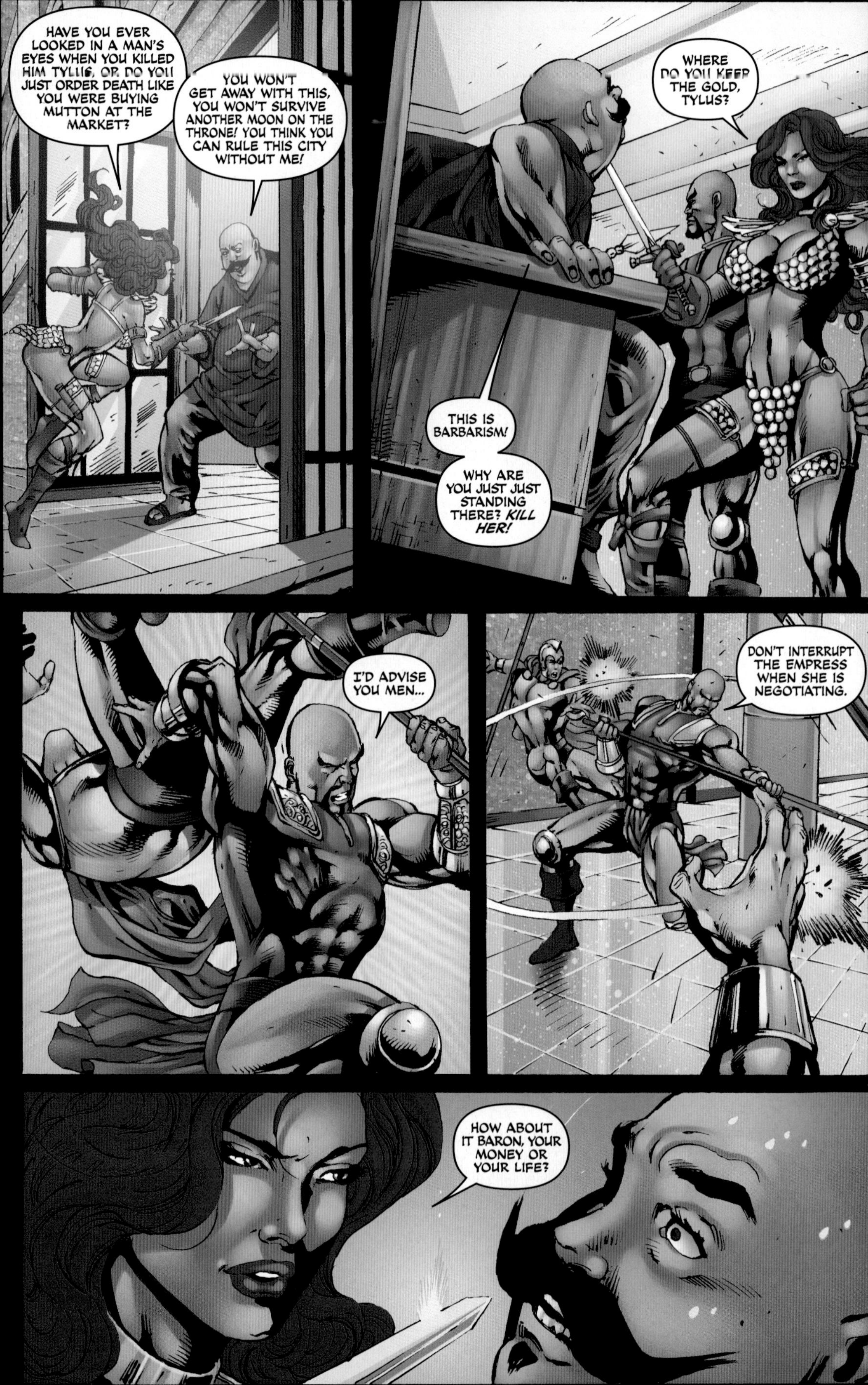
HAVE YOU EVER LOOKED IN A MAN'S EYES WHEN YOU KILLED HIM TYLUS, OR DO YOU JUST ORDER DEATH LIKE YOU WERE BUYING MUTTON AT THE MARKET?
YOU WON'T GET AWAY WITH THIS, YOU WON'T SURVIVE ANOTHER MOON ON THE THRONE! YOU THINK YOU CAN RULE THIS CITY WITHOUT ME!
WHERE DO YOU KEEP THE GOLD, TYLUS?
THIS IS BARBARISM!
WHY ARE YOU JUST JUST STANDING THERE? KILL HER!
I'D ADVISE YOU MEN...
DON'T INTERRUPT THE EMPRESS WHEN SHE IS NEGOTIATING.
HOW ABOUT IT BARON, YOUR MONEY OR YOUR LIFE?

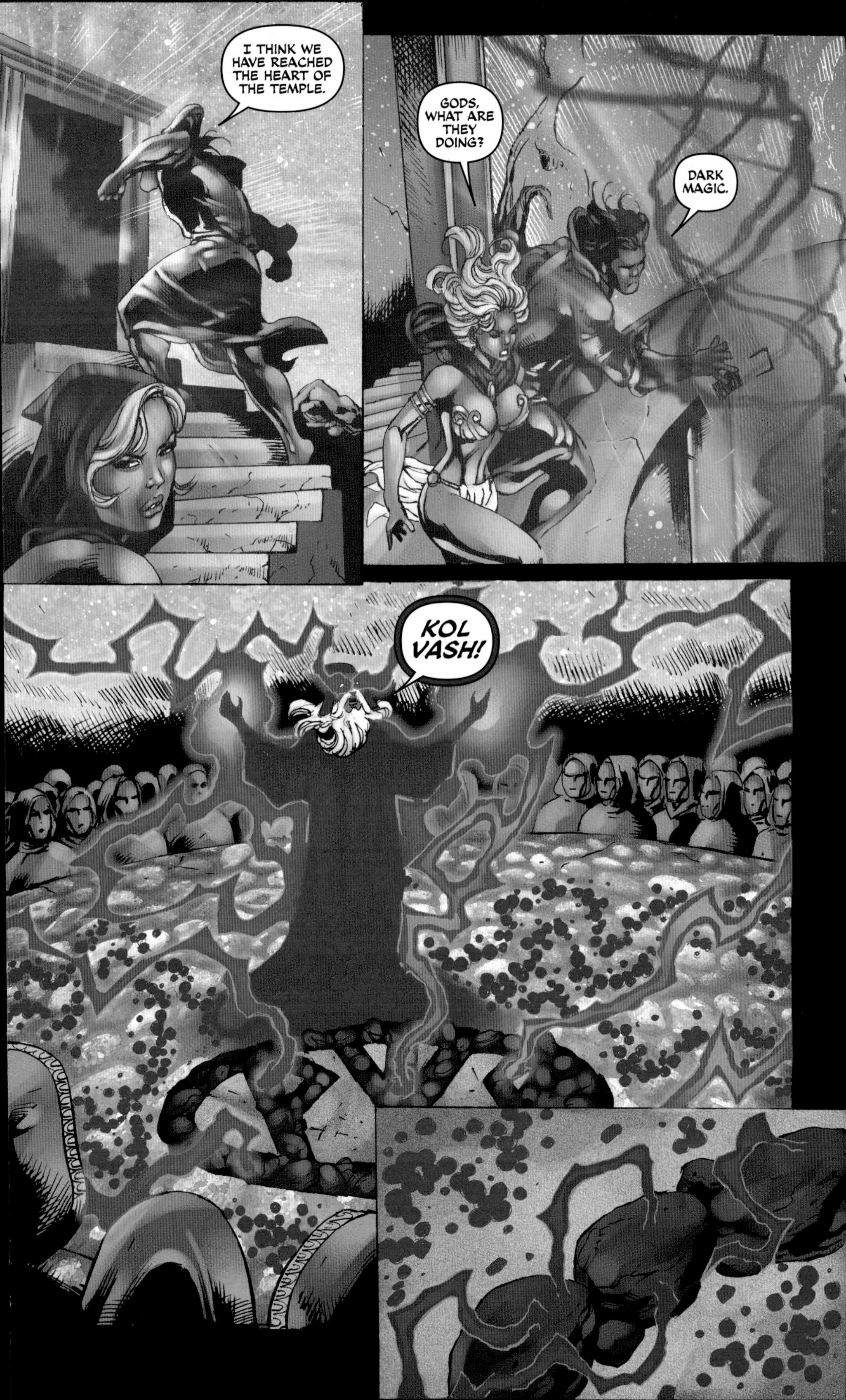
I THINK WE HAVE REACHED THE HEART OF THE TEMPLE.
GODS, WHAT ARE THEY DOING?
DARK MAGIC.
KOL VASH!

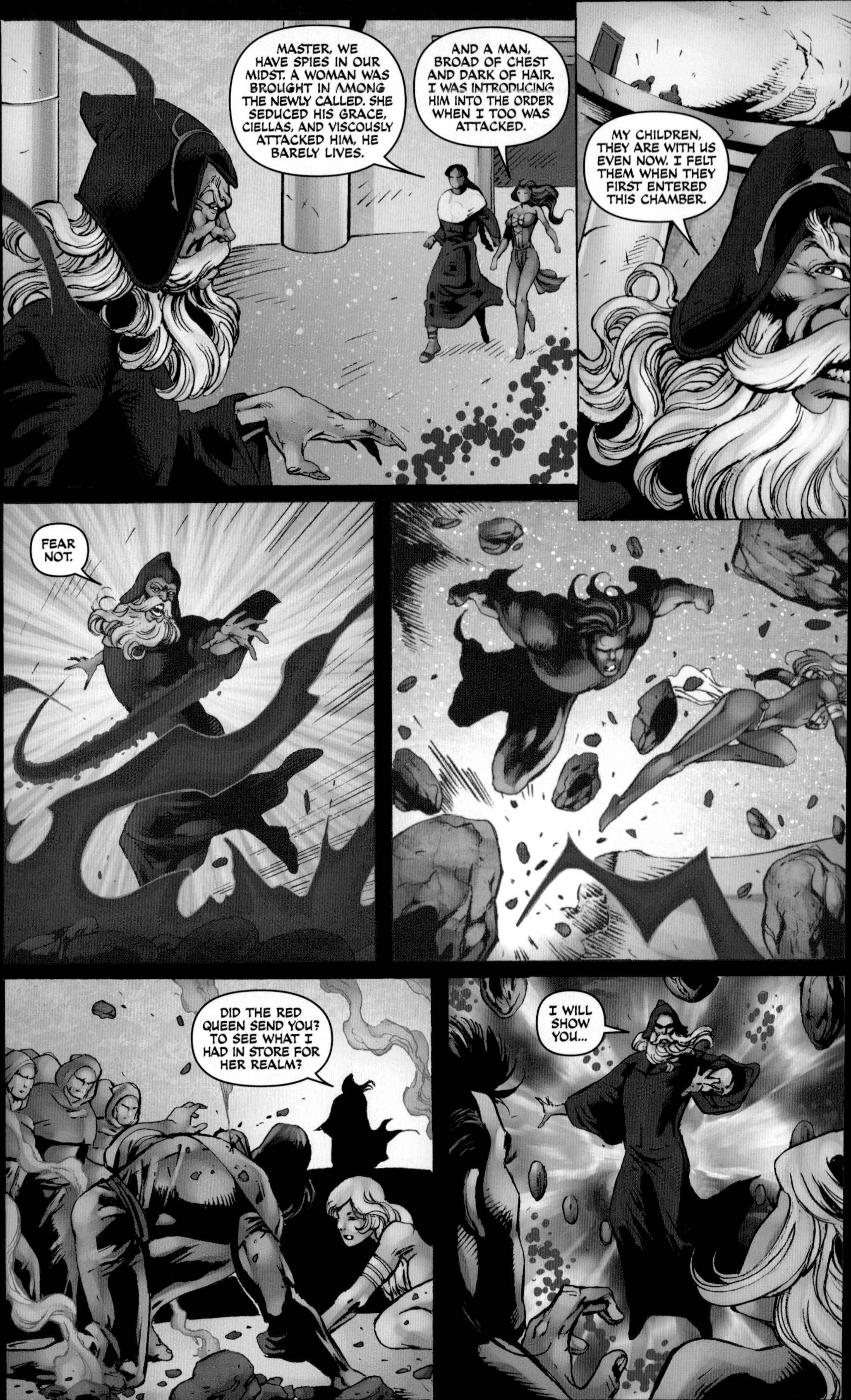
MASTER, WE HAVE SPIES IN OUR MIDST. A WOMAN WAS BROUGHT IN AMONG THE NEWLY CALLED. SHE SEDUCED HIS GRACE, CIELLAS, AND VISCOUSLY ATTACKED HIM, HE BARELY LIVES.
AND A MAN, BROAD OF CHEST AND DARK OF HAIR. I WAS INTRODUCING HIM INTO THE ORDER WHEN I TOO WAS ATTACKED.
MY CHILDREN, THEY ARE WITH US EVEN NOW. I FELT THEM WHEN THEY FIRST ENTERED THIS CHAMBER.
FEAR NOT.
DID THE RED QUEEN SEND YOU? TO SEE WHAT I HAD IN STORE FOR HER REALM?
I WILL SHOW YOU...

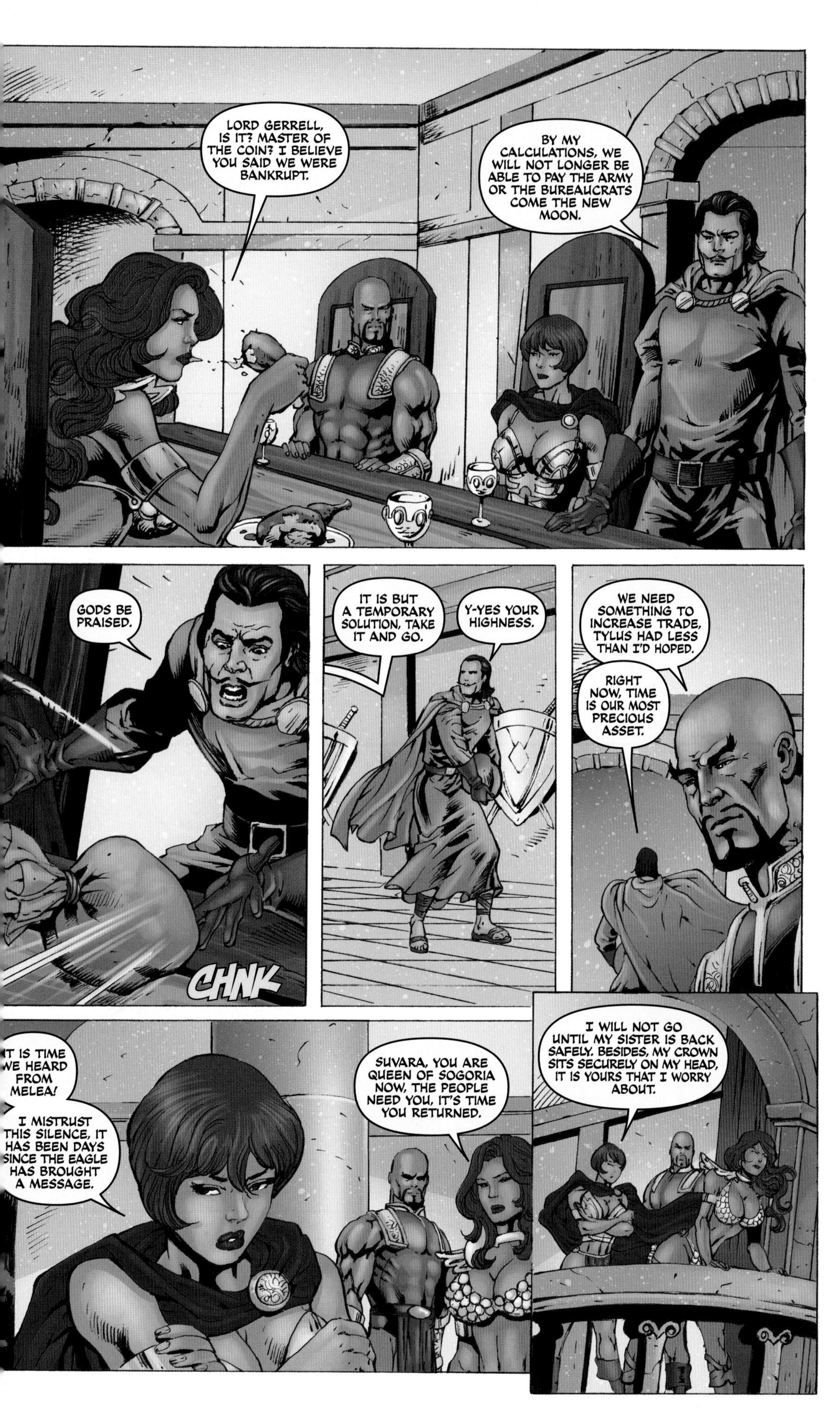
LORD GERRELL, IS IT? MASTER OF THE COIN? I BELIEVE YOU SAID WE WERE BANKRUPT.
BY MY CALCULATIONS, WE WILL NOT LONGER BE ABLE TO PAY THE ARMY OR THE BUREAUCRATS COME THE NEW MOON.
GODS BE PRAISED.
CHNK
IT IS BUT A TEMPORARY SOLUTION, TAKE IT AND GO.
Y-YES YOUR HIGHNESS.
WE NEED SOMETHING TO INCREASE TRADE, TYLUS HAD LESS THAN I'D HOPED.
RIGHT NOW, TIME IS OUR MOST PRECIOUS ASSET.
IT IS TIME WE HEARD FROM MELEA!
I MISTRUST THIS SILENCE, IT HAS BEEN DAYS SINCE THE EAGLE HAS BROUGHT A MESSAGE.
SUVARA, YOU ARE QUEEN OF SOGORIA NOW, THE PEOPLE NEED YOU, IT'S TIME YOU RETURNED.
I WILL NOT GO UNTIL MY SISTER IS BACK SAFELY. BESIDES, MY CROWN SITS SECURELY ON MY HEAD, IT IS YOURS THAT I WORRY ABOUT.

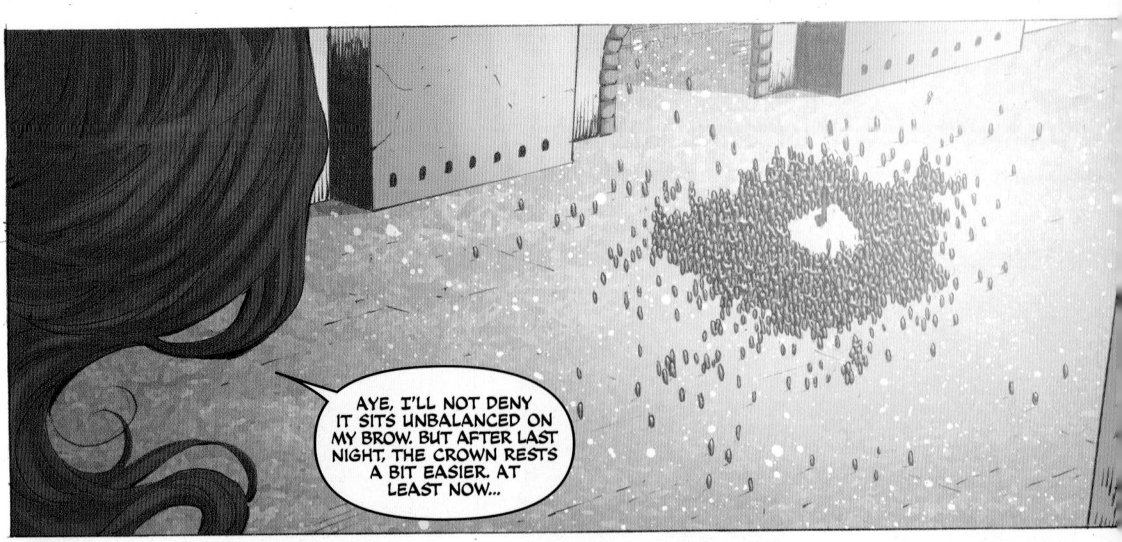
AYE, I'LL NOT DENY IT SITS UNBALANCED ON MY BROW. BUT AFTER LAST NIGHT, THE CROWN RESTS A BIT EASIER. AT LEAST NOW...

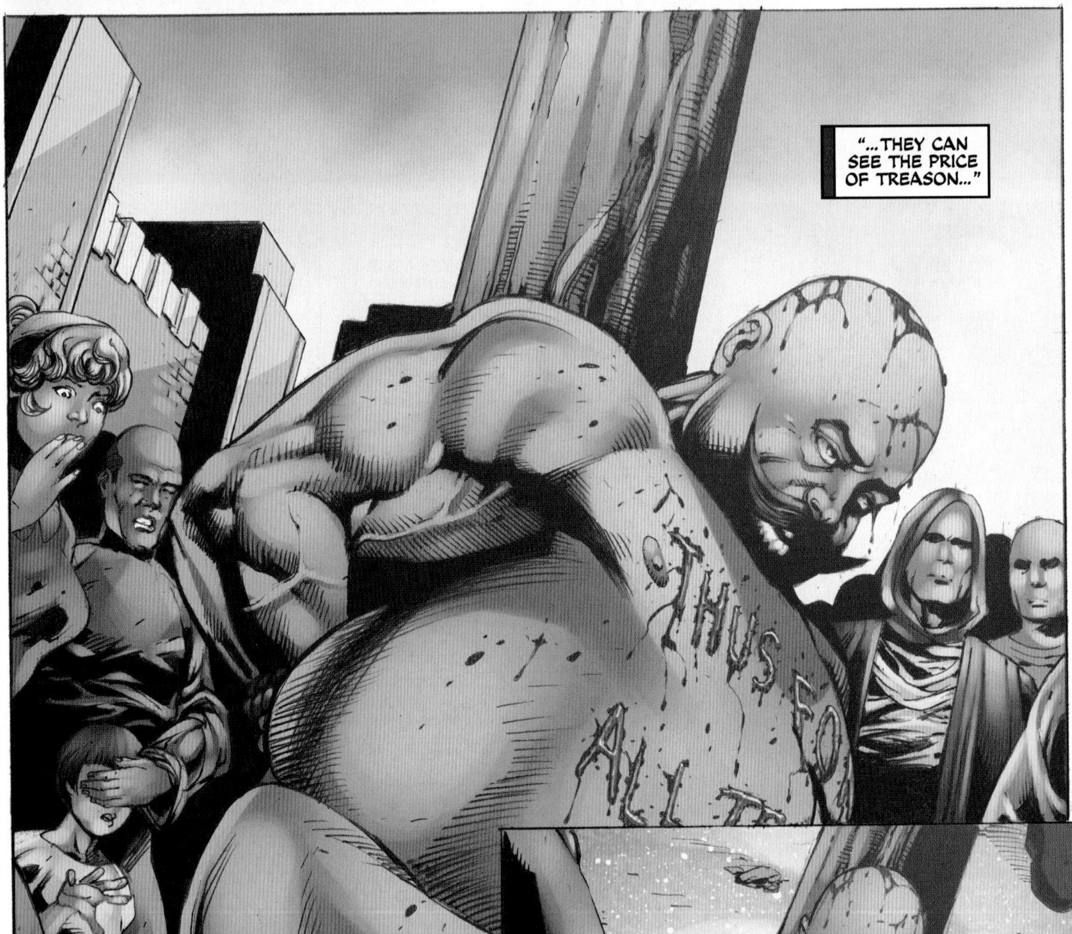
"...THEY CAN SEE THE PRICE OF TREASON..."

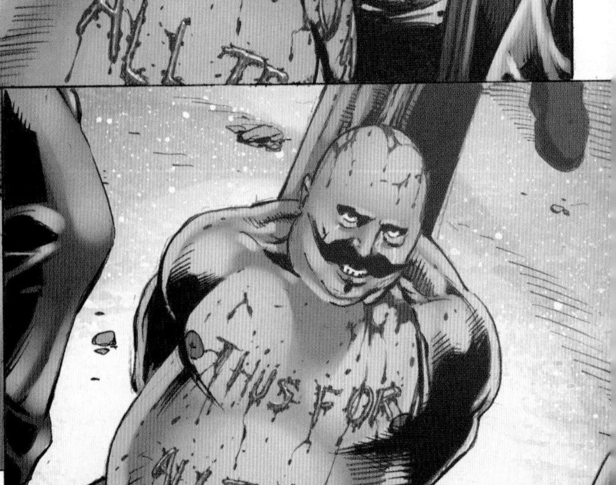
THUS FOR ALL TRAITORS

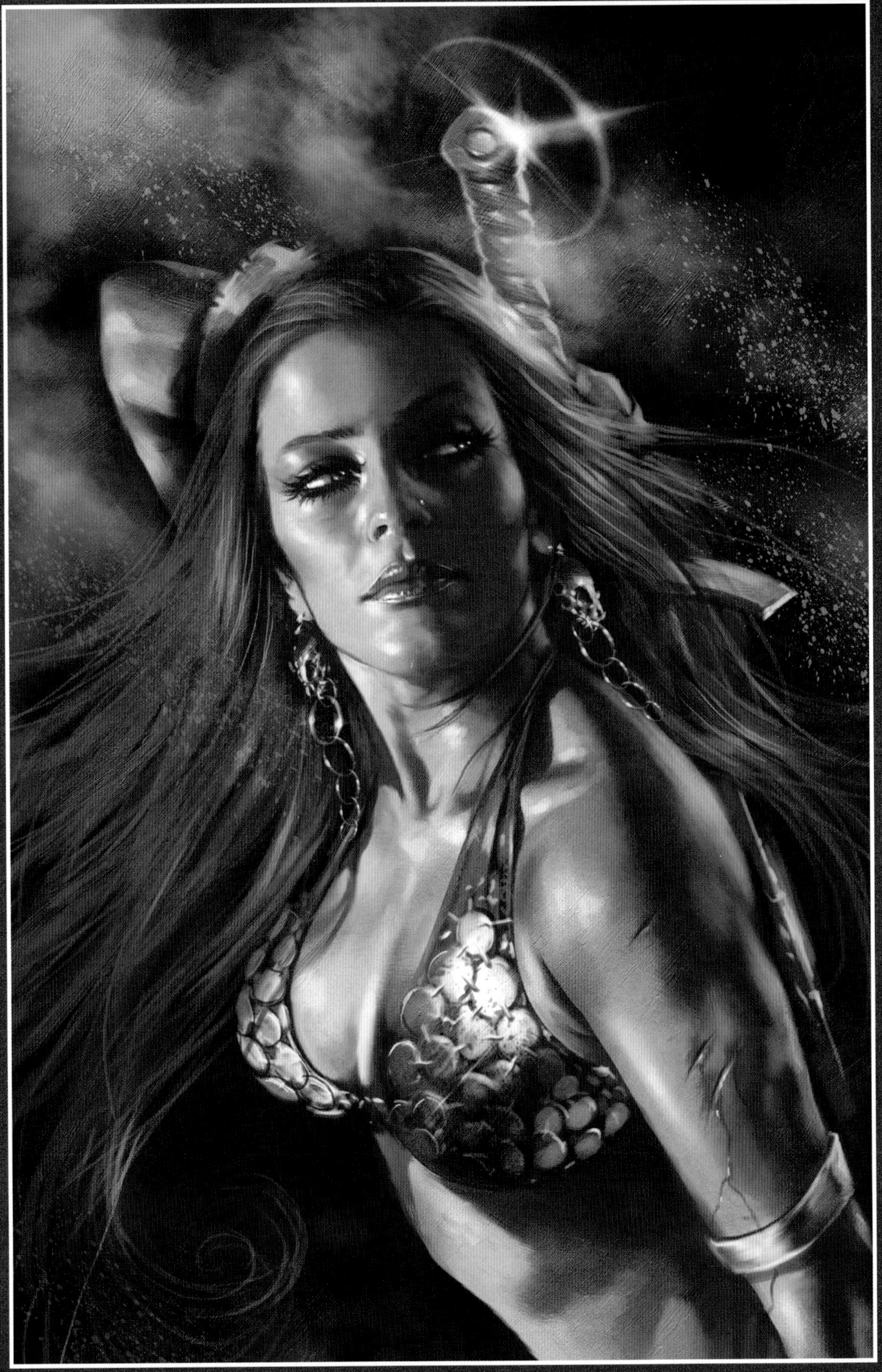

ISSUE #28 COVER BY LUCIO PARRILLO

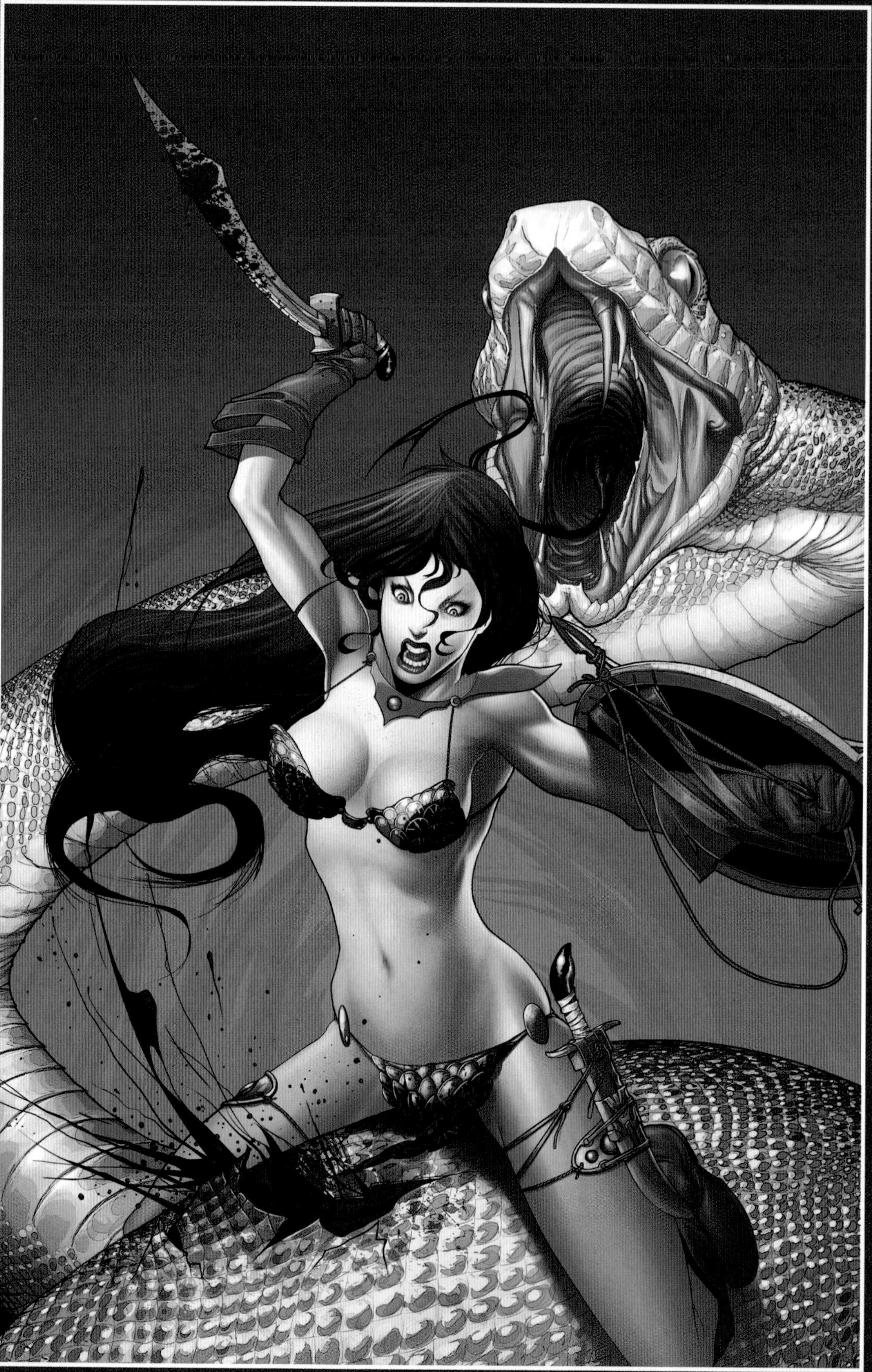

ISSUE #28 COVER BY FRANK MARTIN JR.

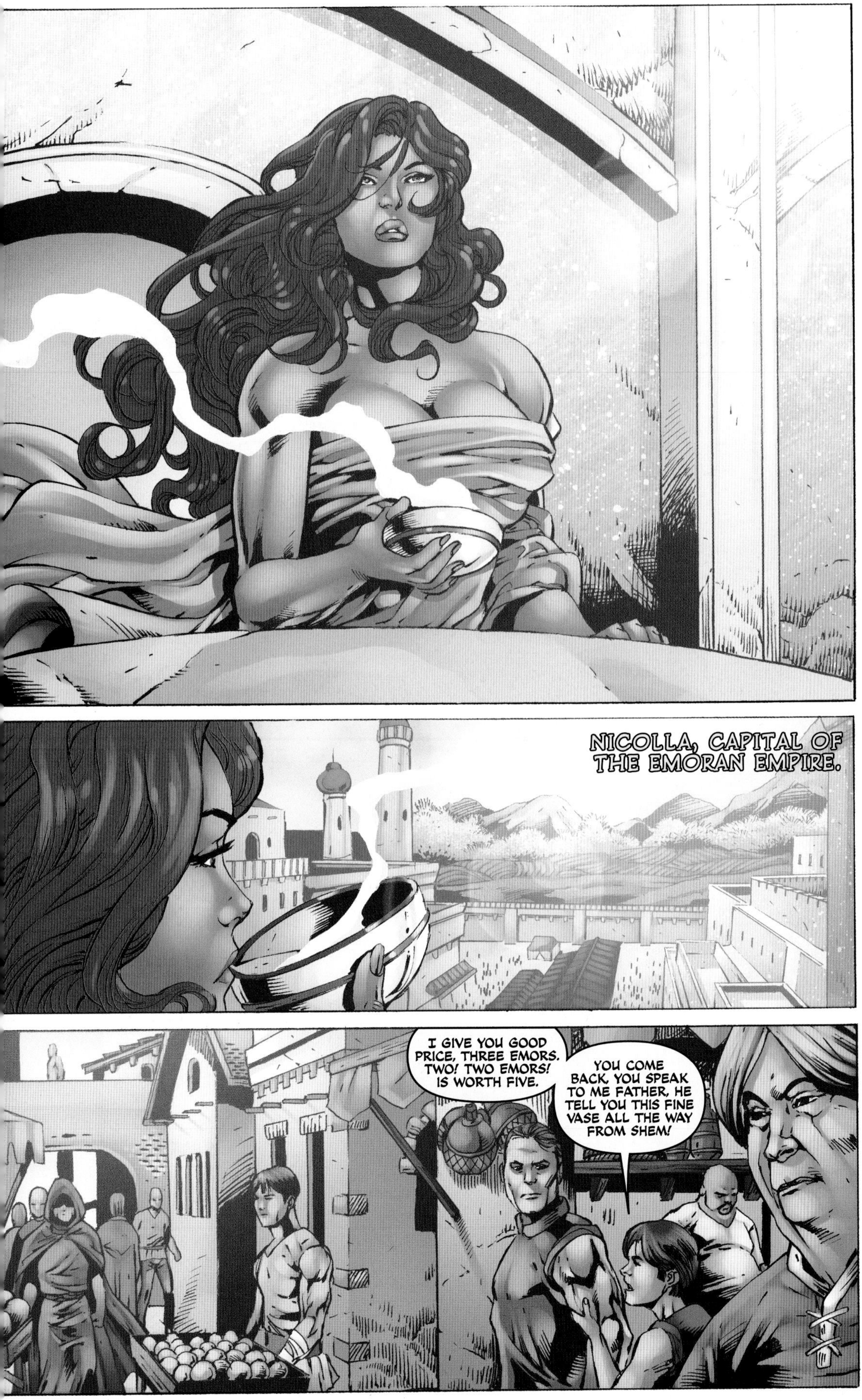
NICOLLA, CAPITAL OF THE EMORAN EMPIRE.
I GIVE YOU GOOD PRICE, THREE EMORS. TWO! TWO EMORS! IS WORTH FIVE.
YOU COME BACK, YOU SPEAK TO ME FATHER, HE TELL YOU THIS FINE VASE ALL THE WAY FROM SHEM!

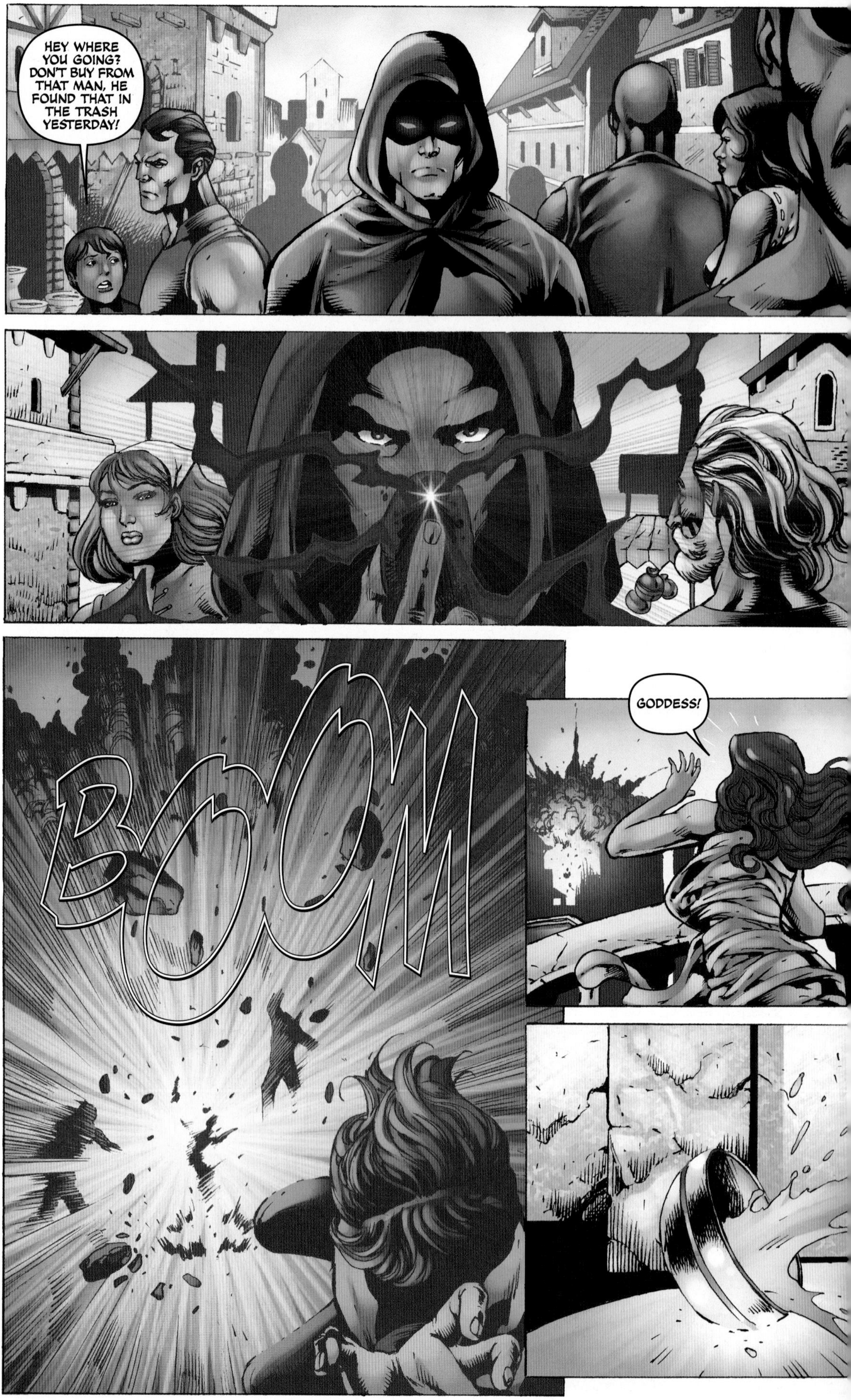
HEY WHERE YOU GOING? DON'T BUY FROM THAT MAN, HE FOUND THAT IN THE TRASH YESTERDAY!
BOOM
GODDESS!

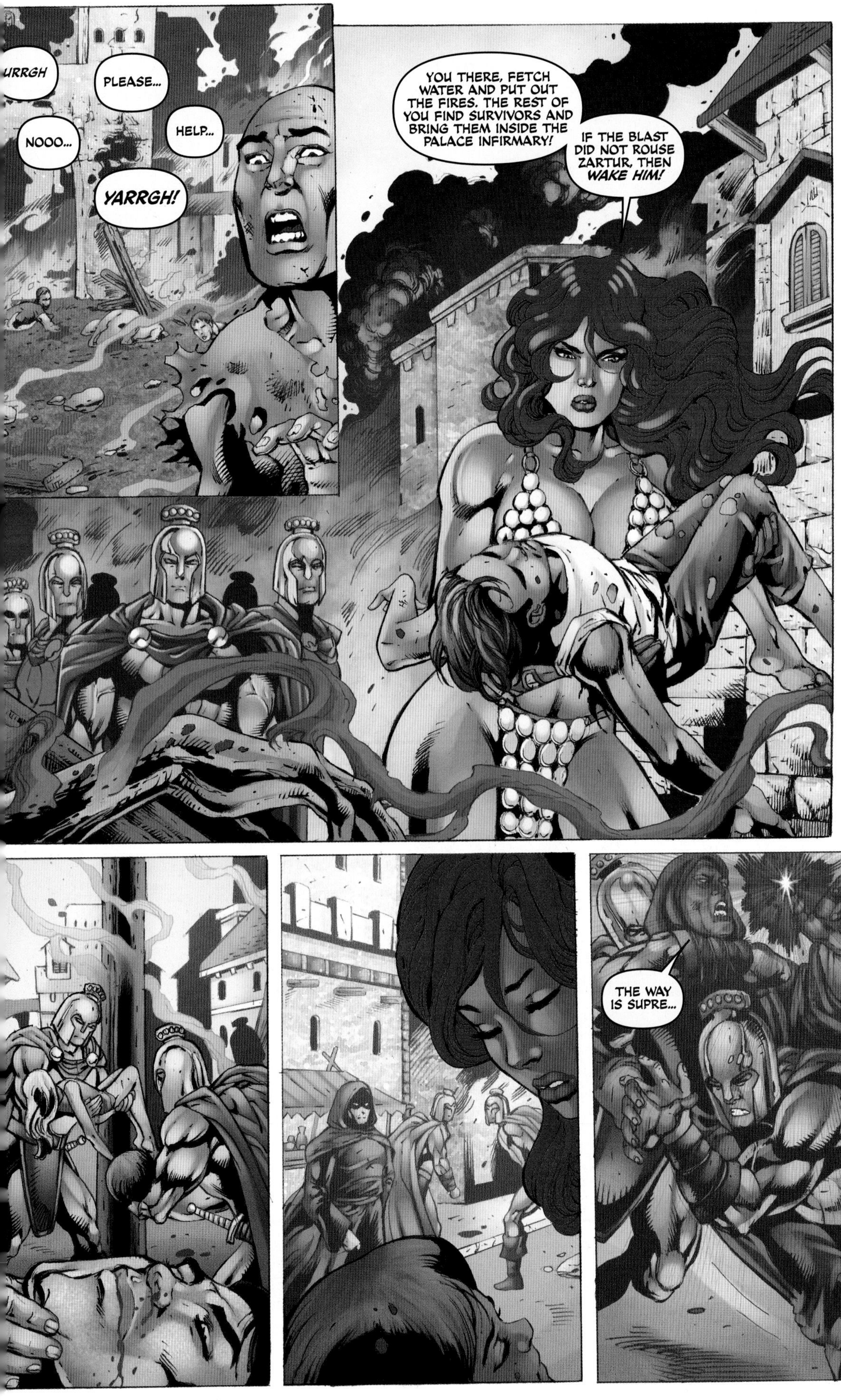
URRGH
PLEASE...
NOOO...
HELP...
YARRGH!
YOU THERE, FETCH WATER AND PUT OUT THE FIRES. THE REST OF YOU FIND SURVIVORS AND BRING THEM INSIDE THE PALACE INFIRMARY!
IF THE BLAST DID NOT ROUSE ZARTUR, THEN *WAKE HIM!*
THE WAY IS SUPRE...

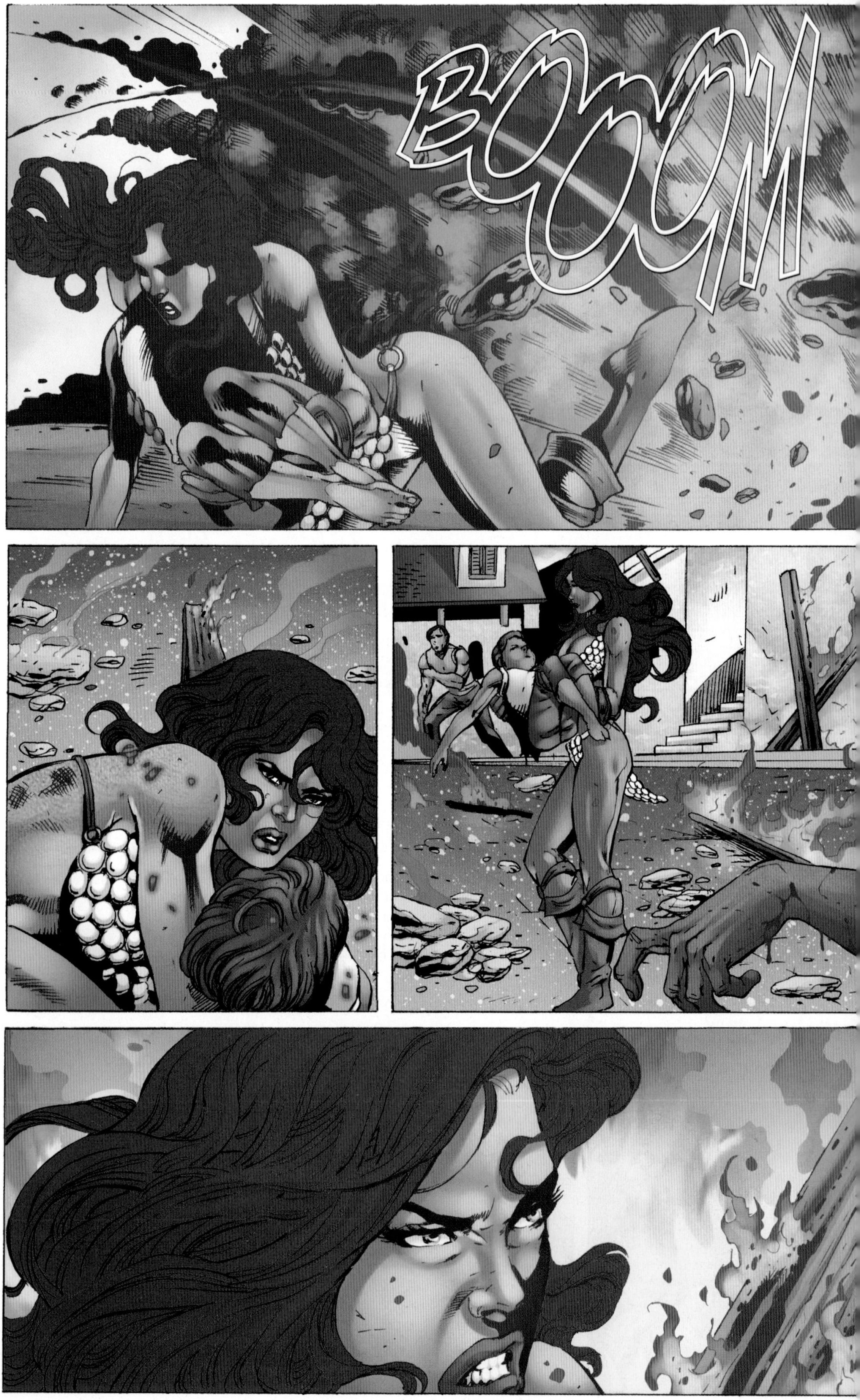
BOOOM

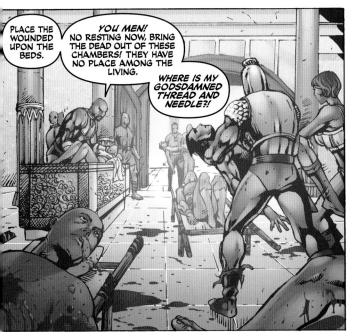

PLACE THE WOUNDED UPON THE BEDS.

YOU MEN! NO RESTING NOW, BRING THE DEAD OUT OF THESE CHAMBERS! THEY HAVE NO PLACE AMONG THE LIVING.

WHERE IS MY GODSDAMNED THREAD AND NEEDLE?!

LOOK AT ME MAIDEN, THE WORST IS PAST NOW THAT I HAVE THIS EVIL THING OUT OF YOU. ALL THAT IS LEFT IS TO SOW YOU UP. BE GLAD, YOU ARE GOING TO LIVE.

MY HUSBAND! WHERE IS MY HUSBAND, WHY IS HE NOT HERE?!

TRUTHFULLY MAIDEN, I KNOW NOT.

PLACE THIS ONE IN A BED, AND BRING ME THE NEXT.

NOT THAT ONE, HE WILL HOLD A WHILE LONGER, BRING ME A...

A CHILD ZARTUR, I HAVE ONE HERE.

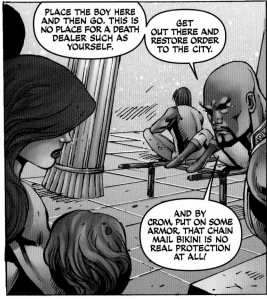

PLACE THE BOY HERE AND THEN GO. THIS IS NO PLACE FOR A DEATH DEALER SUCH AS YOURSELF.

GET OUT THERE AND RESTORE ORDER TO THE CITY.

AND BY CROM, PUT ON SOME ARMOR, THAT CHAIN MAIL BIKINI IS NO REAL PROTECTION AT ALL!

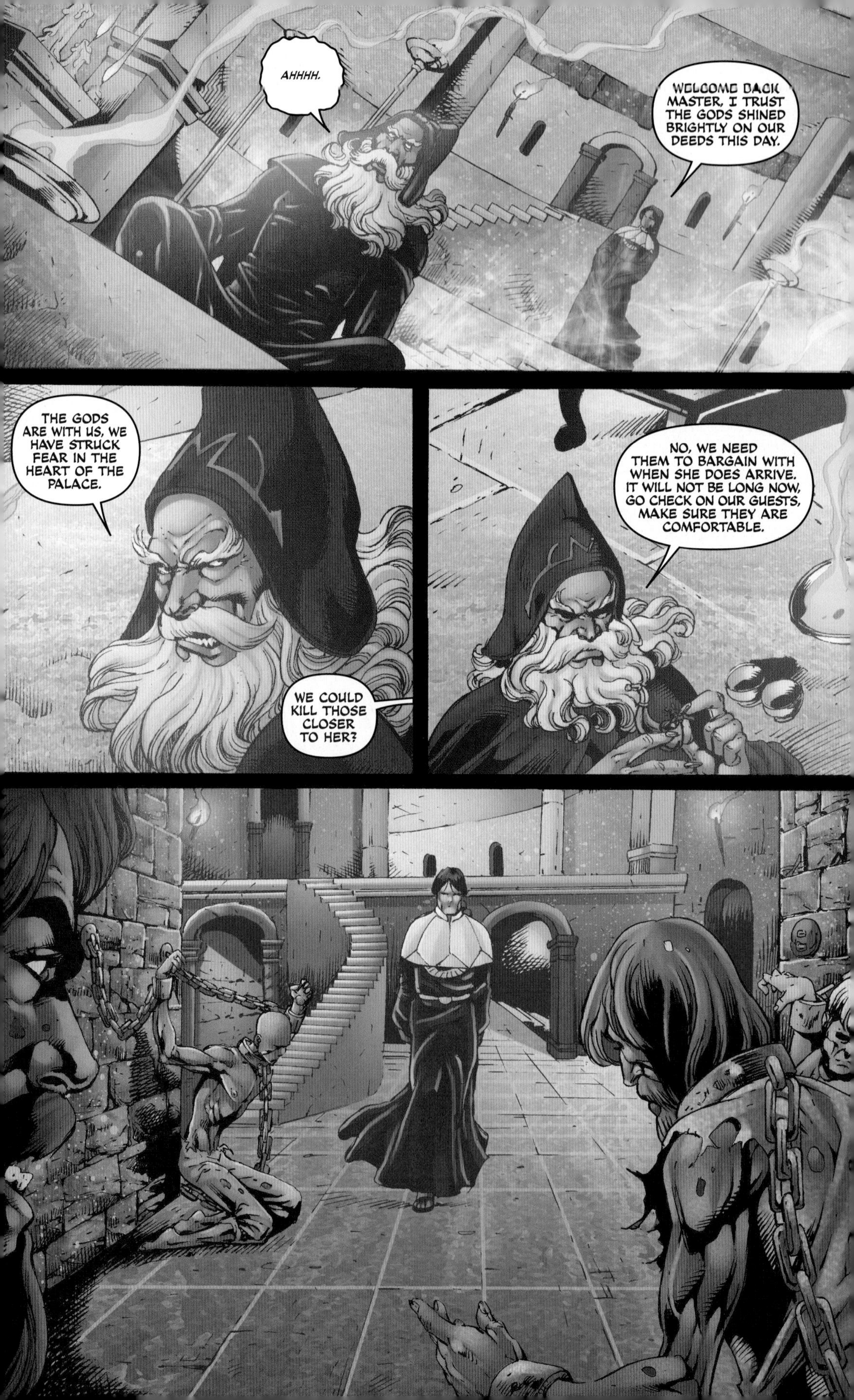
AHHHH.
WELCOME BACK MASTER, I TRUST THE GODS SHINED BRIGHTLY ON OUR DEEDS THIS DAY.
THE GODS ARE WITH US, WE HAVE STRUCK FEAR IN THE HEART OF THE PALACE.
WE COULD KILL THOSE CLOSER TO HER?
NO, WE NEED THEM TO BARGAIN WITH WHEN SHE DOES ARRIVE. IT WILL NOT BE LONG NOW, GO CHECK ON OUR GUESTS, MAKE SURE THEY ARE COMFORTABLE.

GOOD MORNING XANDER, STILL SEARCHING FOR THE WAY, ARE YOU? YOU RODE WITH EMPEROR ANTONIOUS, DID YOU NOT? AND NOW YOU ARE HERE, AT THE BIDDING OF HIS KILLER...CURIOUS...

WHY DID THEY LET YOU LIVE?

THE GODS FORGIVE ALL OF THOSE WITH A CONTRITE HEART. CONFESS YOUR SINS, SAY THE EMPRESS IS A LIAR, AND A TYRANT WHO PERSECUTES THOSE THAT FOLLOW THE WAY. TELL THEM YOU HAVE FOUND THE WAY, AS MUST EVERY CITIZEN OF EMORA. TELL THEM YOU WILL FIGHT THE GODLESS EMPRESS UNTIL YOUR LAST DROP OF BLOOD.

HA HA HA HA HA HA HA!

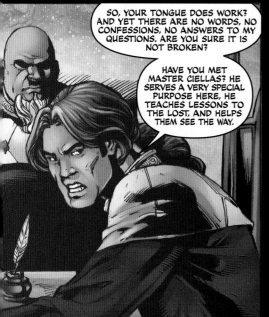

SO, YOUR TONGUE DOES WORK? AND YET THERE ARE NO WORDS, NO CONFESSIONS, NO ANSWERS TO MY QUESTIONS. ARE YOU SURE IT IS NOT BROKEN?

HAVE YOU MET MASTER CIELLAS? HE SERVES A VERY SPECIAL PURPOSE HERE, HE TEACHES LESSONS TO THE LOST, AND HELPS THEM SEE THE WAY.

CIELLAS, THIS ONE HAS A BROKEN TONGUE, FIX IT FOR HIM.

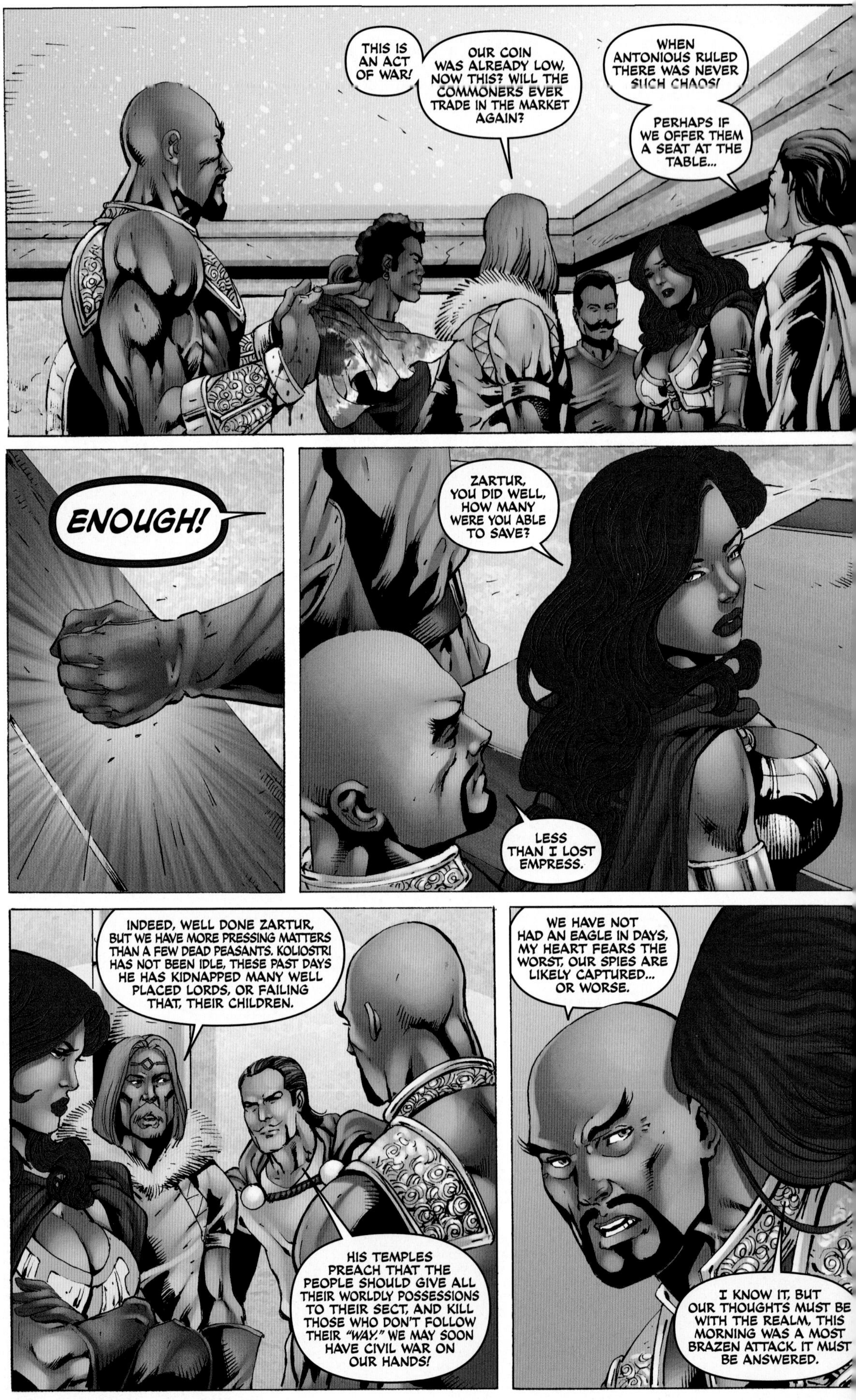

THIS IS AN ACT OF WAR!
OUR COIN WAS ALREADY LOW, NOW THIS? WILL THE COMMONERS EVER TRADE IN THE MARKET AGAIN?
WHEN ANTONIOUS RULED THERE WAS NEVER SUCH CHAOS!
PERHAPS IF WE OFFER THEM A SEAT AT THE TABLE...
ENOUGH!
ZARTUR, YOU DID WELL, HOW MANY WERE YOU ABLE TO SAVE?
LESS THAN I LOST EMPRESS.
INDEED, WELL DONE ZARTUR, BUT WE HAVE MORE PRESSING MATTERS THAN A FEW DEAD PEASANTS. KOLIOSTRI HAS NOT BEEN IDLE, THESE PAST DAYS HE HAS KIDNAPPED MANY WELL PLACED LORDS, OR FAILING THAT, THEIR CHILDREN.
HIS TEMPLES PREACH THAT THE PEOPLE SHOULD GIVE ALL THEIR WORLDLY POSSESSIONS TO THEIR SECT, AND KILL THOSE WHO DON'T FOLLOW THEIR "WAY." WE MAY SOON HAVE CIVIL WAR ON OUR HANDS!
WE HAVE NOT HAD AN EAGLE IN DAYS, MY HEART FEARS THE WORST, OUR SPIES ARE LIKELY CAPTURED... OR WORSE.
I KNOW IT, BUT OUR THOUGHTS MUST BE WITH THE REALM, THIS MORNING WAS A MOST BRAZEN ATTACK. IT MUST BE ANSWERED.

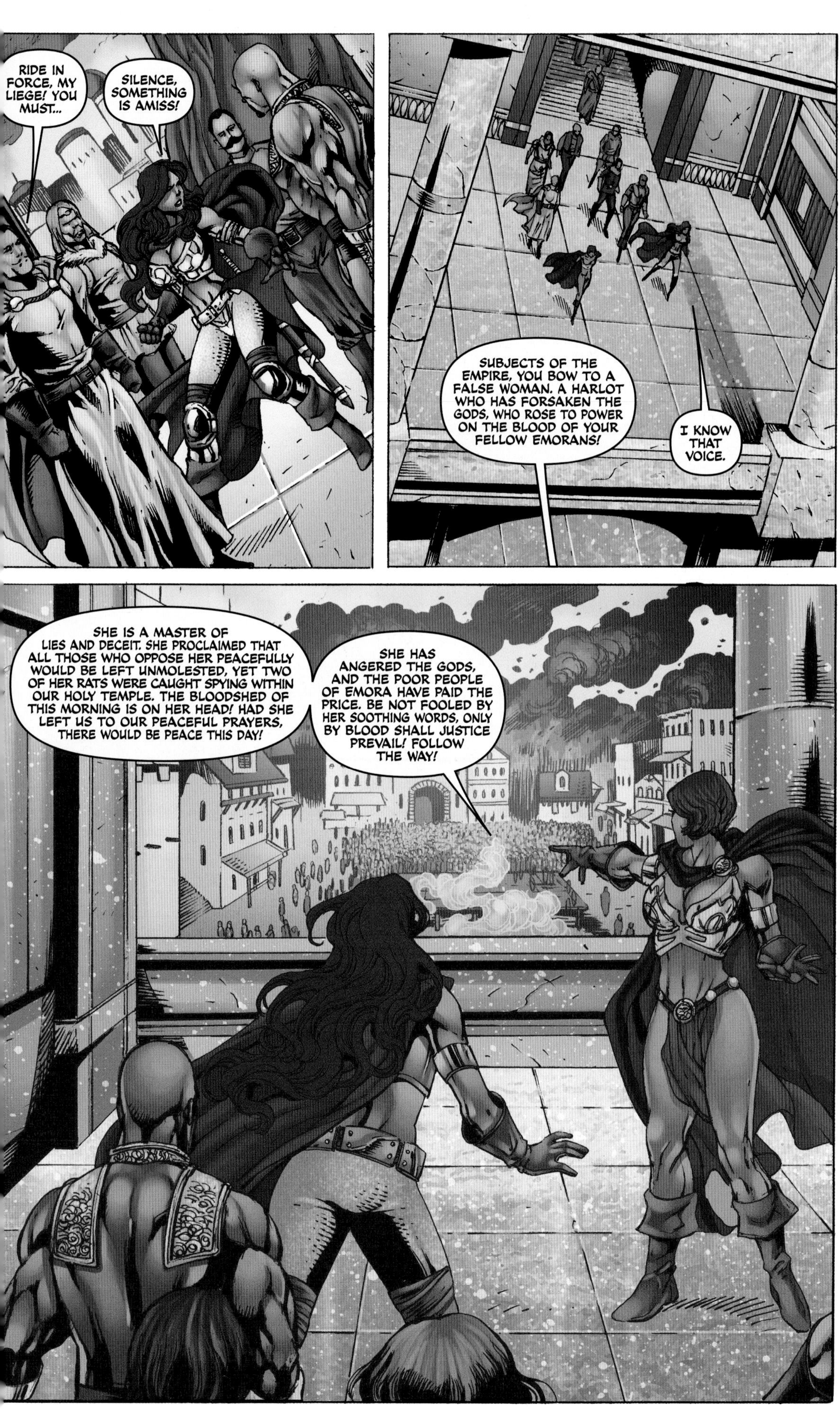
RIDE IN FORCE, MY LIEGE! YOU MUST...
SILENCE, SOMETHING IS AMISS!
SUBJECTS OF THE EMPIRE, YOU BOW TO A FALSE WOMAN. A HARLOT WHO HAS FORSAKEN THE GODS, WHO ROSE TO POWER ON THE BLOOD OF YOUR FELLOW EMORANS!
I KNOW THAT VOICE.
SHE IS A MASTER OF LIES AND DECEIT. SHE PROCLAIMED THAT ALL THOSE WHO OPPOSE HER PEACEFULLY WOULD BE LEFT UNMOLESTED, YET TWO OF HER RATS WERE CAUGHT SPYING WITHIN OUR HOLY TEMPLE. THE BLOODSHED OF THIS MORNING IS ON HER HEAD! HAD SHE LEFT US TO OUR PEACEFUL PRAYERS, THERE WOULD BE PEACE THIS DAY!
SHE HAS ANGERED THE GODS, AND THE POOR PEOPLE OF EMORA HAVE PAID THE PRICE. BE NOT FOOLED BY HER SOOTHING WORDS, ONLY BY BLOOD SHALL JUSTICE PREVAIL! FOLLOW THE WAY!

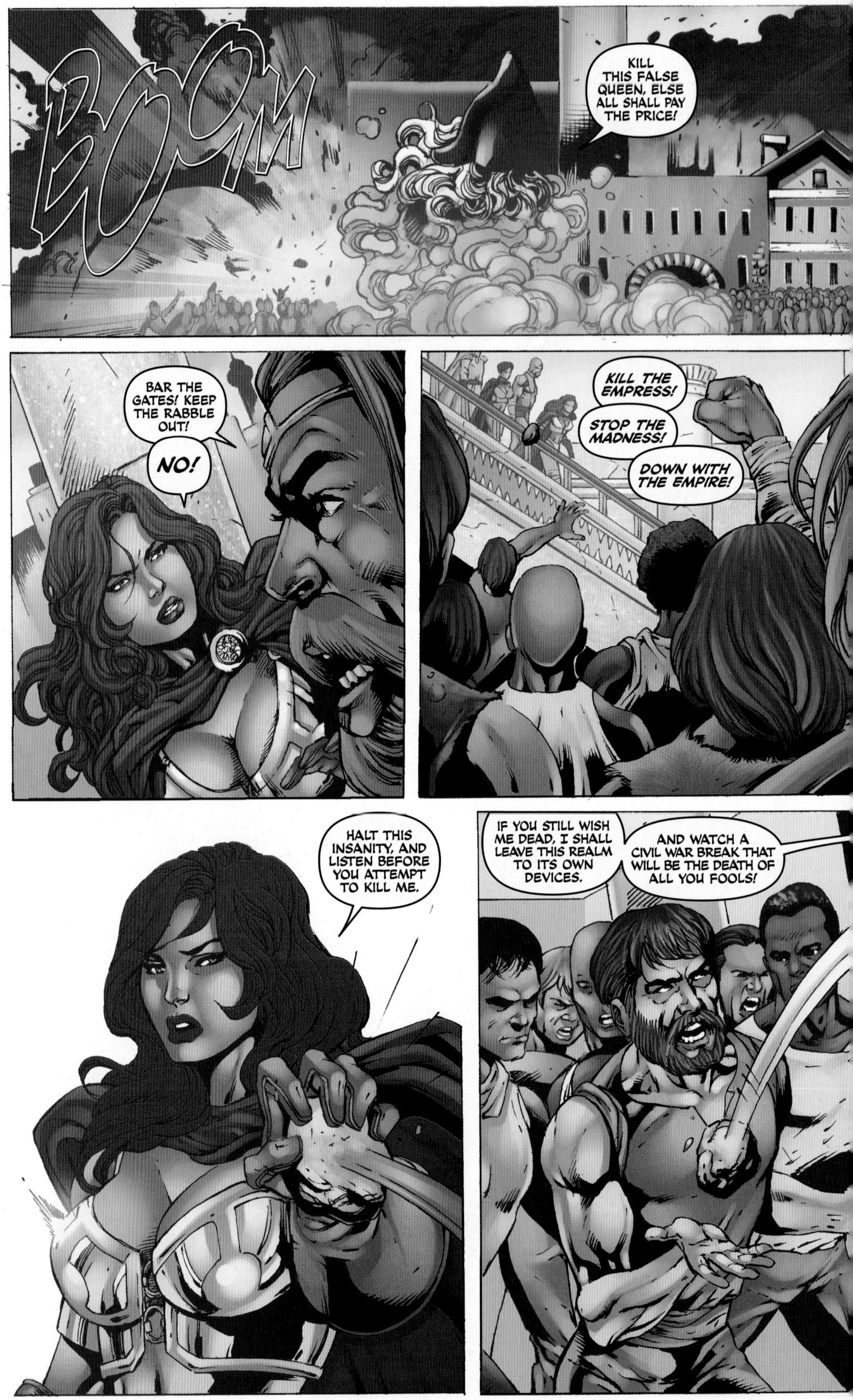
BOOM
KILL THIS FALSE QUEEN, ELSE ALL SHALL PAY THE PRICE!
BAR THE GATES! KEEP THE RABBLE OUT!
NO!
KILL THE EMPRESS!
STOP THE MADNESS!
DOWN WITH THE EMPIRE!
HALT THIS INSANITY, AND LISTEN BEFORE YOU ATTEMPT TO KILL ME.
IF YOU STILL WISH ME DEAD, I SHALL LEAVE THIS REALM TO ITS OWN DEVICES.
AND WATCH A CIVIL WAR BREAK THAT WILL BE THE DEATH OF ALL YOU FOOLS!

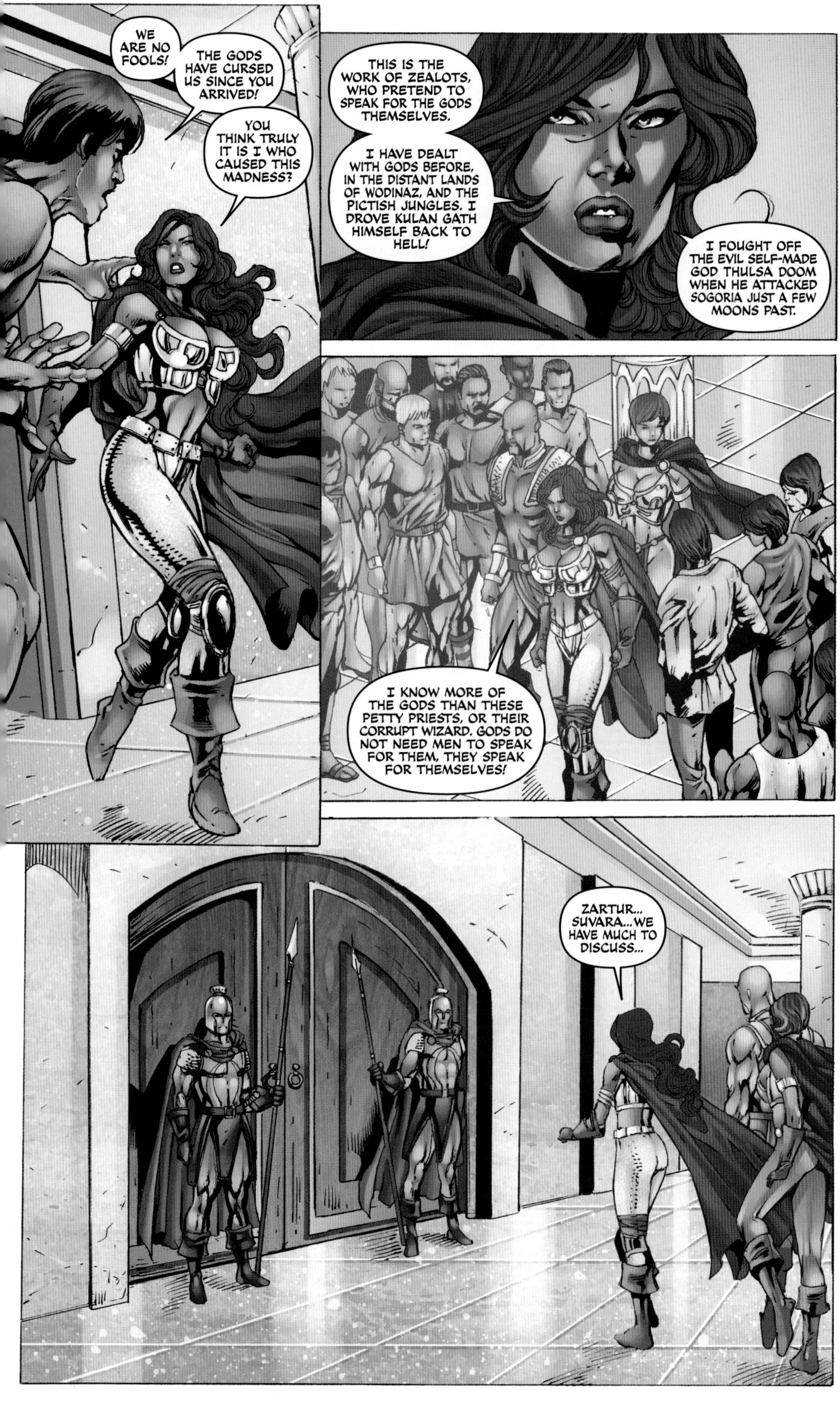
WE ARE NO FOOLS!
THE GODS HAVE CURSED US SINCE YOU ARRIVED!
YOU THINK TRULY IT IS I WHO CAUSED THIS MADNESS?
THIS IS THE WORK OF ZEALOTS, WHO PRETEND TO SPEAK FOR THE GODS THEMSELVES.
I HAVE DEALT WITH GODS BEFORE, IN THE DISTANT LANDS OF WODINAZ, AND THE PICTISH JUNGLES. I DROVE KULAN GATH HIMSELF BACK TO HELL!
I FOUGHT OFF THE EVIL SELF-MADE GOD THULSA DOOM WHEN HE ATTACKED SOGORIA JUST A FEW MOONS PAST.
I KNOW MORE OF THE GODS THAN THESE PETTY PRIESTS, OR THEIR CORRUPT WIZARD. GODS DO NOT NEED MEN TO SPEAK FOR THEM, THEY SPEAK FOR THEMSELVES!
ZARTUR... SUVARA... WE HAVE MUCH TO DISCUSS...

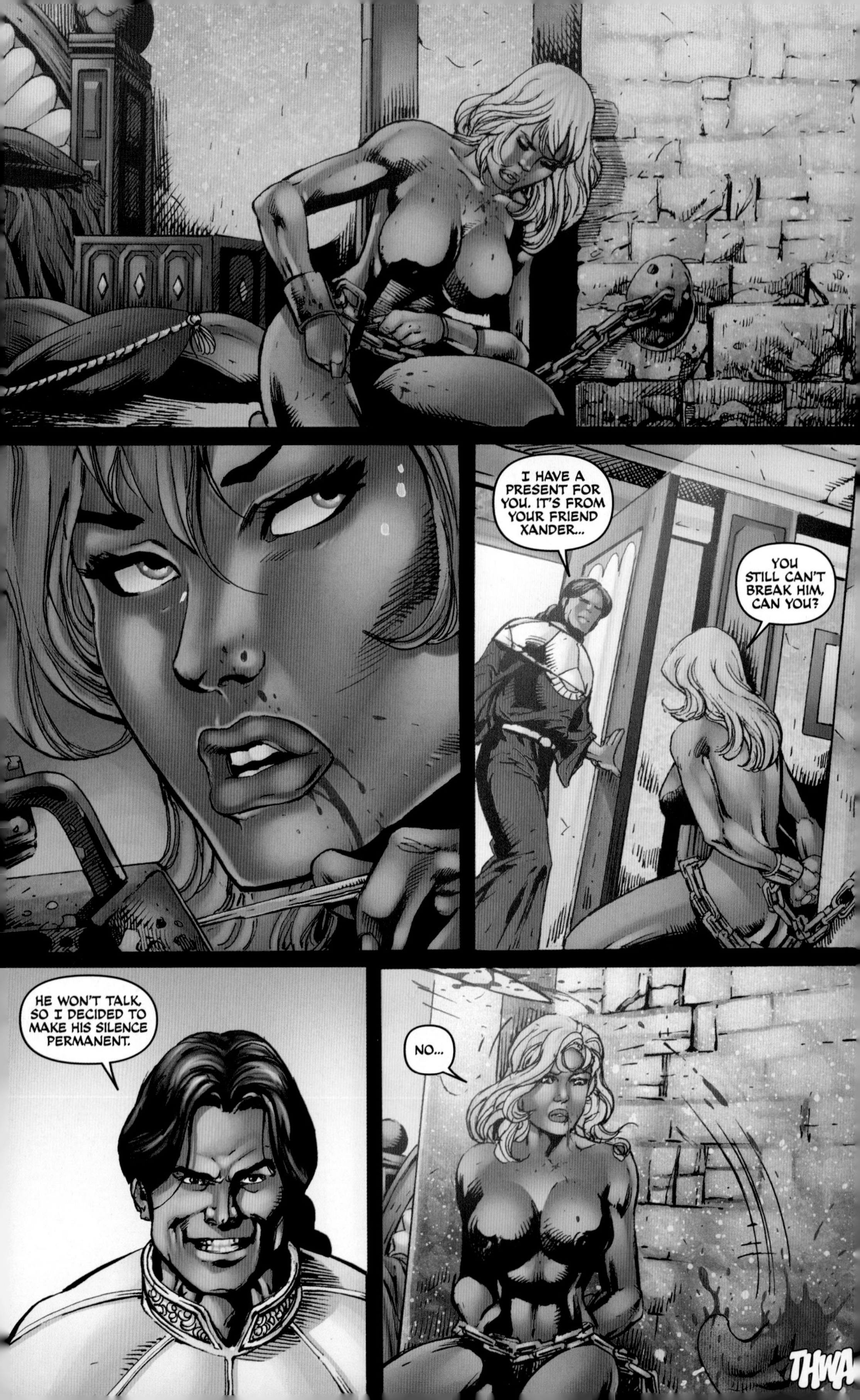
I HAVE A PRESENT FOR YOU. IT'S FROM YOUR FRIEND XANDER...
YOU STILL CAN'T BREAK HIM, CAN YOU?
HE WON'T TALK, SO I DECIDED TO MAKE HIS SILENCE PERMANENT.
NO...
THWA

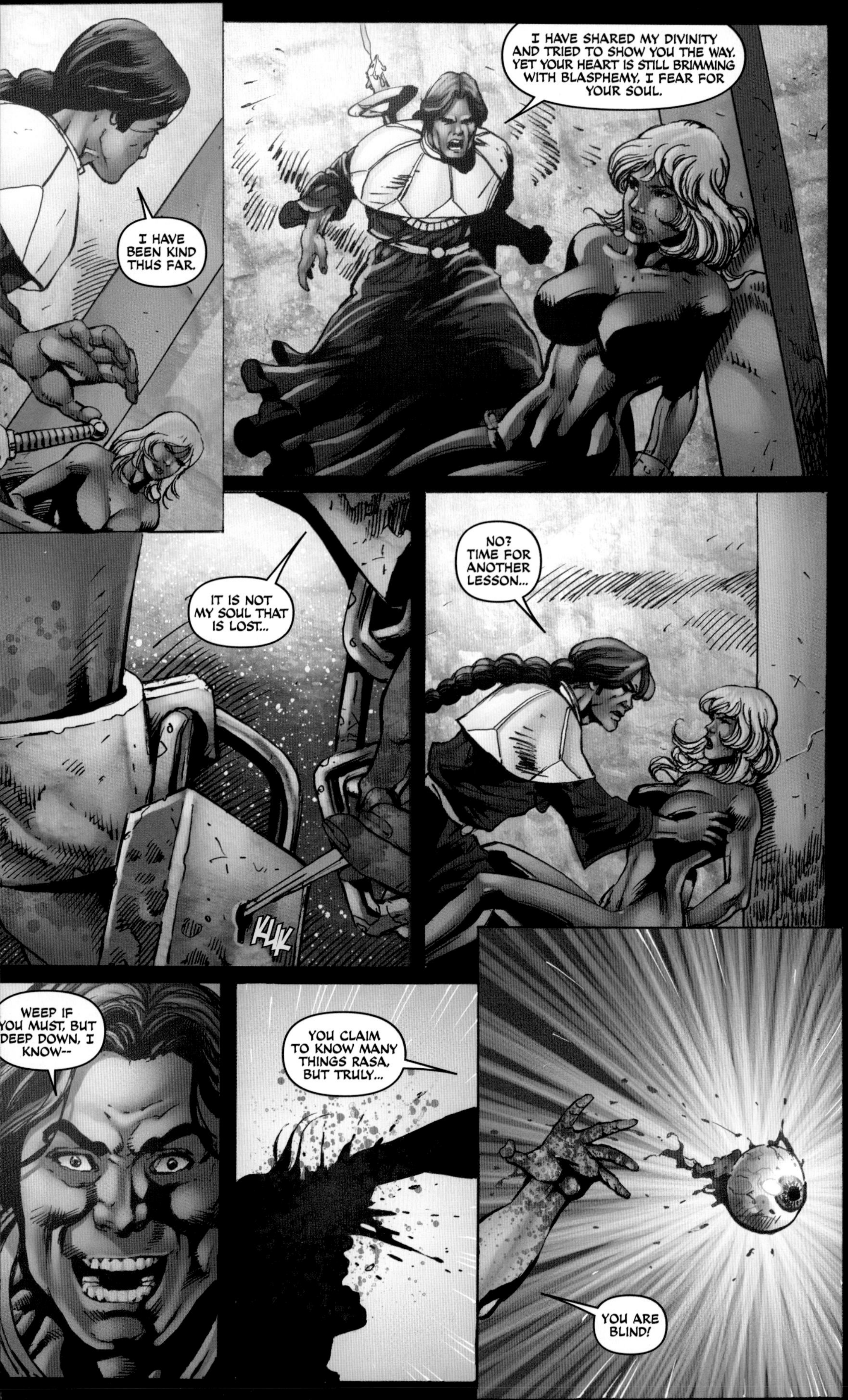
I HAVE BEEN KIND THUS FAR.
I HAVE SHARED MY DIVINITY AND TRIED TO SHOW YOU THE WAY. YET YOUR HEART IS STILL BRIMMING WITH BLASPHEMY, I FEAR FOR YOUR SOUL.
IT IS NOT MY SOUL THAT IS LOST...
KLIK
NO? TIME FOR ANOTHER LESSON...
WEEP IF YOU MUST, BUT DEEP DOWN, I KNOW--
YOU CLAIM TO KNOW MANY THINGS RASA, BUT TRULY...
YOU ARE BLIND!

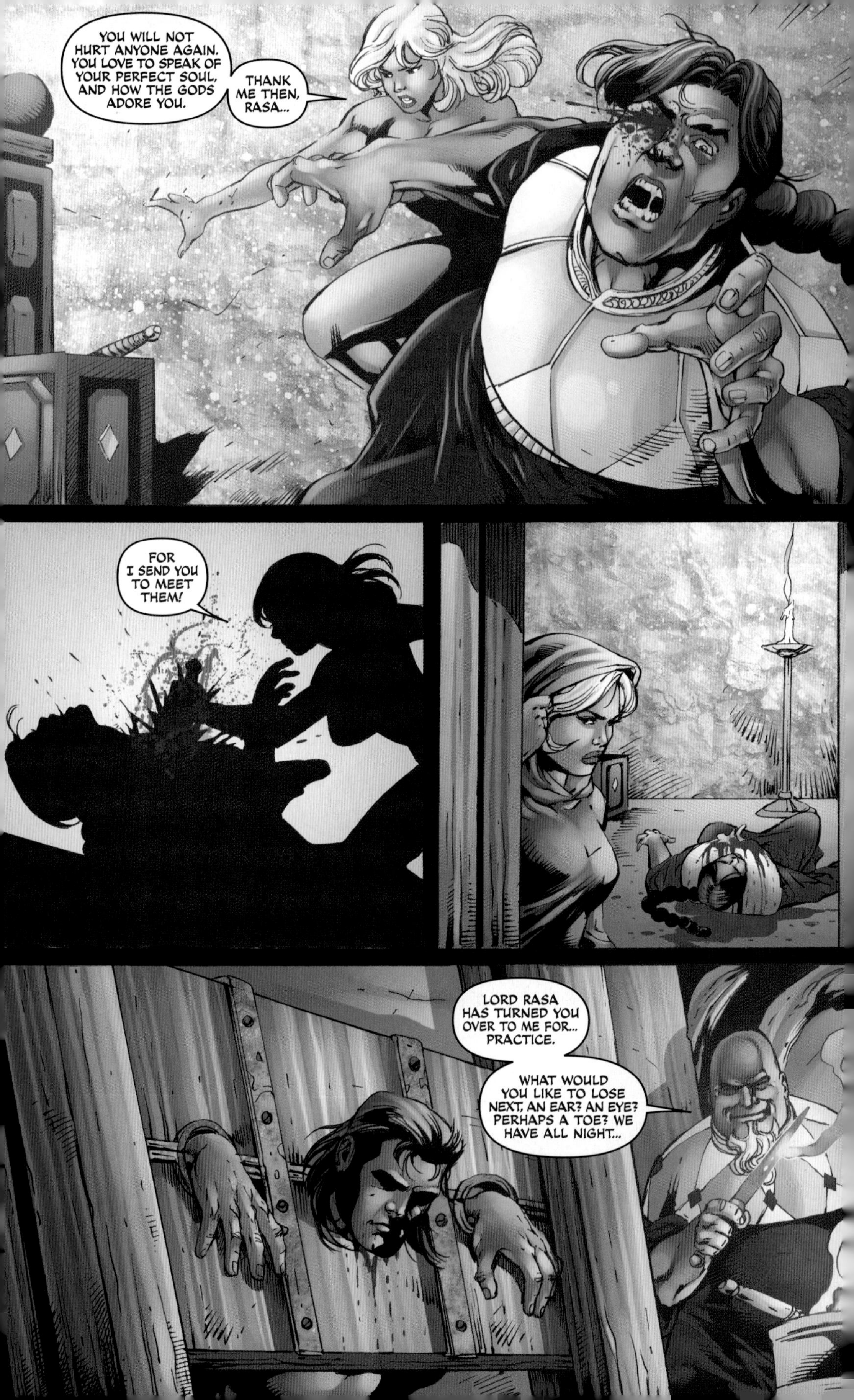
YOU WILL NOT HURT ANYONE AGAIN. YOU LOVE TO SPEAK OF YOUR PERFECT SOUL, AND HOW THE GODS ADORE YOU.
THANK ME THEN, RASA...
FOR I SEND YOU TO MEET THEM!
LORD RASA HAS TURNED YOU OVER TO ME FOR... PRACTICE.
WHAT WOULD YOU LIKE TO LOSE NEXT, AN EAR? AN EYE? PERHAPS A TOE? WE HAVE ALL NIGHT...

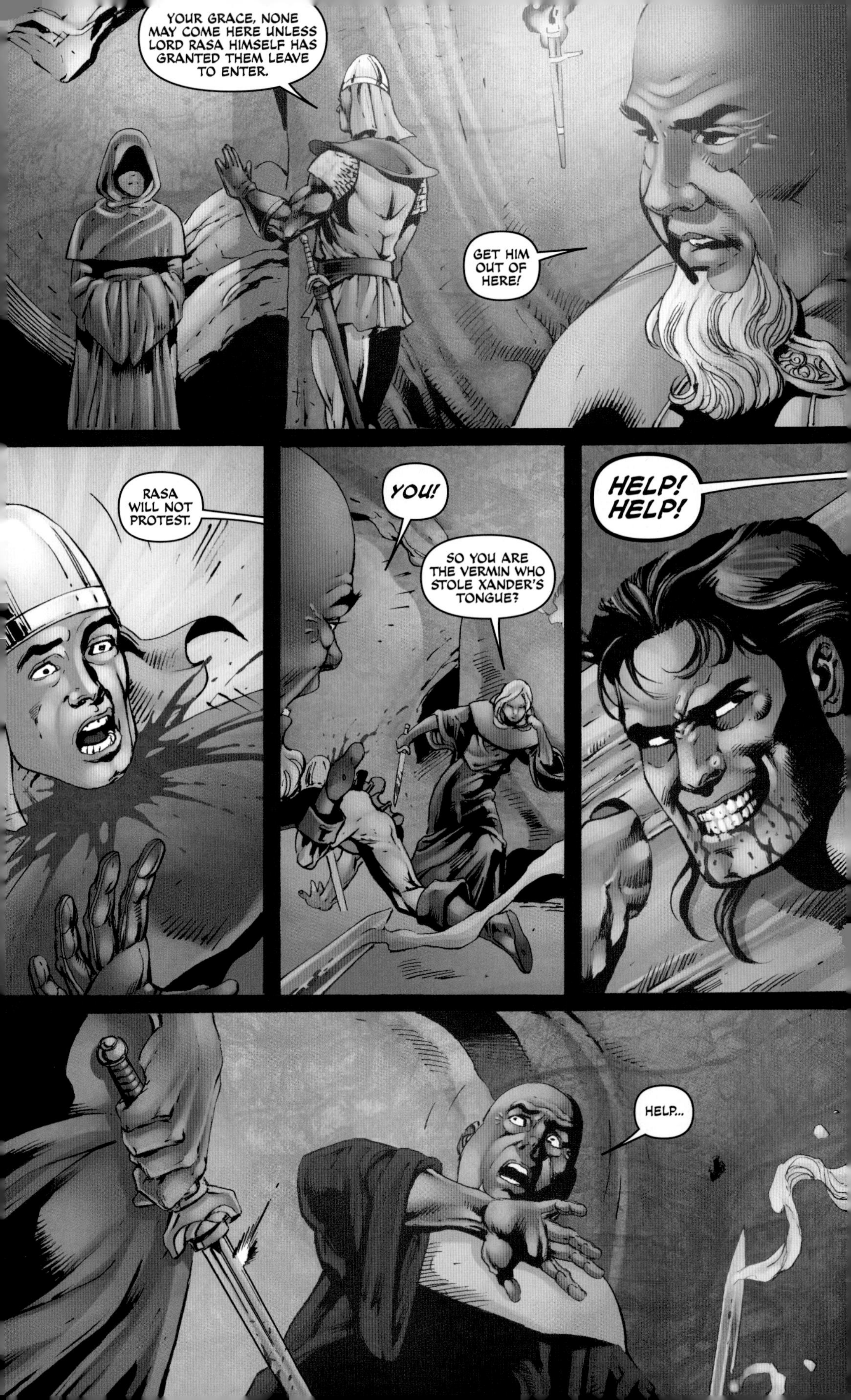
YOUR GRACE, NONE MAY COME HERE UNLESS LORD RASA HIMSELF HAS GRANTED THEM LEAVE TO ENTER.
GET HIM OUT OF HERE!
RASA WILL NOT PROTEST.
YOU!
SO YOU ARE THE VERMIN WHO STOLE XANDER'S TONGUE?
HELP! HELP!
HELP...

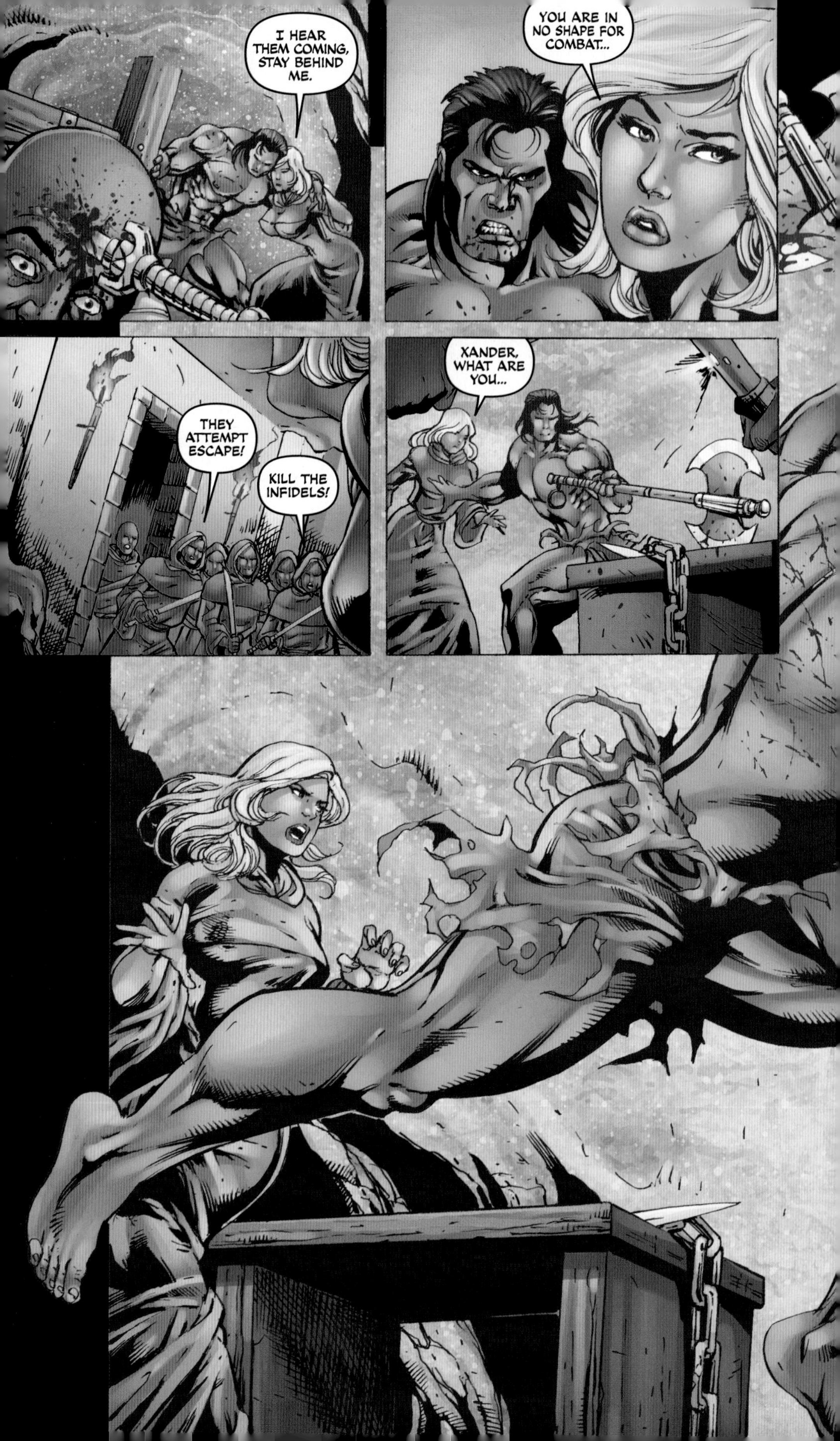

I HEAR THEM COMING, STAY BEHIND ME.
YOU ARE IN NO SHAPE FOR COMBAT...
THEY ATTEMPT ESCAPE!
KILL THE INFIDELS!
XANDER, WHAT ARE YOU...

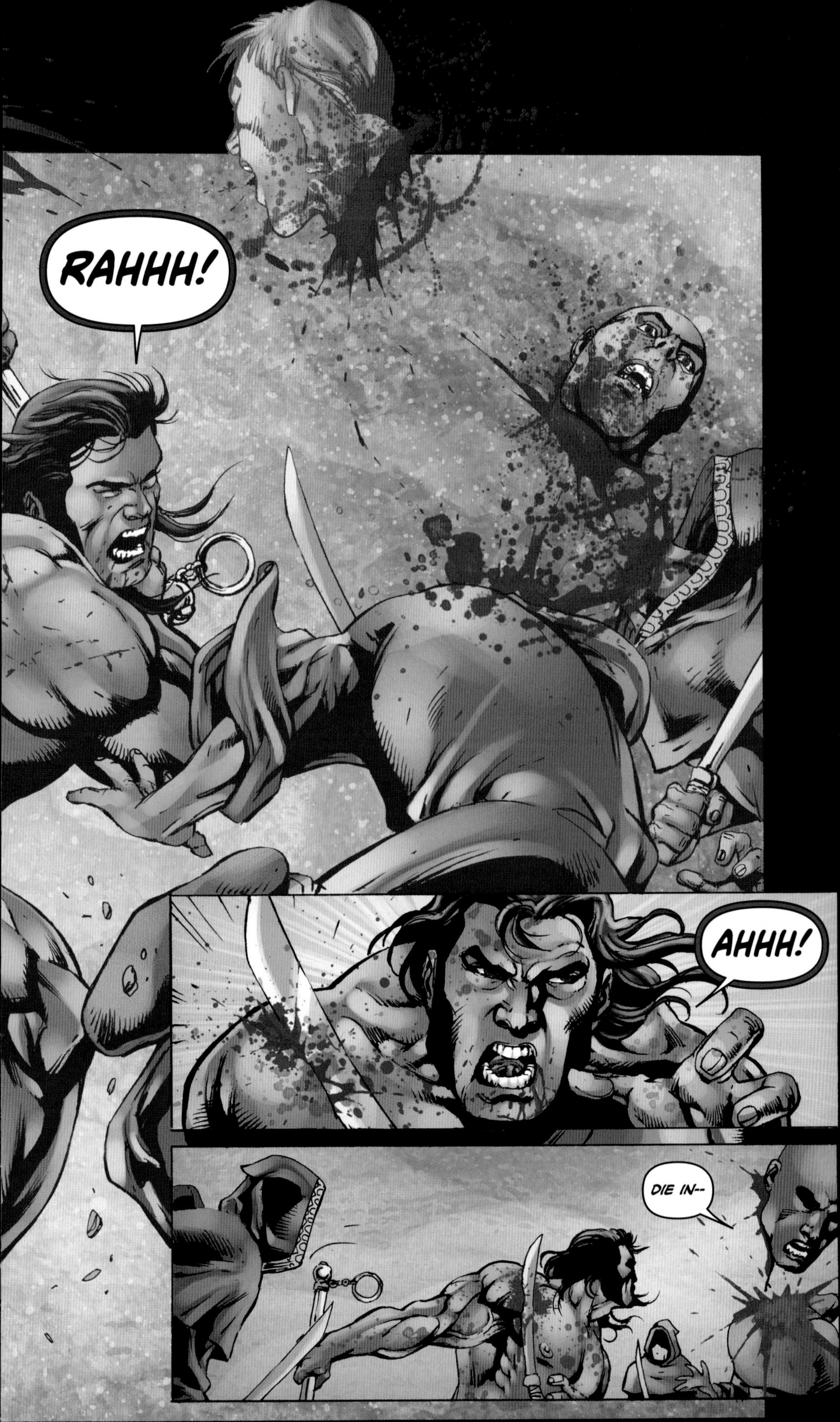
RAHHH!
AHHH!
DIE IN--

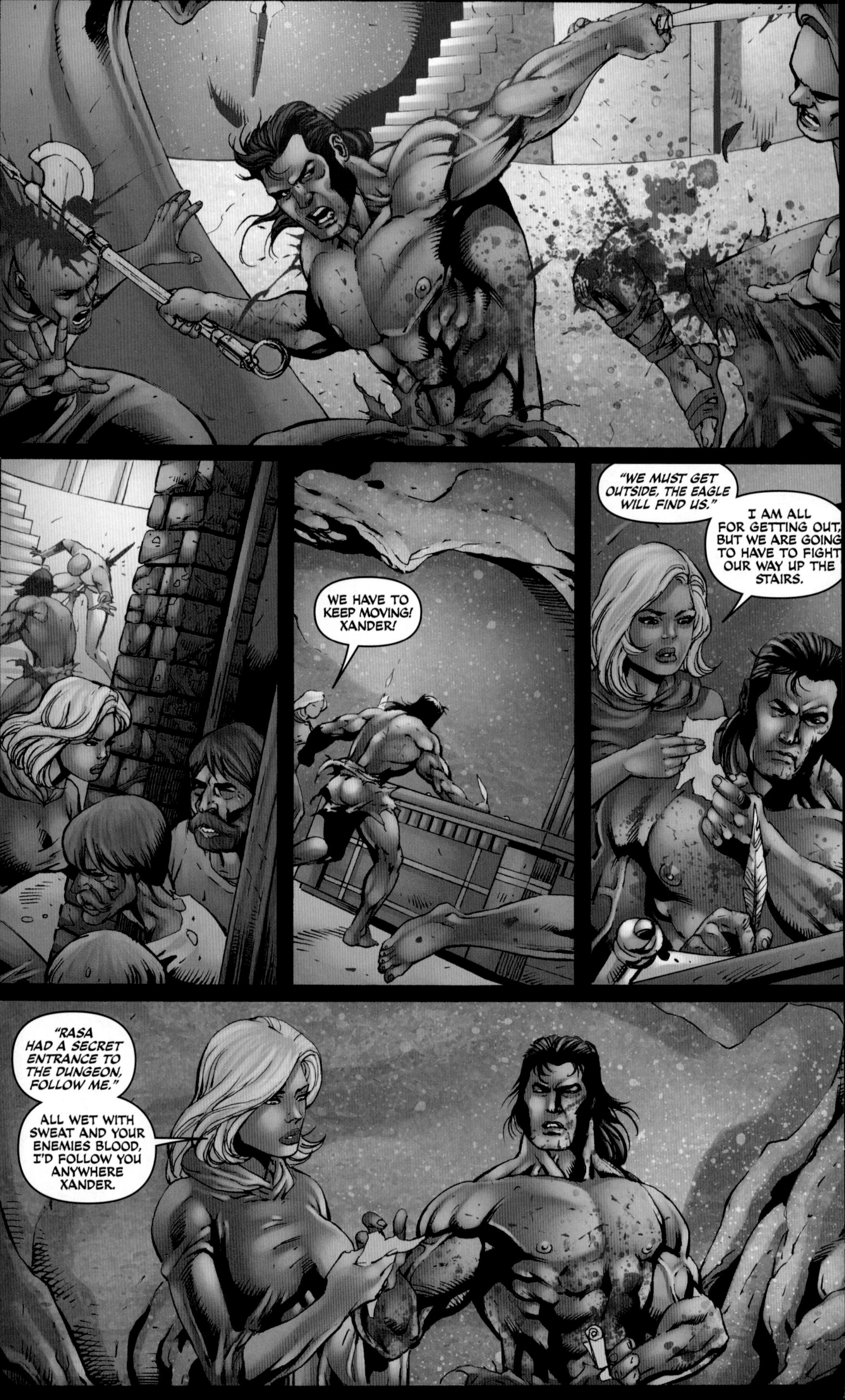
WE HAVE TO KEEP MOVING! XANDER!
"WE MUST GET OUTSIDE, THE EAGLE WILL FIND US."
I AM ALL FOR GETTING OUT, BUT WE ARE GOING TO HAVE TO FIGHT OUR WAY UP THE STAIRS.
"RASA HAD A SECRET ENTRANCE TO THE DUNGEON, FOLLOW ME."
ALL WET WITH SWEAT AND YOUR ENEMIES BLOOD, I'D FOLLOW YOU ANYWHERE XANDER.

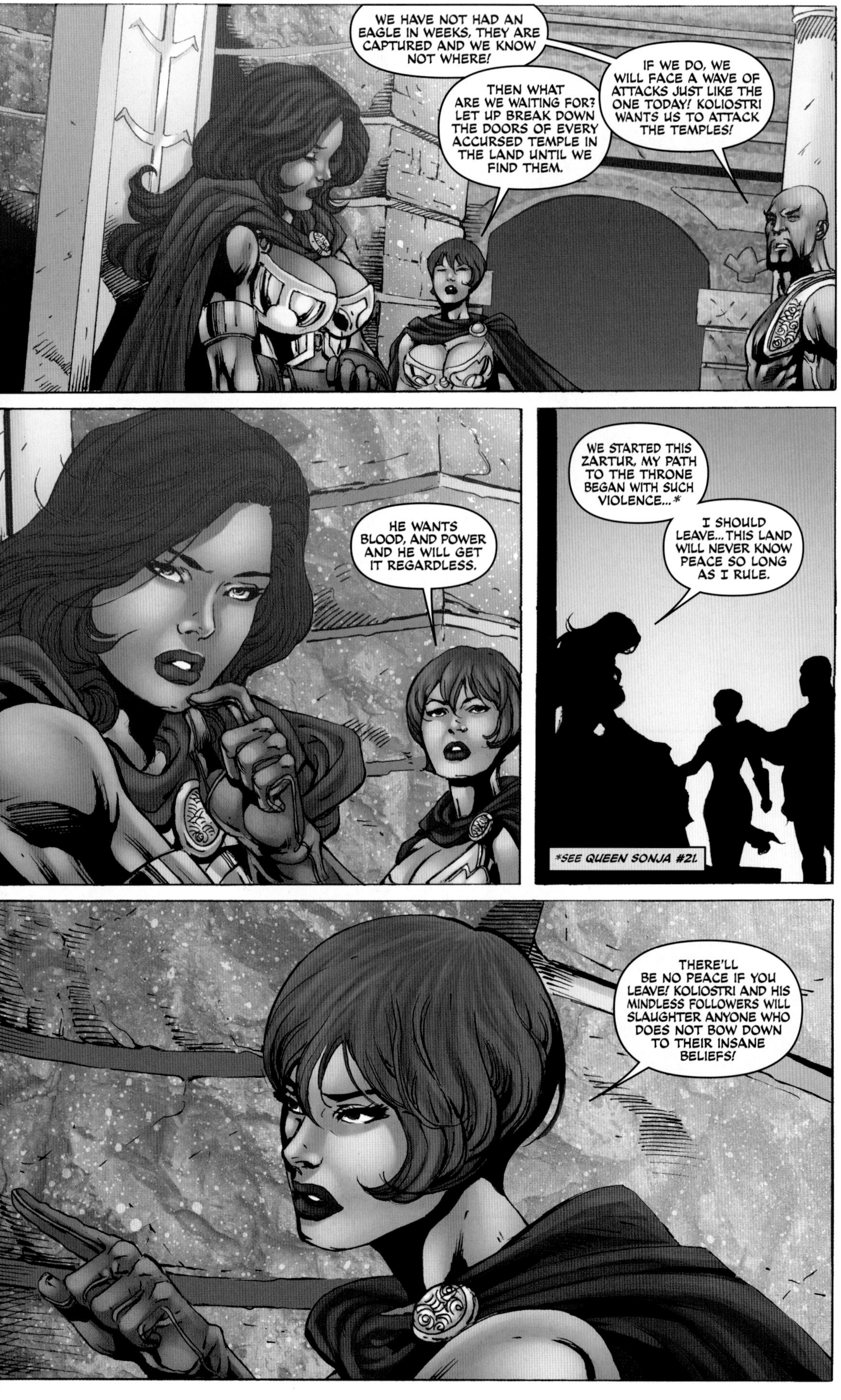
WE HAVE NOT HAD AN EAGLE IN WEEKS, THEY ARE CAPTURED AND WE KNOW NOT WHERE!
THEN WHAT ARE WE WAITING FOR? LET UP BREAK DOWN THE DOORS OF EVERY ACCURSED TEMPLE IN THE LAND UNTIL WE FIND THEM.
IF WE DO, WE WILL FACE A WAVE OF ATTACKS JUST LIKE THE ONE TODAY! KOLIOSTRI WANTS US TO ATTACK THE TEMPLES!
HE WANTS BLOOD, AND POWER AND HE WILL GET IT REGARDLESS.
WE STARTED THIS ZARTUR, MY PATH TO THE THRONE BEGAN WITH SUCH VIOLENCE...*
I SHOULD LEAVE...THIS LAND WILL NEVER KNOW PEACE SO LONG AS I RULE.
*SEE QUEEN SONJA #21.
THERE'LL BE NO PEACE IF YOU LEAVE! KOLIOSTRI AND HIS MINDLESS FOLLOWERS WILL SLAUGHTER ANYONE WHO DOES NOT BOW DOWN TO THEIR INSANE BELIEFS!

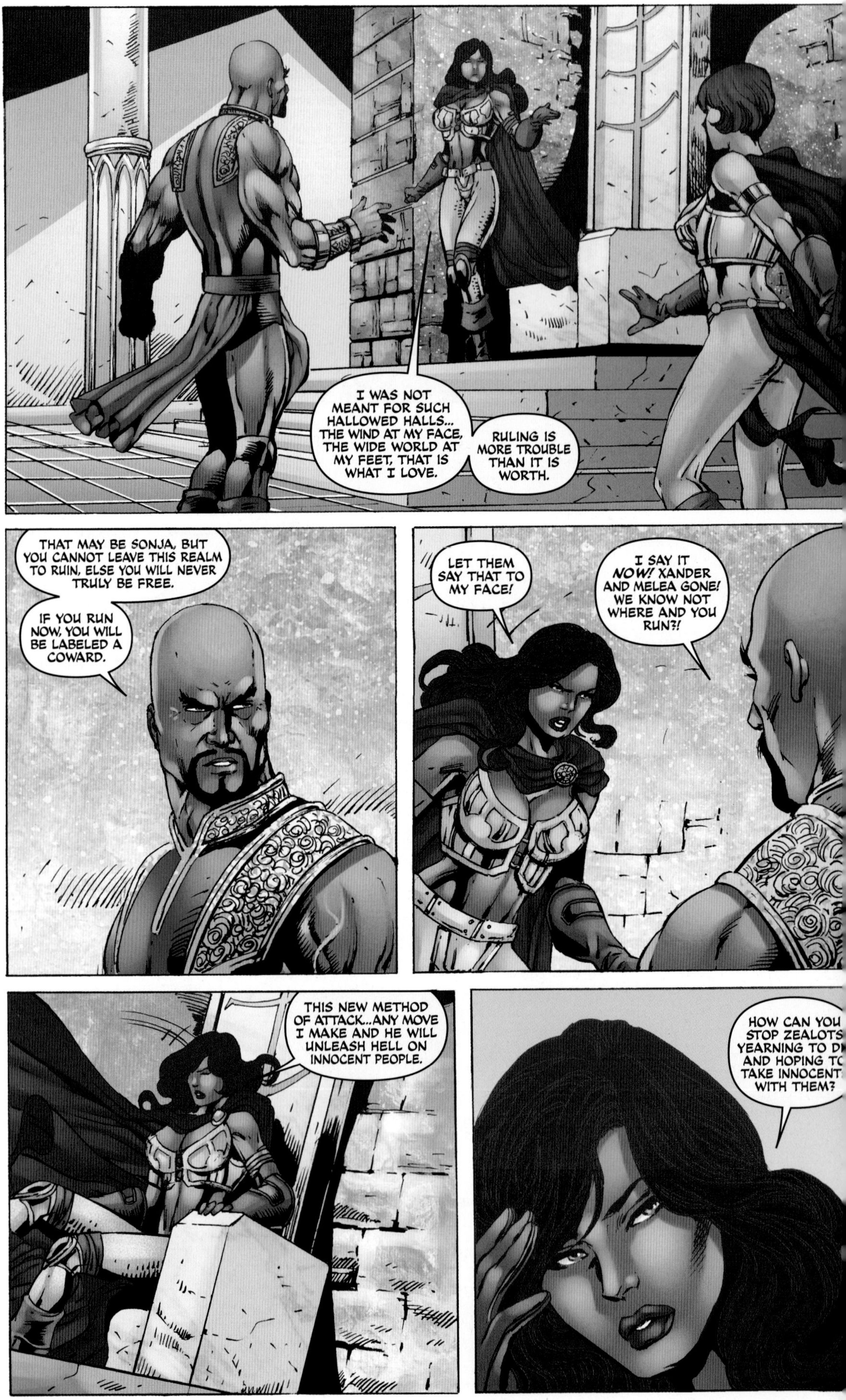
I WAS NOT MEANT FOR SUCH HALLOWED HALLS... THE WIND AT MY FACE, THE WIDE WORLD AT MY FEET, THAT IS WHAT I LOVE.
RULING IS MORE TROUBLE THAN IT IS WORTH.
THAT MAY BE SONJA, BUT YOU CANNOT LEAVE THIS REALM TO RUIN, ELSE YOU WILL NEVER TRULY BE FREE.
IF YOU RUN NOW, YOU WILL BE LABELED A COWARD.
LET THEM SAY THAT TO MY FACE!
I SAY IT *NOW!* XANDER AND MELEA GONE! WE KNOW NOT WHERE AND YOU RUN?!
THIS NEW METHOD OF ATTACK...ANY MOVE I MAKE AND HE WILL UNLEASH HELL ON INNOCENT PEOPLE.
HOW CAN YOU STOP ZEALOTS YEARNING TO D AND HOPING T TAKE INNOCENT WITH THEM?

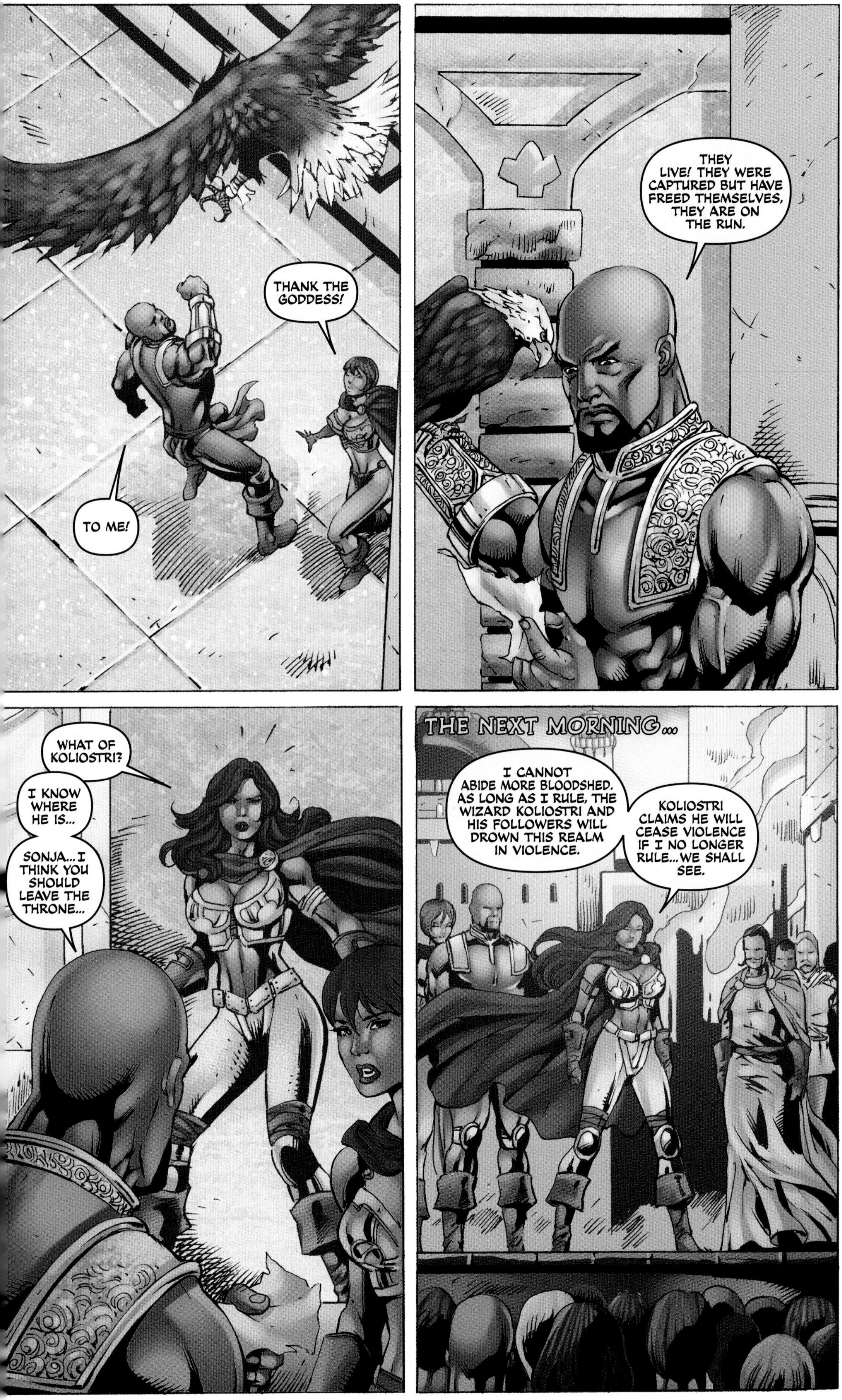
THANK THE GODDESS!
TO ME!
THEY LIVE! THEY WERE CAPTURED BUT HAVE FREED THEMSELVES, THEY ARE ON THE RUN.
WHAT OF KOLIOSTRI?
I KNOW WHERE HE IS...
SONJA... I THINK YOU SHOULD LEAVE THE THRONE...
THE NEXT MORNING...
I CANNOT ABIDE MORE BLOODSHED. AS LONG AS I RULE, THE WIZARD KOLIOSTRI AND HIS FOLLOWERS WILL DROWN THIS REALM IN VIOLENCE.
KOLIOSTRI CLAIMS HE WILL CEASE VIOLENCE IF I NO LONGER RULE...WE SHALL SEE.

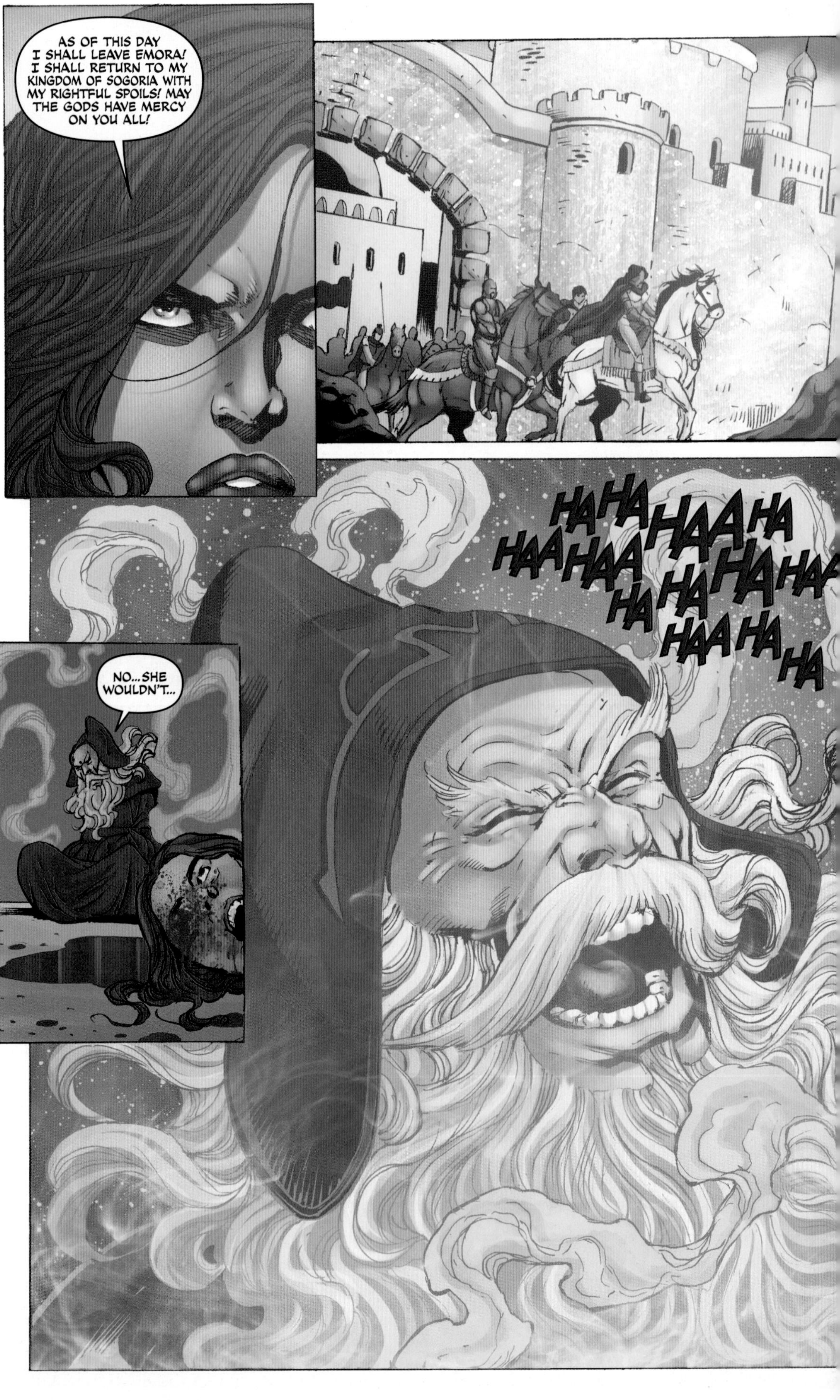
AS OF THIS DAY I SHALL LEAVE EMORA! I SHALL RETURN TO MY KINGDOM OF SOGORIA WITH MY RIGHTFUL SPOILS! MAY THE GODS HAVE MERCY ON YOU ALL!
HAHA HAA HA HAA HAA HA HA HA HA HA HAA HA HAA HA HA
NO...SHE WOULDN'T...

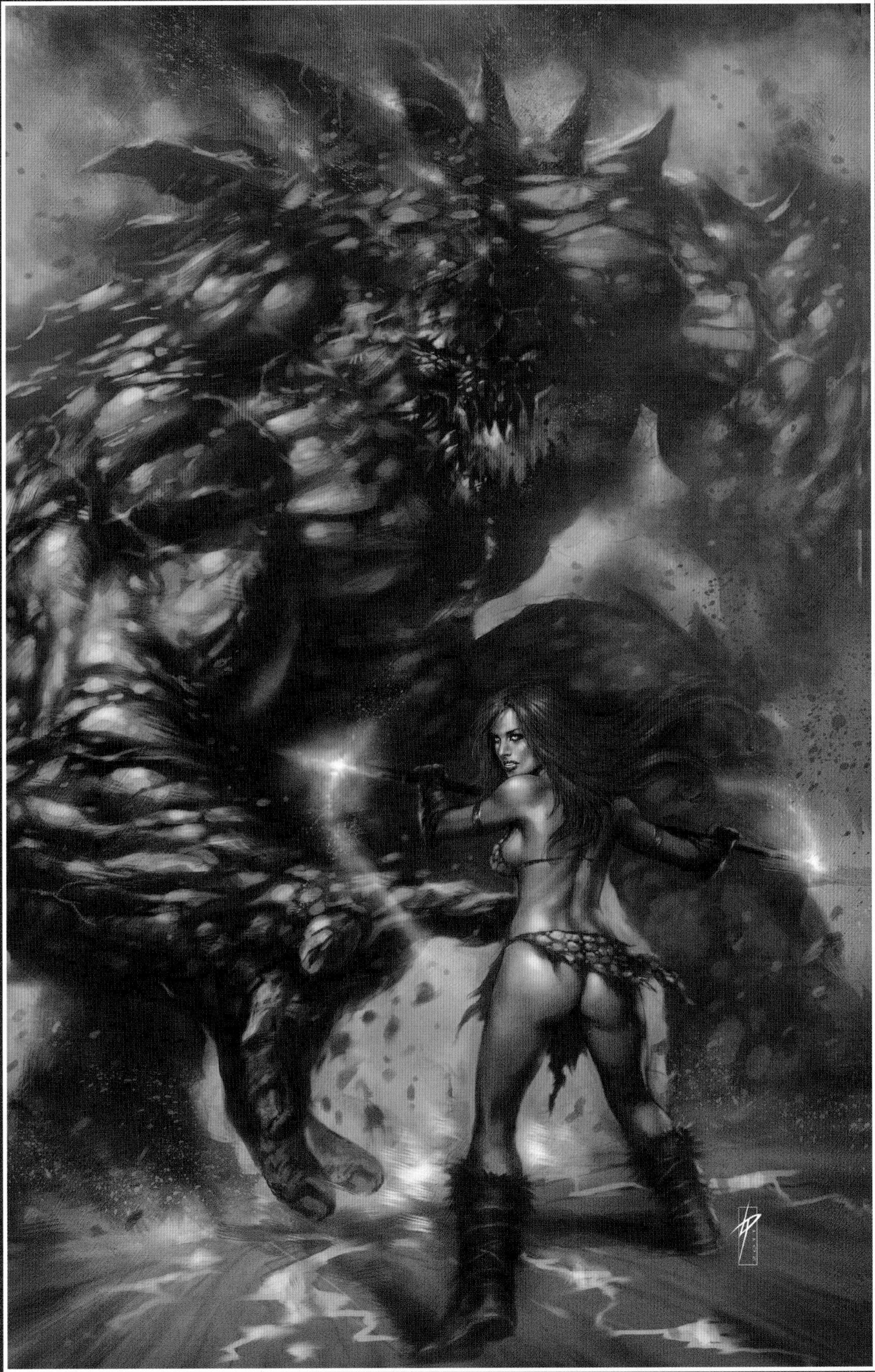

ISSUE #29 COVER BY LUCIO PARRILLO

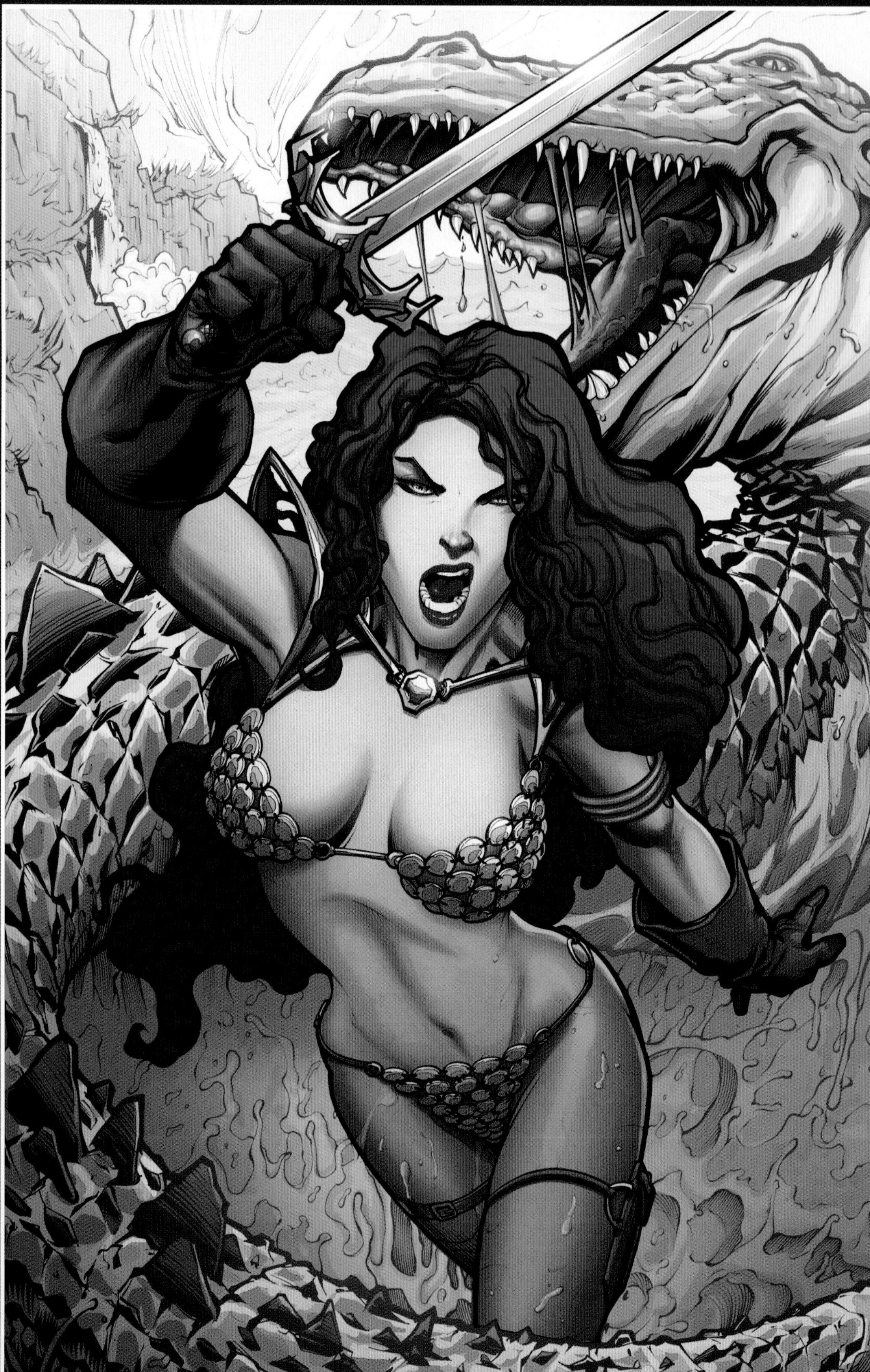

ISSUE #29 COVER BY TOMMY PATTERSON

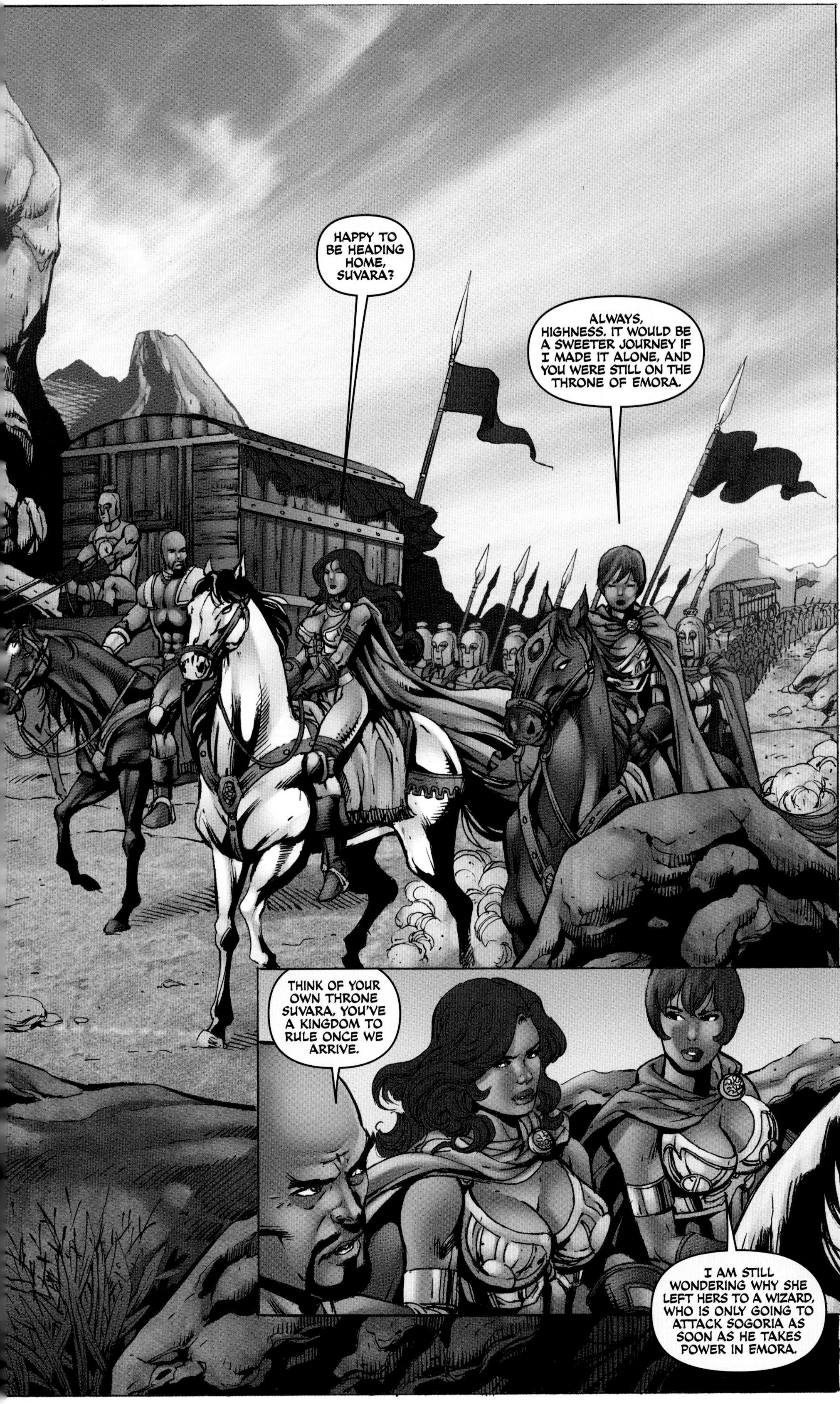
HAPPY TO BE HEADING HOME, SUVARA?
ALWAYS, HIGHNESS. IT WOULD BE A SWEETER JOURNEY IF I MADE IT ALONE, AND YOU WERE STILL ON THE THRONE OF EMORA.
THINK OF YOUR OWN THRONE SUVARA, YOU'VE A KINGDOM TO RULE ONCE WE ARRIVE.
I AM STILL WONDERING WHY SHE LEFT HERS TO A WIZARD, WHO IS ONLY GOING TO ATTACK SOGORIA AS SOON AS HE TAKES POWER IN EMORA.

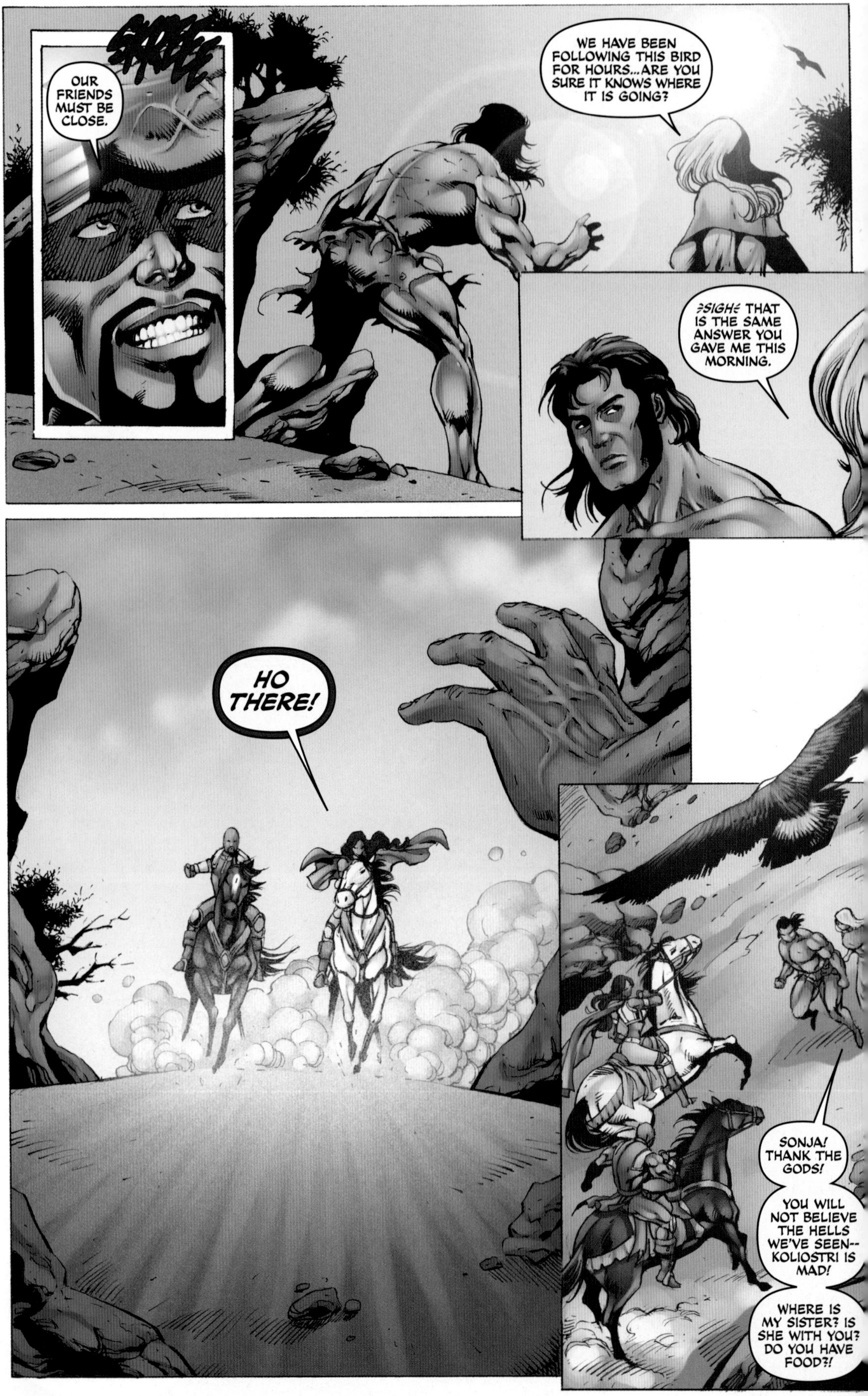
SKREEE
OUR FRIENDS MUST BE CLOSE.
WE HAVE BEEN FOLLOWING THIS BIRD FOR HOURS...ARE YOU SURE IT KNOWS WHERE IT IS GOING?
SIGH THAT IS THE SAME ANSWER YOU GAVE ME THIS MORNING.
HO THERE!
SONJA! THANK THE GODS!
YOU WILL NOT BELIEVE THE HELLS WE'VE SEEN-- KOLIOSTRI IS MAD!
WHERE IS MY SISTER? IS SHE WITH YOU? DO YOU HAVE FOOD?!

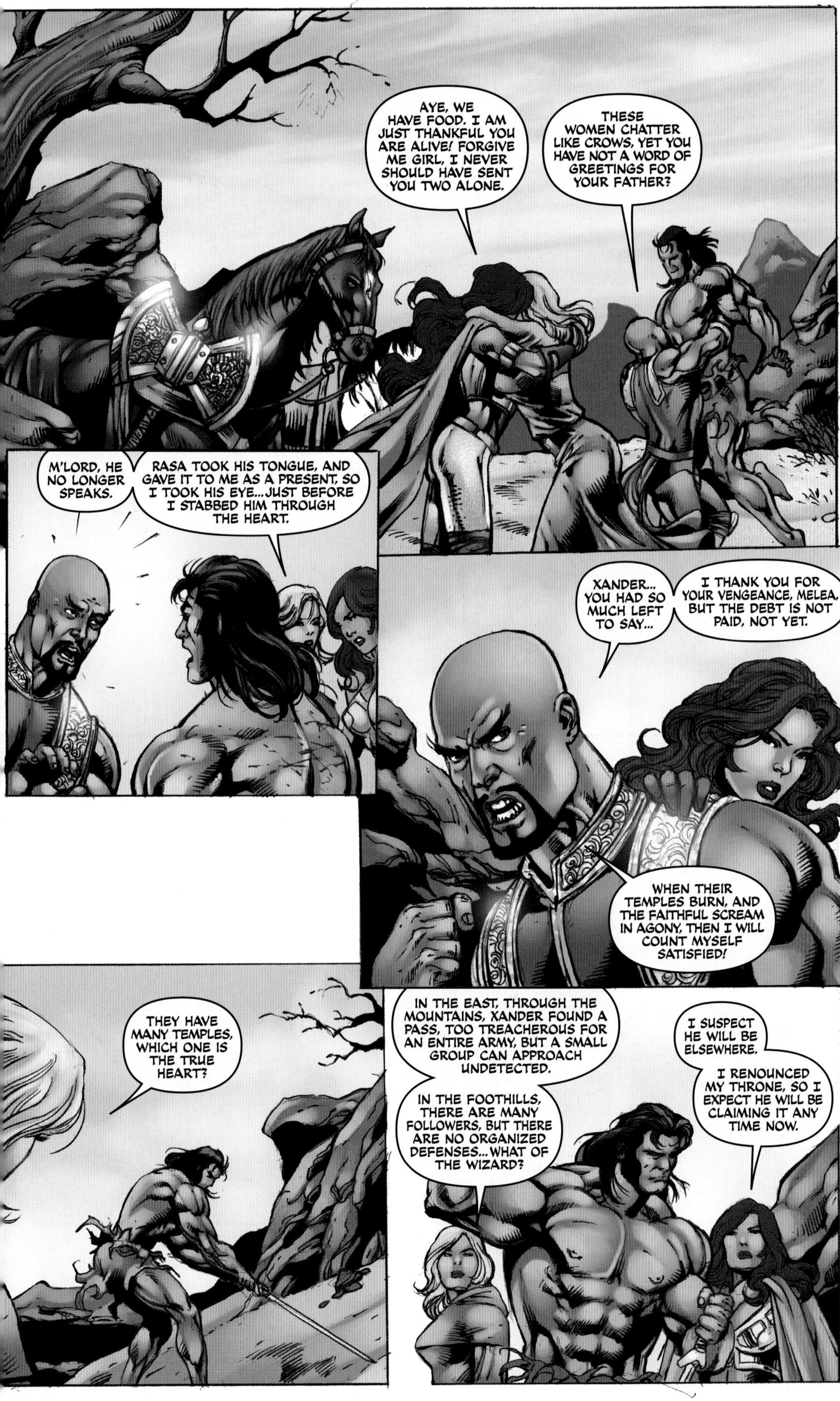
AYE, WE HAVE FOOD. I AM JUST THANKFUL YOU ARE ALIVE! FORGIVE ME GIRL, I NEVER SHOULD HAVE SENT YOU TWO ALONE.
THESE WOMEN CHATTER LIKE CROWS, YET YOU HAVE NOT A WORD OF GREETINGS FOR YOUR FATHER?
M'LORD, HE NO LONGER SPEAKS.
RASA TOOK HIS TONGUE, AND GAVE IT TO ME AS A PRESENT, SO I TOOK HIS EYE...JUST BEFORE I STABBED HIM THROUGH THE HEART.
XANDER... YOU HAD SO MUCH LEFT TO SAY...
I THANK YOU FOR YOUR VENGEANCE, MELEA, BUT THE DEBT IS NOT PAID, NOT YET.
WHEN THEIR TEMPLES BURN, AND THE FAITHFUL SCREAM IN AGONY, THEN I WILL COUNT MYSELF SATISFIED!
THEY HAVE MANY TEMPLES, WHICH ONE IS THE TRUE HEART?
IN THE EAST, THROUGH THE MOUNTAINS, XANDER FOUND A PASS, TOO TREACHEROUS FOR AN ENTIRE ARMY, BUT A SMALL GROUP CAN APPROACH UNDETECTED.
IN THE FOOTHILLS, THERE ARE MANY FOLLOWERS, BUT THERE ARE NO ORGANIZED DEFENSES...WHAT OF THE WIZARD?
I SUSPECT HE WILL BE ELSEWHERE.
I RENOUNCED MY THRONE, SO I EXPECT HE WILL BE CLAIMING IT ANY TIME NOW.

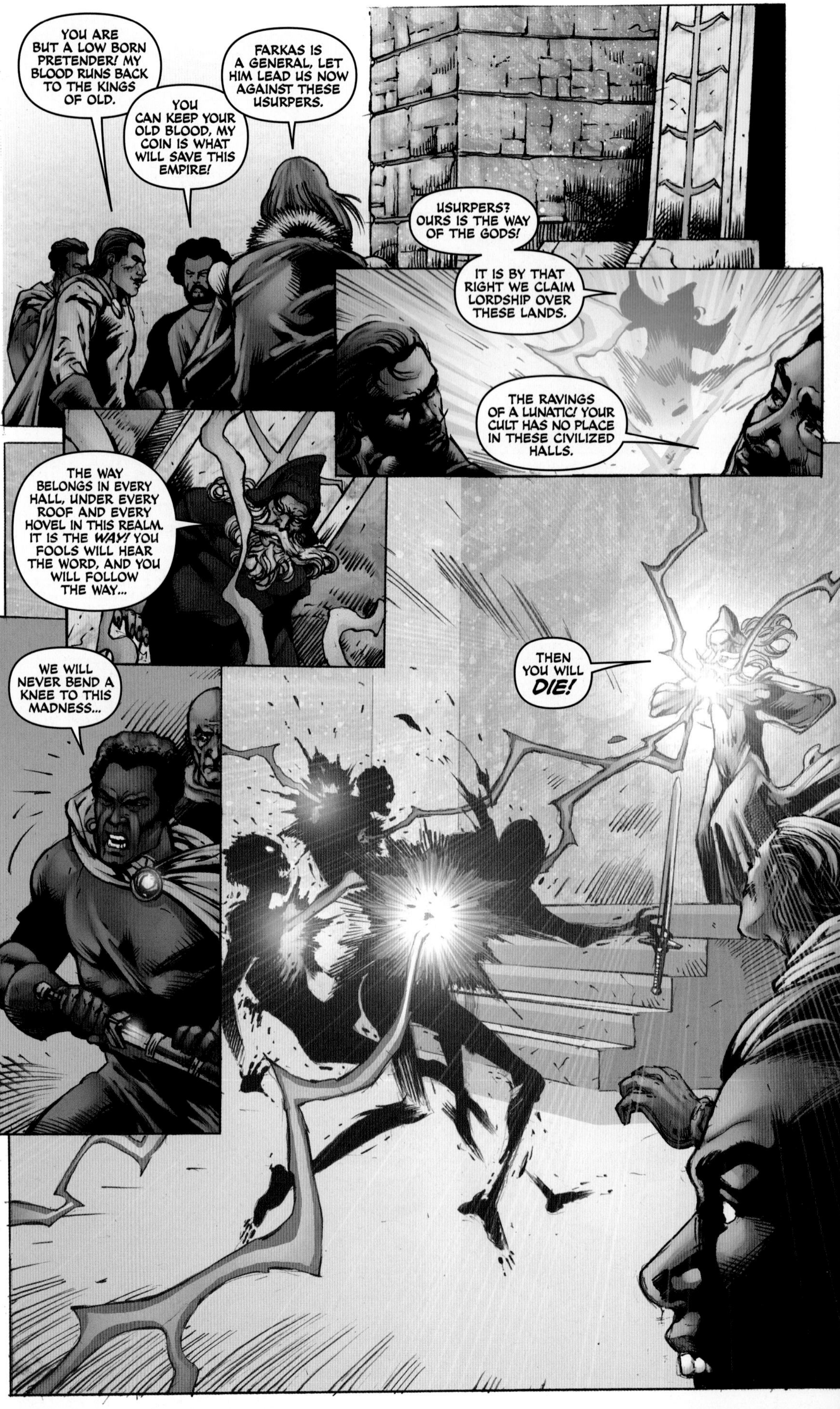
YOU ARE BUT A LOW BORN PRETENDER! MY BLOOD RUNS BACK TO THE KINGS OF OLD.
YOU CAN KEEP YOUR OLD BLOOD, MY COIN IS WHAT WILL SAVE THIS EMPIRE!
FARKAS IS A GENERAL, LET HIM LEAD US NOW AGAINST THESE USURPERS.
USURPERS? OURS IS THE WAY OF THE GODS!
IT IS BY THAT RIGHT WE CLAIM LORDSHIP OVER THESE LANDS.
THE RAVINGS OF A LUNATIC! YOUR CULT HAS NO PLACE IN THESE CIVILIZED HALLS.
THE WAY BELONGS IN EVERY HALL, UNDER EVERY ROOF AND EVERY HOVEL IN THIS REALM. IT IS THE *WAY!* YOU FOOLS WILL HEAR THE WORD, AND YOU WILL FOLLOW THE WAY...
WE WILL NEVER BEND A KNEE TO THIS MADNESS...
THEN YOU WILL *DIE!*

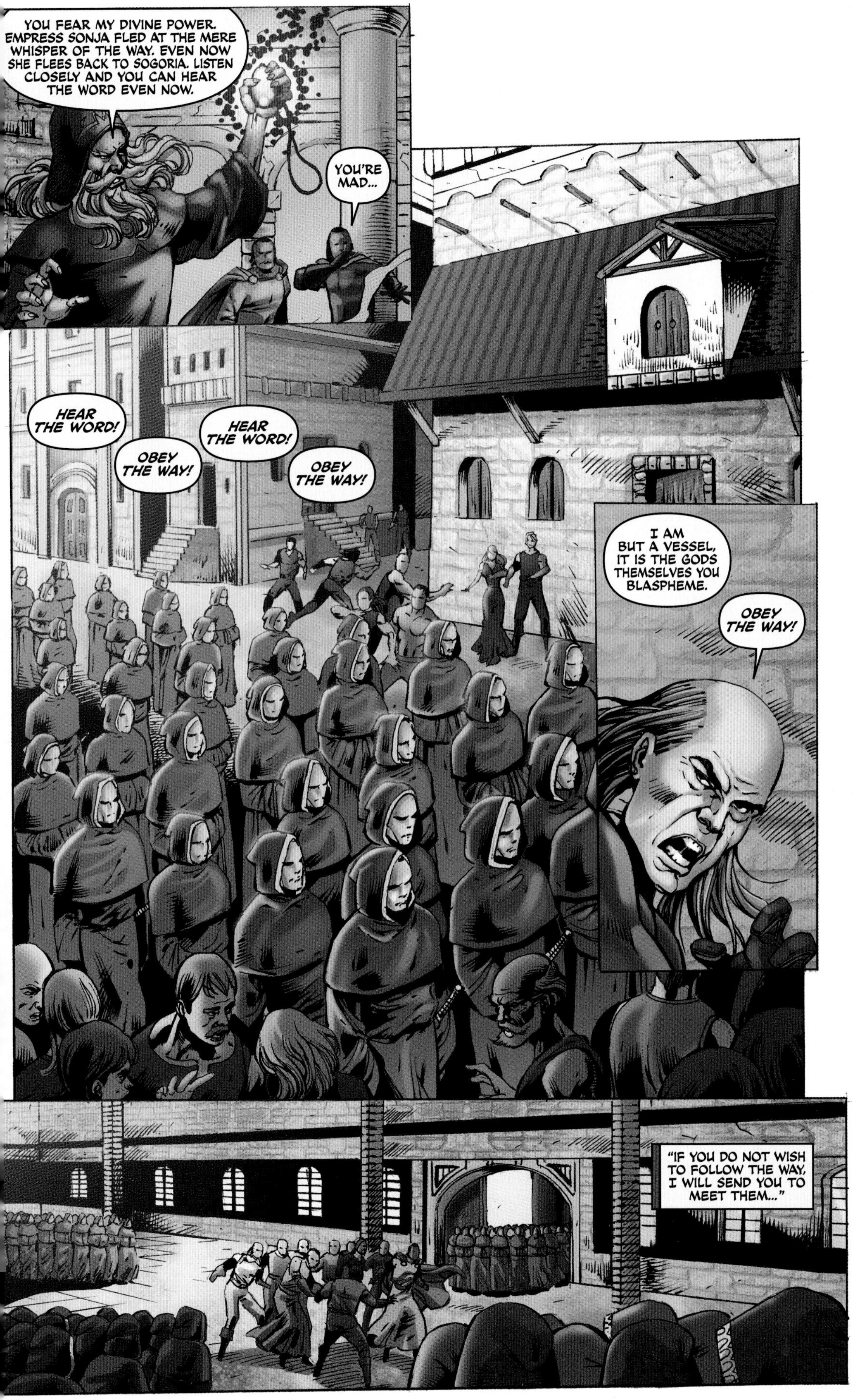

YOU FEAR MY DIVINE POWER. EMPRESS SONJA FLED AT THE MERE WHISPER OF THE WAY. EVEN NOW SHE FLEES BACK TO SOGORIA. LISTEN CLOSELY AND YOU CAN HEAR THE WORD EVEN NOW.
YOU'RE MAD...
HEAR THE WORD!
OBEY THE WAY!
HEAR THE WORD!
OBEY THE WAY!
I AM BUT A VESSEL, IT IS THE GODS THEMSELVES YOU BLASPHEME.
OBEY THE WAY!
"IF YOU DO NOT WISH TO FOLLOW THE WAY, I WILL SEND YOU TO MEET THEM..."

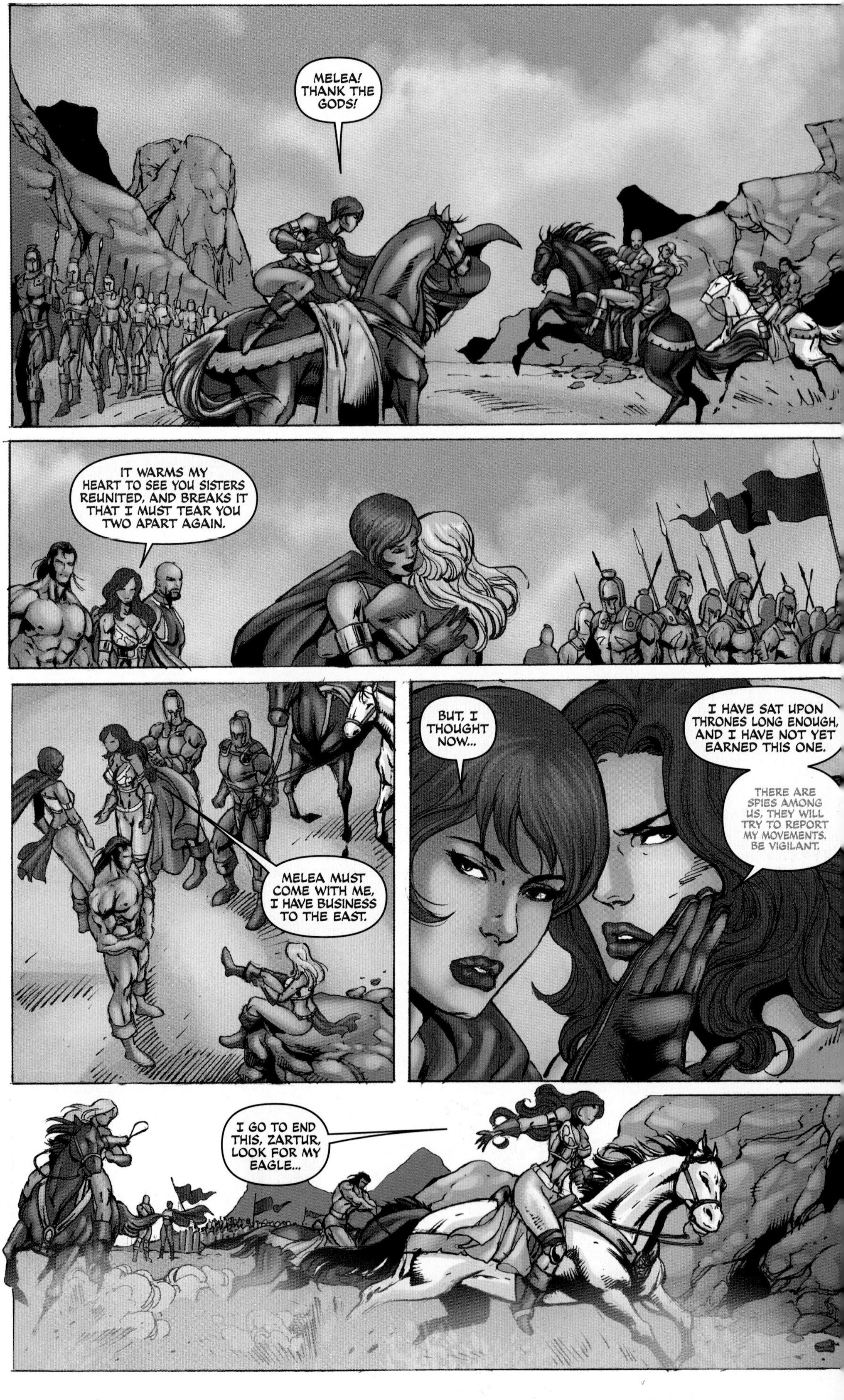
MELEA! THANK THE GODS!
IT WARMS MY HEART TO SEE YOU SISTERS REUNITED, AND BREAKS IT THAT I MUST TEAR YOU TWO APART AGAIN.
MELEA MUST COME WITH ME, I HAVE BUSINESS TO THE EAST.
BUT, I THOUGHT NOW...
I HAVE SAT UPON THRONES LONG ENOUGH, AND I HAVE NOT YET EARNED THIS ONE.
THERE ARE SPIES AMONG US, THEY WILL TRY TO REPORT MY MOVEMENTS. BE VIGILANT.
I GO TO END THIS, ZARTUR, LOOK FOR MY EAGLE...

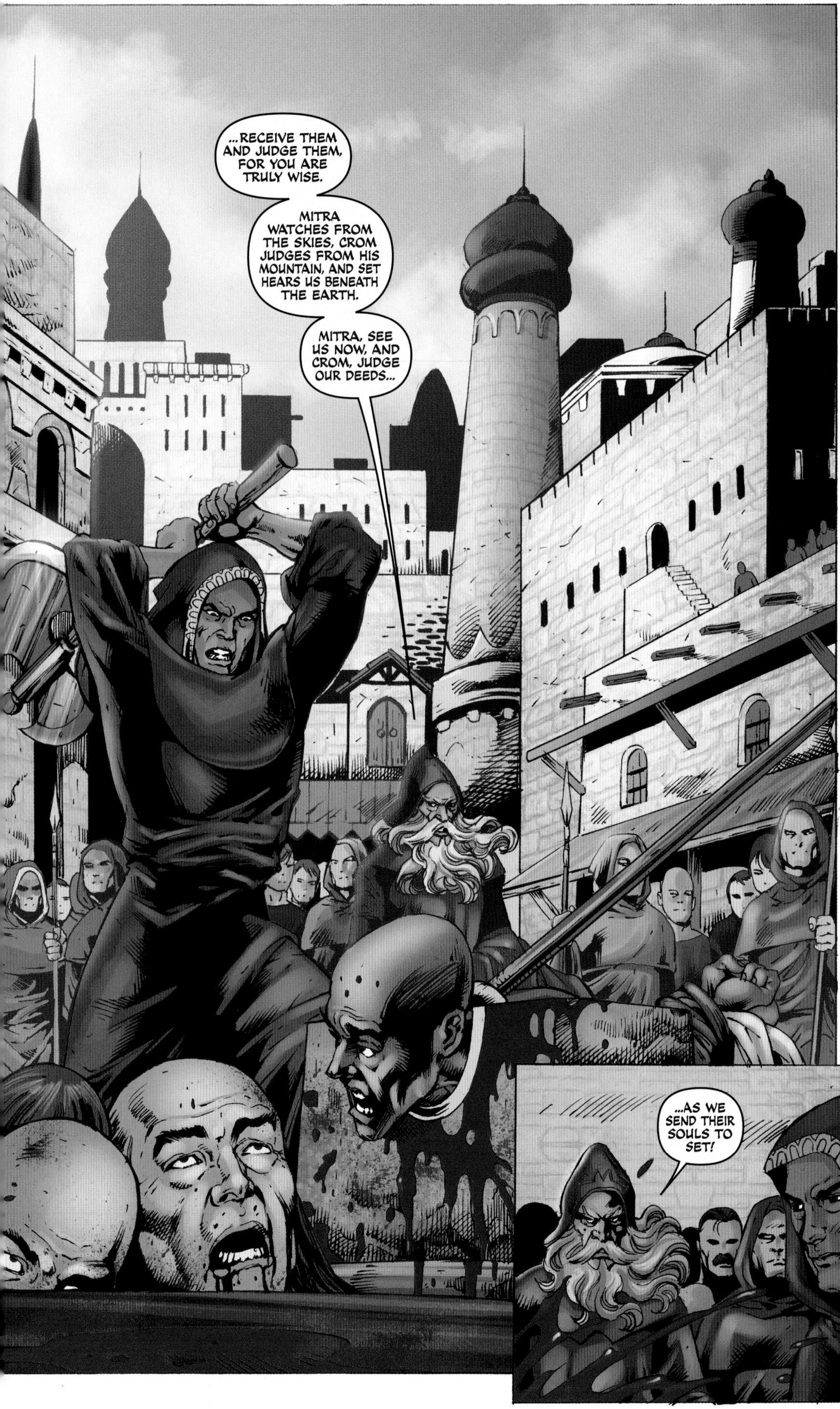
...RECEIVE THEM AND JUDGE THEM, FOR YOU ARE TRULY WISE.
MITRA WATCHES FROM THE SKIES, CROM JUDGES FROM HIS MOUNTAIN, AND SET HEARS US BENEATH THE EARTH.
MITRA, SEE US NOW, AND CROM, JUDGE OUR DEEDS...
...AS WE SEND THEIR SOULS TO SET!

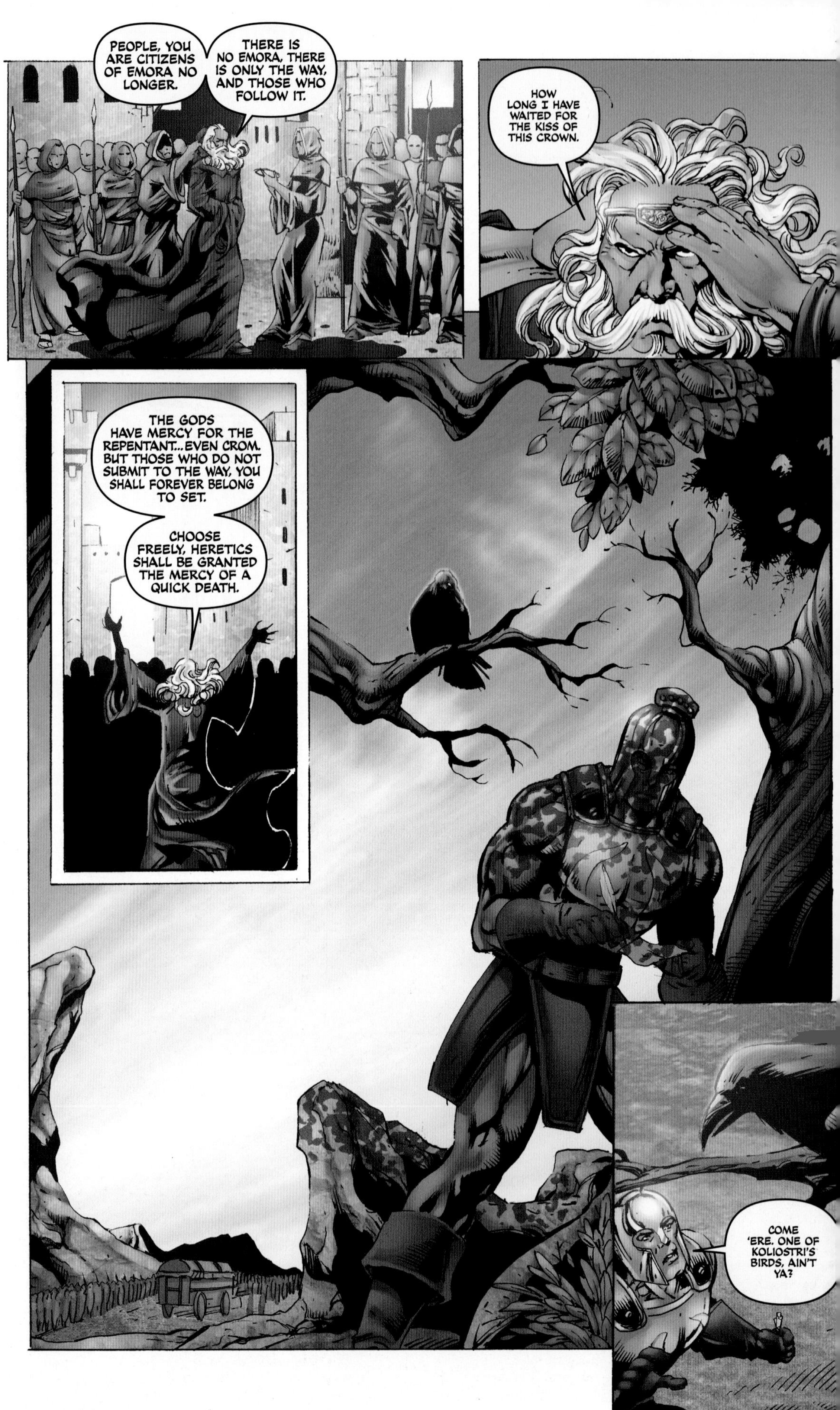
PEOPLE, YOU ARE CITIZENS OF EMORA NO LONGER.
THERE IS NO EMORA, THERE IS ONLY THE WAY, AND THOSE WHO FOLLOW IT.
HOW LONG I HAVE WAITED FOR THE KISS OF THIS CROWN.
THE GODS HAVE MERCY FOR THE REPENTANT...EVEN CROM. BUT THOSE WHO DO NOT SUBMIT TO THE WAY, YOU SHALL FOREVER BELONG TO SET.
CHOOSE FREELY, HERETICS SHALL BE GRANTED THE MERCY OF A QUICK DEATH.
COME 'ERE. ONE OF KOLIOSTRI'S BIRDS, AIN'T YA?

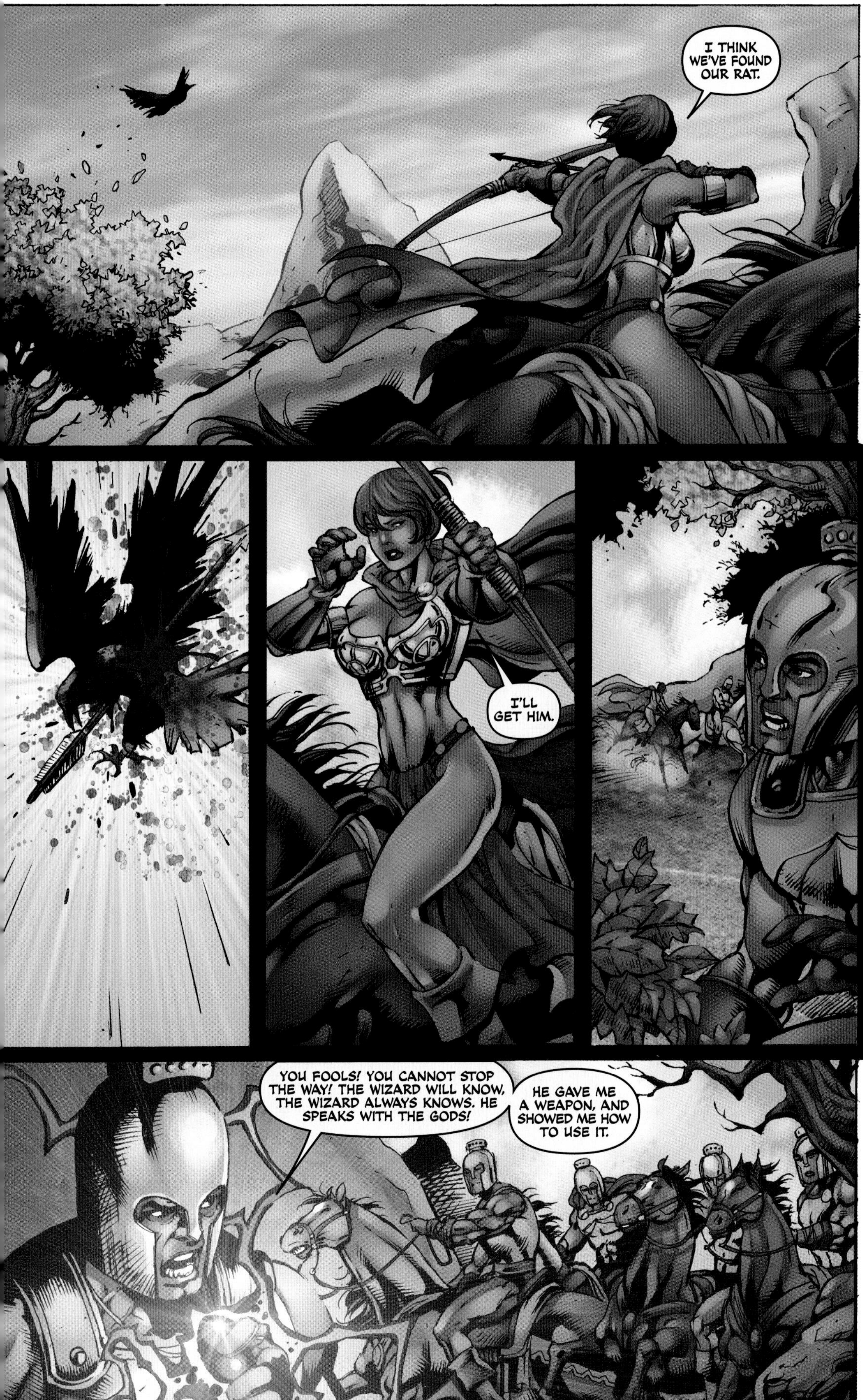
I THINK WE'VE FOUND OUR RAT.
I'LL GET HIM.
YOU FOOLS! YOU CANNOT STOP THE WAY! THE WIZARD WILL KNOW, THE WIZARD ALWAYS KNOWS. HE SPEAKS WITH THE GODS!
HE GAVE ME A WEAPON, AND SHOWED ME HOW TO USE IT.

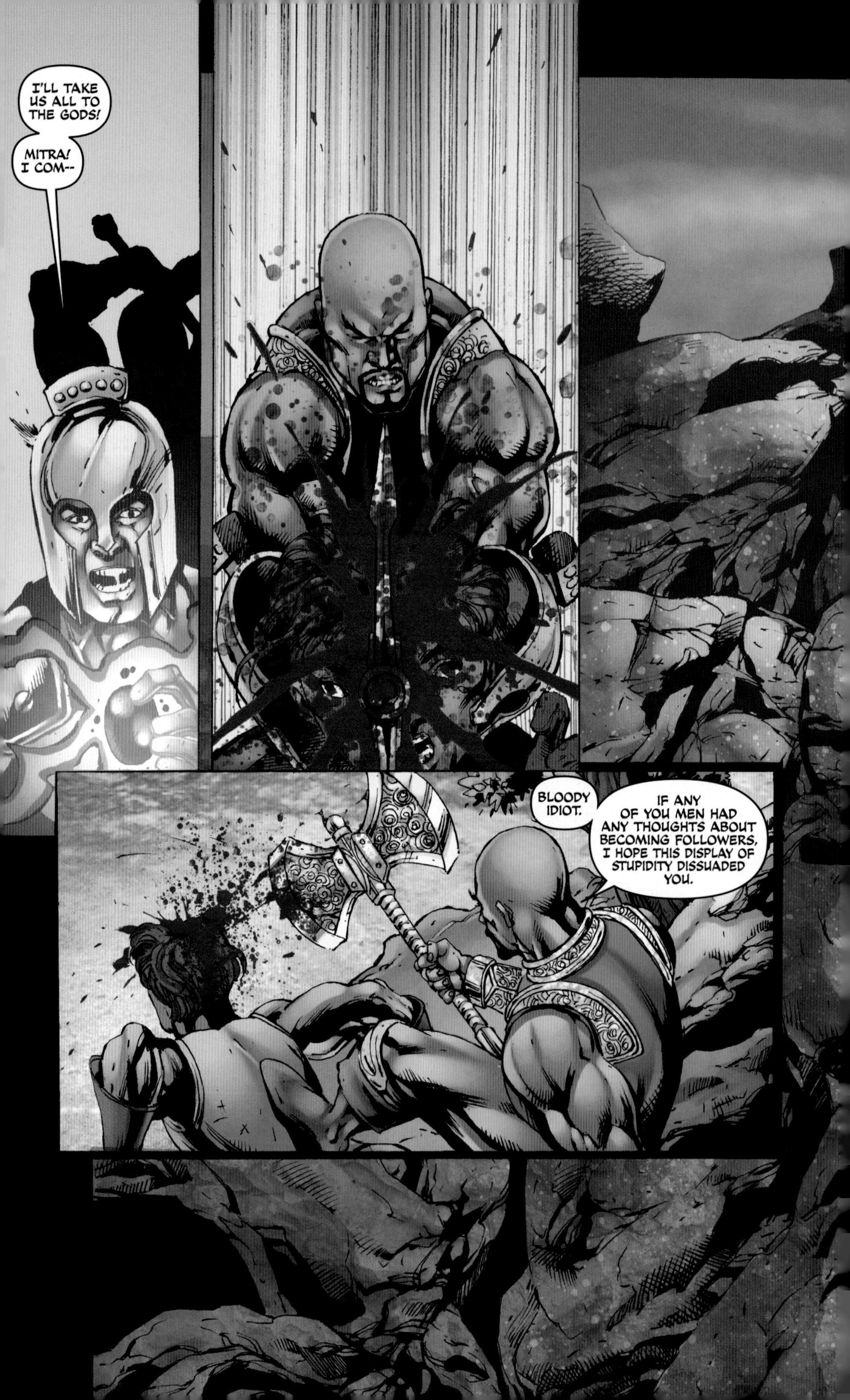
I'LL TAKE US ALL TO THE GODS!
MITRA! I COM--
BLOODY IDIOT.
IF ANY OF YOU MEN HAD ANY THOUGHTS ABOUT BECOMING FOLLOWERS, I HOPE THIS DISPLAY OF STUPIDITY DISSUADED YOU.

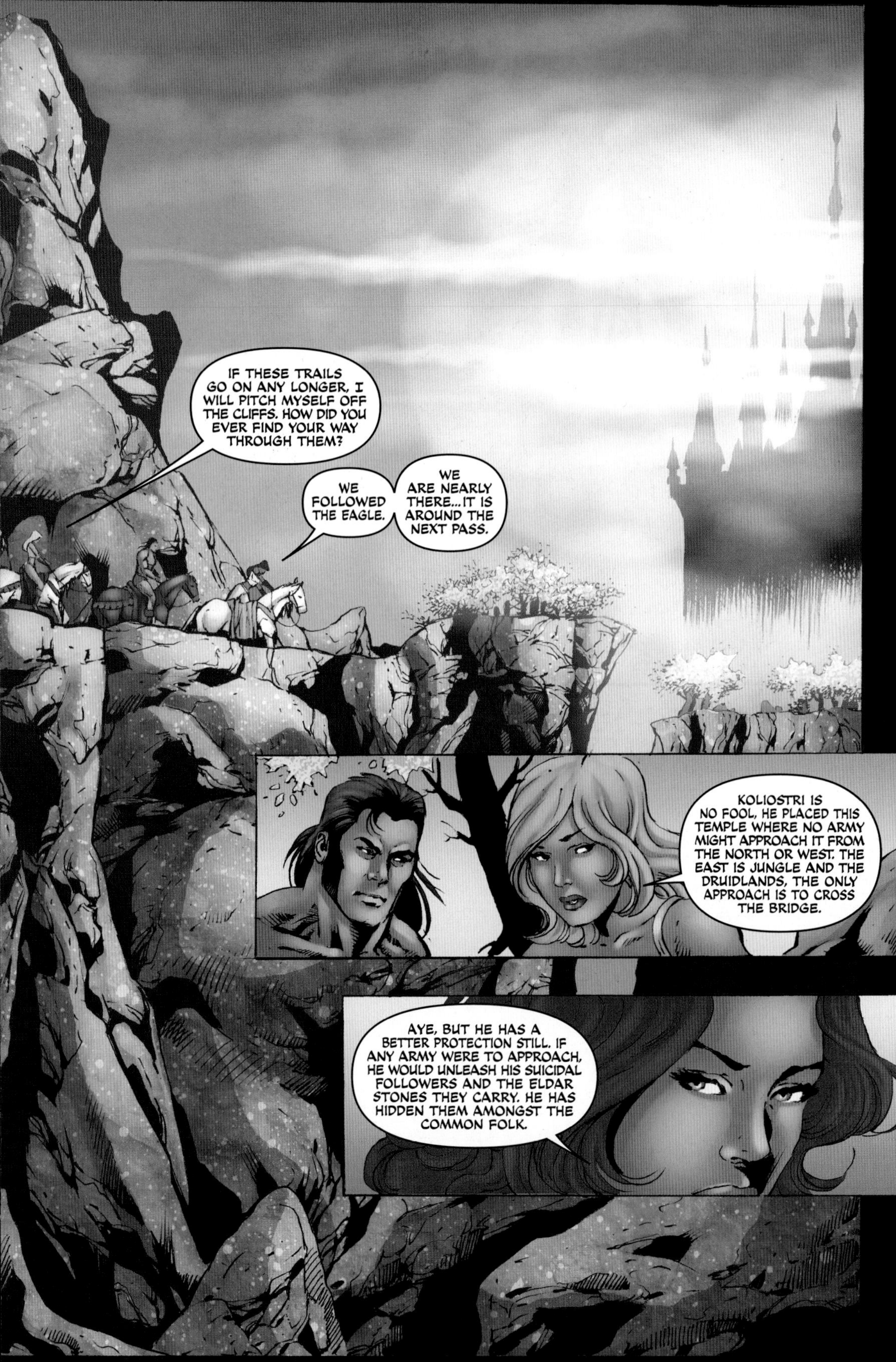

IF THESE TRAILS GO ON ANY LONGER, I WILL PITCH MYSELF OFF THE CLIFFS. HOW DID YOU EVER FIND YOUR WAY THROUGH THEM?
WE FOLLOWED THE EAGLE.
WE ARE NEARLY THERE...IT IS AROUND THE NEXT PASS.
KOLIOSTRI IS NO FOOL, HE PLACED THIS TEMPLE WHERE NO ARMY MIGHT APPROACH IT FROM THE NORTH OR WEST. THE EAST IS JUNGLE AND THE DRUIDLANDS, THE ONLY APPROACH IS TO CROSS THE BRIDGE.
AYE, BUT HE HAS A BETTER PROTECTION STILL. IF ANY ARMY WERE TO APPROACH, HE WOULD UNLEASH HIS SUICIDAL FOLLOWERS AND THE ELDAR STONES THEY CARRY. HE HAS HIDDEN THEM AMONGST THE COMMON FOLK.

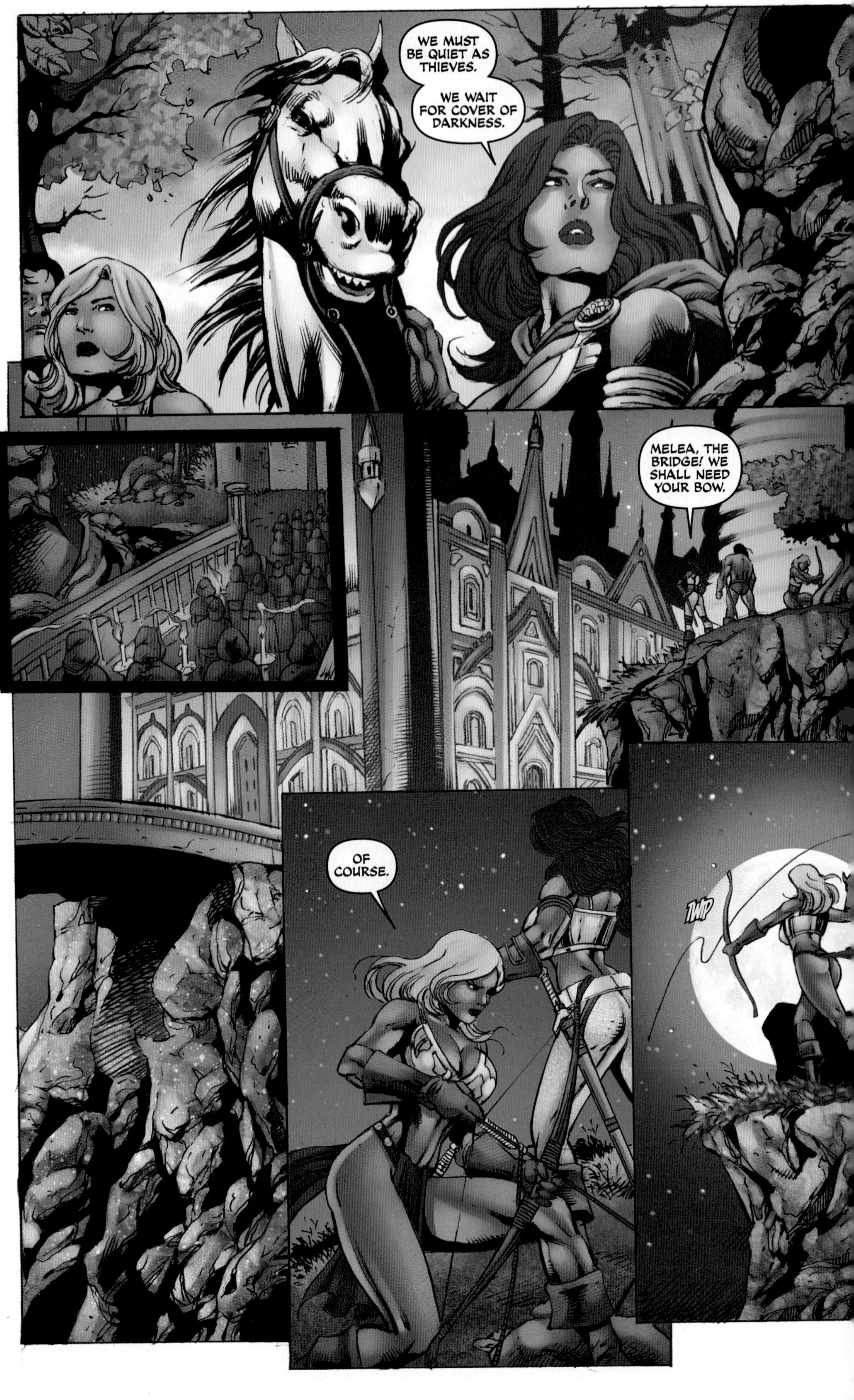
WE MUST BE QUIET AS THIEVES.
WE WAIT FOR COVER OF DARKNESS.
MELEA, THE BRIDGE! WE SHALL NEED YOUR BOW.
OF COURSE.
TWIP

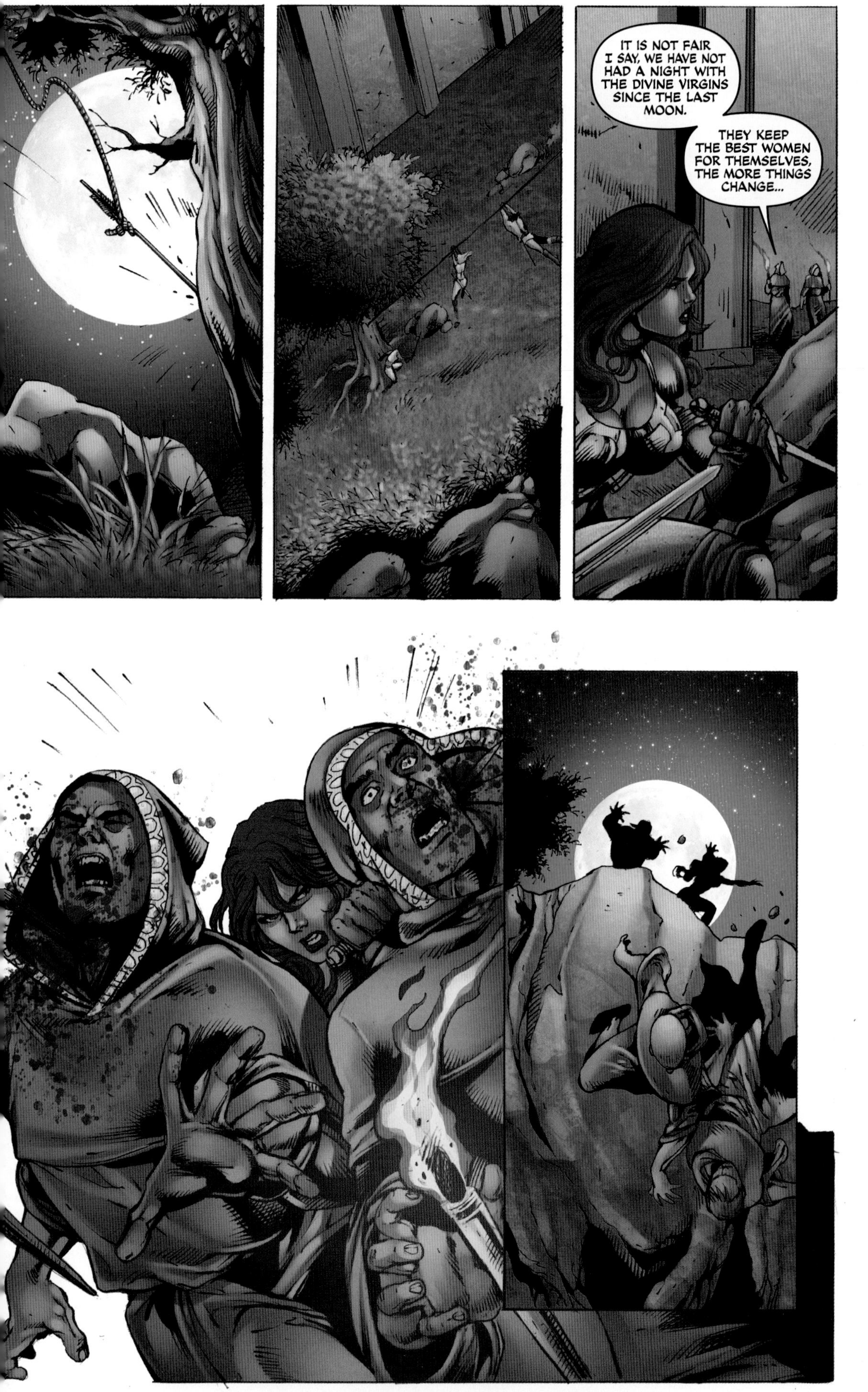
IT IS NOT FAIR I SAY, WE HAVE NOT HAD A NIGHT WITH THE DIVINE VIRGINS SINCE THE LAST MOON.
THEY KEEP THE BEST WOMEN FOR THEMSELVES, THE MORE THINGS CHANGE...

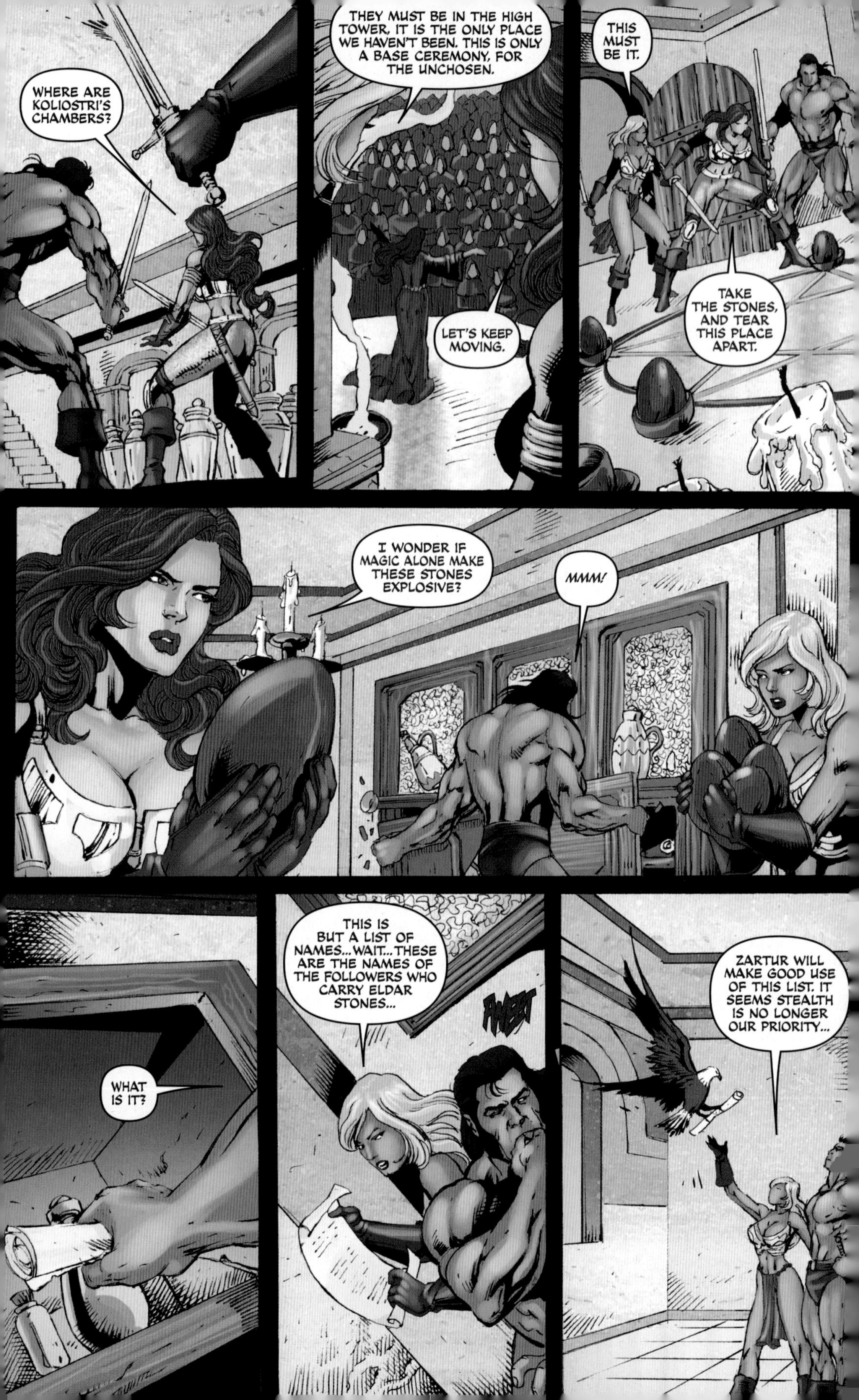
WHERE ARE KOLIOSTRI'S CHAMBERS?
THEY MUST BE IN THE HIGH TOWER, IT IS THE ONLY PLACE WE HAVEN'T BEEN. THIS IS ONLY A BASE CEREMONY, FOR THE UNCHOSEN.
LET'S KEEP MOVING.
THIS MUST BE IT.
TAKE THE STONES, AND TEAR THIS PLACE APART.
I WONDER IF MAGIC ALONE MAKE THESE STONES EXPLOSIVE?
MMM!
WHAT IS IT?
THIS IS BUT A LIST OF NAMES...WAIT...THESE ARE THE NAMES OF THE FOLLOWERS WHO CARRY ELDAR STONES...
FWEET
ZARTUR WILL MAKE GOOD USE OF THIS LIST. IT SEEMS STEALTH IS NO LONGER OUR PRIORITY...

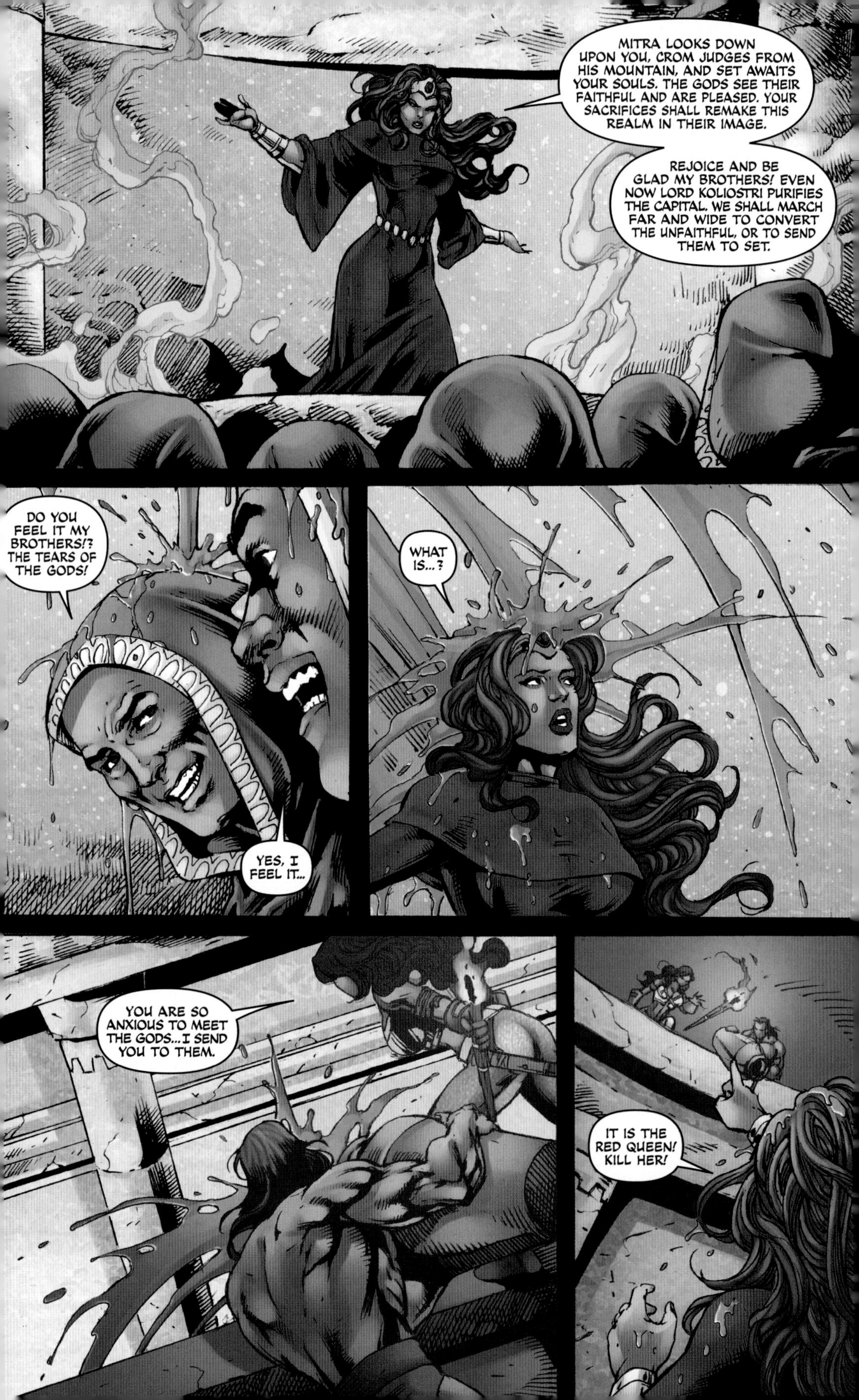
MITRA LOOKS DOWN UPON YOU, CROM JUDGES FROM HIS MOUNTAIN, AND SET AWAITS YOUR SOULS. THE GODS SEE THEIR FAITHFUL AND ARE PLEASED. YOUR SACRIFICES SHALL REMAKE THIS REALM IN THEIR IMAGE.
REJOICE AND BE GLAD MY BROTHERS! EVEN NOW LORD KOLIOSTRI PURIFIES THE CAPITAL. WE SHALL MARCH FAR AND WIDE TO CONVERT THE UNFAITHFUL, OR TO SEND THEM TO SET.
DO YOU FEEL IT MY BROTHERS!? THE TEARS OF THE GODS!
YES, I FEEL IT...
WHAT IS...?
YOU ARE SO ANXIOUS TO MEET THE GODS...I SEND YOU TO THEM.
IT IS THE RED QUEEN! KILL HER!

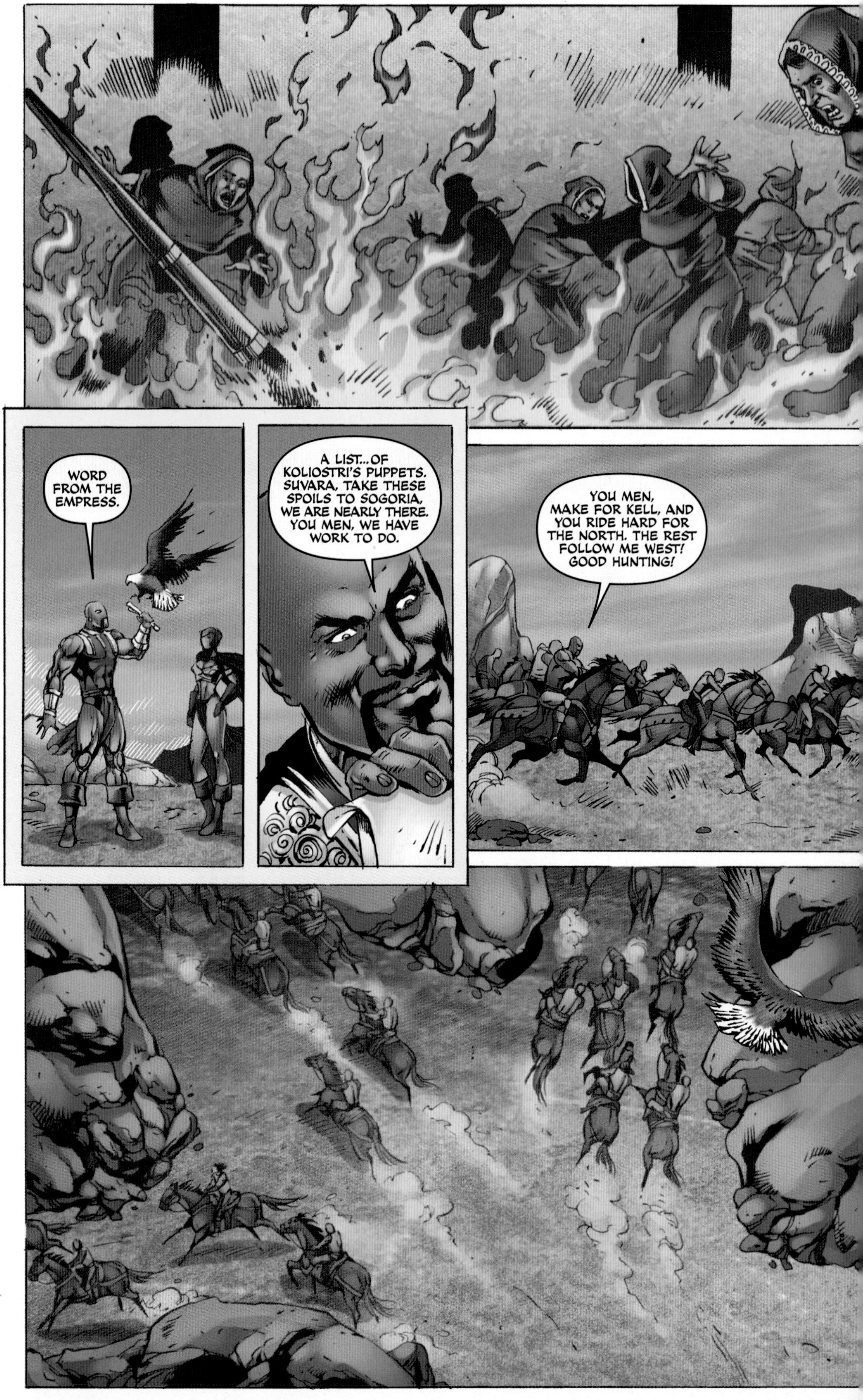
WORD FROM THE EMPRESS.
A LIST...OF KOLIOSTRI'S PUPPETS. SUVARA, TAKE THESE SPOILS TO SOGORIA, WE ARE NEARLY THERE. YOU MEN, WE HAVE WORK TO DO.
YOU MEN, MAKE FOR KELL, AND YOU RIDE HARD FOR THE NORTH. THE REST FOLLOW ME WEST! GOOD HUNTING!

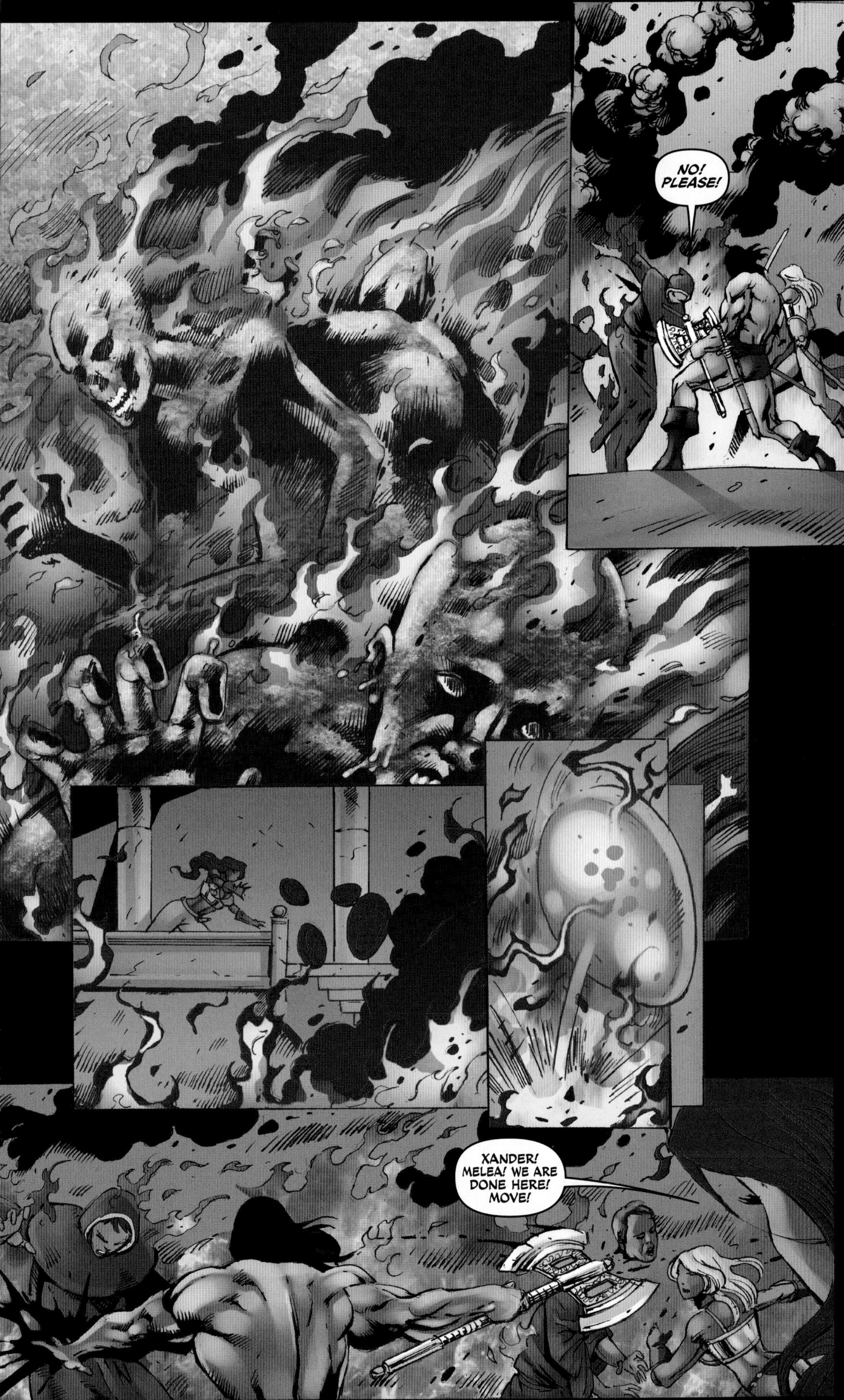
NO! PLEASE!
XANDER! MELEA! WE ARE DONE HERE! MOVE!

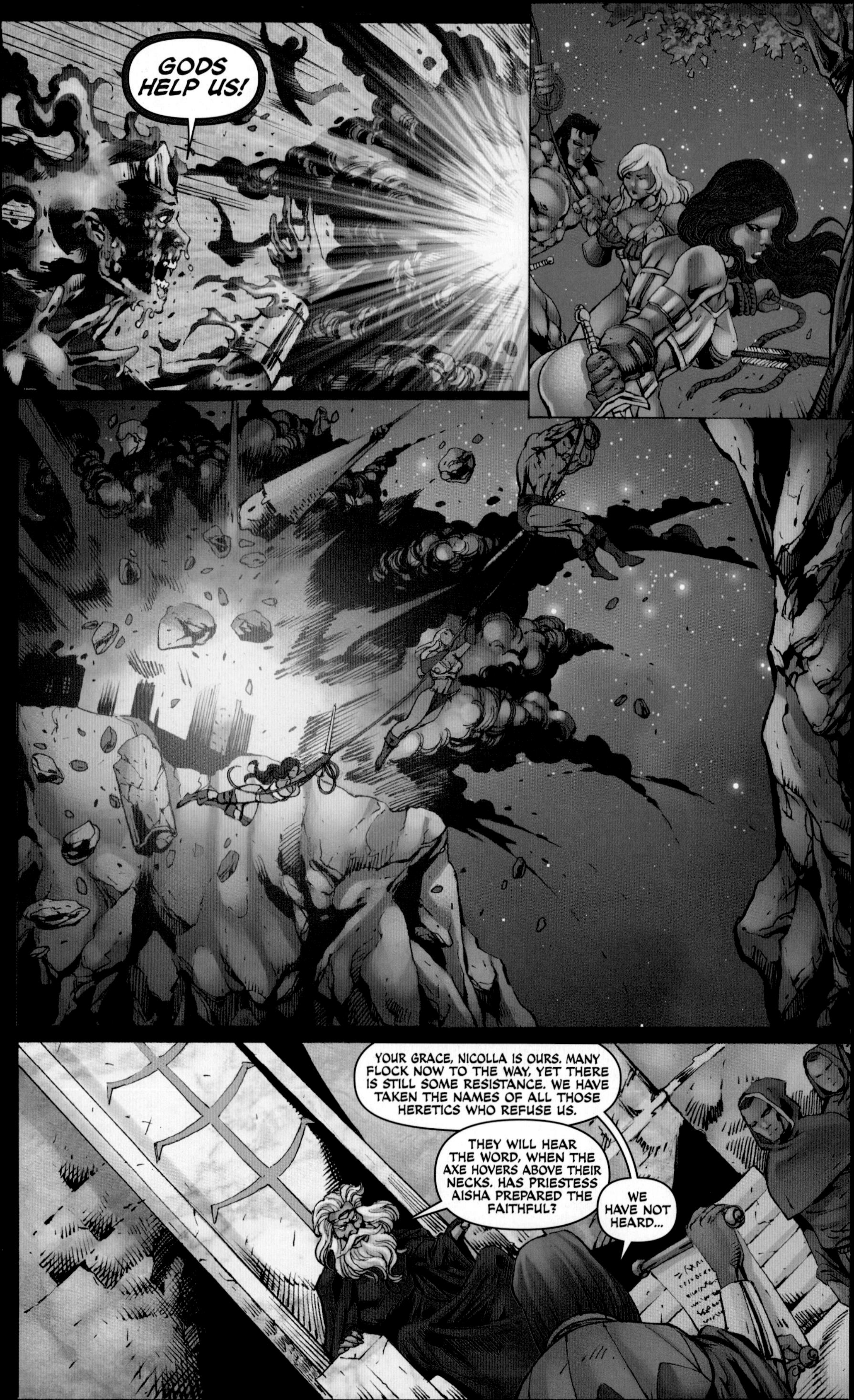
GODS HELP US!
YOUR GRACE, NICOLLA IS OURS. MANY FLOCK NOW TO THE WAY, YET THERE IS STILL SOME RESISTANCE. WE HAVE TAKEN THE NAMES OF ALL THOSE HERETICS WHO REFUSE US.
THEY WILL HEAR THE WORD, WHEN THE AXE HOVERS ABOVE THEIR NECKS. HAS PRIESTESS AISHA PREPARED THE FAITHFUL?
WE HAVE NOT HEARD...

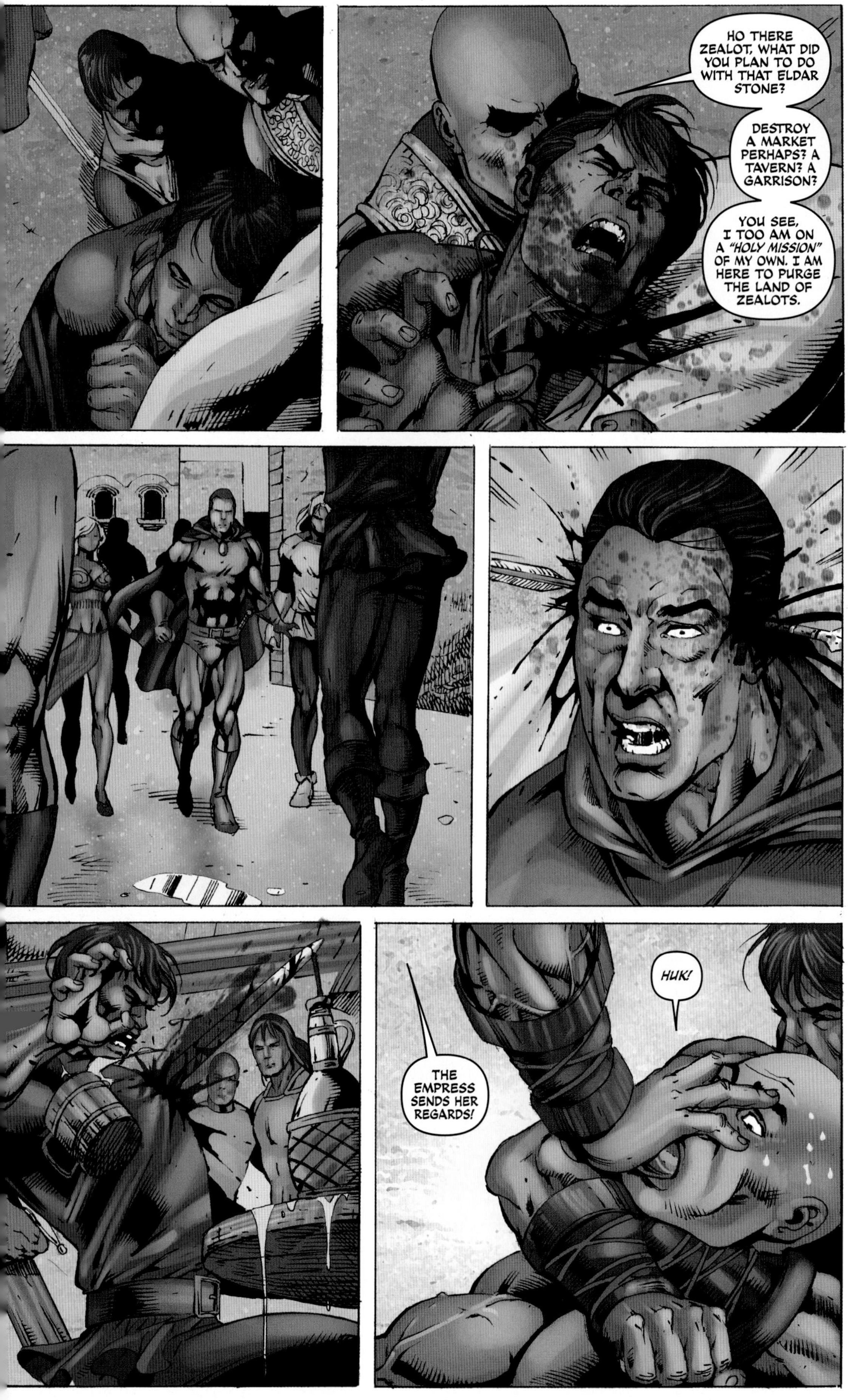
HO THERE ZEALOT, WHAT DID YOU PLAN TO DO WITH THAT ELDAR STONE?
DESTROY A MARKET PERHAPS? A TAVERN? A GARRISON?
YOU SEE, I TOO AM ON A *"HOLY MISSION"* OF MY OWN. I AM HERE TO PURGE THE LAND OF ZEALOTS.
THE EMPRESS SENDS HER REGARDS!
*HUK!*

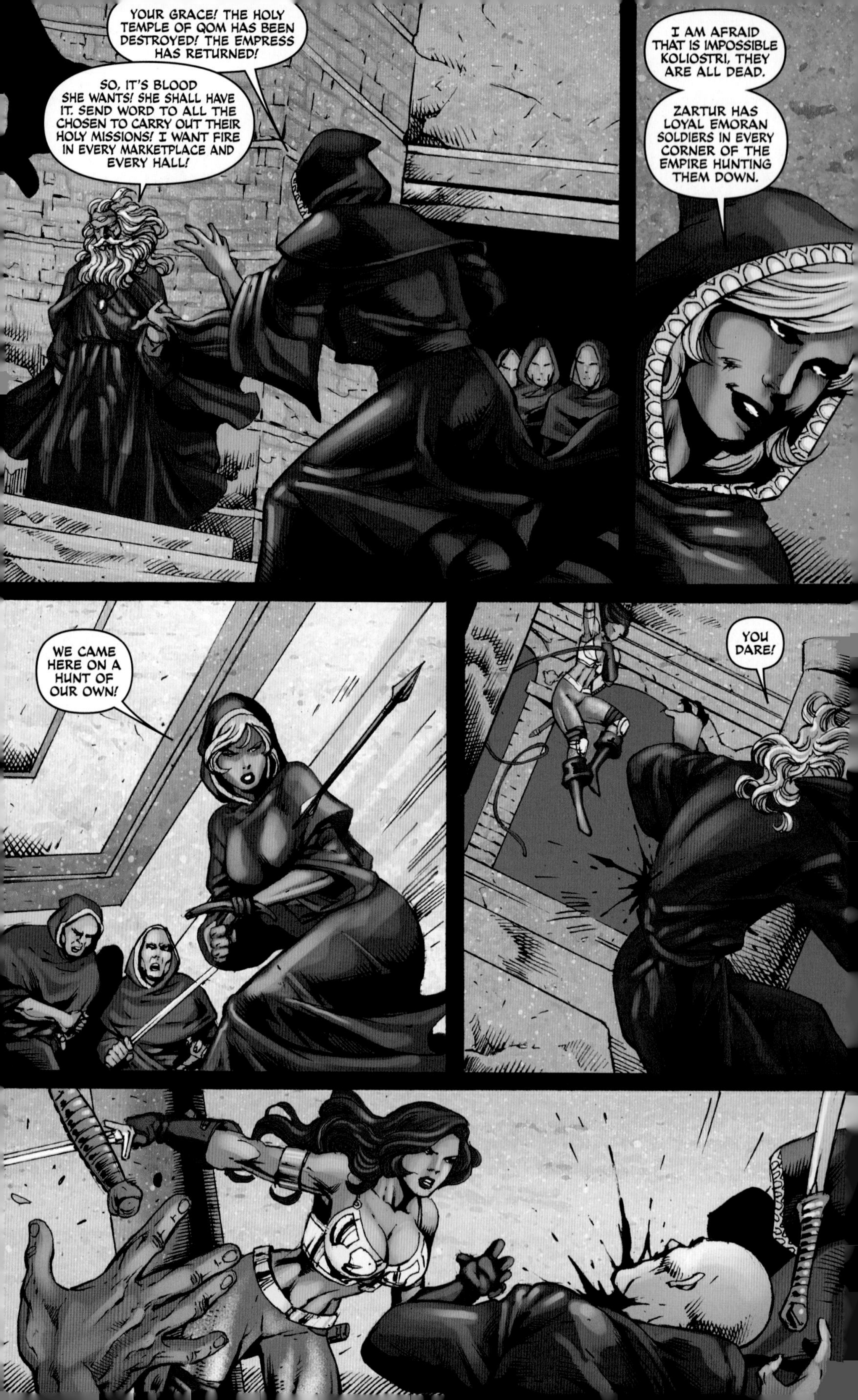

YOUR GRACE! THE HOLY TEMPLE OF QOM HAS BEEN DESTROYED! THE EMPRESS HAS RETURNED!
SO, IT'S BLOOD SHE WANTS! SHE SHALL HAVE IT. SEND WORD TO ALL THE CHOSEN TO CARRY OUT THEIR HOLY MISSIONS! I WANT FIRE IN EVERY MARKETPLACE AND EVERY HALL!
I AM AFRAID THAT IS IMPOSSIBLE KOLIOSTRI, THEY ARE ALL DEAD.
ZARTUR HAS LOYAL EMORAN SOLDIERS IN EVERY CORNER OF THE EMPIRE HUNTING THEM DOWN.
WE CAME HERE ON A HUNT OF OUR OWN!
YOU DARE!

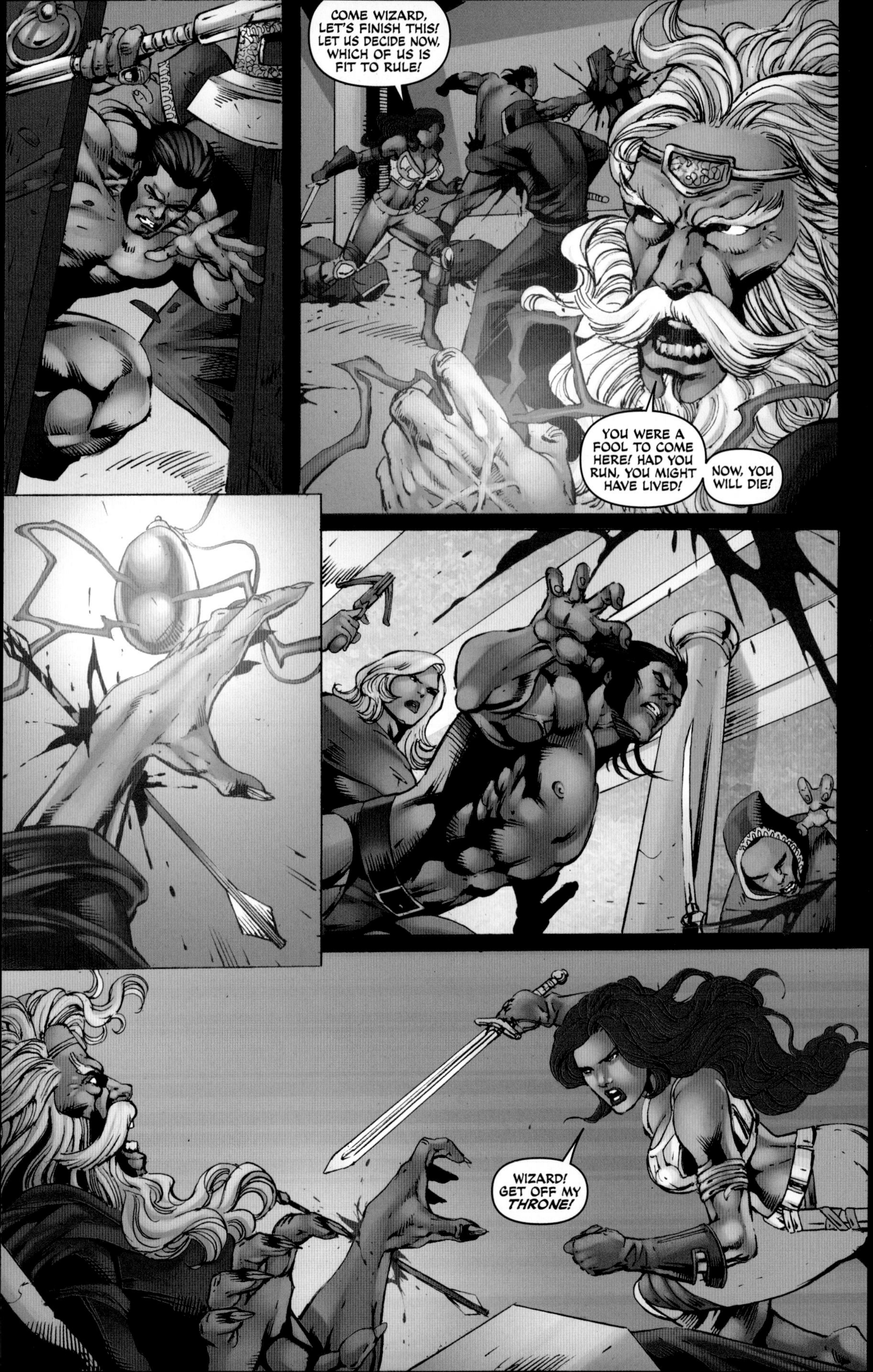
COME WIZARD, LET'S FINISH THIS! LET US DECIDE NOW, WHICH OF US IS FIT TO RULE!
YOU WERE A FOOL TO COME HERE! HAD YOU RUN, YOU MIGHT HAVE LIVED!
NOW, YOU WILL DIE!
WIZARD! GET OFF MY *THRONE!*

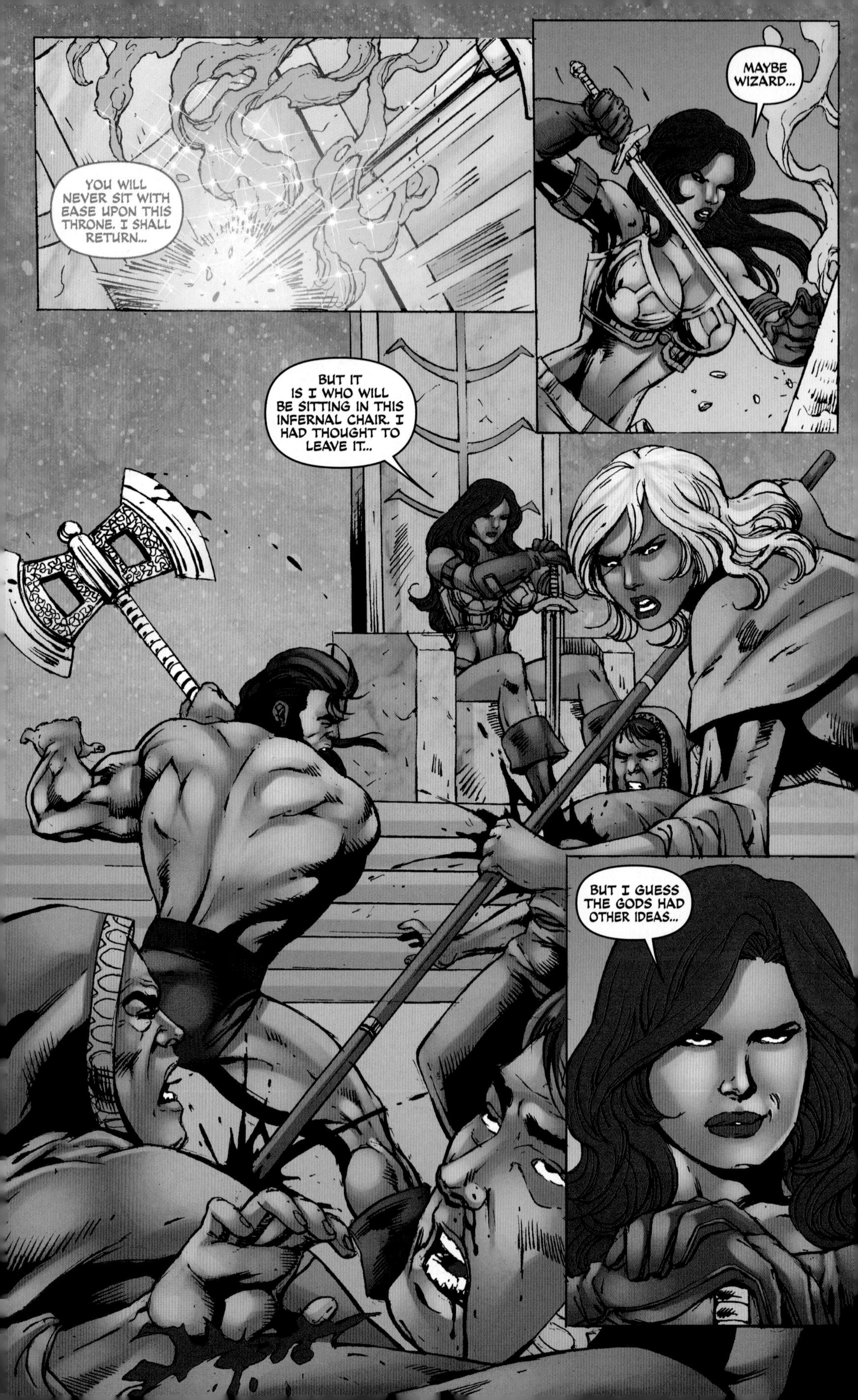
YOU WILL NEVER SIT WITH EASE UPON THIS THRONE. I SHALL RETURN...
MAYBE WIZARD...
BUT IT IS I WHO WILL BE SITTING IN THIS INFERNAL CHAIR. I HAD THOUGHT TO LEAVE IT...
BUT I GUESS THE GODS HAD OTHER IDEAS...

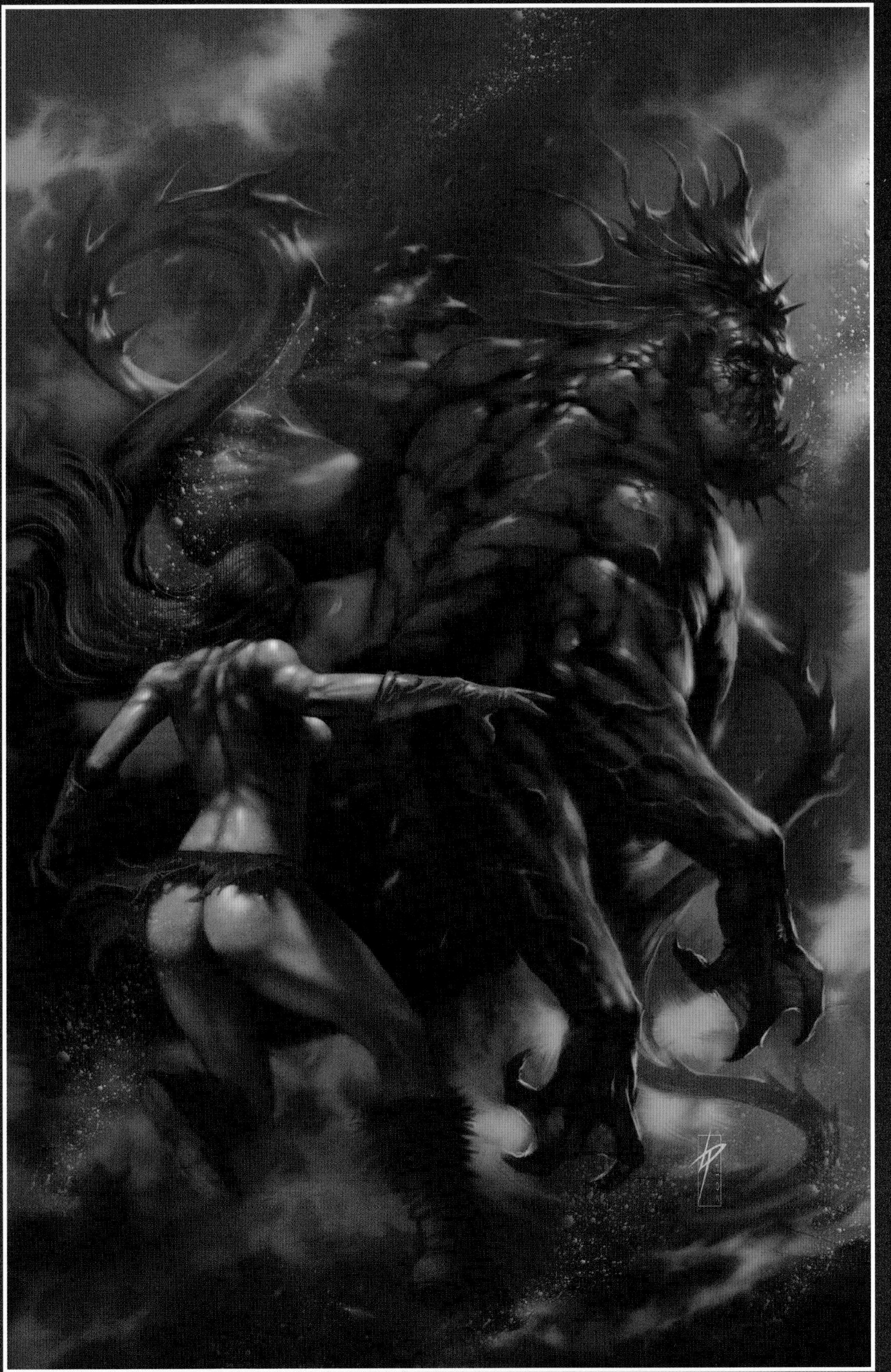

ISSUE #30 COVER BY LUCIO PARRILLO

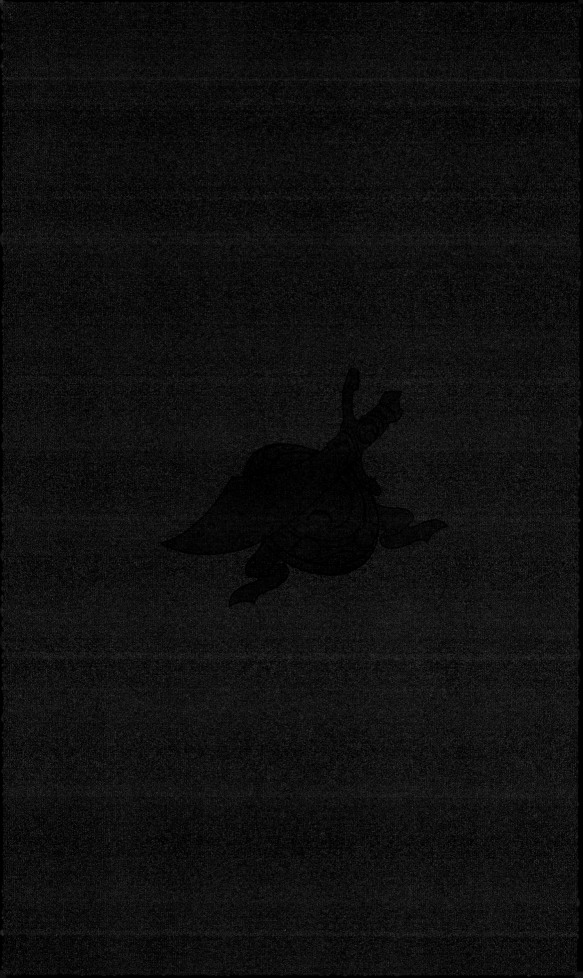

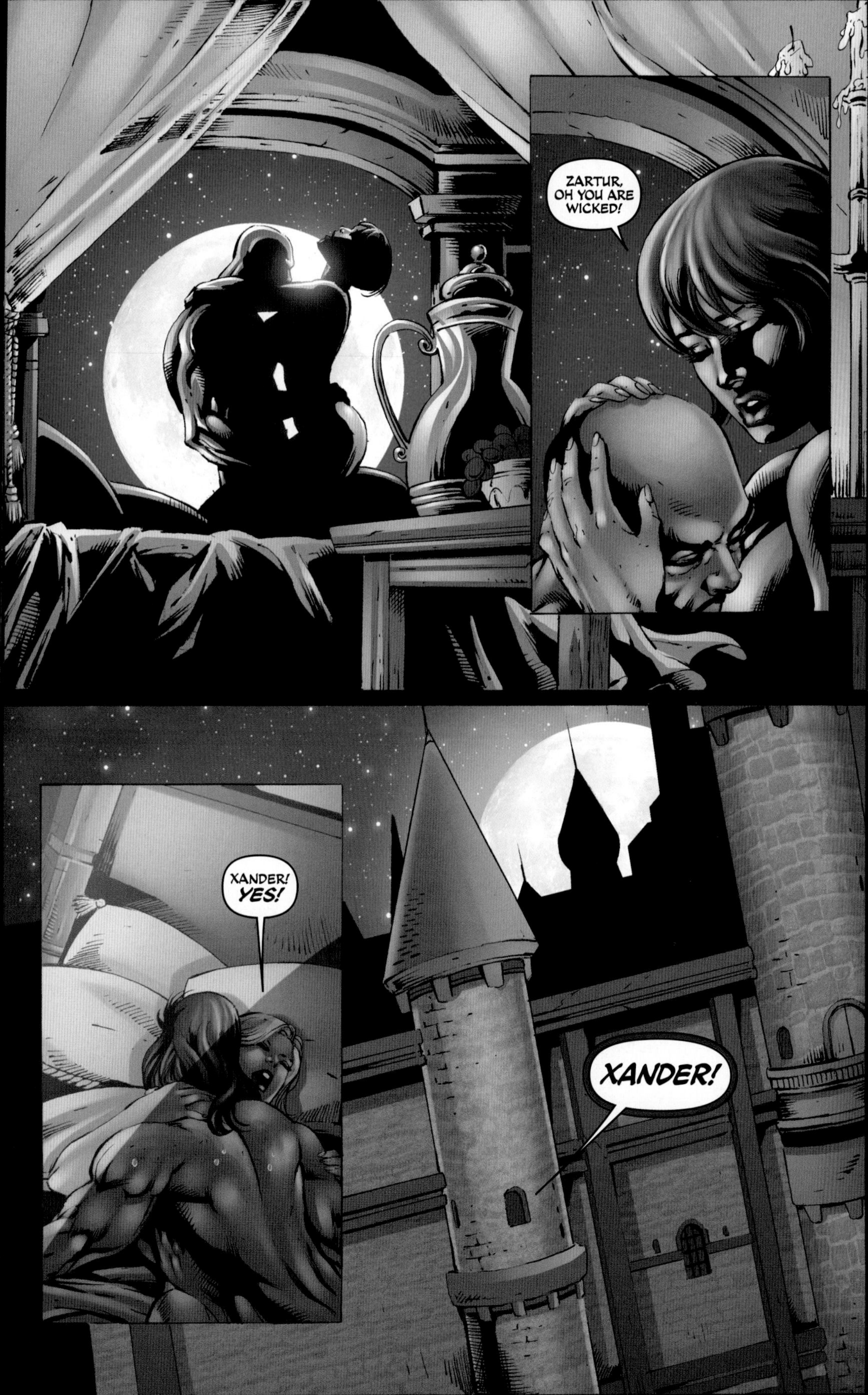
ZARTUR, OH YOU ARE WICKED!
XANDER! YES!
XANDER!

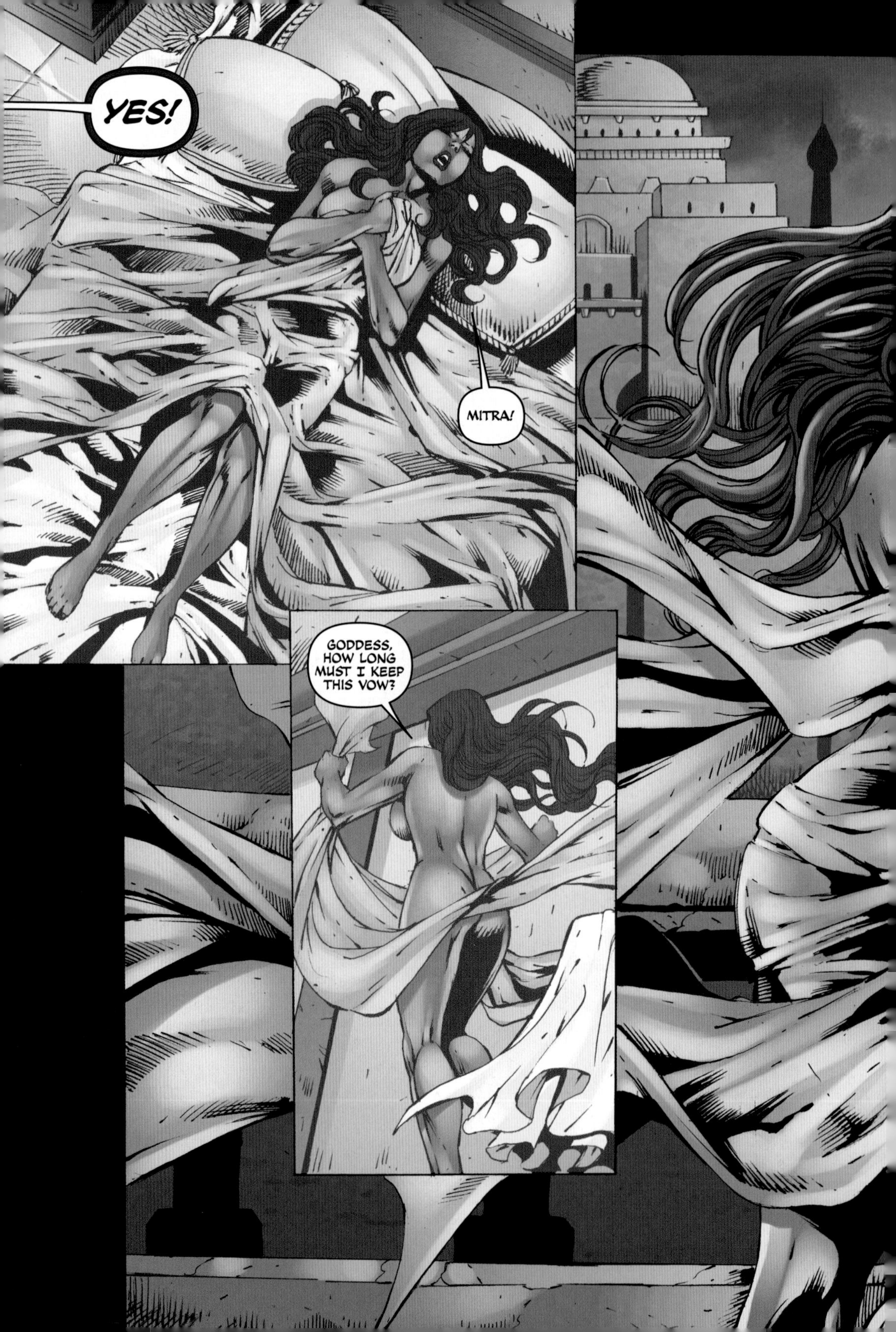
YES!
MITRA!
GODDESS, HOW LONG MUST I KEEP THIS VOW?

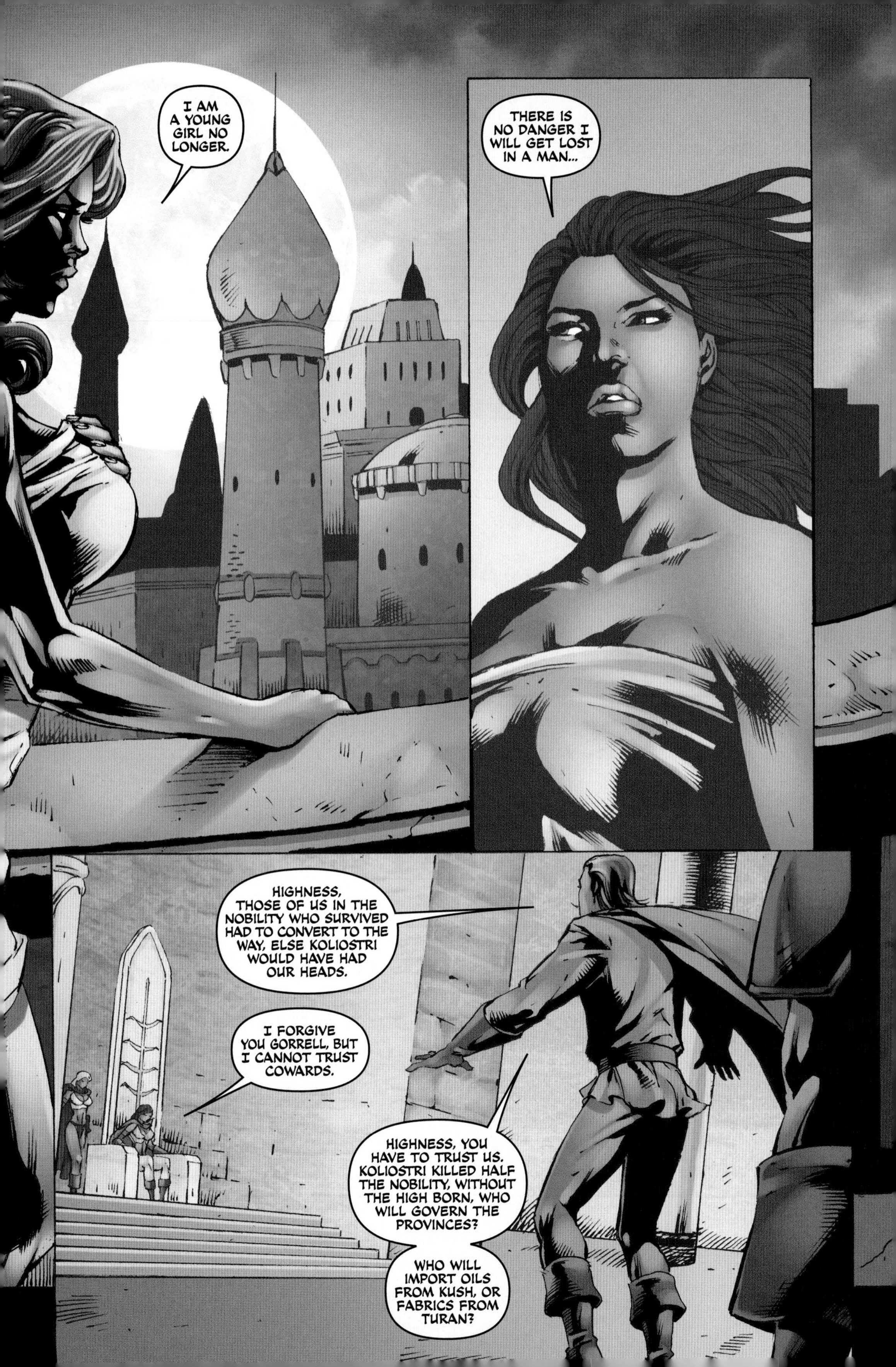
I AM A YOUNG GIRL NO LONGER.
THERE IS NO DANGER I WILL GET LOST IN A MAN...
HIGHNESS, THOSE OF US IN THE NOBILITY WHO SURVIVED HAD TO CONVERT TO THE WAY, ELSE KOLIOSTRI WOULD HAVE HAD OUR HEADS.
I FORGIVE YOU GORRELL, BUT I CANNOT TRUST COWARDS.
HIGHNESS, YOU HAVE TO TRUST US. KOLIOSTRI KILLED HALF THE NOBILITY, WITHOUT THE HIGH BORN, WHO WILL GOVERN THE PROVINCES?
WHO WILL IMPORT OILS FROM KUSH, OR FABRICS FROM TURAN?

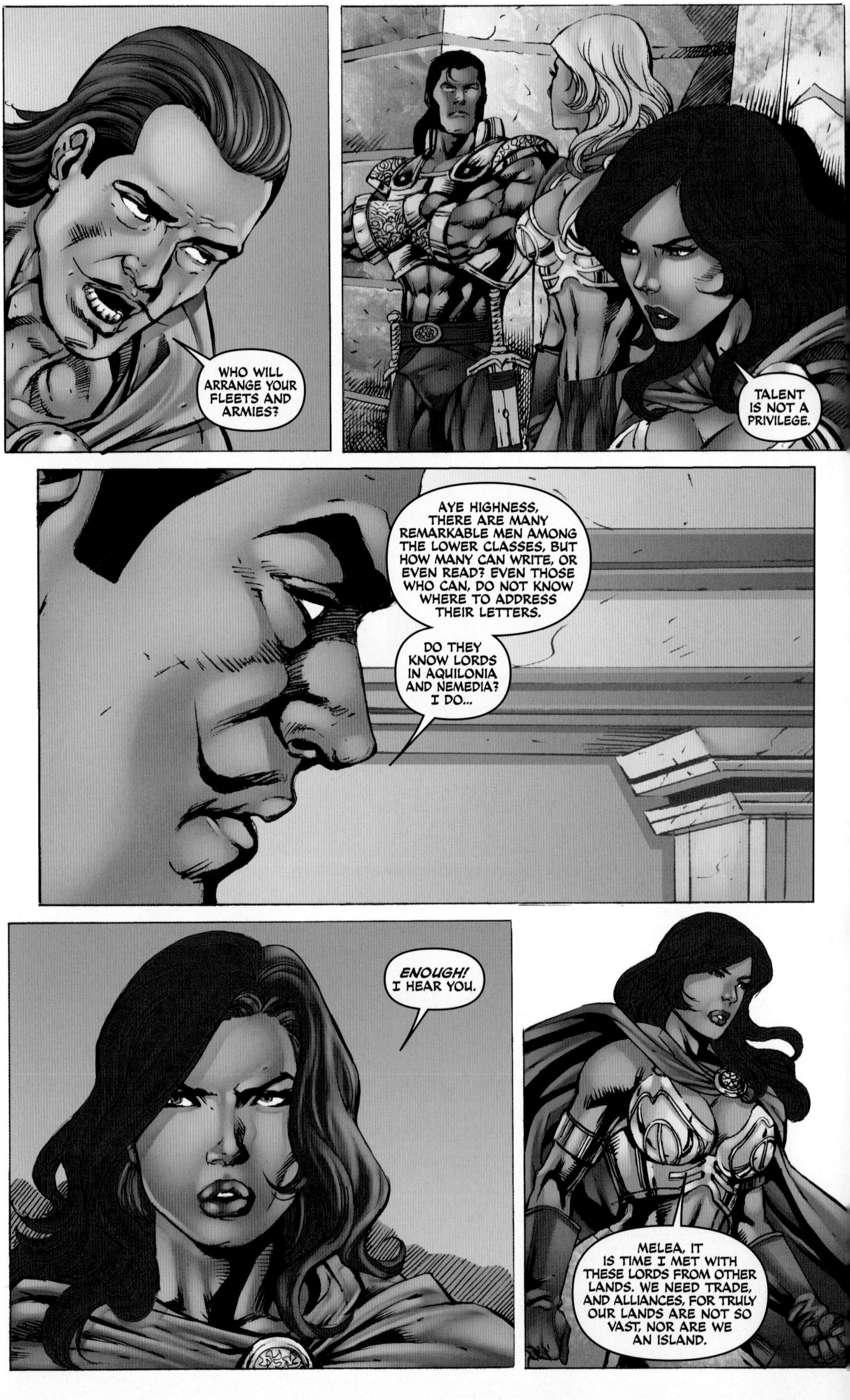
WHO WILL ARRANGE YOUR FLEETS AND ARMIES?
TALENT IS NOT A PRIVILEGE.
AYE HIGHNESS, THERE ARE MANY REMARKABLE MEN AMONG THE LOWER CLASSES, BUT HOW MANY CAN WRITE, OR EVEN READ? EVEN THOSE WHO CAN, DO NOT KNOW WHERE TO ADDRESS THEIR LETTERS.
DO THEY KNOW LORDS IN AQUILONIA AND NEMEDIA? I DO...
ENOUGH! I HEAR YOU.
MELEA, IT IS TIME I MET WITH THESE LORDS FROM OTHER LANDS. WE NEED TRADE, AND ALLIANCES, FOR TRULY OUR LANDS ARE NOT SO VAST, NOR ARE WE AN ISLAND.

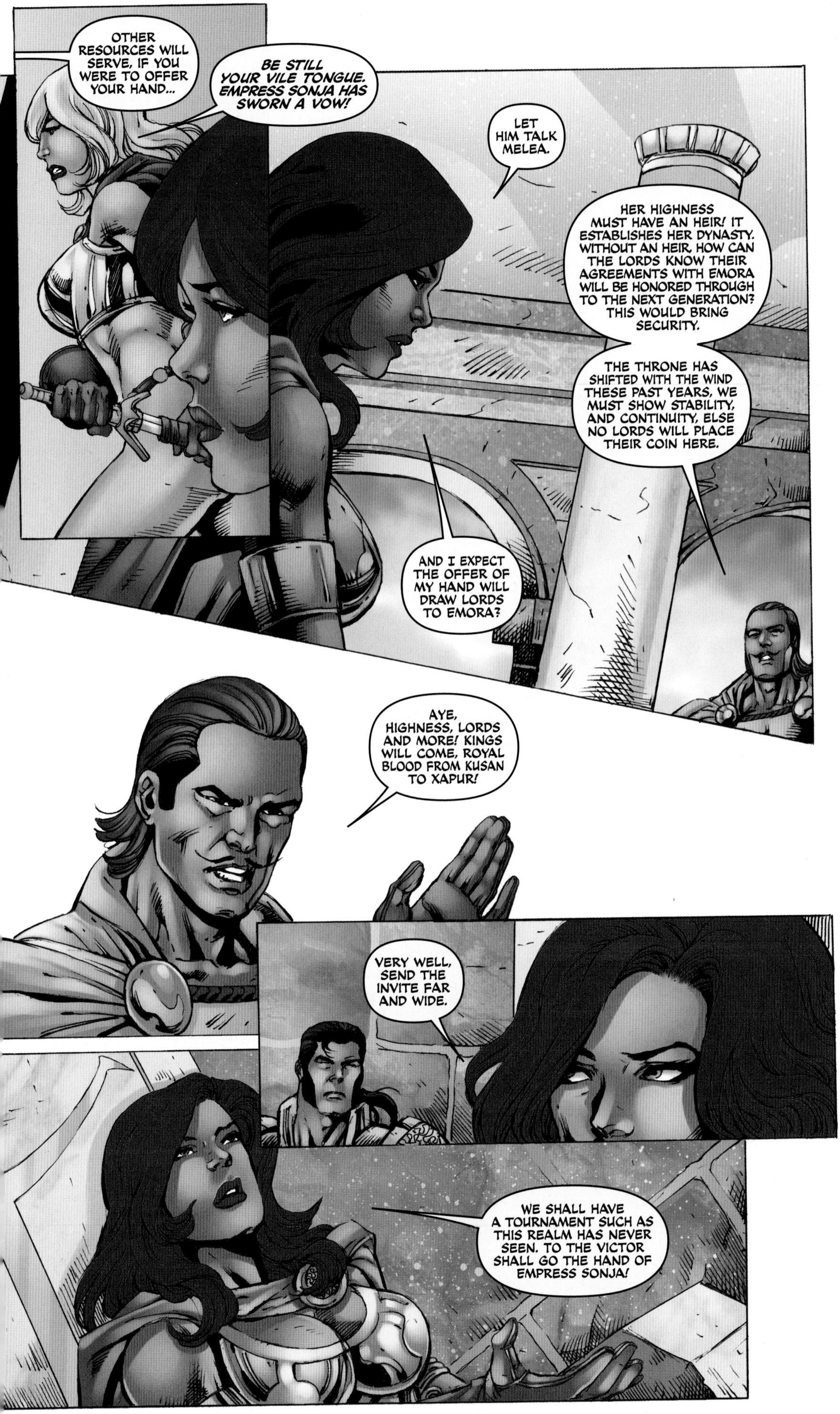
OTHER RESOURCES WILL SERVE, IF YOU WERE TO OFFER YOUR HAND...
BE STILL YOUR VILE TONGUE. EMPRESS SONJA HAS SWORN A VOW!
LET HIM TALK MELEA.
HER HIGHNESS MUST HAVE AN HEIR! IT ESTABLISHES HER DYNASTY. WITHOUT AN HEIR, HOW CAN THE LORDS KNOW THEIR AGREEMENTS WITH EMORA WILL BE HONORED THROUGH TO THE NEXT GENERATION? THIS WOULD BRING SECURITY.
THE THRONE HAS SHIFTED WITH THE WIND THESE PAST YEARS, WE MUST SHOW STABILITY, AND CONTINUITY, ELSE NO LORDS WILL PLACE THEIR COIN HERE.
AND I EXPECT THE OFFER OF MY HAND WILL DRAW LORDS TO EMORA?
AYE, HIGHNESS, LORDS AND MORE! KINGS WILL COME, ROYAL BLOOD FROM KUSAN TO XAPUR!
VERY WELL, SEND THE INVITE FAR AND WIDE.
WE SHALL HAVE A TOURNAMENT SUCH AS THIS REALM HAS NEVER SEEN. TO THE VICTOR SHALL GO THE HAND OF EMPRESS SONJA!

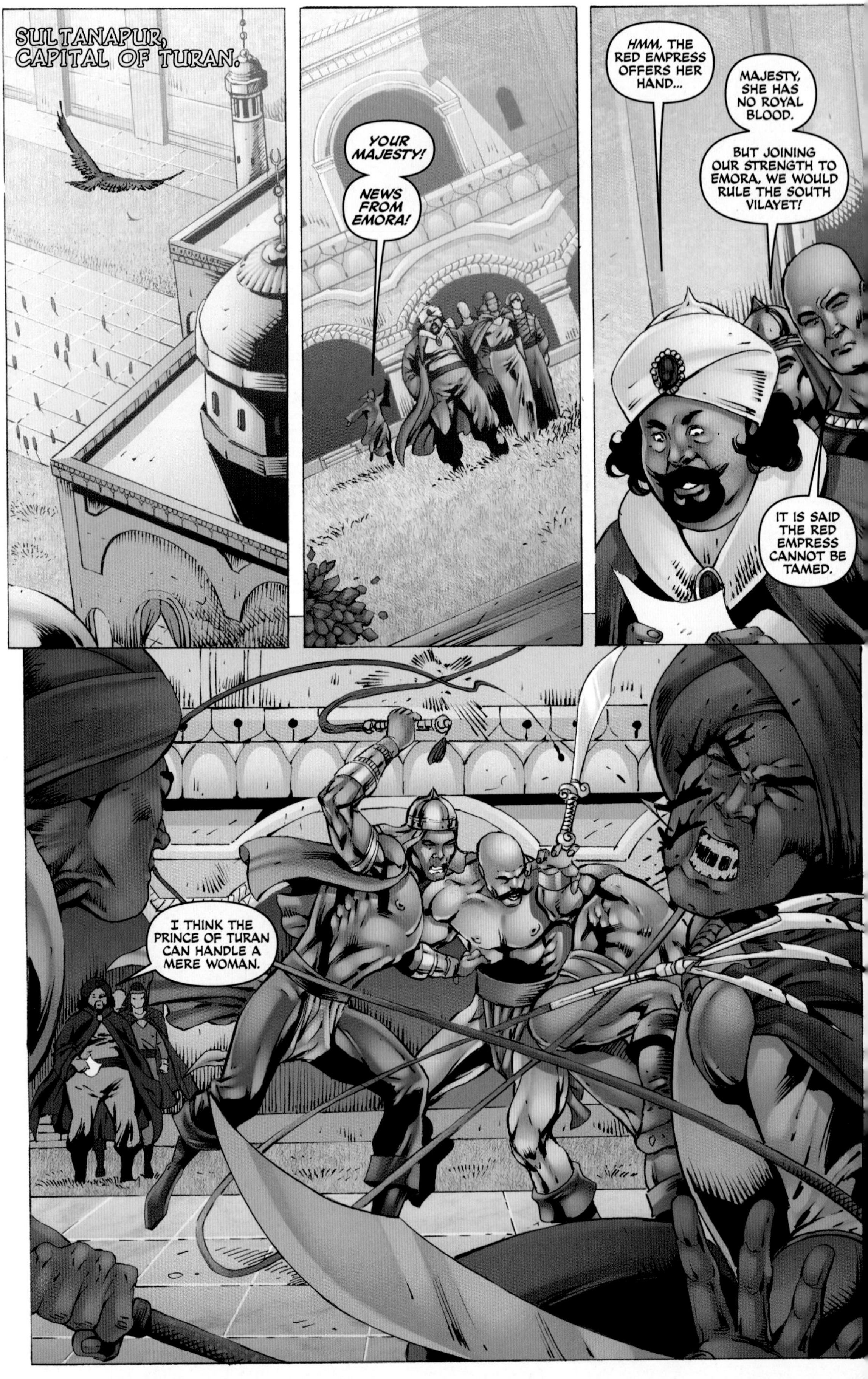
SULTANAPUR, CAPITAL OF TURAN.
YOUR MAJESTY!
NEWS FROM EMORA!
HMM, THE RED EMPRESS OFFERS HER HAND...
MAJESTY, SHE HAS NO ROYAL BLOOD.
BUT JOINING OUR STRENGTH TO EMORA, WE WOULD RULE THE SOUTH VILAYET!
IT IS SAID THE RED EMPRESS CANNOT BE TAMED.
I THINK THE PRINCE OF TURAN CAN HANDLE A MERE WOMAN.

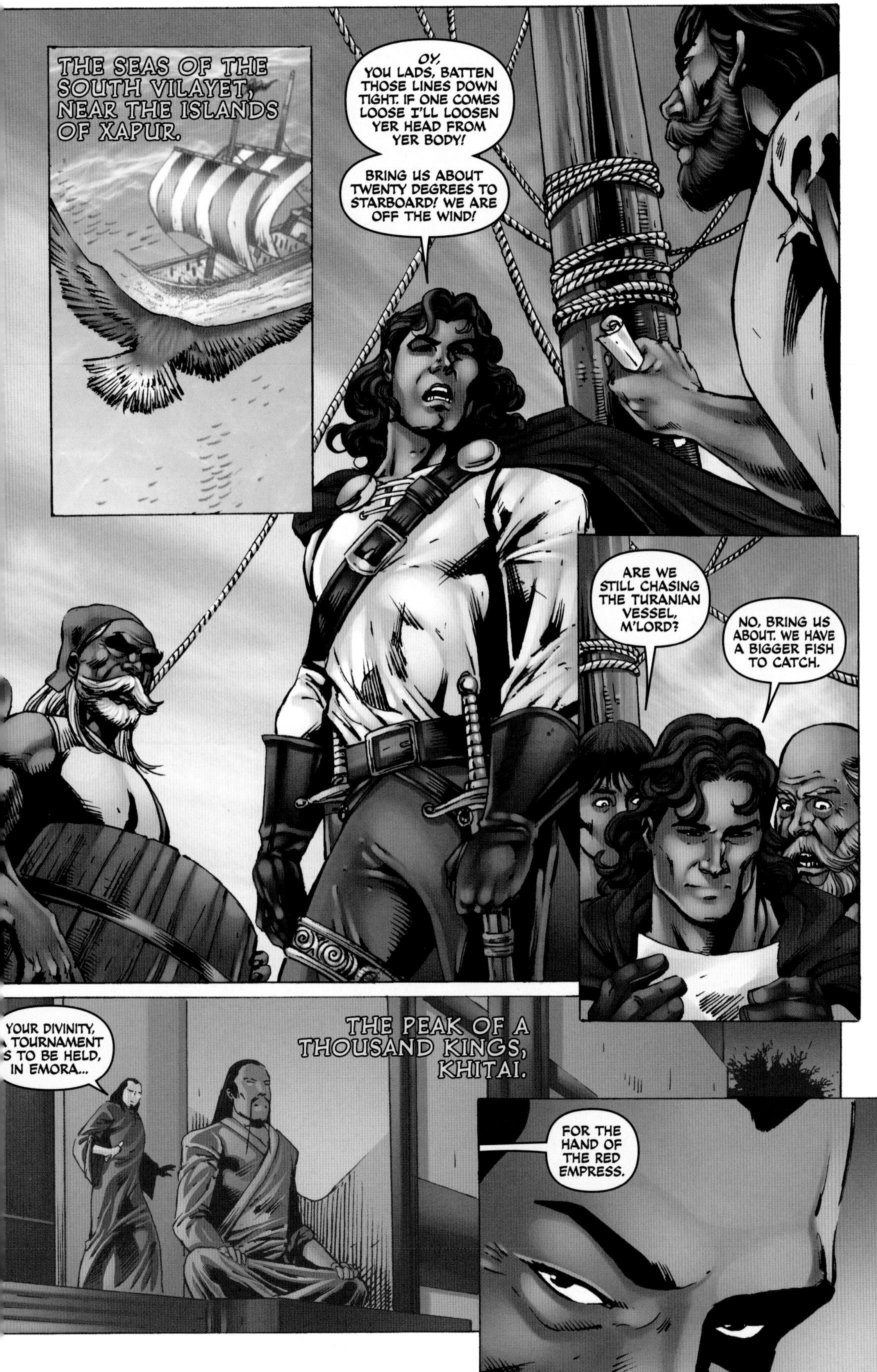
THE SEAS OF THE SOUTH VILAYET, NEAR THE ISLANDS OF XAPUR.
OY, YOU LADS, BATTEN THOSE LINES DOWN TIGHT. IF ONE COMES LOOSE I'LL LOOSEN YER HEAD FROM YER BODY!
BRING US ABOUT TWENTY DEGREES TO STARBOARD! WE ARE OFF THE WIND!
ARE WE STILL CHASING THE TURANIAN VESSEL, M'LORD?
NO, BRING US ABOUT. WE HAVE A BIGGER FISH TO CATCH.
THE PEAK OF A THOUSAND KINGS, KHITAI.
YOUR DIVINITY, TOURNAMENT S TO BE HELD, IN EMORA...
FOR THE HAND OF THE RED EMPRESS.

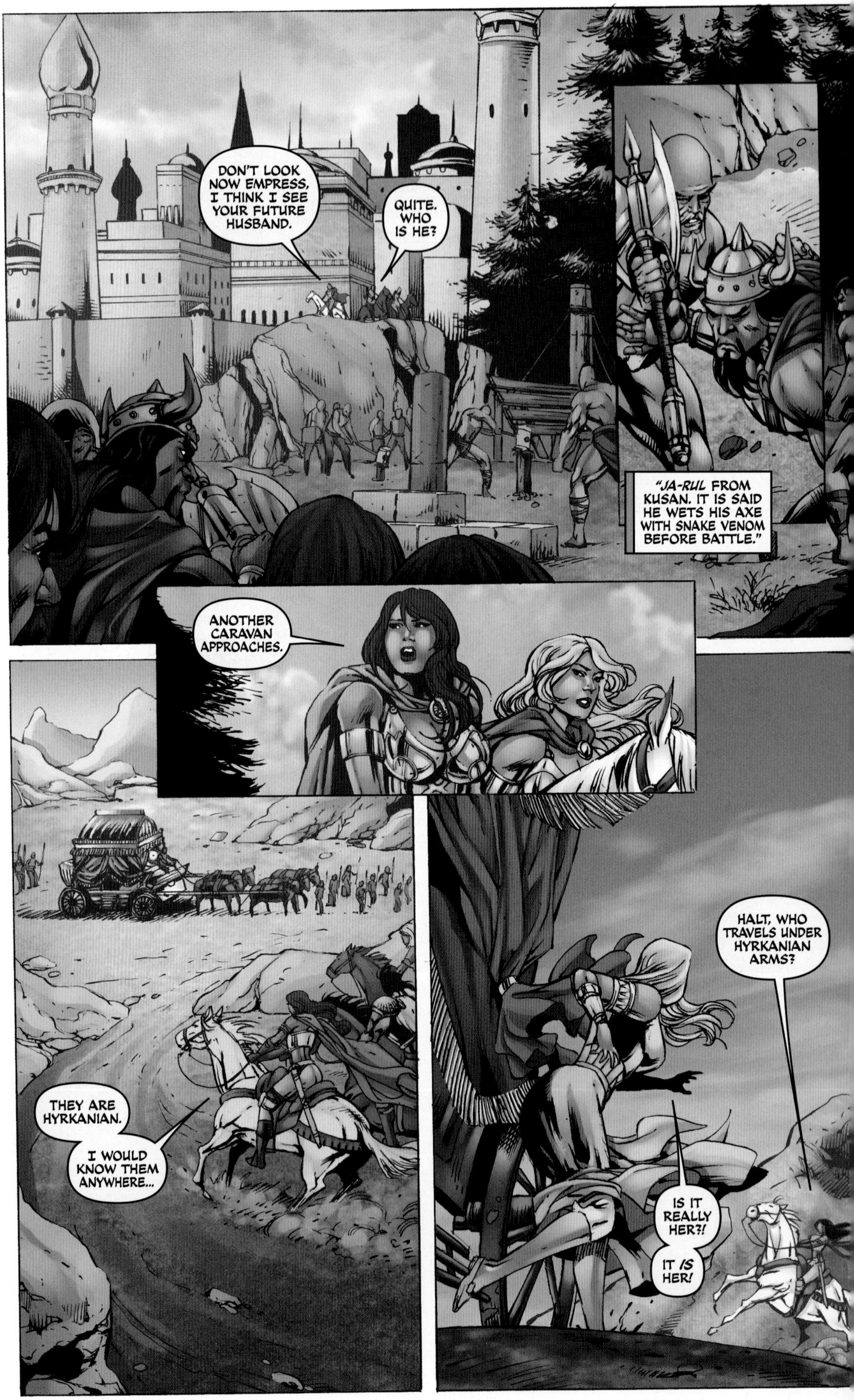
DON'T LOOK NOW EMPRESS, I THINK I SEE YOUR FUTURE HUSBAND.
QUITE. WHO IS HE?
"JA-RUL FROM KUSAN. IT IS SAID HE WETS HIS AXE WITH SNAKE VENOM BEFORE BATTLE."
ANOTHER CARAVAN APPROACHES.
THEY ARE HYRKANIAN.
I WOULD KNOW THEM ANYWHERE...
HALT, WHO TRAVELS UNDER HYRKANIAN ARMS?
IS IT REALLY HER?!
IT IS HER!

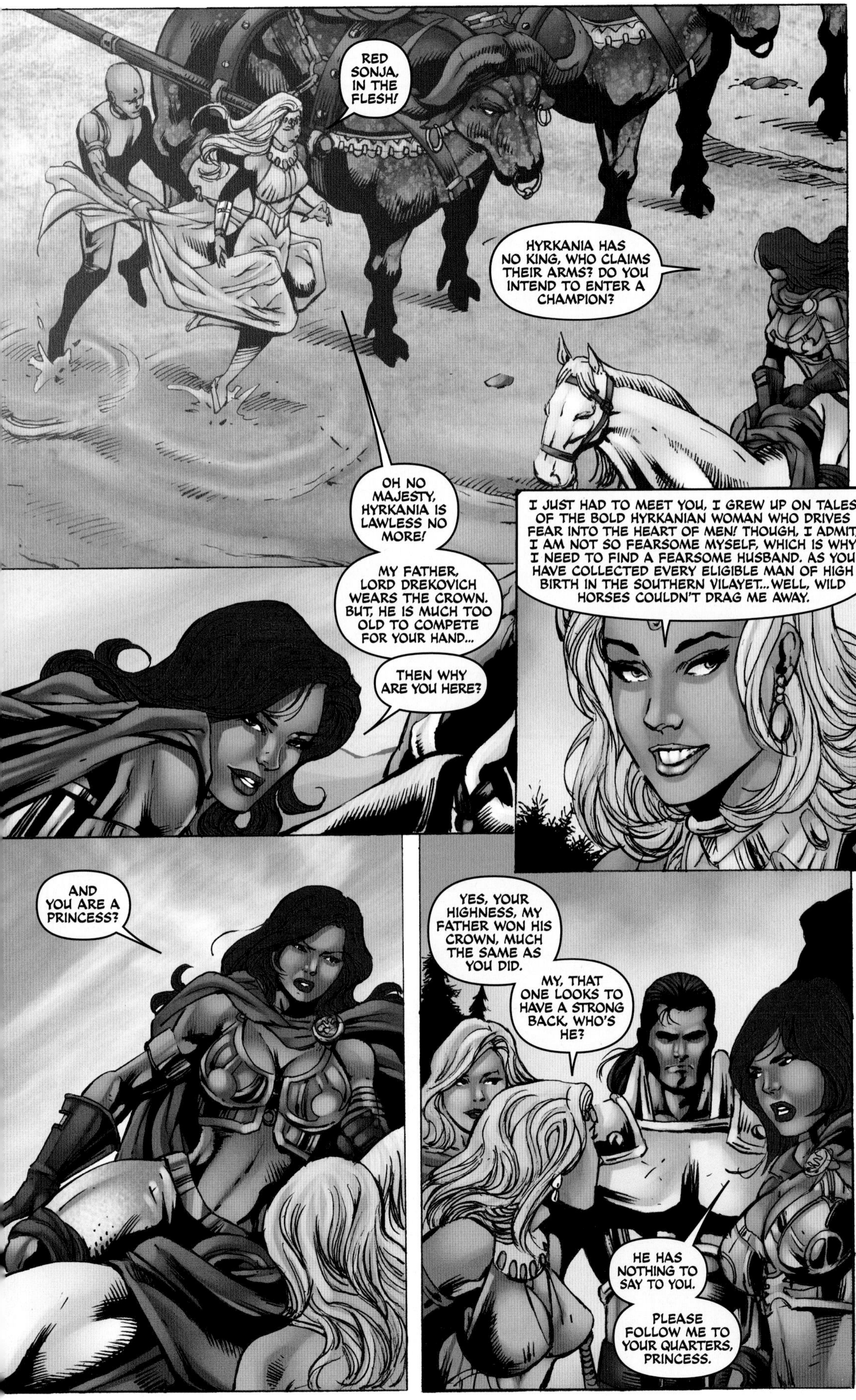
RED SONJA, IN THE FLESH!
HYRKANIA HAS NO KING, WHO CLAIMS THEIR ARMS? DO YOU INTEND TO ENTER A CHAMPION?
OH NO MAJESTY, HYRKANIA IS LAWLESS NO MORE!
MY FATHER, LORD DREKOVICH WEARS THE CROWN. BUT, HE IS MUCH TOO OLD TO COMPETE FOR YOUR HAND...
THEN WHY ARE YOU HERE?
I JUST HAD TO MEET YOU, I GREW UP ON TALES OF THE BOLD HYRKANIAN WOMAN WHO DRIVES FEAR INTO THE HEART OF MEN! THOUGH, I ADMIT, I AM NOT SO FEARSOME MYSELF, WHICH IS WHY I NEED TO FIND A FEARSOME HUSBAND. AS YOU HAVE COLLECTED EVERY ELIGIBLE MAN OF HIGH BIRTH IN THE SOUTHERN VILAYET...WELL, WILD HORSES COULDN'T DRAG ME AWAY.
AND YOU ARE A PRINCESS?
YES, YOUR HIGHNESS, MY FATHER WON HIS CROWN, MUCH THE SAME AS YOU DID.
MY, THAT ONE LOOKS TO HAVE A STRONG BACK, WHO'S HE?
HE HAS NOTHING TO SAY TO YOU.
PLEASE FOLLOW ME TO YOUR QUARTERS, PRINCESS.

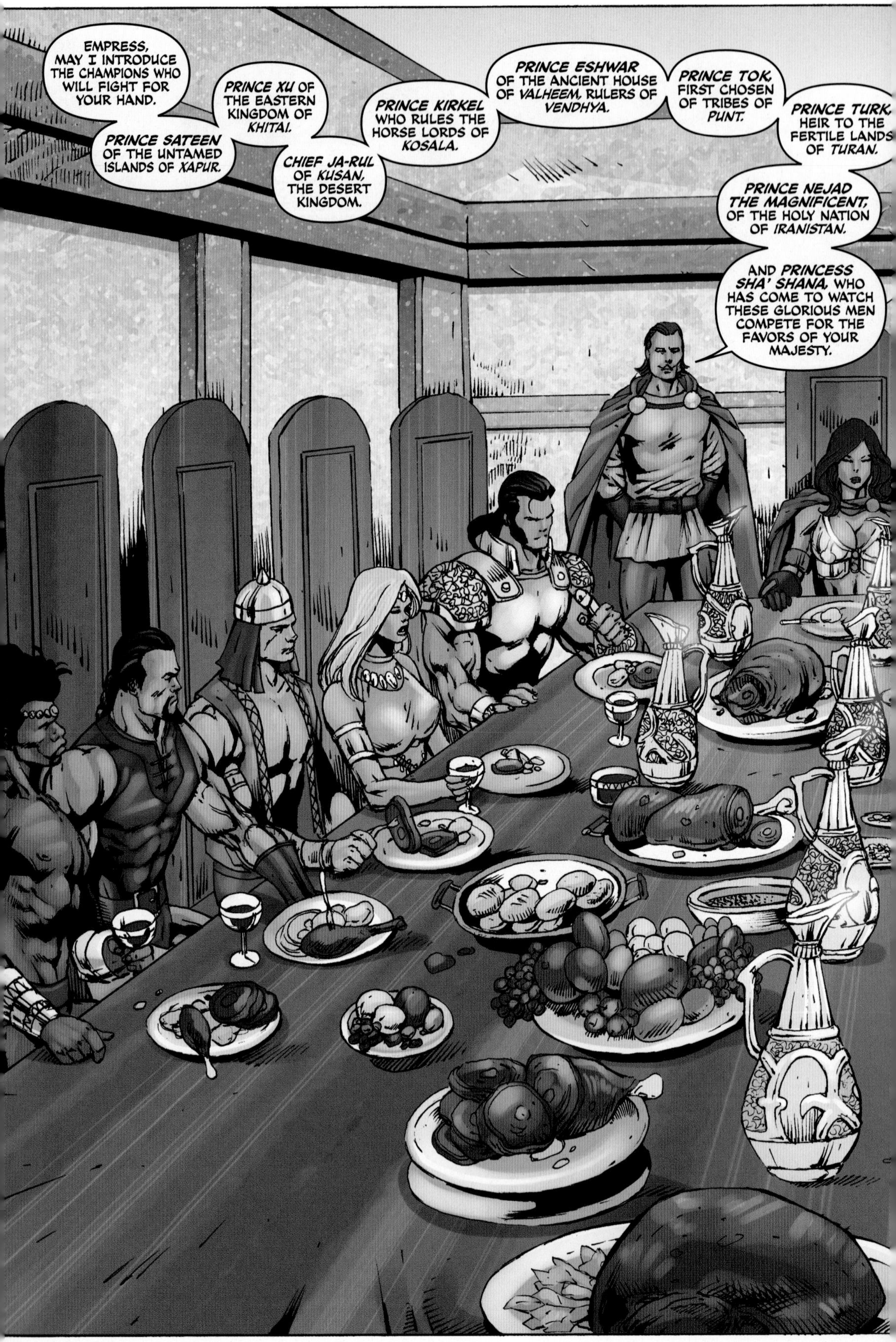
EMPRESS, MAY I INTRODUCE THE CHAMPIONS WHO WILL FIGHT FOR YOUR HAND.
PRINCE SATEEN OF THE UNTAMED ISLANDS OF XAPUR.
PRINCE XU OF THE EASTERN KINGDOM OF KHITAI.
CHIEF JA-RUL OF KUSAN, THE DESERT KINGDOM.
PRINCE KIRKEL WHO RULES THE HORSE LORDS OF KOSALA.
PRINCE ESHWAR OF THE ANCIENT HOUSE OF VALHEEM, RULERS OF VENDHYA.
PRINCE TOK, FIRST CHOSEN OF TRIBES OF PUNT.
PRINCE TURK, HEIR TO THE FERTILE LANDS OF TURAN.
PRINCE NEJAD THE MAGNIFICENT, OF THE HOLY NATION OF IRANISTAN.
AND PRINCESS SHA' SHANA, WHO HAS COME TO WATCH THESE GLORIOUS MEN COMPETE FOR THE FAVORS OF YOUR MAJESTY.

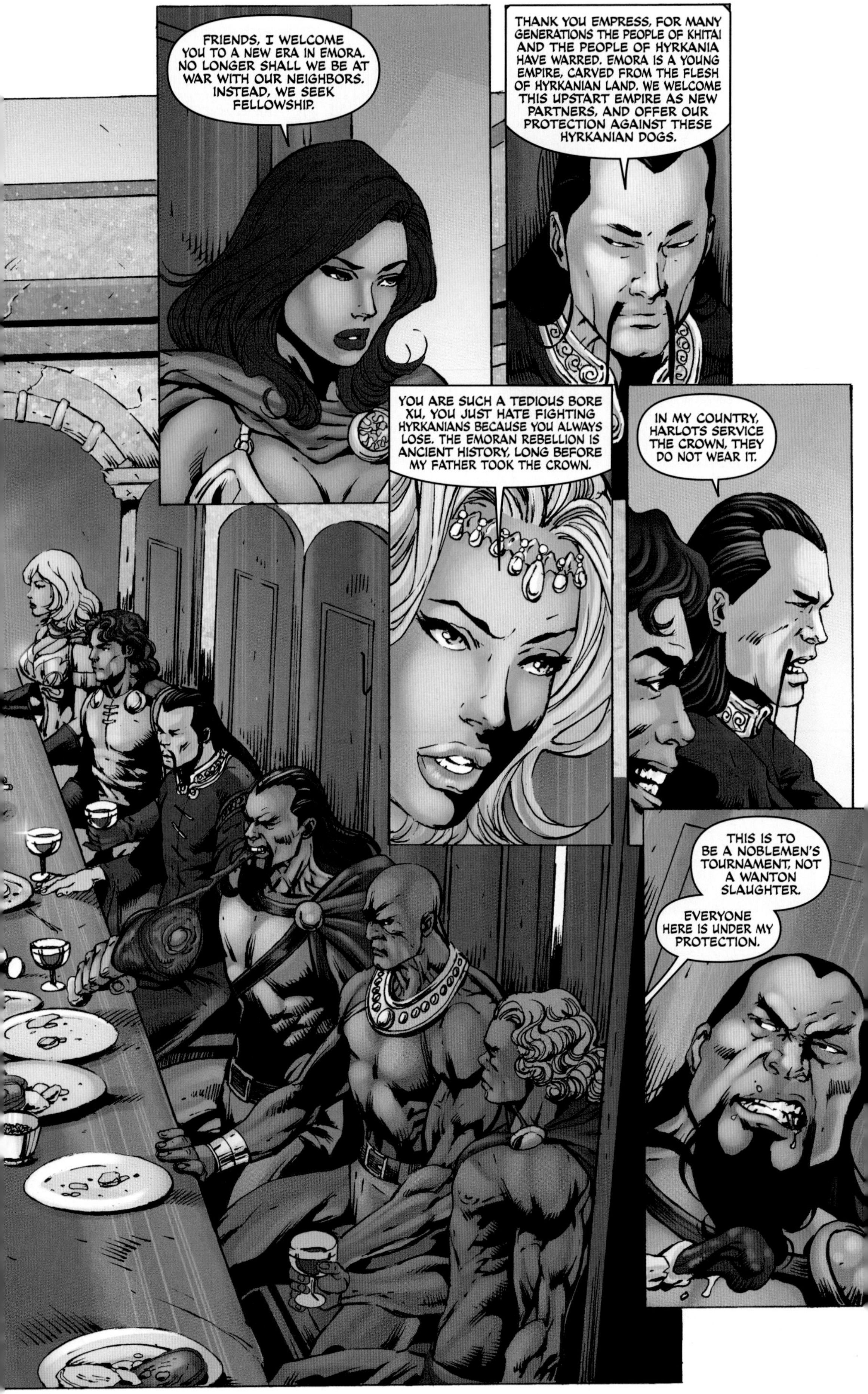
FRIENDS, I WELCOME YOU TO A NEW ERA IN EMORA. NO LONGER SHALL WE BE AT WAR WITH OUR NEIGHBORS. INSTEAD, WE SEEK FELLOWSHIP.
THANK YOU EMPRESS, FOR MANY GENERATIONS THE PEOPLE OF KHITAI AND THE PEOPLE OF HYRKANIA HAVE WARRED. EMORA IS A YOUNG EMPIRE, CARVED FROM THE FLESH OF HYRKANIAN LAND. WE WELCOME THIS UPSTART EMPIRE AS NEW PARTNERS, AND OFFER OUR PROTECTION AGAINST THESE HYRKANIAN DOGS.
YOU ARE SUCH A TEDIOUS BORE XU, YOU JUST HATE FIGHTING HYRKANIANS BECAUSE YOU ALWAYS LOSE. THE EMORAN REBELLION IS ANCIENT HISTORY, LONG BEFORE MY FATHER TOOK THE CROWN.
IN MY COUNTRY, HARLOTS SERVICE THE CROWN, THEY DO NOT WEAR IT.
THIS IS TO BE A NOBLEMEN'S TOURNAMENT, NOT A WANTON SLAUGHTER.
EVERYONE HERE IS UNDER MY PROTECTION.

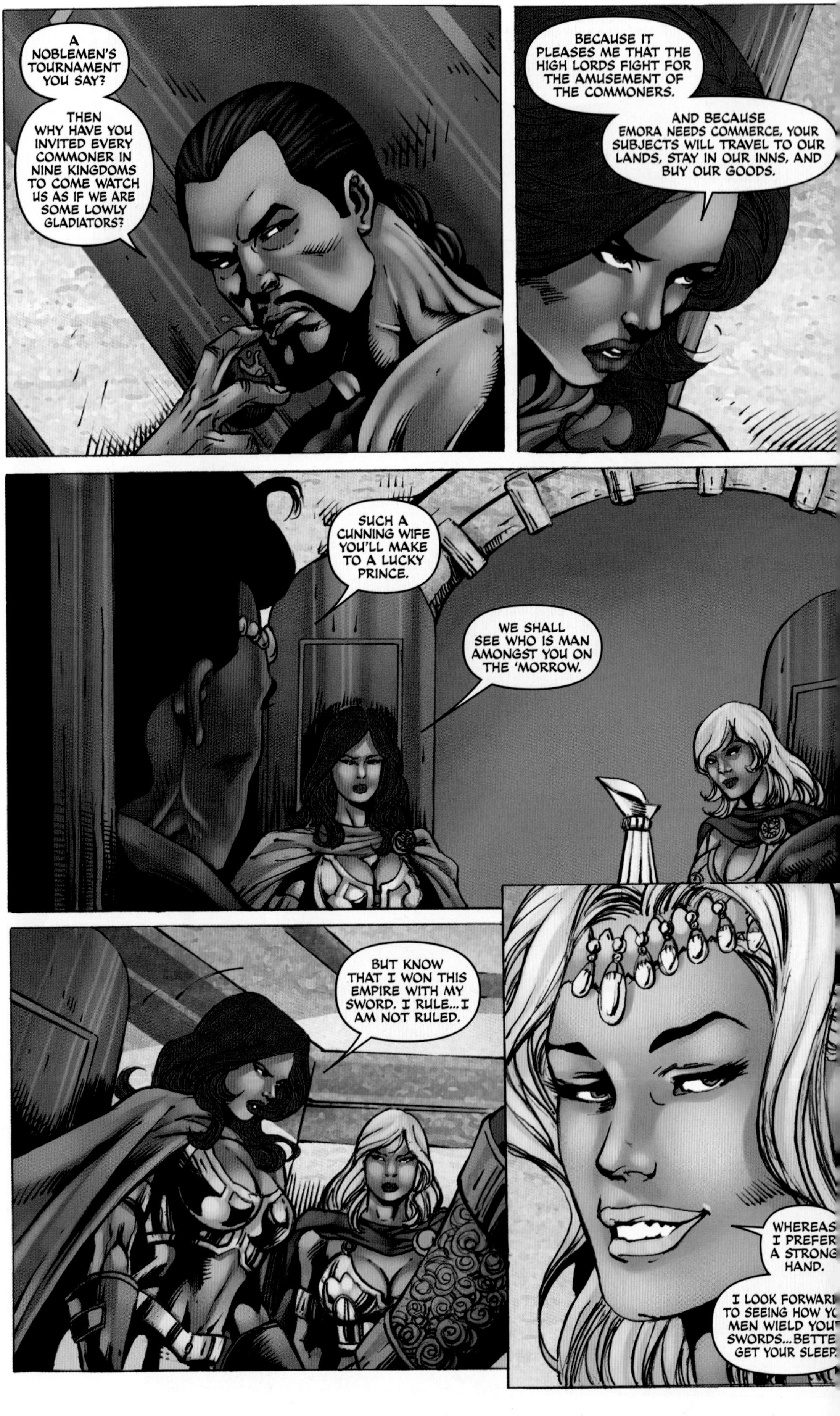
A NOBLEMEN'S TOURNAMENT YOU SAY?
THEN WHY HAVE YOU INVITED EVERY COMMONER IN NINE KINGDOMS TO COME WATCH US AS IF WE ARE SOME LOWLY GLADIATORS?
BECAUSE IT PLEASES ME THAT THE HIGH LORDS FIGHT FOR THE AMUSEMENT OF THE COMMONERS.
AND BECAUSE EMORA NEEDS COMMERCE, YOUR SUBJECTS WILL TRAVEL TO OUR LANDS, STAY IN OUR INNS, AND BUY OUR GOODS.
SUCH A CUNNING WIFE YOU'LL MAKE TO A LUCKY PRINCE.
WE SHALL SEE WHO IS MAN AMONGST YOU ON THE 'MORROW.
BUT KNOW THAT I WON THIS EMPIRE WITH MY SWORD. I RULE... I AM NOT RULED.
WHEREAS I PREFER A STRONG HAND.
I LOOK FORWAR TO SEEING HOW Y MEN WIELD YOU SWORDS... BETTE GET YOUR SLEEP.

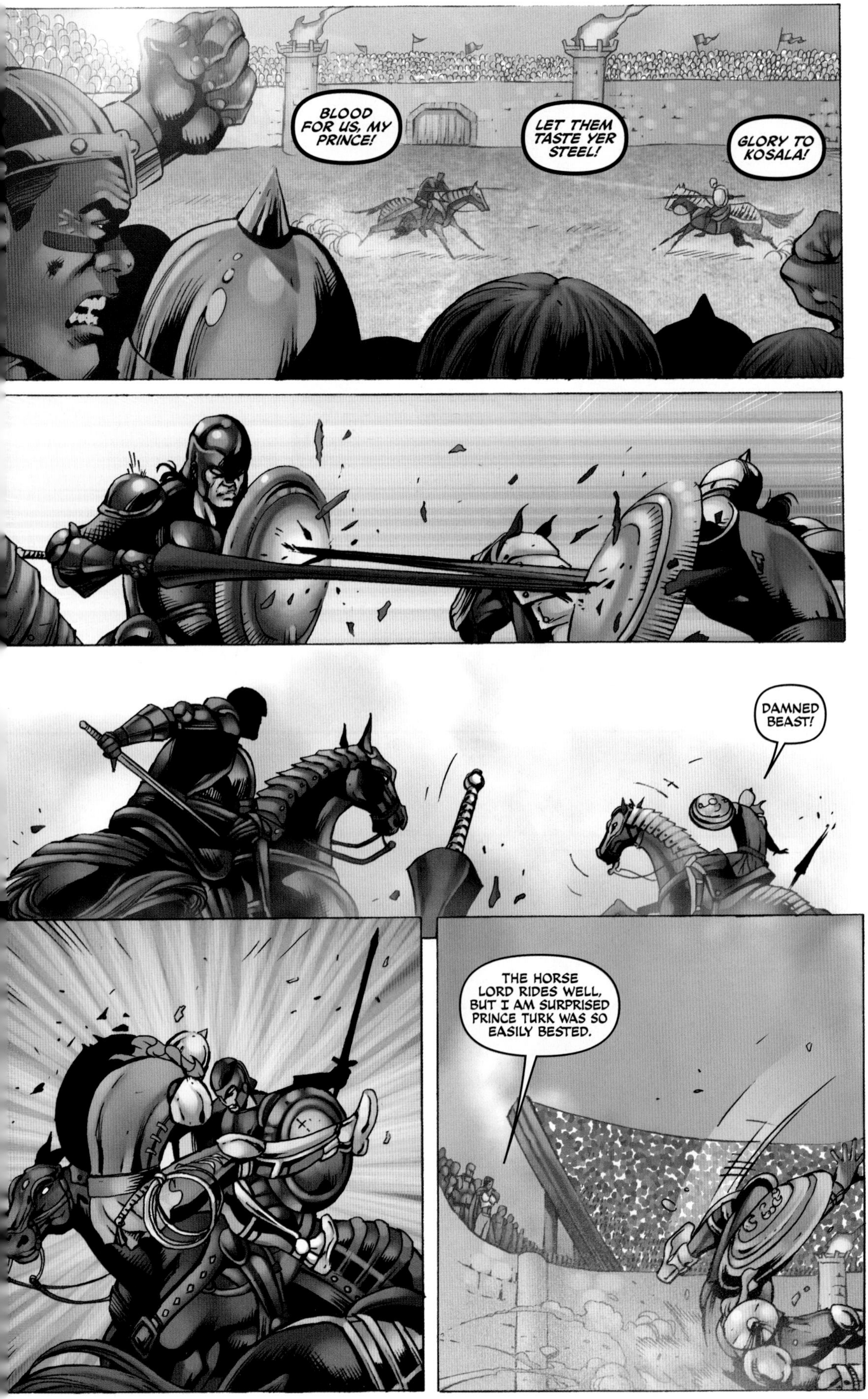
BLOOD FOR US, MY PRINCE!
LET THEM TASTE YER STEEL!
GLORY TO KOSALA!
DAMNED BEAST!
THE HORSE LORD RIDES WELL, BUT I AM SURPRISED PRINCE TURK WAS SO EASILY BESTED.

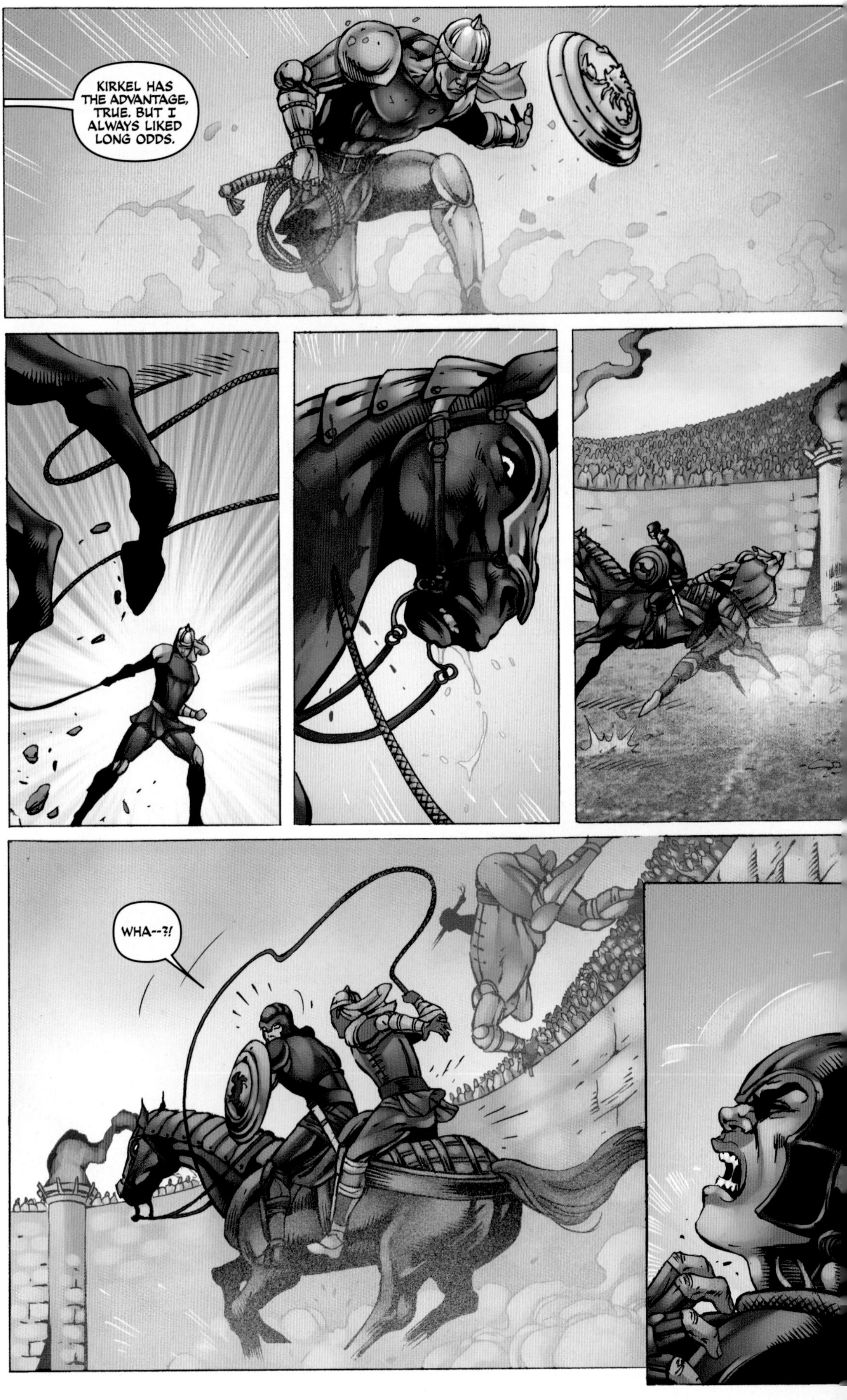
KIRKEL HAS THE ADVANTAGE, TRUE. BUT I ALWAYS LIKED LONG ODDS.
WHA--?!

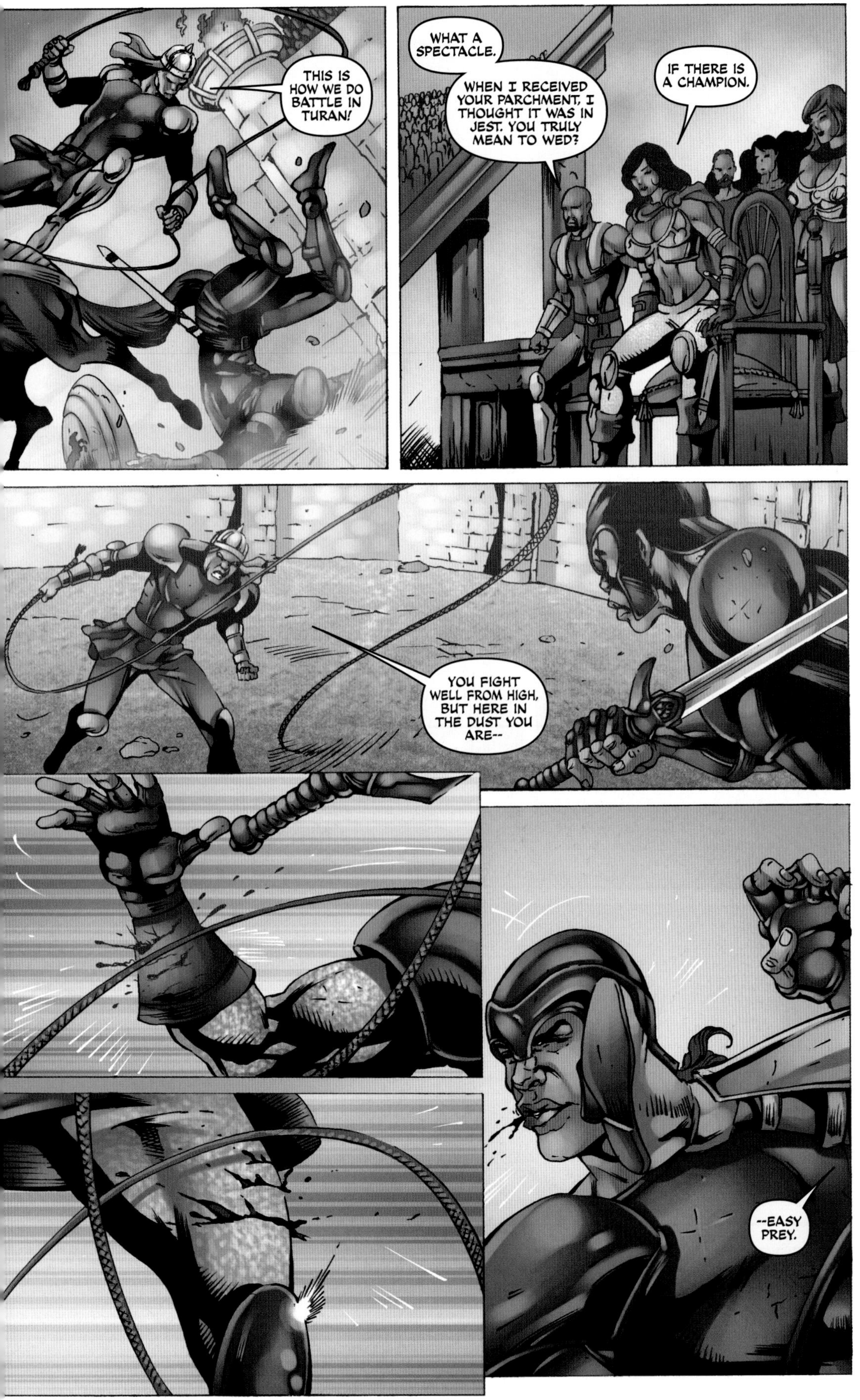
THIS IS HOW WE DO BATTLE IN TURAN!
WHAT A SPECTACLE.
WHEN I RECEIVED YOUR PARCHMENT, I THOUGHT IT WAS IN JEST. YOU TRULY MEAN TO WED?
IF THERE IS A CHAMPION.
YOU FIGHT WELL FROM HIGH, BUT HERE IN THE DUST YOU ARE--
--EASY PREY.

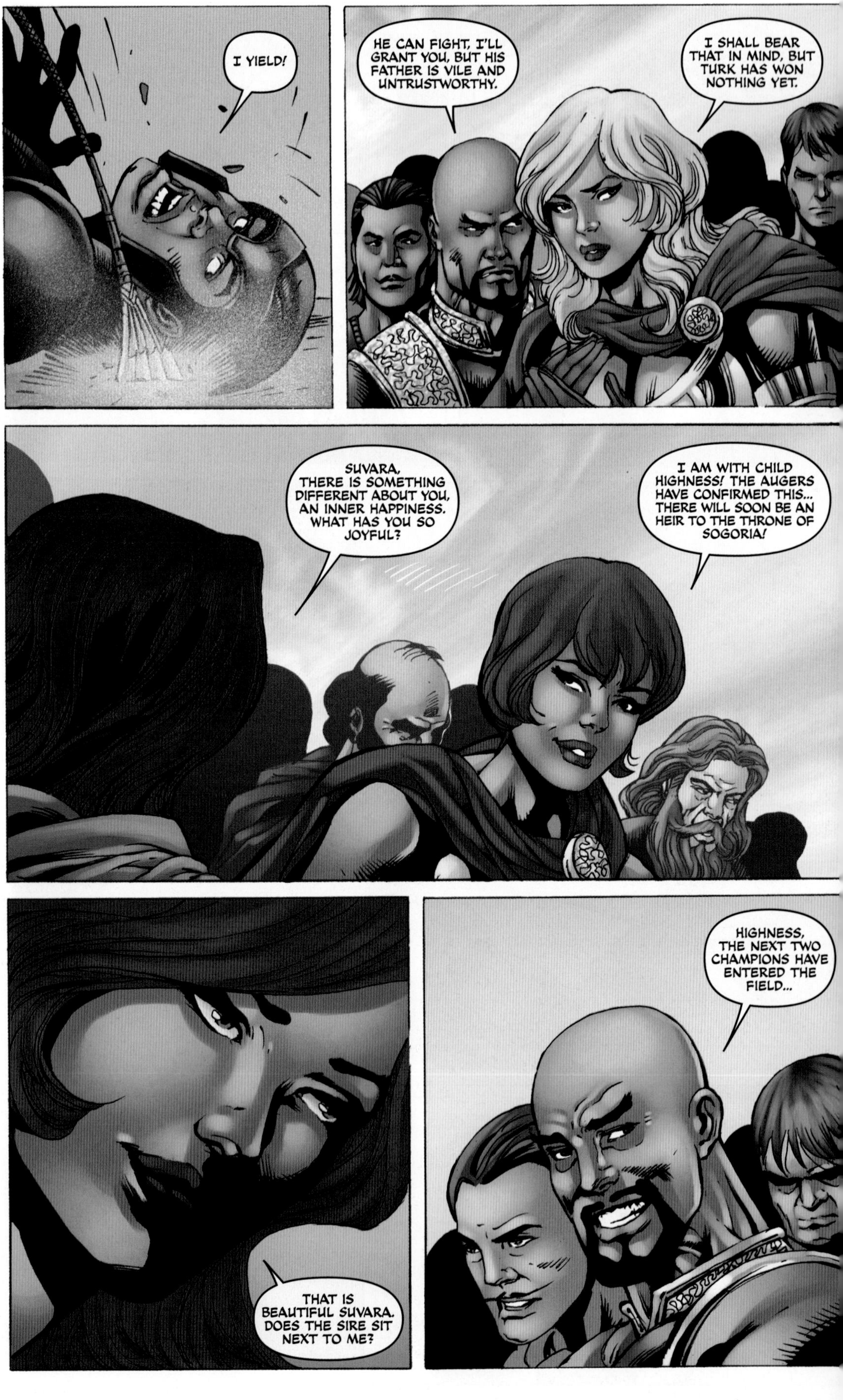
I YIELD!
HE CAN FIGHT, I'LL GRANT YOU, BUT HIS FATHER IS VILE AND UNTRUSTWORTHY.
I SHALL BEAR THAT IN MIND, BUT TURK HAS WON NOTHING YET.
SUVARA, THERE IS SOMETHING DIFFERENT ABOUT YOU, AN INNER HAPPINESS. WHAT HAS YOU SO JOYFUL?
I AM WITH CHILD HIGHNESS! THE AUGERS HAVE CONFIRMED THIS... THERE WILL SOON BE AN HEIR TO THE THRONE OF SOGORIA!
THAT IS BEAUTIFUL SUVARA. DOES THE SIRE SIT NEXT TO ME?
HIGHNESS, THE NEXT TWO CHAMPIONS HAVE ENTERED THE FIELD...

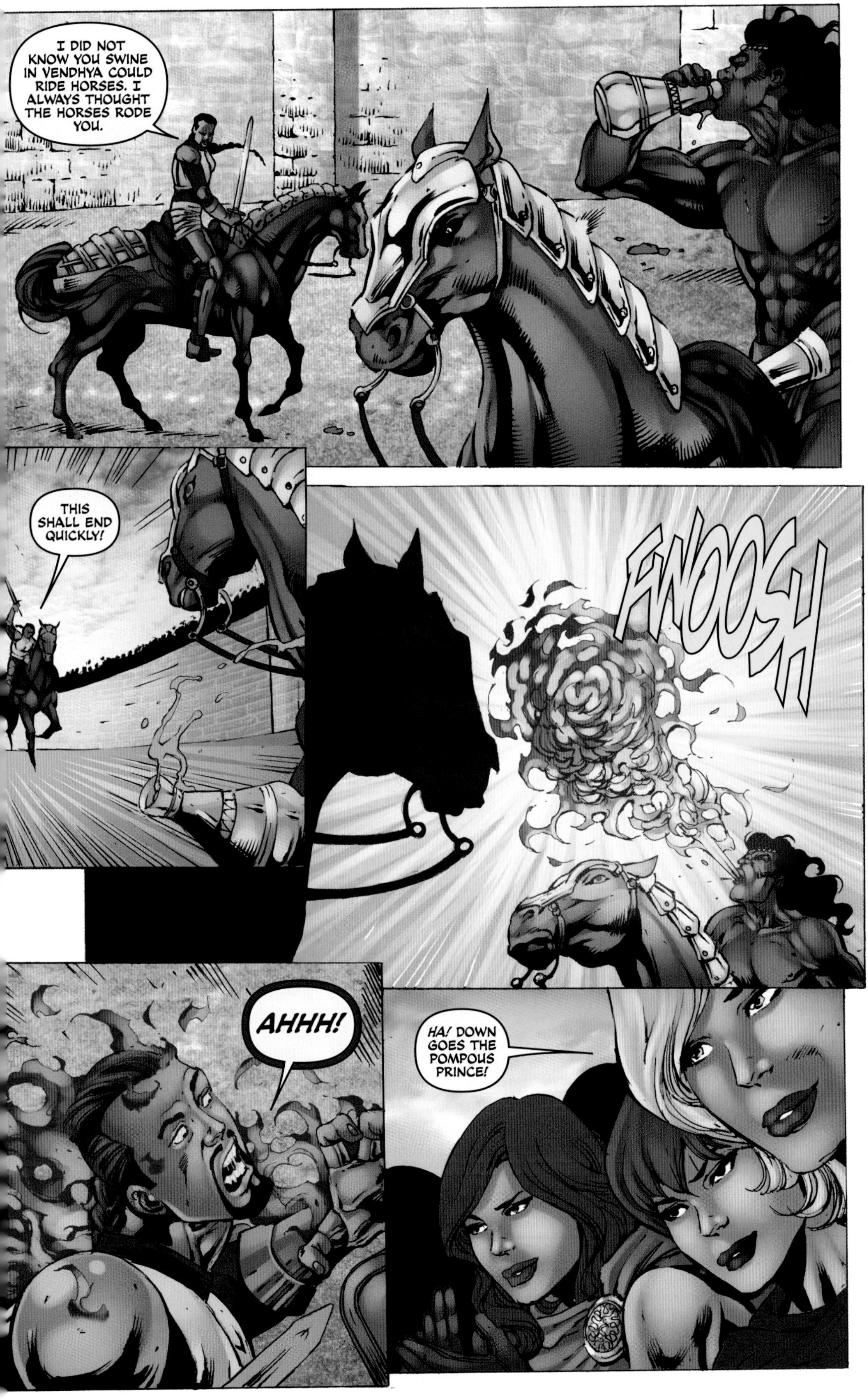
I DID NOT KNOW YOU SWINE IN VENDHYA COULD RIDE HORSES. I ALWAYS THOUGHT THE HORSES RODE YOU.
THIS SHALL END QUICKLY!
FWOOSH
AHHH!
HA! DOWN GOES THE POMPOUS PRINCE!

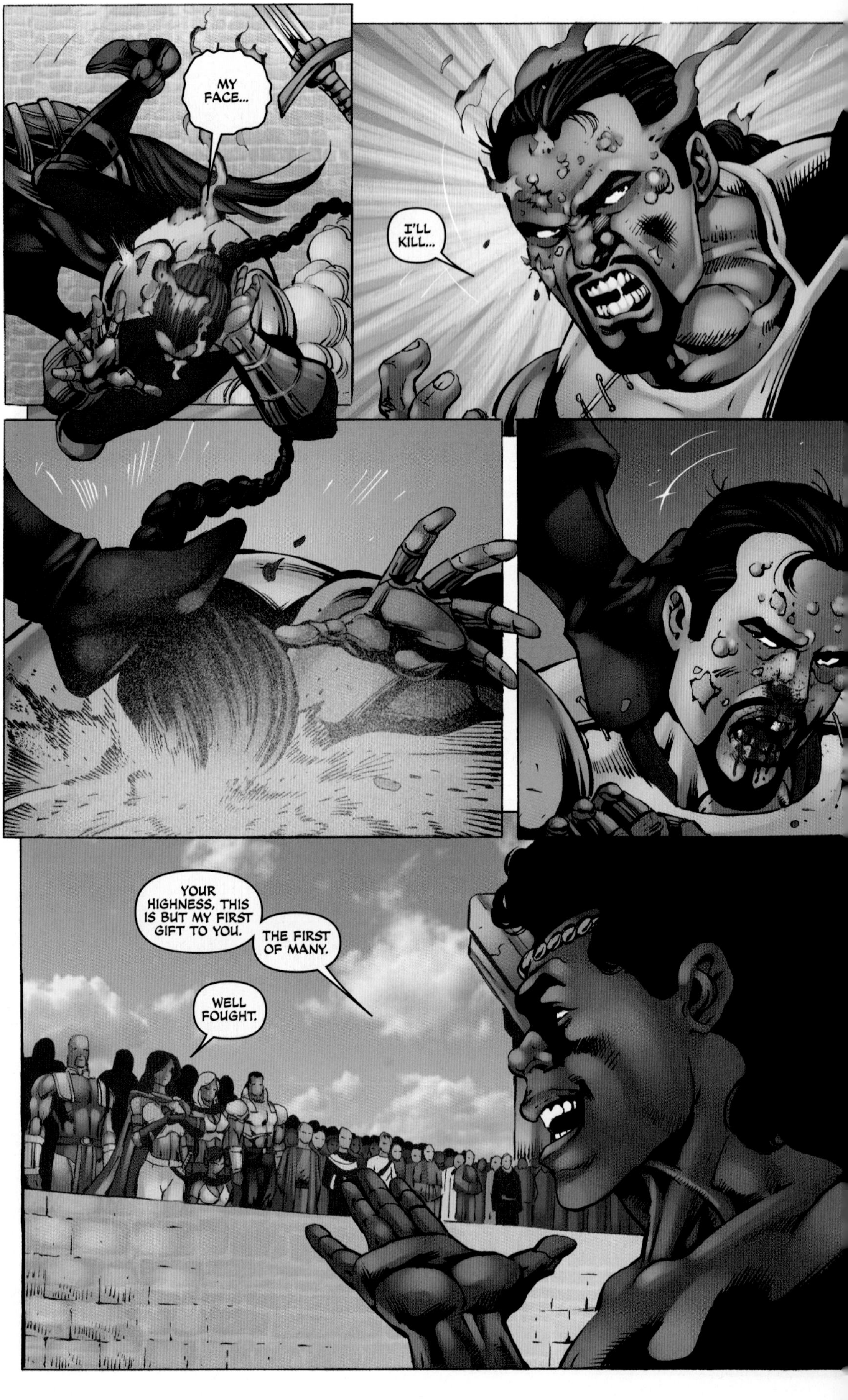
MY FACE...
I'LL KILL...
YOUR HIGHNESS, THIS IS BUT MY FIRST GIFT TO YOU.
THE FIRST OF MANY.
WELL FOUGHT.

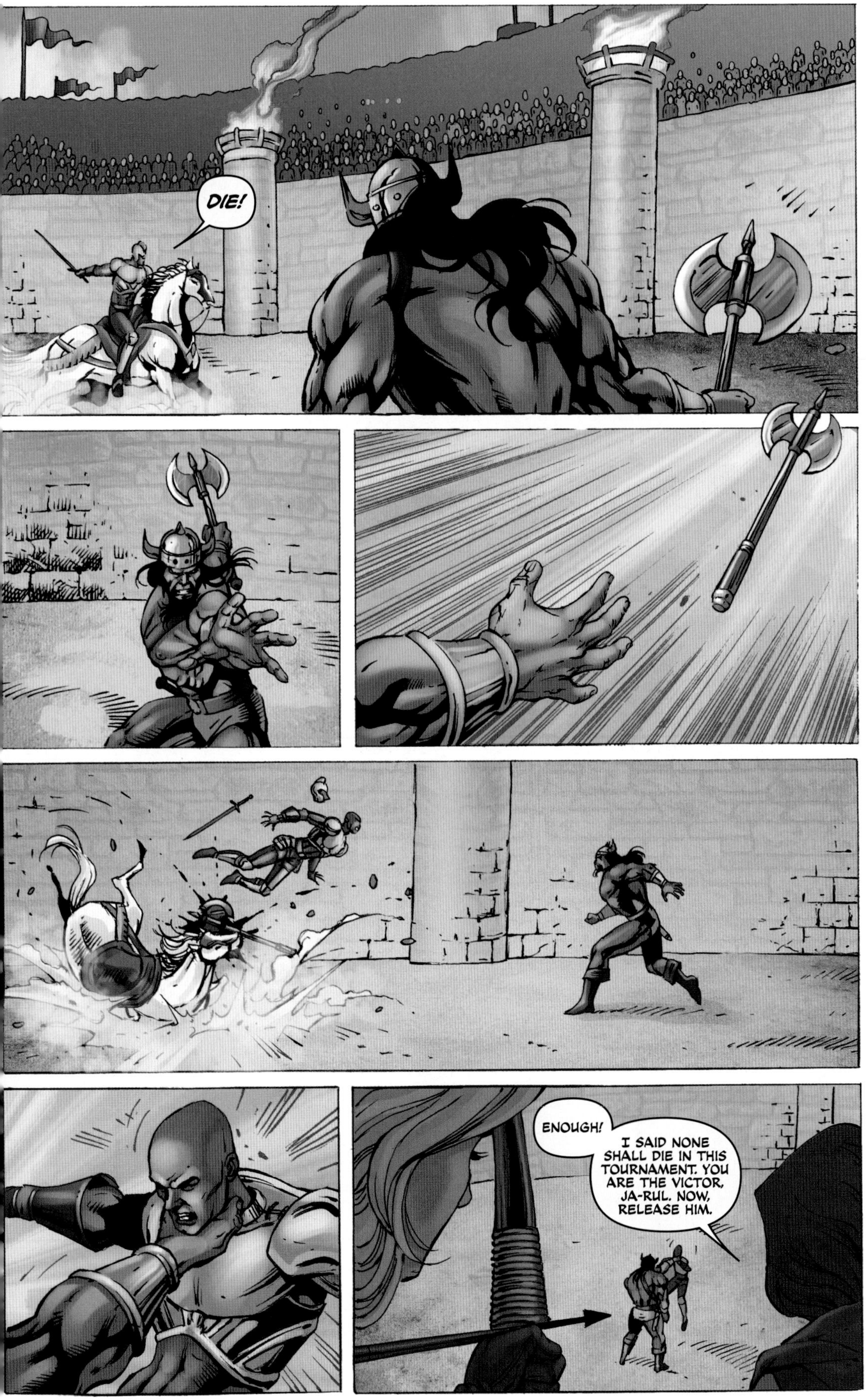
DIE!
ENOUGH!
I SAID NONE SHALL DIE IN THIS TOURNAMENT. YOU ARE THE VICTOR, JA-RUL. NOW, RELEASE HIM.

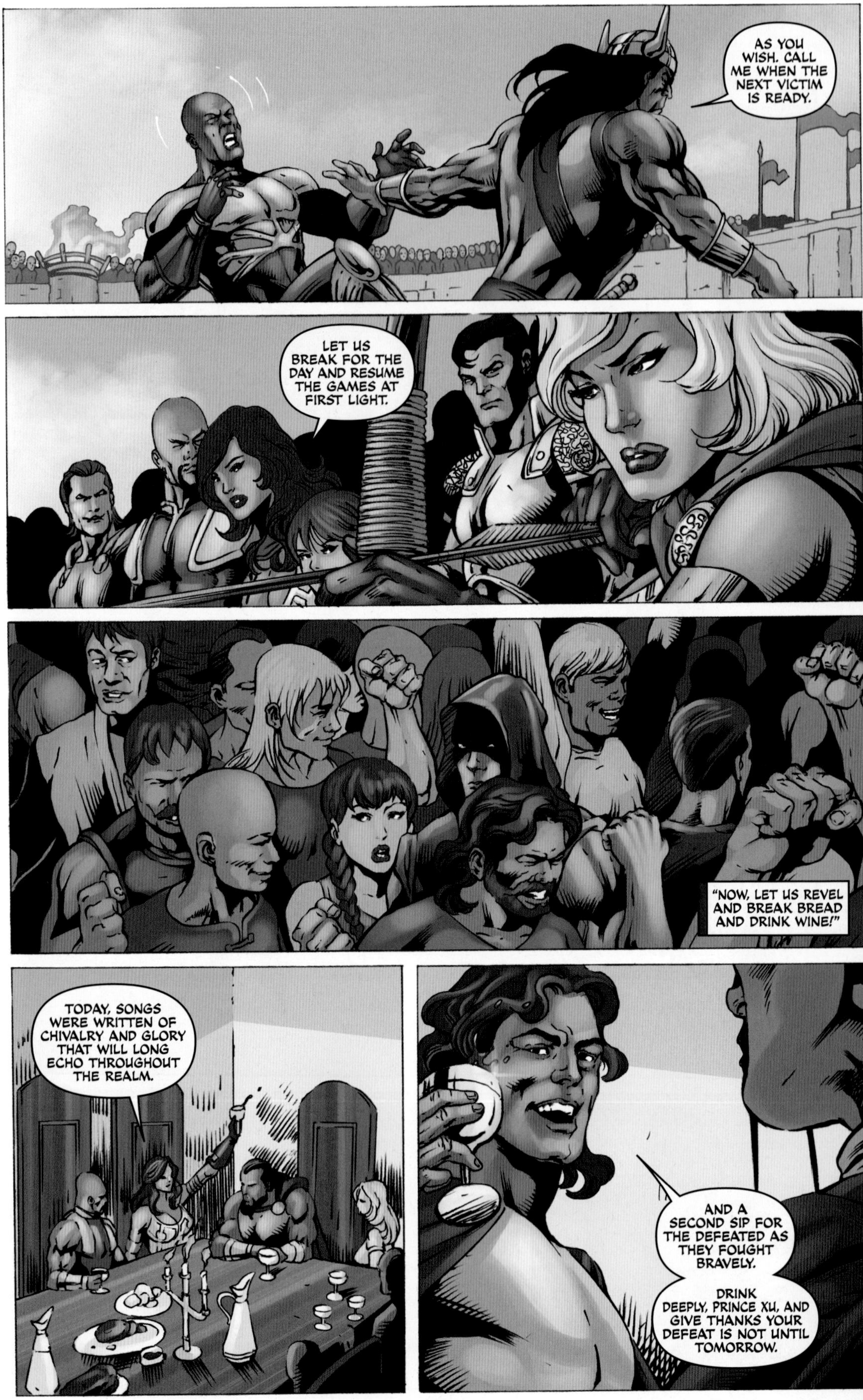
AS YOU WISH. CALL ME WHEN THE NEXT VICTIM IS READY.
LET US BREAK FOR THE DAY AND RESUME THE GAMES AT FIRST LIGHT.
"NOW, LET US REVEL AND BREAK BREAD AND DRINK WINE!"
TODAY, SONGS WERE WRITTEN OF CHIVALRY AND GLORY THAT WILL LONG ECHO THROUGHOUT THE REALM.
AND A SECOND SIP FOR THE DEFEATED AS THEY FOUGHT BRAVELY.
DRINK DEEPLY, PRINCE XU, AND GIVE THANKS YOUR DEFEAT IS NOT UNTIL TOMORROW.

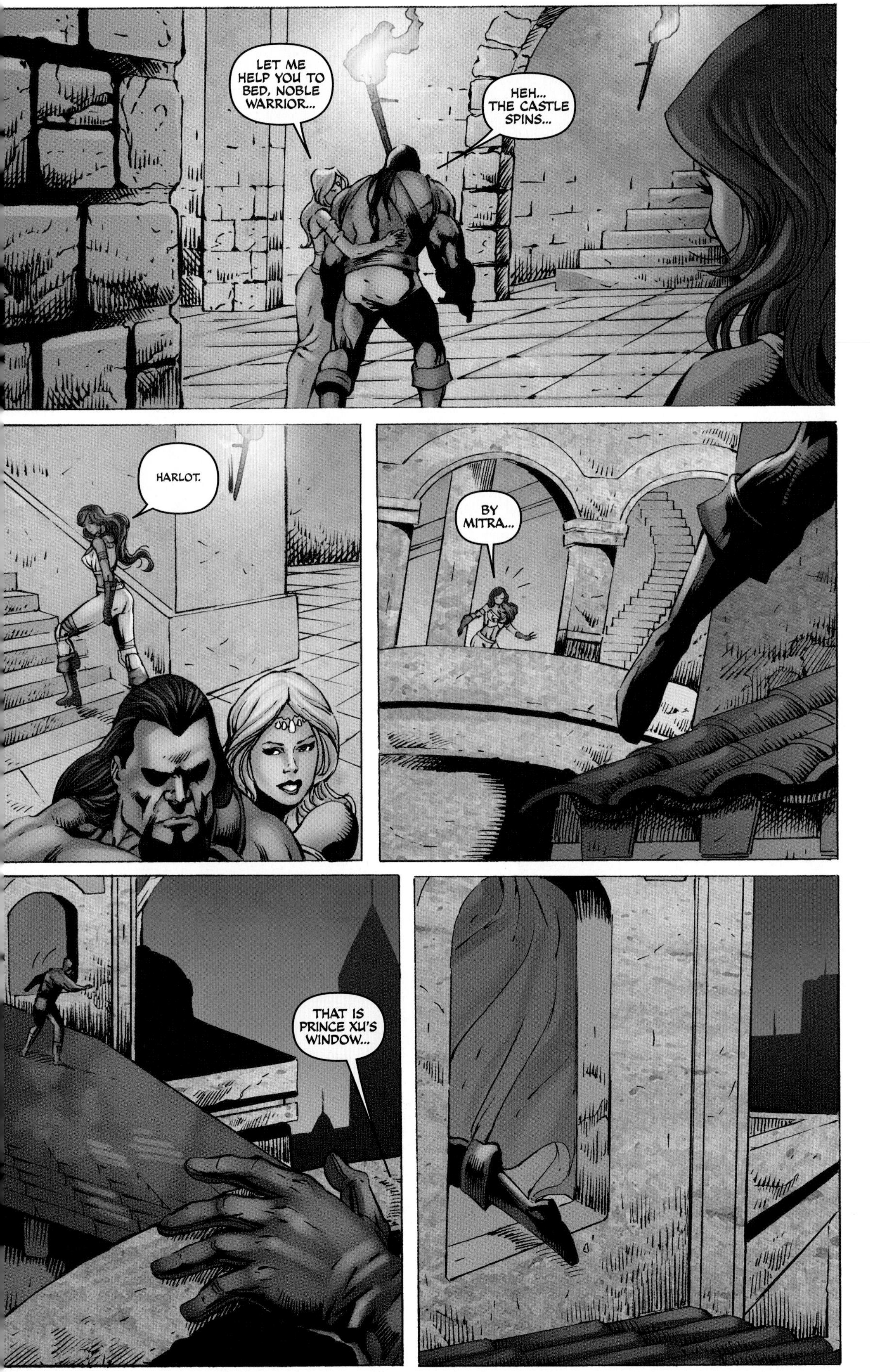
LET ME HELP YOU TO BED, NOBLE WARRIOR...
HEH... THE CASTLE SPINS...
HARLOT.
BY MITRA...
THAT IS PRINCE XU'S WINDOW...

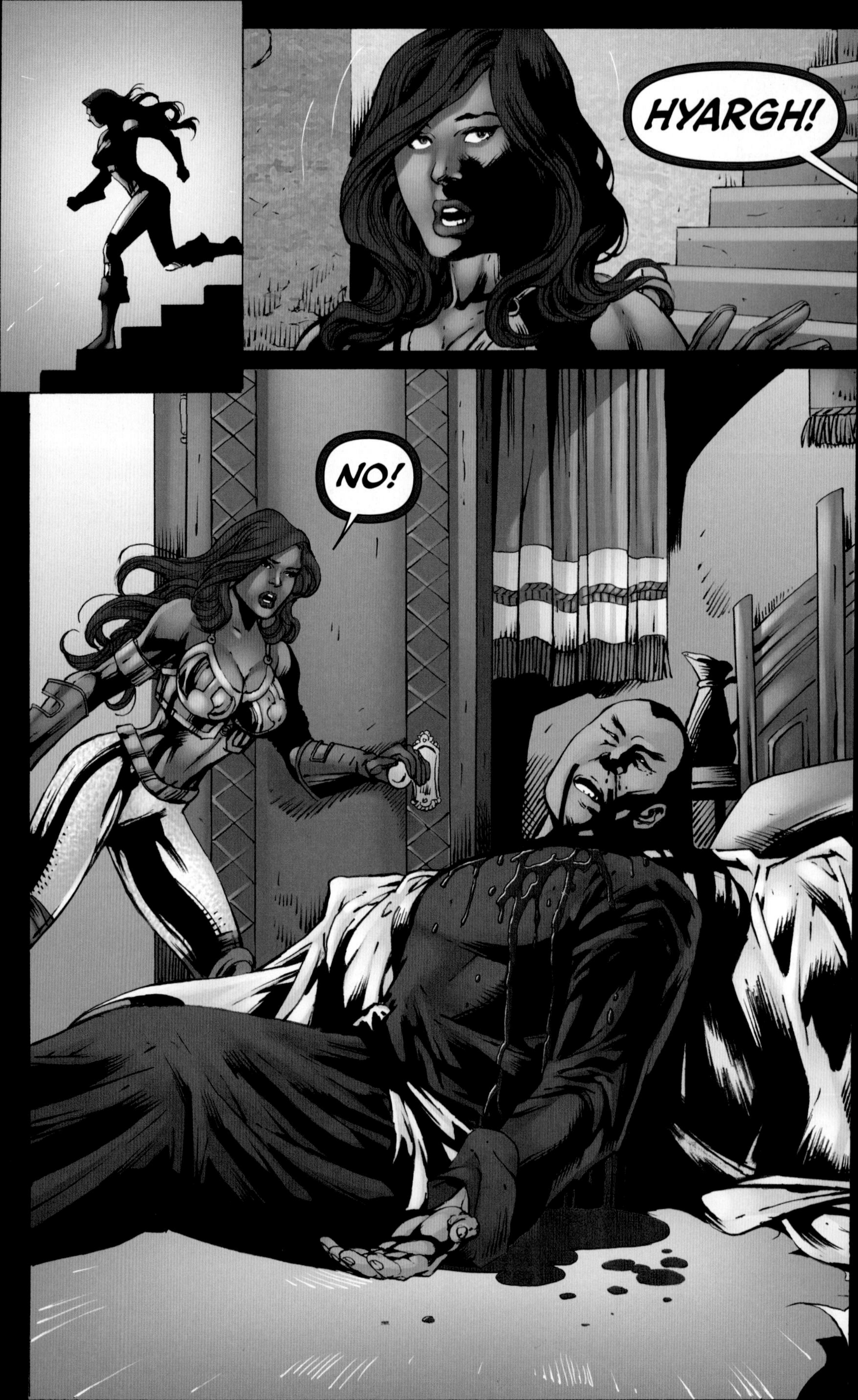
HYARGH!
NO!

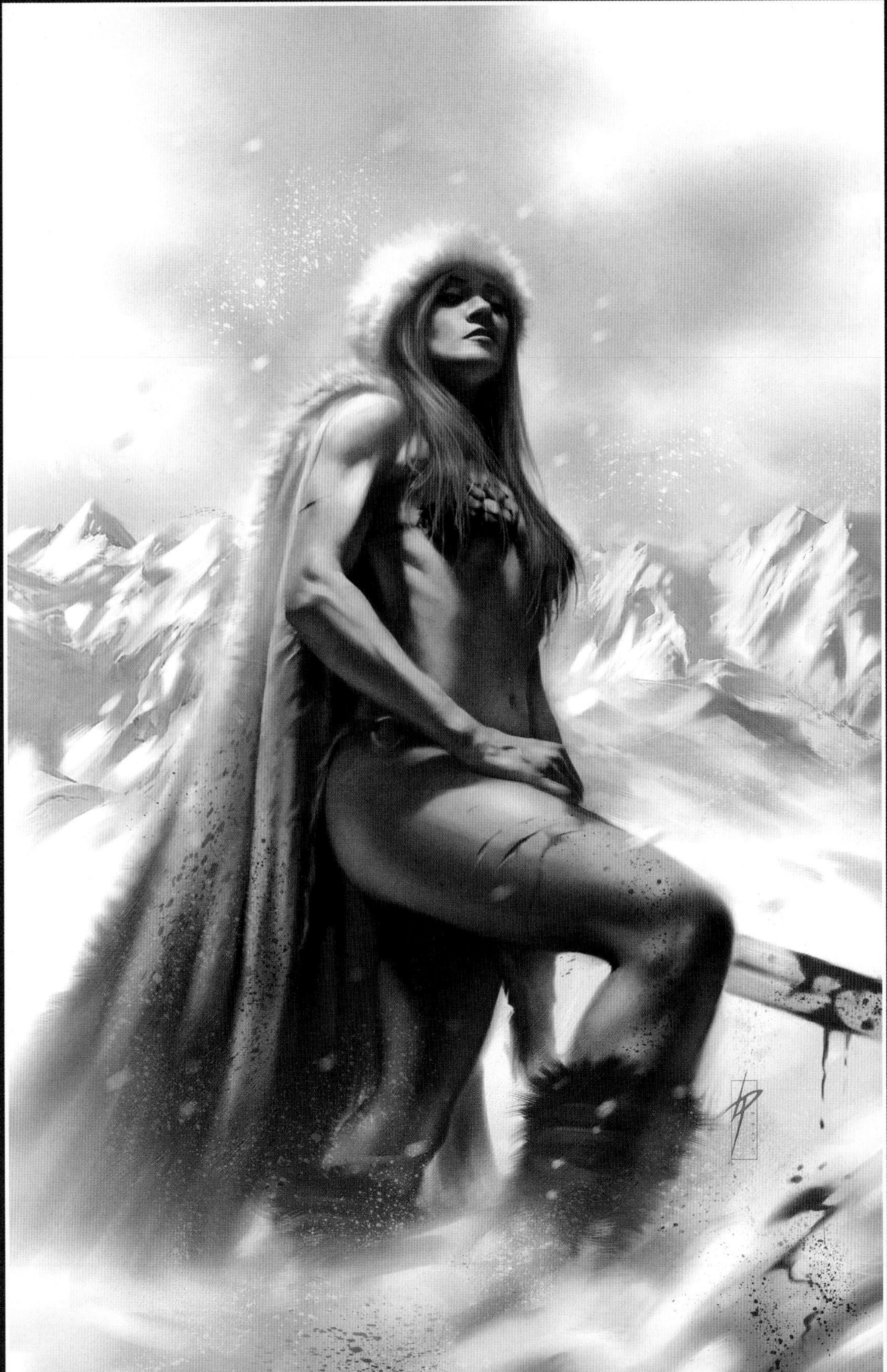

ISSUE #31 COVER BY LUCIO PARRILLO

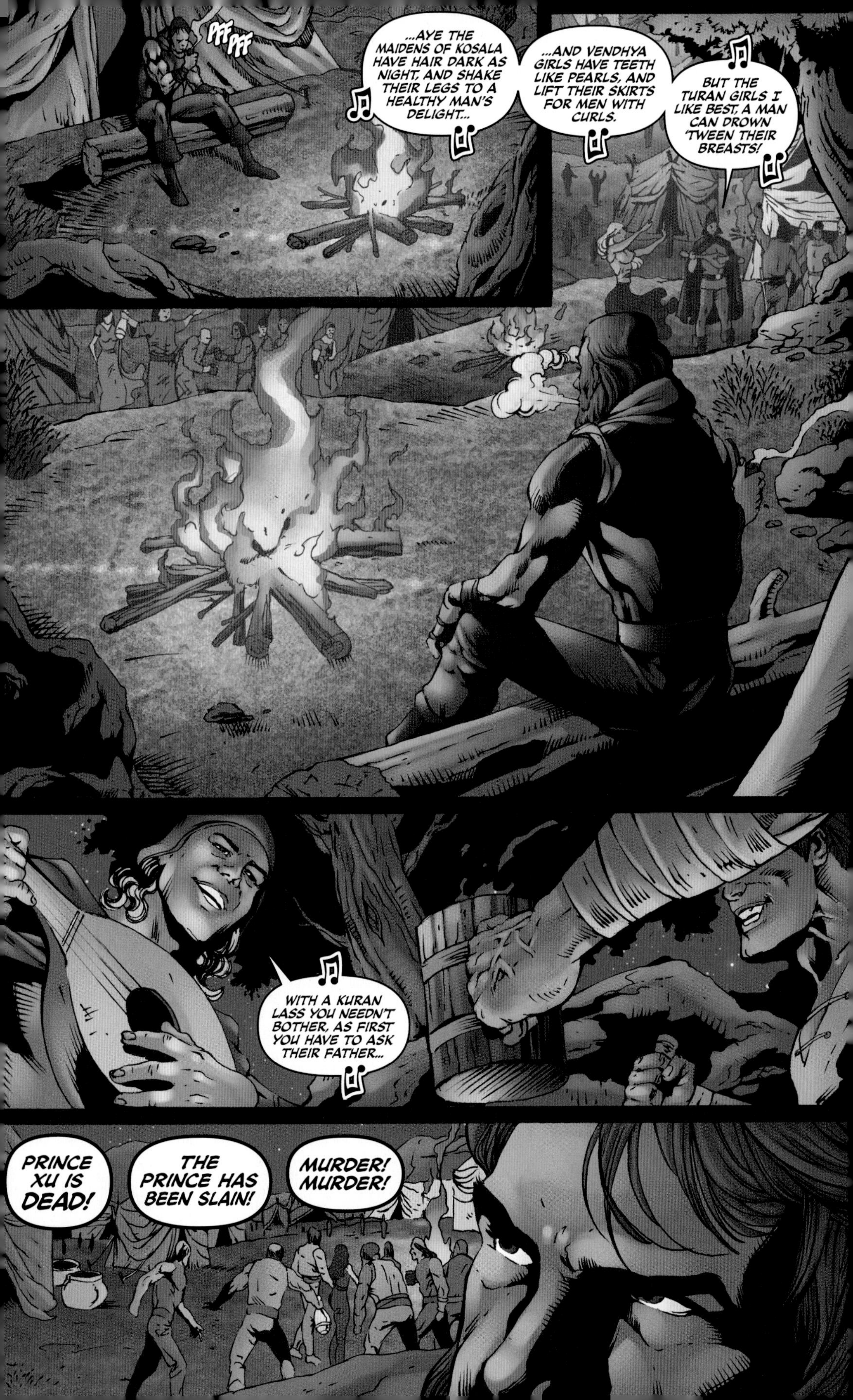
PFF PFF
...AYE THE MAIDENS OF KOSALA HAVE HAIR DARK AS NIGHT, AND SHAKE THEIR LEGS TO A HEALTHY MAN'S DELIGHT...
...AND VENDHYA GIRLS HAVE TEETH LIKE PEARLS, AND LIFT THEIR SKIRTS FOR MEN WITH CURLS.
BUT THE TURAN GIRLS I LIKE BEST, A MAN CAN DROWN 'TWEEN THEIR BREASTS!
WITH A KURAN LASS YOU NEEDN'T BOTHER, AS FIRST YOU HAVE TO ASK THEIR FATHER...
PRINCE XU IS DEAD!
THE PRINCE HAS BEEN SLAIN!
MURDER! MURDER!

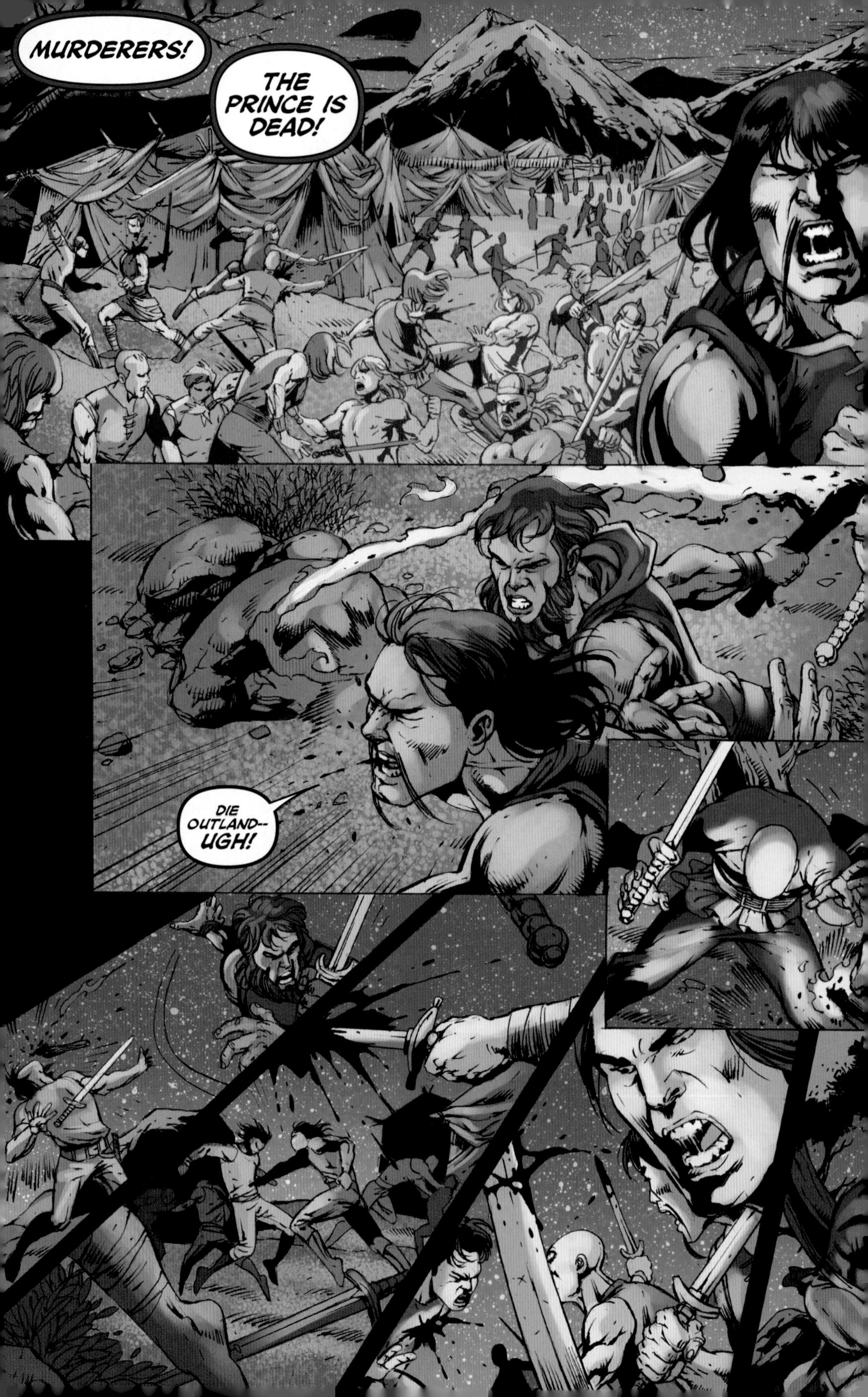
MURDERERS!
THE PRINCE IS DEAD!
DIE OUTLAND-- UGH!

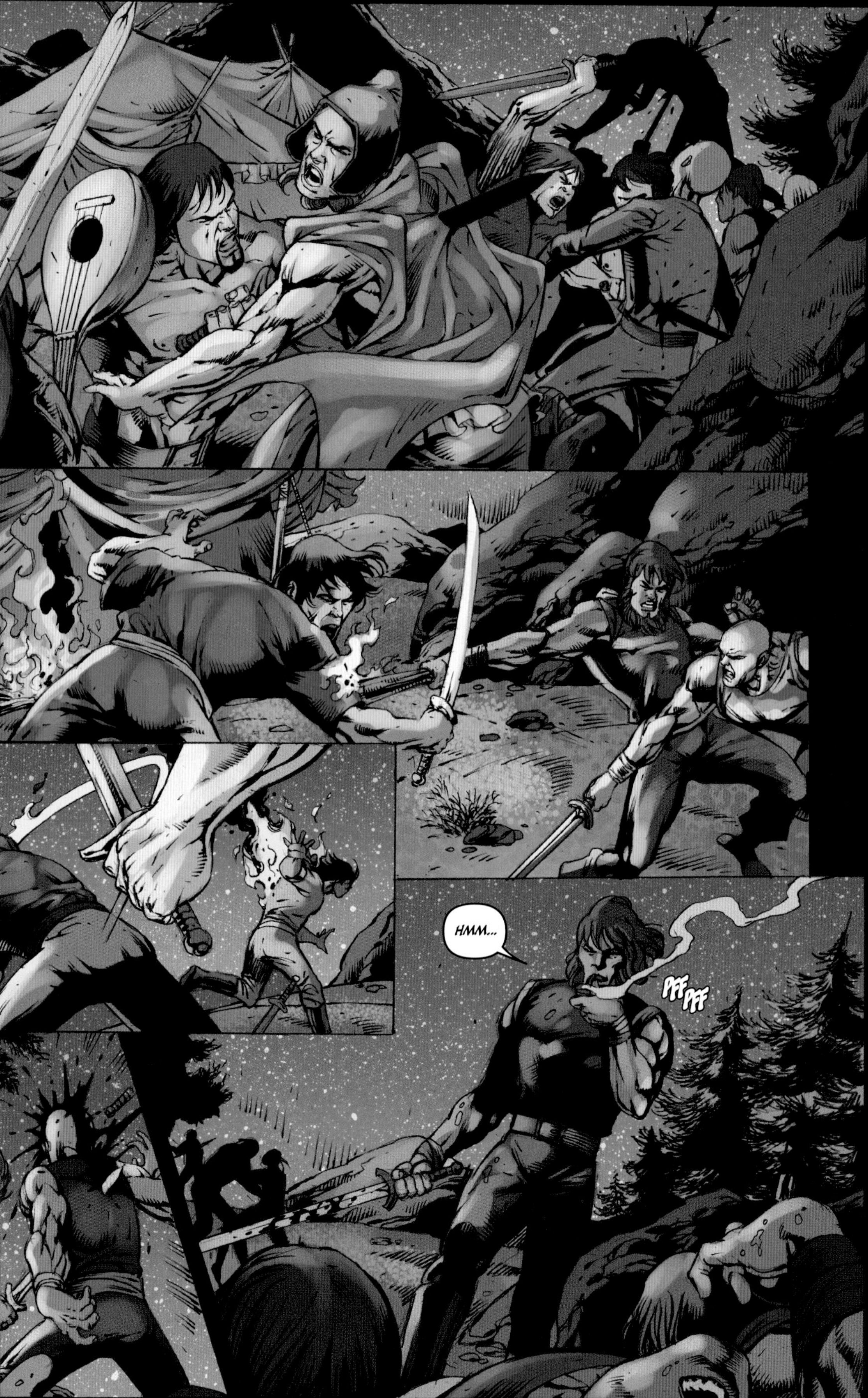
HMM...
PFF PFF

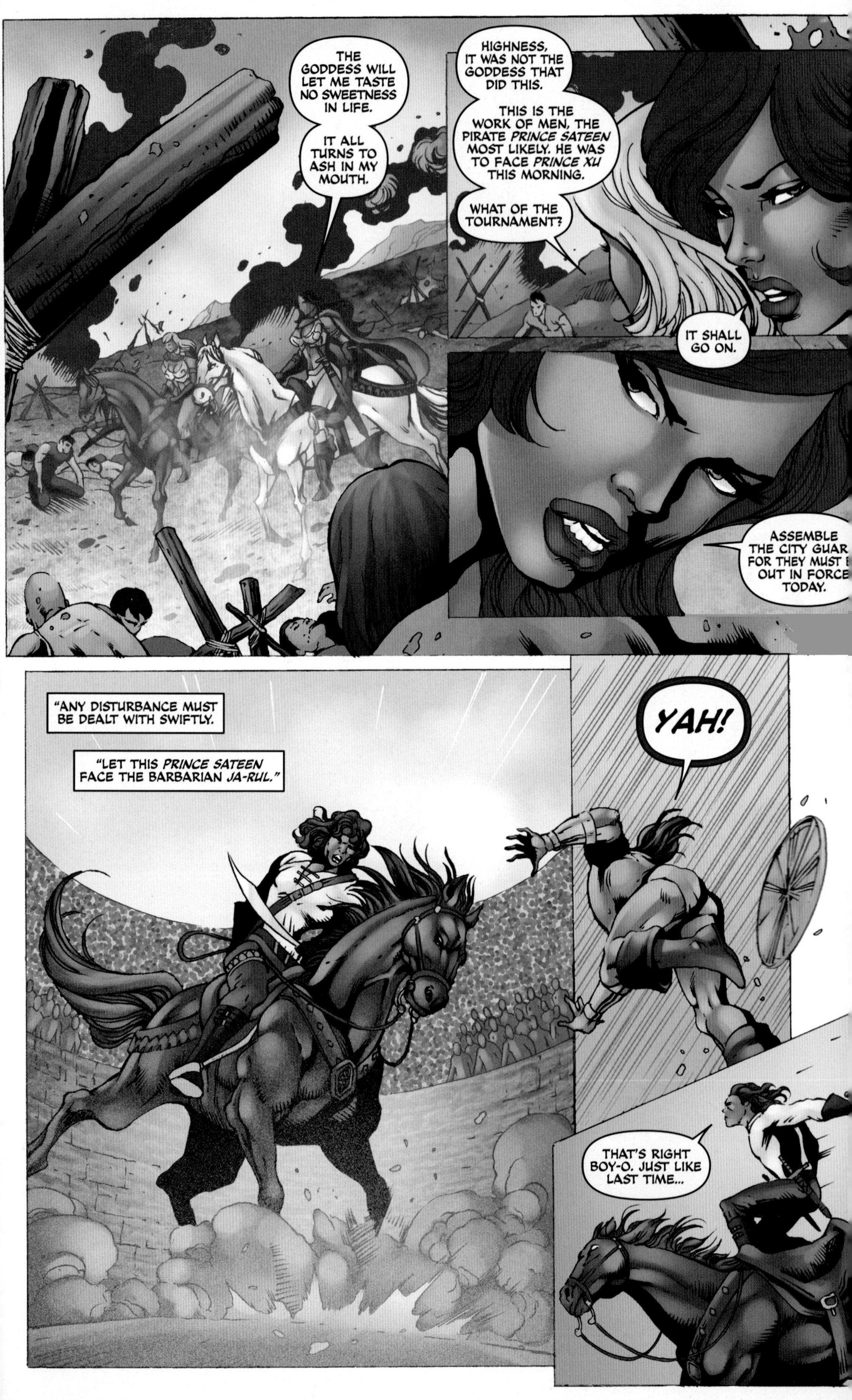

THE GODDESS WILL LET ME TASTE NO SWEETNESS IN LIFE.
IT ALL TURNS TO ASH IN MY MOUTH.
HIGHNESS, IT WAS NOT THE GODDESS THAT DID THIS.
THIS IS THE WORK OF MEN, THE PIRATE PRINCE SATEEN MOST LIKELY. HE WAS TO FACE PRINCE XU THIS MORNING.
WHAT OF THE TOURNAMENT?
IT SHALL GO ON.
ASSEMBLE THE CITY GUAR FOR THEY MUST OUT IN FORCE TODAY.
"ANY DISTURBANCE MUST BE DEALT WITH SWIFTLY.
"LET THIS PRINCE SATEEN FACE THE BARBARIAN JA-RUL."
YAH!
THAT'S RIGHT BOY-O. JUST LIKE LAST TIME...

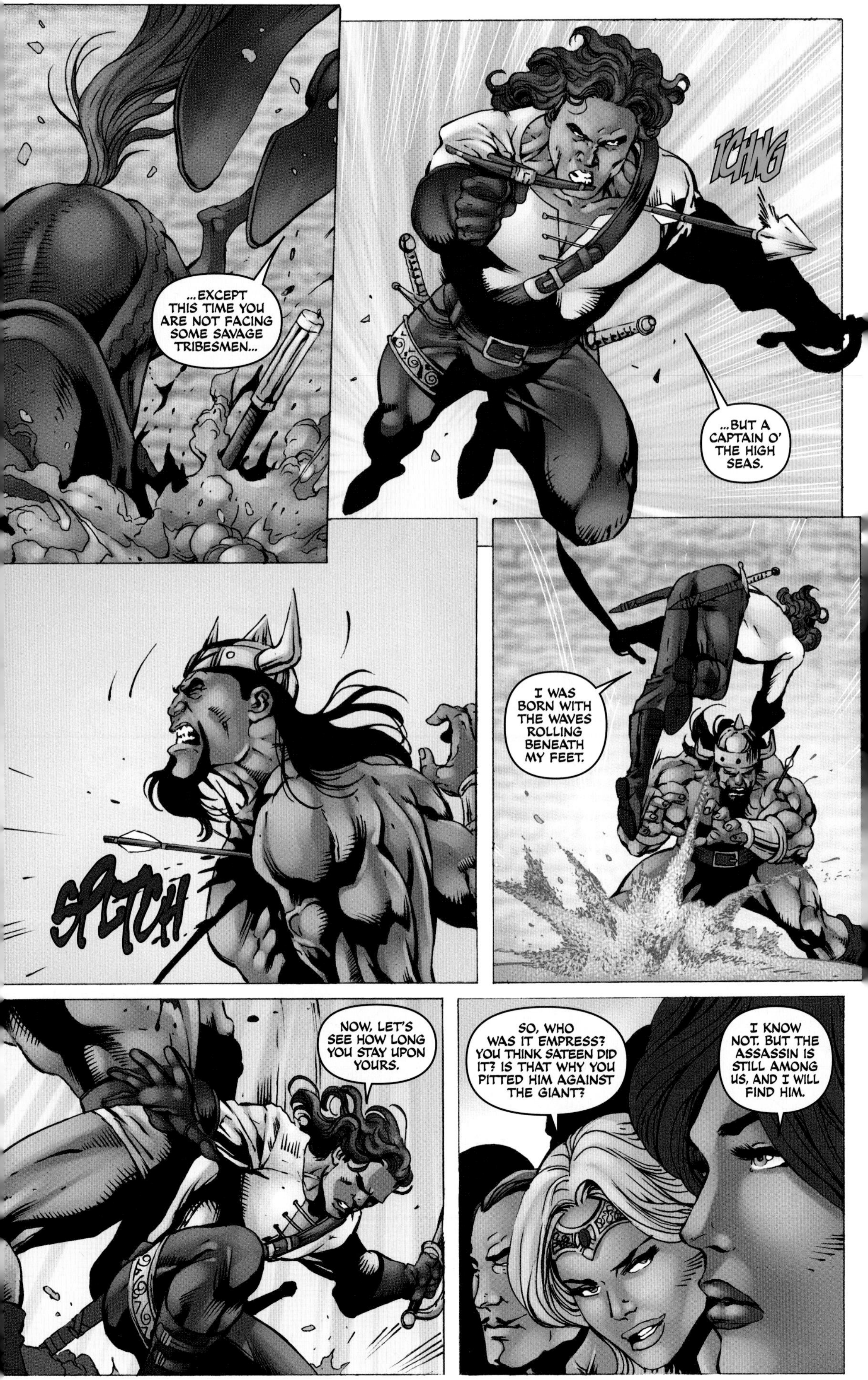

...EXCEPT THIS TIME YOU ARE NOT FACING SOME SAVAGE TRIBESMEN...
TCHNG
...BUT A CAPTAIN O' THE HIGH SEAS.
SPLTCH
I WAS BORN WITH THE WAVES ROLLING BENEATH MY FEET.
NOW, LET'S SEE HOW LONG YOU STAY UPON YOURS.
SO, WHO WAS IT EMPRESS? YOU THINK SATEEN DID IT? IS THAT WHY YOU PITTED HIM AGAINST THE GIANT?
I KNOW NOT. BUT THE ASSASSIN IS STILL AMONG US, AND I WILL FIND HIM.

I DO SO LOVE PALACE INTRIGUE.

I HAD HEARD THERE WAS SOME RUCKUS AMONGST THE COMMONERS, BUT THAT IS TO BE EXPECTED I SUPPOSE.

WHY? BECAUSE THEY ARE COMMON? I WONDER, IF YOU WERE THE NEXT TO DIE, WOULD YOUR COMMONERS RIOT?

FEAR NOT SHA'SHANA, EVERY THREAD IS BEING FOLLOWED...

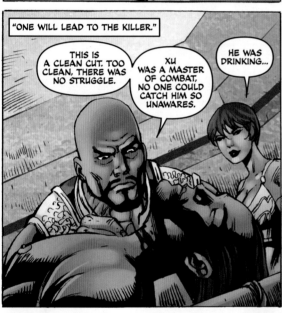

"ONE WILL LEAD TO THE KILLER."

THIS IS A CLEAN CUT. TOO CLEAN, THERE WAS NO STRUGGLE.

XU WAS A MASTER OF COMBAT, NO ONE COULD CATCH HIM SO UNAWARES.

HE WAS DRINKING...

AYE, BUT EVEN SO...

...HE BLEEDS FROM PLACES THAT WERE NOT CUT.

...POISON.

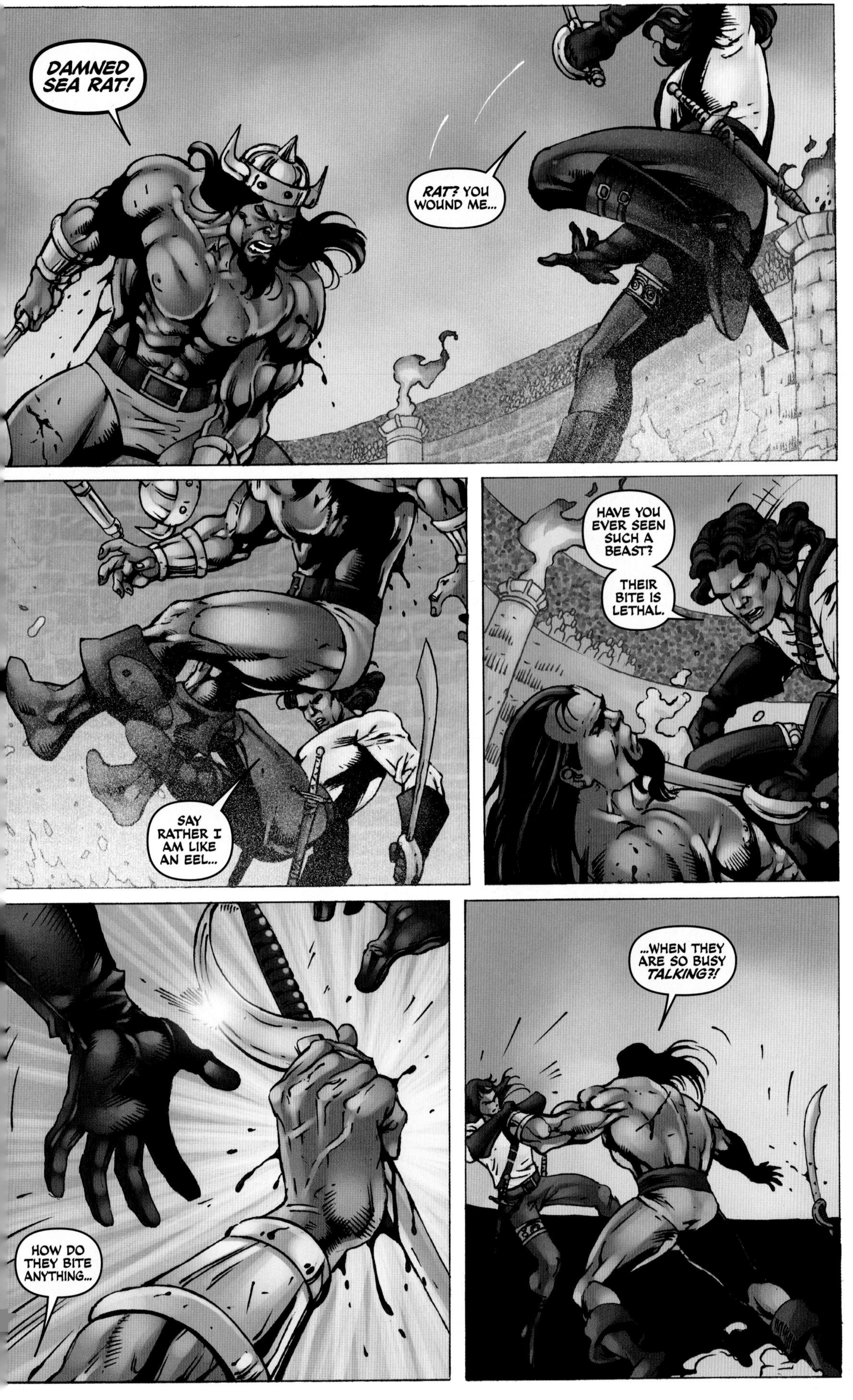
DAMNED SEA RAT!
RAT? YOU WOUND ME...
SAY RATHER I AM LIKE AN EEL...
HAVE YOU EVER SEEN SUCH A BEAST?
THEIR BITE IS LETHAL.
HOW DO THEY BITE ANYTHING...
...WHEN THEY ARE SO BUSY TALKING?!

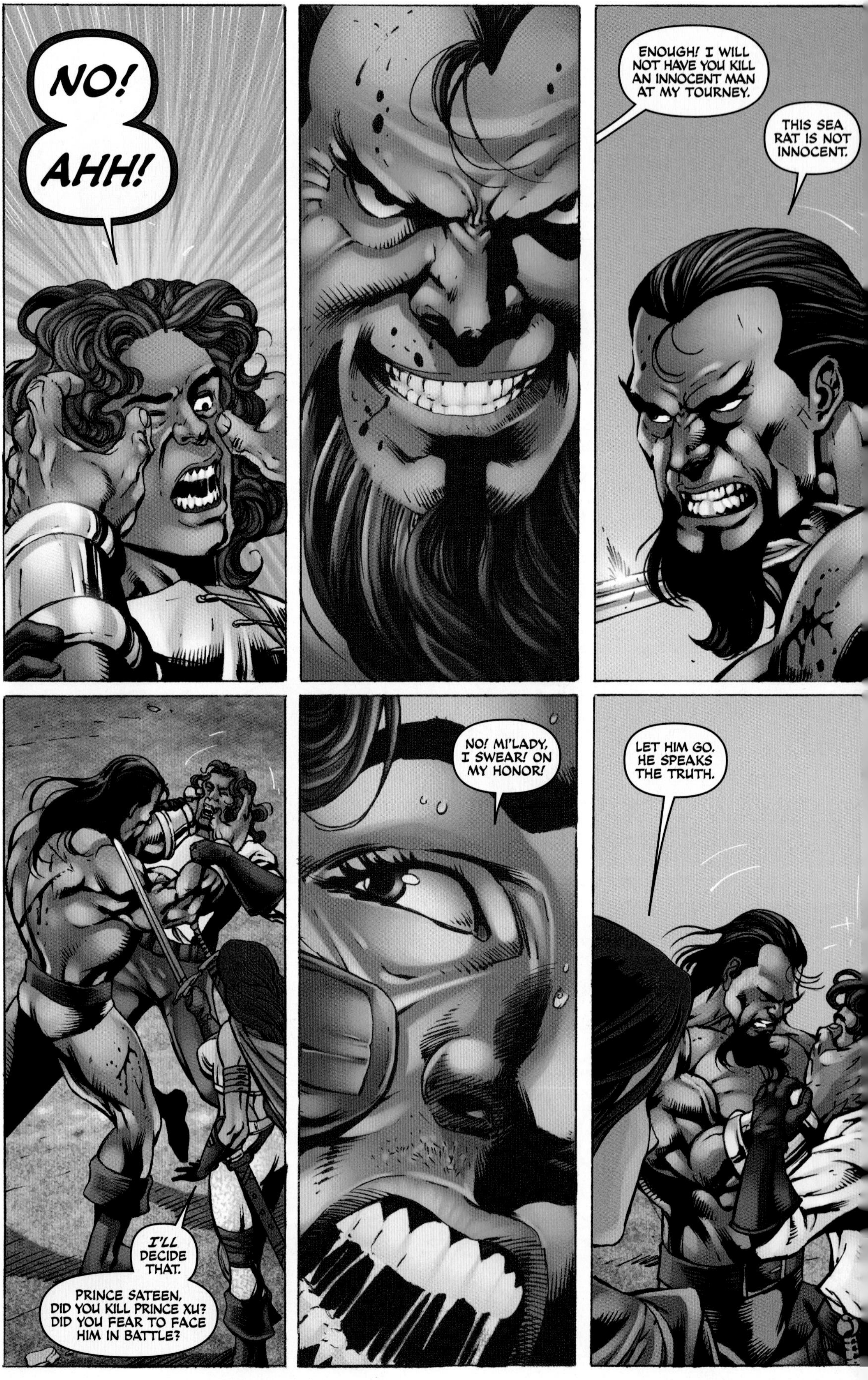
NO!
AHH!
ENOUGH! I WILL NOT HAVE YOU KILL AN INNOCENT MAN AT MY TOURNEY.
THIS SEA RAT IS NOT INNOCENT.
I'LL DECIDE THAT.
PRINCE SATEEN, DID YOU KILL PRINCE XU? DID YOU FEAR TO FACE HIM IN BATTLE?
NO! MI'LADY, I SWEAR! ON MY HONOR!
LET HIM GO. HE SPEAKS THE TRUTH.

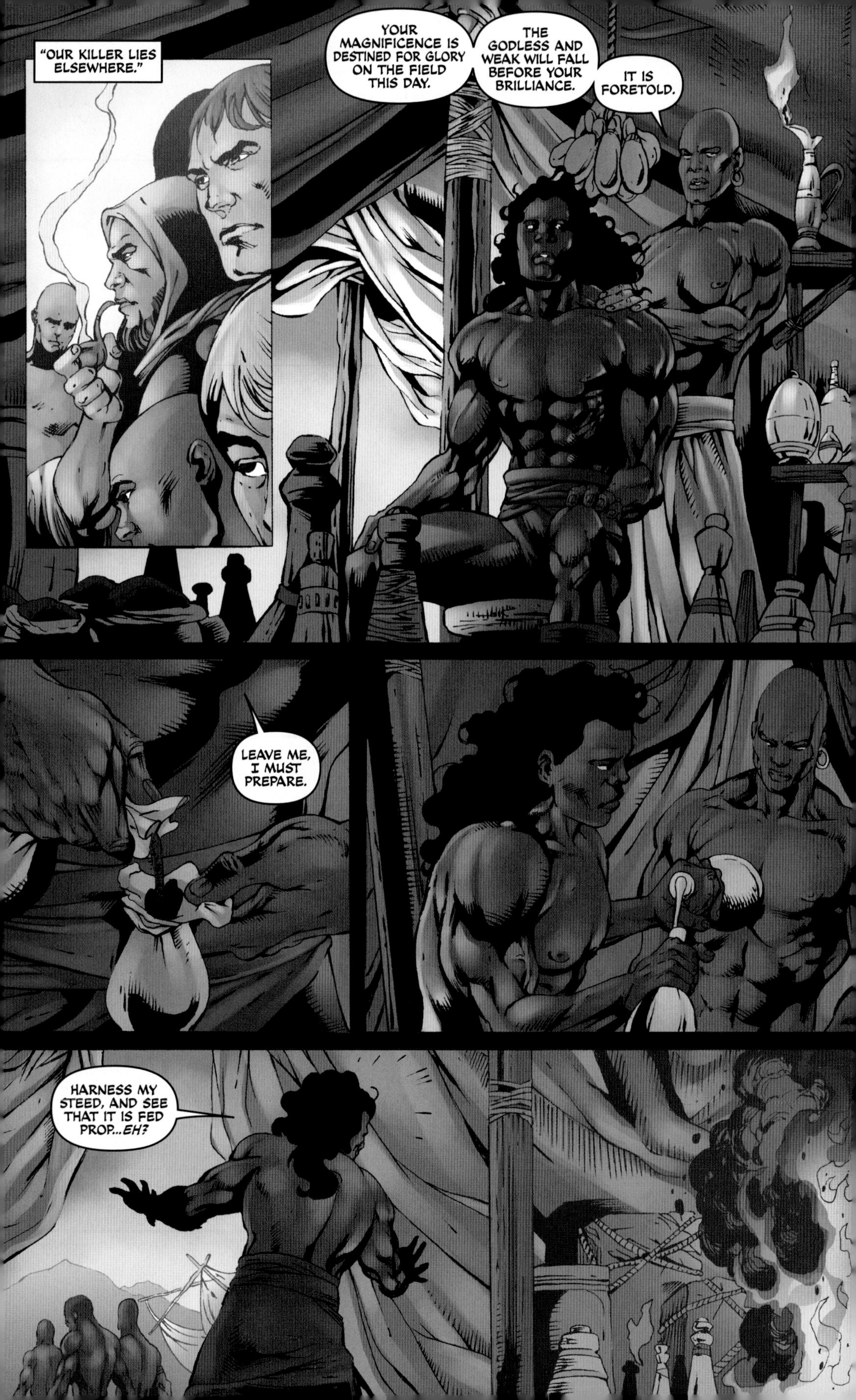
"OUR KILLER LIES ELSEWHERE."
YOUR MAGNIFICENCE IS DESTINED FOR GLORY ON THE FIELD THIS DAY.
THE GODLESS AND WEAK WILL FALL BEFORE YOUR BRILLIANCE.
IT IS FORETOLD.
LEAVE ME, I MUST PREPARE.
HARNESS MY STEED, AND SEE THAT IT IS FED PROP...*EH?*

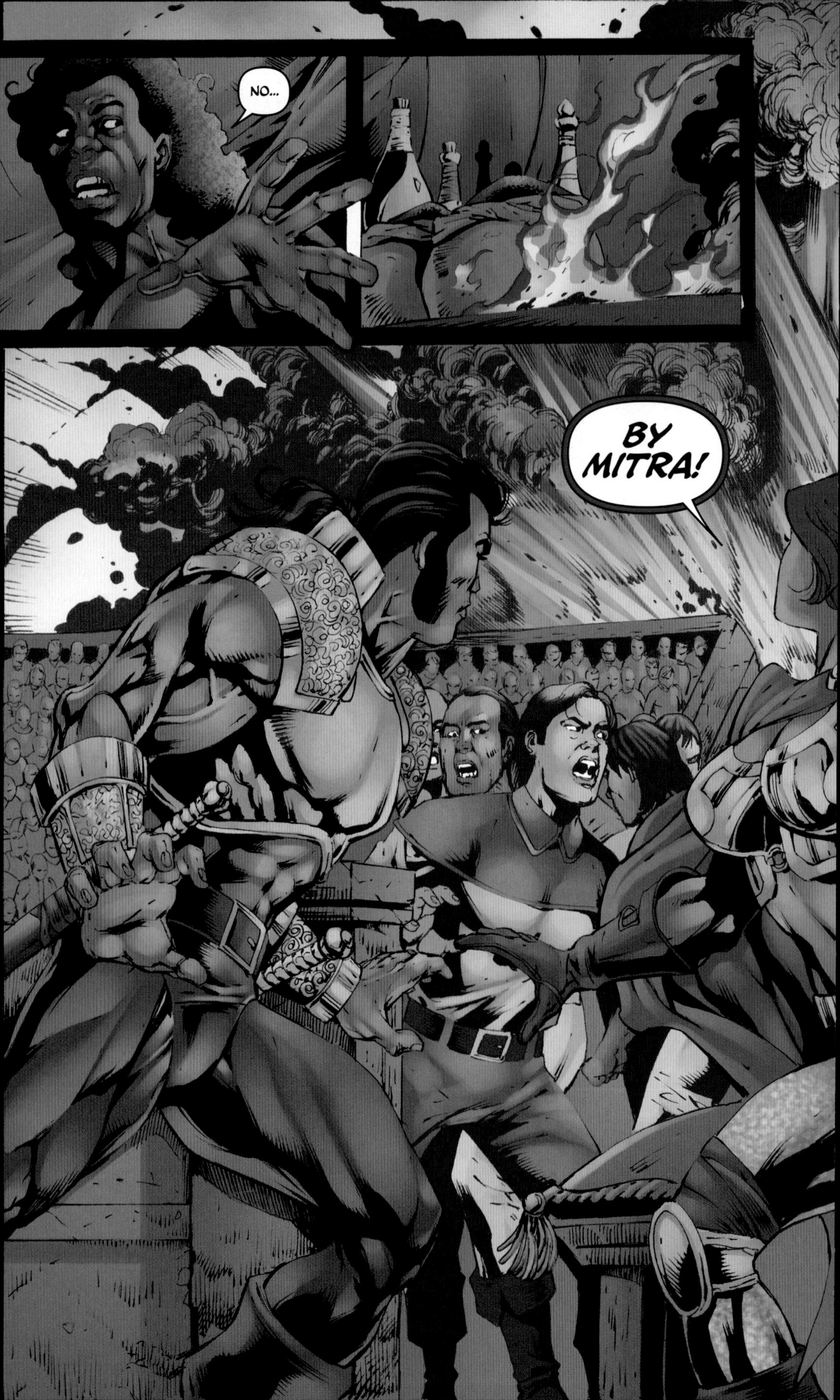
NO...
BY MITRA!

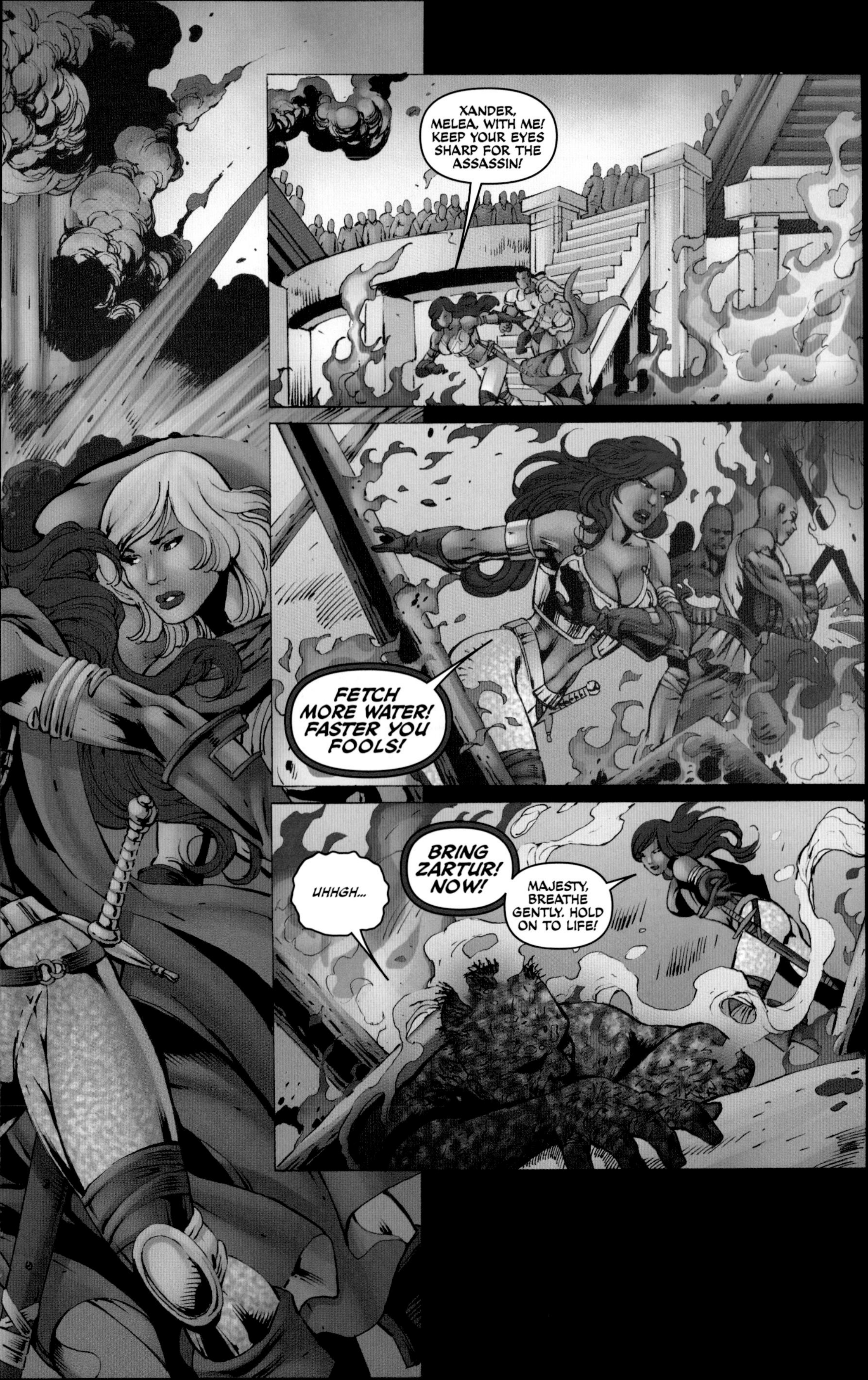

XANDER, MELEA, WITH ME! KEEP YOUR EYES SHARP FOR THE ASSASSIN!
FETCH MORE WATER! FASTER YOU FOOLS!
UHHGH...
BRING ZARTUR! NOW!
MAJESTY, BREATHE GENTLY. HOLD ON TO LIFE!

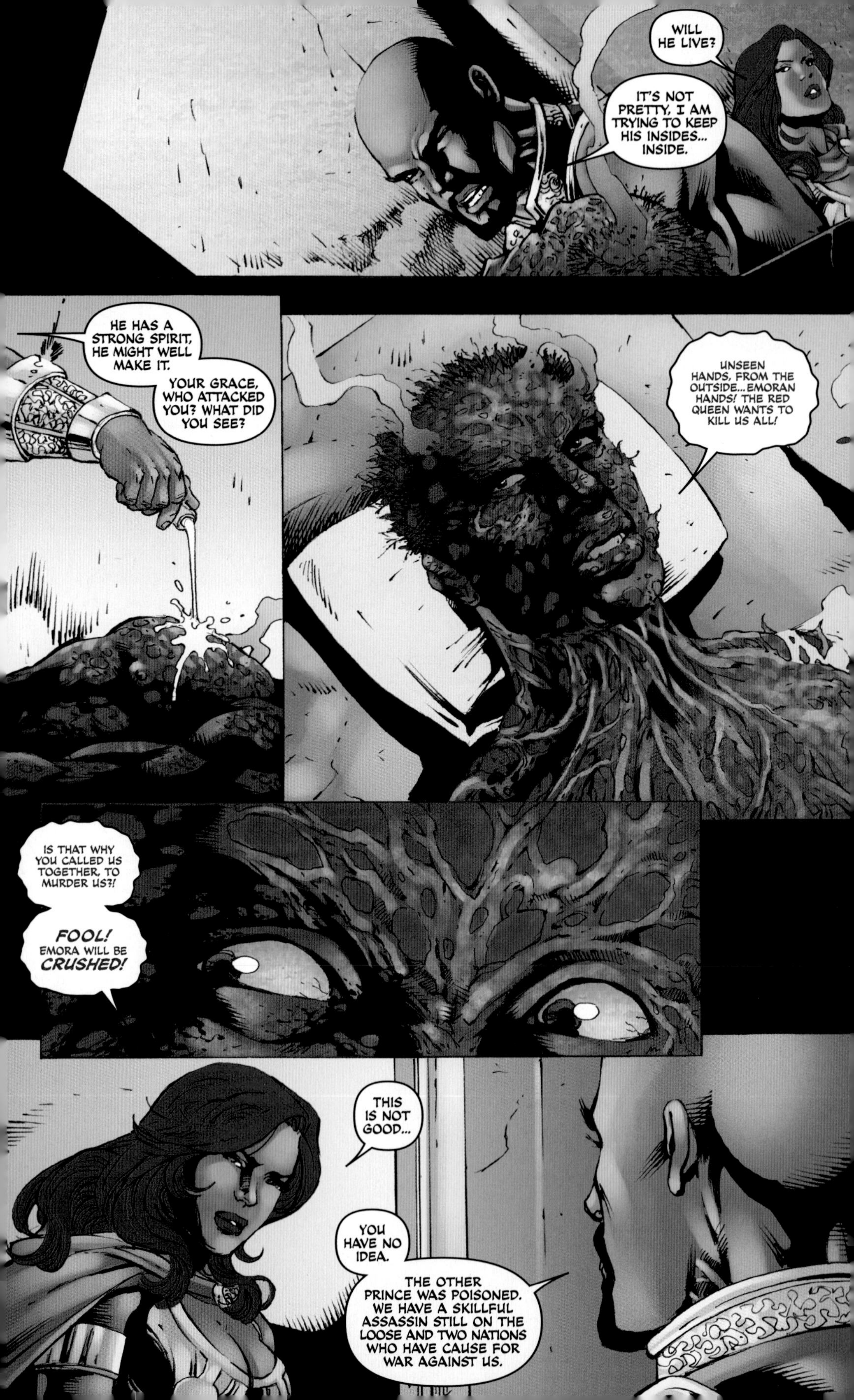
WILL HE LIVE?
IT'S NOT PRETTY, I AM TRYING TO KEEP HIS INSIDES... INSIDE.
HE HAS A STRONG SPIRIT, HE MIGHT WELL MAKE IT.
YOUR GRACE, WHO ATTACKED YOU? WHAT DID YOU SEE?
UNSEEN HANDS, FROM THE OUTSIDE...EMORAN HANDS! THE RED QUEEN WANTS TO KILL US ALL!
IS THAT WHY YOU CALLED US TOGETHER, TO MURDER US?!
FOOL! EMORA WILL BE CRUSHED!
THIS IS NOT GOOD...
YOU HAVE NO IDEA.
THE OTHER PRINCE WAS POISONED. WE HAVE A SKILLFUL ASSASSIN STILL ON THE LOOSE AND TWO NATIONS WHO HAVE CAUSE FOR WAR AGAINST US.

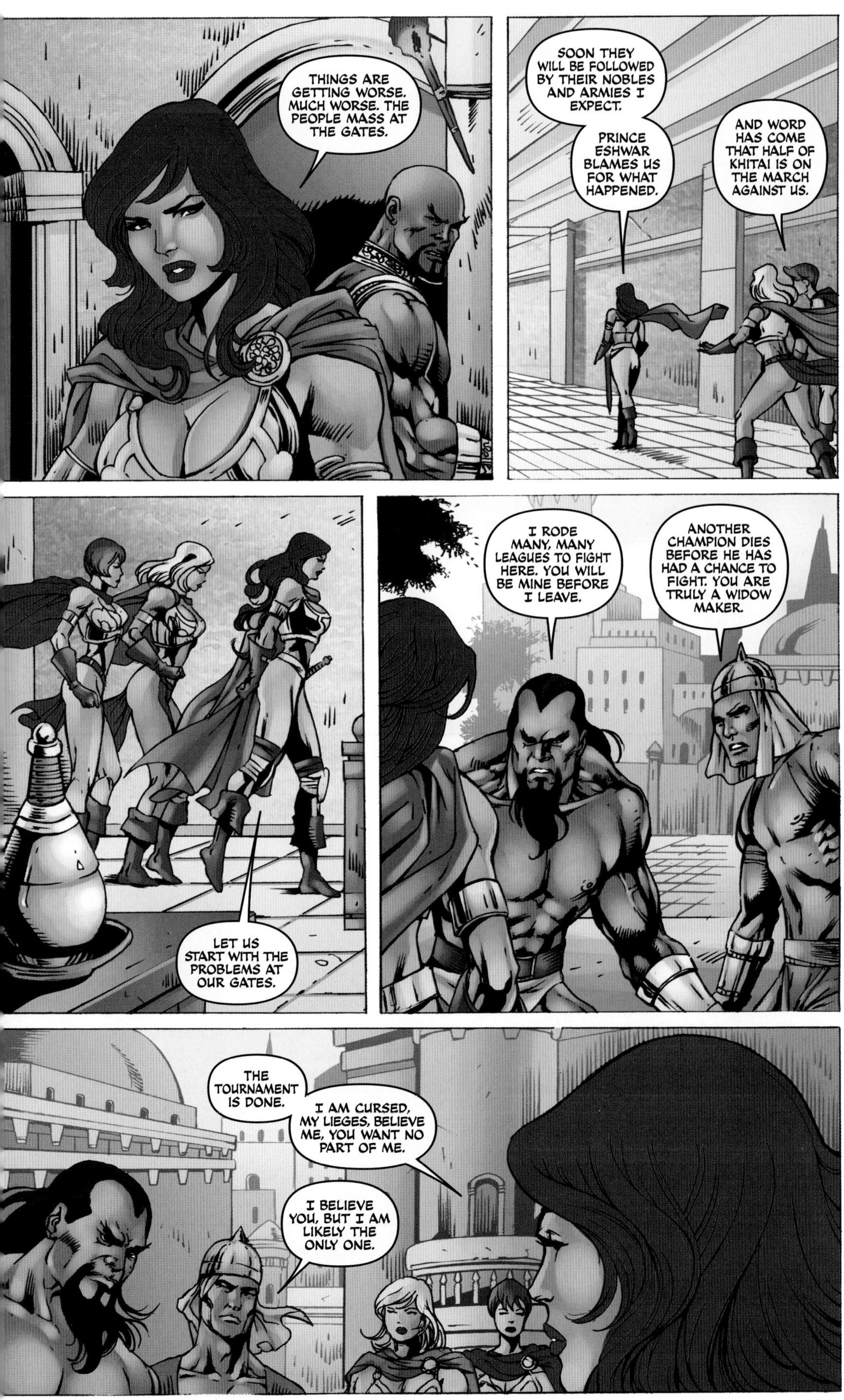
THINGS ARE GETTING WORSE. MUCH WORSE. THE PEOPLE MASS AT THE GATES.
SOON THEY WILL BE FOLLOWED BY THEIR NOBLES AND ARMIES I EXPECT.
PRINCE ESHWAR BLAMES US FOR WHAT HAPPENED.
AND WORD HAS COME THAT HALF OF KHITAI IS ON THE MARCH AGAINST US.
LET US START WITH THE PROBLEMS AT OUR GATES.
I RODE MANY, MANY LEAGUES TO FIGHT HERE. YOU WILL BE MINE BEFORE I LEAVE.
ANOTHER CHAMPION DIES BEFORE HE HAS HAD A CHANCE TO FIGHT. YOU ARE TRULY A WIDOW MAKER.
THE TOURNAMENT IS DONE.
I AM CURSED, MY LIEGES, BELIEVE ME, YOU WANT NO PART OF ME.
I BELIEVE YOU, BUT I AM LIKELY THE ONLY ONE.

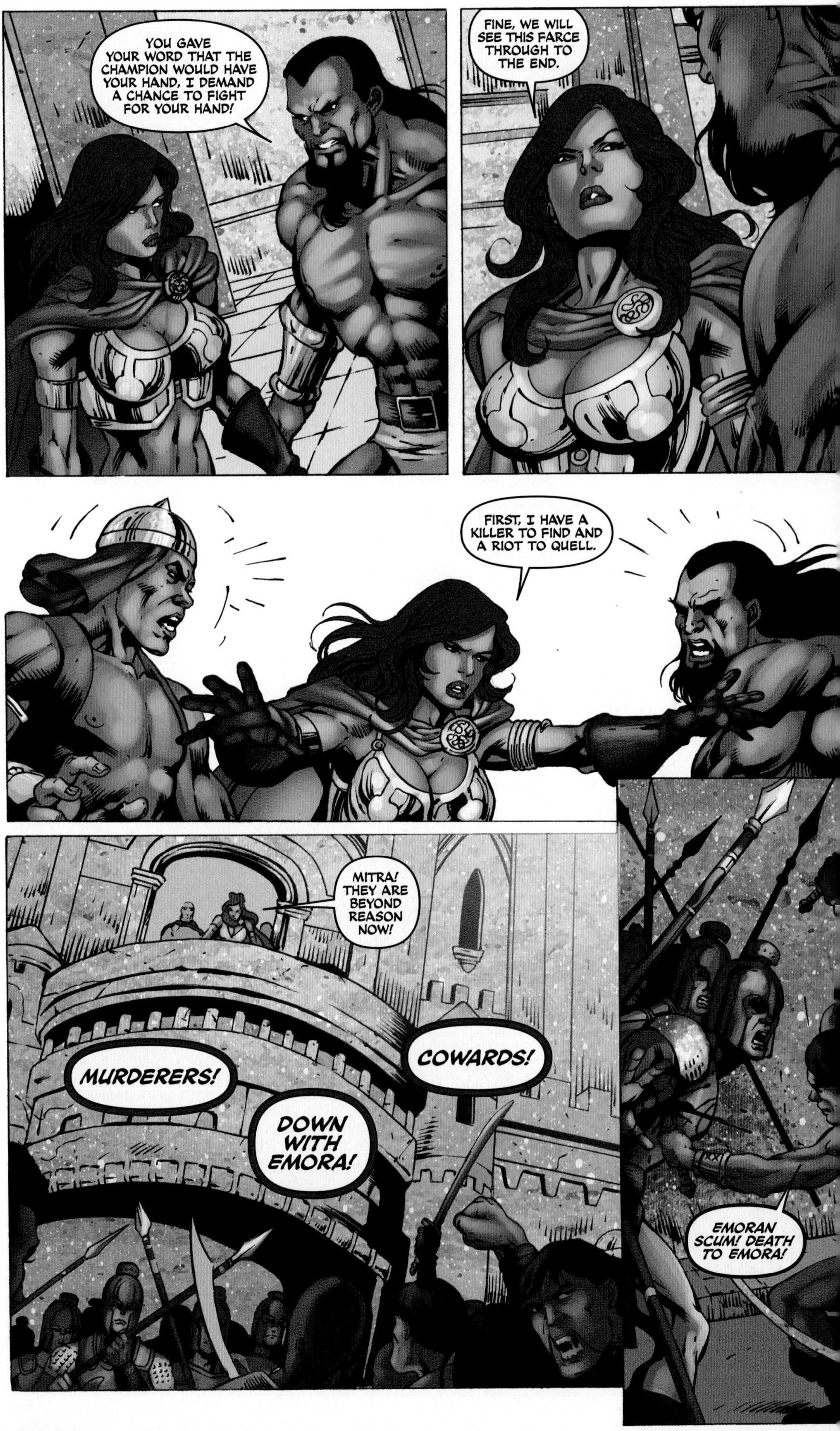
YOU GAVE YOUR WORD THAT THE CHAMPION WOULD HAVE YOUR HAND, I DEMAND A CHANCE TO FIGHT FOR YOUR HAND!
FINE, WE WILL SEE THIS FARCE THROUGH TO THE END.
FIRST, I HAVE A KILLER TO FIND AND A RIOT TO QUELL.
MITRA! THEY ARE BEYOND REASON NOW!
MURDERERS!
COWARDS!
DOWN WITH EMORA!
EMORAN SCUM! DEATH TO EMORA!

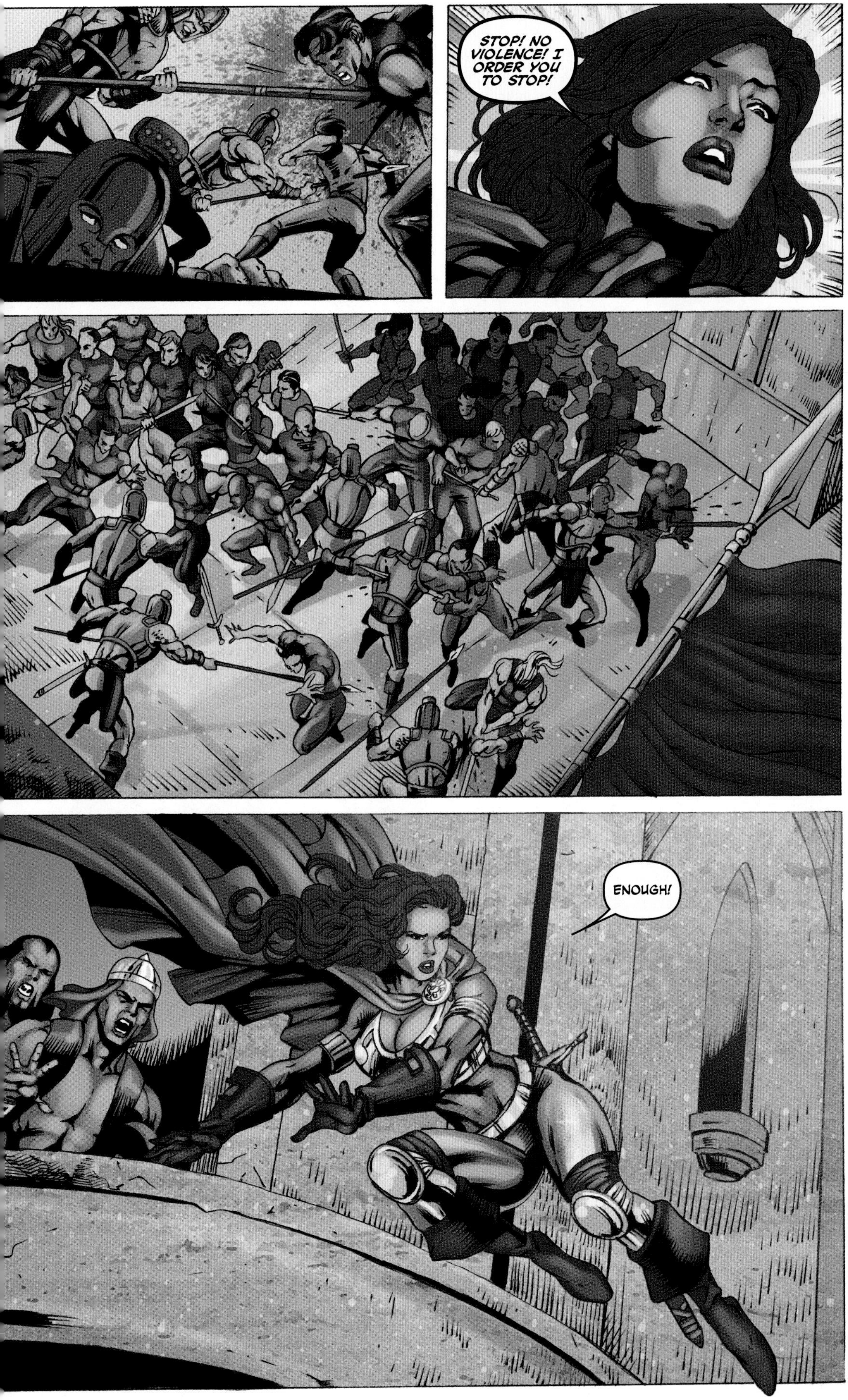
STOP! NO VIOLENCE! I ORDER YOU TO STOP!
ENOUGH!

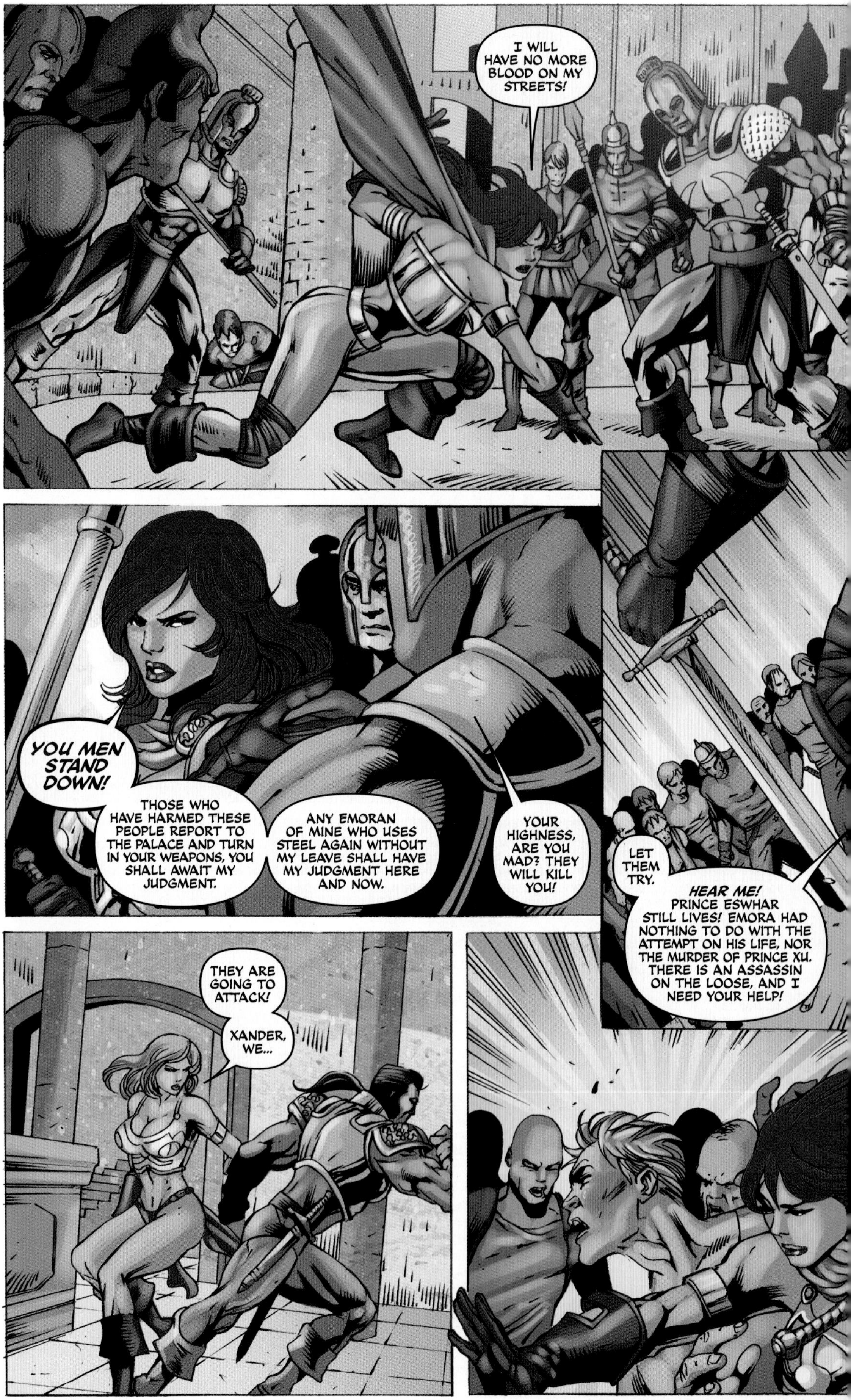
I WILL HAVE NO MORE BLOOD ON MY STREETS!
YOU MEN STAND DOWN!
THOSE WHO HAVE HARMED THESE PEOPLE REPORT TO THE PALACE AND TURN IN YOUR WEAPONS, YOU SHALL AWAIT MY JUDGMENT.
ANY EMORAN OF MINE WHO USES STEEL AGAIN WITHOUT MY LEAVE SHALL HAVE MY JUDGMENT HERE AND NOW.
YOUR HIGHNESS, ARE YOU MAD? THEY WILL KILL YOU!
LET THEM TRY.
HEAR ME! PRINCE ESWHAR STILL LIVES! EMORA HAD NOTHING TO DO WITH THE ATTEMPT ON HIS LIFE, NOR THE MURDER OF PRINCE XU. THERE IS AN ASSASSIN ON THE LOOSE, AND I NEED YOUR HELP!
THEY ARE GOING TO ATTACK!
XANDER, WE...

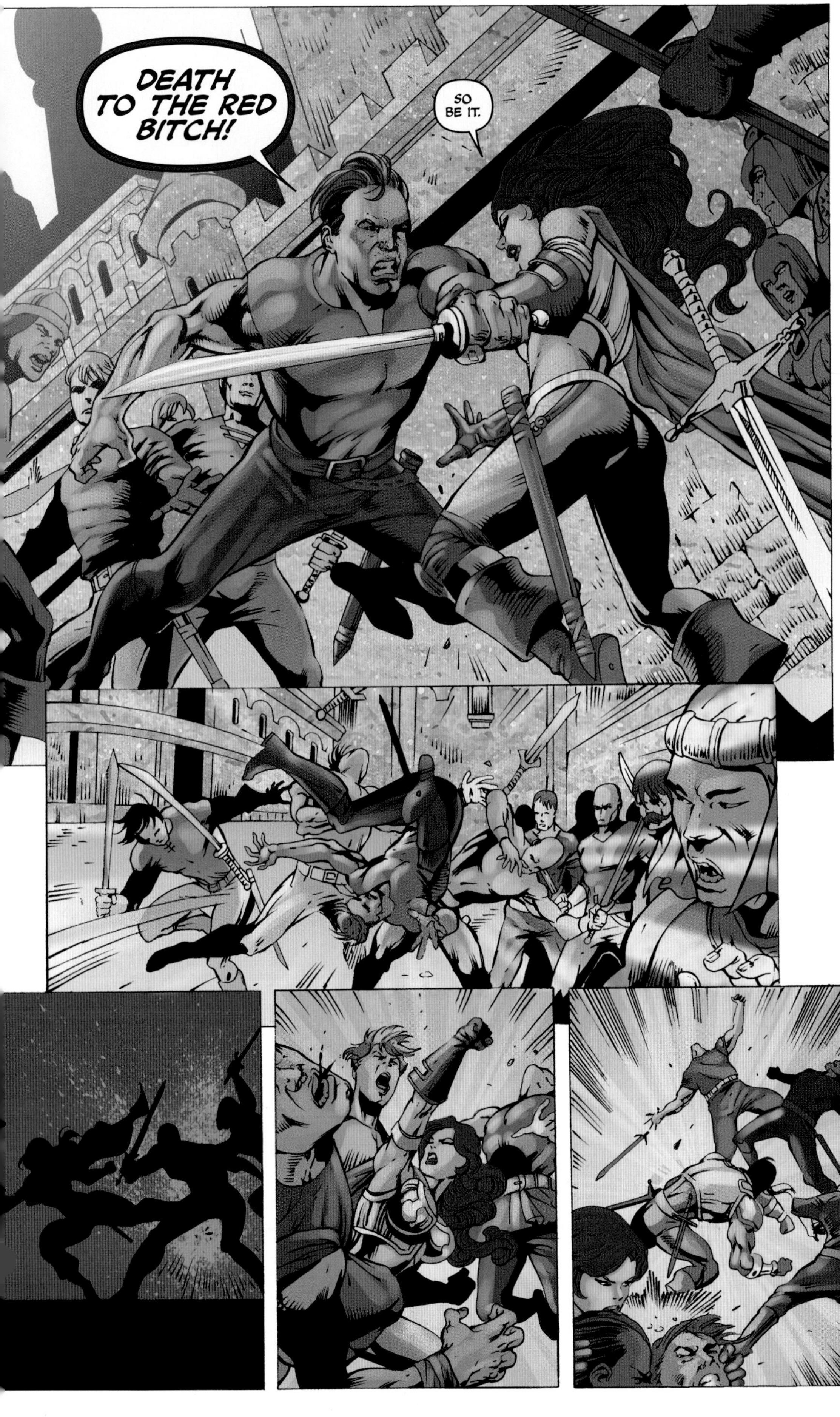
DEATH TO THE RED BITCH!
SO BE IT.

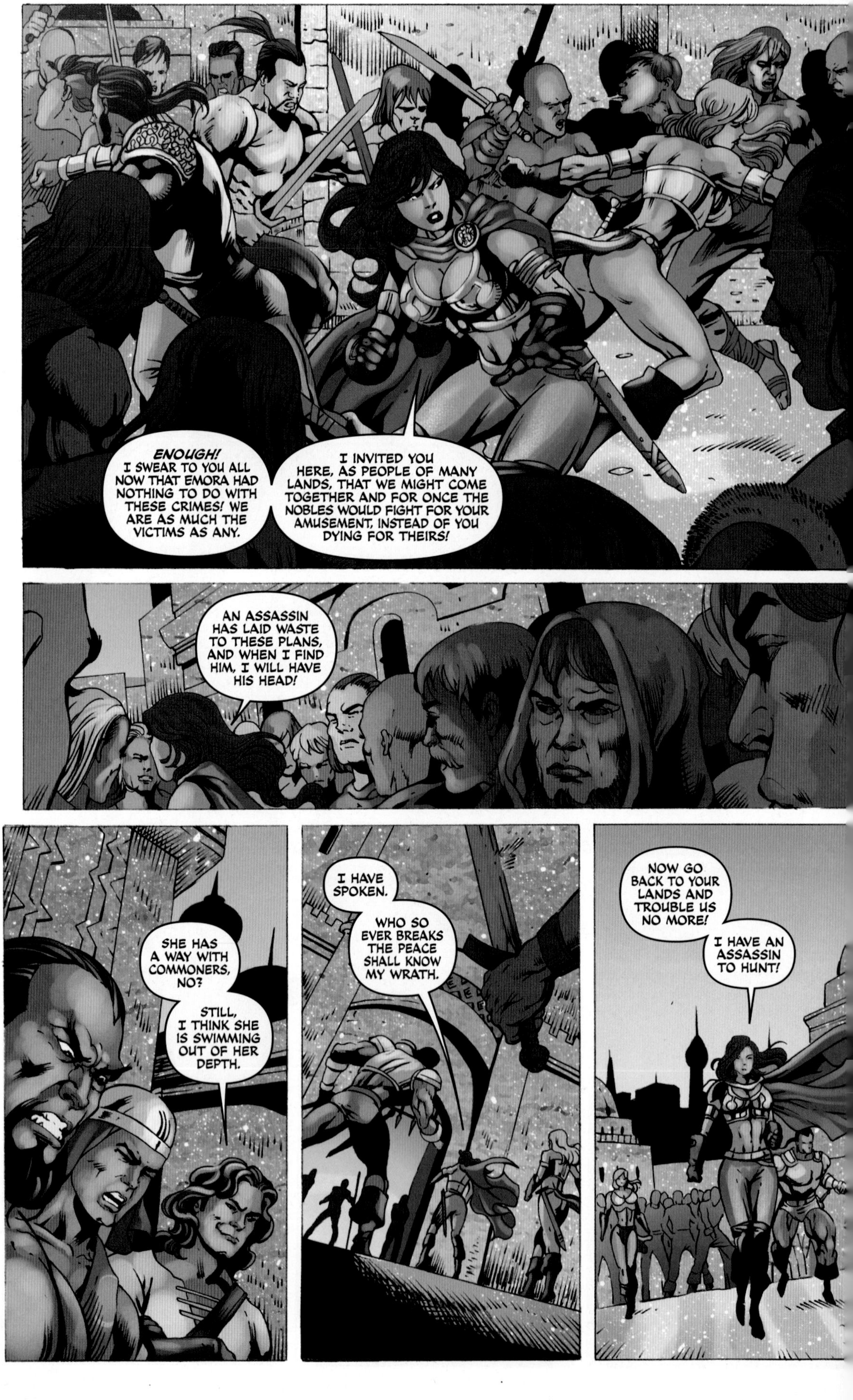
ENOUGH! I SWEAR TO YOU ALL NOW THAT EMORA HAD NOTHING TO DO WITH THESE CRIMES! WE ARE AS MUCH THE VICTIMS AS ANY.
I INVITED YOU HERE, AS PEOPLE OF MANY LANDS, THAT WE MIGHT COME TOGETHER AND FOR ONCE THE NOBLES WOULD FIGHT FOR YOUR AMUSEMENT, INSTEAD OF YOU DYING FOR THEIRS!
AN ASSASSIN HAS LAID WASTE TO THESE PLANS, AND WHEN I FIND HIM, I WILL HAVE HIS HEAD!
SHE HAS A WAY WITH COMMONERS, NO?
STILL, I THINK SHE IS SWIMMING OUT OF HER DEPTH.
I HAVE SPOKEN.
WHO SO EVER BREAKS THE PEACE SHALL KNOW MY WRATH.
NOW GO BACK TO YOUR LANDS AND TROUBLE US NO MORE!
I HAVE AN ASSASSIN TO HUNT!

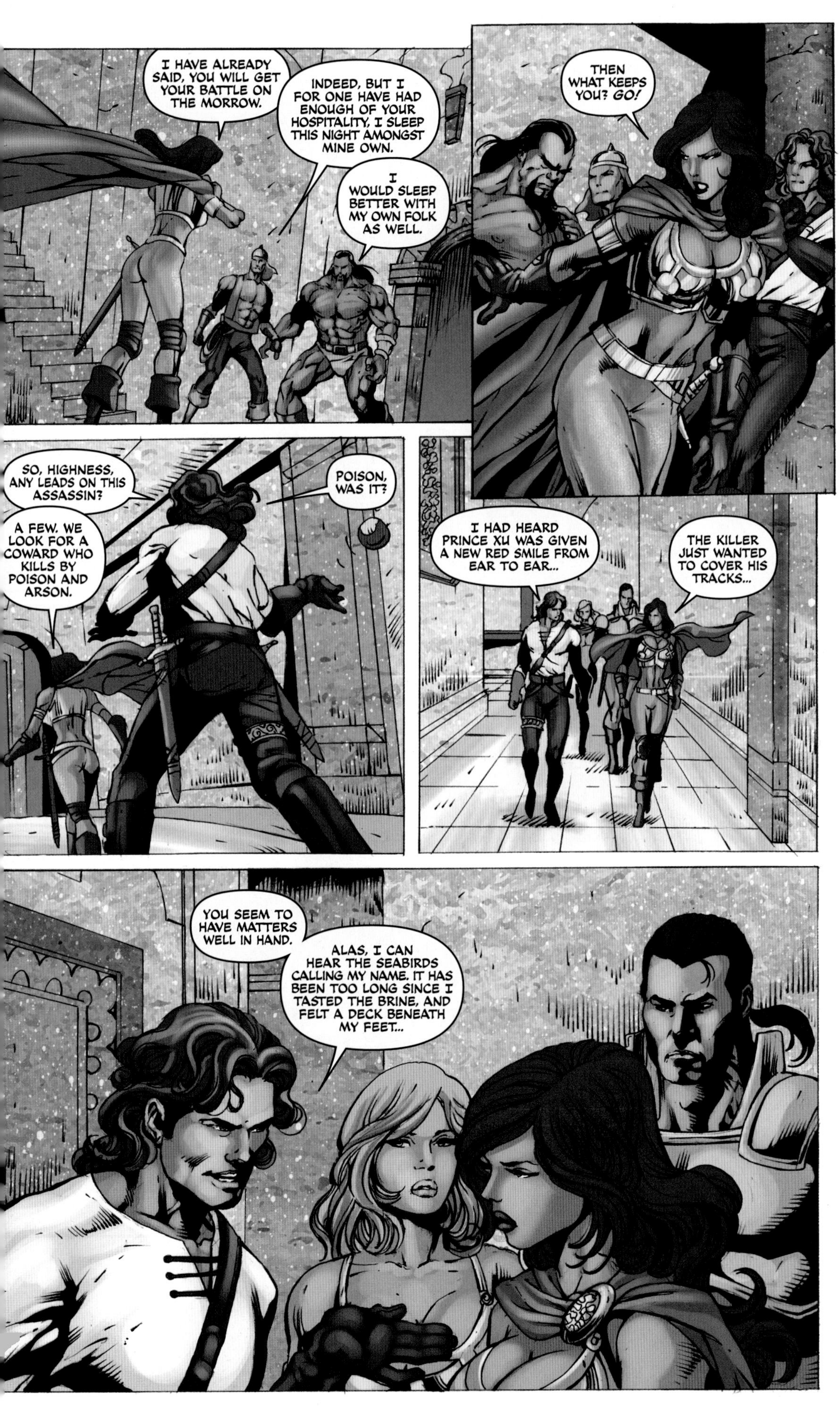

I HAVE ALREADY SAID, YOU WILL GET YOUR BATTLE ON THE MORROW.
INDEED, BUT I FOR ONE HAVE HAD ENOUGH OF YOUR HOSPITALITY, I SLEEP THIS NIGHT AMONGST MINE OWN.
I WOULD SLEEP BETTER WITH MY OWN FOLK AS WELL.
THEN WHAT KEEPS YOU? *GO!*
SO, HIGHNESS, ANY LEADS ON THIS ASSASSIN?
A FEW. WE LOOK FOR A COWARD WHO KILLS BY POISON AND ARSON.
POISON, WAS IT?
I HAD HEARD PRINCE XU WAS GIVEN A NEW RED SMILE FROM EAR TO EAR...
THE KILLER JUST WANTED TO COVER HIS TRACKS...
YOU SEEM TO HAVE MATTERS WELL IN HAND.
ALAS, I CAN HEAR THE SEABIRDS CALLING MY NAME. IT HAS BEEN TOO LONG SINCE I TASTED THE BRINE, AND FELT A DECK BENEATH MY FEET...

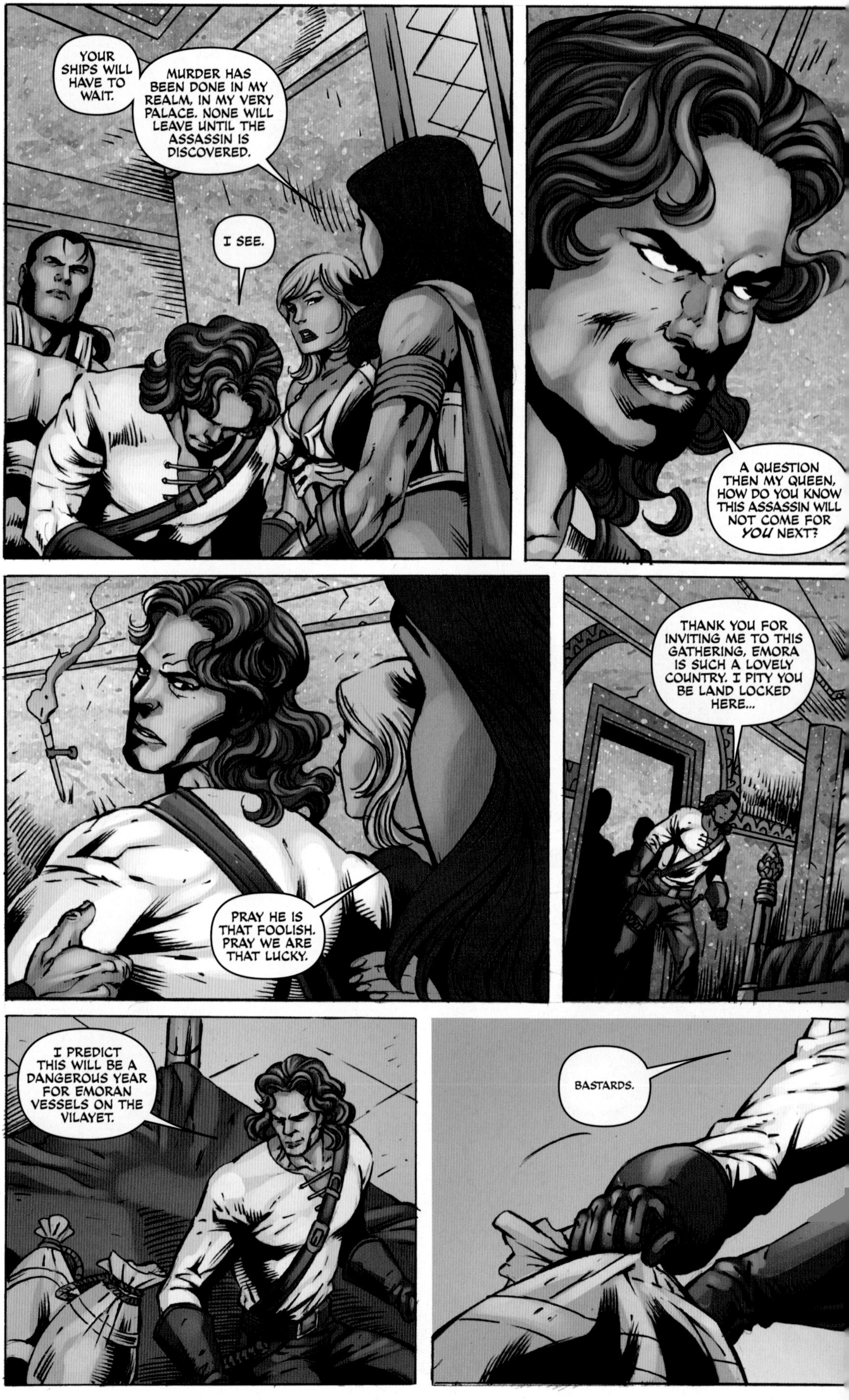
YOUR SHIPS WILL HAVE TO WAIT.
MURDER HAS BEEN DONE IN MY REALM, IN MY VERY PALACE. NONE WILL LEAVE UNTIL THE ASSASSIN IS DISCOVERED.
I SEE.
A QUESTION THEN MY QUEEN, HOW DO YOU KNOW THIS ASSASSIN WILL NOT COME FOR *YOU* NEXT?
PRAY HE IS THAT FOOLISH. PRAY WE ARE THAT LUCKY.
THANK YOU FOR INVITING ME TO THIS GATHERING, EMORA IS SUCH A LOVELY COUNTRY. I PITY YOU BE LAND LOCKED HERE...
I PREDICT THIS WILL BE A DANGEROUS YEAR FOR EMORAN VESSELS ON THE VILAYET.
BASTARDS.

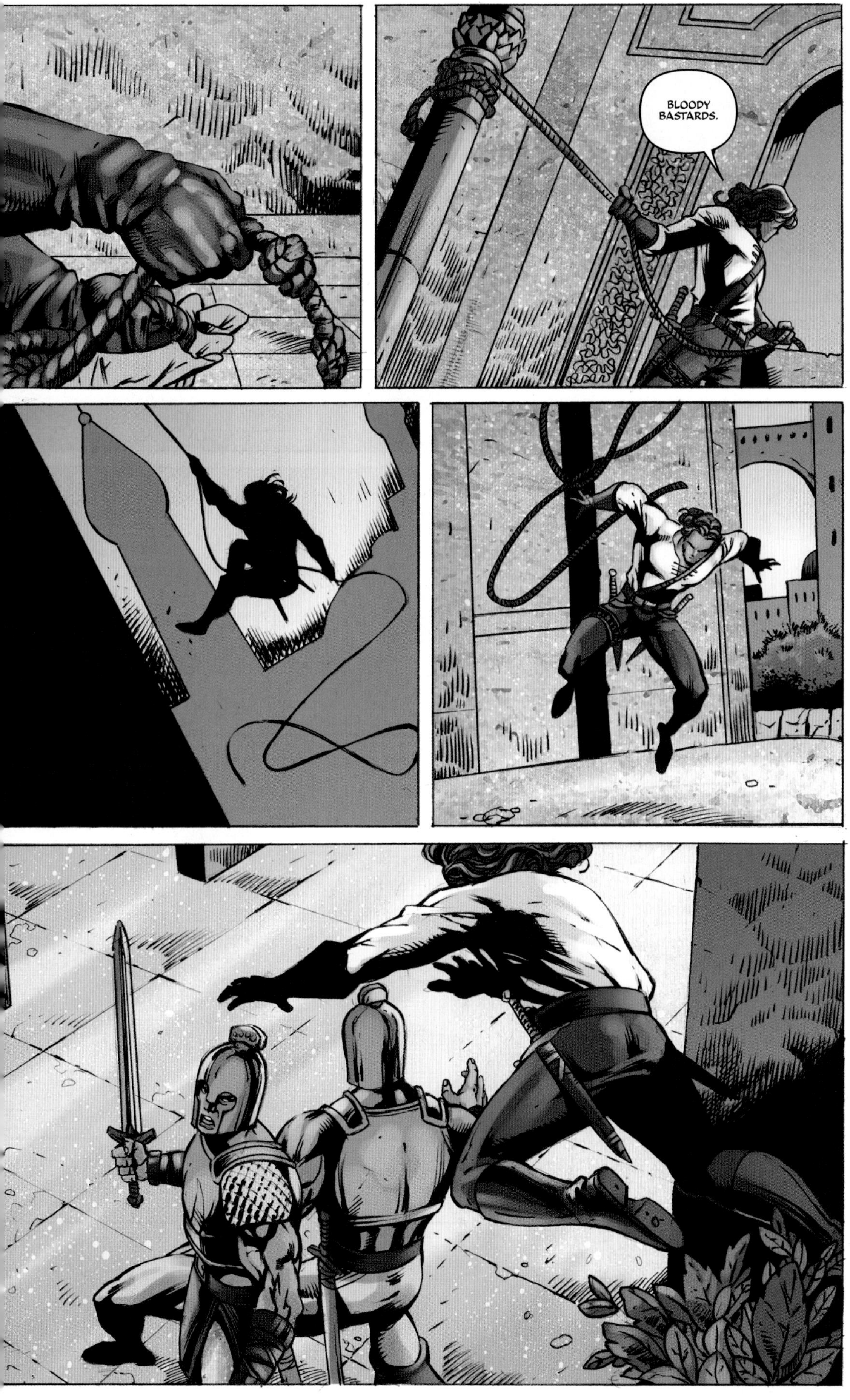
BLOODY BASTARDS.

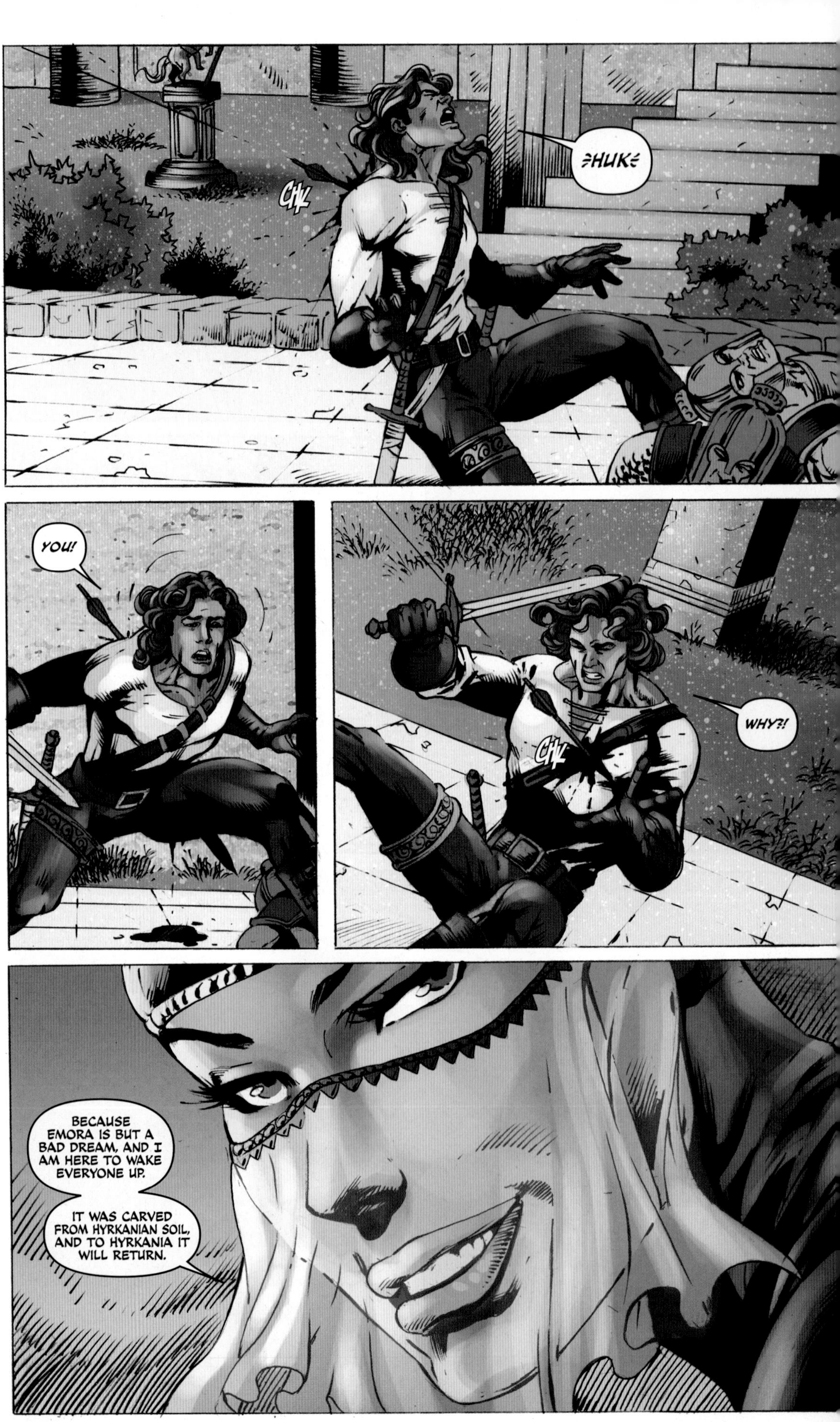
CHK
HUK
YOU!
CHK
WHY?!
BECAUSE EMORA IS BUT A BAD DREAM, AND I AM HERE TO WAKE EVERYONE UP.
IT WAS CARVED FROM HYRKANIAN SOIL, AND TO HYRKANIA IT WILL RETURN.

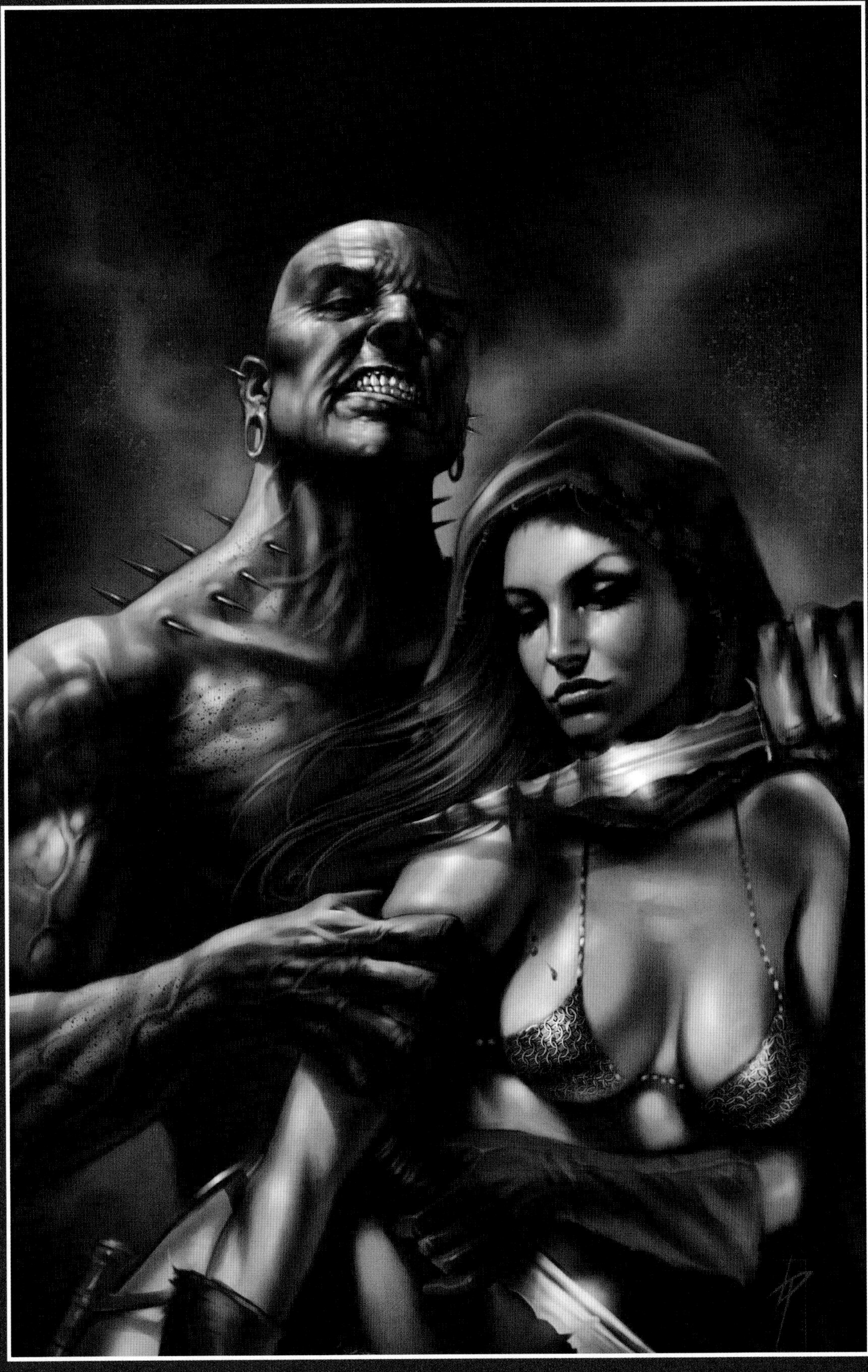

ISSUE #32 COVER BY LUCIO PARRILLO

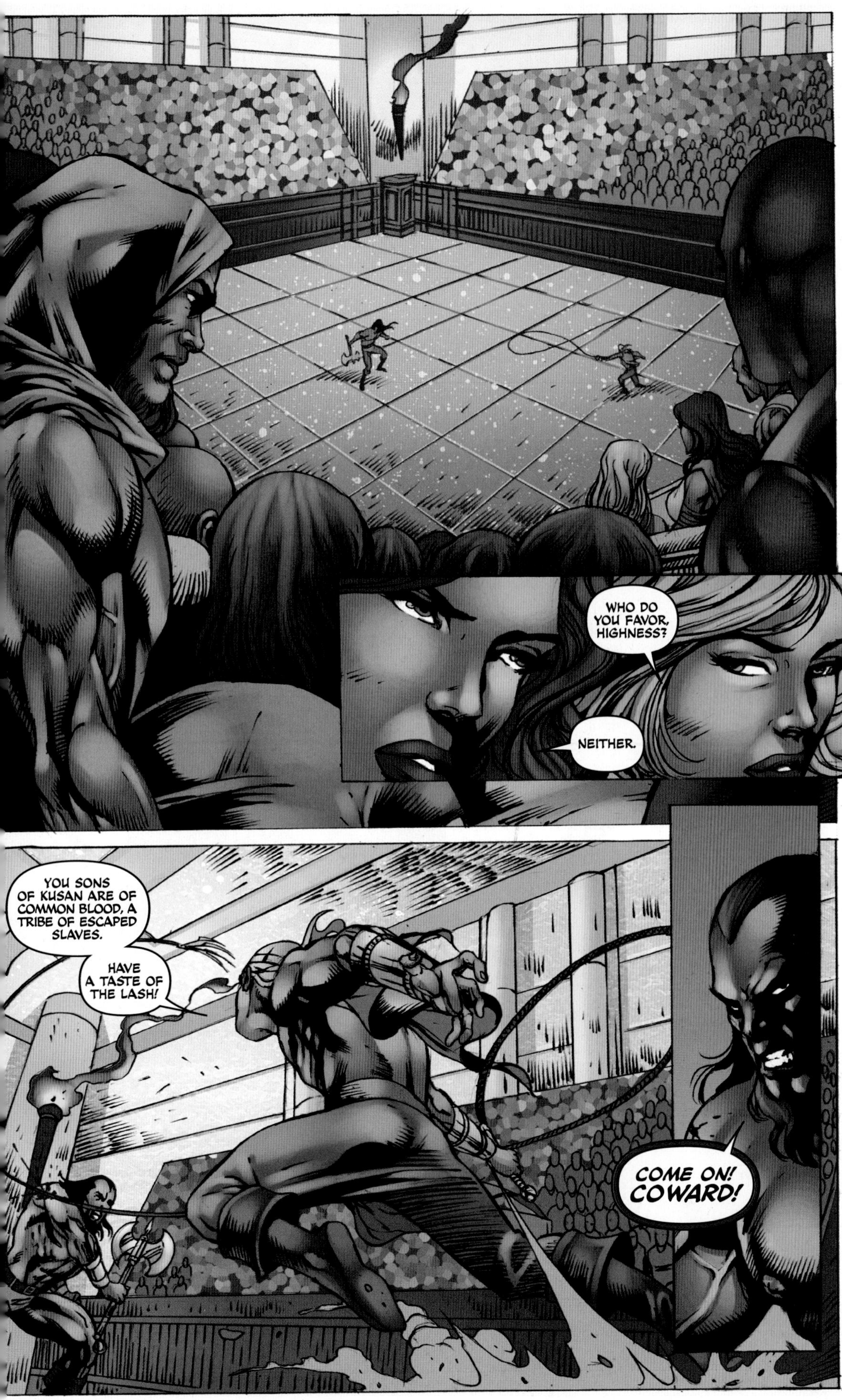
WHO DO YOU FAVOR, HIGHNESS?
NEITHER.
YOU SONS OF KUSAN ARE OF COMMON BLOOD, A TRIBE OF ESCAPED SLAVES.
HAVE A TASTE OF THE LASH!
COME ON! COWARD!

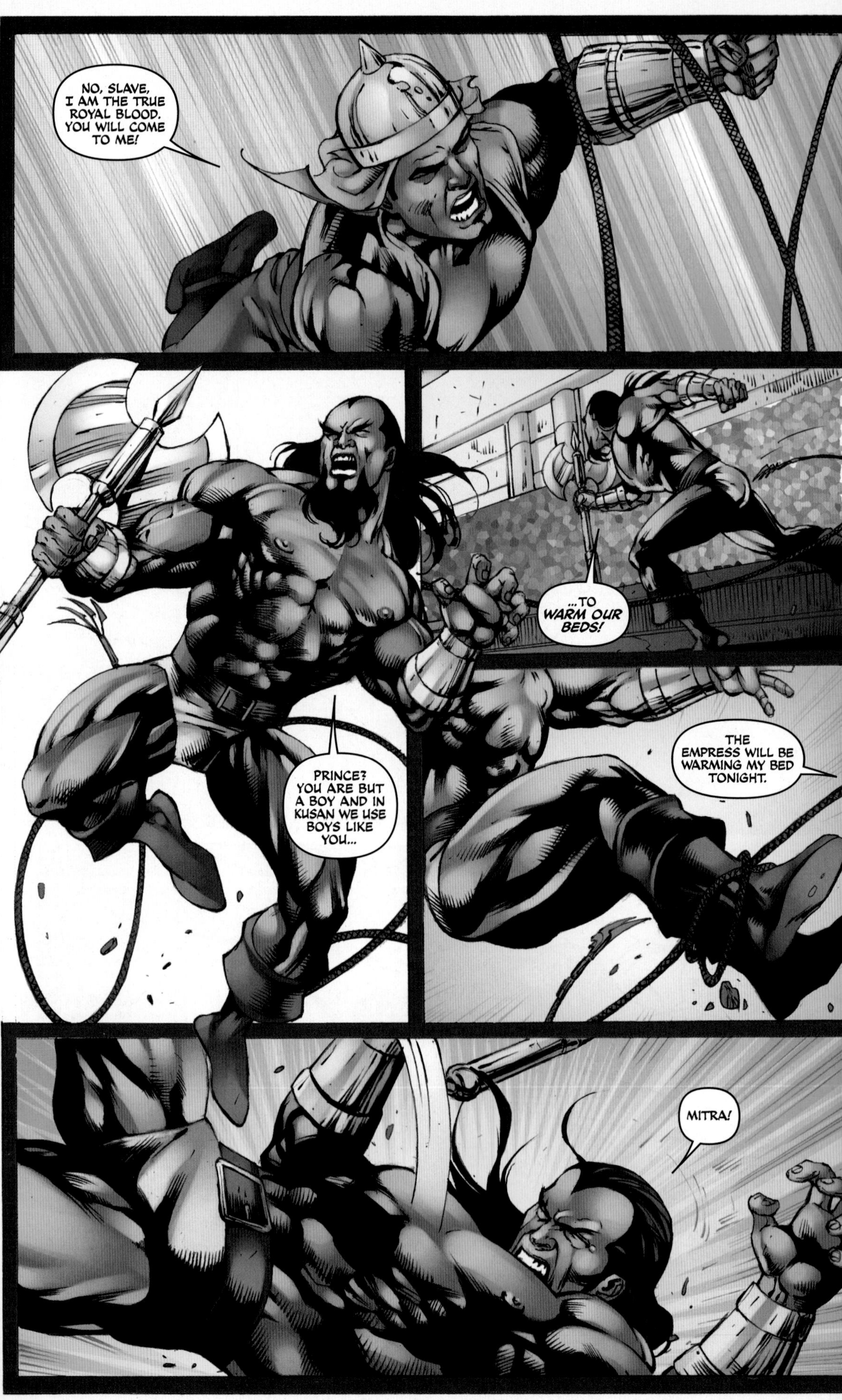
NO, SLAVE, I AM THE TRUE ROYAL BLOOD. YOU WILL COME TO ME!
PRINCE? YOU ARE BUT A BOY AND IN KUSAN WE USE BOYS LIKE YOU...
...TO WARM OUR BEDS!
THE EMPRESS WILL BE WARMING MY BED TONIGHT.
MITRA!

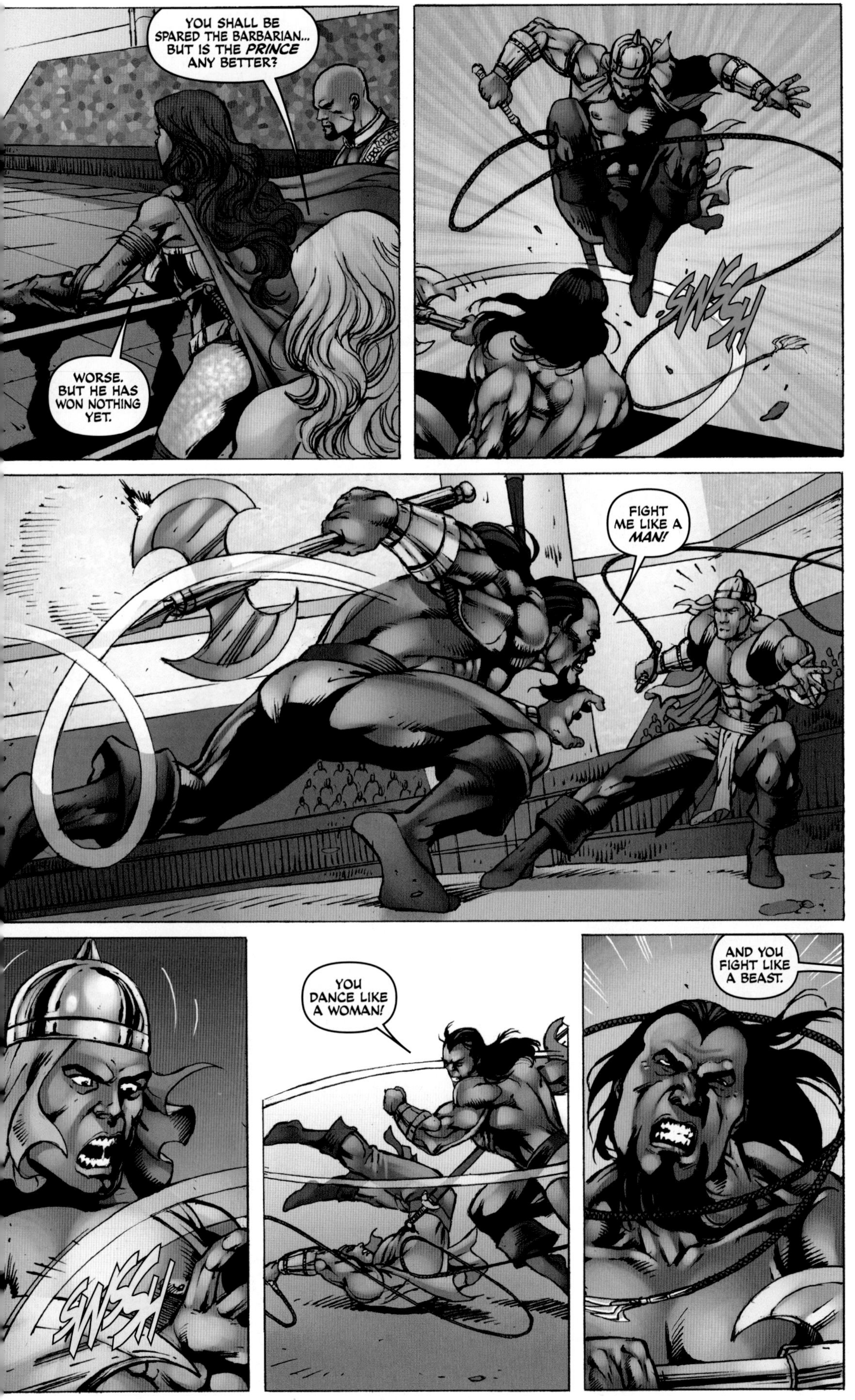

YOU SHALL BE SPARED THE BARBARIAN... BUT IS THE *PRINCE* ANY BETTER?
WORSE. BUT HE HAS WON NOTHING YET.
SNSSH
FIGHT ME LIKE A *MAN!*
YOU DANCE LIKE A WOMAN!
AND YOU FIGHT LIKE A BEAST.
SNSSH

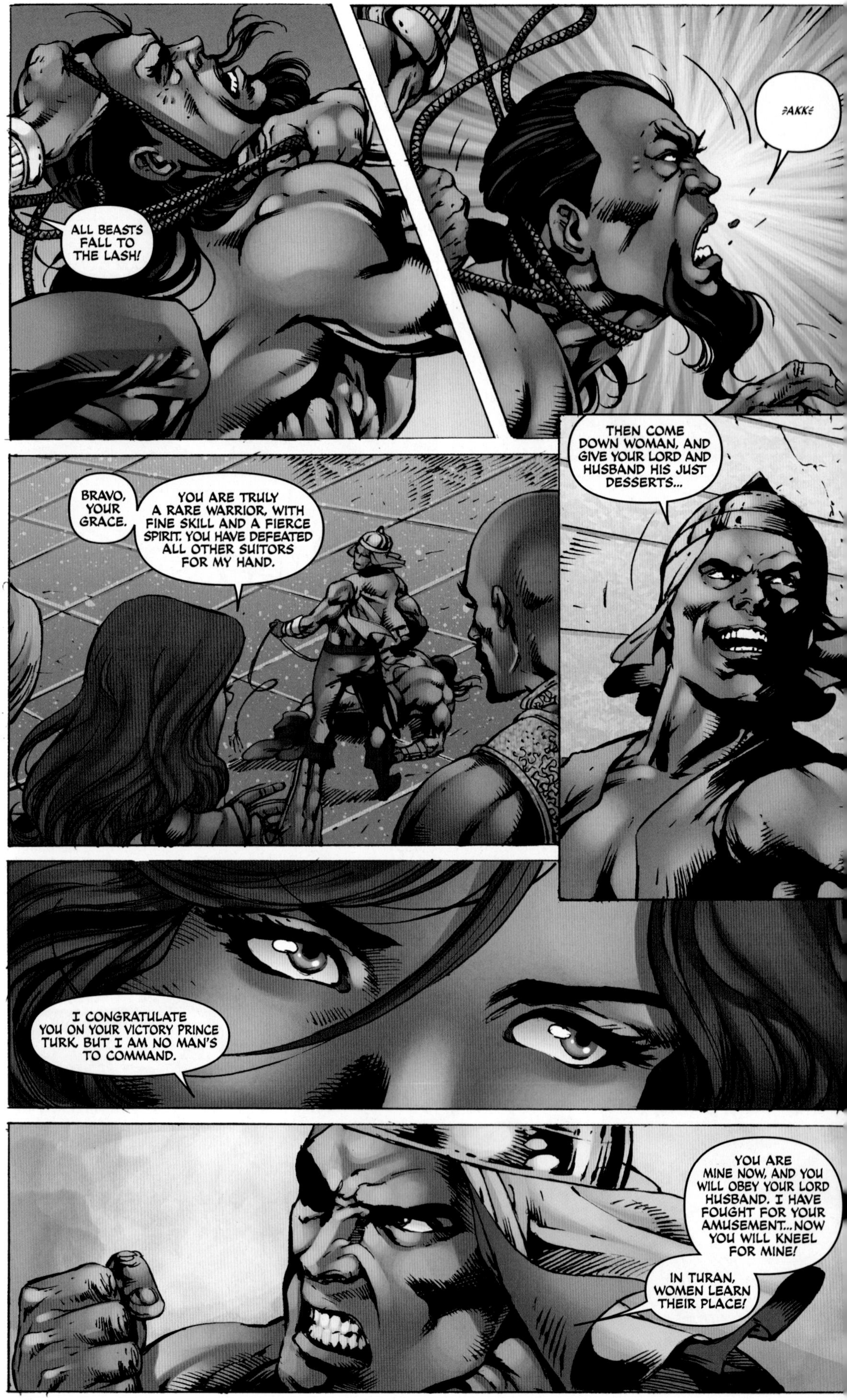
ALL BEASTS FALL TO THE LASH!
≥AKK≤
BRAVO, YOUR GRACE.
YOU ARE TRULY A RARE WARRIOR, WITH FINE SKILL AND A FIERCE SPIRIT. YOU HAVE DEFEATED ALL OTHER SUITORS FOR MY HAND.
THEN COME DOWN WOMAN, AND GIVE YOUR LORD AND HUSBAND HIS JUST DESSERTS...
I CONGRATULATE YOU ON YOUR VICTORY PRINCE TURK, BUT I AM NO MAN'S TO COMMAND.
YOU ARE MINE NOW, AND YOU WILL OBEY YOUR LORD HUSBAND. I HAVE FOUGHT FOR YOUR AMUSEMENT... NOW YOU WILL KNEEL FOR MINE!
IN TURAN, WOMEN LEARN THEIR PLACE!

YOU WISH TO TEACH ME MY PLACE, PRINCE TURK?

"YOU ARE SURROUNDED, MY QUEEN! EVEN NOW, KHITAI *AND* VENDYHA RIDE AGAINST YOU.

"WITHOUT THE STRENGTH OF TURAN YOU WILL BE OVERRUN--YOUR PEOPLE WILL BE PUT TO THE LASH AND YOU WILL BE BURNED AT THE STAKE."

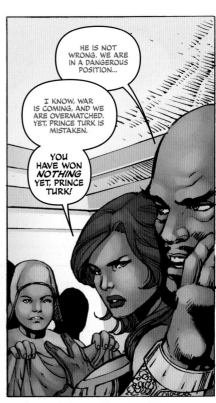

HE IS NOT WRONG. WE ARE IN A DANGEROUS POSITION...

I KNOW, WAR IS COMING, AND WE ARE OVERMATCHED. YET, PRINCE TURK IS MISTAKEN.

YOU HAVE WON *NOTHING* YET, PRINCE TURK!

YOU WOULD BREAK YOUR VOW? YOU WISH TO BE AT WAR WITH TURAN AS WELL?

I SWORE TO GIVE MY HAND TO WHOMEVER WON THIS TOURNAMENT.

THERE IS ONE MORE YOU MUST DEFEAT...

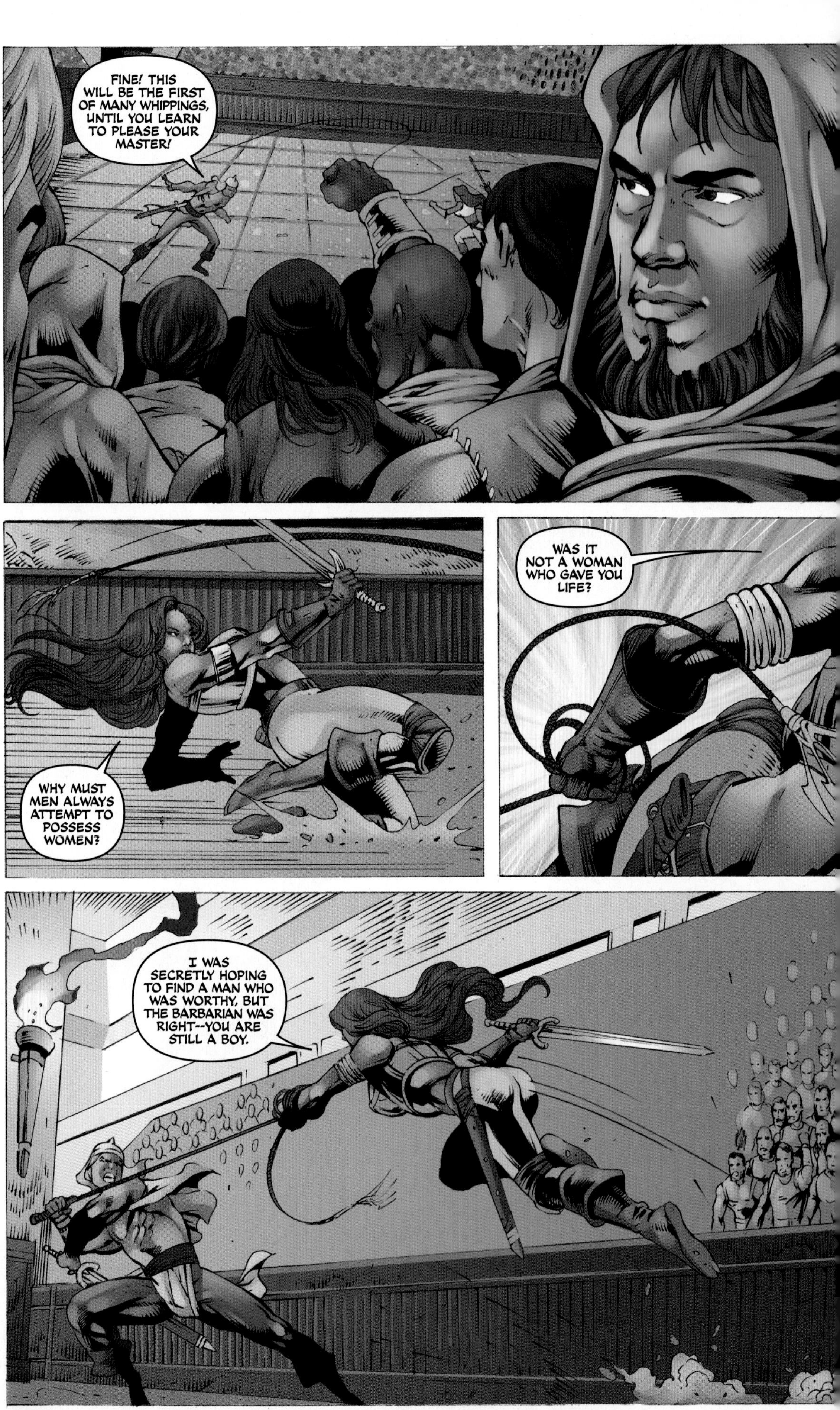
FINE! THIS WILL BE THE FIRST OF MANY WHIPPINGS, UNTIL YOU LEARN TO PLEASE YOUR MASTER!
WHY MUST MEN ALWAYS ATTEMPT TO POSSESS WOMEN?
WAS IT NOT A WOMAN WHO GAVE YOU LIFE?
I WAS SECRETLY HOPING TO FIND A MAN WHO WAS WORTHY, BUT THE BARBARIAN WAS RIGHT--YOU ARE STILL A BOY.

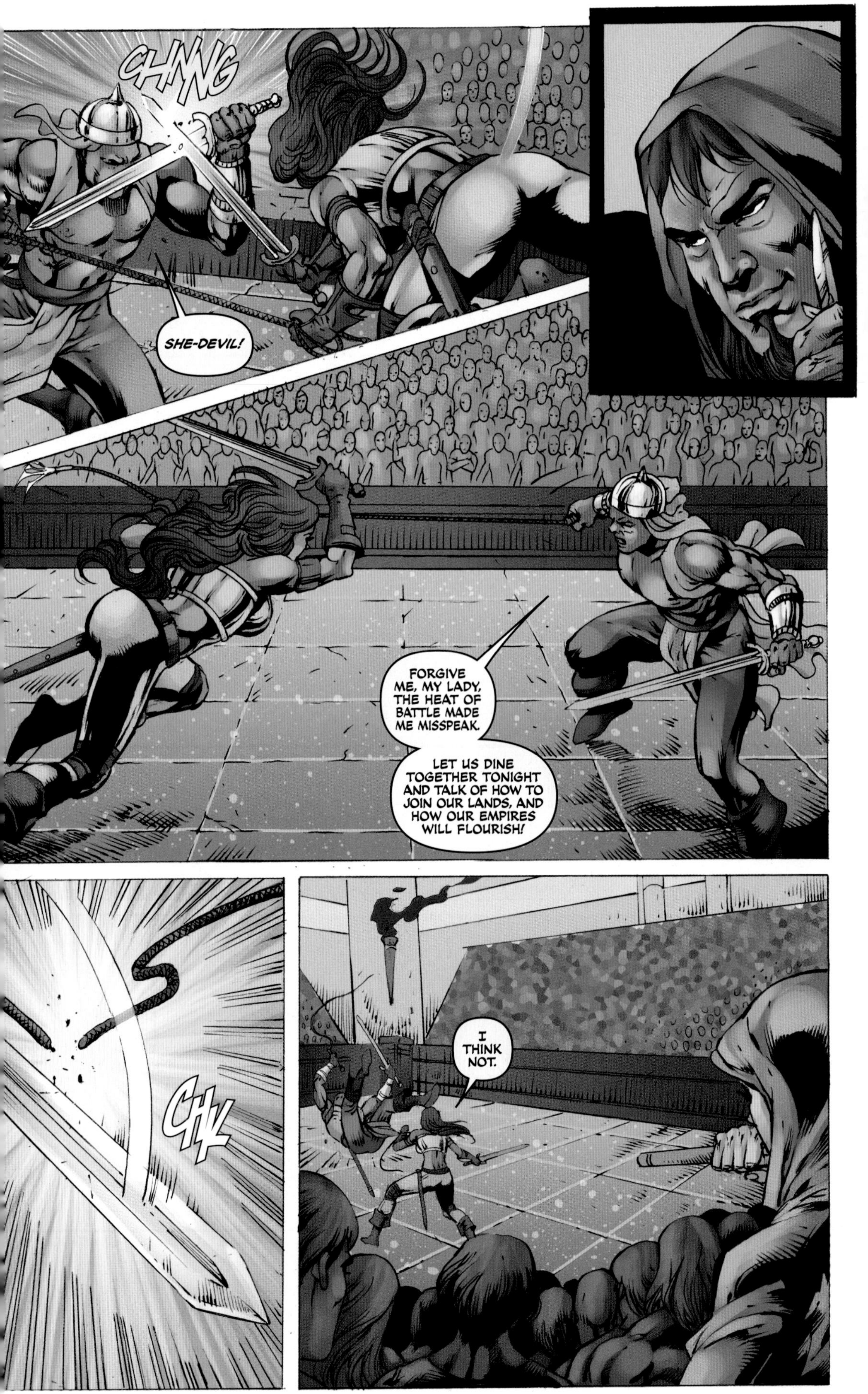
CHNNG
SHE-DEVIL!
FORGIVE ME, MY LADY, THE HEAT OF BATTLE MADE ME MISSPEAK.
LET US DINE TOGETHER TONIGHT AND TALK OF HOW TO JOIN OUR LANDS, AND HOW OUR EMPIRES WILL FLOURISH!
CHK
I THINK NOT.

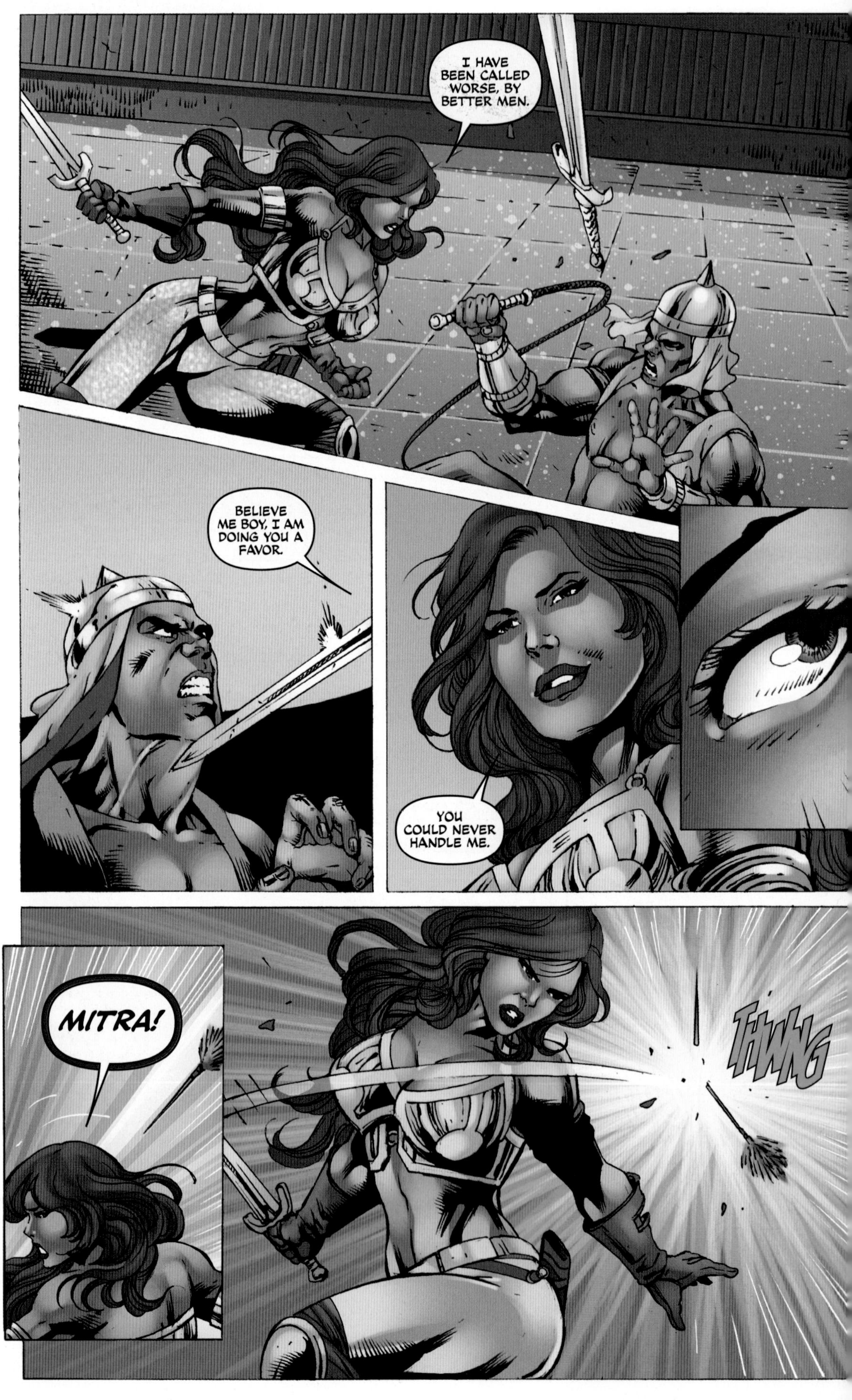
I HAVE BEEN CALLED WORSE, BY BETTER MEN.
BELIEVE ME BOY, I AM DOING YOU A FAVOR.
YOU COULD NEVER HANDLE ME.
MITRA!
THWNG

DAMN.

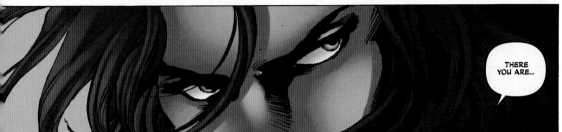

THERE YOU ARE...

YOU WILL PAY FOR THIS!

SHE-DEVIL!

EMORAN BETRAYERS!

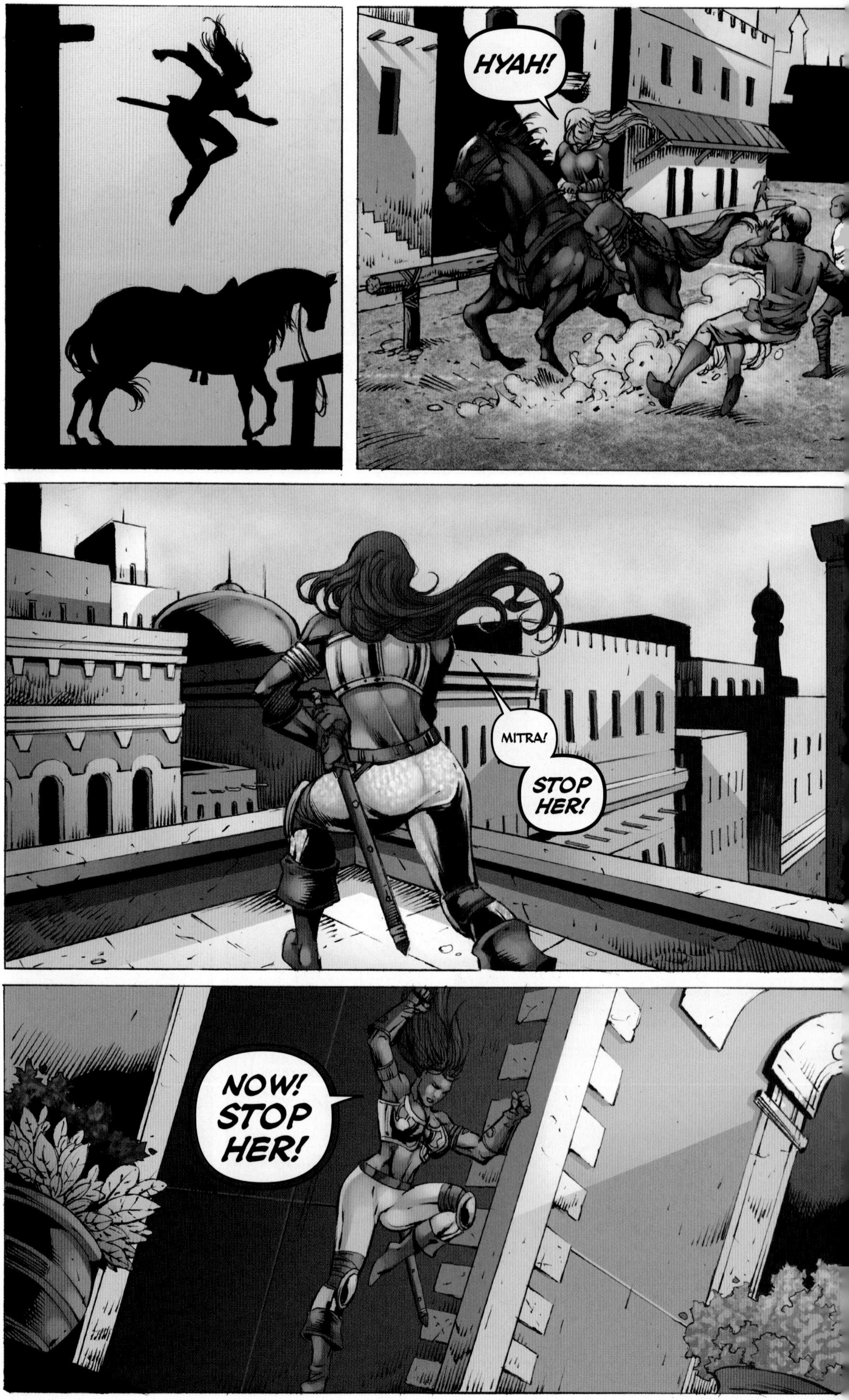
HYAH!
MITRA!
STOP HER!
NOW! STOP HER!

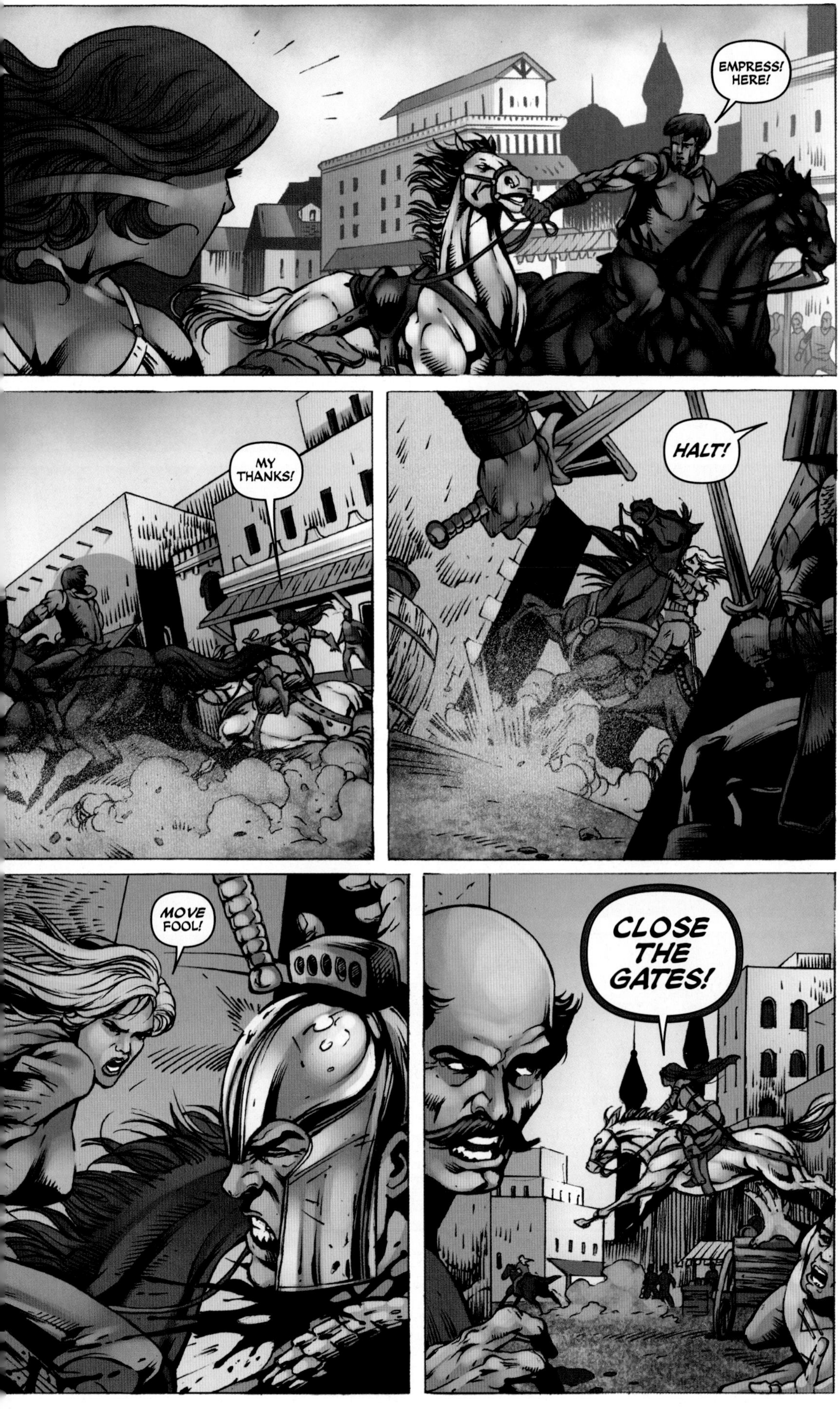
EMPRESS! HERE!
MY THANKS!
HALT!
MOVE FOOL!
CLOSE THE GATES!

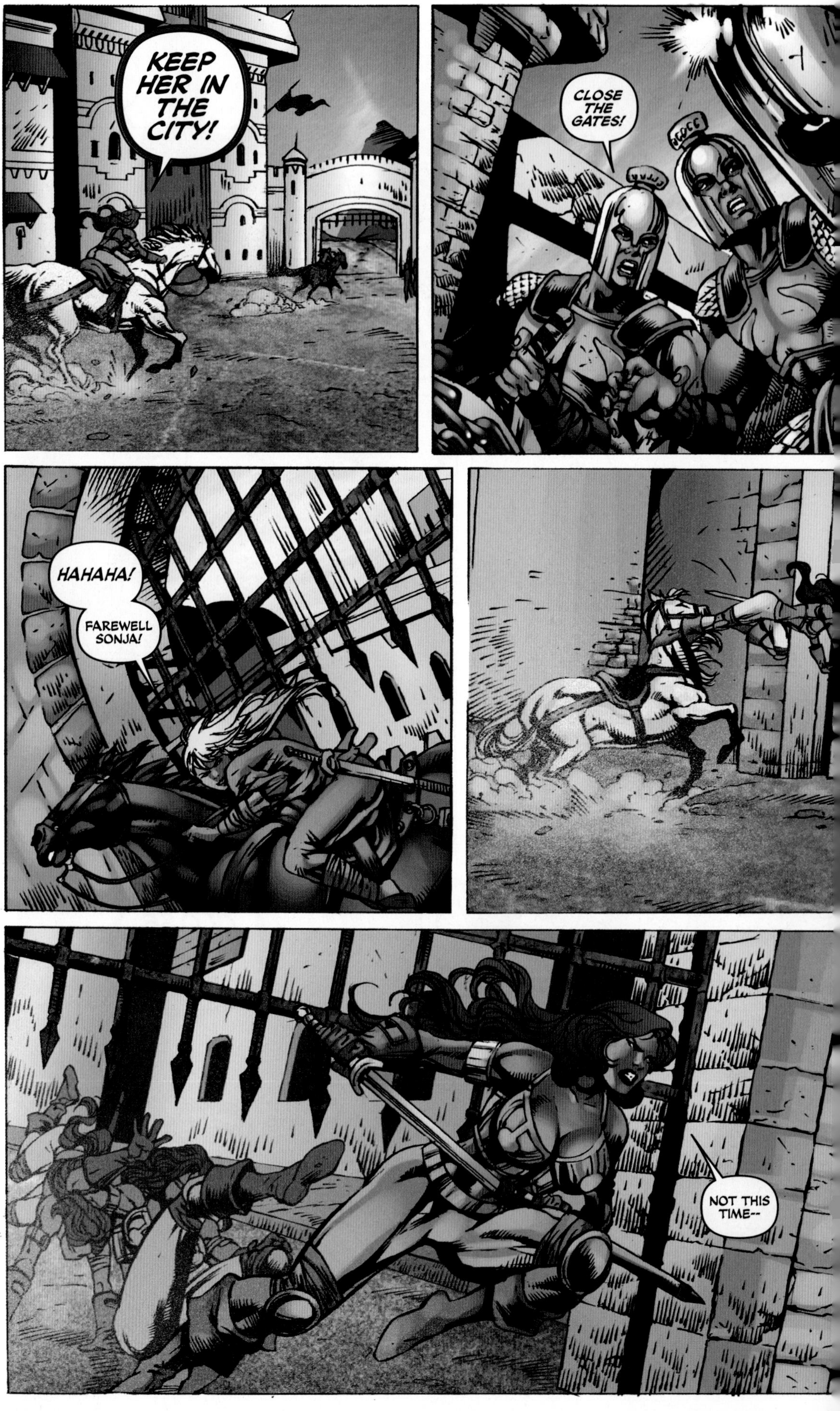
KEEP HER IN THE CITY!
CLOSE THE GATES!
HAHAHA!
FAREWELL SONJA!
NOT THIS TIME--

HMPF!

SHLKK

I MUST ADMIT, YOU HAD ME FOOLED.

I TOOK YOU FOR A SIMPLE TROLLOP WHO SPREAD HER LEGS FOR EVERY MAN WHO CROSSED HER PATH.

BETTER THAN BEING A SHREW AND A TRAITOR. LET ME GO, AND MY FATHER MIGHT JUST LET YOU LIVE WHEN HE CONQUERS EMORA.

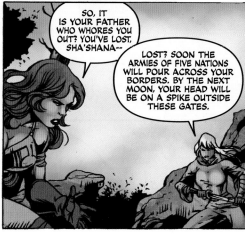

SO, IT IS YOUR FATHER WHO WHORES YOU OUT? YOU'VE LOST, SHA'SHANA—

LOST? SOON THE ARMIES OF FIVE NATIONS WILL POUR ACROSS YOUR BORDERS. BY THE NEXT MOON, YOUR HEAD WILL BE ON A SPIKE OUTSIDE THESE GATES.

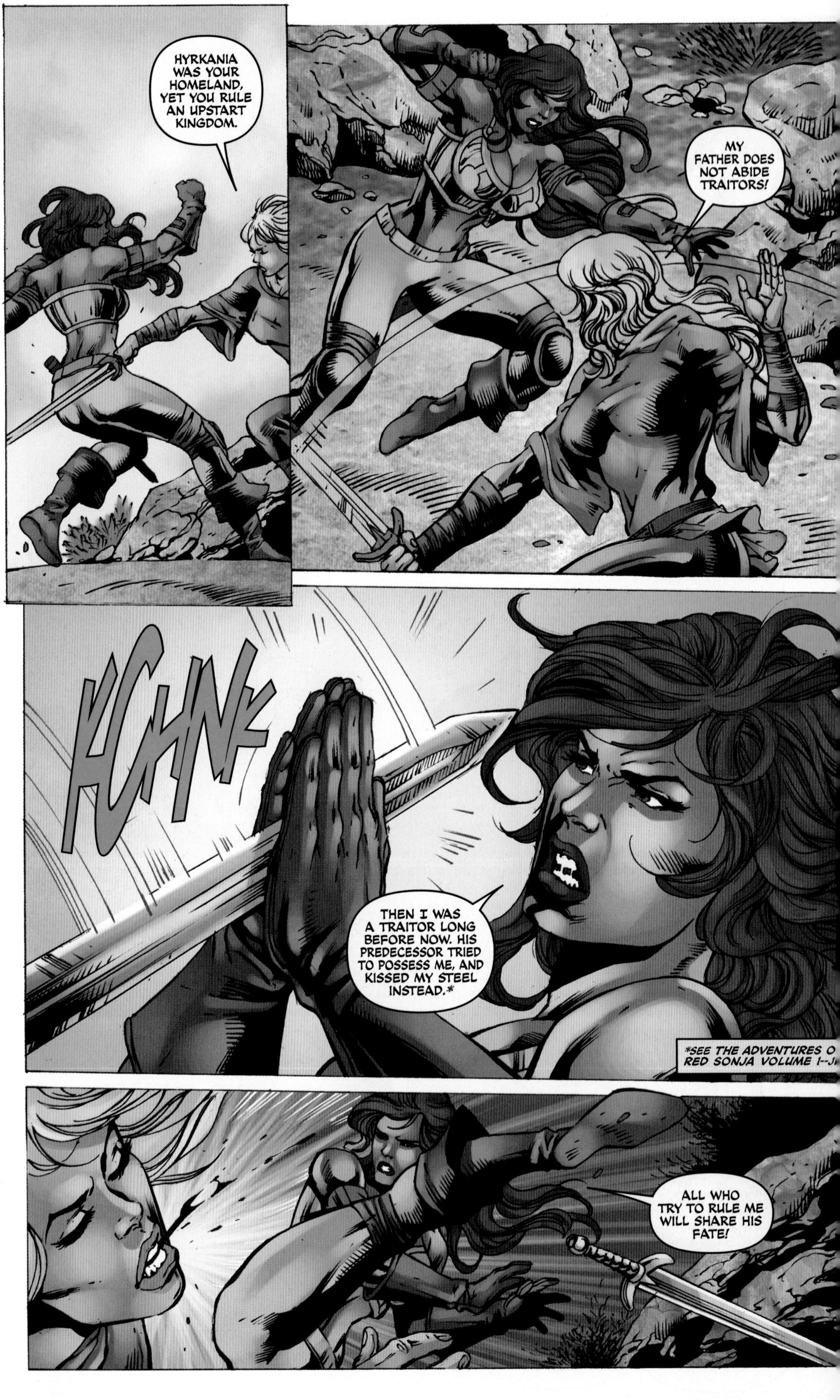
HYRKANIA WAS YOUR HOMELAND, YET YOU RULE AN UPSTART KINGDOM.
MY FATHER DOES NOT ABIDE TRAITORS!
KCHNK
THEN I WAS A TRAITOR LONG BEFORE NOW. HIS PREDECESSOR TRIED TO POSSESS ME, AND KISSED MY STEEL INSTEAD.*
*SEE THE ADVENTURES O
RED SONJA VOLUME 1--J
ALL WHO TRY TO RULE ME WILL SHARE HIS FATE!

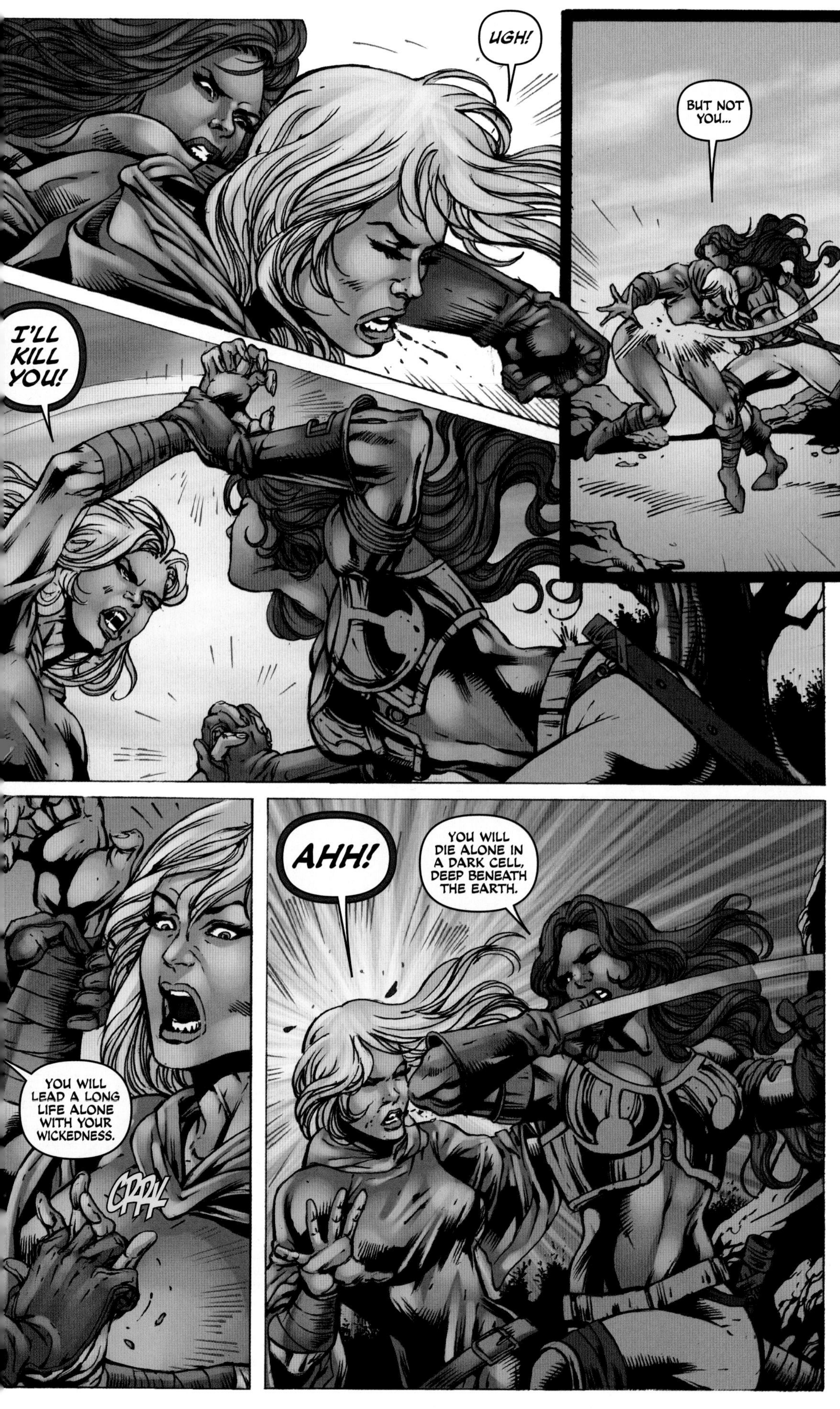
UGH!
BUT NOT YOU...
I'LL KILL YOU!
AHH!
YOU WILL DIE ALONE IN A DARK CELL, DEEP BENEATH THE EARTH.
YOU WILL LEAD A LONG LIFE ALONE WITH YOUR WICKEDNESS.
CRAK

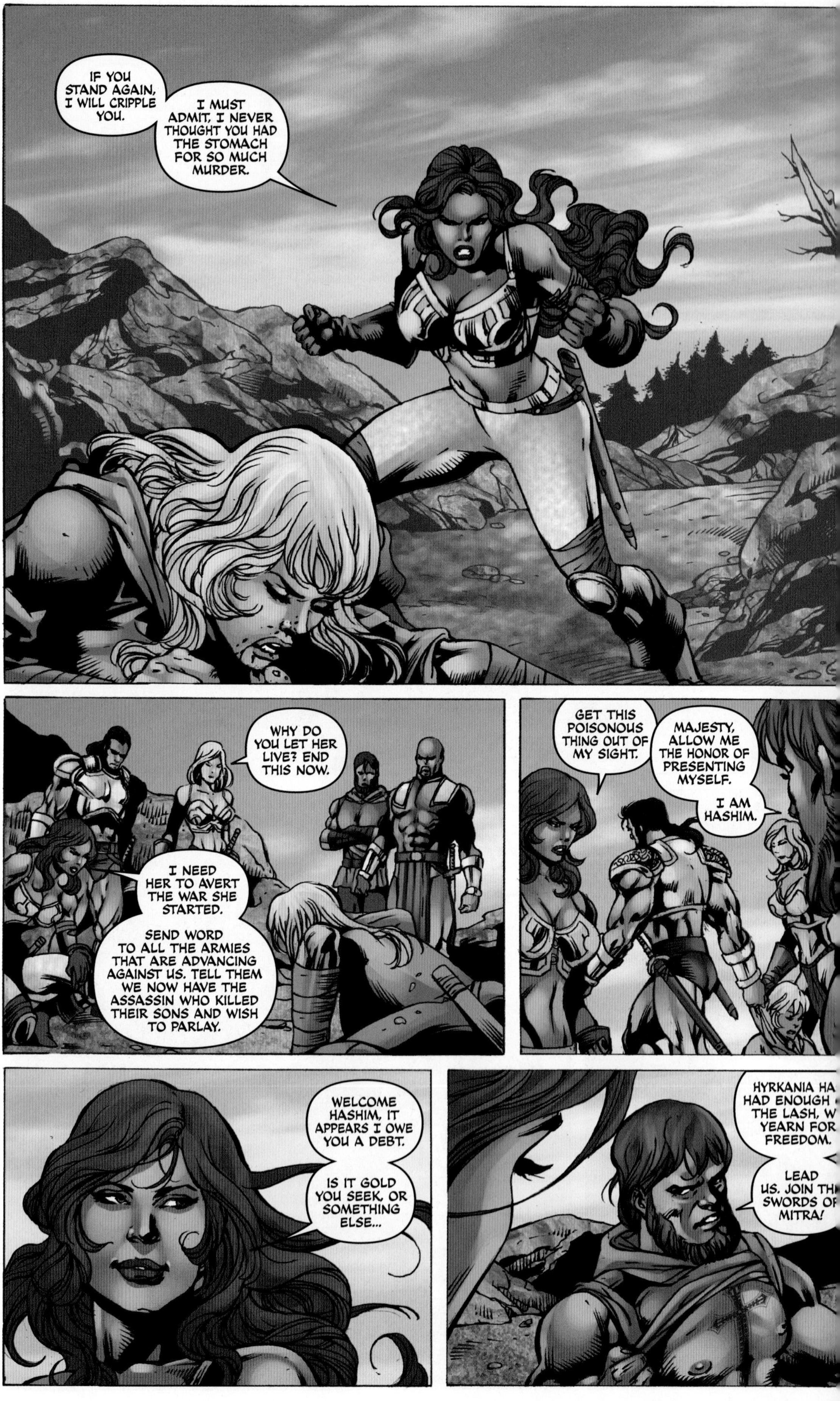
IF YOU STAND AGAIN, I WILL CRIPPLE YOU.
I MUST ADMIT, I NEVER THOUGHT YOU HAD THE STOMACH FOR SO MUCH MURDER.
WHY DO YOU LET HER LIVE? END THIS NOW.
I NEED HER TO AVERT THE WAR SHE STARTED.
SEND WORD TO ALL THE ARMIES THAT ARE ADVANCING AGAINST US. TELL THEM WE NOW HAVE THE ASSASSIN WHO KILLED THEIR SONS AND WISH TO PARLAY.
GET THIS POISONOUS THING OUT OF MY SIGHT.
MAJESTY, ALLOW ME THE HONOR OF PRESENTING MYSELF.
I AM HASHIM.
WELCOME HASHIM, IT APPEARS I OWE YOU A DEBT.
IS IT GOLD YOU SEEK, OR SOMETHING ELSE...
HYRKANIA HA HAD ENOUGH THE LASH, W YEARN FOR FREEDOM.
LEAD US. JOIN TH SWORDS OF MITRA!

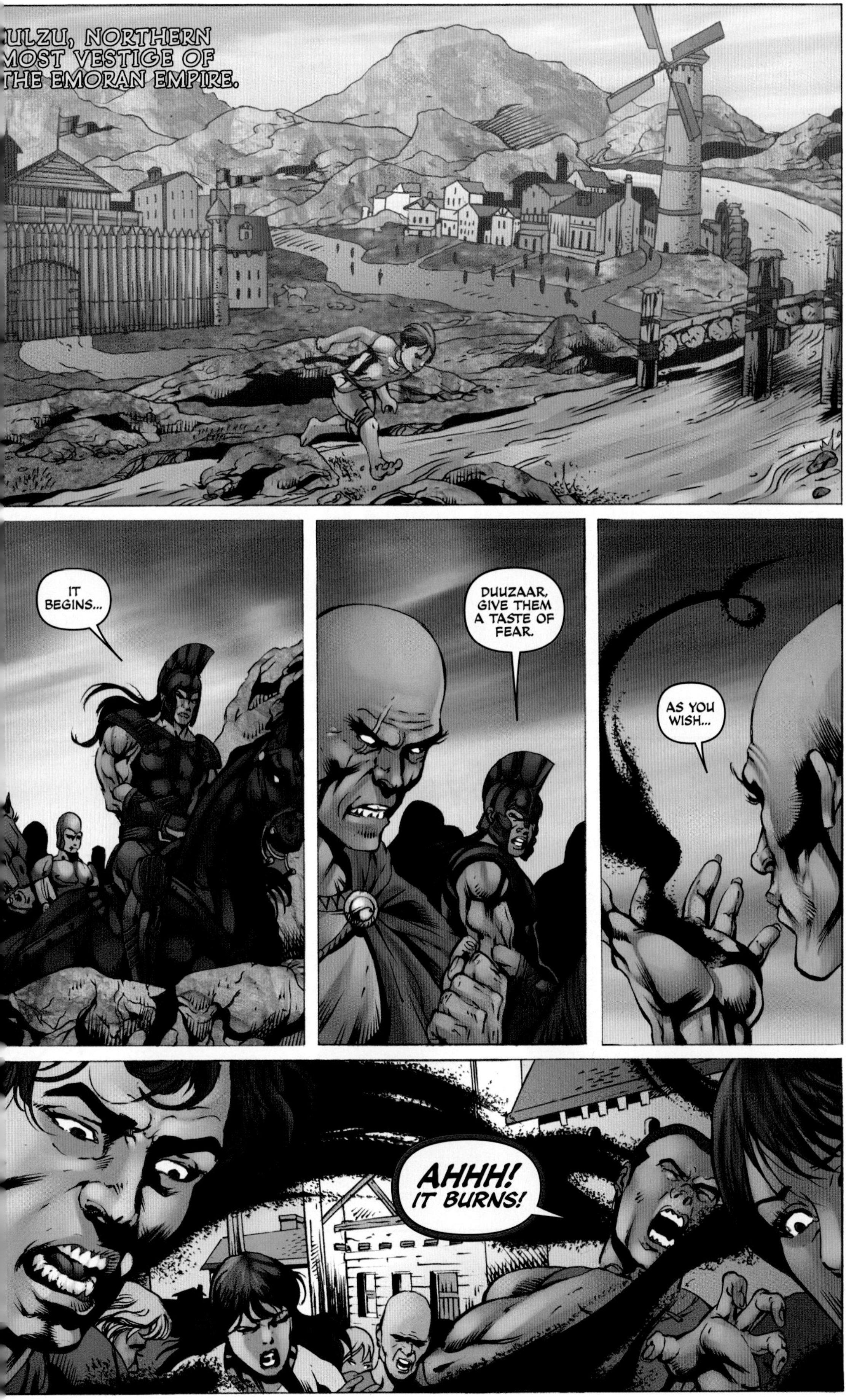
ULZU, NORTHERN MOST VESTIGE OF THE EMORAN EMPIRE.
IT BEGINS...
DUUZAAR, GIVE THEM A TASTE OF FEAR.
AS YOU WISH...
AHHH! IT BURNS!

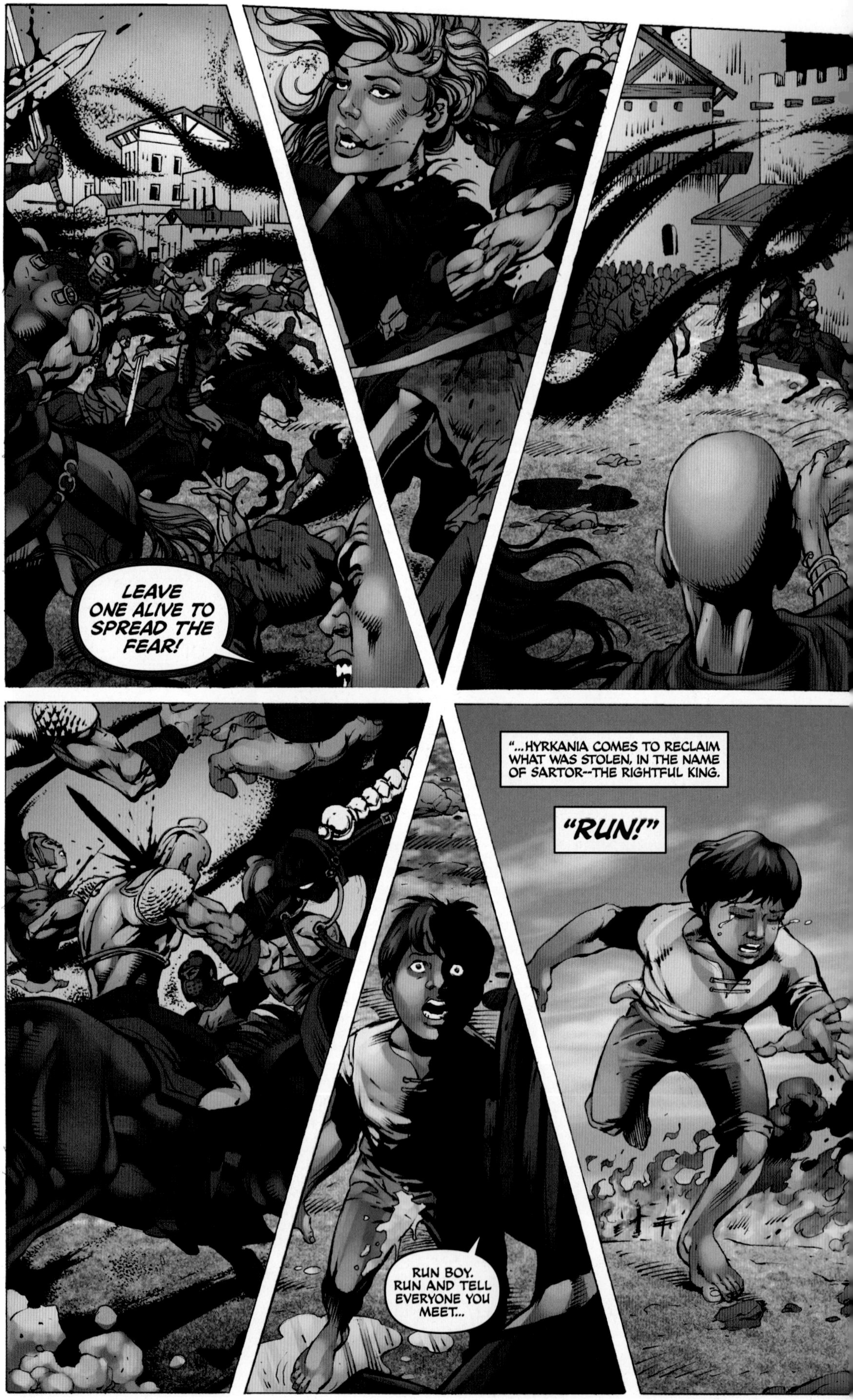
LEAVE ONE ALIVE TO SPREAD THE FEAR!
RUN BOY. RUN AND TELL EVERYONE YOU MEET...
"...HYRKANIA COMES TO RECLAIM WHAT WAS STOLEN, IN THE NAME OF SARTOR--THE RIGHTFUL KING.
"RUN!"

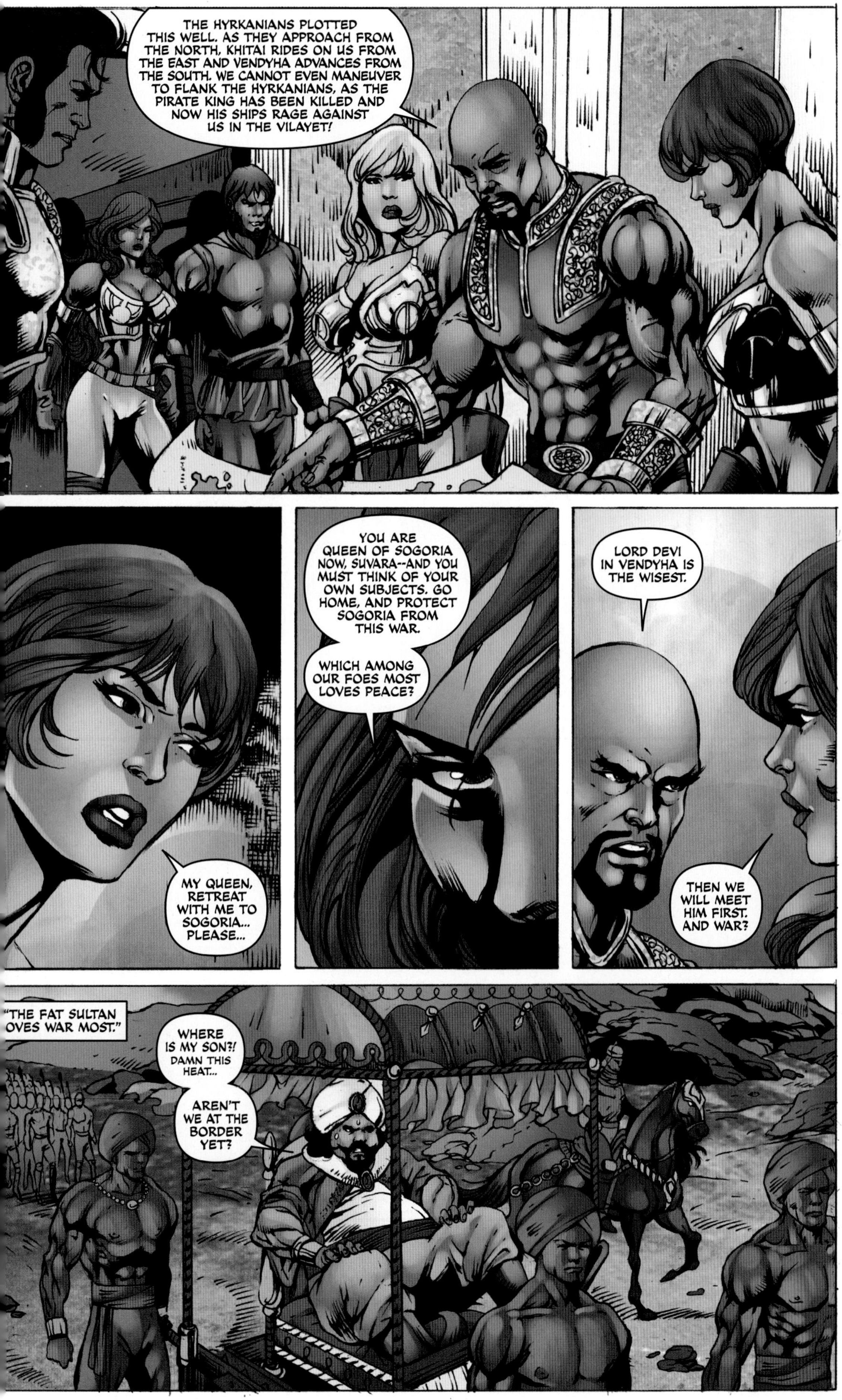

THE HYRKANIANS PLOTTED THIS WELL. AS THEY APPROACH FROM THE NORTH, KHITAI RIDES ON US FROM THE EAST AND VENDYHA ADVANCES FROM THE SOUTH. WE CANNOT EVEN MANEUVER TO FLANK THE HYRKANIANS, AS THE PIRATE KING HAS BEEN KILLED AND NOW HIS SHIPS RAGE AGAINST US IN THE VILAYET!
MY QUEEN, RETREAT WITH ME TO SOGORIA... PLEASE...
YOU ARE QUEEN OF SOGORIA NOW, SUVARA--AND YOU MUST THINK OF YOUR OWN SUBJECTS. GO HOME, AND PROTECT SOGORIA FROM THIS WAR.
WHICH AMONG OUR FOES MOST LOVES PEACE?
LORD DEVI IN VENDYHA IS THE WISEST.
THEN WE WILL MEET HIM FIRST. AND WAR?
"THE FAT SULTAN LOVES WAR MOST."
WHERE IS MY SON?! DAMN THIS HEAT...
AREN'T WE AT THE BORDER YET?

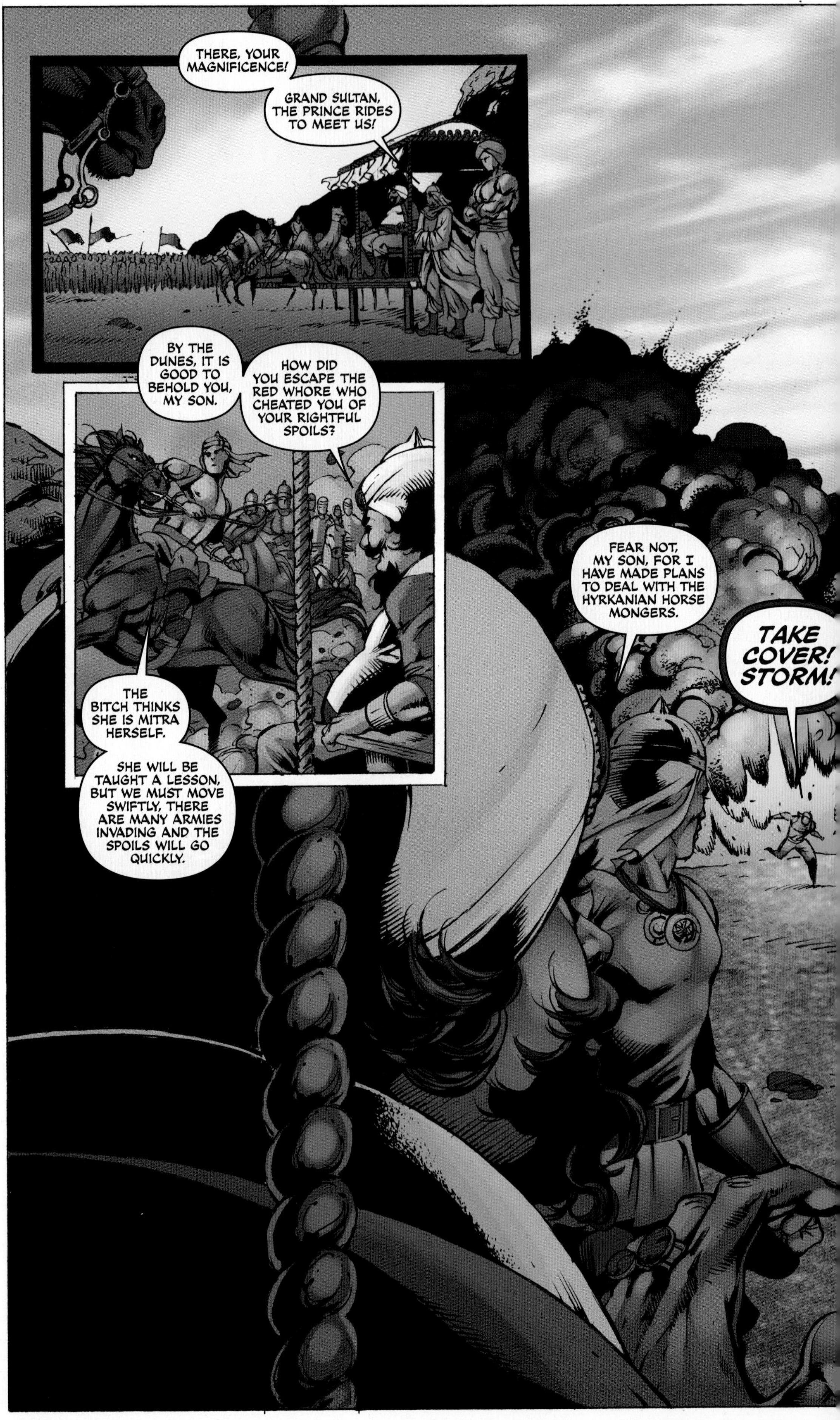
THERE, YOUR MAGNIFICENCE!
GRAND SULTAN, THE PRINCE RIDES TO MEET US!
BY THE DUNES, IT IS GOOD TO BEHOLD YOU, MY SON.
HOW DID YOU ESCAPE THE RED WHORE WHO CHEATED YOU OF YOUR RIGHTFUL SPOILS?
THE BITCH THINKS SHE IS MITRA HERSELF.
SHE WILL BE TAUGHT A LESSON, BUT WE MUST MOVE SWIFTLY, THERE ARE MANY ARMIES INVADING AND THE SPOILS WILL GO QUICKLY.
FEAR NOT, MY SON, FOR I HAVE MADE PLANS TO DEAL WITH THE HYRKANIAN HORSE MONGERS.
TAKE COVER! STORM!

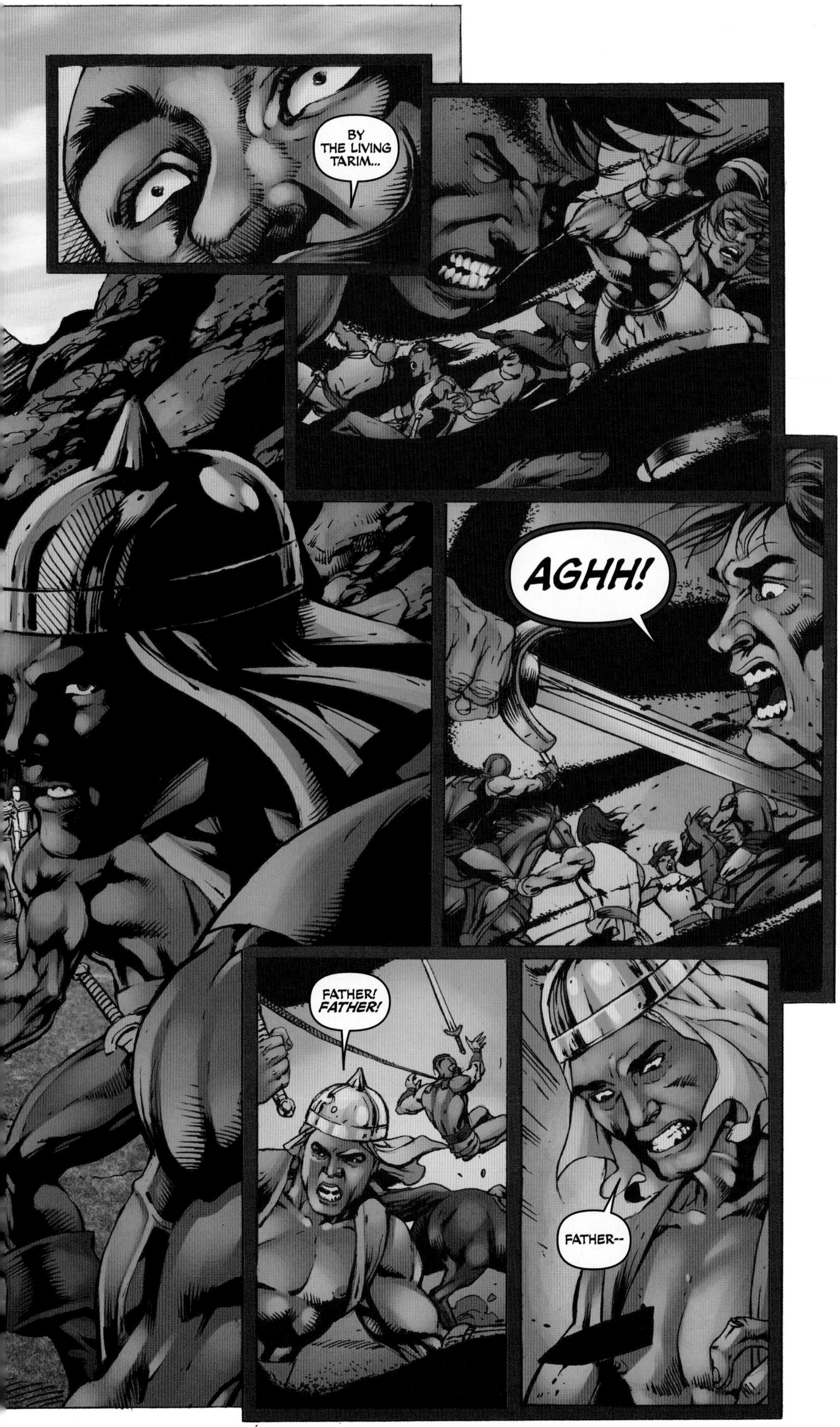
BY THE LIVING TARIM...
AGHH!
FATHER! FATHER!
FATHER--

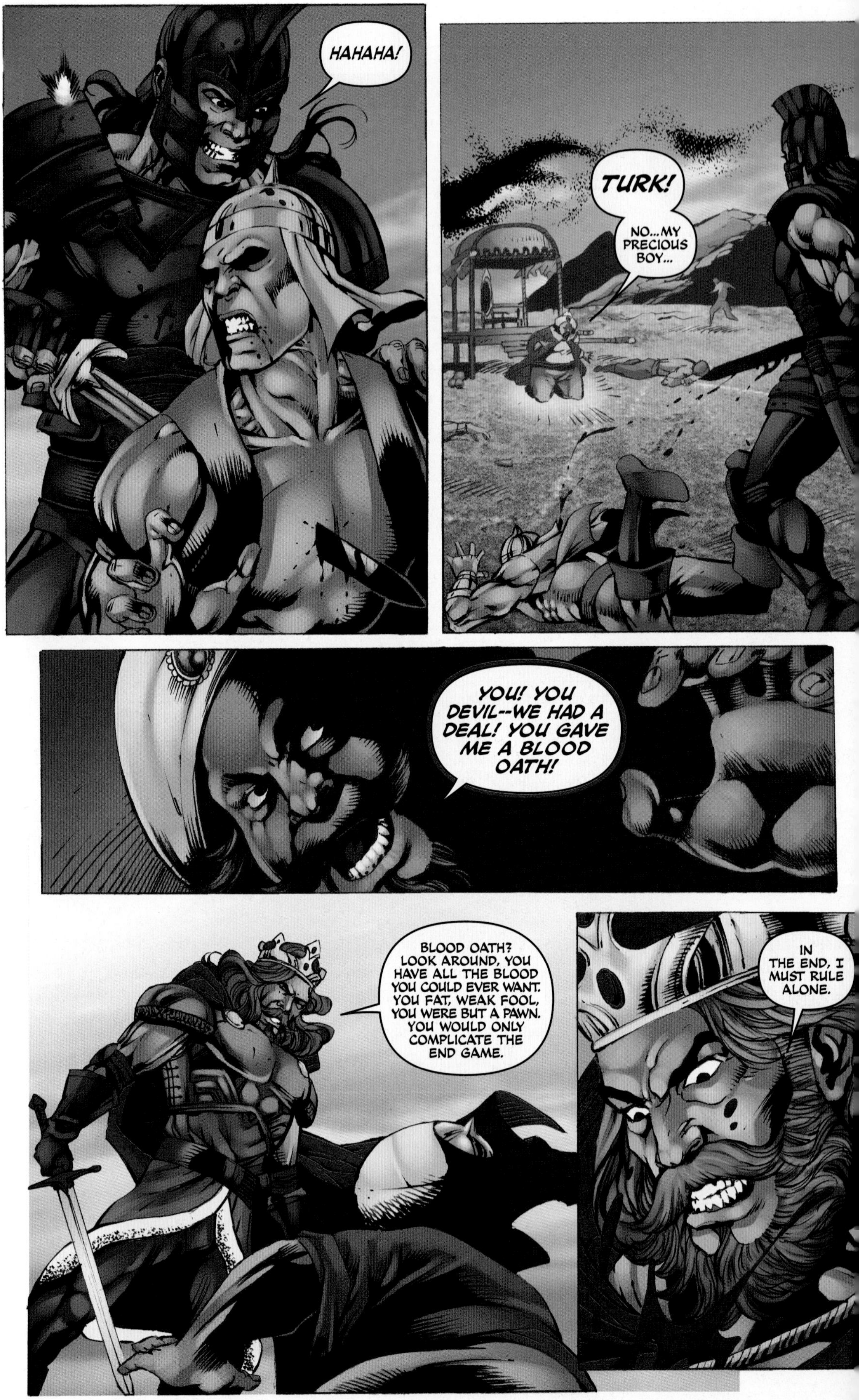
HAHAHA!
TURK!
NO...MY PRECIOUS BOY...
YOU! YOU DEVIL--WE HAD A DEAL! YOU GAVE ME A BLOOD OATH!
BLOOD OATH? LOOK AROUND, YOU HAVE ALL THE BLOOD YOU COULD EVER WANT. YOU FAT, WEAK FOOL, YOU WERE BUT A PAWN. YOU WOULD ONLY COMPLICATE THE END GAME.
IN THE END, I MUST RULE ALONE.

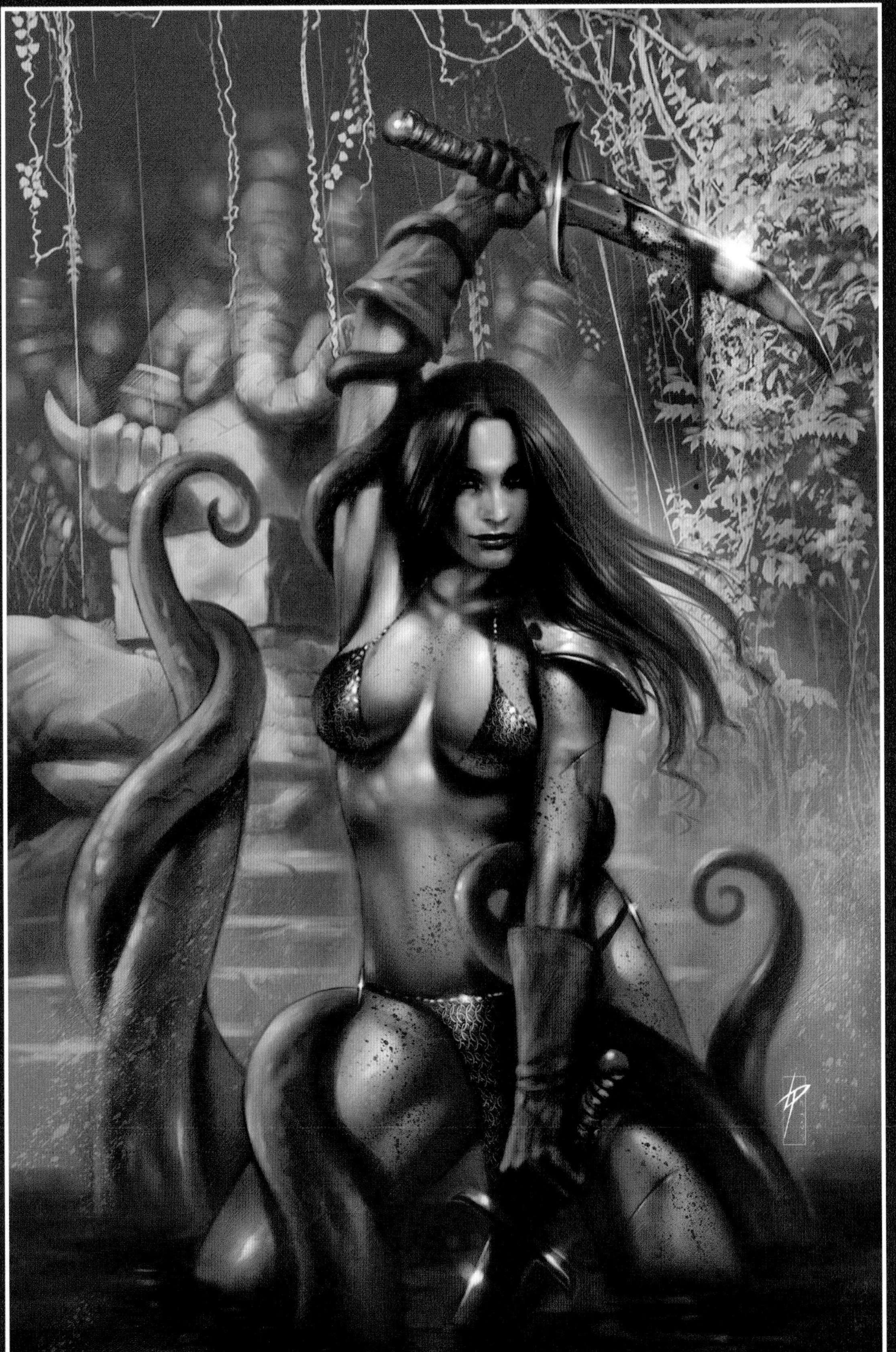

ISSUE #33 COVER BY LUCIO PARRILLO

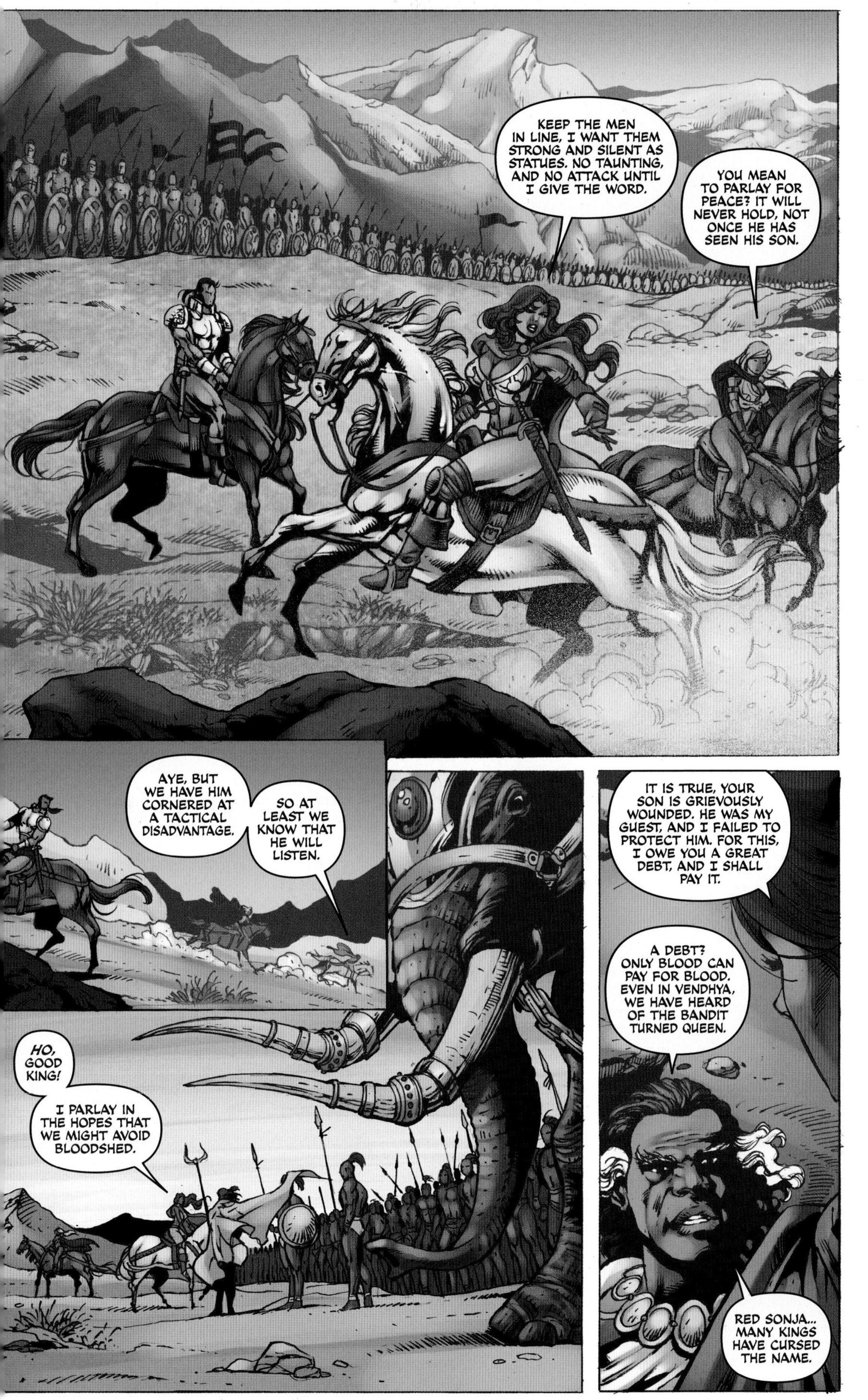
KEEP THE MEN IN LINE, I WANT THEM STRONG AND SILENT AS STATUES. NO TAUNTING, AND NO ATTACK UNTIL I GIVE THE WORD.
YOU MEAN TO PARLAY FOR PEACE? IT WILL NEVER HOLD, NOT ONCE HE HAS SEEN HIS SON.
AYE, BUT WE HAVE HIM CORNERED AT A TACTICAL DISADVANTAGE.
SO AT LEAST WE KNOW THAT HE WILL LISTEN.
*HO,* GOOD KING!
I PARLAY IN THE HOPES THAT WE MIGHT AVOID BLOODSHED.
IT IS TRUE, YOUR SON IS GRIEVOUSLY WOUNDED. HE WAS MY GUEST, AND I FAILED TO PROTECT HIM. FOR THIS, I OWE YOU A GREAT DEBT, AND I SHALL PAY IT.
A DEBT? ONLY BLOOD CAN PAY FOR BLOOD. EVEN IN VENDHYA, WE HAVE HEARD OF THE BANDIT TURNED QUEEN.
RED SONJA... MANY KINGS HAVE CURSED THE NAME.

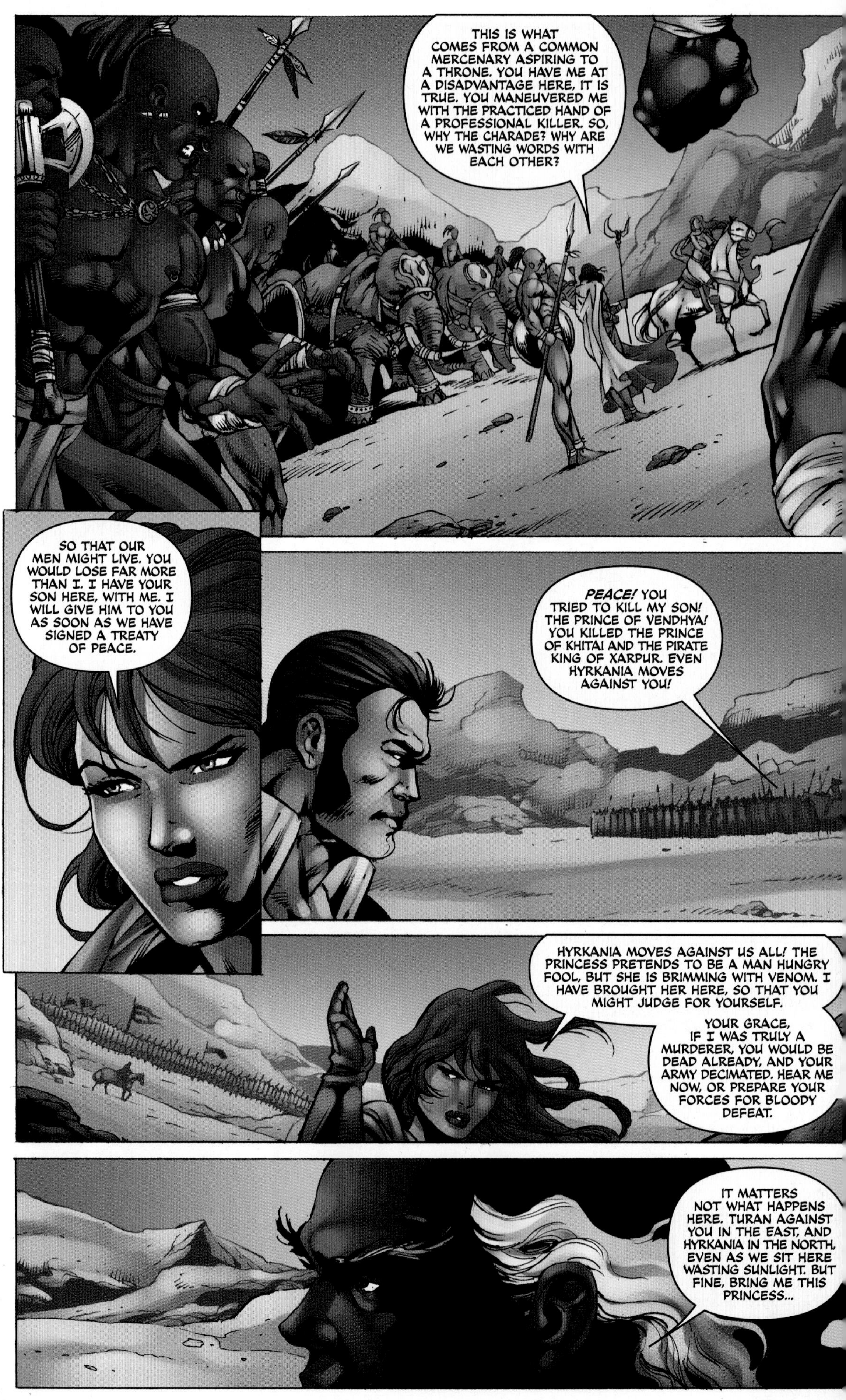
THIS IS WHAT COMES FROM A COMMON MERCENARY ASPIRING TO A THRONE. YOU HAVE ME AT A DISADVANTAGE HERE, IT IS TRUE. YOU MANEUVERED ME WITH THE PRACTICED HAND OF A PROFESSIONAL KILLER. SO, WHY THE CHARADE? WHY ARE WE WASTING WORDS WITH EACH OTHER?
SO THAT OUR MEN MIGHT LIVE. YOU WOULD LOSE FAR MORE THAN I. I HAVE YOUR SON HERE, WITH ME. I WILL GIVE HIM TO YOU AS SOON AS WE HAVE SIGNED A TREATY OF PEACE.
PEACE! YOU TRIED TO KILL MY SON! THE PRINCE OF VENDHYA! YOU KILLED THE PRINCE OF KHITAI AND THE PIRATE KING OF XARPUR. EVEN HYRKANIA MOVES AGAINST YOU!
HYRKANIA MOVES AGAINST US ALL! THE PRINCESS PRETENDS TO BE A MAN HUNGRY FOOL, BUT SHE IS BRIMMING WITH VENOM. I HAVE BROUGHT HER HERE, SO THAT YOU MIGHT JUDGE FOR YOURSELF.
YOUR GRACE, IF I WAS TRULY A MURDERER, YOU WOULD BE DEAD ALREADY, AND YOUR ARMY DECIMATED. HEAR ME NOW, OR PREPARE YOUR FORCES FOR BLOODY DEFEAT.
IT MATTERS NOT WHAT HAPPENS HERE. TURAN AGAINST YOU IN THE EAST, AND HYRKANIA IN THE NORTH, EVEN AS WE SIT HERE WASTING SUNLIGHT. BUT FINE, BRING ME THIS PRINCESS...

WHAT HAVE YOU DONE TO HER?

SHE IS OF ROYAL BLOOD, YET YOU TREAT HER AS A SLAVE?

WHAT SHE DESERVES, FOR SHE IS A PRINCESS NO LONGER.

SHE IS NOW A THRALL OF THE EMORAN EMPIRE.

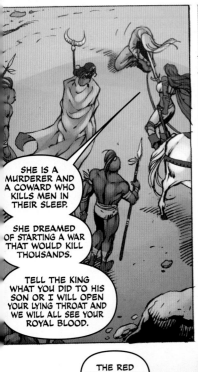

SHE IS A MURDERER AND A COWARD WHO KILLS MEN IN THEIR SLEEP.

SHE DREAMED OF STARTING A WAR THAT WOULD KILL THOUSANDS.

TELL THE KING WHAT YOU DID TO HIS SON OR I WILL OPEN YOUR LYING THROAT AND WE WILL ALL SEE YOUR ROYAL BLOOD.

EMORA IS A USURPER KINGDOM, IT HAD TO FALL. THE PRINCES WERE BUT A SMALL PRICE TO PAY.

MY SON'S LIFE MEANS SO LITTLE TO YOU?

FATHER!

THE RED QUEEN TELLS IT TRUE!

IT WAS HYRKANIA THAT CONSPIRED AGAINST US!

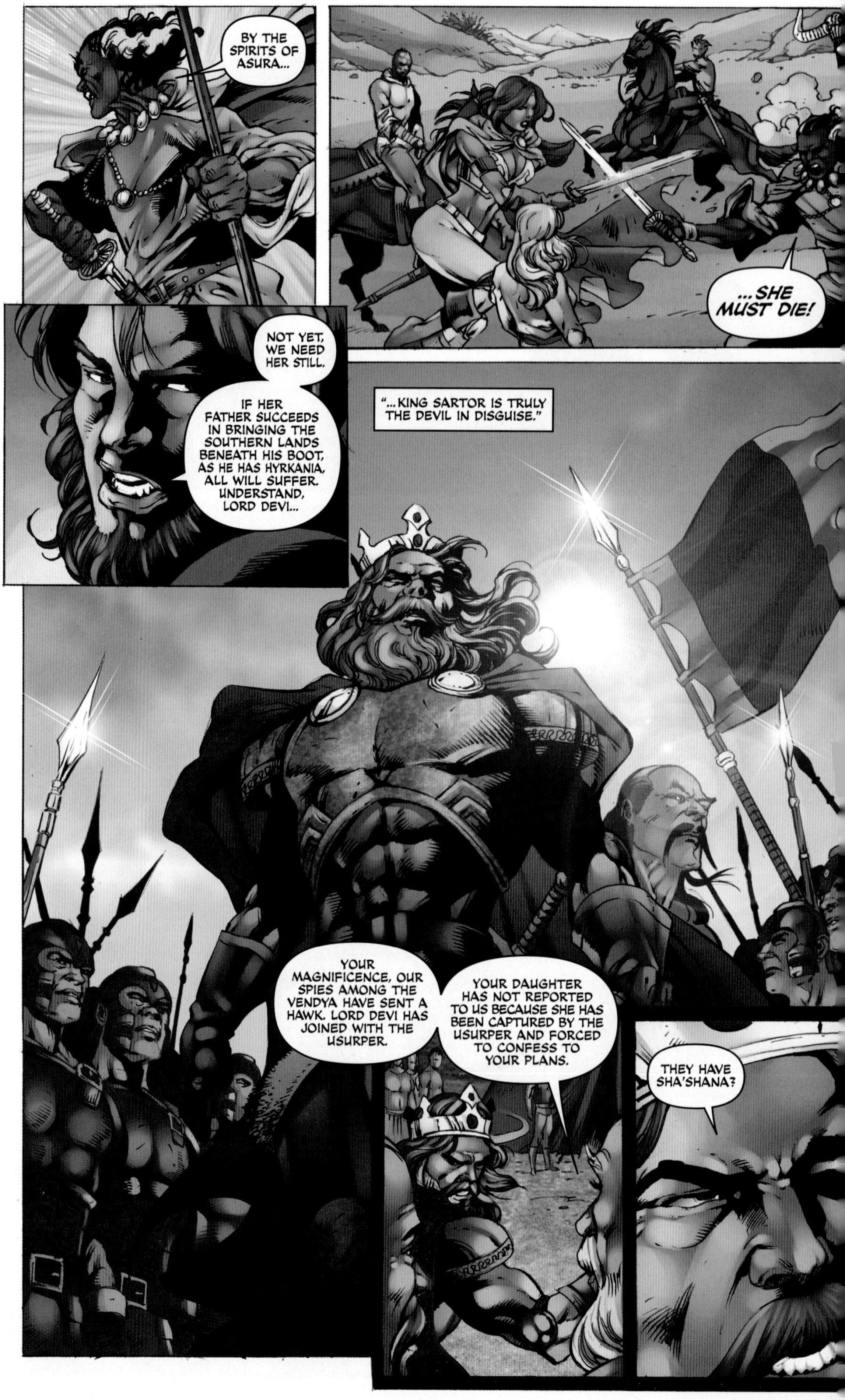
BY THE SPIRITS OF ASURA...
...SHE MUST DIE!
NOT YET, WE NEED HER STILL.
IF HER FATHER SUCCEEDS IN BRINGING THE SOUTHERN LANDS BENEATH HIS BOOT, AS HE HAS HYRKANIA, ALL WILL SUFFER. UNDERSTAND, LORD DEVI...
"...KING SARTOR IS TRULY THE DEVIL IN DISGUISE."
YOUR MAGNIFICENCE, OUR SPIES AMONG THE VENDYA HAVE SENT A HAWK. LORD DEVI HAS JOINED WITH THE USURPER.
YOUR DAUGHTER HAS NOT REPORTED TO US BECAUSE SHE HAS BEEN CAPTURED BY THE USURPER AND FORCED TO CONFESS TO YOUR PLANS.
THEY HAVE SHA'SHANA?

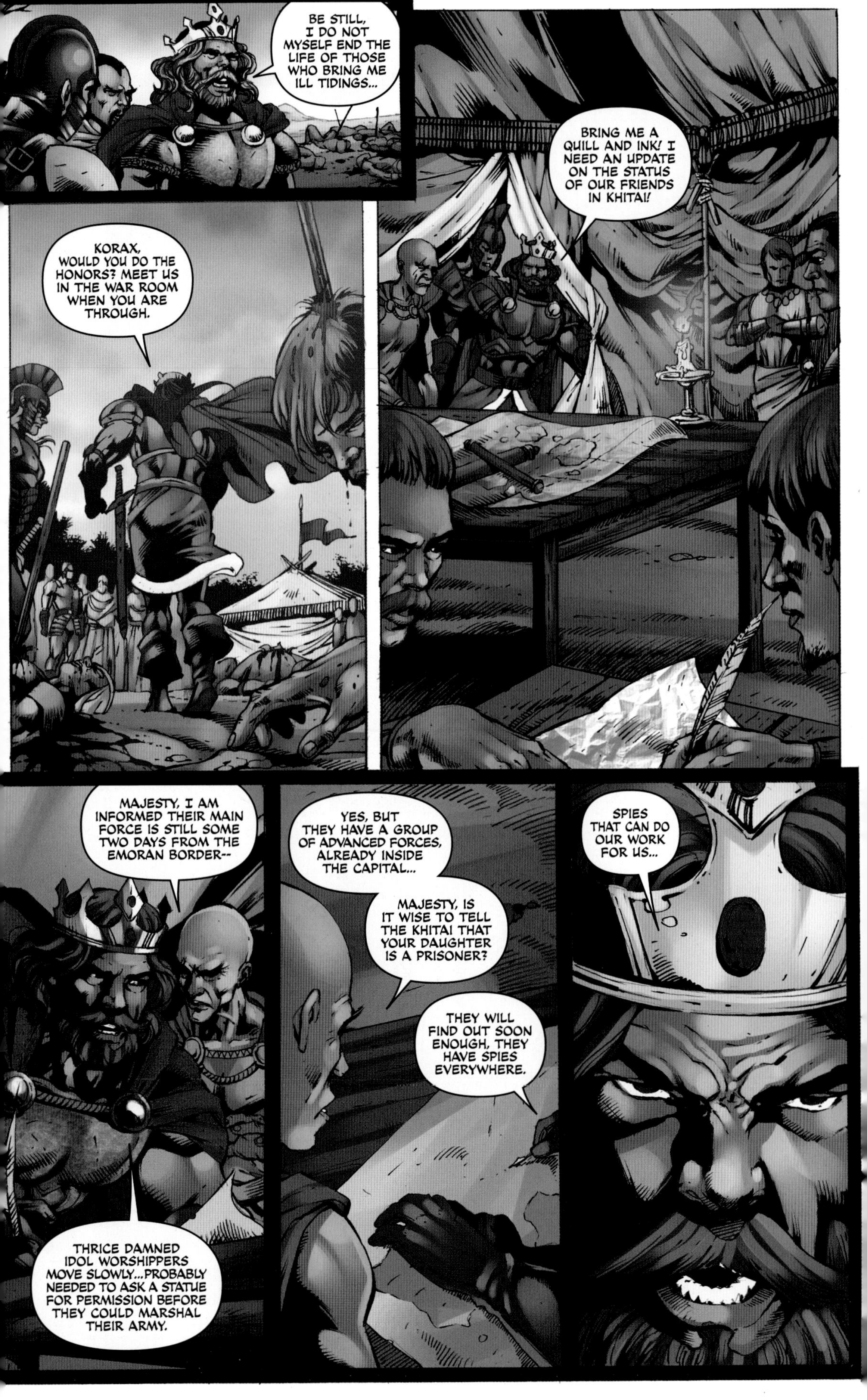
BE STILL, I DO NOT MYSELF END THE LIFE OF THOSE WHO BRING ME ILL TIDINGS...
KORAX, WOULD YOU DO THE HONORS? MEET US IN THE WAR ROOM WHEN YOU ARE THROUGH.
BRING ME A QUILL AND INK! I NEED AN UPDATE ON THE STATUS OF OUR FRIENDS IN KHITAI!
MAJESTY, I AM INFORMED THEIR MAIN FORCE IS STILL SOME TWO DAYS FROM THE EMORAN BORDER--
THRICE DAMNED IDOL WORSHIPPERS MOVE SLOWLY...PROBABLY NEEDED TO ASK A STATUE FOR PERMISSION BEFORE THEY COULD MARSHAL THEIR ARMY.
YES, BUT THEY HAVE A GROUP OF ADVANCED FORCES, ALREADY INSIDE THE CAPITAL...
MAJESTY, IS IT WISE TO TELL THE KHITAI THAT YOUR DAUGHTER IS A PRISONER?
THEY WILL FIND OUT SOON ENOUGH, THEY HAVE SPIES EVERYWHERE.
SPIES THAT CAN DO OUR WORK FOR US...

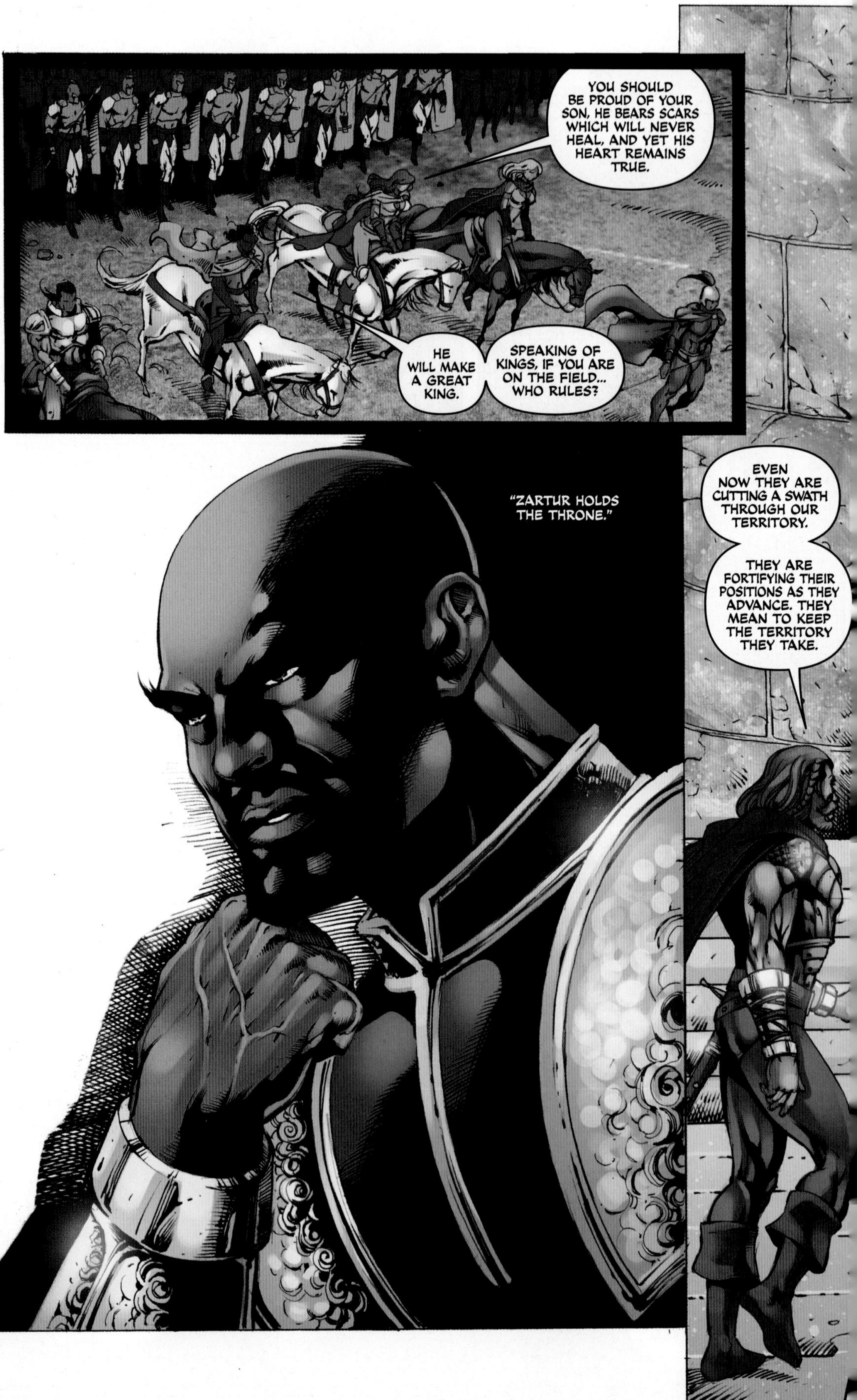
YOU SHOULD BE PROUD OF YOUR SON, HE BEARS SCARS WHICH WILL NEVER HEAL, AND YET HIS HEART REMAINS TRUE.
HE WILL MAKE A GREAT KING.
SPEAKING OF KINGS, IF YOU ARE ON THE FIELD... WHO RULES?
"ZARTUR HOLDS THE THRONE."
EVEN NOW THEY ARE CUTTING A SWATH THROUGH OUR TERRITORY.
THEY ARE FORTIFYING THEIR POSITIONS AS THEY ADVANCE. THEY MEAN TO KEEP THE TERRITORY THEY TAKE.

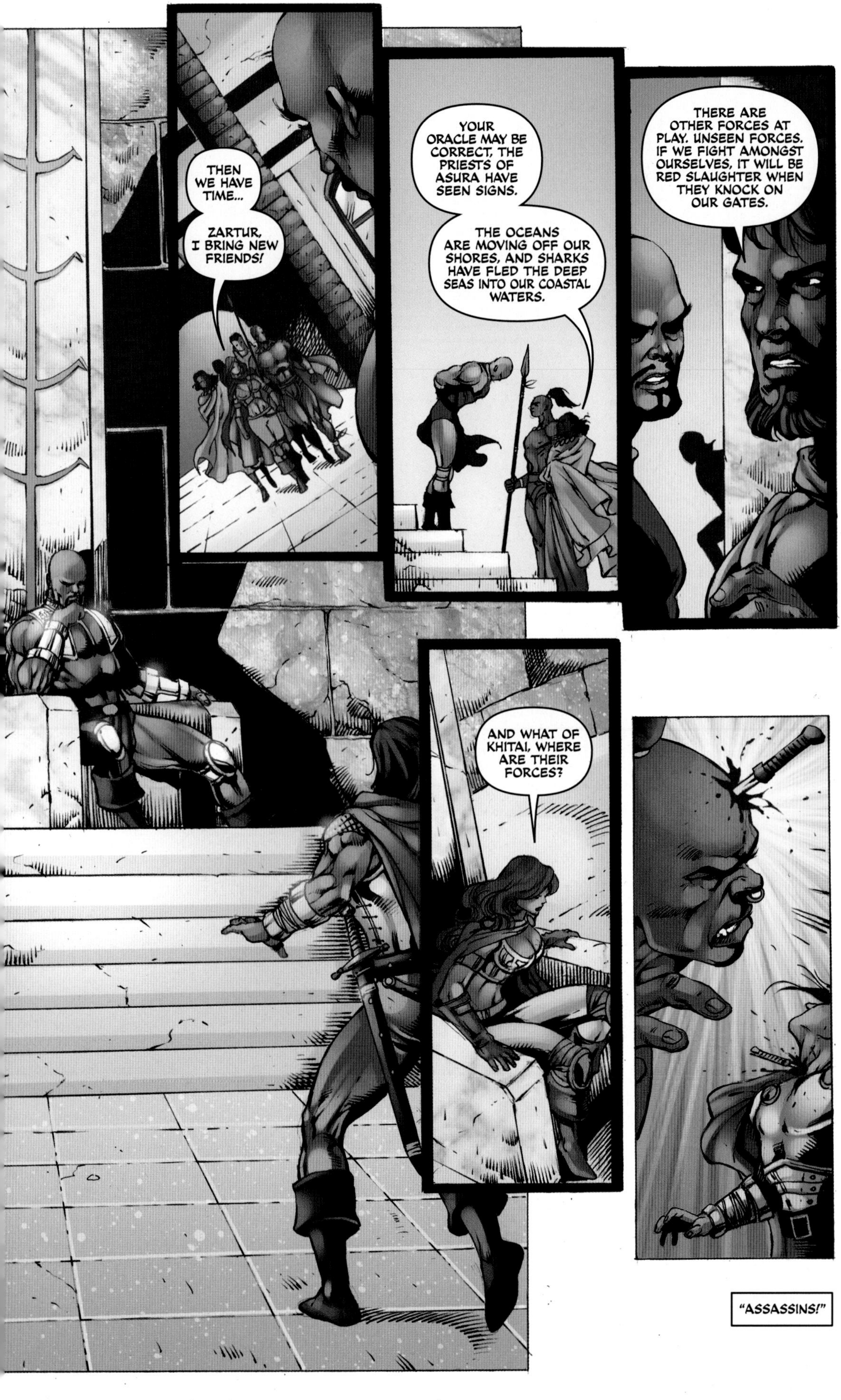
THEN WE HAVE TIME...
ZARTUR, I BRING NEW FRIENDS!
YOUR ORACLE MAY BE CORRECT, THE PRIESTS OF ASURA HAVE SEEN SIGNS.
THE OCEANS ARE MOVING OFF OUR SHORES, AND SHARKS HAVE FLED THE DEEP SEAS INTO OUR COASTAL WATERS.
THERE ARE OTHER FORCES AT PLAY. UNSEEN FORCES. IF WE FIGHT AMONGST OURSELVES, IT WILL BE RED SLAUGHTER WHEN THEY KNOCK ON OUR GATES.
AND WHAT OF KHITAI, WHERE ARE THEIR FORCES?
"ASSASSINS!"

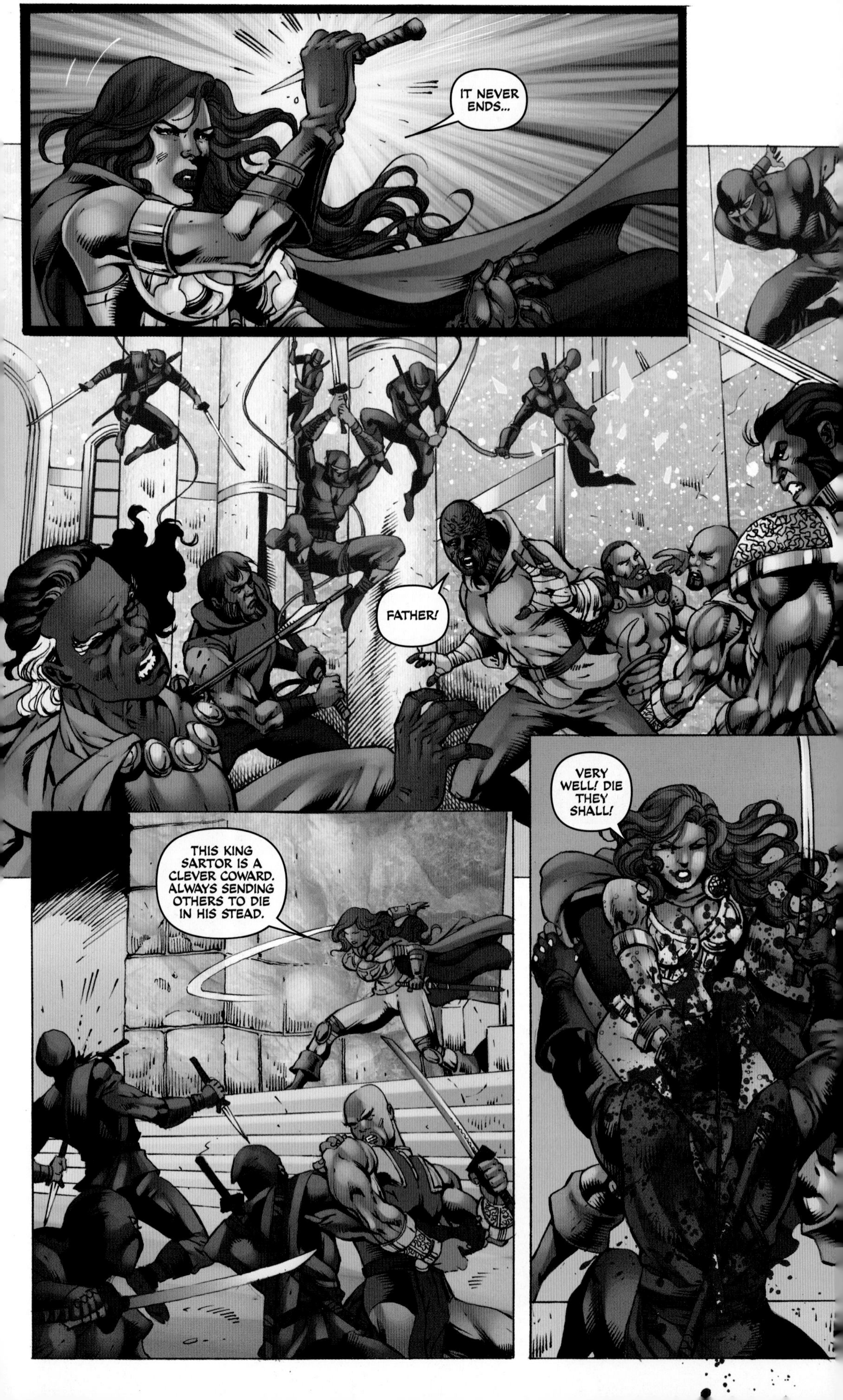
IT NEVER ENDS...
FATHER!
THIS KING SARTOR IS A CLEVER COWARD. ALWAYS SENDING OTHERS TO DIE IN HIS STEAD.
VERY WELL! DIE THEY SHALL!

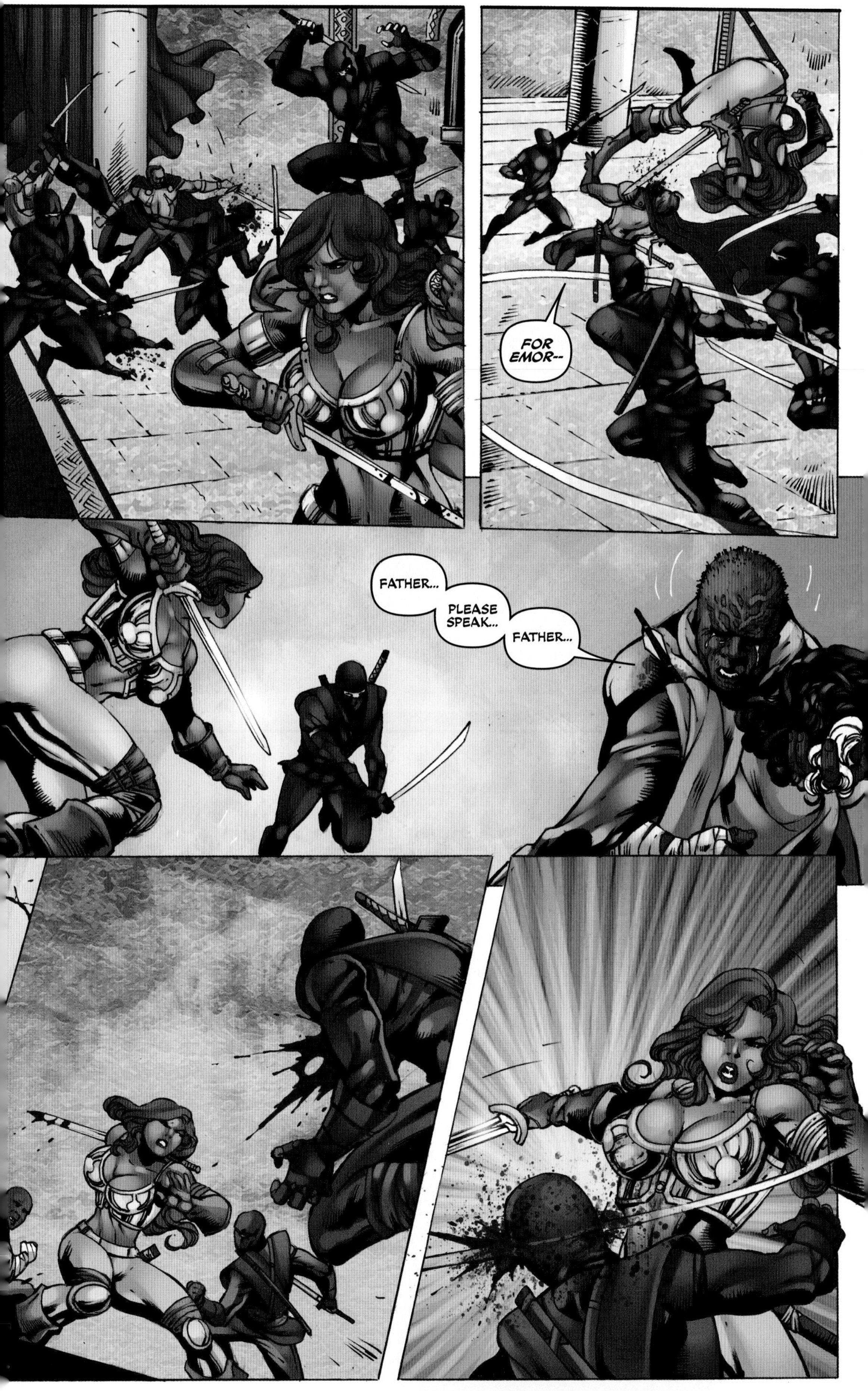
FOR EMOR--
FATHER...
PLEASE SPEAK...
FATHER...

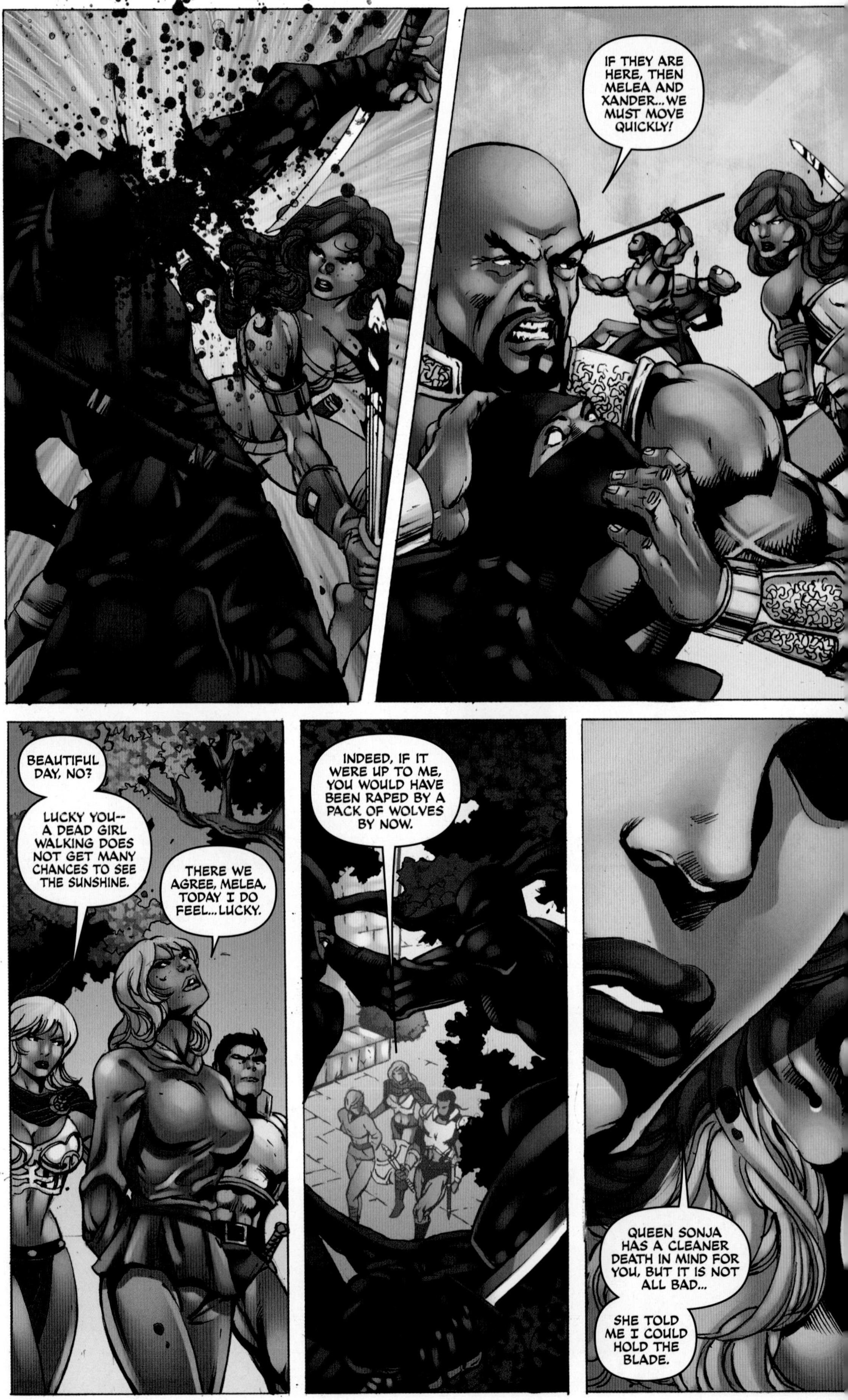

IF THEY ARE HERE, THEN MELEA AND XANDER...WE MUST MOVE QUICKLY!
BEAUTIFUL DAY, NO?
LUCKY YOU-- A DEAD GIRL WALKING DOES NOT GET MANY CHANCES TO SEE THE SUNSHINE.
THERE WE AGREE, MELEA. TODAY I DO FEEL...LUCKY.
INDEED, IF IT WERE UP TO ME, YOU WOULD HAVE BEEN RAPED BY A PACK OF WOLVES BY NOW.
QUEEN SONJA HAS A CLEANER DEATH IN MIND FOR YOU, BUT IT IS NOT ALL BAD...
SHE TOLD ME I COULD HOLD THE BLADE.

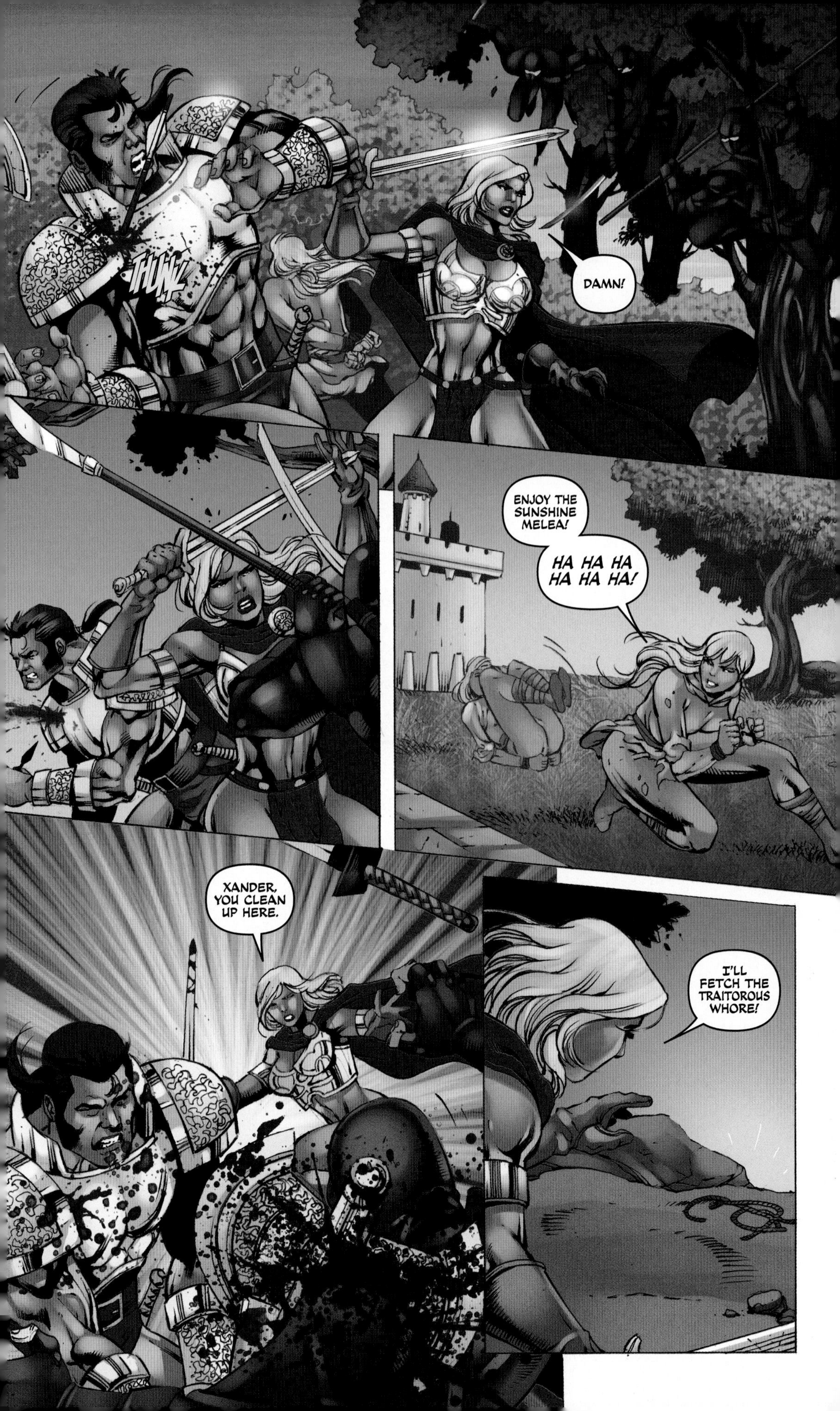
THUNK
DAMN!
ENJOY THE SUNSHINE MELEA!
HA HA HA HA HA HA!
XANDER, YOU CLEAN UP HERE.
I'LL FETCH THE TRAITOROUS WHORE!

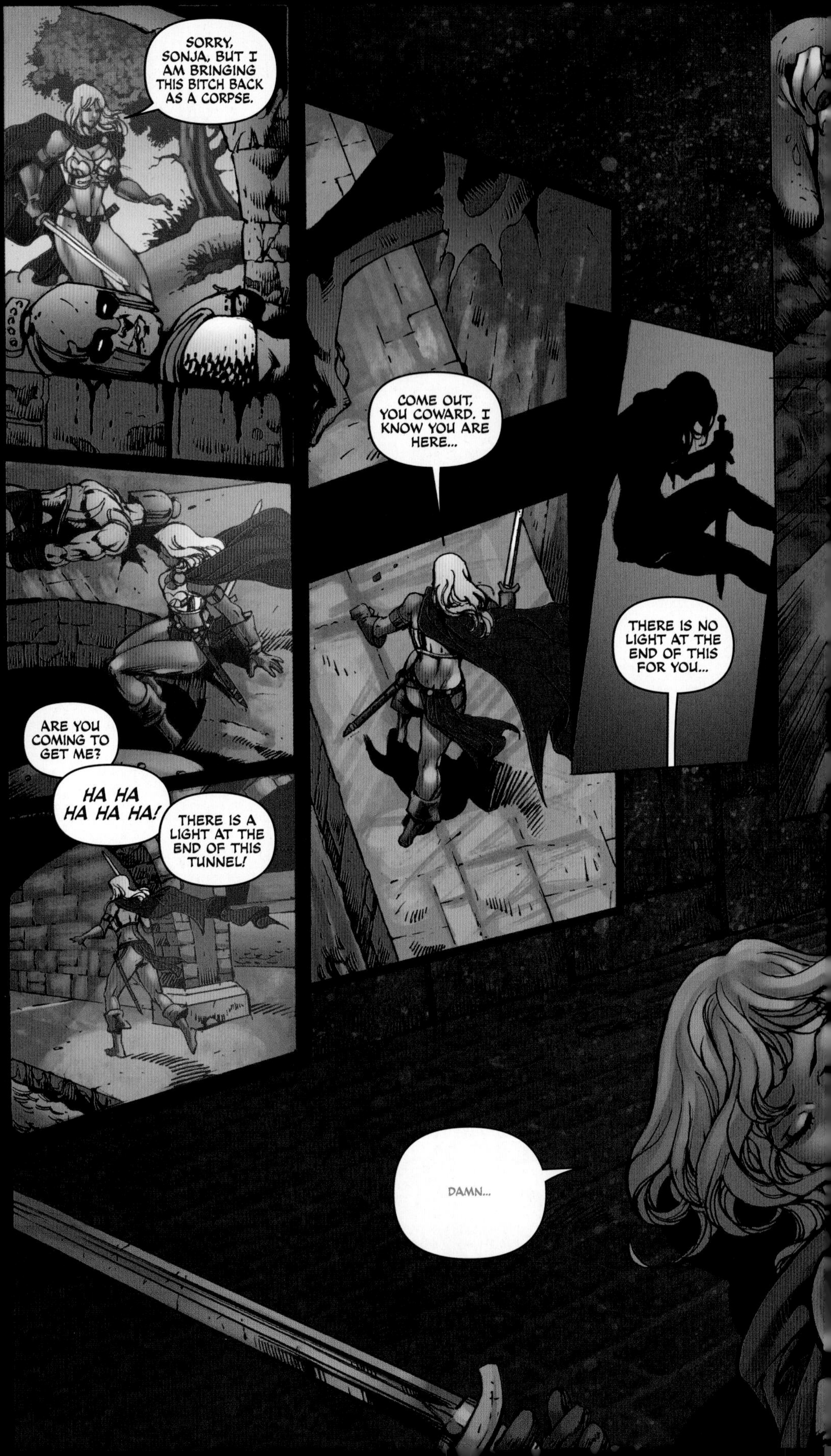
SORRY, SONJA, BUT I AM BRINGING THIS BITCH BACK AS A CORPSE.
COME OUT, YOU COWARD. I KNOW YOU ARE HERE...
THERE IS NO LIGHT AT THE END OF THIS FOR YOU...
ARE YOU COMING TO GET ME?
HA HA HA HA HA!
THERE IS A LIGHT AT THE END OF THIS TUNNEL!
DAMN...

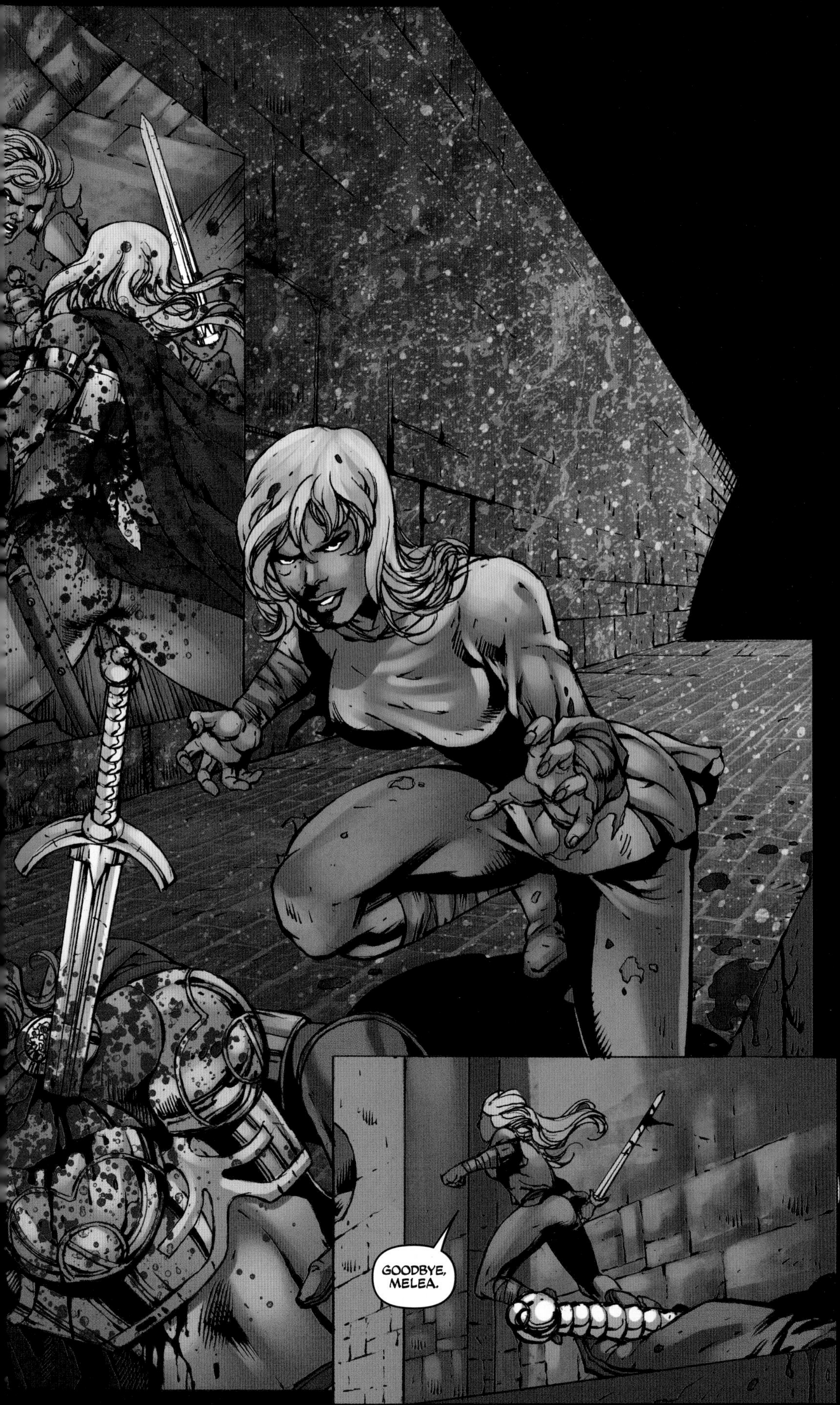
GOODBYE, MELEA.

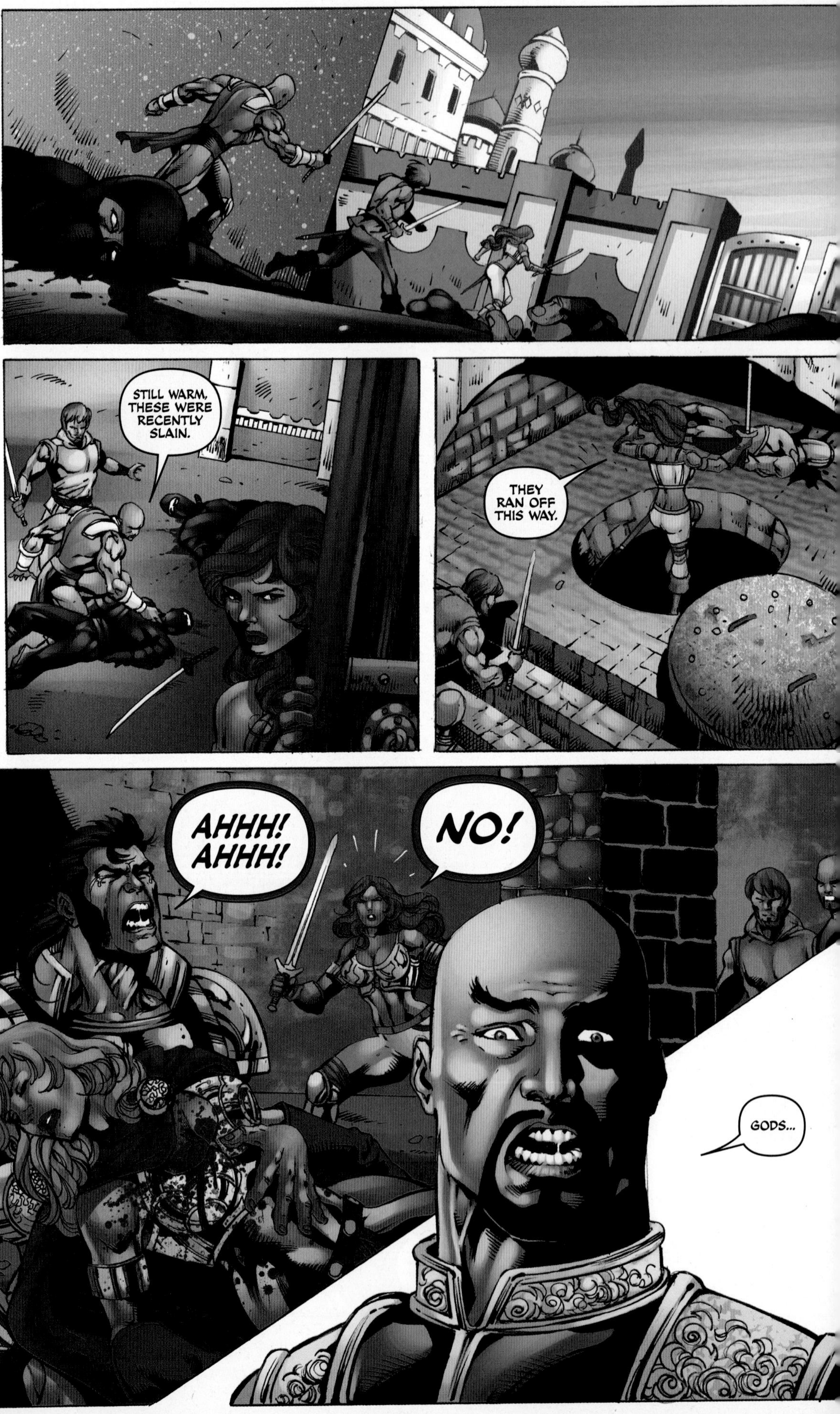
STILL WARM, THESE WERE RECENTLY SLAIN.
THEY RAN OFF THIS WAY.
AHHH! AHHH!
NO!
GODS...

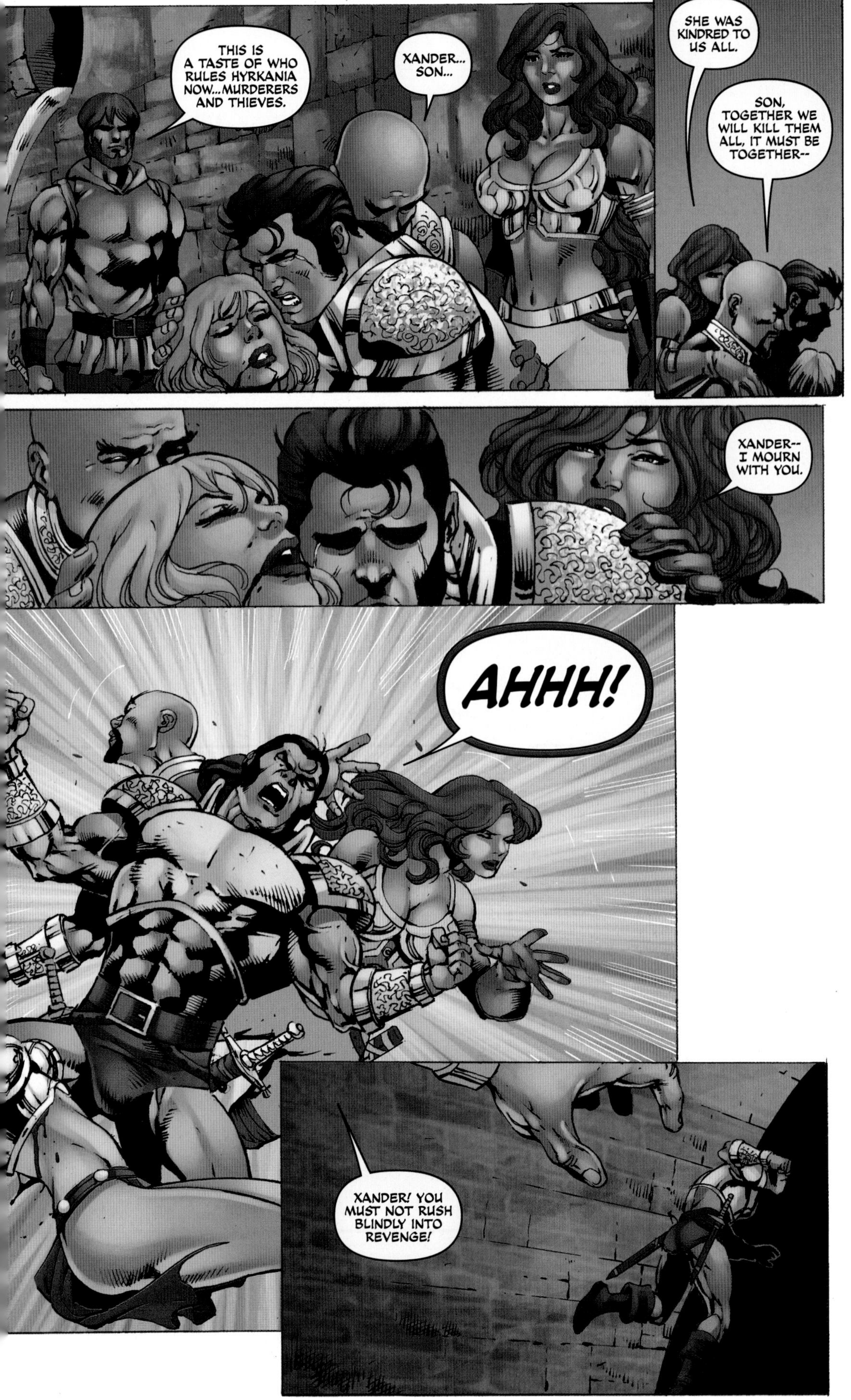
THIS IS A TASTE OF WHO RULES HYRKANIA NOW...MURDERERS AND THIEVES.
XANDER... SON...
SHE WAS KINDRED TO US ALL.
SON, TOGETHER WE WILL KILL THEM ALL, IT MUST BE TOGETHER--
XANDER-- I MOURN WITH YOU.
AHHH!
XANDER! YOU MUST NOT RUSH BLINDLY INTO REVENGE!

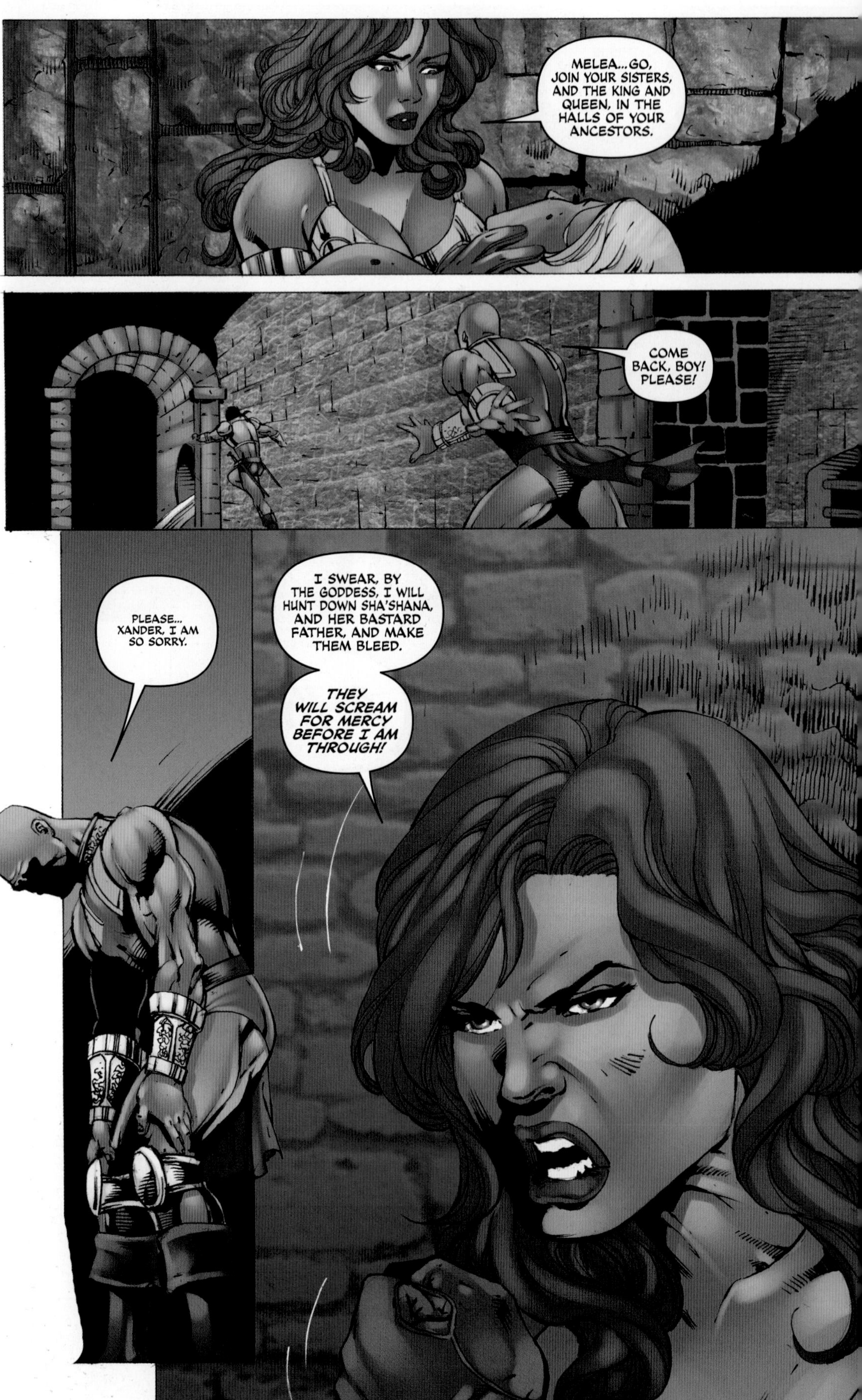
MELEA...GO, JOIN YOUR SISTERS, AND THE KING AND QUEEN, IN THE HALLS OF YOUR ANCESTORS.
COME BACK, BOY! PLEASE!
PLEASE... XANDER, I AM SO SORRY.
I SWEAR, BY THE GODDESS, I WILL HUNT DOWN SHA'SHANA, AND HER BASTARD FATHER, AND MAKE THEM BLEED.
THEY WILL SCREAM FOR MERCY BEFORE I AM THROUGH!

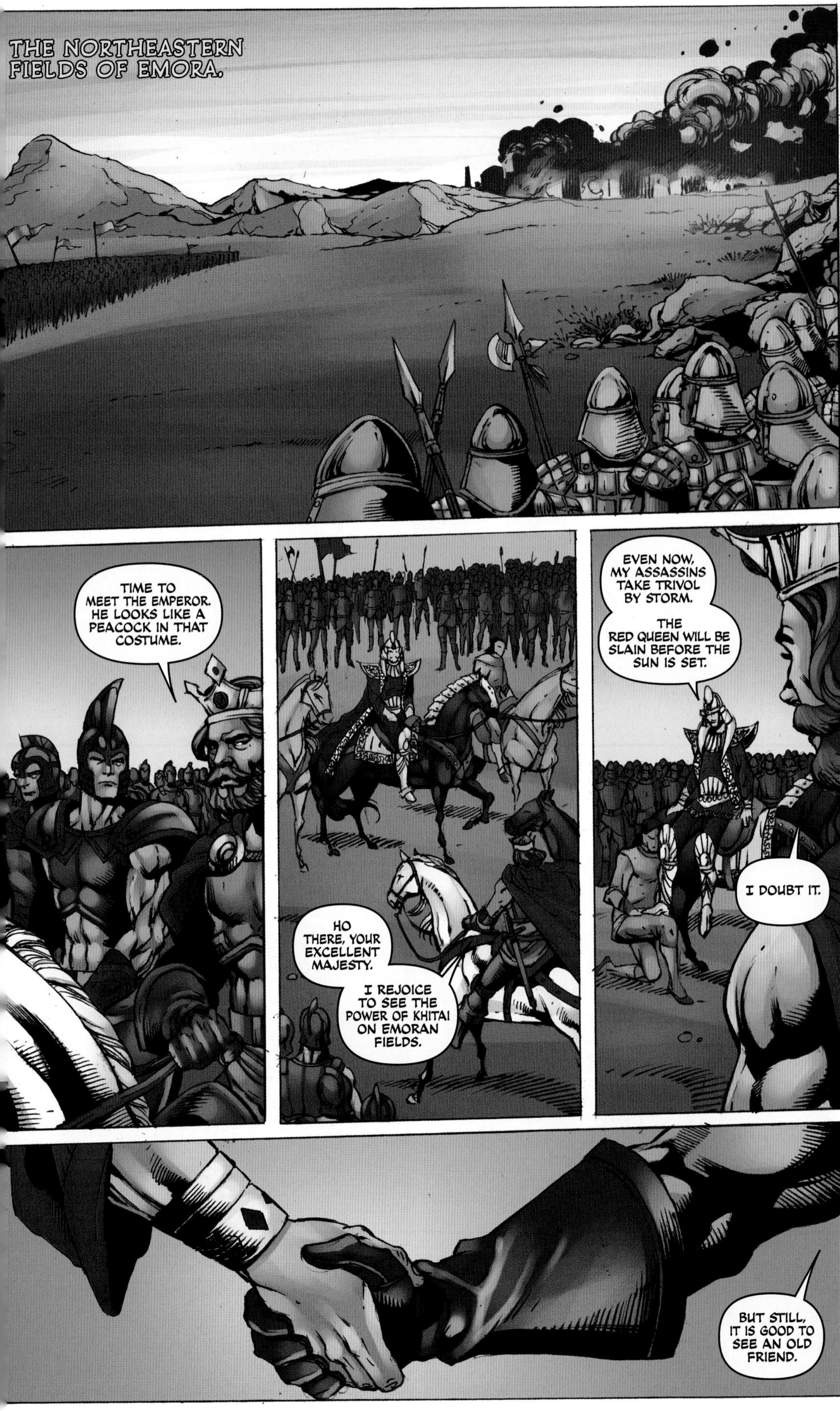
THE NORTHEASTERN FIELDS OF EMORA.
TIME TO MEET THE EMPEROR. HE LOOKS LIKE A PEACOCK IN THAT COSTUME.
HO THERE, YOUR EXCELLENT MAJESTY.
I REJOICE TO SEE THE POWER OF KHITAI ON EMORAN FIELDS.
EVEN NOW, MY ASSASSINS TAKE TRIVOL BY STORM.
THE RED QUEEN WILL BE SLAIN BEFORE THE SUN IS SET.
I DOUBT IT.
BUT STILL, IT IS GOOD TO SEE AN OLD FRIEND.

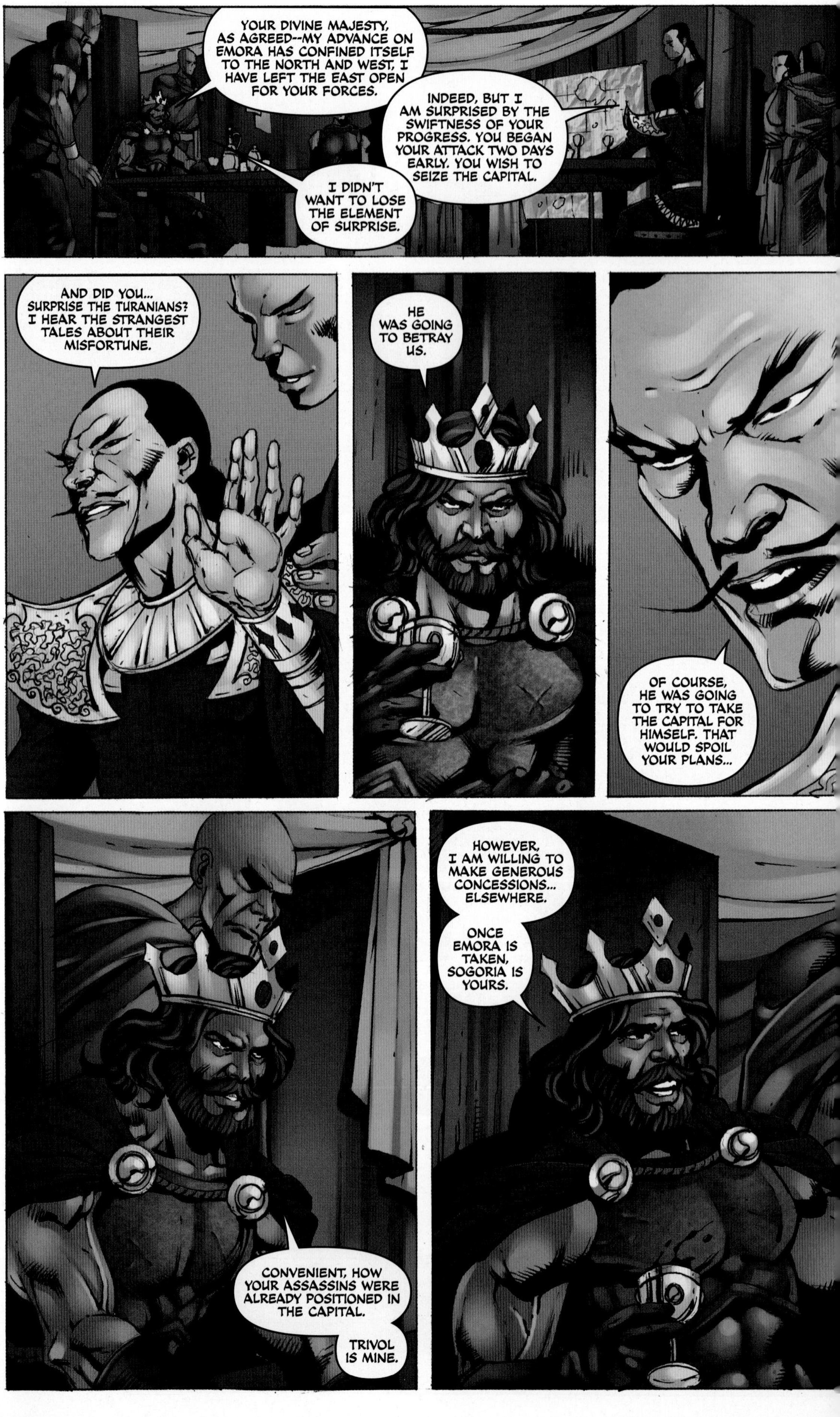
YOUR DIVINE MAJESTY, AS AGREED--MY ADVANCE ON EMORA HAS CONFINED ITSELF TO THE NORTH AND WEST, I HAVE LEFT THE EAST OPEN FOR YOUR FORCES.
INDEED, BUT I AM SURPRISED BY THE SWIFTNESS OF YOUR PROGRESS. YOU BEGAN YOUR ATTACK TWO DAYS EARLY. YOU WISH TO SEIZE THE CAPITAL.
I DIDN'T WANT TO LOSE THE ELEMENT OF SURPRISE.
AND DID YOU... SURPRISE THE TURANIANS? I HEAR THE STRANGEST TALES ABOUT THEIR MISFORTUNE.
HE WAS GOING TO BETRAY US.
OF COURSE, HE WAS GOING TO TRY TO TAKE THE CAPITAL FOR HIMSELF. THAT WOULD SPOIL YOUR PLANS...
CONVENIENT, HOW YOUR ASSASSINS WERE ALREADY POSITIONED IN THE CAPITAL.
TRIVOL IS MINE.
HOWEVER, I AM WILLING TO MAKE GENEROUS CONCESSIONS... ELSEWHERE.
ONCE EMORA IS TAKEN, SOGORIA IS YOURS.

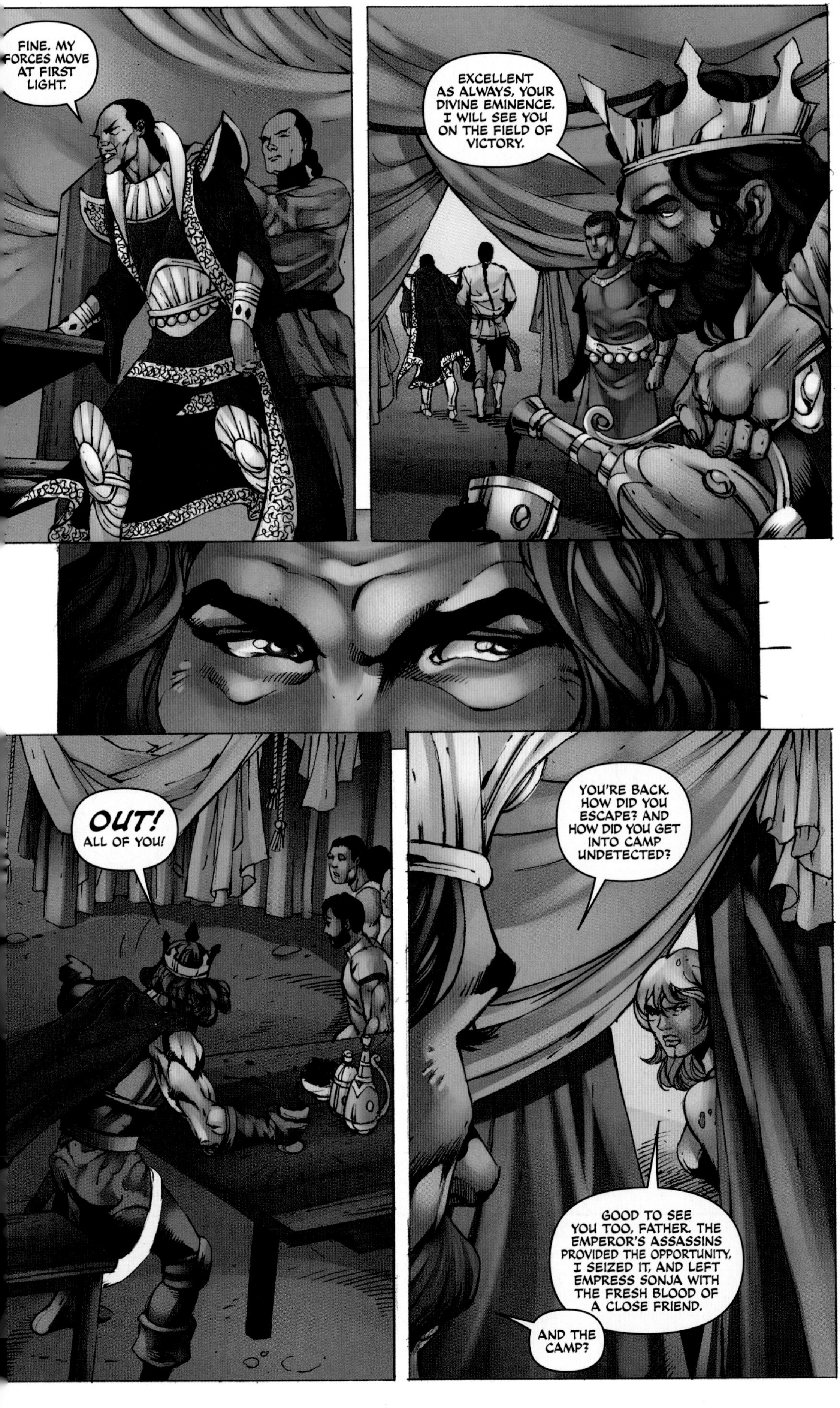
FINE. MY FORCES MOVE AT FIRST LIGHT.
EXCELLENT AS ALWAYS, YOUR DIVINE EMINENCE. I WILL SEE YOU ON THE FIELD OF VICTORY.
OUT! ALL OF YOU!
YOU'RE BACK. HOW DID YOU ESCAPE? AND HOW DID YOU GET INTO CAMP UNDETECTED?
GOOD TO SEE YOU TOO, FATHER. THE EMPEROR'S ASSASSINS PROVIDED THE OPPORTUNITY, I SEIZED IT, AND LEFT EMPRESS SONJA WITH THE FRESH BLOOD OF A CLOSE FRIEND.
AND THE CAMP?

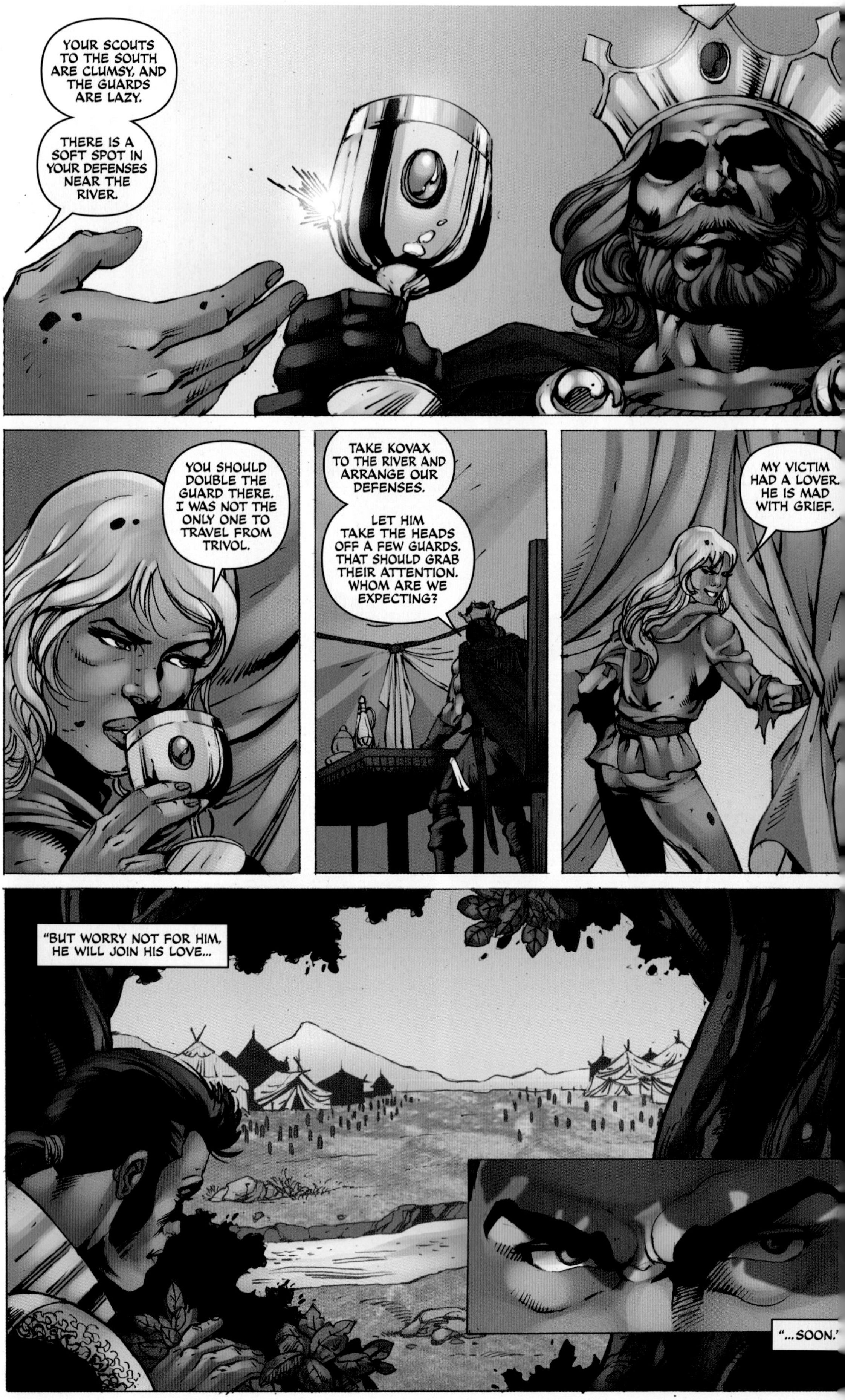

YOUR SCOUTS TO THE SOUTH ARE CLUMSY, AND THE GUARDS ARE LAZY.
THERE IS A SOFT SPOT IN YOUR DEFENSES NEAR THE RIVER.
YOU SHOULD DOUBLE THE GUARD THERE. I WAS NOT THE ONLY ONE TO TRAVEL FROM TRIVOL.
TAKE KOVAX TO THE RIVER AND ARRANGE OUR DEFENSES.
LET HIM TAKE THE HEADS OFF A FEW GUARDS. THAT SHOULD GRAB THEIR ATTENTION. WHOM ARE WE EXPECTING?
MY VICTIM HAD A LOVER. HE IS MAD WITH GRIEF.
"BUT WORRY NOT FOR HIM, HE WILL JOIN HIS LOVE...
"...SOON."

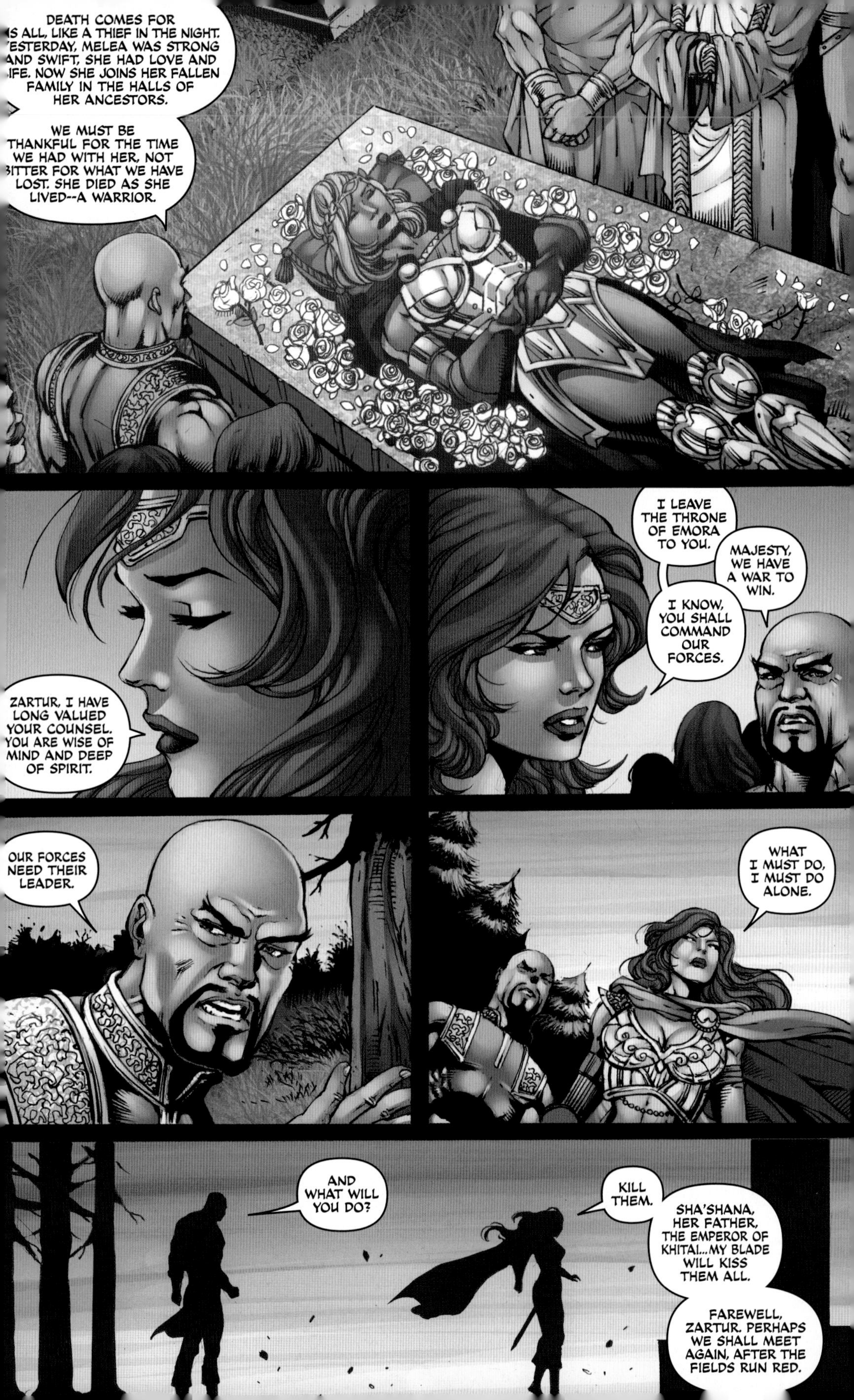
DEATH COMES FOR US ALL, LIKE A THIEF IN THE NIGHT. YESTERDAY, MELEA WAS STRONG AND SWIFT. SHE HAD LOVE AND LIFE. NOW SHE JOINS HER FALLEN FAMILY IN THE HALLS OF HER ANCESTORS.
WE MUST BE THANKFUL FOR THE TIME WE HAD WITH HER, NOT BITTER FOR WHAT WE HAVE LOST. SHE DIED AS SHE LIVED--A WARRIOR.
ZARTUR, I HAVE LONG VALUED YOUR COUNSEL. YOU ARE WISE OF MIND AND DEEP OF SPIRIT.
I LEAVE THE THRONE OF EMORA TO YOU.
MAJESTY, WE HAVE A WAR TO WIN.
I KNOW. YOU SHALL COMMAND OUR FORCES.
OUR FORCES NEED THEIR LEADER.
WHAT I MUST DO, I MUST DO ALONE.
AND WHAT WILL YOU DO?
KILL THEM.
SHA'SHANA, HER FATHER, THE EMPEROR OF KHITAI...MY BLADE WILL KISS THEM ALL.
FAREWELL, ZARTUR. PERHAPS WE SHALL MEET AGAIN, AFTER THE FIELDS RUN RED.

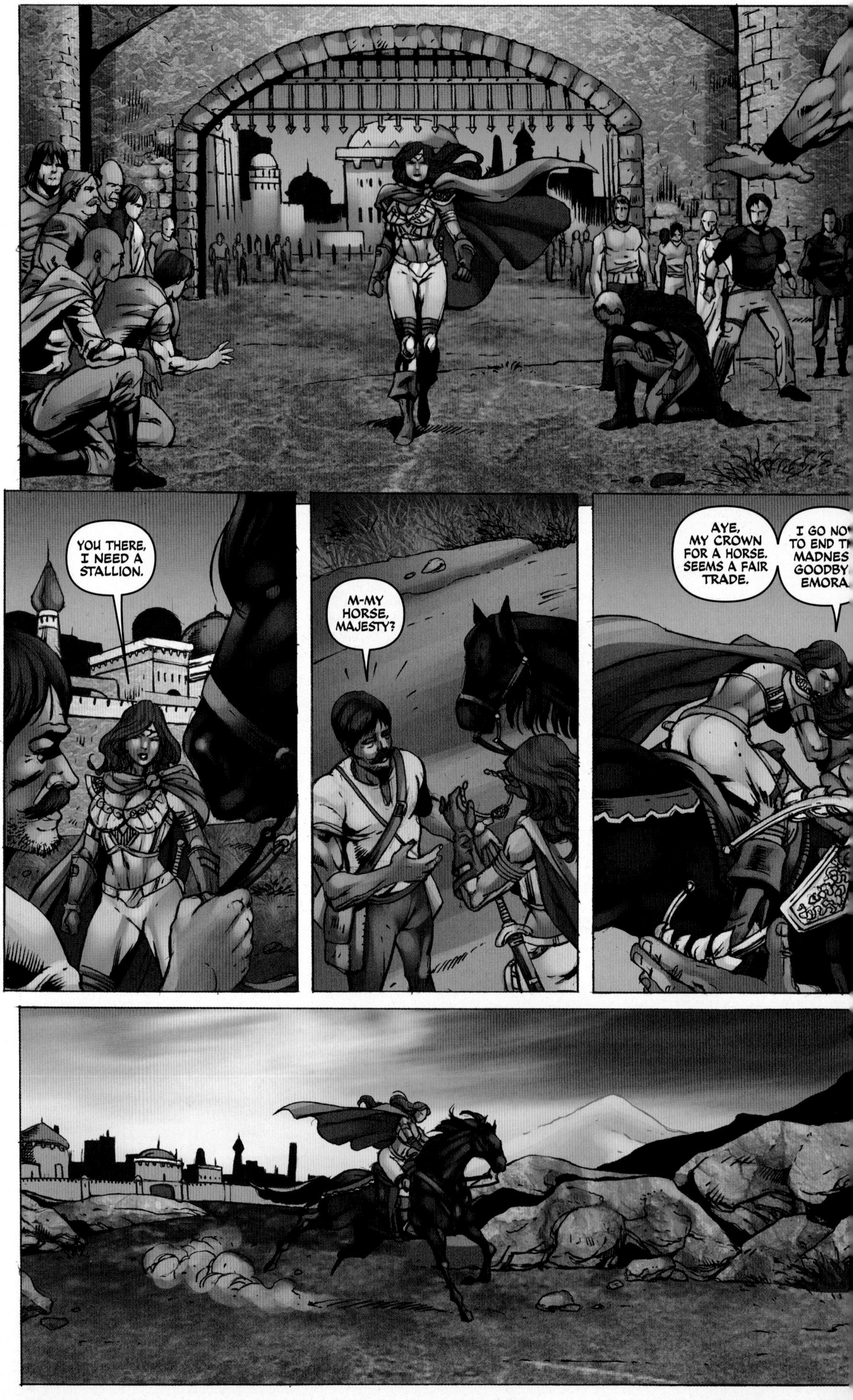
YOU THERE, I NEED A STALLION.
M-MY HORSE, MAJESTY?
AYE, MY CROWN FOR A HORSE. SEEMS A FAIR TRADE.
I GO NO TO END T MADNES GOODBY EMORA

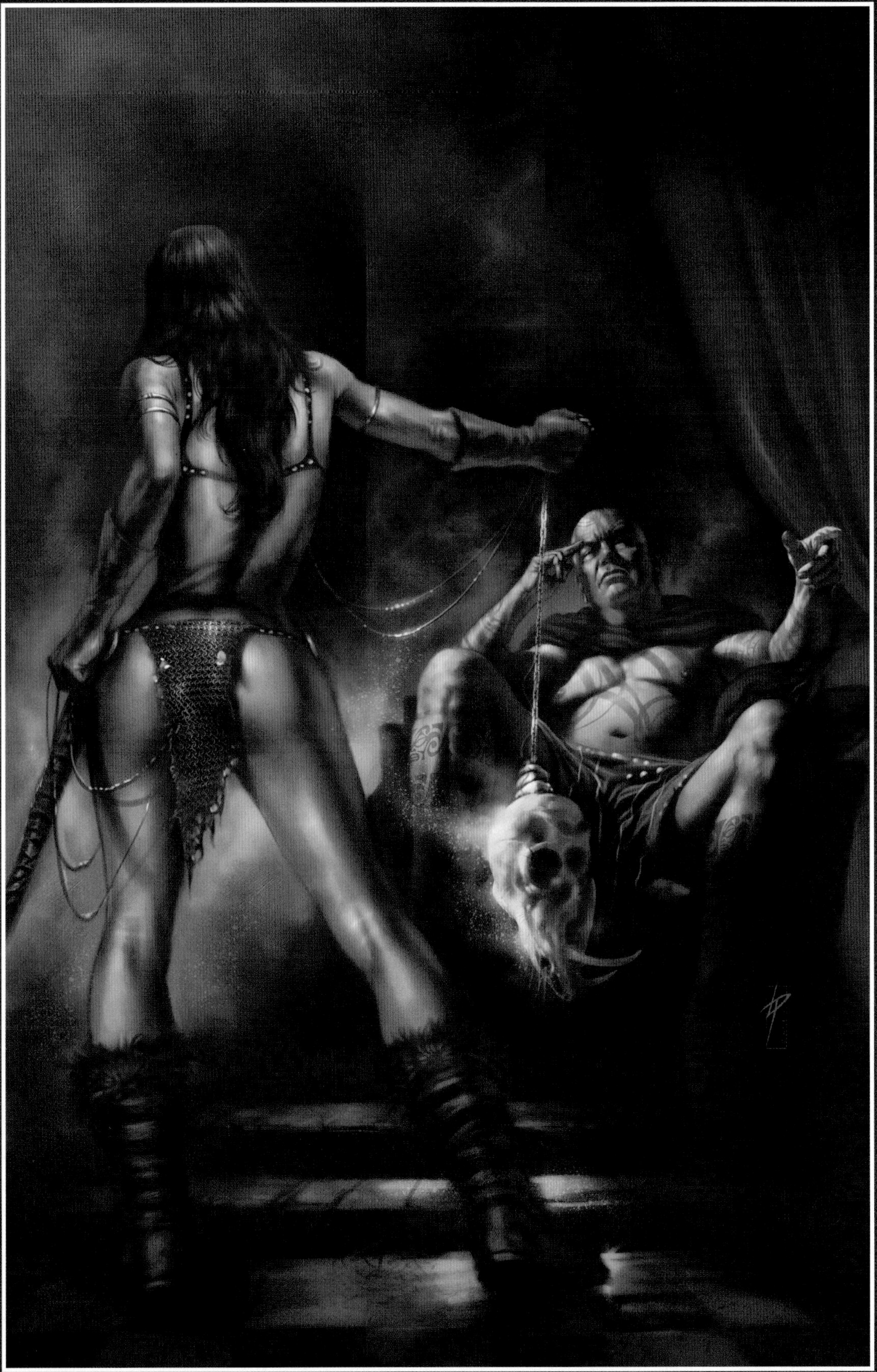

ISSUE #34 COVER BY LUCIO PARRILLO

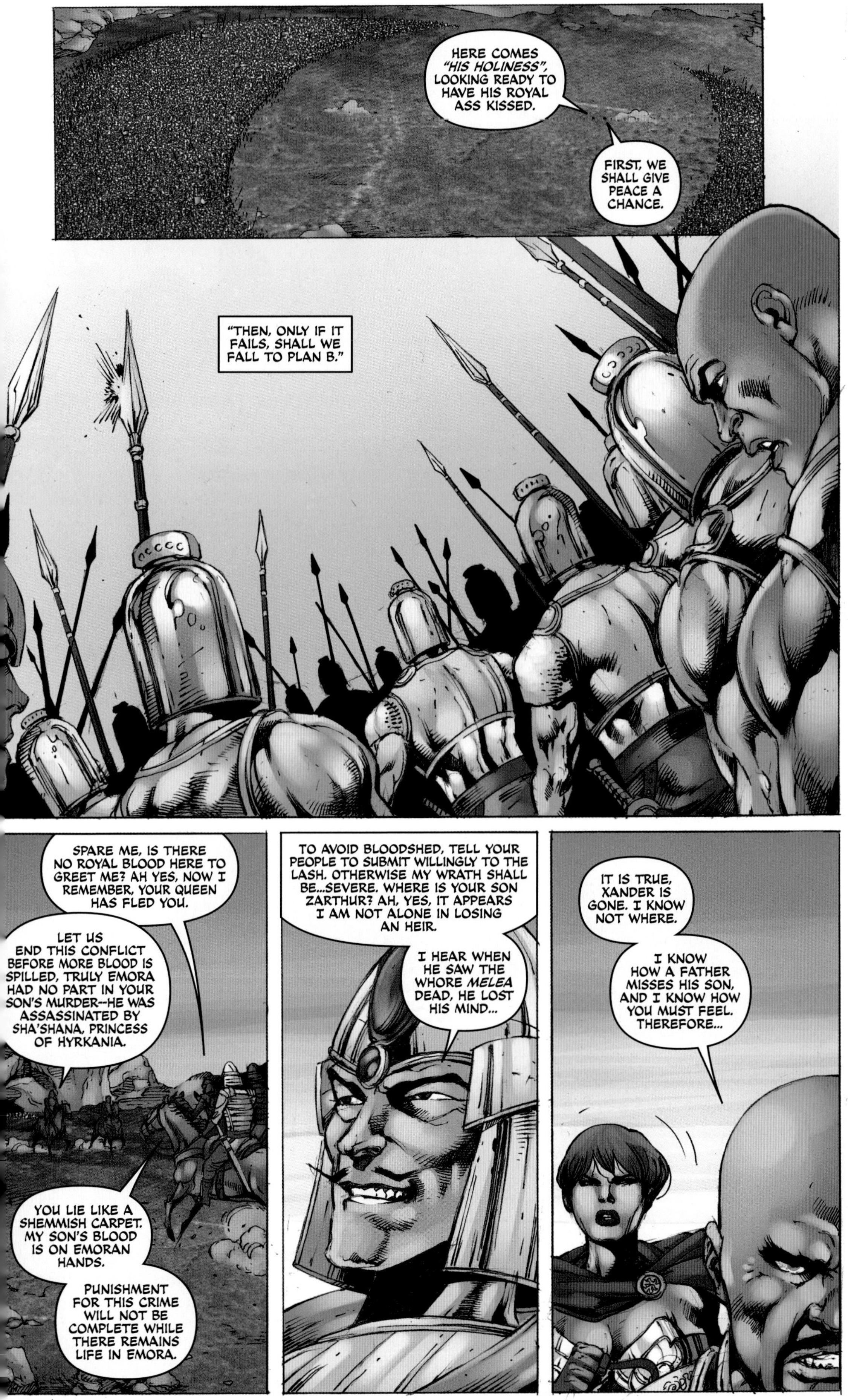
HERE COMES "HIS HOLINESS", LOOKING READY TO HAVE HIS ROYAL ASS KISSED.
FIRST, WE SHALL GIVE PEACE A CHANCE.
"THEN, ONLY IF IT FAILS, SHALL WE FALL TO PLAN B."
SPARE ME, IS THERE NO ROYAL BLOOD HERE TO GREET ME? AH YES, NOW I REMEMBER, YOUR QUEEN HAS FLED YOU.
LET US END THIS CONFLICT BEFORE MORE BLOOD IS SPILLED, TRULY EMORA HAD NO PART IN YOUR SON'S MURDER--HE WAS ASSASSINATED BY SHA'SHANA, PRINCESS OF HYRKANIA.
YOU LIE LIKE A SHEMMISH CARPET. MY SON'S BLOOD IS ON EMORAN HANDS.
PUNISHMENT FOR THIS CRIME WILL NOT BE COMPLETE WHILE THERE REMAINS LIFE IN EMORA.
TO AVOID BLOODSHED, TELL YOUR PEOPLE TO SUBMIT WILLINGLY TO THE LASH. OTHERWISE MY WRATH SHALL BE...SEVERE. WHERE IS YOUR SON ZARTHUR? AH, YES, IT APPEARS I AM NOT ALONE IN LOSING AN HEIR.
I HEAR WHEN HE SAW THE WHORE MELEA DEAD, HE LOST HIS MIND...
IT IS TRUE, XANDER IS GONE. I KNOW NOT WHERE.
I KNOW HOW A FATHER MISSES HIS SON, AND I KNOW HOW YOU MUST FEEL. THEREFORE...

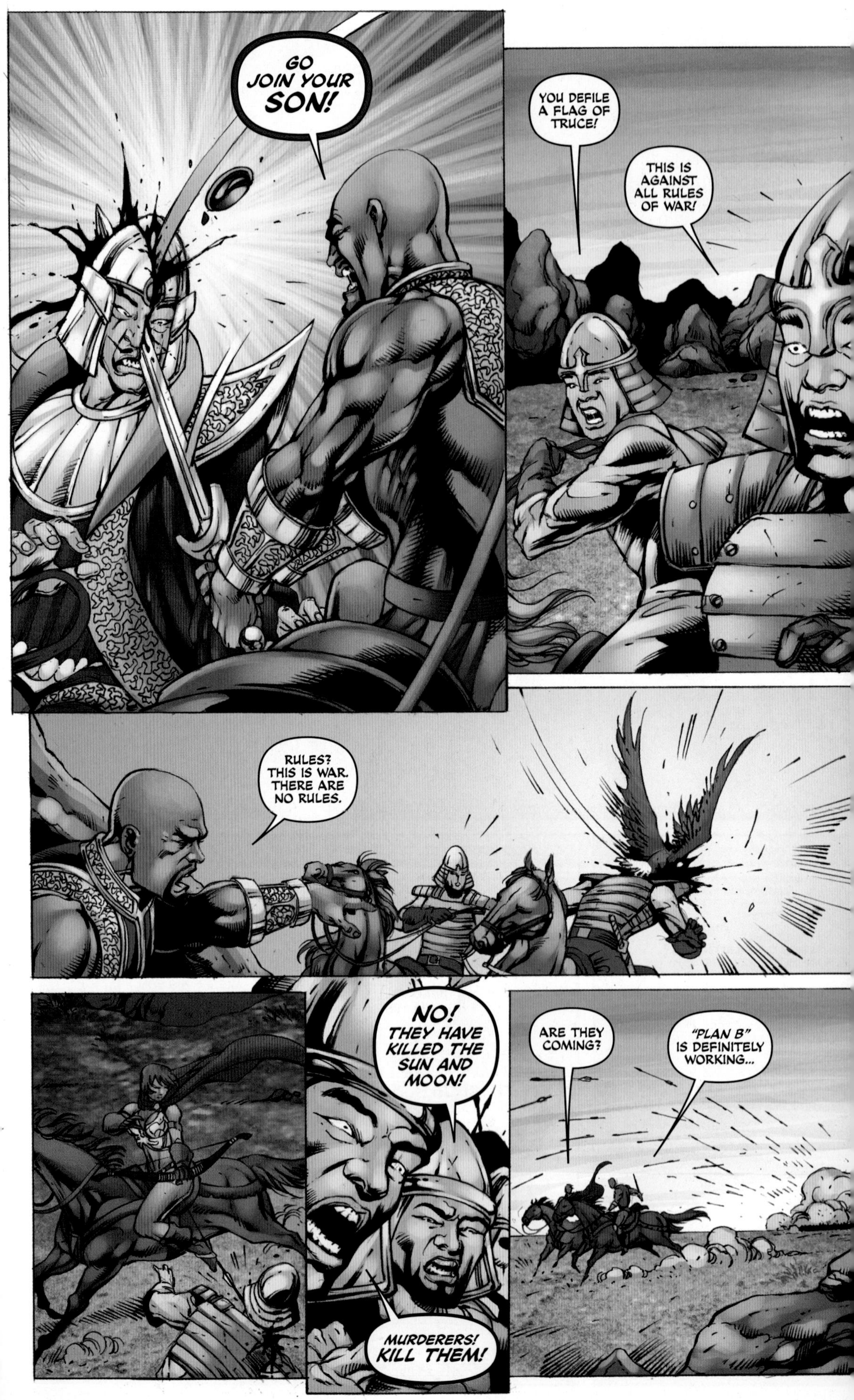
GO JOIN YOUR SON!
YOU DEFILE A FLAG OF TRUCE!
THIS IS AGAINST ALL RULES OF WAR!
RULES? THIS IS WAR. THERE ARE NO RULES.
NO! THEY HAVE KILLED THE SUN AND MOON!
MURDERERS! KILL THEM!
ARE THEY COMING?
"PLAN B" IS DEFINITELY WORKING...

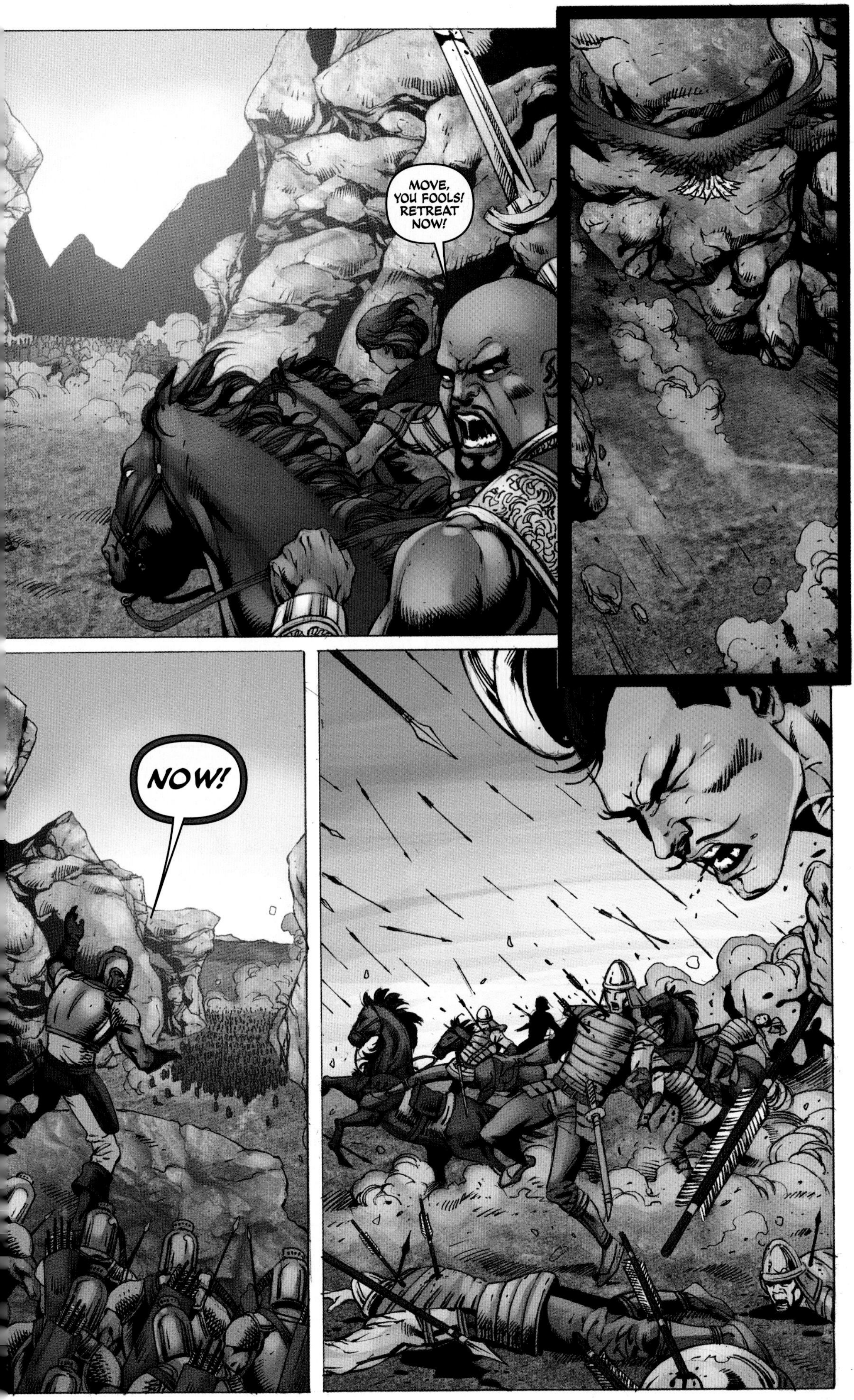
MOVE, YOU FOOLS! RETREAT NOW!
NOW!

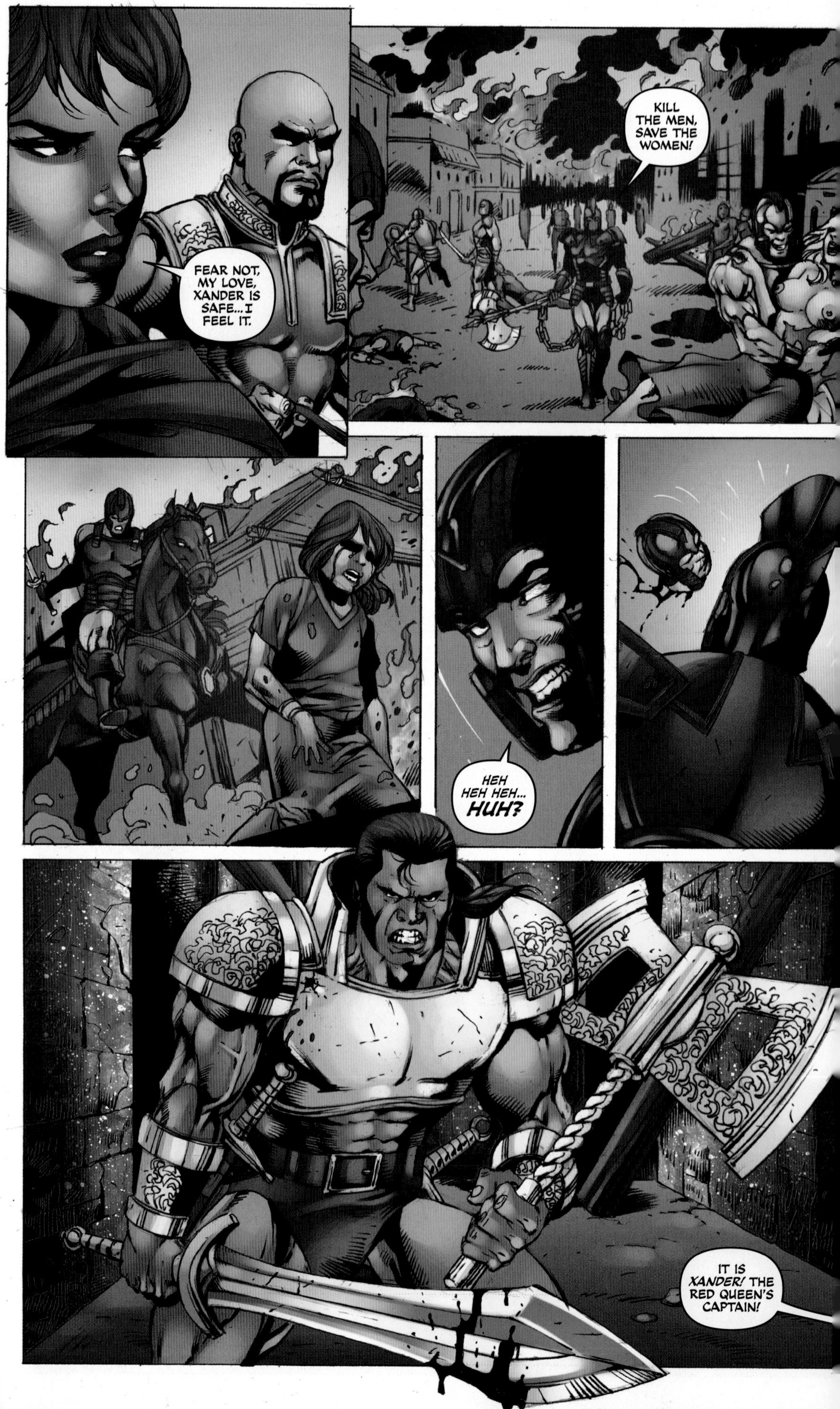
FEAR NOT, MY LOVE, XANDER IS SAFE...I FEEL IT.
KILL THE MEN, SAVE THE WOMEN!
HEH HEH HEH... HUH?
IT IS XANDER! THE RED QUEEN'S CAPTAIN!

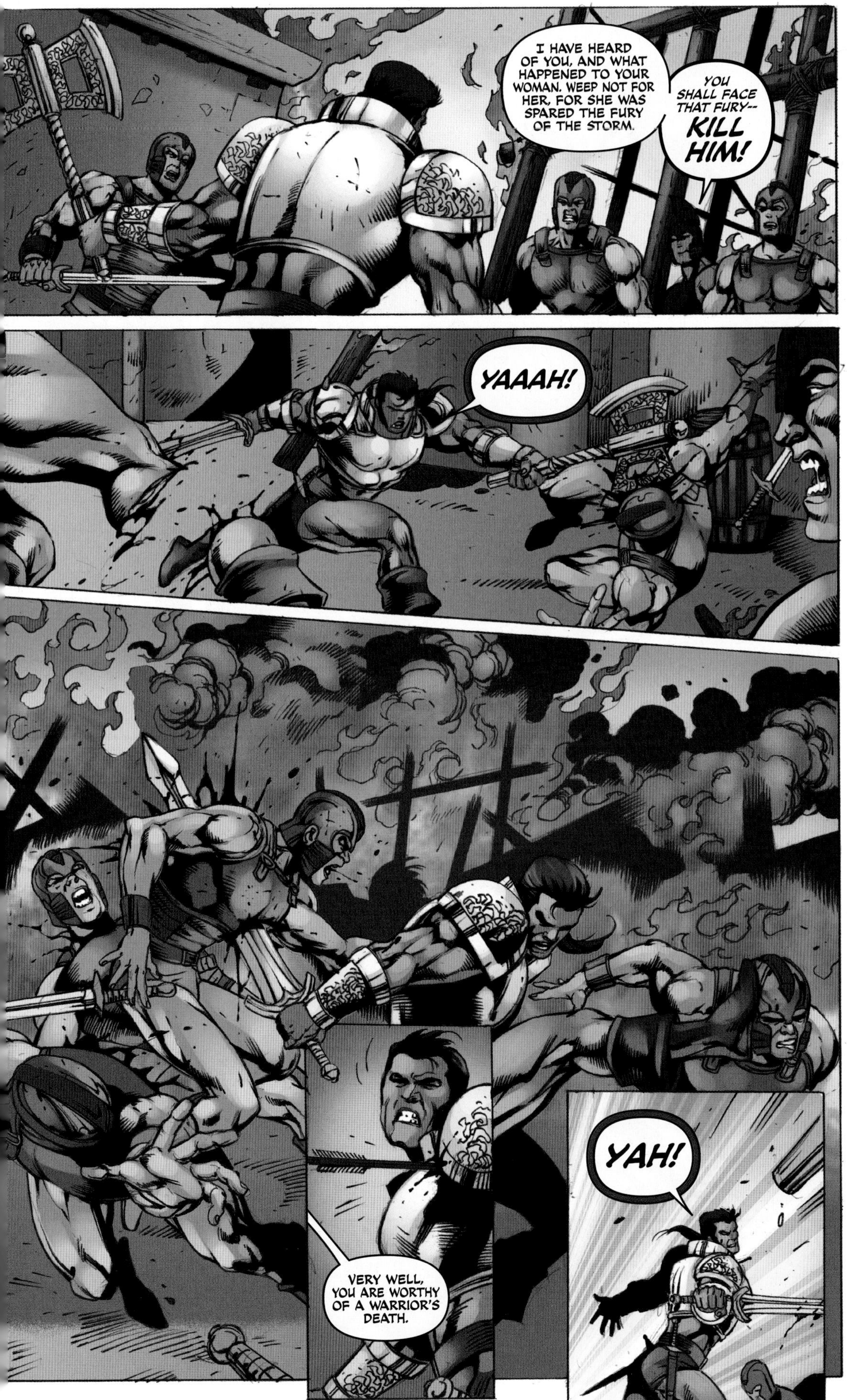
I HAVE HEARD OF YOU, AND WHAT HAPPENED TO YOUR WOMAN. WEEP NOT FOR HER, FOR SHE WAS SPARED THE FURY OF THE STORM.
YOU SHALL FACE THAT FURY-- KILL HIM!
YAAAH!
VERY WELL, YOU ARE WORTHY OF A WARRIOR'S DEATH.
YAH!

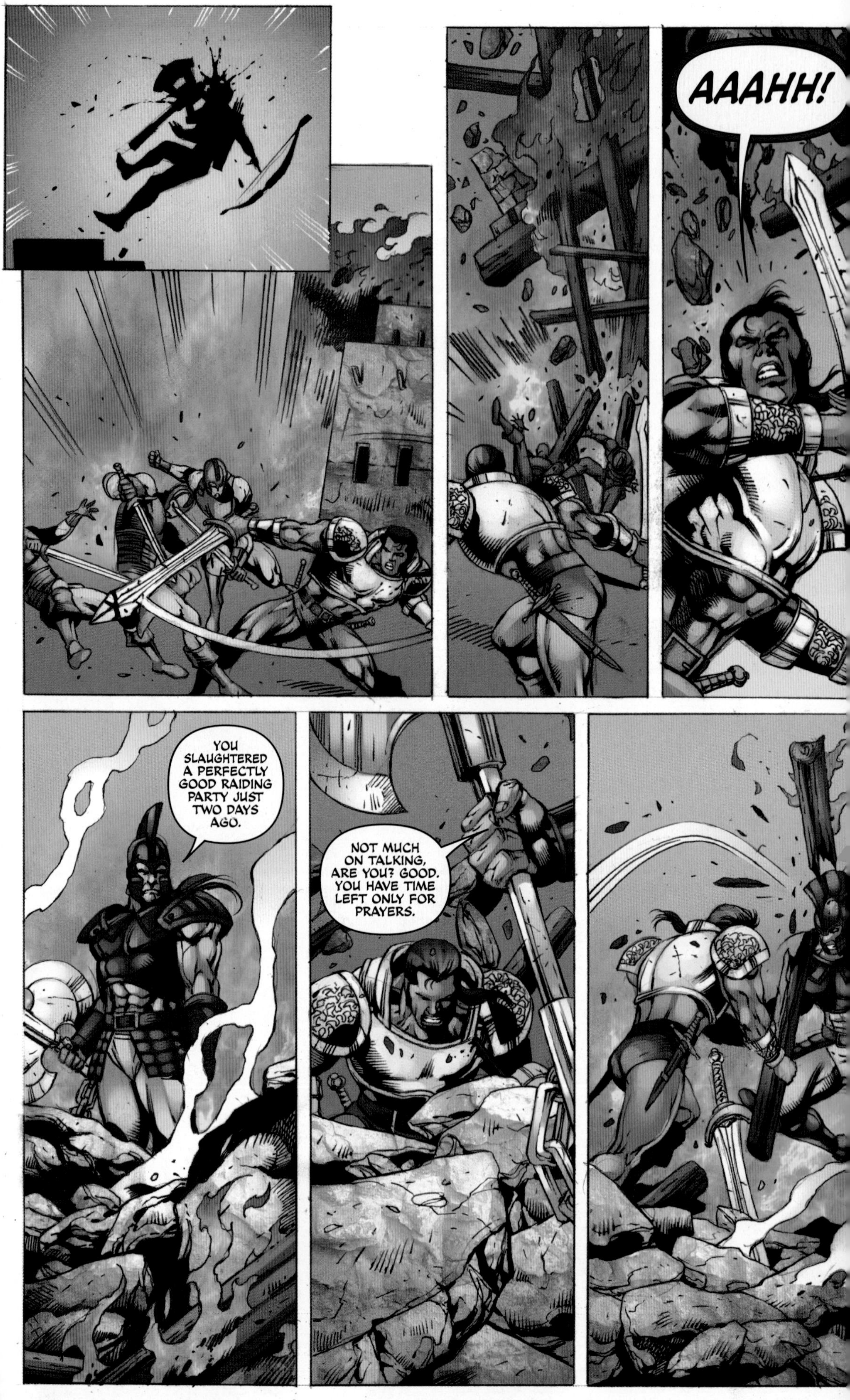
AAAHH!
YOU SLAUGHTERED A PERFECTLY GOOD RAIDING PARTY JUST TWO DAYS AGO.
NOT MUCH ON TALKING, ARE YOU? GOOD. YOU HAVE TIME LEFT ONLY FOR PRAYERS.

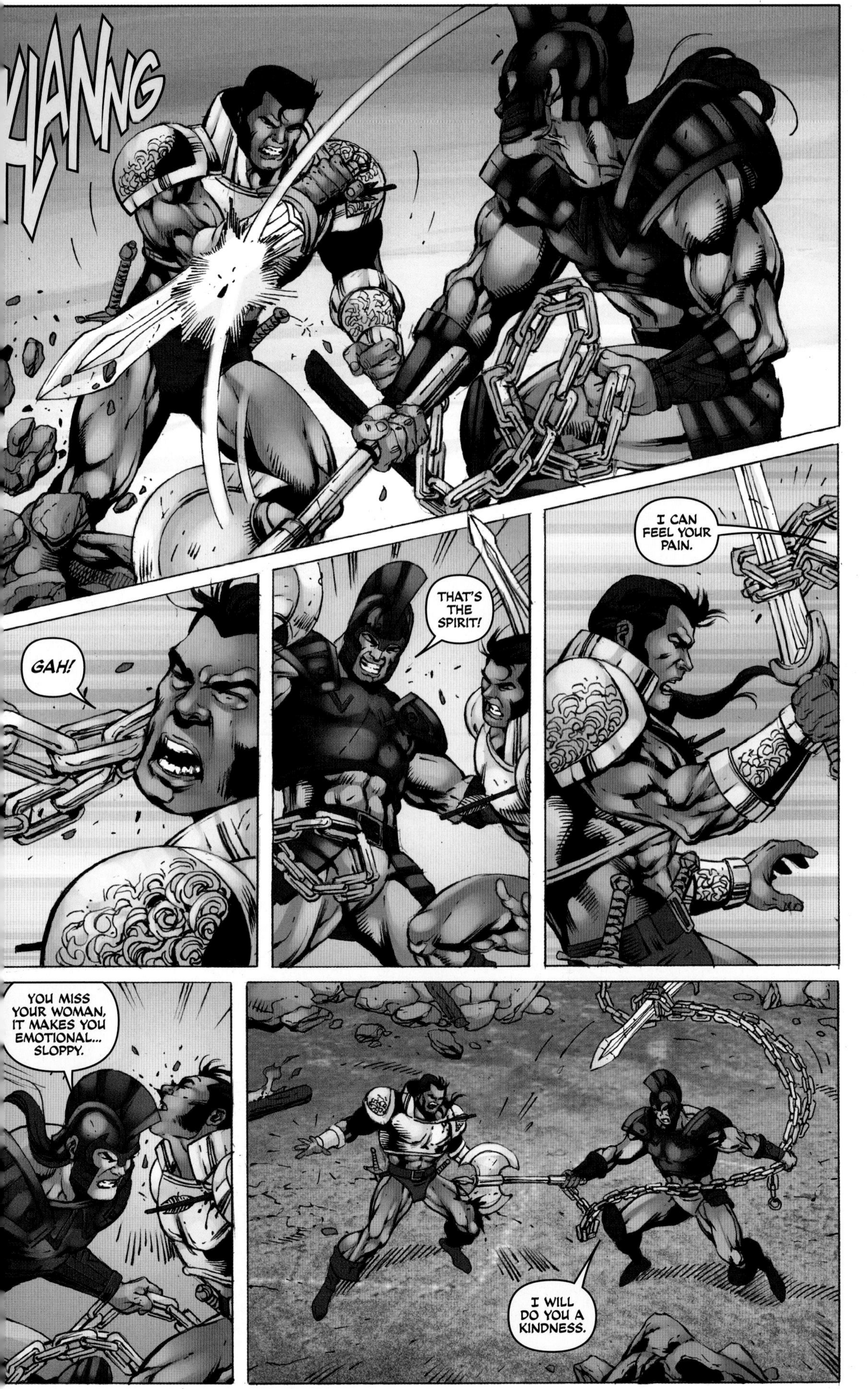
KLANNG
GAH!
THAT'S THE SPIRIT!
I CAN FEEL YOUR PAIN.
YOU MISS YOUR WOMAN, IT MAKES YOU EMOTIONAL... SLOPPY.
I WILL DO YOU A KINDNESS.

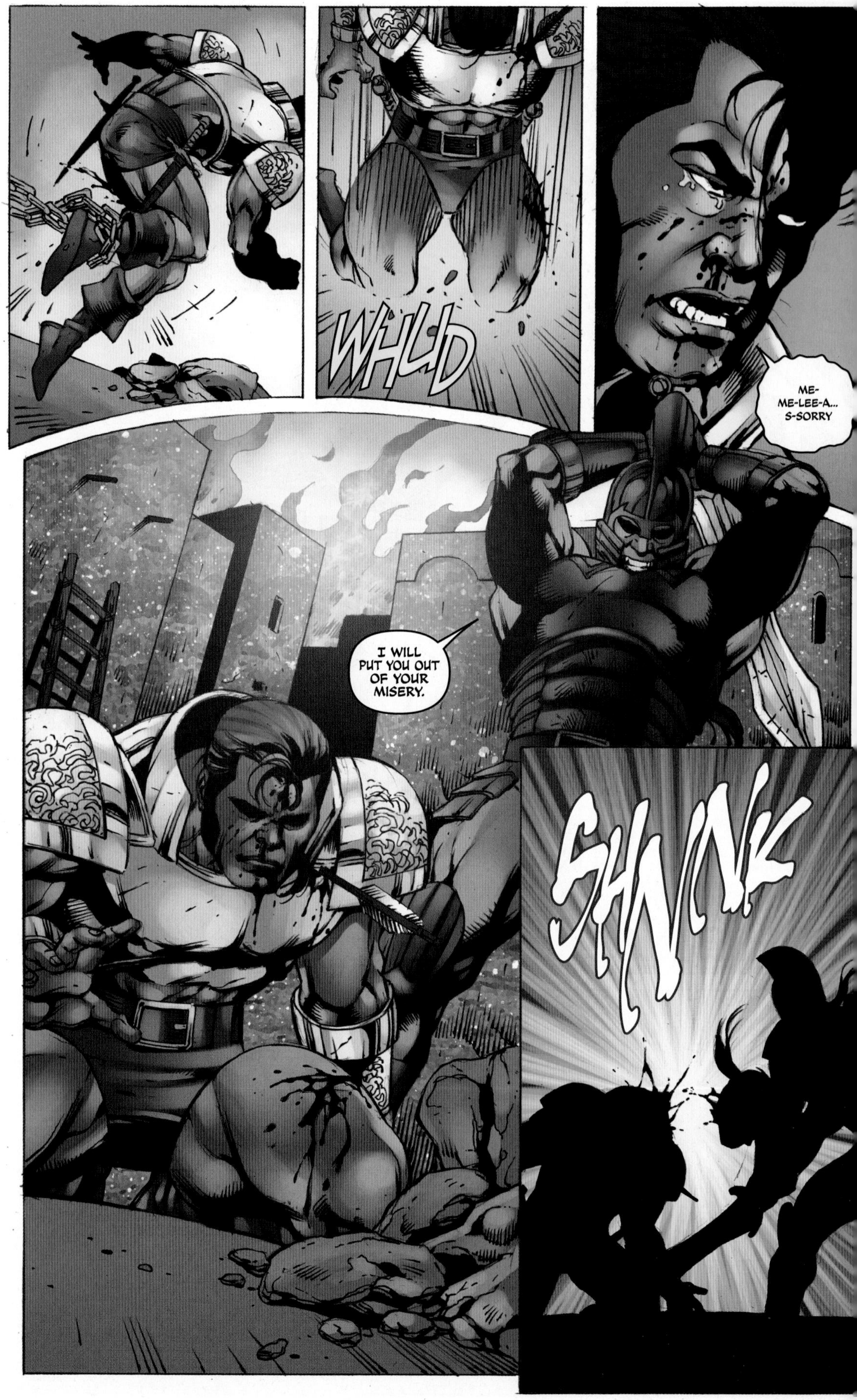
WHUD
ME-
ME-LEE-A...
S-SORRY
I WILL
PUT YOU OUT
OF YOUR
MISERY.
SHNNK

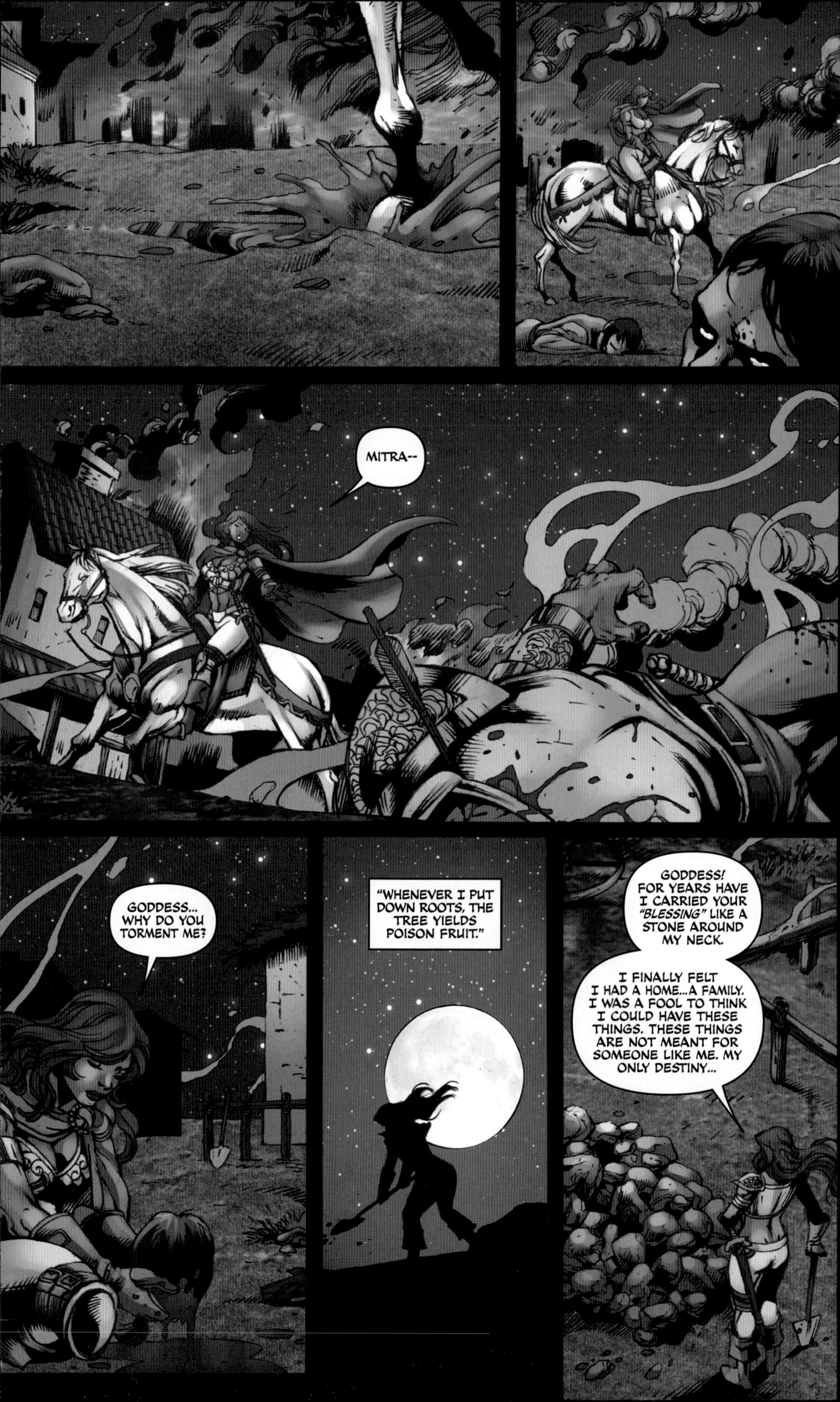
MITRA--
GODDESS... WHY DO YOU TORMENT ME?
"WHENEVER I PUT DOWN ROOTS, THE TREE YIELDS POISON FRUIT."
GODDESS! FOR YEARS HAVE I CARRIED YOUR "BLESSING" LIKE A STONE AROUND MY NECK.
I FINALLY FELT I HAD A HOME...A FAMILY. I WAS A FOOL TO THINK I COULD HAVE THESE THINGS. THESE THINGS ARE NOT MEANT FOR SOMEONE LIKE ME. MY ONLY DESTINY...

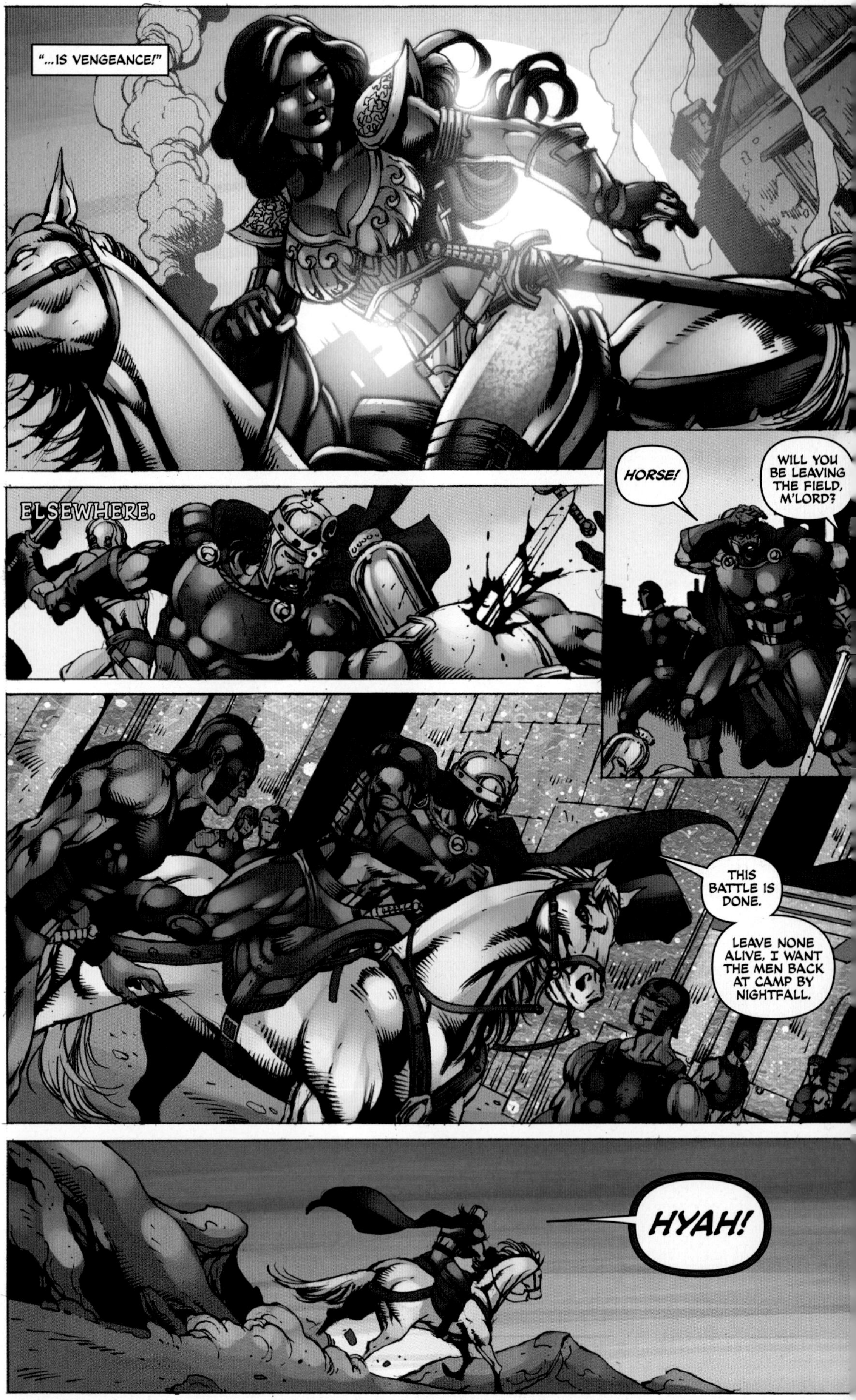
"...IS VENGEANCE!"
ELSEWHERE.
HORSE!
WILL YOU BE LEAVING THE FIELD, M'LORD?
THIS BATTLE IS DONE.
LEAVE NONE ALIVE, I WANT THE MEN BACK AT CAMP BY NIGHTFALL.
HYAH!

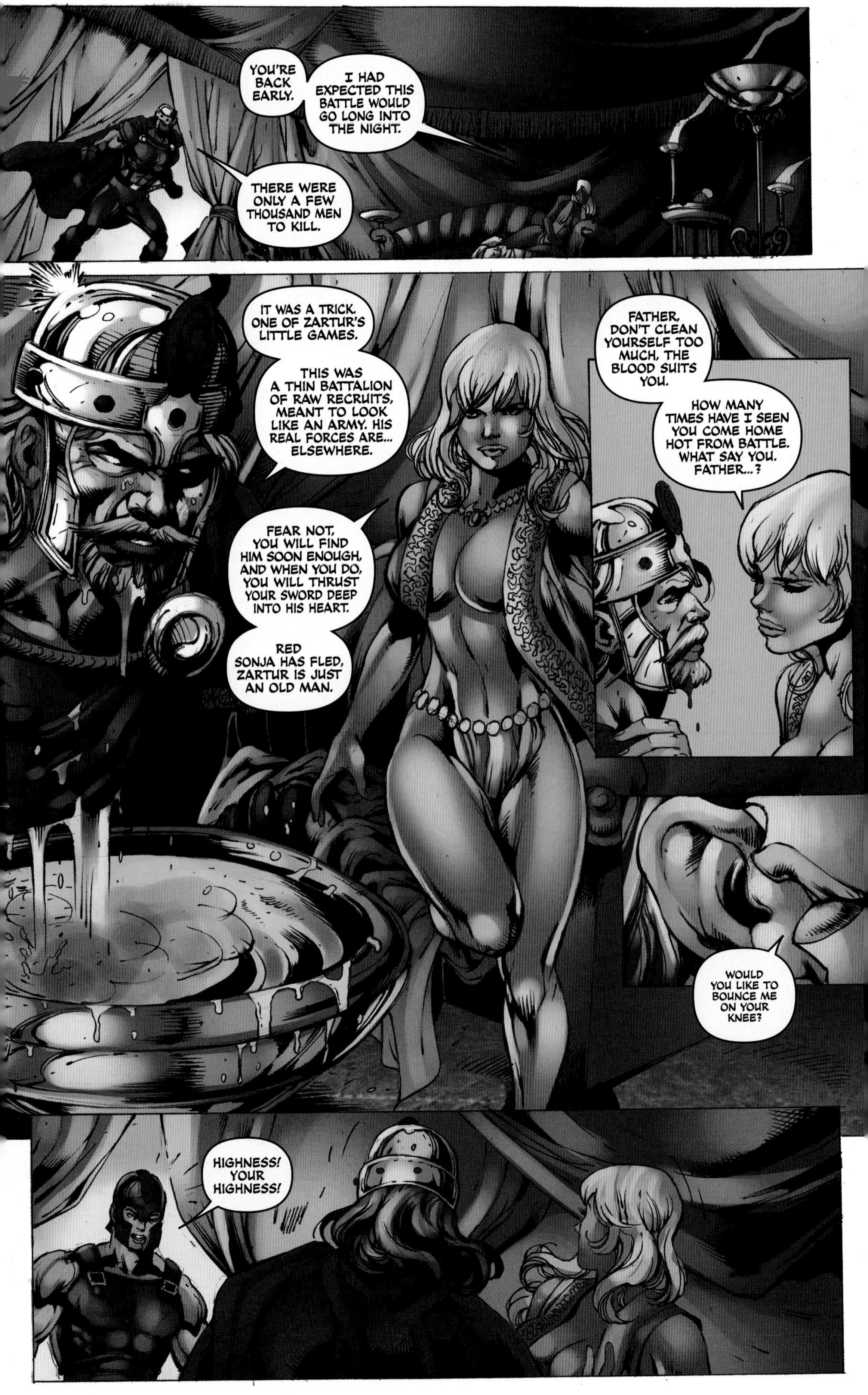
YOU'RE BACK EARLY.
I HAD EXPECTED THIS BATTLE WOULD GO LONG INTO THE NIGHT.
THERE WERE ONLY A FEW THOUSAND MEN TO KILL.
IT WAS A TRICK. ONE OF ZARTUR'S LITTLE GAMES.
THIS WAS A THIN BATTALION OF RAW RECRUITS, MEANT TO LOOK LIKE AN ARMY. HIS REAL FORCES ARE... ELSEWHERE.
FEAR NOT, YOU WILL FIND HIM SOON ENOUGH, AND WHEN YOU DO, YOU WILL THRUST YOUR SWORD DEEP INTO HIS HEART.
RED SONJA HAS FLED, ZARTUR IS JUST AN OLD MAN.
FATHER, DON'T CLEAN YOURSELF TOO MUCH, THE BLOOD SUITS YOU.
HOW MANY TIMES HAVE I SEEN YOU COME HOME HOT FROM BATTLE. WHAT SAY YOU. FATHER...?
WOULD YOU LIKE TO BOUNCE ME ON YOUR KNEE?
HIGHNESS! YOUR HIGHNESS!

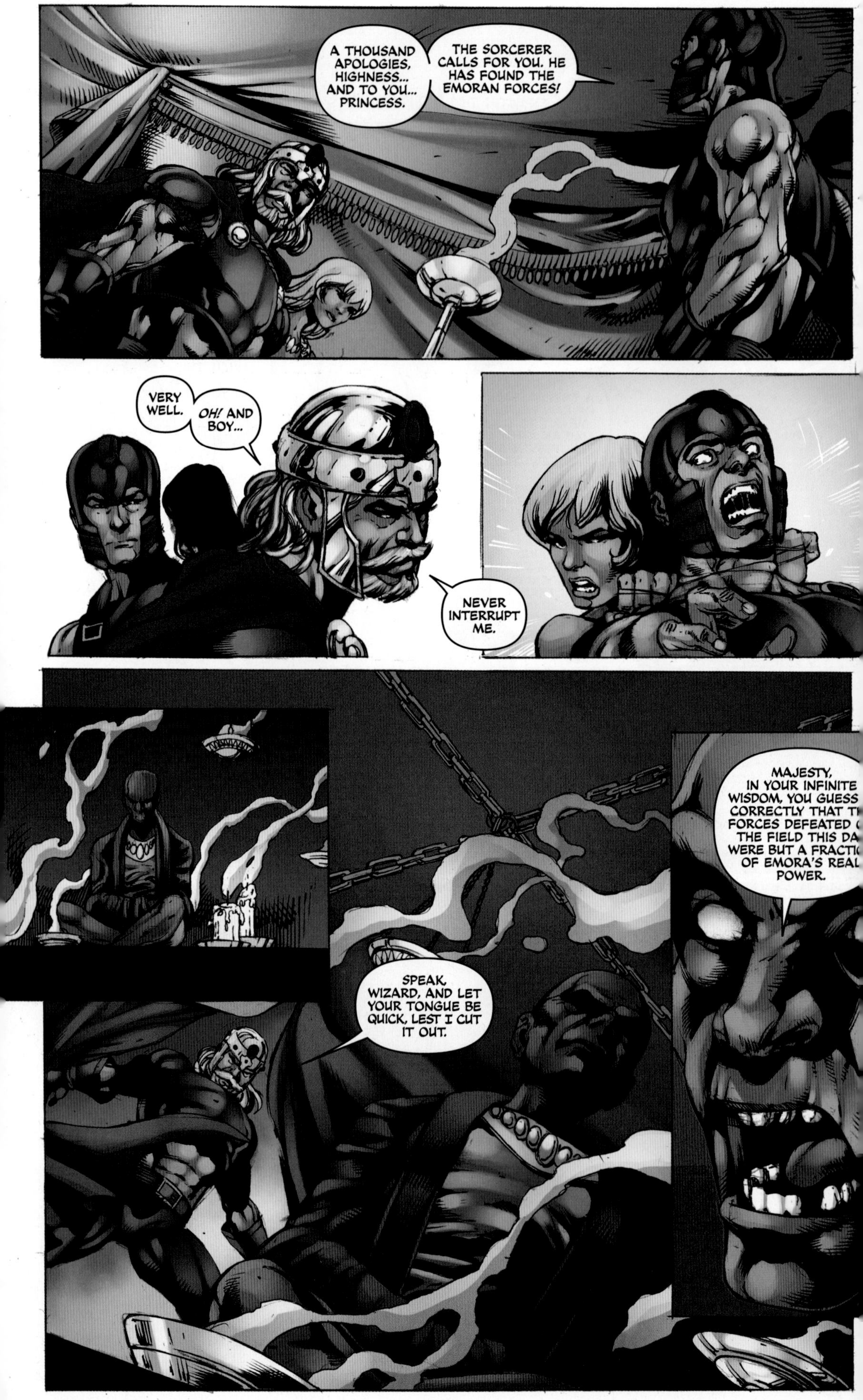
A THOUSAND APOLOGIES, HIGHNESS... AND TO YOU... PRINCESS.
THE SORCERER CALLS FOR YOU. HE HAS FOUND THE EMORAN FORCES!
VERY WELL.
OH! AND BOY...
NEVER INTERRUPT ME.
SPEAK, WIZARD, AND LET YOUR TONGUE BE QUICK, LEST I CUT IT OUT.
MAJESTY, IN YOUR INFINITE WISDOM, YOU GUESS CORRECTLY THAT T FORCES DEFEATED THE FIELD THIS DA WERE BUT A FRACTI OF EMORA'S REAL POWER.

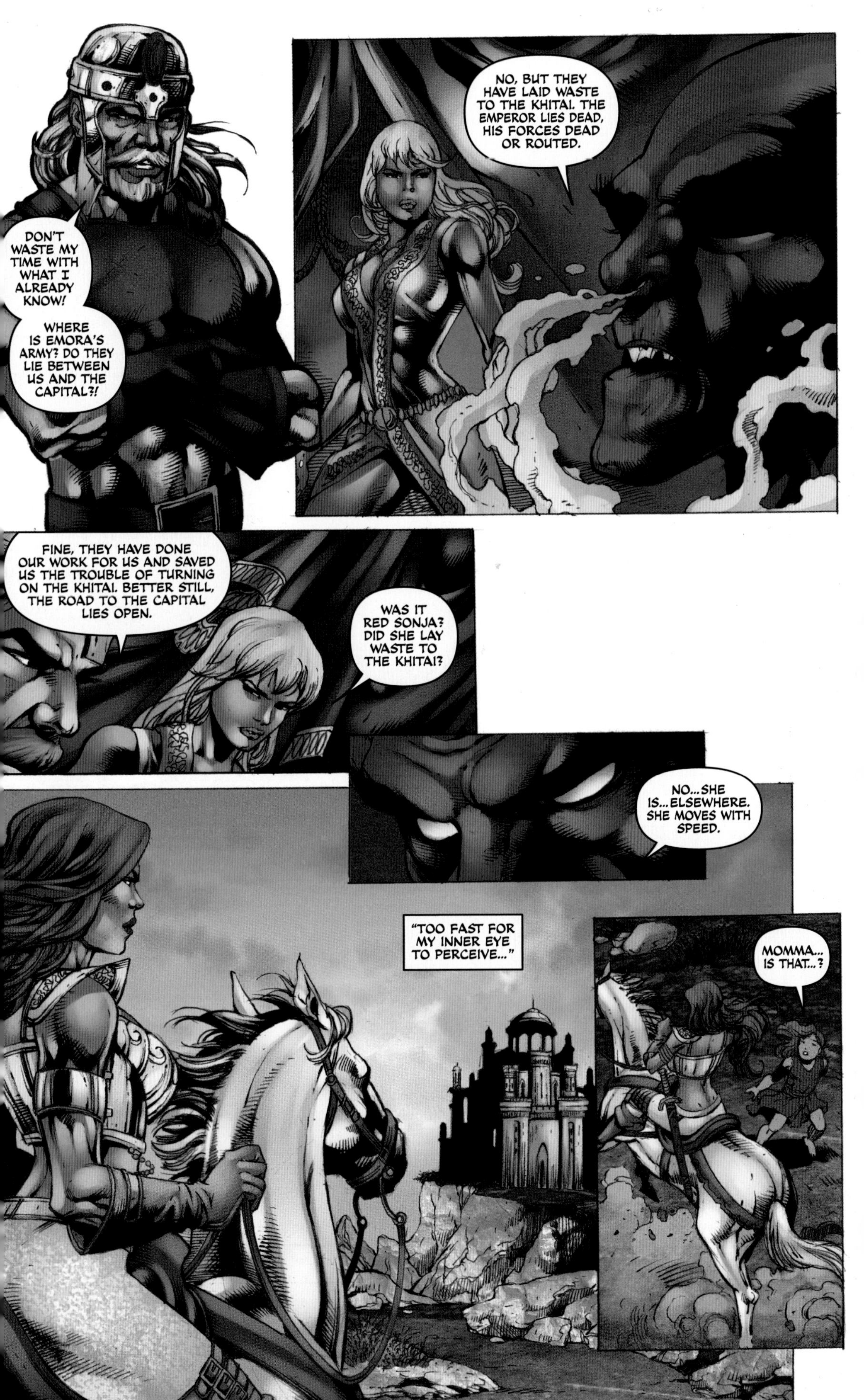
DON'T WASTE MY TIME WITH WHAT I ALREADY KNOW!
WHERE IS EMORA'S ARMY? DO THEY LIE BETWEEN US AND THE CAPITAL?!
NO, BUT THEY HAVE LAID WASTE TO THE KHITAI. THE EMPEROR LIES DEAD, HIS FORCES DEAD OR ROUTED.
FINE, THEY HAVE DONE OUR WORK FOR US AND SAVED US THE TROUBLE OF TURNING ON THE KHITAI. BETTER STILL, THE ROAD TO THE CAPITAL LIES OPEN.
WAS IT RED SONJA? DID SHE LAY WASTE TO THE KHITAI?
NO...SHE IS...ELSEWHERE. SHE MOVES WITH SPEED.
"TOO FAST FOR MY INNER EYE TO PERCEIVE..."
MOMMA... IS THAT...?

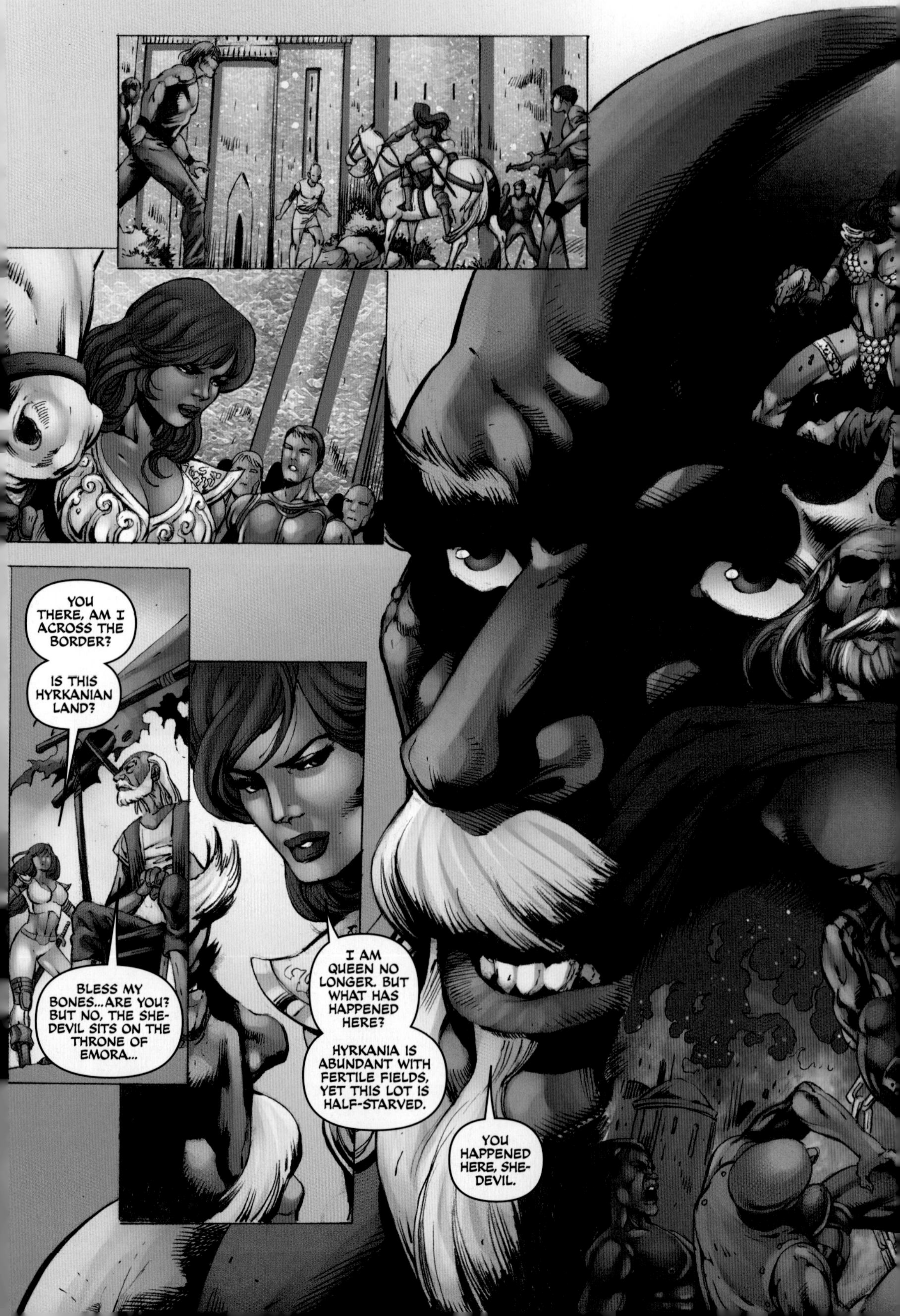
YOU THERE, AM I ACROSS THE BORDER?
IS THIS HYRKANIAN LAND?
BLESS MY BONES...ARE YOU? BUT NO, THE SHE-DEVIL SITS ON THE THRONE OF EMORA...
I AM QUEEN NO LONGER. BUT WHAT HAS HAPPENED HERE?
HYRKANIA IS ABUNDANT WITH FERTILE FIELDS, YET THIS LOT IS HALF-STARVED.
YOU HAPPENED HERE, SHE-DEVIL.

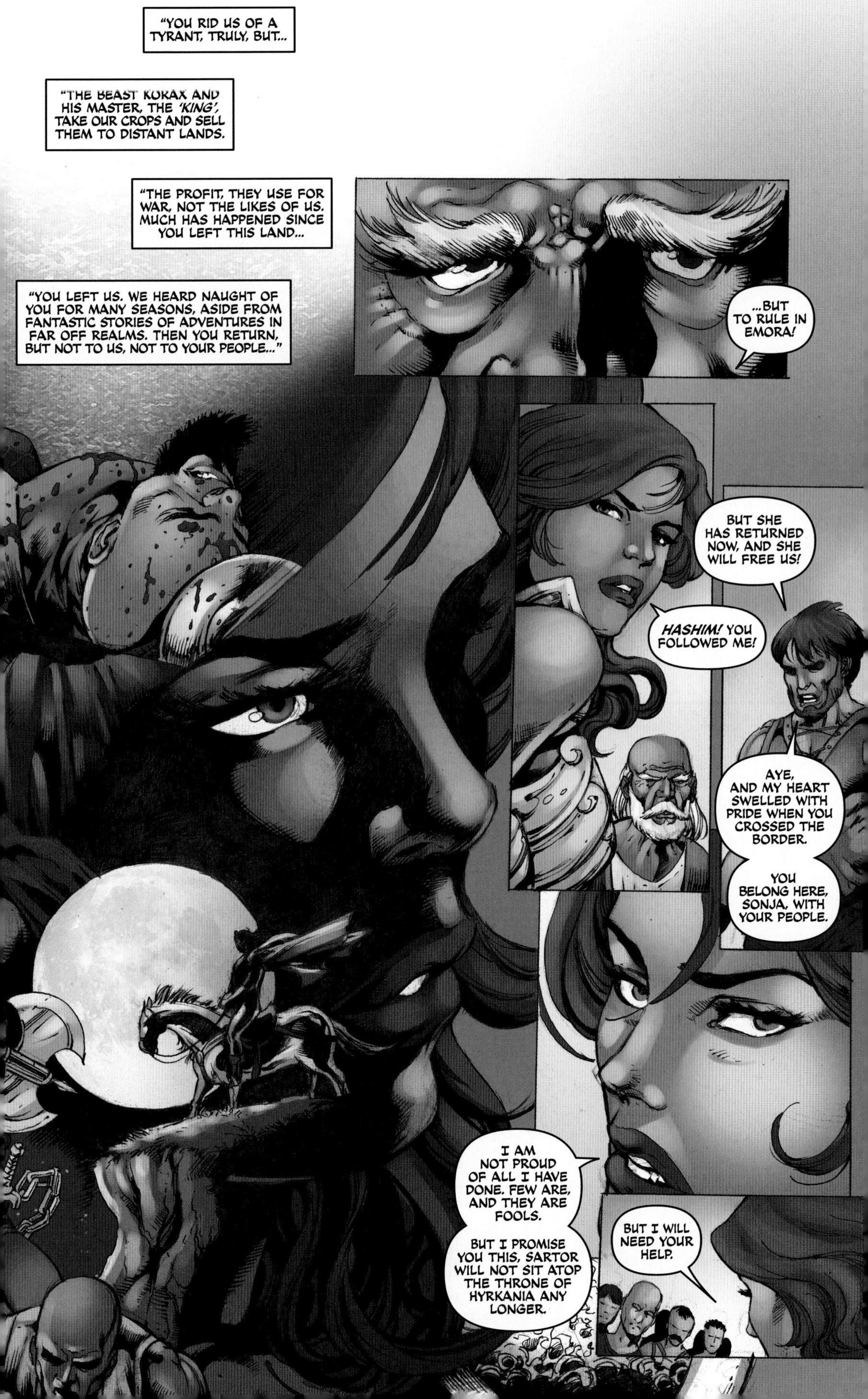
"YOU RID US OF A TYRANT, TRULY, BUT...
"THE BEAST KORAX AND HIS MASTER, THE 'KING', TAKE OUR CROPS AND SELL THEM TO DISTANT LANDS.
"THE PROFIT, THEY USE FOR WAR, NOT THE LIKES OF US. MUCH HAS HAPPENED SINCE YOU LEFT THIS LAND...
"YOU LEFT US. WE HEARD NAUGHT OF YOU FOR MANY SEASONS, ASIDE FROM FANTASTIC STORIES OF ADVENTURES IN FAR OFF REALMS. THEN YOU RETURN, BUT NOT TO US, NOT TO YOUR PEOPLE..."
...BUT TO RULE IN EMORA!
BUT SHE HAS RETURNED NOW, AND SHE WILL FREE US!
HASHIM! YOU FOLLOWED ME!
AYE, AND MY HEART SWELLED WITH PRIDE WHEN YOU CROSSED THE BORDER.
YOU BELONG HERE, SONJA, WITH YOUR PEOPLE.
I AM NOT PROUD OF ALL I HAVE DONE. FEW ARE, AND THEY ARE FOOLS.
BUT I PROMISE YOU THIS, SARTOR WILL NOT SIT ATOP THE THRONE OF HYRKANIA ANY LONGER.
BUT I WILL NEED YOUR HELP.

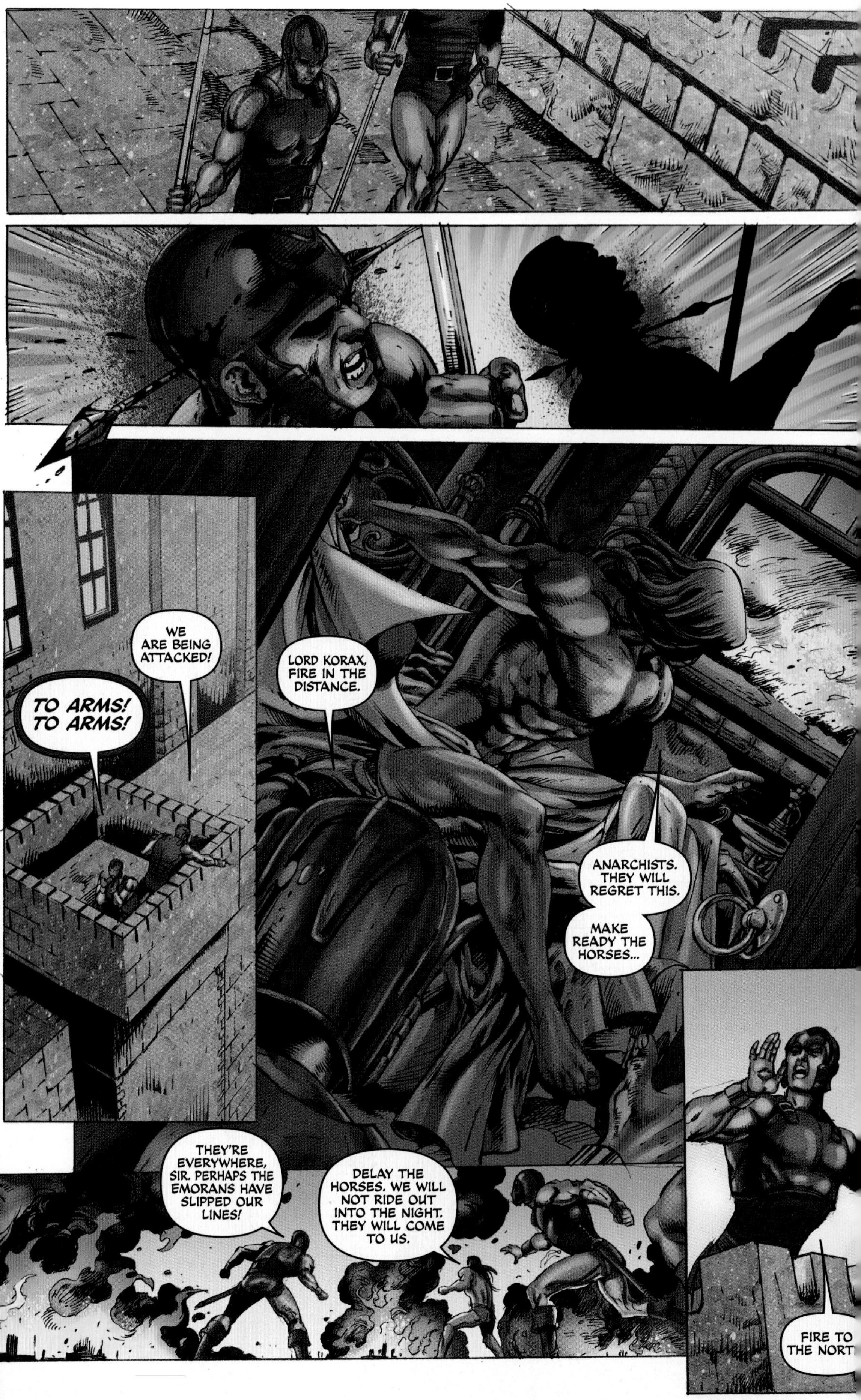
WE ARE BEING ATTACKED!
TO ARMS! TO ARMS!
LORD KORAX, FIRE IN THE DISTANCE.
ANARCHISTS. THEY WILL REGRET THIS.
MAKE READY THE HORSES...
FIRE TO THE NORT
THEY'RE EVERYWHERE, SIR. PERHAPS THE EMORANS HAVE SLIPPED OUR LINES!
DELAY THE HORSES. WE WILL NOT RIDE OUT INTO THE NIGHT. THEY WILL COME TO US.

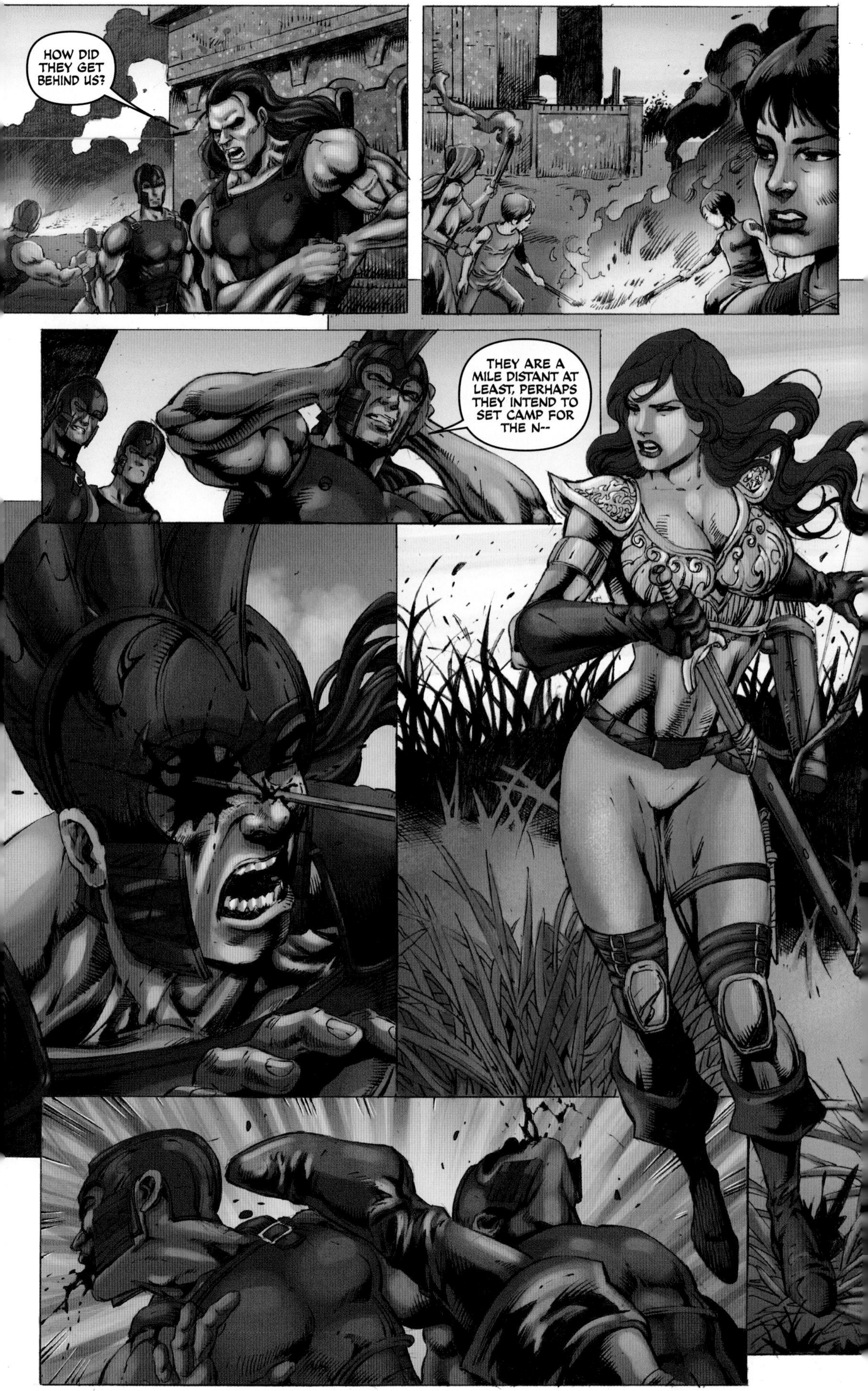
HOW DID THEY GET BEHIND US?
THEY ARE A MILE DISTANT AT LEAST, PERHAPS THEY INTEND TO SET CAMP FOR THE N--

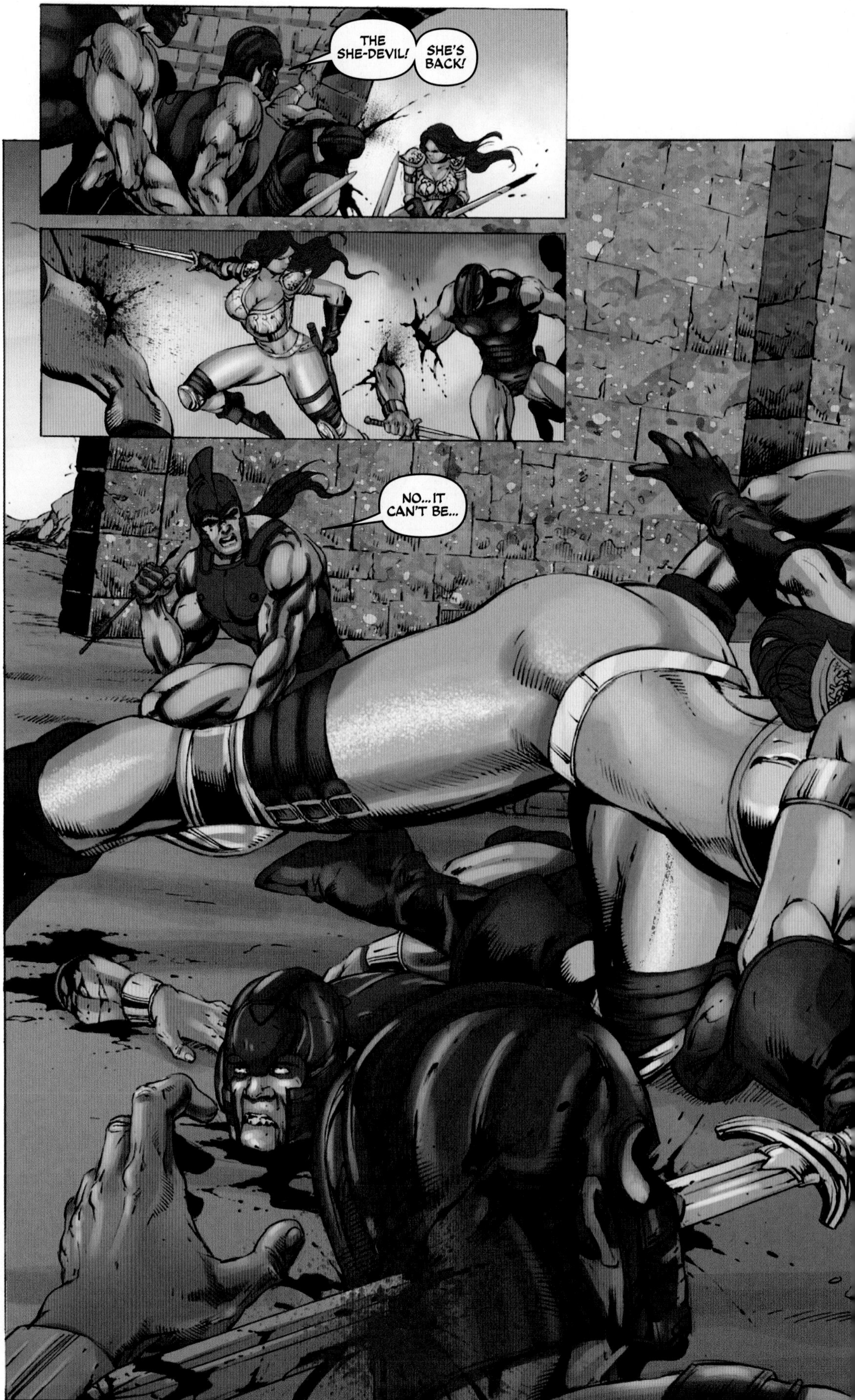
THE SHE-DEVIL!
SHE'S BACK!
NO...IT CAN'T BE...

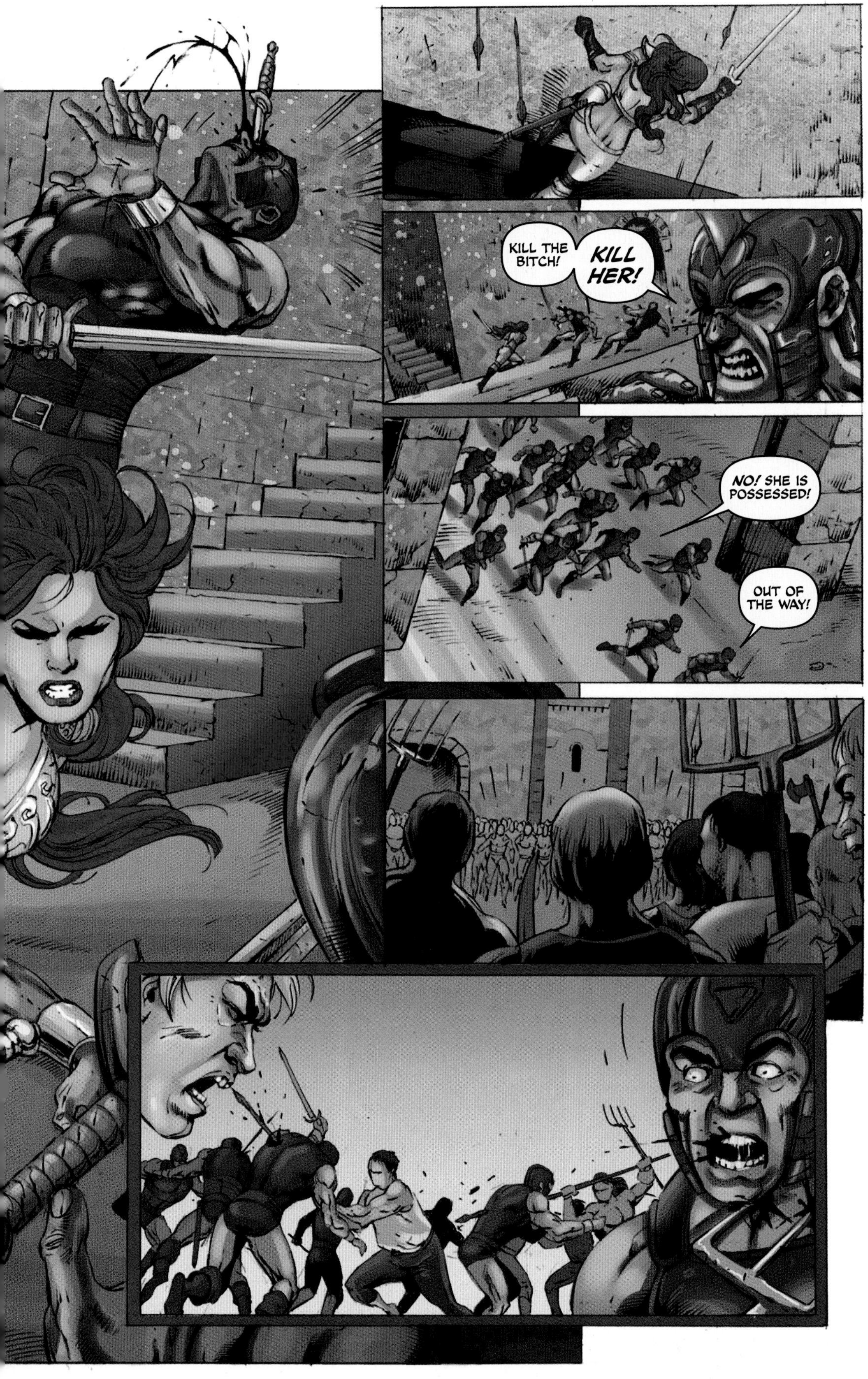

KILL THE BITCH!
KILL HER!
NO! SHE IS POSSESSED!
OUT OF THE WAY!

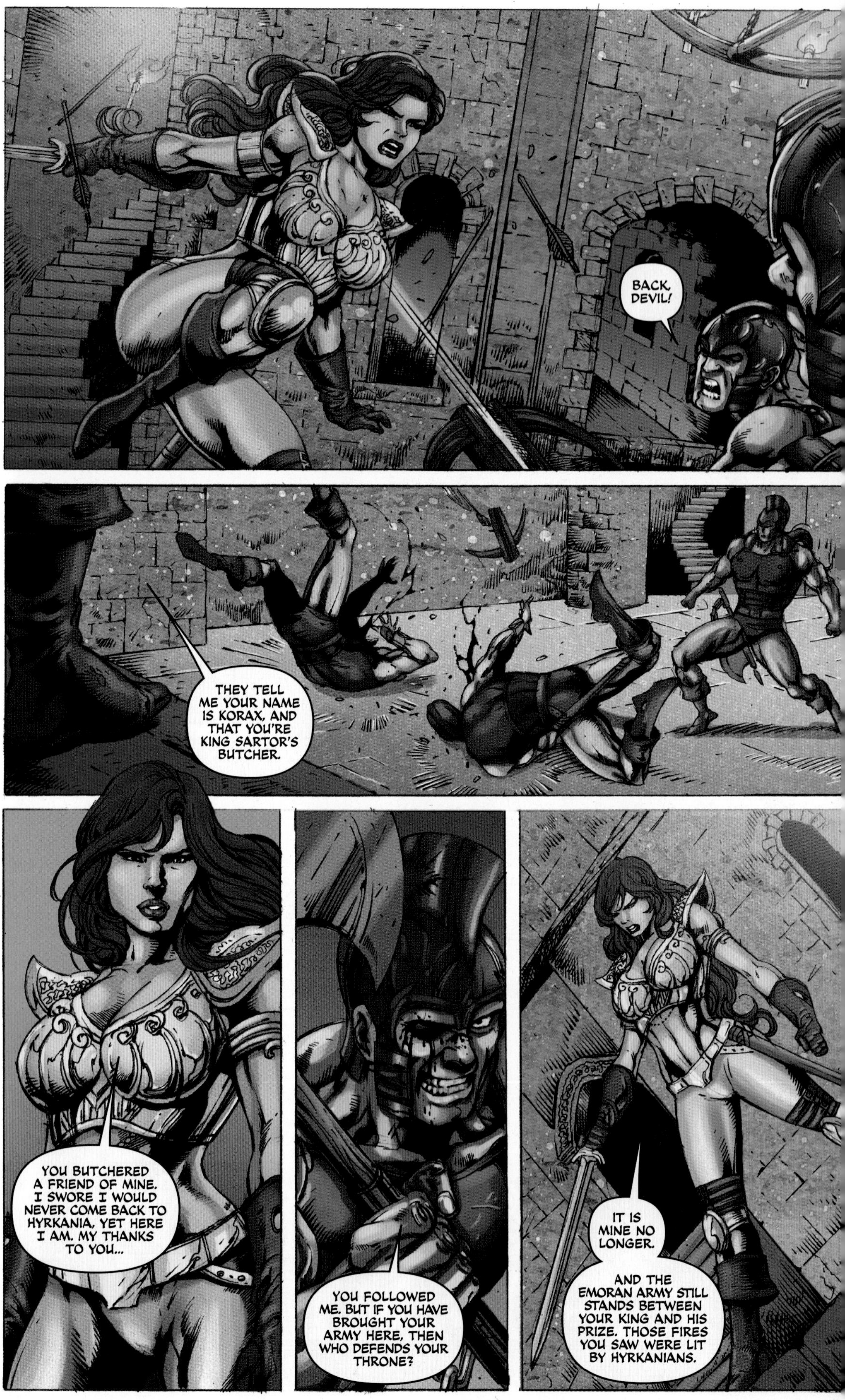
BACK, DEVIL!
THEY TELL ME YOUR NAME IS KORAX, AND THAT YOU'RE KING SARTOR'S BUTCHER.
YOU BUTCHERED A FRIEND OF MINE. I SWORE I WOULD NEVER COME BACK TO HYRKANIA, YET HERE I AM. MY THANKS TO YOU...
YOU FOLLOWED ME. BUT IF YOU HAVE BROUGHT YOUR ARMY HERE, THEN WHO DEFENDS YOUR THRONE?
IT IS MINE NO LONGER.
AND THE EMORAN ARMY STILL STANDS BETWEEN YOUR KING AND HIS PRIZE. THOSE FIRES YOU SAW WERE LIT BY HYRKANIANS.

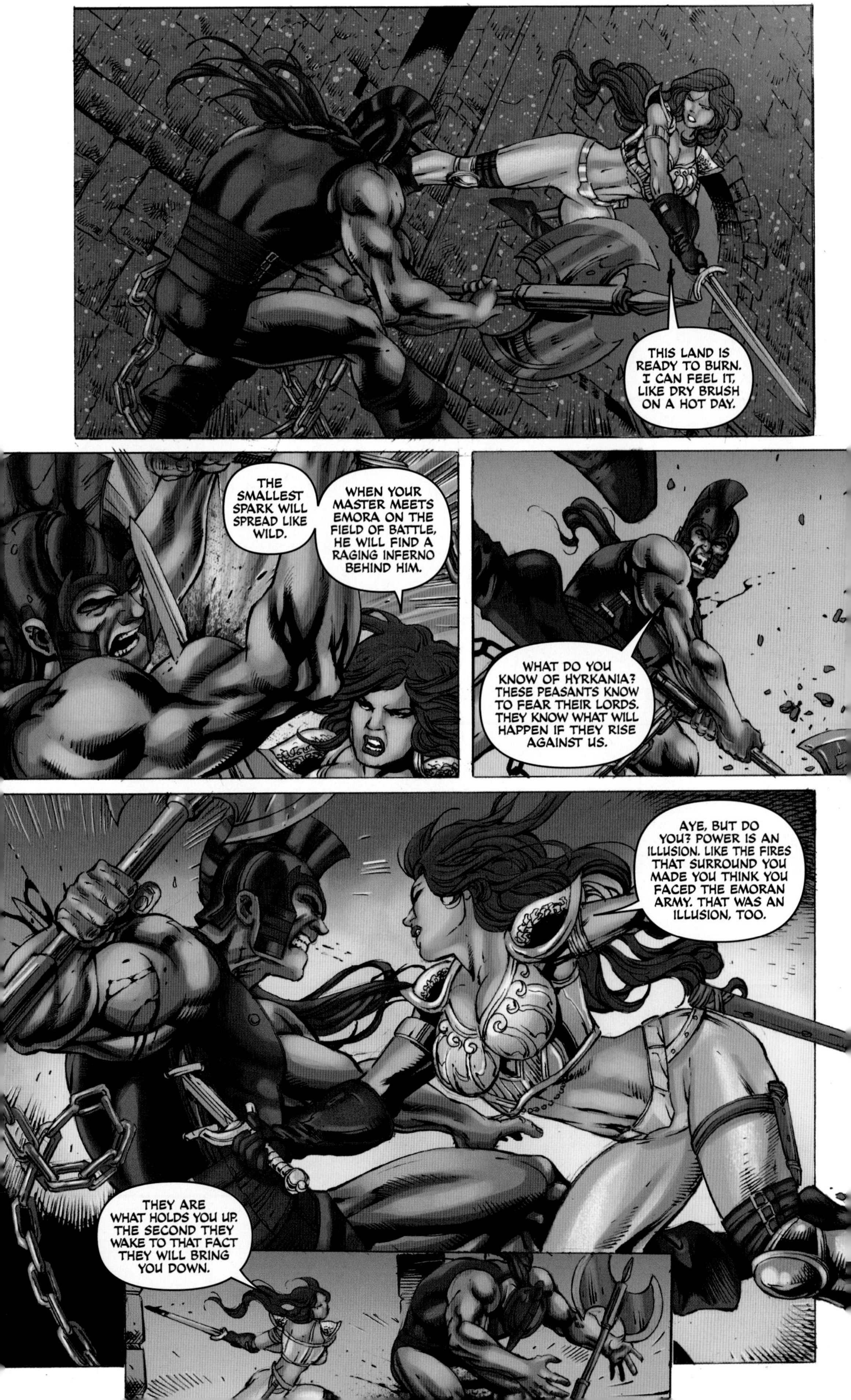

THIS LAND IS READY TO BURN. I CAN FEEL IT, LIKE DRY BRUSH ON A HOT DAY.
THE SMALLEST SPARK WILL SPREAD LIKE WILD.
WHEN YOUR MASTER MEETS EMORA ON THE FIELD OF BATTLE, HE WILL FIND A RAGING INFERNO BEHIND HIM.
WHAT DO YOU KNOW OF HYRKANIA? THESE PEASANTS KNOW TO FEAR THEIR LORDS. THEY KNOW WHAT WILL HAPPEN IF THEY RISE AGAINST US.
AYE, BUT DO YOU? POWER IS AN ILLUSION. LIKE THE FIRES THAT SURROUND YOU MADE YOU THINK YOU FACED THE EMORAN ARMY. THAT WAS AN ILLUSION, TOO.
THEY ARE WHAT HOLDS YOU UP. THE SECOND THEY WAKE TO THAT FACT THEY WILL BRING YOU DOWN.

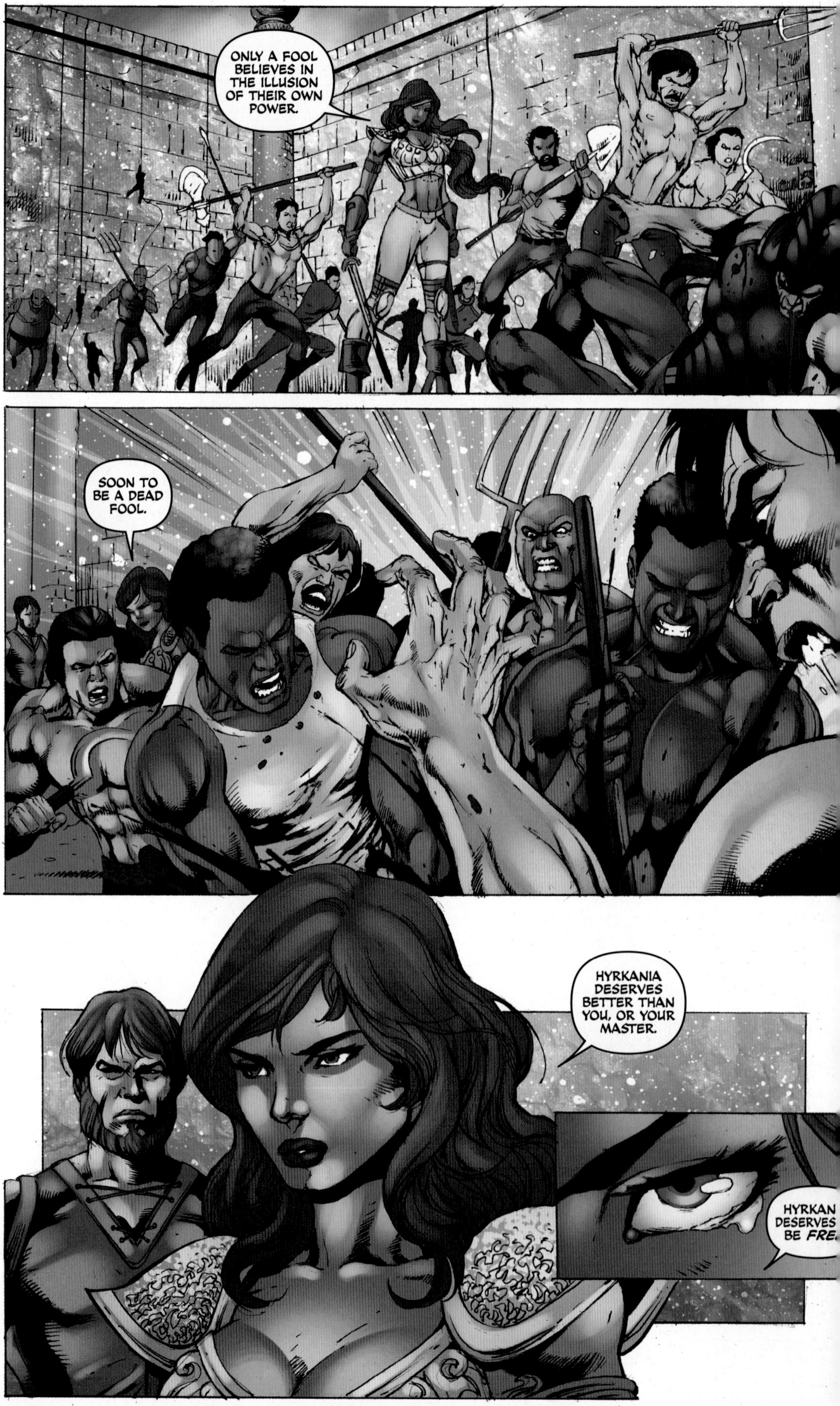
ONLY A FOOL BELIEVES IN THE ILLUSION OF THEIR OWN POWER.
SOON TO BE A DEAD FOOL.
HYRKANIA DESERVES BETTER THAN YOU, OR YOUR MASTER.
HYRKAN DESERVES BE FRE

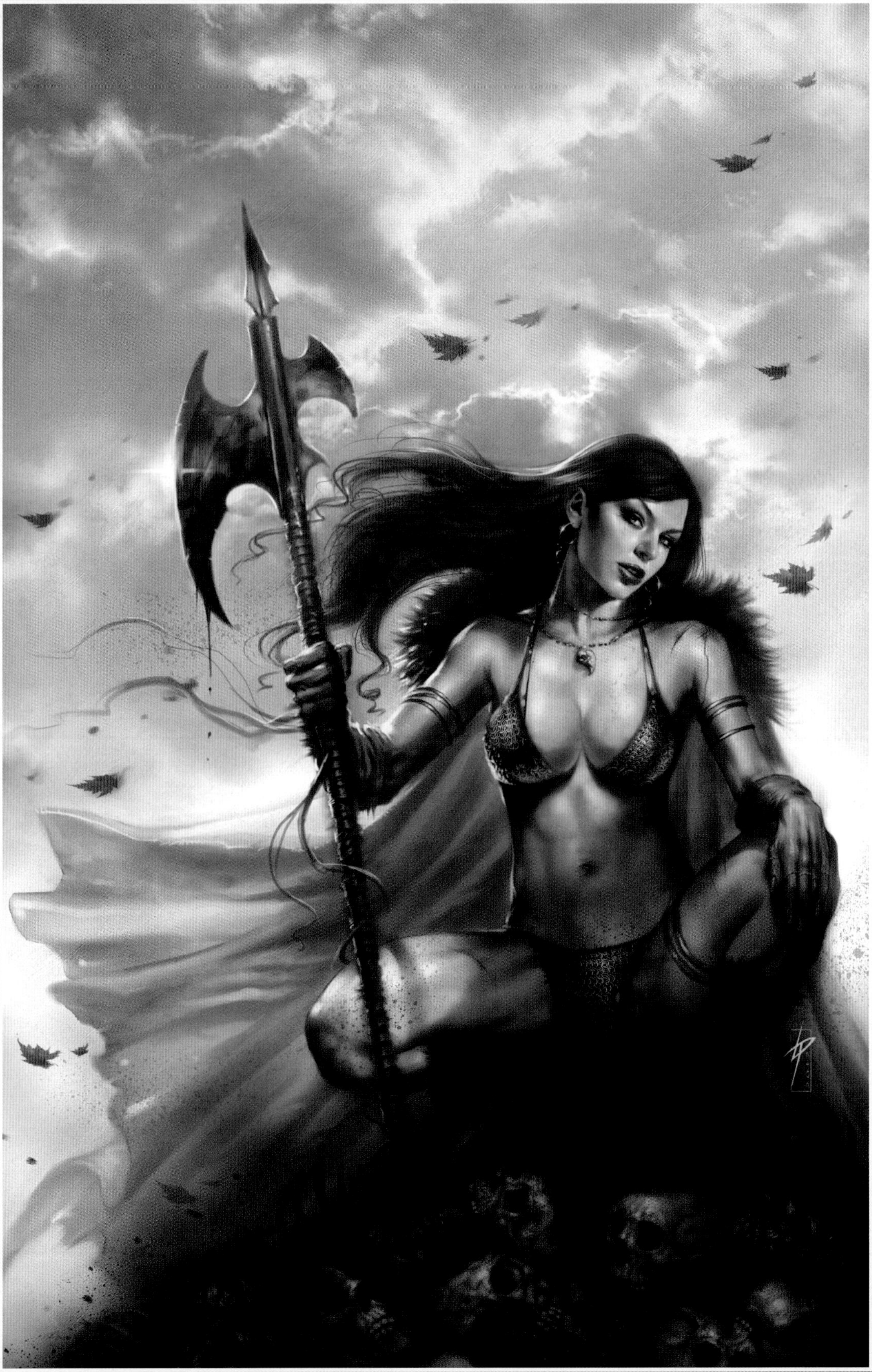

ISSUE #35 COVER BY LUCIO PARRILLO

THE SHE-DEVIL RETURNED HOME, TO HILLS LONG FORGOTTEN, SHROUDED IN THE PAINFUL MISTS OF TRAGEDY. YET, WHILE SHE HERSELF HAS FORGOTTEN, HYRKANIA REMEMBERS.

THE LEGEND OF RED SONJA ENDURED, IN WHISPERED TALES OF THE BOLD WOMAN WHO SLEW THE HATED KING, THEN TRAVELED THE WIDE WORLD.

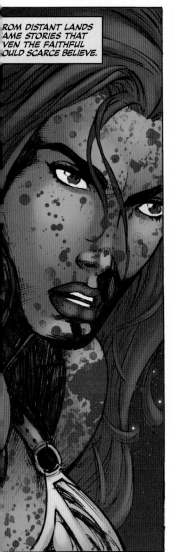

ROM DISTANT LANDS AME STORIES THAT VEN THE FAITHFUL OULD SCARCE BELIEVE.

BUT AT THE SIGHT OF RED SONJA IN THE FLESH, THE WEAKEST AMONG THEM FOUND COURAGE.

SHE HAD ALREADY KILLED ONE KING, SO WHY NOT TWO?

SO THEY CAME, YOUNG AND OLD, COMMON MAN AND WOMAN, TO RETAKE THEIR LAND.

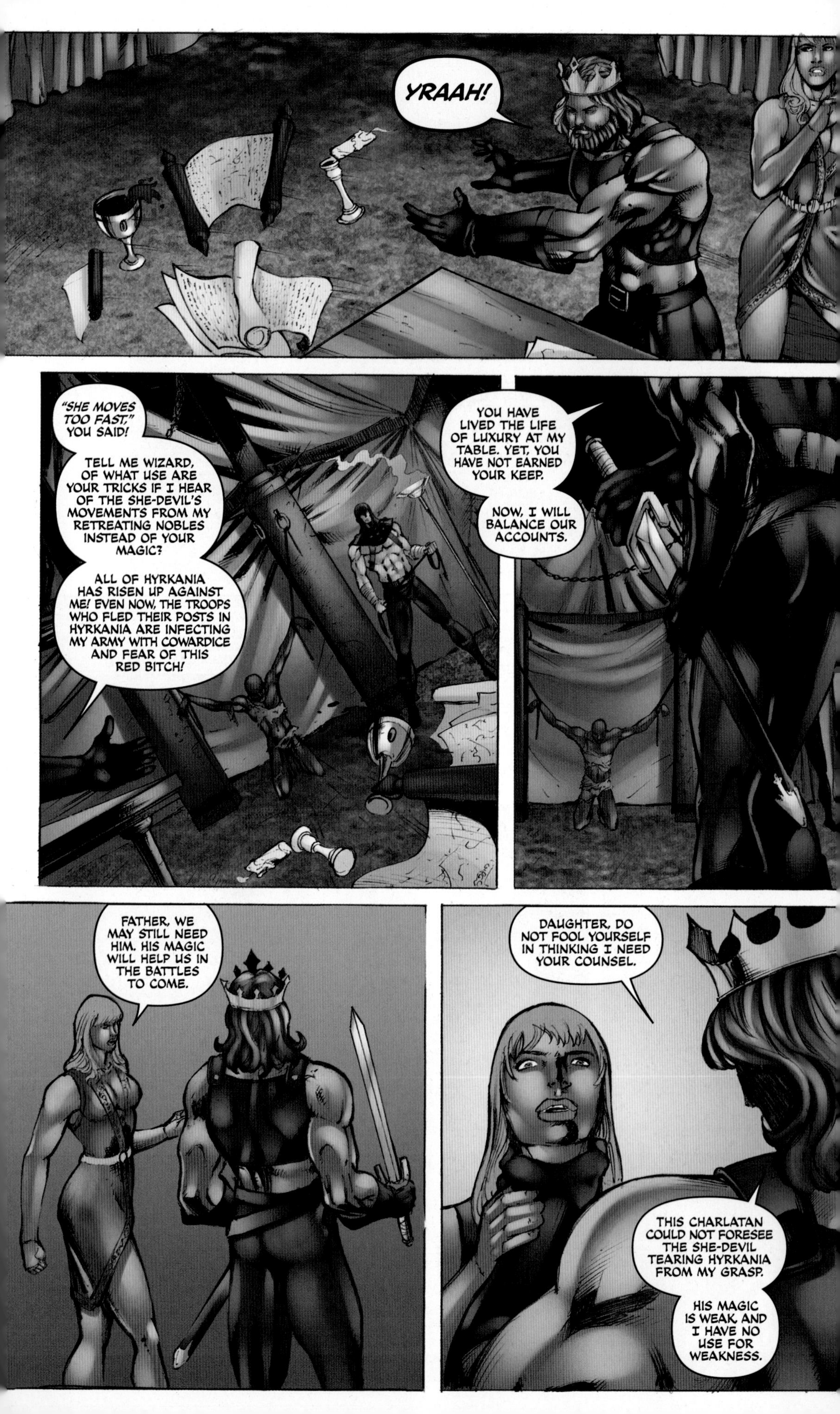
YRAAH!
"SHE MOVES TOO FAST," YOU SAID!
TELL ME WIZARD, OF WHAT USE ARE YOUR TRICKS IF I HEAR OF THE SHE-DEVIL'S MOVEMENTS FROM MY RETREATING NOBLES INSTEAD OF YOUR MAGIC?
ALL OF HYRKANIA HAS RISEN UP AGAINST ME! EVEN NOW, THE TROOPS WHO FLED THEIR POSTS IN HYRKANIA ARE INFECTING MY ARMY WITH COWARDICE AND FEAR OF THIS RED BITCH!
YOU HAVE LIVED THE LIFE OF LUXURY AT MY TABLE. YET, YOU HAVE NOT EARNED YOUR KEEP.
NOW, I WILL BALANCE OUR ACCOUNTS.
FATHER, WE MAY STILL NEED HIM. HIS MAGIC WILL HELP US IN THE BATTLES TO COME.
DAUGHTER, DO NOT FOOL YOURSELF IN THINKING I NEED YOUR COUNSEL.
THIS CHARLATAN COULD NOT FORESEE THE SHE-DEVIL TEARING HYRKANIA FROM MY GRASP.
HIS MAGIC IS WEAK, AND I HAVE NO USE FOR WEAKNESS.

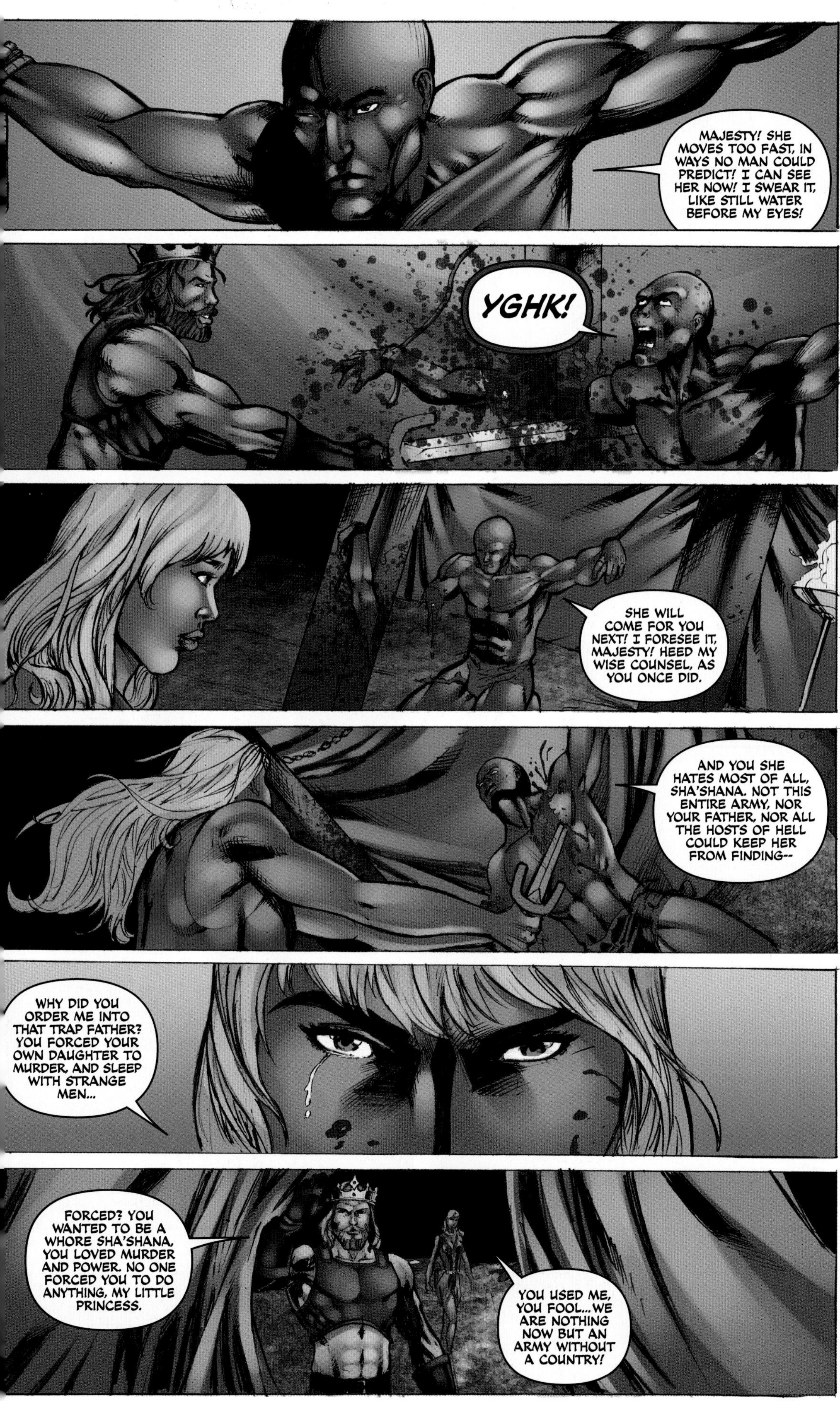
MAJESTY! SHE MOVES TOO FAST, IN WAYS NO MAN COULD PREDICT! I CAN SEE HER NOW! I SWEAR IT, LIKE STILL WATER BEFORE MY EYES!
YGHK!
SHE WILL COME FOR YOU NEXT! I FORESEE IT, MAJESTY! HEED MY WISE COUNSEL, AS YOU ONCE DID.
AND YOU SHE HATES MOST OF ALL, SHA'SHANA. NOT THIS ENTIRE ARMY, NOR YOUR FATHER, NOR ALL THE HOSTS OF HELL COULD KEEP HER FROM FINDING--
WHY DID YOU ORDER ME INTO THAT TRAP FATHER? YOU FORCED YOUR OWN DAUGHTER TO MURDER, AND SLEEP WITH STRANGE MEN...
FORCED? YOU WANTED TO BE A WHORE SHA'SHANA, YOU LOVED MURDER AND POWER. NO ONE FORCED YOU TO DO ANYTHING, MY LITTLE PRINCESS.
YOU USED ME, YOU FOOL...WE ARE NOTHING NOW BUT AN ARMY WITHOUT A COUNTRY!

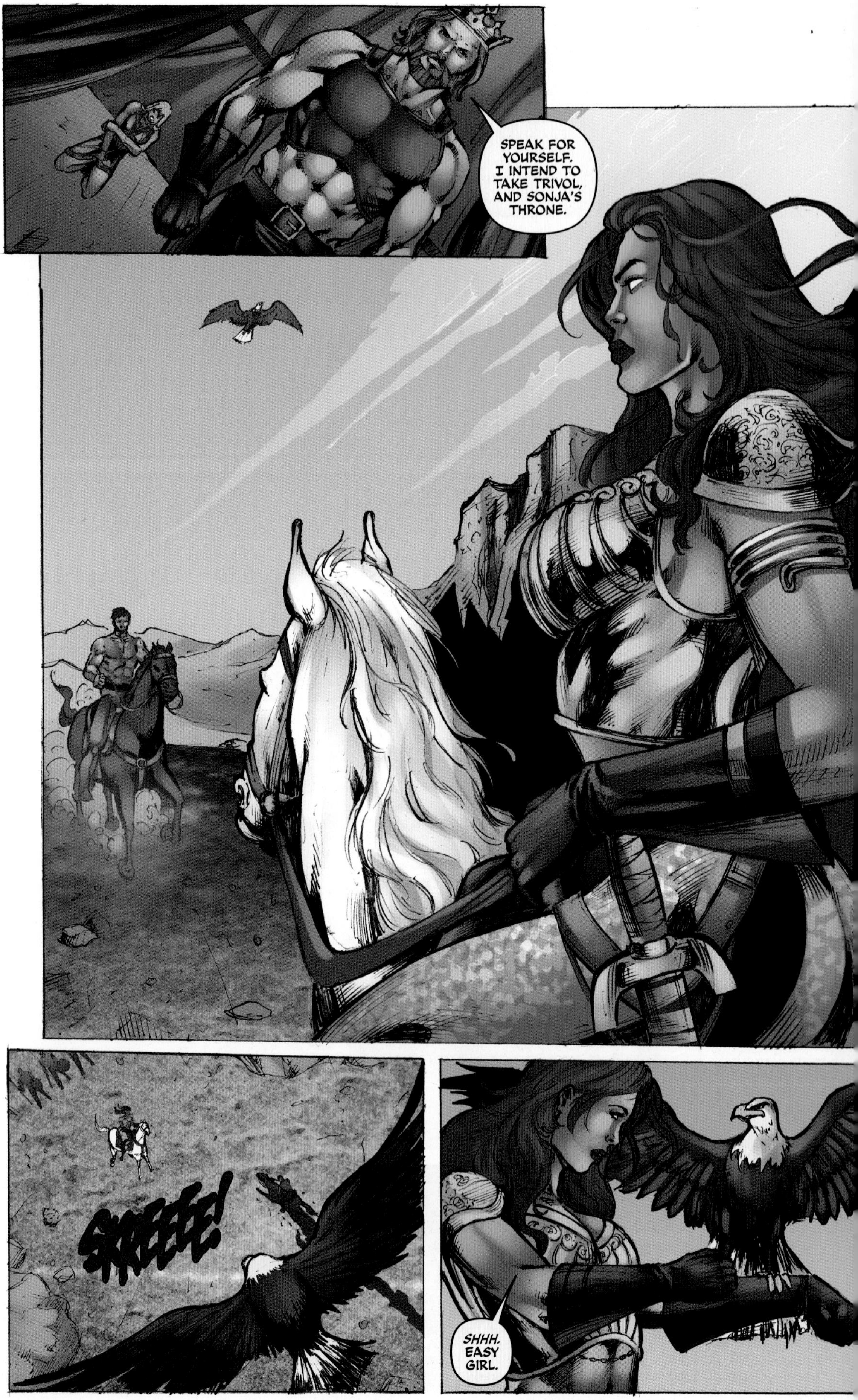
SPEAK FOR YOURSELF. I INTEND TO TAKE TRIVOL, AND SONJA'S THRONE.
SKREEEE!
SHHH. EASY GIRL.

KHITAI HAS BEEN SCATTERD TO THE FOUR WINDS...ZARTUR IS STILL OVER-MATCHED BY THE HYRKANIAN JUGGERNAUT.

THEY ARE TWO DAYS FROM TRIVOL.

SARTOR'S ARMY MOVES AWAY FROM US.

SARTOR HAS DESIGNS ON THE CAPITAL, AND THAT IS WHERE ZARTUR SHOULD MAKE HIS STAND, BEHIND THOSE HIGH WALLS.

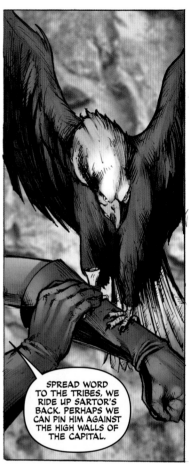

SPREAD WORD TO THE TRIBES, WE RIDE UP SARTOR'S BACK. PERHAPS WE CAN PIN HIM AGAINST THE HIGH WALLS OF THE CAPITAL.

LET HIM FIGHT IT OUT WITH THE EMORANS-- ENOUGH HYRKANIAN BLOOD WILL BE SPILLED!

YOU ASK US TO FIGHT OUR OWN BROTHERS.

WHAT HAVE YOU BEEN DOING THIS PAST MOON, IF NOT FIGHTING OTHER HYRKANIANS, HASHIM?

BESIDES, SARTOR'S ARMY IS MANNED BY MERCENARIES FROM ALL OVER THE WORLD.

"THE SCUM FROM TWELVE NATIONS GATHER UNDER HIS WRETCHED BANNER."

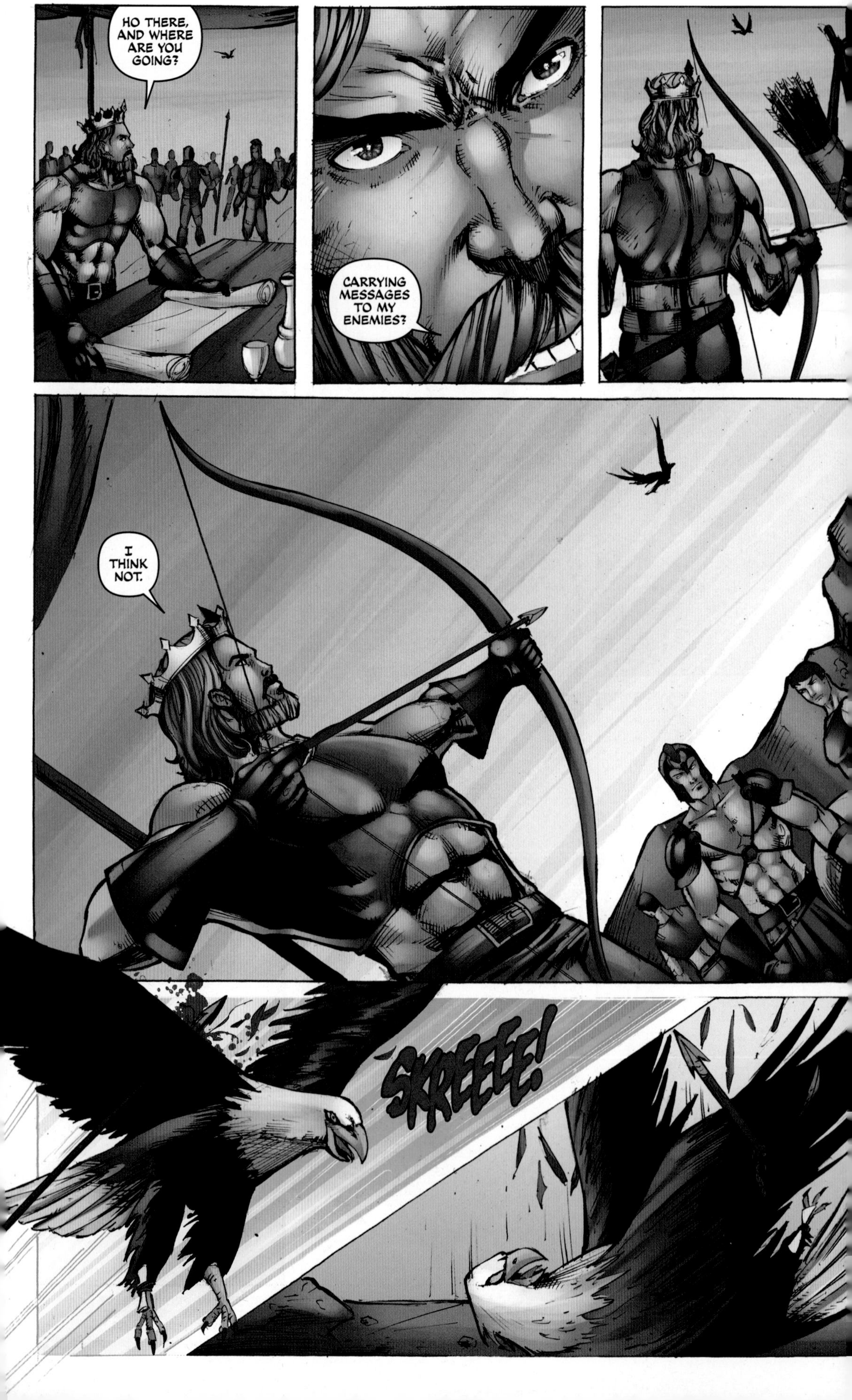
HO THERE, AND WHERE ARE YOU GOING?
CARRYING MESSAGES TO MY ENEMIES?
I THINK NOT.
SKREEEE!

ELSEWHERE.

LORD ZARTUR! THERE ARE MORE OF THEM! TOO MANY!

RETREAT!

FOLLOW ME!

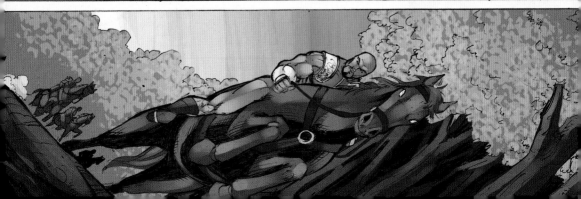

QUICKLY, ON YOUR HORSES, MEN, WE RETREAT TO THE CAPITAL. ONLY DEATH AWAITS US ON THE OPEN FIELD OF BATTLE!

SET AMBUSHES EVERY HALF LEAGUE ALL THE WAY TO TRIVOL.

MY LOVE, YOU RETURN TOO SOON, AND YET, NOT SOON ENOUGH.

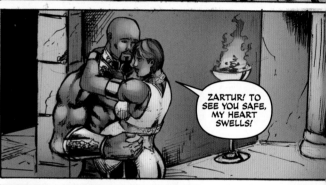

ZARTUR! TO SEE YOU SAFE, MY HEART SWELLS!

THAT IS NOT ALL THAT SWELLS, YOU LOOK RIPE TO BURST.

GODS, SUVARA! THE CHILD IS READY... YOU MUST BE IN BED. WE HAVE ONLY A FEW SHORT HOURS.

YOU RETURN NOT IN VICTORY, BUT IN RETREAT. I WILL NOT LEAVE YOUR SIDE TO FIGHT ALONE!

SARTOR WILL NEVER SEE THE INSIDE OF THESE GATES.

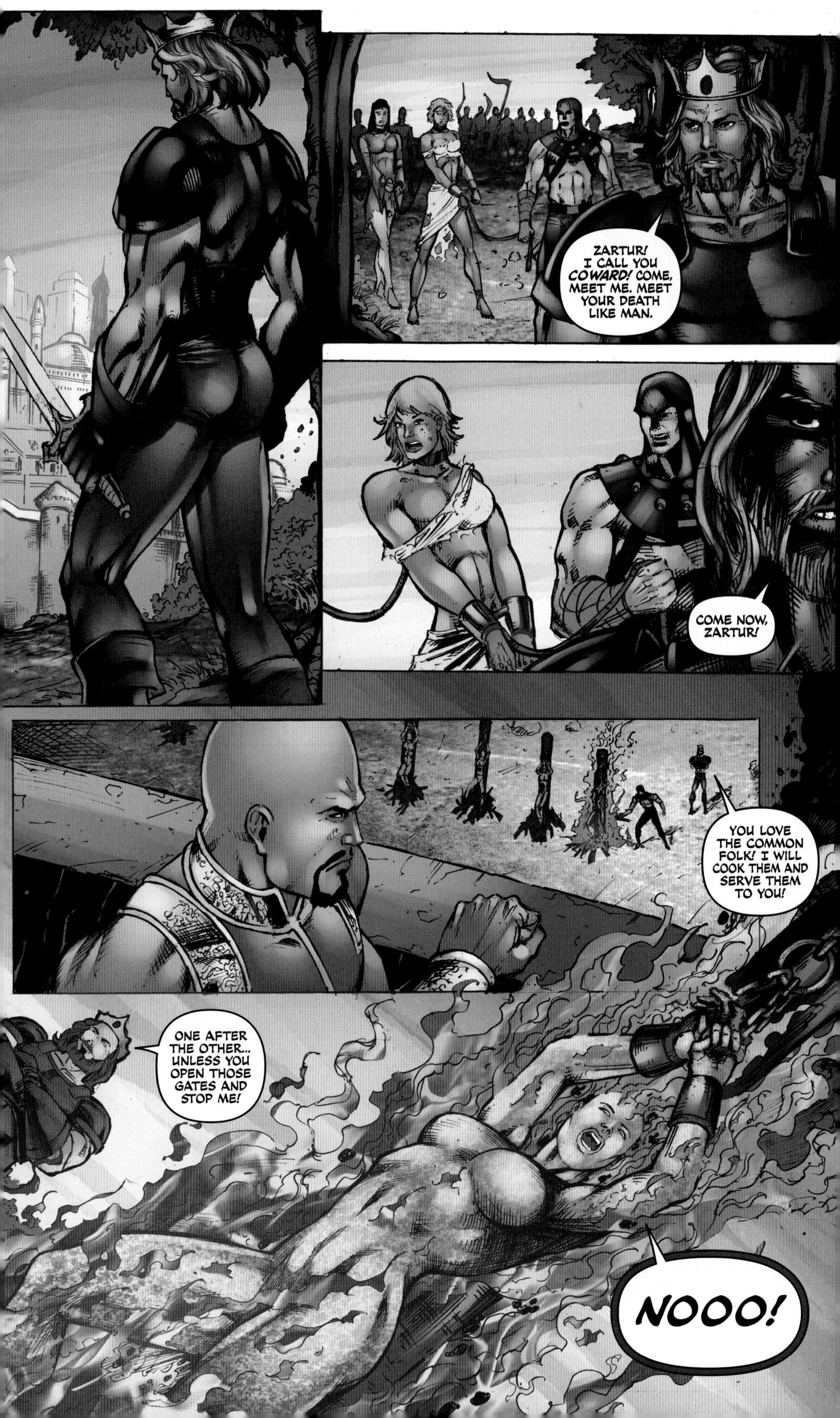

ZARTUR! I CALL YOU COWARD! COME, MEET ME. MEET YOUR DEATH LIKE MAN.
COME NOW, ZARTUR!
YOU LOVE THE COMMON FOLK! I WILL COOK THEM AND SERVE THEM TO YOU!
ONE AFTER THE OTHER... UNLESS YOU OPEN THOSE GATES AND STOP ME!
NOOO!

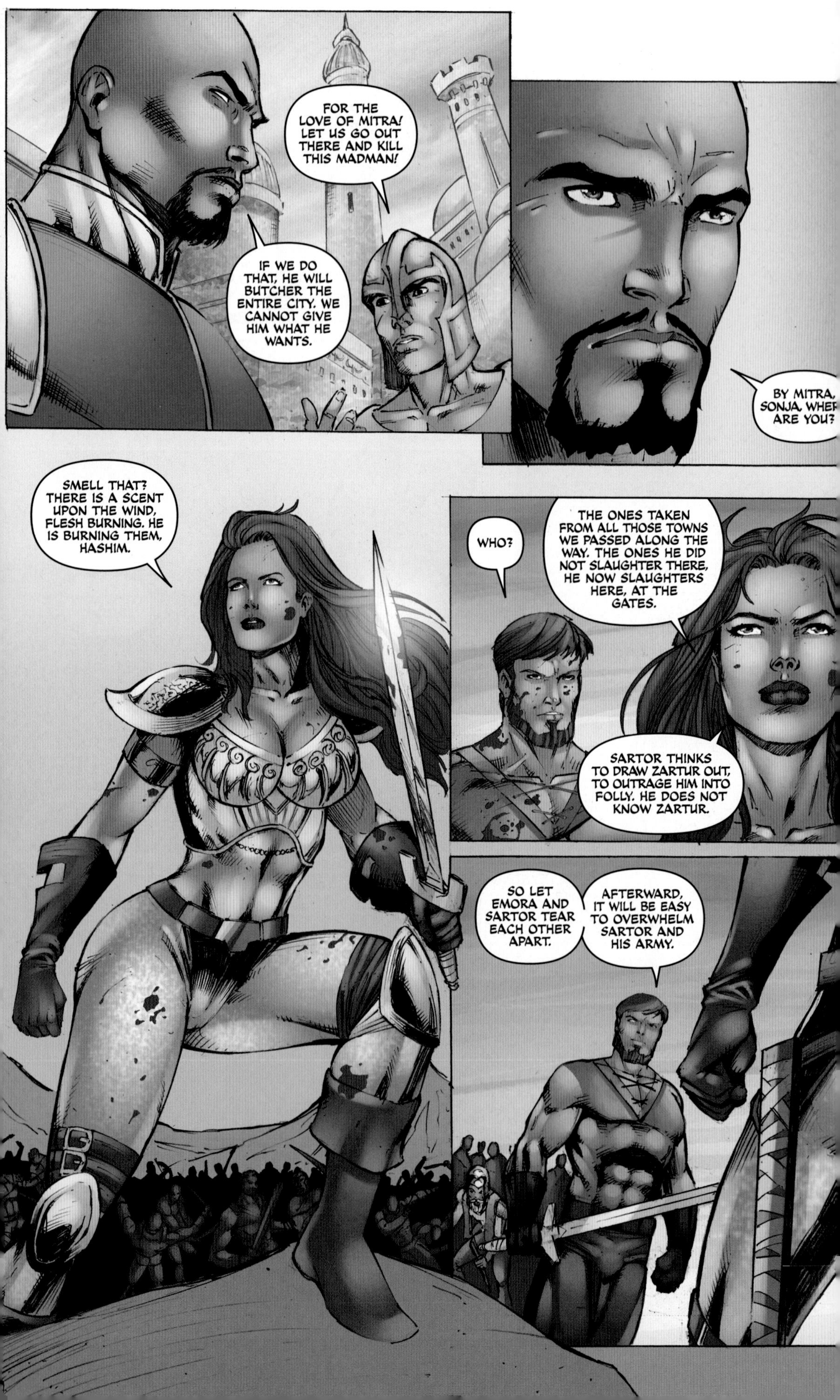
FOR THE LOVE OF MITRA! LET US GO OUT THERE AND KILL THIS MADMAN!
IF WE DO THAT, HE WILL BUTCHER THE ENTIRE CITY. WE CANNOT GIVE HIM WHAT HE WANTS.
BY MITRA, SONJA, WHER ARE YOU?
SMELL THAT? THERE IS A SCENT UPON THE WIND, FLESH BURNING. HE IS BURNING THEM, HASHIM.
WHO?
THE ONES TAKEN FROM ALL THOSE TOWNS WE PASSED ALONG THE WAY. THE ONES HE DID NOT SLAUGHTER THERE, HE NOW SLAUGHTERS HERE, AT THE GATES.
SARTOR THINKS TO DRAW ZARTUR OUT, TO OUTRAGE HIM INTO FOLLY. HE DOES NOT KNOW ZARTUR.
SO LET EMORA AND SARTOR TEAR EACH OTHER APART.
AFTERWARD, IT WILL BE EASY TO OVERWHELM SARTOR AND HIS ARMY.

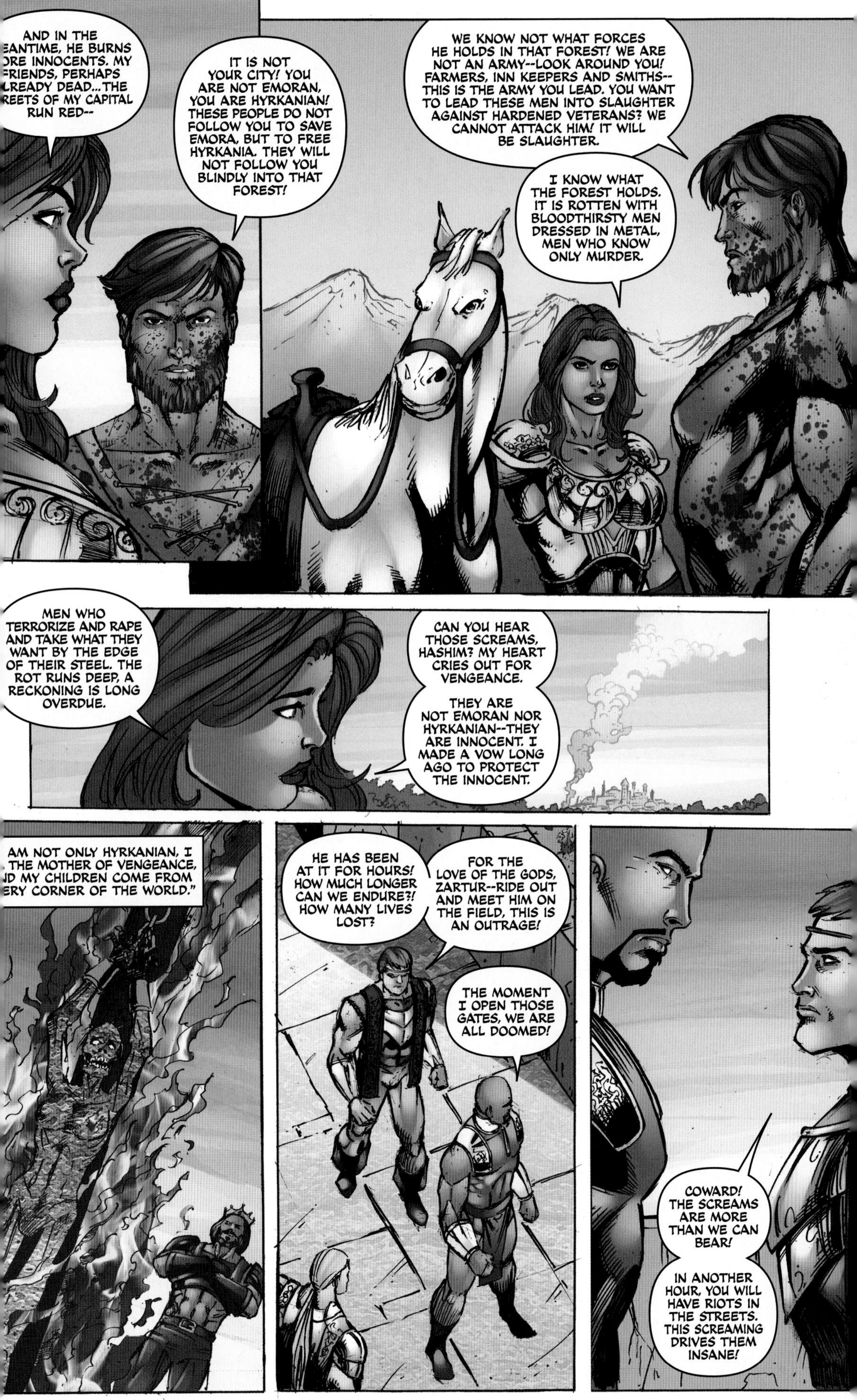

AND IN THE EANTIME, HE BURNS ORE INNOCENTS. MY FRIENDS, PERHAPS LREADY DEAD...THE REETS OF MY CAPITAL RUN RED--
IT IS NOT YOUR CITY! YOU ARE NOT EMORAN, YOU ARE HYRKANIAN! THESE PEOPLE DO NOT FOLLOW YOU TO SAVE EMORA, BUT TO FREE HYRKANIA. THEY WILL NOT FOLLOW YOU BLINDLY INTO THAT FOREST!
WE KNOW NOT WHAT FORCES HE HOLDS IN THAT FOREST! WE ARE NOT AN ARMY--LOOK AROUND YOU! FARMERS, INN KEEPERS AND SMITHS--THIS IS THE ARMY YOU LEAD. YOU WANT TO LEAD THESE MEN INTO SLAUGHTER AGAINST HARDENED VETERANS? WE CANNOT ATTACK HIM! IT WILL BE SLAUGHTER.
I KNOW WHAT THE FOREST HOLDS. IT IS ROTTEN WITH BLOODTHIRSTY MEN DRESSED IN METAL, MEN WHO KNOW ONLY MURDER.
MEN WHO TERRORIZE AND RAPE AND TAKE WHAT THEY WANT BY THE EDGE OF THEIR STEEL. THE ROT RUNS DEEP, A RECKONING IS LONG OVERDUE.
CAN YOU HEAR THOSE SCREAMS, HASHIM? MY HEART CRIES OUT FOR VENGEANCE.
THEY ARE NOT EMORAN NOR HYRKANIAN--THEY ARE INNOCENT. I MADE A VOW LONG AGO TO PROTECT THE INNOCENT.
AM NOT ONLY HYRKANIAN, I THE MOTHER OF VENGEANCE, D MY CHILDREN COME FROM ERY CORNER OF THE WORLD."
HE HAS BEEN AT IT FOR HOURS! HOW MUCH LONGER CAN WE ENDURE?! HOW MANY LIVES LOST?
FOR THE LOVE OF THE GODS, ZARTUR--RIDE OUT AND MEET HIM ON THE FIELD, THIS IS AN OUTRAGE!
THE MOMENT I OPEN THOSE GATES, WE ARE ALL DOOMED!
COWARD! THE SCREAMS ARE MORE THAN WE CAN BEAR!
IN ANOTHER HOUR, YOU WILL HAVE RIOTS IN THE STREETS. THIS SCREAMING DRIVES THEM INSANE!

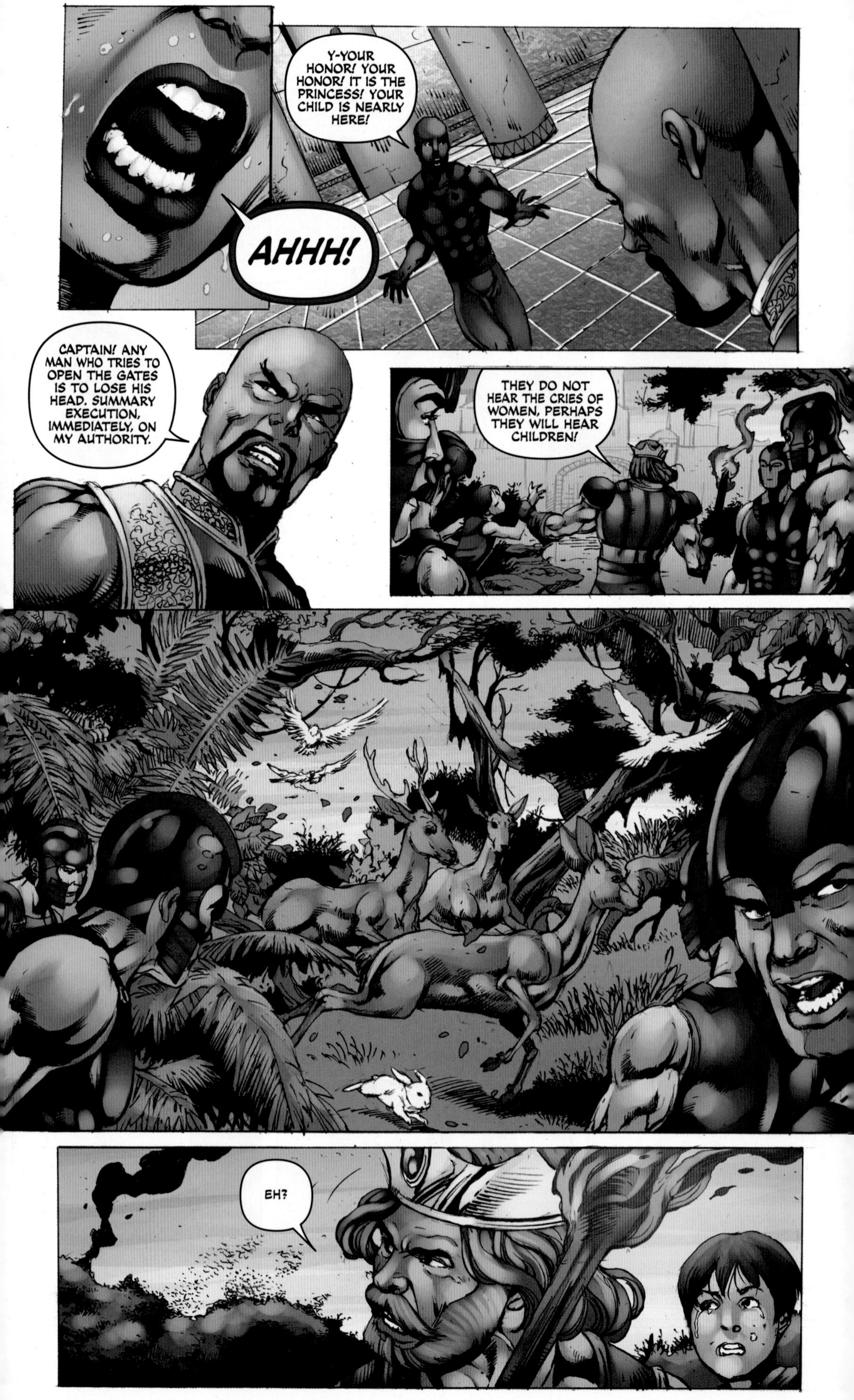
AHHH!
Y-YOUR HONOR! YOUR HONOR! IT IS THE PRINCESS! YOUR CHILD IS NEARLY HERE!
CAPTAIN! ANY MAN WHO TRIES TO OPEN THE GATES IS TO LOSE HIS HEAD. SUMMARY EXECUTION, IMMEDIATELY, ON MY AUTHORITY.
THEY DO NOT HEAR THE CRIES OF WOMEN, PERHAPS THEY WILL HEAR CHILDREN!
EH?

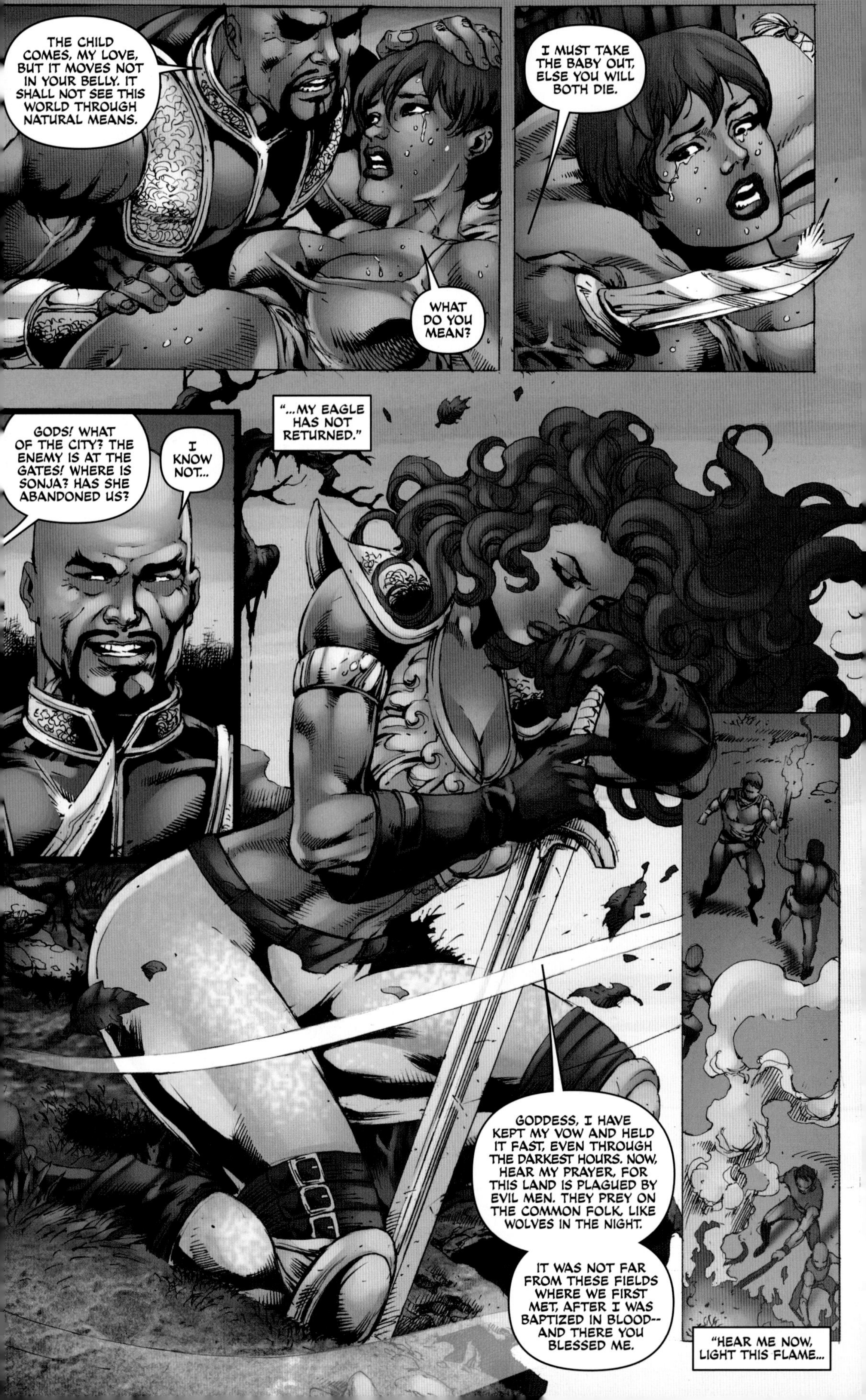
THE CHILD COMES, MY LOVE, BUT IT MOVES NOT IN YOUR BELLY. IT SHALL NOT SEE THIS WORLD THROUGH NATURAL MEANS.
WHAT DO YOU MEAN?
I MUST TAKE THE BABY OUT, ELSE YOU WILL BOTH DIE.
GODS! WHAT OF THE CITY? THE ENEMY IS AT THE GATES! WHERE IS SONJA? HAS SHE ABANDONED US?
I KNOW NOT...
"...MY EAGLE HAS NOT RETURNED."
GODDESS, I HAVE KEPT MY VOW AND HELD IT FAST, EVEN THROUGH THE DARKEST HOURS. NOW, HEAR MY PRAYER, FOR THIS LAND IS PLAGUED BY EVIL MEN. THEY PREY ON THE COMMON FOLK, LIKE WOLVES IN THE NIGHT.
IT WAS NOT FAR FROM THESE FIELDS WHERE WE FIRST MET, AFTER I WAS BAPTIZED IN BLOOD-- AND THERE YOU BLESSED ME.
"HEAR ME NOW, LIGHT THIS FLAME...

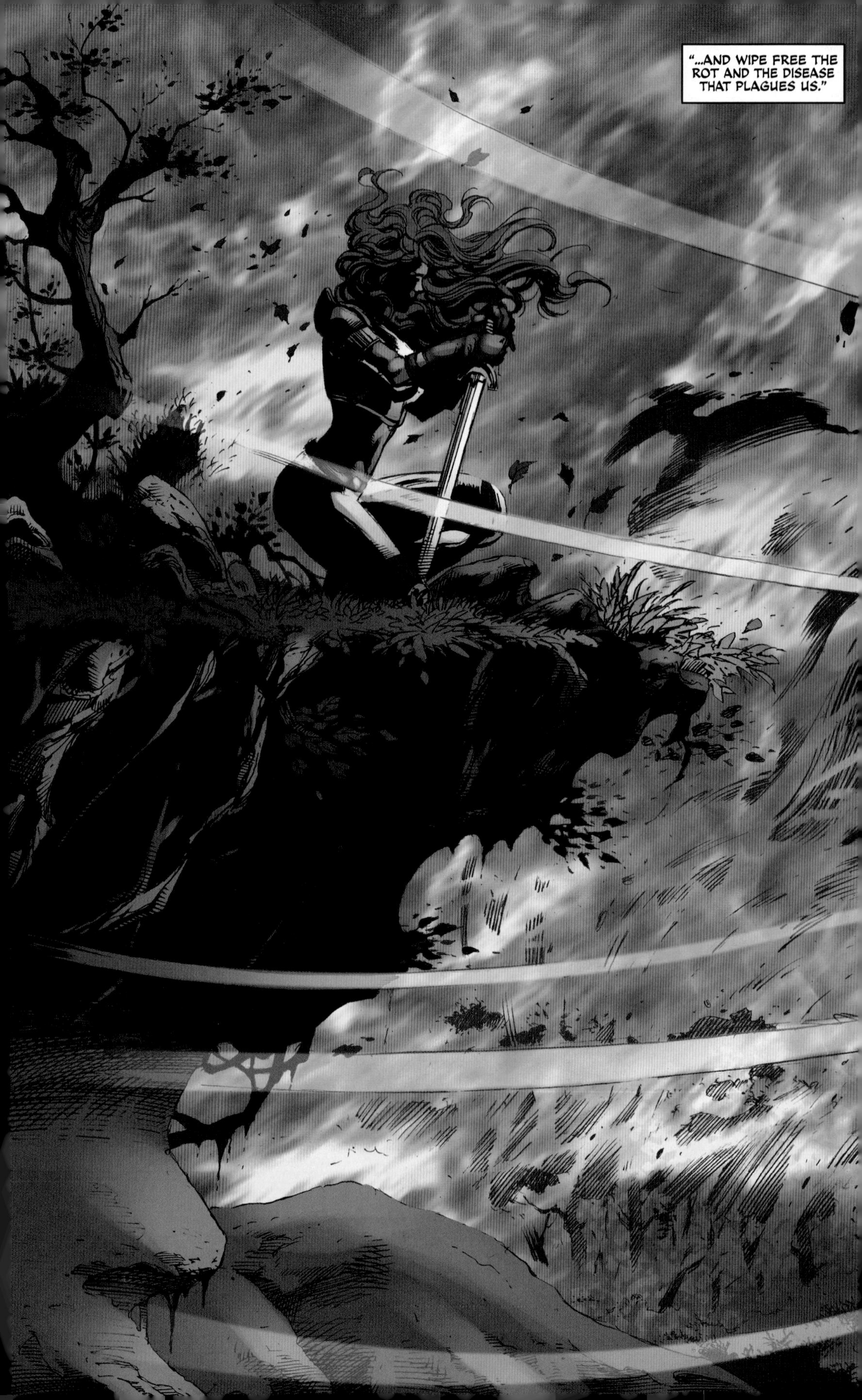
"...AND WIPE FREE THE ROT AND THE DISEASE THAT PLAGUES US."

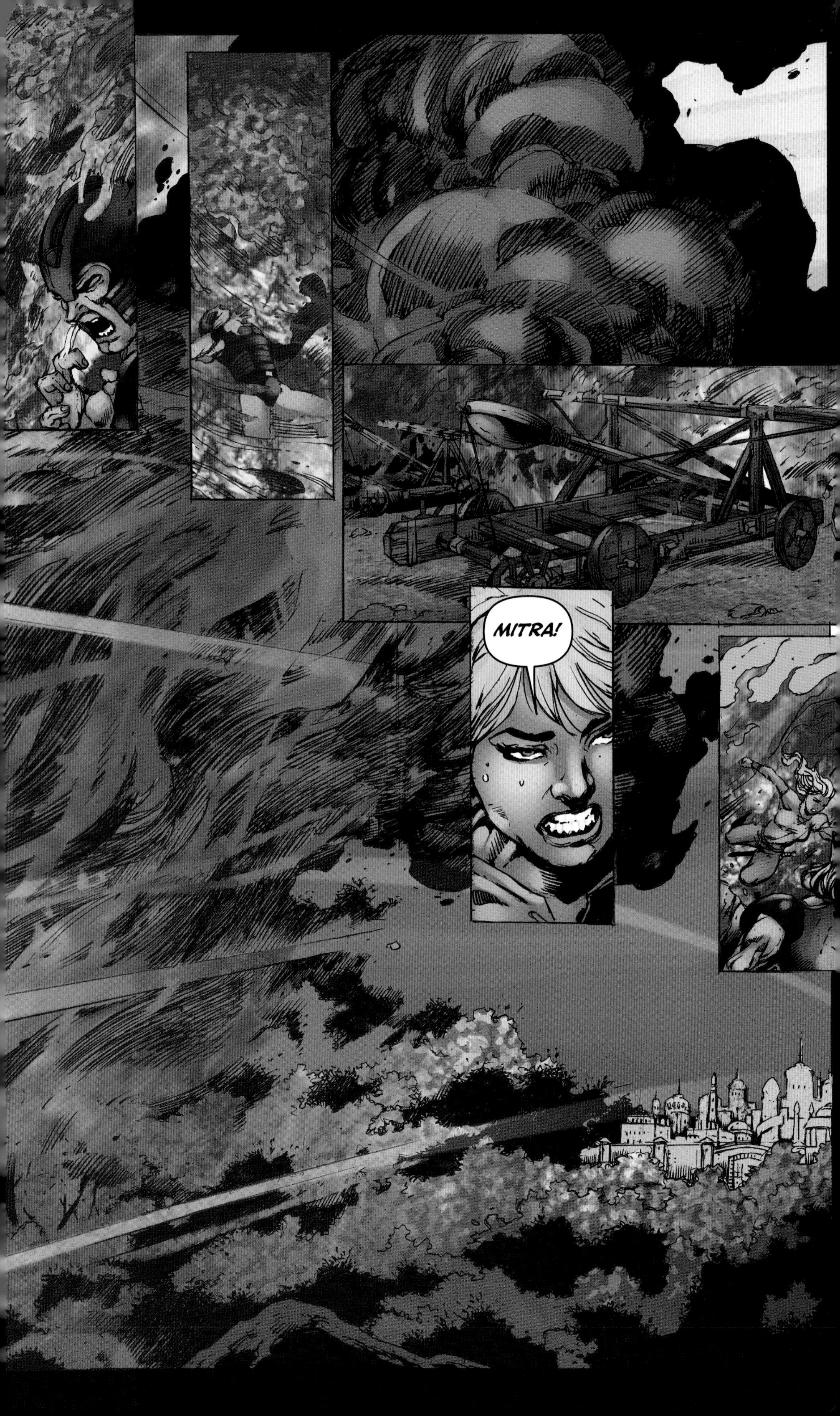
MITRA!

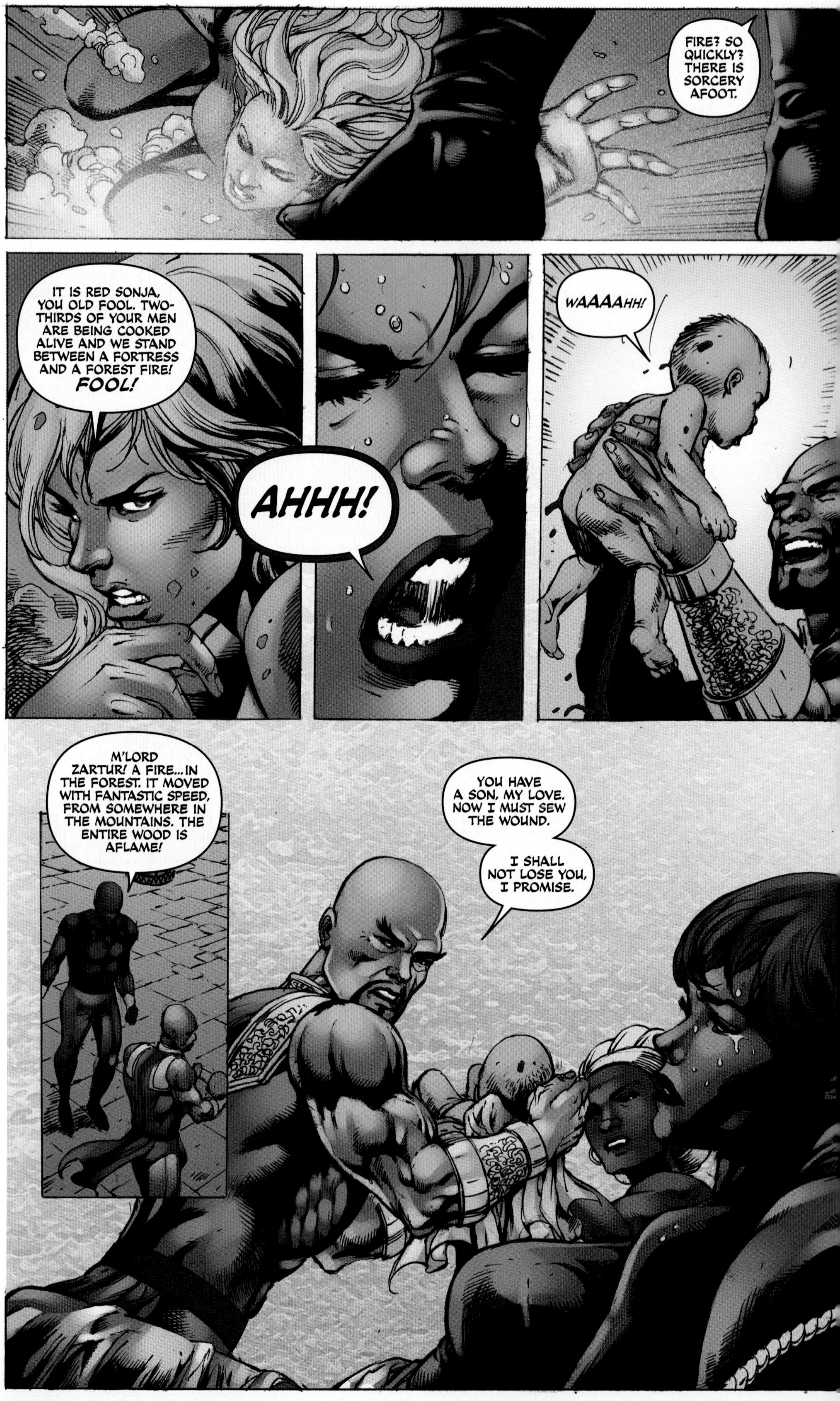
FIRE? SO QUICKLY? THERE IS SORCERY AFOOT.
IT IS RED SONJA, YOU OLD FOOL. TWO-THIRDS OF YOUR MEN ARE BEING COOKED ALIVE AND WE STAND BETWEEN A FORTRESS AND A FOREST FIRE! FOOL!
AHHH!
WAAAAHH!
M'LORD ZARTUR! A FIRE...IN THE FOREST. IT MOVED WITH FANTASTIC SPEED, FROM SOMEWHERE IN THE MOUNTAINS. THE ENTIRE WOOD IS AFLAME!
YOU HAVE A SON, MY LOVE. NOW I MUST SEW THE WOUND.
I SHALL NOT LOSE YOU, I PROMISE.

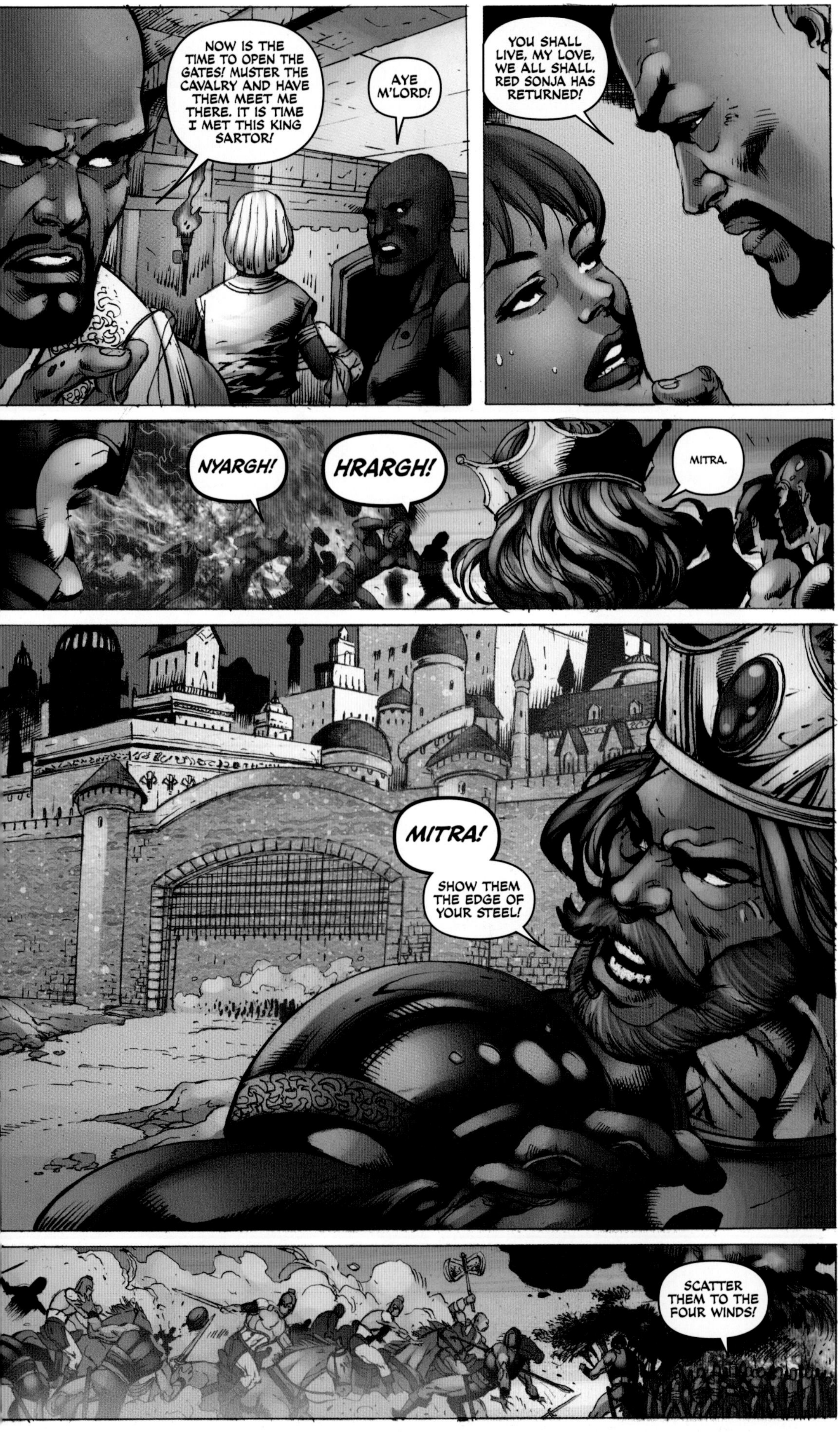
NOW IS THE TIME TO OPEN THE GATES! MUSTER THE CAVALRY AND HAVE THEM MEET ME THERE. IT IS TIME I MET THIS KING SARTOR!
AYE M'LORD!
YOU SHALL LIVE, MY LOVE, WE ALL SHALL. RED SONJA HAS RETURNED!
NYARGH!
HRARGH!
MITRA.
MITRA!
SHOW THEM THE EDGE OF YOUR STEEL!
SCATTER THEM TO THE FOUR WINDS!

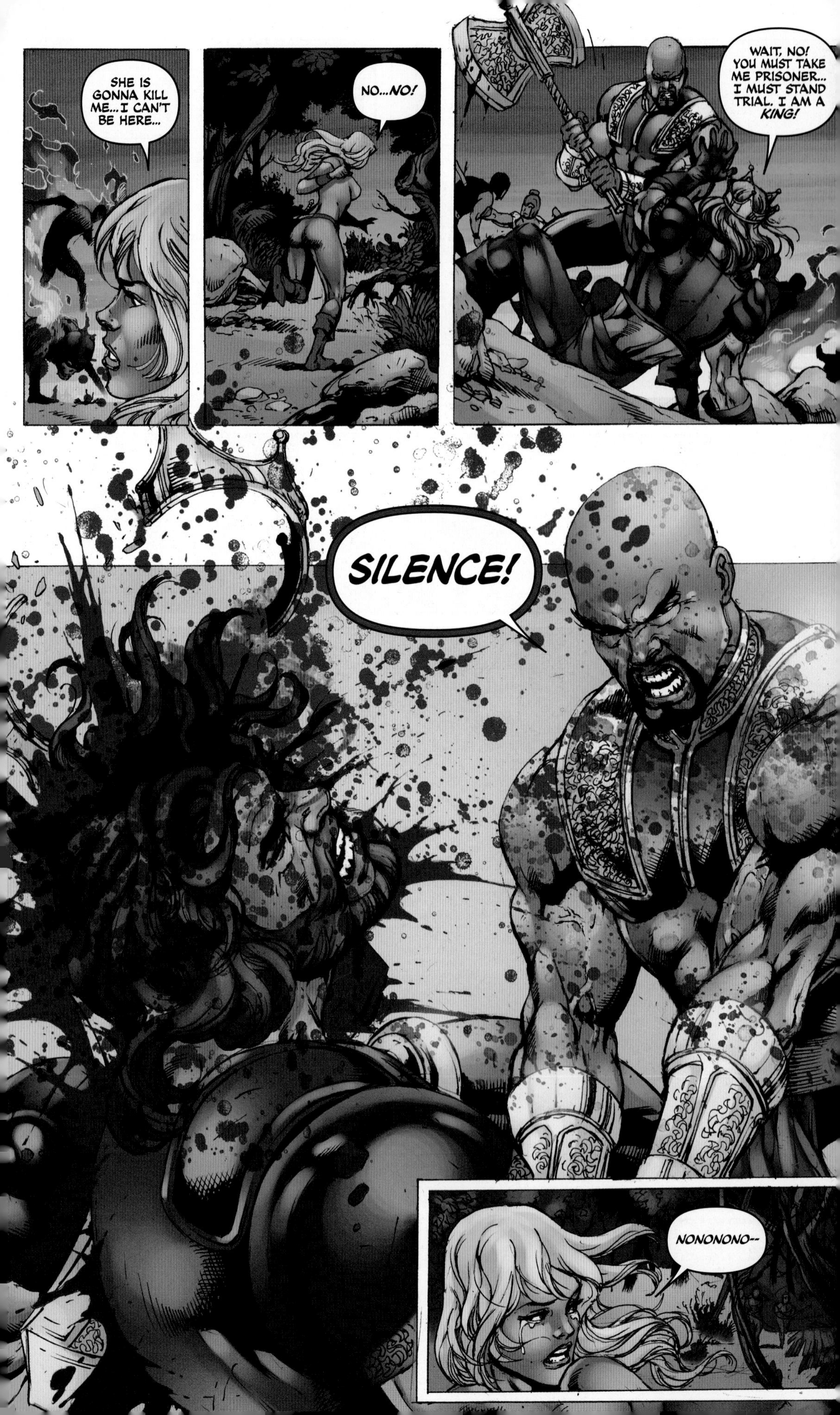
SHE IS GONNA KILL ME... I CAN'T BE HERE...
NO...NO!
WAIT, NO! YOU MUST TAKE ME PRISONER... I MUST STAND TRIAL. I AM A KING!
SILENCE!
NONONONO--

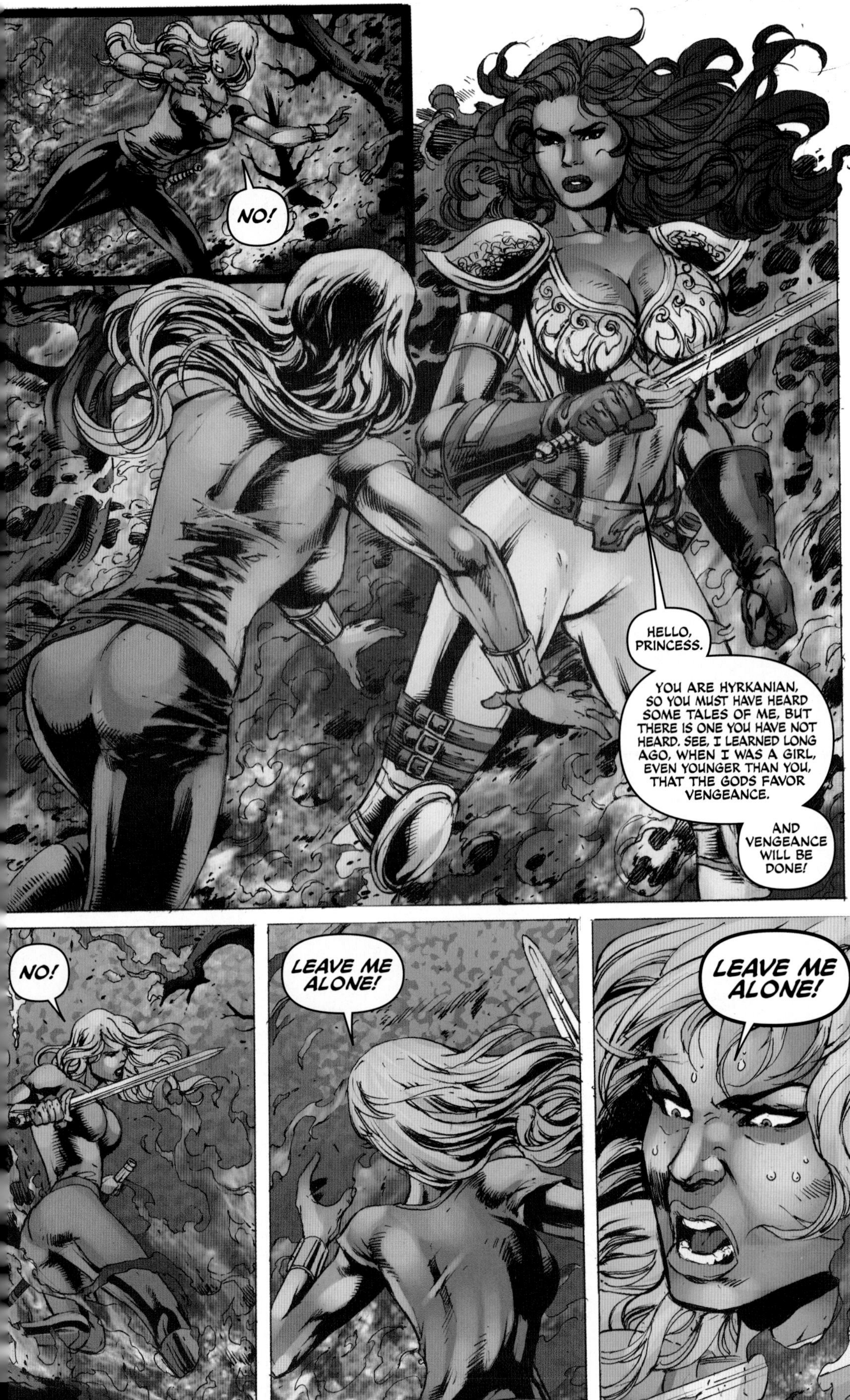
NO!
HELLO, PRINCESS.
YOU ARE HYRKANIAN, SO YOU MUST HAVE HEARD SOME TALES OF ME, BUT THERE IS ONE YOU HAVE NOT HEARD. SEE, I LEARNED LONG AGO, WHEN I WAS A GIRL, EVEN YOUNGER THAN YOU, THAT THE GODS FAVOR VENGEANCE.
AND VENGEANCE WILL BE DONE!
NO!
LEAVE ME ALONE!
LEAVE ME ALONE!

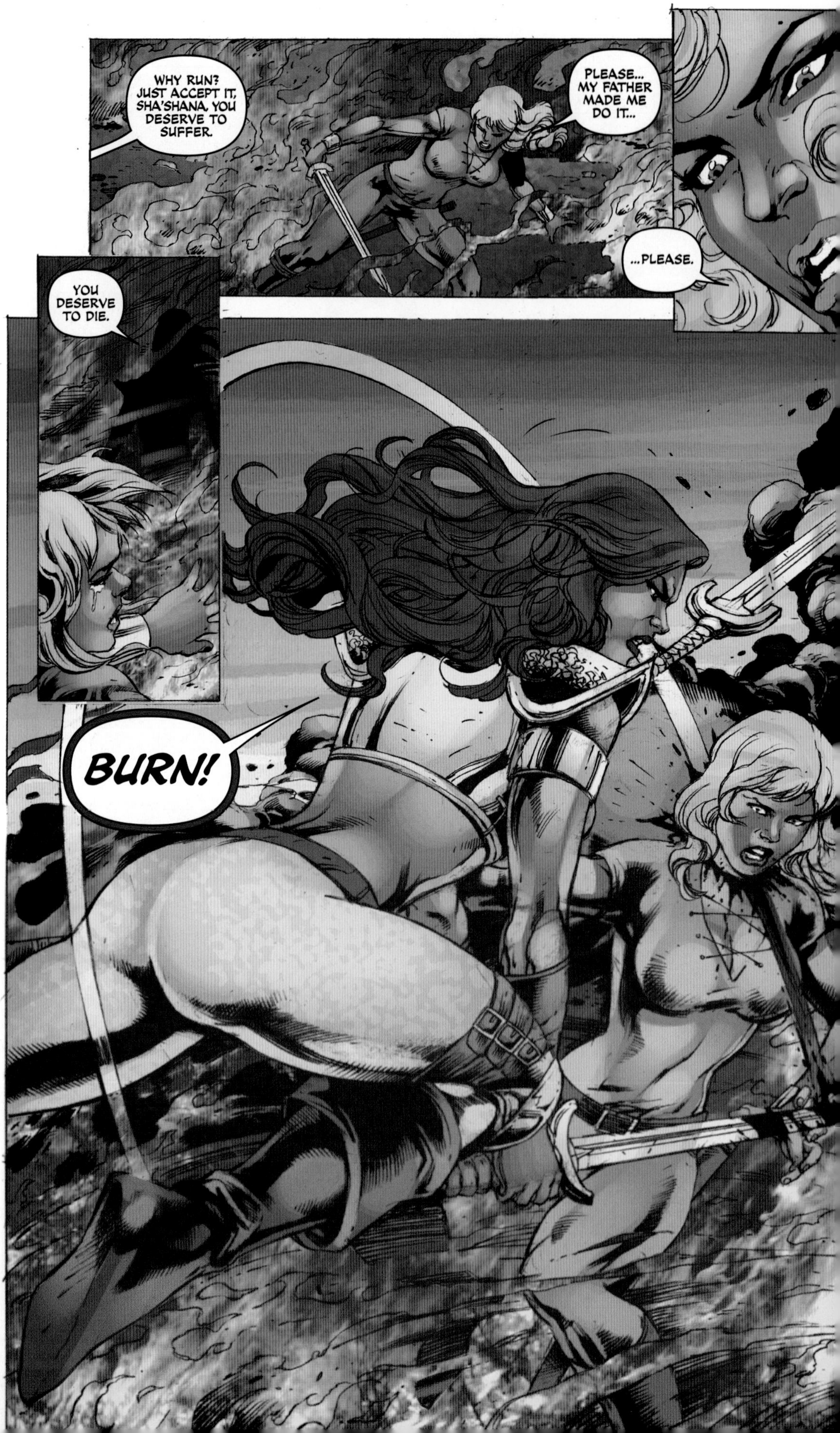

WHY RUN? JUST ACCEPT IT, SHA'SHANA. YOU DESERVE TO SUFFER.
PLEASE... MY FATHER MADE ME DO IT...
...PLEASE.
YOU DESERVE TO DIE.
BURN!

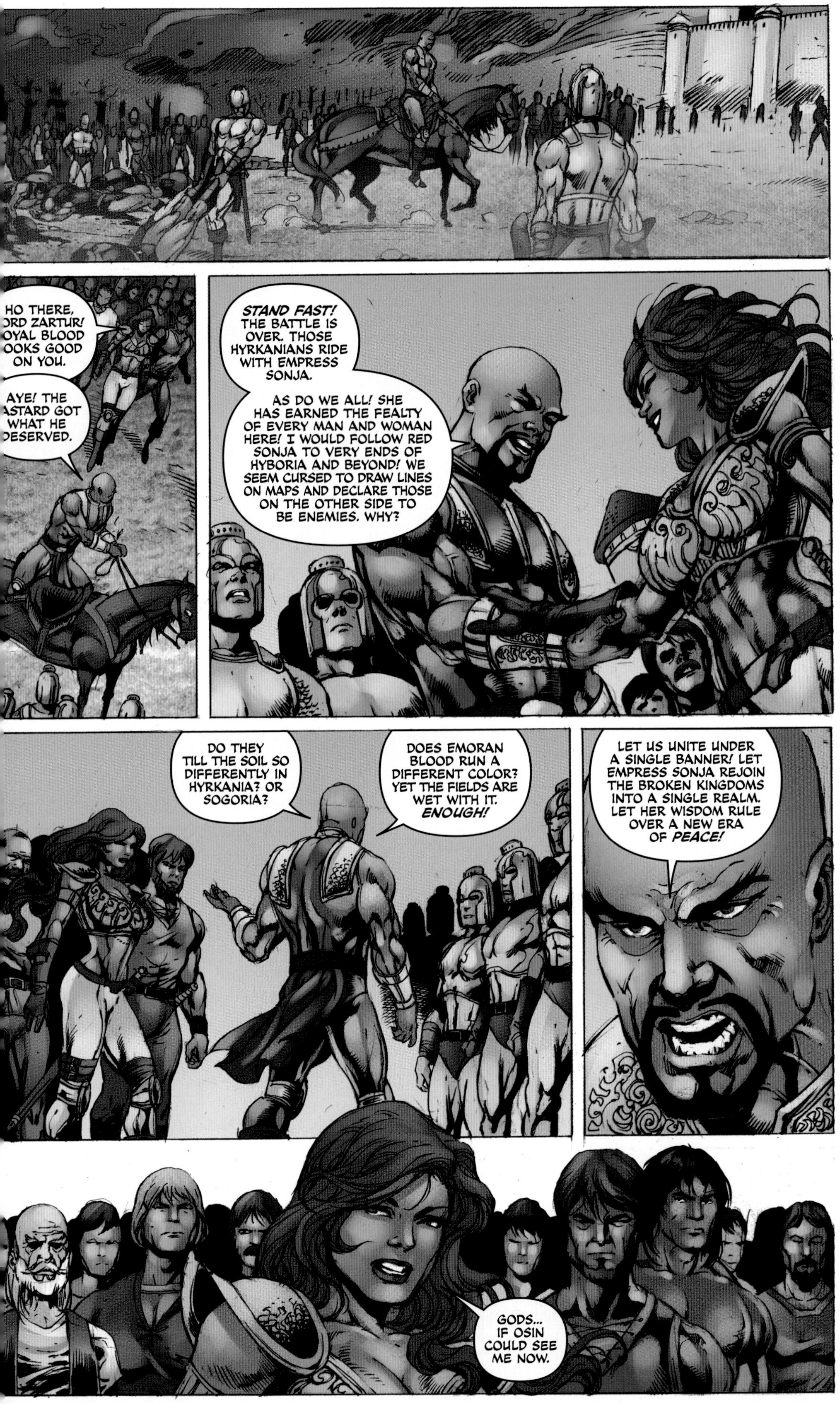
HO THERE, ORD ZARTUR! OYAL BLOOD OOKS GOOD ON YOU.
AYE! THE ASTARD GOT WHAT HE DESERVED.
STAND FAST! THE BATTLE IS OVER. THOSE HYRKANIANS RIDE WITH EMPRESS SONJA.
AS DO WE ALL! SHE HAS EARNED THE FEALTY OF EVERY MAN AND WOMAN HERE! I WOULD FOLLOW RED SONJA TO VERY ENDS OF HYBORIA AND BEYOND! WE SEEM CURSED TO DRAW LINES ON MAPS AND DECLARE THOSE ON THE OTHER SIDE TO BE ENEMIES. WHY?
DO THEY TILL THE SOIL SO DIFFERENTLY IN HYRKANIA? OR SOGORIA?
DOES EMORAN BLOOD RUN A DIFFERENT COLOR? YET THE FIELDS ARE WET WITH IT. ENOUGH!
LET US UNITE UNDER A SINGLE BANNER! LET EMPRESS SONJA REJOIN THE BROKEN KINGDOMS INTO A SINGLE REALM. LET HER WISDOM RULE OVER A NEW ERA OF PEACE!
GODS... IF OSIN COULD SEE ME NOW.

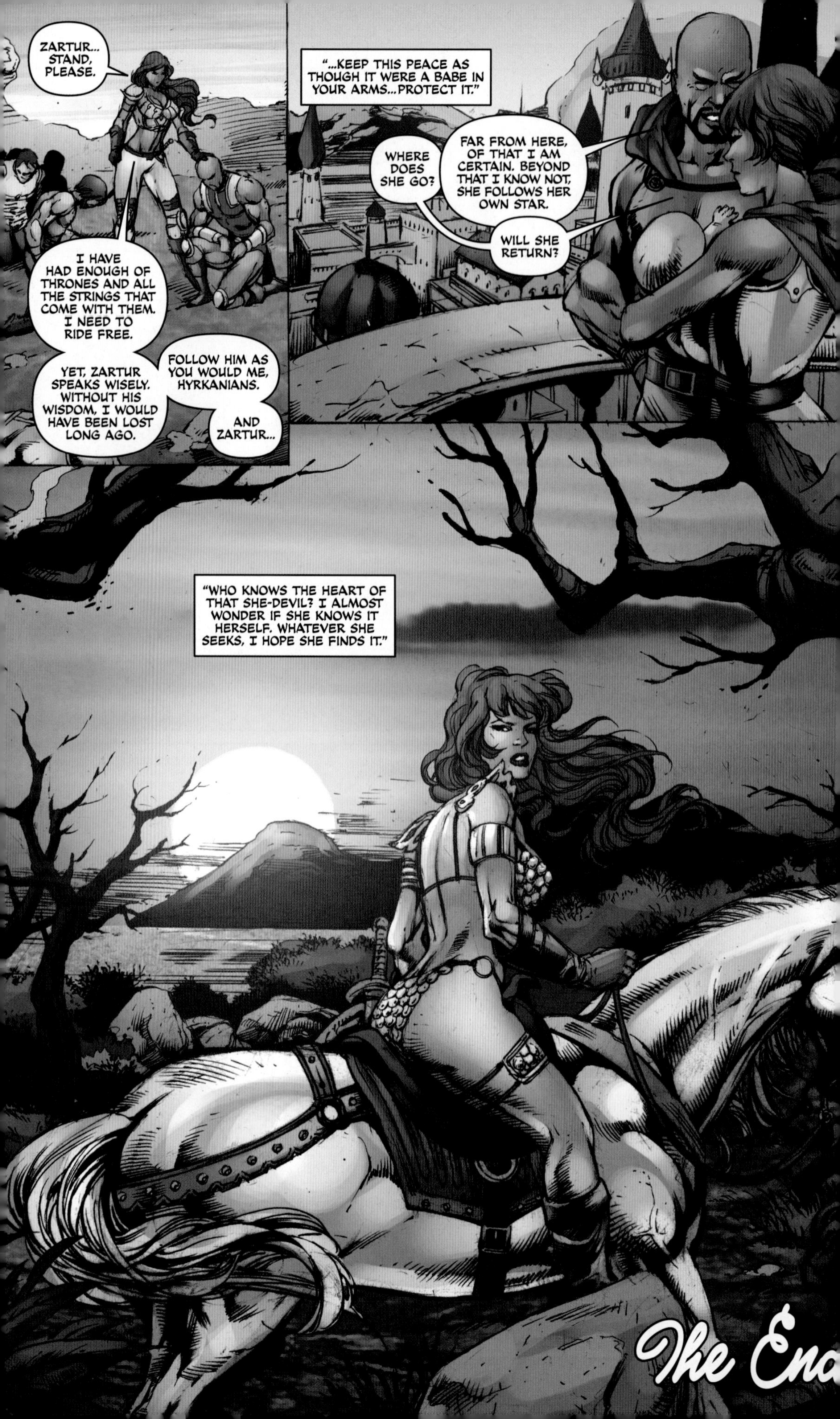
ZARTUR... STAND, PLEASE.
I HAVE HAD ENOUGH OF THRONES AND ALL THE STRINGS THAT COME WITH THEM. I NEED TO RIDE FREE.
YET, ZARTUR SPEAKS WISELY. WITHOUT HIS WISDOM, I WOULD HAVE BEEN LOST LONG AGO.
FOLLOW HIM AS YOU WOULD ME, HYRKANIANS.
AND ZARTUR...
"...KEEP THIS PEACE AS THOUGH IT WERE A BABE IN YOUR ARMS...PROTECT IT."
WHERE DOES SHE GO?
FAR FROM HERE, OF THAT I AM CERTAIN. BEYOND THAT I KNOW NOT, SHE FOLLOWS HER OWN STAR.
WILL SHE RETURN?
"WHO KNOWS THE HEART OF THAT SHE-DEVIL? I ALMOST WONDER IF SHE KNOWS IT HERSELF. WHATEVER SHE SEEKS, I HOPE SHE FINDS IT."

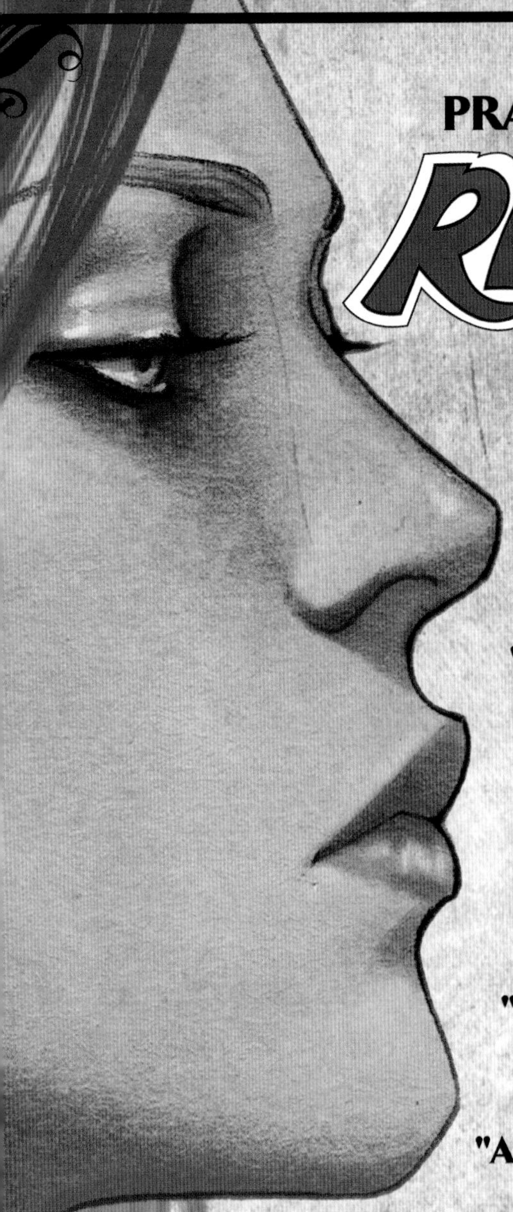

# PRAISE FOR GAIL SIMONE'S RED SONJA

**Newsarama**
"A strong and promising debut."

**Comic Book Resources**
"Sword and sorcery adventure done right... Great fun!"

**IGN**
"This is a great comic book and it deserves your attention."

**Comic Vine**
"5 stars out of 5."

**Comic Book Therapy**
"Lives up to the hype."

**Comicosity**
"A fun, action-packed, violent and humorous adventure."

**Unleash The Fanboy**
"Absolutely spectacular to behold."

**Geeks of Doom**
"Comic fans, what are you waiting for?!"

**Major Spoilers**
"I'm desperate for the next installment."

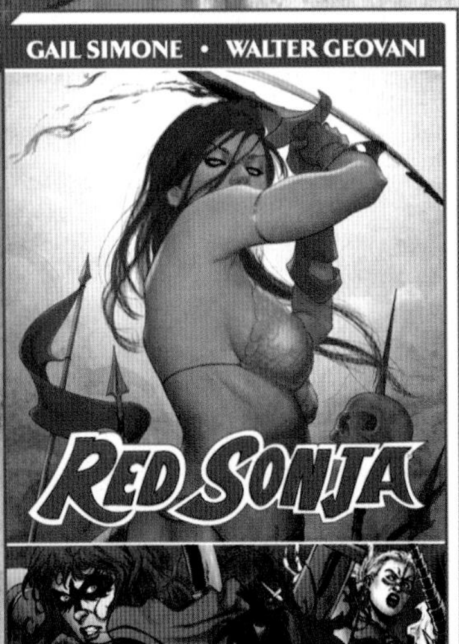
GAIL SIMONE • WALTER GEOVANI
RED SONJA
1

## RED SONJA VOL. 1:

**"QUEEN OF PLAGUES" TRADE PAPERBACK**
**written by GAIL SIMONE**
**art by WALTER GEOVANI**

**Collection in stores February 2014**
**Ongoing series in stores now!**

DYNAMITE. DYNAMITE.COM • TWITTER: @DYNAMITECOMICS • FACEBOOK: /DYNAMITECOMICS

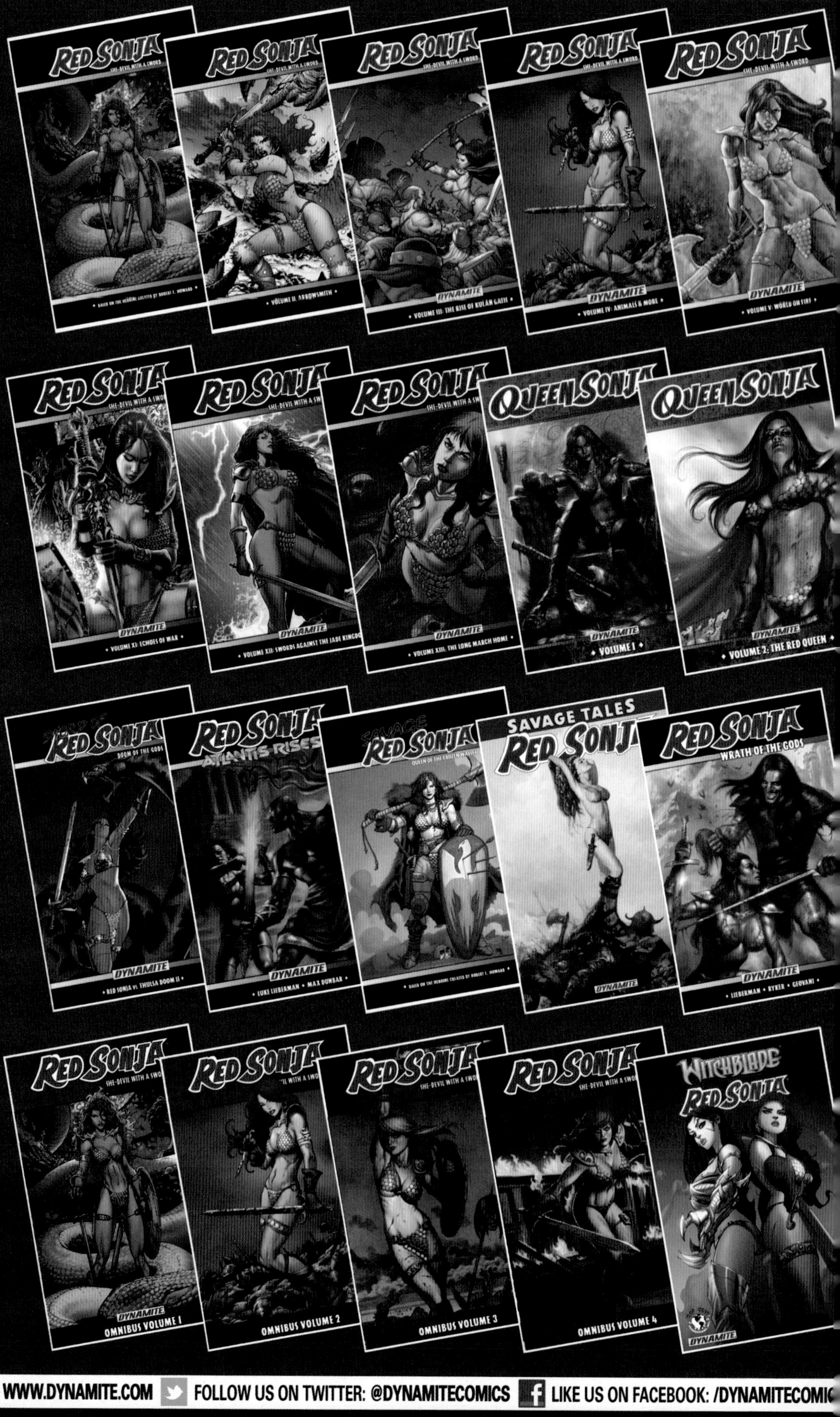

RED SONJA
SHE-DEVIL WITH A SWORD
RED SONJA
SHE-DEVIL WITH A SWORD
VOLUME II: ARROWSMITH
RED SONJA
SHE-DEVIL WITH A SWORD
DYNAMITE
VOLUME III: THE RISE OF KULAN GATH
RED SONJA
SHE-DEVIL WITH A SWORD
DYNAMITE
VOLUME IV: ANIMALS & MORE
RED SONJA
SHE-DEVIL WITH A SWORD
DYNAMITE
VOLUME V: WORLD ON FIRE
RED SONJA
SHE-DEVIL WITH A SWORD
DYNAMITE
VOLUME XI: ECHOES OF WAR
RED SONJA
DYNAMITE
VOLUME XII: SWORDS AGAINST THE JADE KINGDO
RED SONJA
DYNAMITE
VOLUME XIII: THE LONG MARCH HOME
QUEEN SONJA
DYNAMITE
VOLUME 1
QUEEN SONJA
DYNAMITE
VOLUME 2: THE RED QUEEN
RED SONJA
DOOM OF THE GODS
DYNAMITE
RED SONJA vs. THULSA DOOM II
RED SONJA
ATLANTIS RISES
DYNAMITE
LUKE LIEBERMAN • MAX DUNBAR
SAVAGE
RED SONJA
DYNAMITE
SAVAGE TALES
RED SONJA
DYNAMITE
RED SONJA
WRATH OF THE GODS
DYNAMITE
LIEBERMAN • RYKER • GEOVANI
RED SONJA
SHE-DEVIL WITH A SWO
DYNAMITE
OMNIBUS VOLUME 1
RED SONJA
OMNIBUS VOLUME 2
RED SONJA
SHE-DEVIL WITH A SW
OMNIBUS VOLUME 3
RED SONJA
SHE-DEVIL WITH A SWO
OMNIBUS VOLUME 4
WITCHBLADE
RED SONJA
DYNAMITE

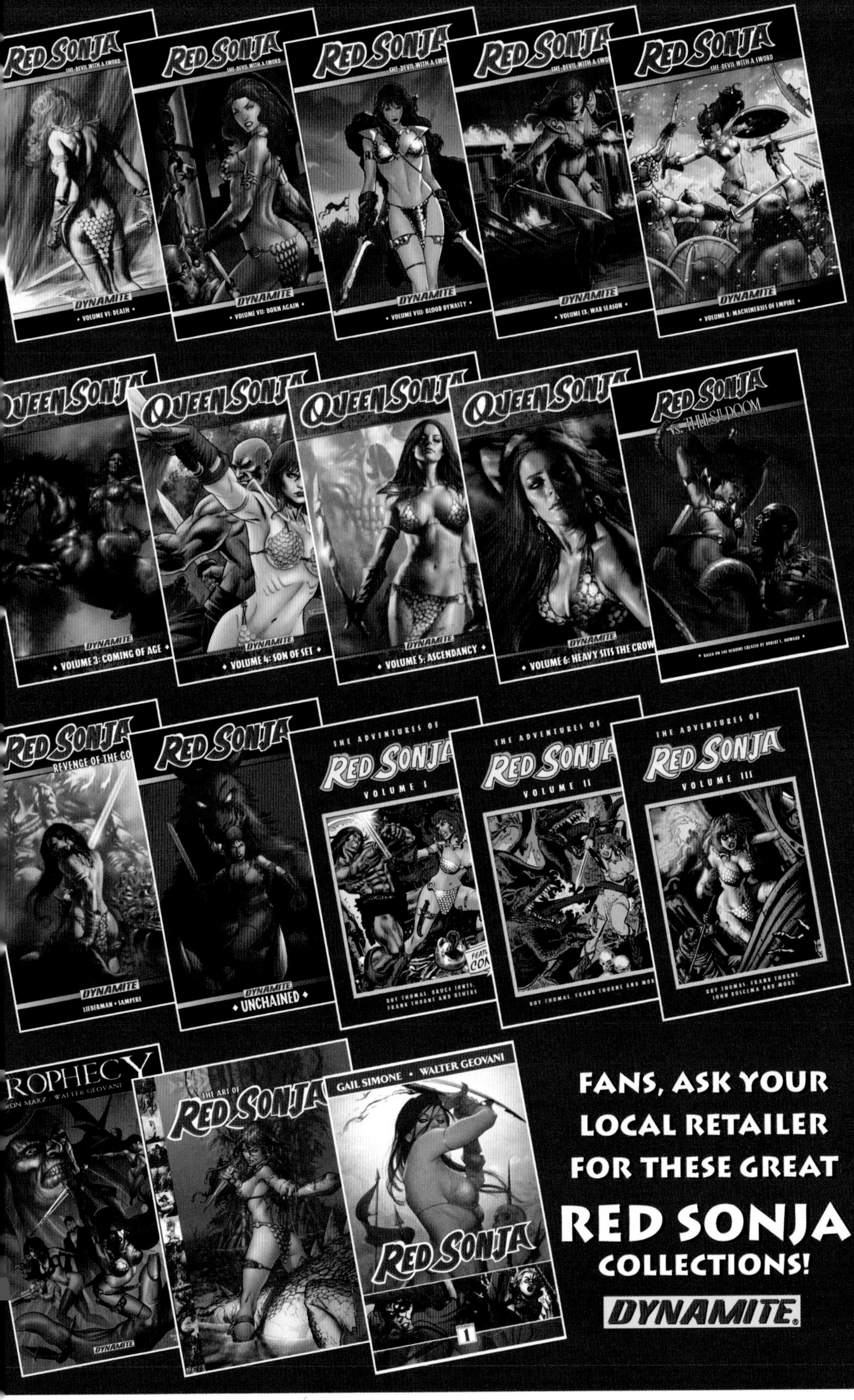
RED SONJA
SHE-DEVIL WITH A SWORD
DYNAMITE
VOLUME VI: DEATH
VOLUME VII: BORN AGAIN
VOLUME VIII: BLOOD DYNASTY
VOLUME IX: WAR SEASON
VOLUME X: MACHINERIES OF EMPIRE
QUEEN SONJA
VOLUME 3: COMING OF AGE
VOLUME 4: SON OF SET
VOLUME 5: ASCENDANCY
VOLUME 6: HEAVY SITS THE CROW
RED SONJA VS. THULSA DOOM
REVENGE OF THE GO
LIEBERMAN • SAMPERE
UNCHAINED
THE ADVENTURES OF RED SONJA
VOLUME I
VOLUME II
VOLUME III
ROY THOMAS, BRUCE JONES, FRANK THORNE AND OTHERS
ROY THOMAS, FRANK THORNE AND MORE
ROY THOMAS, FRANK THORNE, JOHN BUSCEMA AND MORE
ROPHECY
RON MARZ • WALTER GEOVANI
THE ART OF RED SONJA
GAIL SIMONE • WALTER GEOVANI
1